Seventeenth-Century Europe

HISTORY OF EUROPE

PUBLISHED

Early Medieval Europe 300–1000 (3rd edn)
Roger Collins

Sixteenth Century Europe
Richard Mackenney

Seventeenth Century Europe 1598–1700 (2nd edn)
Thomas Munck

Eighteenth Century Europe (2nd edn)
Jeremy Black

Nineteenth Century Europe
Michael Rapport

History of Europe
Series Standing Order
ISBN 0–333–71699–X hardcover
ISBN 0–333–69381–7 paperback
(*outside North America only*)

You can receive future titles in this series as they are published by placing a standing order. Please contact your bookseller or, in the case of difficulty, write to us at the address below with your name and address, the title of the series and the ISBN quoted above.

Customer Services Department, Macmillan Distribution Ltd
Houndmills, Basingstoke, Hampshire RG21 6XS, England

Seventeenth-Century Europe

State, Conflict and the
Social Order in Europe,
1598–1700

Thomas Munck

Second Edition

palgrave
macmillan

First published 2005 by
PALGRAVE MACMILLAN
Houndmills, Basingstoke, Hampshire RG21 6XS and
175 Fifth Avenue, New York, N.Y. 10010
Companies and representatives throughout the world

PALGRAVE MACMILLAN is the global academic imprint of the
Palgrave Macmillan division of St. Martin's Press, LLC and of Palgrave
Macmillan Ltd. Macmillan® is a registered trademark in the United
States, United Kingdom and other countries. Palgrave is a registered
trademark in the European Union and other countries.

ISBN-13: 978–1–4039–3618–9 hardback
ISBN 10: 1–4039–3618–8   hardback
ISBN-13: 978–1–4039–3619–6 paperback
ISBN 10: 1–4039–3619–6   paperback

This book is printed on paper suitable for recycling and made from
fully managed and sustained forest sources. Logging, pulping and
manufacturing processes are expected to conform to the
environmental regulations of the country of origin.

A catalogue record for this book is available from the British Library.

A catalog record for this book is available from the Library of Congress.

Printed in Great Britain by the MPG Books Group, Bodmin and King's Lynn

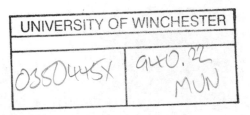

Contents

Chronology of main events, 1598–1700

The West	C. & N. Europe	The East
1598: Peace of Vervins between France and Spain	Swedes depose Sigismund: Charlés IX (–1611)	Boris Godunov Tsar (–1605)
Edict of Nantes protects French Huguenots		
Philip III of Spain (–1621)		
1600: English E. India Co.	Giordano Bruno burnt (Rome)	
1602: Dutch E. India Co.		
1603: Death of Elizabeth I: Scottish James VI/I (–1625)		
Shakespeare: *Hamlet*		
1605: Gunpowder plot in Westminster	Caravaggio: *Death of the Virgin*	Muscovy: Time of Troubles (–1613)
1606: Papal interdict vs Venice	Habsburg peace with Turks; Emperor Rudolf II (1576–1612) loses power to his brother Matthias	Bolotnikov revolt in Ukraine
1607: Ulster Plantation begun	Occupation of Donauwörth by Maximilian of Bavaria (1597–1651)	
Virginia founded	Monteverdi: *Orfeo*	
1608: Quebec founded by French	Diet of Regensburg fails	
	Protestant union formed	

The West	C. & N. Europe	The East
1609: 12-year truce between Spain and United Provinces	Jülich–Cleves dispute Letter of Majesty issued to Bohemian Protestants	Swedes and Poles in Muscovy
Moors expelled from Spain	German Catholic League formed	
Amsterdam Exchange Bank		
1610: Henry IV murdered: Louis XIII (–1643) under regent Marie de Medici	Frederick V Elector in Palatinate Galileo uses telescope	Sigismund III (1587–1632) of Poland garrisons Moscow
1611: English authorised version of Bible	Christian IV (1588–1648) vs Sweden (Kalmar war)	
	Gustav Adolf King of Sweden (–1632)	
	Saxony: Johann Georg I (–1656)	
1612:	Death of Emperor Rudolf II: Matthias (–1619)	
1613: Amsterdam Exchange	Peace between Denmark and Sweden at Knäröd	Michael Romanov Tsar (–1645)
	Elector of Brandenburg adopts Calvinism	
1614: Estates General called in France	Treaty of Xanten splits Jülich and Cleves	
1615: Dutch take Moluccas		
1616: Death of Shakespeare and of Cervantes		
1617: Regency in France terminated by force		Peace of Stolbova between Sweden & Muscovy
		Swedish–Polish war

The West	C. & N. Europe	The East
1618: Synod of Dordrecht narrows Dutch Church	Defenestration of Prague starts Bohemian war	
1619: Oldenbarneveldt executed in The Hague	Death of Emperor Matthias: Ferdinand II (–1637)	Bethlen Gabor invades Hungary
Black slaves in North America	Hamburg bank set up	
	Andrea: *Christianopolis*	
1620: Bacon: *Novum Organum*	Battle of White Mountain: 'Winter King' loses Bohemia	
Mayflower sails		
1621: Death of Philip III: Philip IV (–1665)	Empire heads for financial chaos, *Kipper- und Wipperzeit*	
	Swedes take Riga	
1622: French peace with Huguenots (Montpellier)	Re-Catholicisation begins in Habsburg lands	
Olivares first minister in Madrid (–1643)	Recurrent peasant revolts (–1627)	
1623:	Maffeo Barberini elected Pope Urban VIII (–1644)	
1624: Anglo–French war	Monteverdi: *Il combattimento*	
Richelieu increasingly influential in French government (–1642)		
1625: Death of James VI/I: Charles I (–1649)	Wallenstein hired by Emperor	
Death of Maurits of Orange, Dutch surrender Breda	Christian IV intervenes in Empire (–1629	
Grotius: *De jure belli ac pacis*		

The West	C. & N. Europe	The East
1627: Siege of La Rochelle	Wallenstein and Tilly extend imperial control north	
Wat of Mantuan succession	Swedish peasant revolt (Dalarna)	
1628: Duke of Buckingham assassinated	Wallenstein 'general of the Baltic Sea'	
Petition of Right	Swedish control of Baltic trade tightened	
Harvey: *De motu cordis*		
1629: Huguenots accept durable peace at Alais	Peace of Lübeck takes Christian IV out of war	Truce of Altmark between Sweden and Poland
English parliament dissolved		
1630: Day of Dupes in Paris	Gustav Adolf enters German war	
Rubens: *Peace and War*	Wallenstein dismissed	
	Plague virulent in Europe	
1631: *Gazette de France*	Magdeburg sacked by Tilly	
	Treaty of Bärwalde between France and Sweden	
	Leipzig colloquium	
	Swedish victory at Breitenfeld	
	Fall of Prague to von Arnim	
1632: Wentworth in Ireland	Gustav Adolf killed at Lützen; Christina queen (–1654)	Muscovy attacks Poland
Major rebellions in France continuing into 1640s	Oxenstierna dominant (–1644)	Wladyslaw IV King of Poland (–1644)
	Galileo: *Dialogue*, then trial in Rome	Muscovite expansion into Siberia

The West	C. & N. Europe	The East
1633: Baptists in England Charles I visits Edinburgh	Protestant league of Heilbronn	
1634: Ship-money first collected in London	Wallenstein again dismissed, then assassinated Protestant defeat at Nördlingen Swedish Form of Government	Polish–Muscovite peace
1635: France and Spain at war (–1659) Académie française set up	Peace of Prague between Emperor and Saxony	
1636: France invaded by Habsburg army	Saxons defeated by Swedes at Wittstock	
1637: Spain loses Breda Prayer book riots in Scotland Descartes: *Discourse on method*	Ferdinand III Emperor (–1657) Public opera house opens in Venice	Muscovite expedition through Siberia to Pacific
1638: National Covenant in Scotland		
1639: Spanish navy defeated by Dutch off Downs		
1640: Revolts in Catalonia and Portugal Short and Long Parliaments called in England (Scots invasion)	Frederick William Elector of Brandenburg–Prussia (–1688): peace with Sweden	

The West	C. & N. Europe	The East
1641: Irish rebellion Strafford beheaded in London Grand Remonstrance		
1642: Civil war in England Death of Richelieu, Mazarin first minister Hobbes: *De cive* Rembrandt: *Night Watch*		
1643: Death of Louis XIII: Louis XIV (–1715) under regency Spain defeated at Rocroi Assembly of Westminster	Danish–Swedish war (–1645)	
1644: English battle at Marston Moor	German peace conferences start in Westphalia (–1648) Pope Innocent X (–1655)	Colloquy of Torun
1645: Cromwell wins at Naseby Laud beheaded		Alexis Tsar (–1676)
1646: End of first civil war in England (–1648)		
1647: Willem II Dutch stadholder (–1650)	Revolt of Masaniello in Naples	
1648: Parlement of Paris starts Frondes (–1653) 2nd English civil war Pride's Purge of Parliament	Dutch–Spanish peace Prague taken by Swedes Peace of Westphalia Frederick III King of Denmark (–1670)	Jan II Kazimierz King of Poland (abdic. 1668) Riots in Moscow *zemsky* called

The West	C. & N. Europe	The East
1649: Charles I beheaded Cromwell to Ireland, later also Scotland Leveller *Third Agreement*	Europe-wide harvest failures (–1652)	Russian *Ulozheniye* (law code)
1650: Dutch power struggle until Willem II d.: Joh. de Witt takes over (–1672)	Swedish Estates in conflict	
1651: First Navigation Act Hobbes: *Leviathan*		
1652: Anglo–Dutch war		Irkutsk founded
1653: Barebones Parliament, Cromwell Lord Protector Ormée (Bordeaux) ends, princes' Fronde collapses, Mazarin back from exile	Imperial diet reconvenes Swiss peasant revolt starts in Lucerne	Nikon's reforms of Russian Orthodox Church
1654:	Abdication of Christina of Sweden: Charles X (–1660)	Ukrainian revolt of Khmelnytsky Polish–Russian war Smolensk falls to Tsar
1655: Anglo-Spanish war (–1659)	Charles X invades Poland Pope Alexander VII (–1667)	
1656: General hospital set up in Paris Huygens: pendulum clock	Saxony: Johann Georg II (–1680)	Mohammed Küprülü Grand Vizier in Ottoman Empire
1657: Humble Petition and Advice to Cromwell	Death of Emperor Ferdinand III; First Danish–Swedish war	

The West	C. & N. Europe	The East
1658: Cromwell dies: son Richard ineffective	Leopold I Emperor (–1705)	
	Second Danish– Swedish war	
1659: French–Spanish peace at Pyrenees	Europe-wide harvest failures (–1661)	
Pepys: *Diary* (–1669)		
1660: English Restoration: Charles II (–1685)	Death of Charles X of Sweden: Charles XI (–1697) under regency: peace with Danes	Swedish–Polish war ended by peace of Oliva
	'Coup' makes crown hereditary in Denmark	
1661: Death of Mazarin: Colbert minister (–1683)		Russo-Swedish peace at Kardis
		Ahmed Küprülü Ottoman Grand Vizier (–1676)
1662: English Press Acts and 'Clarendon code'		Copper riots in Muscovy
Royal Society in London		
1663:	Diet of Regensburg in permanent session	
1664: Anglo-Dutch war (–1667)	Turkish–Habsburg truce at Vasvar	
1665: London Plague	Danish Royal Law	
Carlos II of Spain (1700)		
1666: Louvois minister of war		Schism in Russian Orthodox Church
Great Fire of London		
Moliére: *Le Misanthrope*		
1667: Milton: *Paradise Lost*		Truce of Andrusovo between Poland and Muscovy

The West	C. & N. Europe	The East
French War of Devolution in Flanders (–1668)		Stenka Rasin rebellion
La Reynie chief of Paris police		
1668: Spanish partition treaty	Grimmelshausen: *Simplicissimus*	Abdication of John Casimir Vasa from the Polish throne
Rembrandt: *Jewish Bride*		
1670: Secret treaty of Dover	Death of Frederick III: Christian V (–1699)	Hungarian Wesselenyi revolt suppressed
Spinoza: *Tractatus th.*		
1672: Franco–Dutch war (–1678): de Witt killed, power to William III of Orange		Cossack–Turkish attack on Poland
Stop of English Exchequer		
1673: English Test Act passed		
1674: Peace of Westminster: England out of war	Swdes invade North Germany	John Sobieski King of Poland (–1696)
1675: Rebuilding of St Paul's under way	Swedish defeat at Fehrbellin	Ottoman forces reach Lvov
Revolt in Brittany crushed	Danish–Swedish war (–1679)	
	Fall of Griffenfeld (Denmark)	
1676:	Pope Innocent XI (–1689)	Fiodor III Tsar (–1682) under regency
		Kara Mustafa Grand Vizier
1677: William of Orange m. Stuart Princess Mary		Russo–Turkish war (–1681)
Spinoza: *Ethics*		

The West	C. & N. Europe	The East
1678: Peace of Nijmegen ends war in west	Hamburg opera house	
'Popish plot' in England		
1679: Habeas Corpus Act	N. European wars end	
English Exclusion Crisis		
Scottish Covenanters defeated		
1680: Réunions start on French Rhine frontier	Saxony: Johann Georg III (–1690)	
	Swedish comn. examines regency: crown strengthened	
Purcell: *Dido & Aeneas*	Bohemian peasant revolt	
1681: French seize Strassburg		
1682: Four articles launch French church vs Papacy	Thököli rebellion in Hungary	Peter I Tsar (–1725), under Sofya's regency
French court to Versailles	Swedish *reduktion* under way	
1683: Franco–Spanish war	Siege of Veinna by Turks fails	Austro–Polish war vs Turks (–1699)
Death of Colbert: Louvois dominant minister	Danish law code published	
1684: Truce at Regensburg		
1685: Death of Charles II: James II/VII (–1688) Argyll and Monmouth rebellions		
Revocation of Edict of Nantes, Huguenot exodus from France		
1686: League of Augsburg vs Louis XIV		Ottoman surrender of Breda

The West	C. & N. Europe	The East
1687: Louis excommunicated		Turks defeated at Mohacs
Newton: *Principia M.*	Habsburg control of Hungary improved (Diet of Pressburg)	
1688: French launch war of League of Augsburg (–1697)	Frederick III Elector of Brandenburg–Prussia (–1713)	Turks lose Belgrade
William lands in England, James flees to France		
1689: William & Mary given English crown: Bill of Rights	French devastate Palatinate	Tsar Peter I takes power
England join war on France		
Huguenot revolt in southern France		
James lands in Ireland		
Locke: *Two Treaties*		
1690: James defeated at Boyne		Mustafa Küprülü leads Ottoman recovery
1691: Death of Louvois	Saxony: Johann Georg IV (–1694)	Ottoman recapture of Belgrade
1692: Massacre at Glencoe	Hanover becomes electorate	
1693: National debt set up in England	Swedish absolutism complete	
1694: Bank of England	Saxony: Augustus the Strong (–1733)	
Famine starts in much of Europe (–1697)	Halle University founded	
1695: End of effective censorship in England		
1696: Bayle: *Dictionnaire historique*		Peter takes Azov

The West	C. & N. Europe	The East
1697: Treaty of Rijswick ends war in west	Augustus also King of Poland	Habsburg victory over Turks (Zenta)
	Charles XII King of Sweden (–1718)	Peter I visits west
1698: Spanish partition treaty		Streltsy revolt suppressed by Peter
Fénelon: *Télémaque*		
1699: Scottish Darien project fails		Peace of Karlowitz ends Turkish war
Vauban: *Dîme royale* (not yet published)	Frederick IV of Denmark (–1730)	
1700: Spanish Habsburg line extinct	Great northern war (–1721)	

Acknowledgements

This volume has taken much longer to write than originally anticipated, but in the process I have benefited from the help and advice of many. I owe most of all to my family – especially to my wife Margaret, who has not only for all her married life had to put up with someone perpetually reluctant to take a break from successive time-consuming projects, but has cheerfully encouraged and helped me along, and to my children, without whom this book would have appeared much sooner!

Any historian attempting a wide-ranging survey has an enormous debt to the countless scholars in whose work he has sought evidence, ideas and interpretative guidance – and whose findings he may in the process have been rash enough to compress out of recognition. There are some areas covered by this book where I have detailed research experience of my own, but many more where I have necessarily had to rely entirely on the work of others. The endnote references and the bibliography will, I hope, serve as some acknowledgement of where my greatest debts lie, but such is the vitality and range of work in the early modern period that neither of these can, within the confines of a textbook, be comprehensive. I have been able to include references only to what seemed to me most important and most helpful for anyone wishing to pursue particular themes in greater depth, but have added a number of works of a slightly more specialised nature, where more thorough guidance is given on recent developments in the field. If there is a heavy weighting towards work completed in the last ten or fifteen years, that is because perceptions of many central aspects of the period have in fact changed dramatically within that time-span.

I am grateful to the University of Glasgow for leaves of absence, and for providing what is still a congenial and stimulating environment for students and staff alike. Many colleagues and friends deserve personal acknowledgement, but I owe a particular debt to the following: to Hamish Scott at the University of St Andrews, whose detailed and invariably helpful comments were both a great encouragement, when the enterprise seemed daunting, and of enormous practical assistance; and at my own university to Christopher F. Black and Alan G. R. Smith, whose expertise in areas outside my usual range proved particularly invaluable. For chapter 10 I have unashamedly pirated ideas from a Special Subject which Chris Black and I have run jointly for some years, and his thorough knowledge, especially of Roman Catholic Italy, has been of as much benefit to me as to our students. No less generous with his time was G. V. R. Grant, always willing to help by commenting on drafts at any stage of the work. I need hardly say that these friends and colleagues, whilst generously spending much time and effort on improving both structure and detail, in no way take on any responsibility for inadequacies in the final text.

In a less direct but important way I have also gained a great deal from certain colleagues outside the field of early modern Europe: in particular, Evan Mawdsley and Rick Trainor, whose enthusiasm brought me into the age of the microcomputer, in the process changing my outlook both on teaching and on research. That this book shows so little obvious sign of quantitative analysis is something that I regret, but which the nature of the project made inevitable. At least its production was greatly eased (the excellent earlier typing of Pat Ferguson notwithstanding) by means of the new technology, which has also enabled me to remedy some of the accruing defects of long gestation. And on that note I must thank my publishers for their forbearance with more overshot deadlines than I would care to admit to in print.

University of Glasgow
October 1988

Thomas Munck

This second (revised) edition seeks to take account of a great deal of new work which has appeared during the 15 years that have elapsed since this book was first published. Although the overall structure of the book has been retained, some chapters have been substantially reorganised, and others have had new sections added where simple rewriting proved insufficient. My own research agenda has changed significantly over this period, and the work of many other early modern European historians has brought out a number of new perspectives to which readers will want to be alerted. As with the first edition, some of my most important scholarly debts are tracked either in the extensively reworked Further Reading, or in the notes. Since the Further Reading has had to be selective, the index will, I hope, allow readers to locate relevant additional material in the notes. There is no sign that innovative new work on the early modern period is in any danger of drying up, and if a book such as this cannot do justice to it all, it may at least encourage readers to pursue further searches.

On a personal note, I wish once more to thank my colleagues in the History Department at Glasgow University for providing a lively and friendly environment in which to work. This revised edition was completed while I was well into, but not yet through, my four years as Head of Department – a period in which I came to appreciate even more how fortunate I was to have, as friends, historians who between them are actively working in fields spanning across fifteen centuries and several continents. Their enthusiasm, the angelic patience of the secretarial staff (especially Alison Peden and Margo Hunter) and of my family, and the constant challenge from students at all levels have all contributed to make this book better in ways which may not be as obvious to them as they are to me.

University of Glasgow
November 2004

TM

Introduction

No attempted synthesis of a whole century of European history could hope to be fully comprehensive, given the amount of stimulating work that is being done in the field of early modern studies. The structure of this book has accordingly been based on two broad principles. First, while the narrative framework is covered in some detail in the key political chapters of the book (namely chapters 1, 2, 7, 11 and 12), the rest of the text is centred on themes which are crucial to an understanding of the period but which do not necessarily lend themselves to either chronologically or geographically structured treatment. The aim has been to survey areas where more recent work has led to reassessments of the period and its meaning, and to outline some of the ideas which have guided historians in their attempts to solve crucial difficulties. The index will help readers to locate individuals and countries on which they may wish to concentrate; the book as a whole will, it is hoped, provide some guidance for those seeking an overall understanding of the relationship between state and subject, of the structure of society, of the location of power and the nature of status and influence, of the mental and cultural world of the early modern period, of the urban and rural communities, and of the demographic and economic realities that shaped society.

Secondly, the book has been written in the belief that the British Isles are part of Europe. This is not to say that English or Scottish developments are necessarily comparable to what happens on the continent; indeed, one obvious thread running through this book is the significance of the local and the particular all over the continent, and the extent to which even smaller states in this period were still far from being coherent entities in themselves in any meaningful sense. But the fact that the British Isles were surrounded by sea, while ensuring a natural advantage in avoiding the worst excesses of continental military development, also ensured ready commercial, cultural and even political contact with continental states – despite that legendary streak of insularity and xenophobia for which at least the English were renowned. During the seventeenth century, as newspapers and travel made Europeans more aware of what was happening beyond their immediate horizons, some observers also became more aware of the potential repercussions of developments in other countries. Nowhere is this more strikingly revealed than in the horror all over the continent which greeted the news of the execution of Charles I, or in the growing awareness later in the century that Louis XIV was becoming both a model of the grandeur of monarchy and a warning of the dangers of military arrogance.

French and English material necessarily forms a large part of any survey of early modern Europe, partly because French- and English-language scholars have led the way towards a re-evaluation of the social and economic history of the period. Given the strengths of recent publications in these fields, however, the aim of this book has been to try to broaden the perspective by emphasising central, north-ern and eastern Europe as far as possible. This may at times lead to some unusual choices of examples and case-studies; in the process, however, it is hoped that a more balanced view of European develop-ments will emerge. Absolute monarchy, to return to an earlier point, may have had its most grandiose exponent in the form of Louis XIV, but it is the history of smaller states, as well as the reluctance of the English to follow suit, that throw the clearest light on what govern-ments could and could not achieve in practice during this period.

As a period the seventeenth century itself requires some justifica-tion. It stands in transition between on the one hand the relatively prosperous and dynamic sixteenth century, with its major religious debates, its overseas expansion and the economic growth which lasted into the 1590s or even to 1620, and on the other hand the more relaxed and expansive eighteenth century, where aristocratic society was at its height yet where many intellectual and cultural trends came to fruition in the enlightenment. Boxed in by the Muslim world in the Mediterranean, threatened by recurrent warfare both amongst the European powers and overseas, and at times overwhelmed by disease and starvation of extraordinary ferocity, seventeenth-century Europe was under siege. Chapter 7 is a central part of this story, covering the middle decades of the century when to many Europeans the whole structure seemed about to collapse. This chapter provides the resolu-tion of the growing tensions of wartime Europe discussed in the first two chapters, but also helps to explain why those with any influence were so insistent after 1660 on the preservation of the social order and the consolidation of stable monarchy. This consolidation is discussed in chapter 11, whilst some of its negative sides, together with the continuing limitations of classic absolutism, are outlined in the final chapter.

Only rarely is the story taken beyond the last decade of the seven-teenth century. This is a departure from earlier historical traditions, where 1715 has been the point of termination. I am not convinced that the latter date is helpful; by that stage the War of the Spanish Succession had drastically altered the balance of power in a way that belongs to the eighteenth century, not the seventeenth. No less impor-tant, many of the central themes of the seventeenth century reach a natural conclusion in the last years of the century rather than after an additional half-generation of European war; this applies to the witch-craze as well as to the completion of the scientific and intellectual revolutions, to the commercial reorientation of Europe in favour of the north-west, and to the resolution of the last trailers of the 'mid-century crisis' in England in 1688–9 and in Sweden in the period 1680–97. French absolutism itself makes best sense if seen as an organic development from the end of the civil war in 1598, through Henry IV and the ministers of Louis XIII to a culmination (after the brief interlude of the Fronde) in the fully-developed but hardly innovative approach of Louis XIV's ministers, Colbert and Louvois. In the last years of his reign, however, the French crown had to rely on emergency expedients, abandoning any long-term planning in favour of what at times seemed simple survival in an all-out European war. The legacy of those last years was apparent through much of the eighteenth century.

In the broader cultural area there are equally good reasons to stop short of the turn of the century. Chapter 10 attempts to analyse the period in terms of the arts. In the arts, too – whether one examines the changes in literary tastes, away from the grandeur and passion of Milton and Racine towards the lighter entertainment of the Restoration theatre, whether one turns from the dramatic master-pieces of Monteverdi to the more formal conventions of court music during the last years of Lully and after his death, or whether one looks at the relative decline of Italian artistic innovation after the age of Bernini – the conclusion must once more be that a natural point of summation comes in the last quarter of the seventeenth century. By then the demands of patrons and the tastes of the public were coming to favour the idyllic rather than the dramatic or the emotional. By then, too, the new 'aristocratic' standards of the *ancien régime* were becoming apparent even in the paintings of the Dutch. There is no longer any general agreement about the relationship between elite and popular culture, or whether the two can be separated in any meaning-ful way, but, as we will note, the dynamics of cultural development changed significantly in the last years of the century.

In terms of the social history of the period, a century is perhaps less meaningful. Continuity is often more apparent than change, and the historian must try to avoid overdramatising what is often a very gradual and almost imperceptible process. Nowhere is this more obvi-ous than with respect to the peasantry and to peasant–seigneur rela-tions. Nevertheless, chapter 8 has been placed after that on the 'mid-century crisis' because the consolidation of serfdom in parts of eastern and east-central Europe clearly was in part conditioned by the resolution not just of the Thirty Years War but also of the bitter conflict in northern Europe and the Ukraine in the 1650s. In Poland, in particular, the Crown then lost what with hindsight may have been its last chance of playing a decisive regulative role in the style of other European monarchies. As we shall note, it is simplistic to see rural Europe as divided into east and west, enserfed and 'free'; ultimately landowners had a natural interest in preserving the productive capacity of their peasants, even if they might interpret that interest in different ways. In the long-term perspective, peasant–seigneur relations formed an essential and fundamental part of the social hierarchy all over early modern Europe, and contemporaries recognised the mutual dependence that such a relationship involved. It is difficult to avoid the conclusion, however, that at some stage the market-orientation and exclusive privileges of some east-central European landowners would reinforce a fundamental divergence of approach from the more divided motivations of the western elite, concerned as they were with status based both on the *rentier* income of landed estates and on the juggling for position in the office-holding ranks of increasingly intricate bureaucracies and court circles.

What exactly was 'Europe' in this period? The term itself was used, but less frequently than today, and it would be hard to argue that contemporaries had a very clear idea of what it meant. Concepts of nationality were less precise than they became later, and more readily confused with local or regional loyalties. Since, as we shall see, government was far less intrusive and omnipresent than it is in modern Europe, most people would probably have been more conscious of their links with their particular community and their social network – defining themselves in terms of their membership of a specific parish, of a privileged corporation or guild, and (if wealthy) of one of the infinite number of finely divided ranks into which contemporaries liked to categorise the strictly hierarchical society which they saw around them. If a wider perspective was adopted, the prevailing frame of reference would have been that of Christianity – or rather one of its many, usually mutually hostile, variants. To contemporaries in the West, Russian Orthodox Christianity, in particular, was very remote and utterly different, whilst much of the Greek Orthodox community had been absorbed into the Ottoman Empire, traditionally the most obvious 'other' in European culture.

Until recently, there was a paucity of historical literature in Western languages regarding the Ottoman state, its Islamic ideology and its political structures. This situation is now changing, and historians have been able to start making more informed comparisons across Europe. They have also been better placed to understand that Muslim and Christian cultures were in fact not always as far removed from each other as contemporary (and more recent) polemicists might lead us to believe. There were of course major differences, many of them defined (as amongst the various Christian Churches themselves) by differences in religious beliefs. But, as this book will indicate, the barrier was far from impermeable, and the sheer size of the Christian communities settled within the Ottoman Empire should remind us that that state was in many ways more tolerant, more efficient and more secure than many of its European neighbours. Contemporaries on both sides, however, were seldom open-minded about such comparisons. The existence of slavery in the Ottoman Empire is a case in point: held up as a form of oppression which might appear to victimise children from non-Muslim families who were 'conscripted' into, and trained for, state service, it was not quite what it appeared to be. First, it operated in spite of, rather than because of, Islamic law itself; secondly, in practice it appears to have created considerable social mobility and career opportunities, so much so that it tended to be a sign of status rather than of oppression. Whether Ottoman slavery was better or worse than serfdom elsewhere in Europe will perhaps become apparent, once more research has been done, but clearly we should not accept at face value descriptions designed to maximise the contrast between systems and traditions in Christian and Muslim parts of Europe. Europe was a deeply divided continent, but its divisions were social, political and economic as well as religious, and far more complicated than the political map would at first sight suggest.

At the beginning of the seventeenth century, a well-informed European would have had a very different perception of his political and social environment than that of his grandson or great-grandson after the peace settlements of 1648, 1659 and 1660. The Thirty Years War, for all its tortuous meanderings, had inescapable and decisive consequences everywhere – not just in central Europe but also, as even the sheer length of chapter 2 suggests, in every part of the continent. The slowness with which the conflict got off the ground, however, suggests that 1618 did not mark the culminating release of long-accumulating tensions and imbalances in Europe. On the contrary, one could argue that at the turn of the century the outlook was in some respects quite positive.

On the economic front, despite the catastrophic harvest failures and consequent unrest of the 1590s, there were not yet any clear indications of the long-term stagnation and recession which had unmistakably set in by the early 1620s. Overseas long-distance trade was buoyant if unpredictable, and while the Dutch access to the east via the Cape in 1595 warned of a change of balance to come, the longstanding Spanish and Portuguese positions in the Americas were still secure. New trade openings were being developed at the turn of the century, the optimism that they generated clearly shown in the trading companies and banking facilities springing up in different cities in the first decades of our period. And, whilst the rise in prices had far outstripped that of wages during the sixteenth century, thereby damaging sections of the skilled and unskilled urban populations, there were signs of prosperity both in the older ports of the Mediterranean and in the more recently developing coastal regions of the United Provinces and north-western Germany.

On the political front the outlook seemed particularly good in 1598. The death of Philip II of Spain, the conclusion of peace with France at Vervins, and the compromise settlement at Nantes of the long and bitter French religious wars all helped to create some ground for optimism. The balance of power in Europe had not shifted significantly. While the Habsburgs clearly dominated Europe with the combined strengths of their Spanish and German imperial branches, neither wing aimed at major aggrandisement within Europe. Emperor Maximilan II had demonstrated his tolerance of (and interest in) Protestantism during the third quarter of the sixteenth century, and while his son and heir, Rudolf II, was much more encouraging of Counter-Reformation work in the German lands, he progressively lost control of the political situation there. Although the collateral line on the Spanish throne was rigidly and grimly orthodox, it was in no position to use substantial force; the Spanish system was already stretched to capacity to hold its widely scattered European and vast overseas possessions. Apart from the long-standing and now irreconcilable conflict with the rebellious United Provinces in the northern Netherlands, Philip II had also had to face severe threats from the Arab world in the Mediterranean at various times throughout his reign, not to mention the native Morisco population in the Iberian peninsula itself, and growing Algiers-based piracy. It was the need to deal with two fronts at once, divided though each was, that prevented Philip II from winning decisively on either. The strain could be observed by anyone in Europe, including the Dutch rebels themselves: most obviously, the financial reputation of the Spanish crown was ruined by recurrent state bankruptcies in 1575, 1596 and 1607. So, while the Spanish position in the Netherlands recovered somewhat in the last years before the 12-year truce of 1609, and Spain could still call on sizeable resources from, for example, its Italian possessions, the advisers of Philip III were no doubt correct in their cautious evaluation of long-term prospects.

The first decade of the seventeenth century, therefore, was in some respects a period of recovery from exhaustion on several fronts. As we shall note, smouldering religious-based discords in the German lands remained intractable, but in large areas of Europe political and religious stability of a kind had at last been achieved. Both Scandinavian monarchies were under new and effective leadership, and were solidly Lutheran. In the British Isles the death of Elizabeth I in 1603 brought a personal union of Scotland and England in the hands of the experienced if eccentric James. In France the reign of Henry IV, later recalled as a 'golden age', very nearly catapulted Europe into another war, but his assassination in 1610 resulted in a cautious regency. East-central and eastern Europe looked less promising, with growing tensions in Bohemia and open confrontation along the Baltic between the Swedish and Polish branches of the Vasa royal family. But there was no immediate risk of these problems overspilling into the rest of Europe, and, in the east, Muscovy was so torn by internal problems that both Sweden and Poland diverted their attentions in that direction. Conflict in Europe, therefore, was not a foregone conclusion. Initially it even looked as if the Bohemian war of 1618 might produce no sequel, just as many hoped that the 12-year truce between Spain and the United Provinces might be extended indefinitely. Neither turned out to be the case: the Thirty Years War acquired a momentum of its own, which left both the political and the social structure of Europe fundamentally changed.

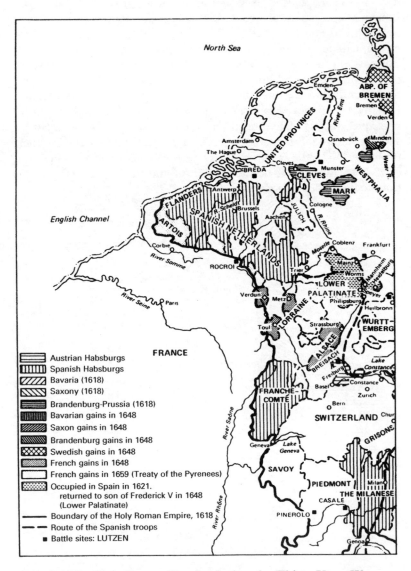

Map 1   The Holy Roman Empire during the Thirty Years War

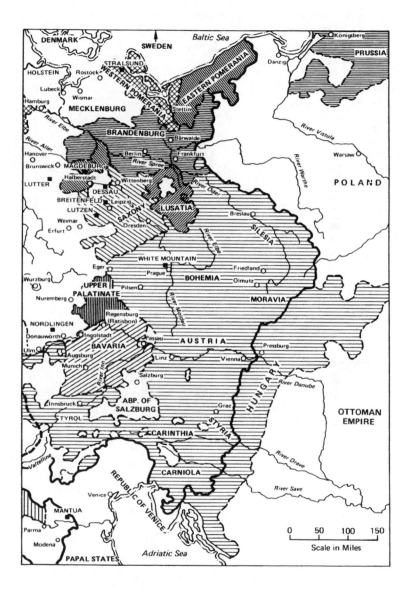

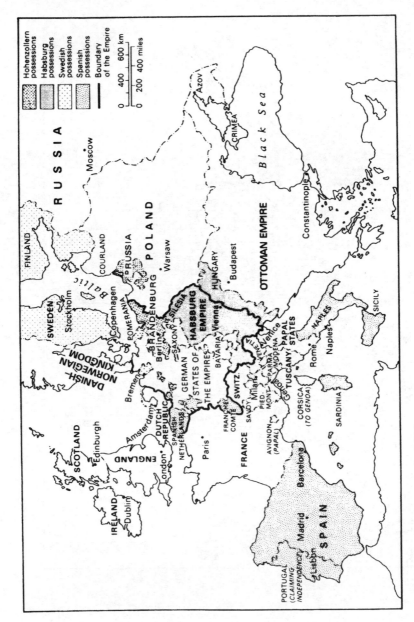

Map 2   European states in 1660

1 The Thirty Years War in the German lands

The early seventeenth century was a period of such complex and widespread warfare that few parts of Europe remained unscathed. Ever since, the motives of the major protagonists have been disputed, the overall significance of religious, economic and diplomatic factors debated, the severity of the material destructiveness reviewed, and the long-term significance of the concluding peace settlements re-assessed – even the very existence of a definable 'Thirty Years War' between 1618 and 1648 has been challenged.[1] Without denying the usefulness of this revisionism, historians have more recently concentrated on detailed studies of individual regions and localities within the Holy Roman Empire, in order to provide more finely drawn analyses appropriate to the territorial particularism which became so prominent a feature of the Empire during the course of the war and thereafter. Interestingly, however, many of these studies have revealed the continuing strengths and positive aspects of the imperial machinery, especially after 1648. What older generations of historians, taking their cue from an out-of-context phrase from Pufendorf's *De statu imperii Germanici* of 1667, regarded as a monstrous medieval constitutional anachronism in fact remained a loose but in many respects beneficial confederative framework capable of protecting the independence and security of the smaller states, at least in the western and south-western parts of the Empire. It has also become apparent that it is meaningless to generalise about the causes and effects of the war in terms of the Empire as a whole: experiences varied enormously from one part to another, and contemporary observers, like some historians later on, tended to portray the conflict in extreme terms.

The Thirty Years War, therefore, can be examined in a number of different ways. Earlier generations of twentieth-century historians naturally saw the conflict through their own experiences, as a major European conflict and perhaps the first 'general war' – as a conflict which had its roots in issues going back to the Reformation, a conflict where 1648 brought only partial resolution, but which nonetheless brought profound shifts in the balance of power and in the nature of 'authority' all over Europe. In that sense it included not only the conflicts between the Habsburg emperors and their rebellious subjects between 1618 and 1635, but also a decisive stage in the long-term conflict between the ruling dynasties of France and both branches of the Habsburg family. Closely related to these was the French search for 'secure' frontiers (a longer-lasting quest, thanks to Louis XIV), Spanish efforts to protect their north Italian possessions, and the second phase of the Dutch struggle for independence from Habsburg Spain between 1621 and 1648. Equally, the war encompassed attempts by various princes (and their spiritual or lay advisors) to promote or arrest the Catholic Counter-Reformation, consolidate or stamp out Calvinism in the German lands and elsewhere, or protect Lutheranism from both. Within the Empire, this in some instances led to a growth in aggressive princely territorialism which permanently altered the balance of political power in central Europe. To these scenarios must be added the chronic rivalry between Denmark and Sweden; the struggle between Sweden, Poland and Muscovy; and, of great importance when we turn to the economic history of the period too, the clash of strategic and commercial interests in the Baltic, involving the Dutch, the English and others; not to mention the wider context of overseas rivalry, centring especially on the increasingly insecure defensive position of the Spanish Empire. Given all these genuinely interrelated conflicts, it is almost a surprise to find that the Hungarian–Ottoman frontier was, for a while after 1606, relatively quiet, even though Transylvanian independence movements led by Bethlen Gabor (sometimes in association with the northern belligerents) created recurrent worries for the Habsburgs. It is indisputable that, for conflicting political and religious reasons, the Thirty Years War was a highly disjointed conflict which at some stage significantly affected nearly every part of Europe. In some areas (such as Magdeburg) wartime destruction was so severe that much historical evidence has itself disappeared. The conflict also left deep scars which, given the lack of effective leadership in many areas after 1648, were slower in healing than in some early modern war zones.

The German lands before 1618

Although the Empire did not conform to seventeenth-century European ideals of strong and centralising monarchy, its institutions do not appear inherently moribund when seen in their own perspective of stable conservatism. But much of the imperial machinery had, by the beginning of the period, become blocked with jurisdictional and judicial disputes arising from political exploitation of confessional differences. The Peace of Augsburg of 1555 had recognised a division of Germany between Catholicism and Lutheranism according to the decision of each prince, and had acknowledged the secularisation of that church property which had become part of the Lutheran areas by 1552. An additional imperial edict, the Ecclesiastical Reservation, had insisted that if a ruler of an independent ecclesiastical territory (for example a prince-bishop) converted to another denomination, he should lose his benefice and privileges, so that they might remain Catholic through the election of a new incumbent. The Protestants did not agree to this edict, although it was attached to the Peace, but they acquiesced in a kind of truce, owing to a secret imperial declaration guaranteeing toleration for those ecclesiastical dominions already practising Protestantism. In the long run, however, as soon as there was further prospect of the secularisation of church property on an important scale after 1582, the Ecclesiastical Reservation became a central bone of contention in confessional disputes. Even where it was accepted that a Protestant could act as 'administrator' of a see or benefice, the question of his precise rights and entitlements (not least his voting right in the *Reichstag* or imperial assembly) was disputed. The validity of the *ius reformandi* (right of reform) for imperial cities which had been Catholic in 1555 was also soon questioned. Moreover, the growing strength of Calvinism radically changes the dynamics of confrontation in the Empire.

It was only in the last decades of the sixteenth century that attitudes hardened on all sides. Emperor Rudolf II (1576–1612), whilst hardly 'orthodox' or even normal by the standards of his age, was less ambivalent in religious matters than his father Maximilian II had been. Although always constrained by the Habsburg family traditions, Maximilian, accused of crypto-Lutheranism, had tolerated the growth of Protestantism, even in the Austrian and Bohemian lands which were outside the terms of the Peace of Augsburg. As a result, Calvinism and Anabaptism had spread freely in the eastern reaches of the Habsburg lands. By the 1580s Moravia and Lusatia were almost entirely Lutheran, Habsburg Hungary was almost totally Protestant of some kind, and even in Upper and Lower Austria Catholicism appeared moribund, requiring major remedial action. There was growing pressure on Rudolf from the Wittelsbach dynasty in Bavaria, who were supporters of Tridentine Counter-Reforming Catholicism from 1569 and remained so through the long reign of the fiercely autocratic Duke Maximilian I (1591–1651). The effective (if rival) work of the Jesuits and the Capuchins in the southern parts of the empire added momentum, and in the years from 1578 Rudolf ordered the expulsion of Protestant preachers from Vienna and the imposition of restrictions on worship elsewhere. An Austrian peasant revolt of 1595 failed to reverse this trend, but continuing anti-Protestant measures from the government led to mounting resistance in most of the territorial Estates in the first decade of the seventeenth century, and even open revolt in Hungary. Rudolf's growing mental derangement, however, caused family rifts and led to the open rivalry for power by his younger brother, Archduke Matthias. A compromise between them in 1608 did not prevent the territorial Estates within the

Habsburg dominions from extracting political and religious concessions, the most significant of which, ultimately, was Rudolf's Letter of
Majesty granting religious autonomy to the Estates of Bohemia in
1609 (subsequently confirmed by Matthias).

On the Protestant side, the most serious challenge no longer came
from the Lutherans but from Calvinism. Luther's followers had split
into two basically incompatible groups, with the fundamentalist or
Gnesio-Lutheran tendency gaining ground in many parts of
Germany over the more liberal but less determined Philipists (followers of Philip Melancthon). The Formula of Concord reached in
1578–80 had attempted to reunify Lutheranism, but did so by direct-
ing it towards a narrow and uninspiring fundamentalist orthodoxy
torn by theological factionalism. Basic to Lutheranism was the acceptance of the secular supremacy of the state or the prince, and this gave
religious justification for the kind of conservative or defensive militancy adopted notably by the Electors of Saxony around and after the
turn of the century. By contrast, Calvinism (as already demonstrated
in France and the Netherlands) was far less subservient politically, and
because it had not been recognised in the Peace of Augsburg, became
the greatest challenge to the existing confessional balance. A presbyterian form of church organisation was probably too decentralised to
appeal to the Erastian mood in much of Germany, but Reformed or
Calvinist theology had gained some important footholds. It had
become established in the Palatinate since 1556, and had spread to the
ruling families of a number of smaller territories by the beginning of
the seventeenth century, including Nassau, Anhalt, Hessen-Kassel
(where Landgrave Moritz established the University of Marburg as a
Calvinist centre in 1604), Württemberg and, finally, Brandenburg
itself in 1613. These princes became increasingly concerned to arrest
what they saw as the defeatism of the Lutheran princes at the imperial assembly, notably over issues such as the grant of taxation for an
army to fight the Turks. Such a force, they feared, could equally well
be used by the Emperor against Protestantism. There appeared to be
clear warnings of that in the successful use of military means to
restore Catholicism in Cologne between 1582 and 1588 in favour of
another member of the Wittelsbach family, whilst in some other cities,
like Strassburg in 1604, the Protestants had to give in peacefully in the
face of superior power.

By the early years of the seventeenth century most of the imperial
machinery had been paralysed by this political–confessional
confrontation. The imperial assembly (*Reichstag*) felt it particularly
clearly. The first of its three houses, the House of Electors, consisted
of the Archbishop of Mainz (who was also its leader), the
Archbishops of Trier and Cologne, the Count Palatine, the Duke of
Saxony, the Margrave of Brandenburg and the King of Bohemia. The

first six of these (that is, omitting the Habsburg King of Bohemia, who was also Holy Roman Emperor) often acted as an electoral council, without whose consent the imperial assembly could not be convened. This council also determined the wording of the electoral capitulation which each Habsburg had to accept on taking up the imperial dignity, and had powers of initiative which the lower houses did not. It was, however, equally divided between Catholics and Protestants, with the latter group split between Lutherans and Calvinists. The second house, that of the princes of the empire (*Reichsfürsten*) who did not have electoral status, was presided over by a Habsburg agent, and tended to lean in favour of the Catholic side. Because its hundred or so voting delegates represented a large number of divergent interests (with some votes exercised collectively by a group of smaller territories, each of whom were entitled to representation in an observer capacity), this house was particularly prone to procedural difficulties over specific rights and privileges. The third house, consisting of the 51 free imperial cities, had a Protestant majority, but was empowered only to accept or reject resolutions passed on to it by the upper two houses and the Emperor. The overall procedures of the imperial assembly were slow at the best of times, but became virtually paralysed by 1603 because block voting according to confessional lines became the norm, with the *corpus catholicorum* pitted against the *corpus evangelicorum*. Political events soon made any compromise out of the question. In 1606, for example, rioting occurred in the imperial city of Donauwörth between the Protestant citizenry and a very small group of Catholic families encouraged by Benedictine monks and the Jesuits. Maximilian of Bavaria, with imperial blessing, used this in 1607 as an invitation to occupy the city with an army of 5000, impose Catholicism, and demand an indemnity so large that the city could not free itself. When the imperial assembly met in 1608, this breach of the 1555 compromise was not put right, and the Palatinate withdrew from the assembly in protest, followed by a substantial number of the other Protestant delegates. A further meeting of the imperial assembly was held in 1613, but it merely confirmed that the institution was no longer workable. Apart from a session in 1640, the full assembly did not function properly again until after the end of the war.

The imperial machinery of justice was also directly affected by the disputes, many of which ended up before the highest court of the Empire, the *Reichskammergericht* (imperial chamber court). Very long delays amounting to stalemate led the Emperor to refer cases to the Habsburg appellate court, the *Reichshofrat* (Aulic Council), but the Protestants refused to recognise such a strengthening of Catholic jurisdiction. In effect, there was no longer any means of settling disputes by law at the highest level.

The predictable consequence of this was the formation of armed leagues on each side. In May 1608 the Union of Auhausen was formed by a group of Protestant rulers, primarily those of Calvinist allegiance led by the Elector Palatine's ambitious advisor, Prince Christian of Anhalt. This Union, however, was weakened by the abstention of certain Lutheran princes, first and foremost Johann Georg of Saxony (influenced by his violently anti-Calvinist court preacher, Matthias Hoe van Hoënegg), and disintegration set in even before 1618. Meanwhile, the Catholic princes had responded by reviving an older League in Munich in 1609 and placing it under the leadership of the determined Maximilian of Bavaria. But it too had inherent weaknesses, revealed in the fact that the Emperor himself did not join, for political reasons. The two alliances were soon put to the test in a drawn-out dispute over the succession to the territories of Jülich, Cleves, Mark, Berg and Ravensberg in north-western Germany in 1609, to which there were several claimants. A complex sequence of far-reaching dynastic chess moves followed. The Union approached Henry IV of France, himself interested in breaking the Habsburg hold on the Rhine and in northern Italy, and war was only narrowly averted by the assassination of Henry IV and the *de facto* occupation of the territories by a joint anti-Habsburg force. The disputed claims soon flared up again when one of the claimants converted to Catholicism and gained the support of the League, whilst the other, the Elector of Brandenburg, Johann Sigismund, in 1613 turned to Calvinism (without, however, attempting to use his *ius reformandi* over his staunchly Lutheran subjects). The involvement of the Genoese-born Spanish commander Spinola and his formidable Army of Flanders on one side, and Maurits of Orange-Nassau commanding the Dutch forces on the other, created an immediate risk of international escalation, only averted by means of mediation and partition of the territories (Treaty of Xanten, 1614).

There was clearly no longer any way of disguising the international ramifications of political and confessional conflict between German princes, especially since imperial institutions were manifestly incapable of handling such problems and warding off external manipulation. No progress could be made in terms of reactivating the imperial institutions either. Emperor Matthias (1612–19) was himself not an active leader, and his most influential advisor, Melchior Khlesl, Bishop of Vienna and cardinal, could not realise his ostensible plans for conferences to settle the German disputes as long as Maximilian of Bavaria pressed a more belligerent stance. By 1617 the imperial succession itself was becoming an urgent issue, complicated by the knowledge that the Dutch–Spanish truce of 1609 would expire in 1621. Spain would consequently have a major interest in Germany, especially in the areas affecting the security of the 'Spanish Road' from northern Italy to the Netherlands.[2]

Bohemia and the Rhine (1617–28)

Despite the clear international implications of even lesser political and confessional clashes in central Europe, a Bohemian revolt did not at one level seem the most likely route to major war. Bohemia had accepted the Habsburg dynasty as elected kings for nearly a century, and the constitutional claims of its assemblies of Estates met little sympathy outside the Habsburg lands. Conflicts between princes and their territorial Estates were common everywhere at the beginning of the century, and rarely turned conclusively either way. In Bavaria the dukes had brought their Estates under firm control in the later sixteenth century, but elsewhere, for instance in Württemberg and in Electoral Saxony, the Estates continued to exercise an important influence on the grant and administration of taxation, on religious matters and on the conduct of war during the early seventeenth century and beyond. Habsburg policy towards the Bohemian Estates could thus be regarded as one of many examples of intended government consolidation over an area which, in the later sixteenth century, had enjoyed considerable economic prosperity. Admittedly the Letter of Majesty of 1609 had made substantial concessions to the large Hussite, Lutheran, Calvinist and other religious groups under the Bohemian Crown, increasing their feeling of security against Counter-Reformation (and especially Jesuit) pressures, whilst creating a very complex constitutional situation. But religious interests apart, the differences were not clear-cut: Rudolf II himself had preferred Prague as his capital and residential city, and even when he became an eccentric recluse much of the Bohemian nobility was still bound to the Habsburgs by strong ties of loyalty or, as in the case of the Chancellor of Bohemia, Zdenek Lobkovic, by self-interest.

That Bohemian aspirations were more threatening, however, became apparent in the last years of Matthias's reign. Archduke Ferdinand, educated by the Jesuits and inclined towards the Spanish party at court, had already shown his determination in the Counter-Reformation cause as a ruler of Styria and Carinthia since 1595. He was recognised as King of Bohemia in 1617 and King of Hungary the following year only by means of heavy pressure from Vienna. By then, Habsburg intentions of destroying the religious compromise of 1609 in Bohemia had become clear: censorship, closure of Protestant churches and other forms of harassment eventually brought about an opposition move in the form of the calling of a Protestant assembly in Prague in 1618 in accordance with the terms of the Letter of Majesty. When a petition to the Emperor was rejected, and there were further indications of the annulment of the rights accorded in 1609, a delegation from the assembly went to the governor's rooms in the Hradschin Palace in Prague. After a kind of token 'hearing', the two governors,

Martinic and Slavata, and their protesting secretary, were ritually thrown out of a high window; the political challenge was unmistakable.

The Defenestration of Prague[3] was followed in due course by the formation of a confederation of all the lands under the Bohemian Crown (including Moravia, Silesia and the two Lusatias), based on the Letter of Majesty and granting religious toleration to Protestants as well as Catholics (but banning Jesuits). A directory was set up, and a military force organised by Count Matthias von Thurn. An Apology was issued to explain the revolt abroad, and diplomatic contacts initiated. The revolt soon spread to Upper and Lower Austria, and valuable assistance was obtained, notably from Bethlen Gabor in Transylvania. After the death of Emperor Matthias in March 1619, the Estates General of the Bohemian Kingdom formally deposed Ferdinand on 22 August, going back on their earlier recognition. In his place they chose as king the Calvinist Elector Palatine, Frederick V. This was a serious mistake: Frederick had no connection with Bohemia, was not respected abroad, and, totally lacking political ability, was manipulated by the ambitious and militant Prince Christian of Anhalt. Not only was this a direct challenge to the Emperor and to Spanish imperial interests on the Rhine, it is also significant that although the rebels gained some support from other Estates within the Habsburg lands, the reaction in the rest of the Empire was lukewarm. Apart from the Duke of Savoy, who put some troops at the disposal of the mercenary adventurer Ernst von Mansfeld, commander on behalf of the Evangelical Union, few princes responded beyond verbal expressions of sympathy. Indeed, after the election – unanimously – of Ferdinand as Emperor on 28 August 1619, he was promised support not only by the Spanish government and Maximilian of Bavaria (supplying a solid army under the Flemish-born veteran commander, Johann T'Serclaes von Tilly), but also by the Lutheran Elector Johann Georg of Saxony, who had territorial ambitions in the Lusatias at the eastern end of his frontier with Bohemia. The division between Lutherans and Calvinists in the Empire, the desistance of the Union and, after a preliminary defeat, of Mansfeld, the disarray of opposition groups within the Habsburg lands, and the lack of political acumen of Frederick himself (and in a different way of his father-in-law, James VI of Scotland/I of England), all contributed to the disintegration of the Bohemian revolt. The Battle of the White Mountains in November 1620, and the flight of Frederick, the 'Winter King', effectively ended the war and paved the way for the emphatic imposition of Habsburg rule.

Deep disillusionment spread rapidly amongst the Bohemian leaders and their predominantly noble sympathisers, both because of their international isolation and because of their signal failure to overcome internal differences and win popular support, particularly amongst the rural population. But the way the Habsburgs made use of this opportunity to establish 'territorial absolutism' in the lands of the Bohemian crown has been extensively debated amongst historians. Encouraged notably by the Spanish party and the many clerics at court, Ferdinand authorised the establishment of commissions to confiscate the lands of those associated with the rebellion and of the growing number of refugees leaving for nearby Protestant areas such as Saxony and Silesia. In June 1621 the execution of 26 of the noble leaders of the rebellion took place and, in spite of a general pardon in February 1632, further penalties were imposed by the governor, Liechtenstein, on those members of the Estates who had not resisted the directory. In one and a half years some 680 noble families in Bohemia, 250 in Moravia and many more burgher families suffered confiscations and other penalties designed to replenish the Habsburg treasury, but in fact mostly enriching others.

During the next decades, just over half the total number of landed estates in Bohemia, especially the larger ones, were expropriated. The main beneficiaries were a number of Bohemian Catholic magnate families, including the Liechtensteins, the Lobkovics and the near-martyrs Martinic and Slavata, as well as some outsiders, such as Eggenberg, and a number of mercenaries. Another beneficiary was the greedy native-Bohemian landowner Albrecht von Wallenstein (Waldstein), who had gone over to the Habsburg side and was already playing a significant role as commander and military entrepreneur for Ferdinand II: he acquired landed estates worth 1.9 million florins. Non-Catholic landowners were forced to sell their property even if they had not been involved in the rebellion and, in Prague, fines were imposed indiscriminately on Catholics and Protestants, since a number of the former had backed the rebels. The confiscations, controlled pillaging, and army exactions not only caused acute inflation, but also knocked the bottom out of the real-estate market. Economic damage in both the rural and the urban sectors was aggravated by the influx of adventurers and crown creditors trying to exploit the situation. A semblance of administrative order was achieved only from 1623, when crippling new tax rates were also imposed following a period of growing monetary instability.

The papal nuncio in Vienna, Carlo Carafa, and others backed Ferdinand's decision to pursue in Bohemia a policy of total suppression not only of Calvinism (from 1621), but soon even of Lutheranism – a process which was extended into Moravia in 1624. The peasantry, although not so directly affected in the first instance, reacted to the recatholicisation programme and the increased fiscal exactions by attempting rebellions in 1621, 1622 and 1624. A further revolt in 1627 received assistance from Lower Saxon forces, but nevertheless also collapsed. The new Forms of Government promulgated in Bohemia in 1627 and in Moravia the following year formally terminated religious coexistence. These constitutional documents also made the Bohemian Crown hereditary in the Habsburg family, and circumscribed the Estates so narrowly that the foundation for territorial absolutism was effectively laid (if not immediately exploited to the full).

Silesia escaped more lightly, since its proximity to Lusatia and to Electoral Saxony made a less brutal religious policy expedient in order to avoid alienating Elector Johann Georg. But that was clearly an exception, for even in the older lands Ferdinand adopted stricter policies, perhaps under the influence of his belligerent Jesuit confessor, Lamormaini.[4] He authorised repressive measures designed to force Catholicism back on to what were by then predominantly Protestant provinces, and to ensure more direct control over all the hereditary lands. Even Upper Austria, temporarily administered by Maximilian of Bavaria to cover his war expenditure, felt the effects of this form of confessional absolutism through the governor, Adam von Herbertsdorff. A peasant revolt broke out there around Easter 1626 after a group of Protestant leaders objecting to the expulsion of Protestant preachers were forced to cast lots to decide who would be hanged. All other non-Catholics were ordered to convert or leave the country. A well-organised peasant army lead by Stefan Fadinger vom Fattinghof, motivated both by these religious grievances and by the Bavarian military exactions, took over the entire province except Linz. Despite the sympathy of some noble families, and further victories over Bavarian forces, the rebels were finally massacred by an army of 8000 commanded by von Pappenheim. The prospect of further insurgence did not deter Ferdinand from ordering the expulsion of all Protestant preachers and teachers from Lower Austria as well, in 1627. The following year an expulsion order was issued for all nobles in Inner Austria who did not convert within a year. Altogether, an estimated 100,000 refugees sold up and left the Austrian parts of the Habsburg dominions at this time.

There has been some debate about the actual longer-term political and social impact of these policies – whether they caused a substantial deterioration in agrarian conditions (see chapter 8), and whether the impact on the landed elite in Bohemia was as dramatic as it appeared, allowing for the ability of leading Catholic magnate families to accommodate themselves to the new regime and thereby adapt it to their own interests. Contemporaries were not slow to exploit the sensationalist dimensions both in text and in images, in an effort to alert a wider European opinion to the perceived dangers both of further conflict and of compromise.[5] Nevertheless, the severity of Habsburg policies in Bohemia, and to a lesser extent in Moravia, was

notable even by the standards of that harsh generation, when toleration was considered a sign of weakness. The emigration of an estimated 150,000 refugees from Bohemia alone gives some indication of
the post-war conditions created by government militancy, cynicism
and military self-help.

These years also brought economic chaos. Much of Europe experienced monetary dislocation in the early 1620s, only partially or
remotely related to warfare, but in the Empire political uncertainty
contributed to a period of particularly rampant inflation and uncontrolled speculation, known as the '*Kipper- und Wipperjahre*' ('snipper
and weigher years') from all the coinage manipulation. A number of
private and seigneurial mints were set up, flooding the market with a
profusion of copper and tin coins of decreasing intrinsic value. The
poorer urban classes were particularly badly affected, since they were
rarely in a position to barter effectively, but international traders were
also severely hit because exchange rates were badly destabilised.
Numerous but sporadic riots occurred, for example in a number of
towns in Brandenburg required to pay taxes in old sound money. The
coinage edicts of Duke Frederick III of Holstein-Gottorp and of
Christian IV of Denmark reveal how anxious neighbouring princes
were to avoid the worst destabilising effects.[6] But in Bohemia those in
power made the most of the opportunity, in some instances with
striking cynicism: a major swindle was perpetrated in 1621–3, when
a minting consortium including Liechtenstein, Wallenstein, his
Calvinist Antwerp-born banker Jan de Witte and the Jewish
merchant Bassevi exploited the economic confusion after the Battle
of the White Mountain to make a huge profit, thereby also precipitating the state bankruptcy of 1623. Characteristically for such
upheavals, the main imperial officials took their own cuts of the
proceeds.

But protests over Bohemia from non-Catholic Europe remained
verbal only, and the Emperor did not face serious international repercussions. The war was soon extended westwards, since there was some
agreement that religious Counter-Reformation measures were
compatible with the political objectives of Maximilian of Bavaria and
even of the Spanish government. The Palatinate itself suffered heavy
human and material losses from both Mansfeld's and Tilly's armies,
but by 1622 Tilly and Spinola had occupied the remaining parts of the
electorate. The electoral title was transferred to Maximilian as a
reward for his leadership of the League.[7] Further north, the next
Catholic objectives were the Westphalian and Lower Saxon Circles,[8]
where there was a large number of secularised bishoprics, some of
them of considerable political and international significance. Tilly's
move in that direction by 1625 emphasised the urgency of defensive
reorganisation amongst the Protestant princes.

Christian IV, Gustav Adolf and Wallenstein (1625–30)

The later 1620s and early 1630s are a particularly complex phase in the Thirty Years War because of rapid military movement within Germany itself and shifting international interference. Ferdinand had recognised that he could not continue to rely on Maximilian's army after the end of the Bohemian War, and in 1625 accepted Wallenstein's offer of a mercenary imperial army which, given his lack of resources, the Emperor could only hope to control indirectly, if at all. A new force was thus introduced in the German conflict, with aims different from those of Tilly. The Spanish contingents in the Empire were also still sizeable, but Philip IV (like his father) considered the Netherlands his primary objective, for which the security of the military routes from northern Italy to Brussels (either through Franche Comté and Lorraine or through the Valtellina, round Lake Constance and through the Palatinate) were essential. In France, Louis XIII's government, by 1624 increasingly influenced by Richelieu, gradually abandoned its pacific attitude towards Spain, in favour of policies seeking to break the Habsburg hold in northern Italy with the help of the Duke of Savoy and the Doge of Venice. Richelieu even tentatively associated with the Protestant flank, through the Dutch – in spite of the domestic implications of such religious ambivalence. James VI/I, after the humiliation of the unpopular Spanish marriage plans for the Prince of Wales in 1623, turned towards the French, but the accession of the now French-married Charles in 1625 did not make Stuart policy any more predictable or reliable. In fact, popular resentment in England was readily aroused against closer contact either with Catholic France or with the Dutch commercial rivals, and Charles played a diminishing role on the continent thereafter, particularly as his domestic difficulties increased (see chapter 2). Even the United Provinces themselves, agreed though they might be on the need for defence of some kind, hardly presented a particularly solid front. This was one of the few states in Europe where a kind of 'public opinion' could exert decisive influence against dynastic interests: religious–political opposition to the foreign policy of the Orange-Nassau family never quite disappeared, not even during the crisis leading up to and following the long-awaited Spanish onslaught and the loss of Breda to Spinola in 1625. Maurits of Orange-Nassau died shortly before its fall, and only later in the 1620s did his successor, Frederik Hendrik, begin to win the initiative against the experienced Spanish forces in the Netherlands.

The involvement of the Scandinavian monarchies made this highly fluid situation more complex. Although Christian IV and Gustav Adolf were both staunch Lutherans, traditional rivalry between the two dynasties had ensured that relations had been anything but cordial for a very long time (see chapter 2). The personal meeting between the two monarchs at Halmstad in late February and early March 1619, at a time when their relations were relatively calm, had been cordial but politically unproductive because of their incompatible interests. By the mid-1620s, in spite of growing awareness of the threat to Protestantism in Germany, each monarch was committed very much to his own territorial and personal dynastic ambitions, making co-operation quite unthinkable. Denmark–Norway was still regarded as the dominant economic and military power, but Christian's policies in pursuit of control of the Baltic since 1613 had led to the formation of a defensive alliance between the United Provinces, Gustav Adolf and a number of Hansa cities[9] led by Lübeck and Hamburg. Christian therefore turned his main attention to his north-German interests, by means of which he might counterbalance Swedish expansion in the eastern Baltic. First, he needed to look after his position as Duke of Holstein (in which capacity he had a seat in the German imperial assembly and a leading role in the Lower Saxon Circle). Secondly, he claimed administration on behalf of his younger son, Frederik, of the secularised bishoprics of Bremen, Verden, Osnabrück and Halberstadt, which would give him political and fiscal control over the lower Elbe and Weser rivers – an ambition he had entertained since at least 1616, when he founded the fortified port of Glückstadt on the mouth of the Elbe. By 1624 Prince Frederik had indeed become administrator or coadjutor of the bishoprics, and the hostility of many north-German princes and Hansa towns had diminished with the growing imperial threat. The United Provinces, too, were turning to Denmark rather than the preoccupied Swedes for help against the Habsburgs. But Christian's plans for using this to consolidate his position against what he saw as the continuing Swedish threat led him into an overhasty military involvement. In order to pre-empt an encircling alliance between the western powers and Gustav, he accepted an ill-defined offer of assistance from James VI/I and the Dutch (the Hague Coalition) and, against the advice of the Danish aristocratic council, entered the Thirty Years War in 1625 as commander of the Lower Saxon Circle and at the head of a mercenary army hired for the defence of Protestantism.

Christian's decision has long been regarded as a typical example of political cynicism, self-delusion and ineptitude combined. The anti-Habsburg alliance never materialised, nor did much of the expected English subsidies, so Christian had to commit far greater personal and state resources than he originally intended. The warnings of the Danish aristocratic council soon seemed entirely justified, in that Christian could not act merely in his capacity as duke without drag-ging in his kingdoms. A man of great impulsive energy who seems to have lacked a clear long-term strategy, Christian overestimated his own abilities as politician and commander. His military intervention in the Empire ended in disaster at the Battle of Lutter against Tilly in 1626, and eventually brought severe retaliation in the shape of an occupation of the whole of Jutland and parts of Mecklenburg and Pomerania by the recently formed imperial army supplied by Wallenstein. Only the nomination of Wallenstein as 'general of the oceanic and baltic sea' in 1628 induced Christian and Gustav to overcome their deep mutual antagonisms and collaborate in the defence of Stralsund, and even this did not last. Wallenstein persuaded Christian to accept a generous peace at Lübeck in 1629, which restored the status quo (except for the administration of the bishoprics) in return for the king's promise not to intervene in the war again.

This brief so-called 'Danish phase' of the war caused severe physical damage and hardship in the Lower Saxon Circle (as well as having major repercussions in Denmark, outlined in chapter 2). It also showed up all the weaknesses in the anti-Habsburg front, to the point of making the collapse of Protestantism in northern Germany appear a real possibility. Responsibility has overwhelmingly been laid on Christian IV personally, but recent work suggests that, while the broad picture is basically correct, the king had two major disadvantages in addition to his own temperament. The western allies proved unreliable, and the Danish aristocratic council itself, concerned about Christian's domineering tendencies, failed to appreciate the genuine security interests of the kingdom to the extent of refusing to give him adequate backing.[10] In both these respects Gustav showed his greater statesmanship. He would not in 1625 commit himself before securing a stronger diplomatic position, and at home he had the backing of a relatively united aristocratic council, over which he was in any case dominant (since, in contrast to Denmark, Swedish kingship was no longer elective).

By 1628 the Habsburg position was as strong as it would ever be. With plans for control of the southern coast of the Baltic and for an alliance with Catholic Poland, it seemed likely that they might block the Dutch commercial artery in the Baltic: Dutch trade had already been seriously disrupted by Swedish advances against Poland and the imposition of tolls. Within the Empire Ferdinand felt sufficiently confident to promulgate the long-planned Edict of Restitution on 6 March 1629. This document, resulting partly from Jesuit pressure (via Ferdinand's confessor Lamormaini and others), partly from the Emperor's political aspirations and his own genuinely firm religious convictions, called for the restitution of all secularised church land lost by the Catholic Church since 1552, and for the enforcement of the Ecclesiastical Reservation of 1555, without any recognition of Calvinist claims and without concessions for religiously mixed towns. This could only be regarded as an outright challenge: an enforcement of the edict would have affected two archbishoprics, a dozen bish-oprics and hundreds of lesser church territories, and the Reformation itself could become threatened. The forces of Wallenstein did indeed initiate steps to secure military implementation, whilst Habsburg and Wittelsbach administrators were put forward to take over from the Protestants. Resistance was at first slight, but the sweeping potential political consequences of this policy soon caused grave reservations amongst the German princes, including Johann Georg of Saxony and even (for practical reasons) Wallenstein himself.

In addition, the Spanish position did not hold. Spinola was recalled in 1627, and the military effort was further disrupted by the Dutch capture of the Spanish treasure-fleet off Cuba the following year, upsetting Philip IV's system of revenue anticipation (see p. 37). Both branches of the Habsburg family also had to commit troops to the war of succession in Mantua (resulting from the decline of the senior line of the Gonzaga family and its extinction with the death of Duke Vincenzo II in December 1627). One of the claimants, Carlo Gonzaga, Duke of Nevers (descendant of a younger branch of the family) had the support of France, whilst the Habsburgs attempted (unsuccessfully in the end) to back a more distant relative, Prince Cesare Gonzaga of Molfetta. The crucial strategic position of Mantua for Spain's European military position, and the ability of Louis XIII to lead an army there in person in 1629 (after the fall of La Rochelle and the end of the Huguenot rebellion at home, to which we shall return in chapter 2), ensured a bitter and destructive war lasting until 1631, during which Mantua itself was sacked and hit by the plague.

The Mantuan war drew off considerable forces from Germany itself, and encouraged the French government to consolidate its diplomatic position. But it also added to the divisions on the imperial side within Germany, where the Catholic electors were opposed to foreign diver-sions and on the whole unsympathetic to Spanish interests. In addition, Wallenstein himself was regarded with growing resentment from 1627, partly because of his heavy-handed conscription and military entrepre-neurship, partly because of his elevation to the Duchy of Mecklenburg in place of an old German family. His critical attitude to the Edict of Restitution also brought him into complete opposition to Ferdinand's confessor, Lamormaini, and indeed to the only slightly less militant Maximilian of Bavaria – whose League army Wallenstein was over-shadowing, and whose confessor, Adam Contzen, was a Jesuit as inflex-ible as Lamormaini. By 1630 Wallenstein had command of around 130,000 troops, a colossal army for the period. It was supplied to a considerable extent from industrial enterprises on his Friedland estates, and financed by means of complex dealings with Ferdinand which the general used to secure his material and political strength. Enemy and allied territory alike had to bear quartering and contributions, enabling the Emperor's advisers to cast doubts on Wallenstein's reliability in the Counter-Reformation cause. At the 1630 rump meeting of electors at Regensburg (where the Protestants were represented by delegates only, in protest against the Edict), Maximilian made a formal demand for the dismissal of Wallenstein, while at the same time conducting negotiations with Richelieu's advisor, Père Joseph, should the need arise. Ferdinand, hoping that the end of the war was in sight and seeking support for the election of his eldest son as King of the Romans (heir-apparent to the imperial title), reluctantly gave in and dismissed Wallenstein on 13 August 1630, transferring the imperial army to Tilly. Wallenstein's banker, Jan de Witte, committed suicide at the prospect of bankruptcy. But contacts at the Habsburg court and the offer of a new army (at the time of a growing threat from Sweden) secured Wallenstein's return to imperial service late in 1631. Ultimately, his failure against the Swedes at Lützen in 1632, his growing ambivalence to the Habsburg cause, his hesitation and military caution, and eventually his over-indulgence in secret negotiations with all the major belligerents on both sides in 1633, made him so distrusted a figure that his opponents at court could accuse him (with considerable justification) of treason, and press the Emperor once more. Wallenstein, feared, disliked and isolated, was dismissed a second time in January 1634 and murdered in Eger six weeks later by some officers acting with the connivance of Vienna. His huge and relatively prosperous landed estates were divided between other opportunists: the bottomless imperial treasury, as always, seemed little better off, for all its attempts to prove that the general had been guilty of conspiratorial treason and his possessions thus liable to forfeiture.

Gustav Adolf and Swedish grand designs (1629–34)

Gustav Adolf (not unlike his Danish counterpart, Christian IV) was a lively, well-educated and domineering king. However, as well as being rather more abstemious in his drinking habits, Gustav was also a better politician. He had convinced the Swedish political nation of the need for his broadening foreign policy, and the Swedish hold on the Baltic coast from Karelia and Riga to Danzig was sufficient (especially after the conclusion of a six-year truce with Poland at Altmark in 1629, thanks to French mediation) to give Sweden a relatively free hand. Christian had already recognised the growing military strength of Sweden in 1624, and was hardly in a position to challenge it after 1629. Even the crucial port of Stralsund had recognised the new situation by accepting a permanent Swedish garrison in lieu of the Danish one. Gustav had also secured an industrial base for his war effort by developing Sweden's copper and iron industry, making Sweden as nearly self-sufficient in armaments as any European country. The existing recruitment system had been updated to provide a well-trained national army, and although Gustav continued to rely on a large supplementary contingent of mercenaries in his campaigns, he tried to discipline these as well. Finally, he developed new battlefield tactics derived from Maurits of Orange-Nassau's Dutch patterns, and introduced lighter effective field artillery to achieve better co-ordination of offensive and defensive strategies in action, giving the Swedes a durable advantage even after they had lost their charismatic commander.[11]

All of these factors help to explain the spectacular successes of Gustav after his landing in July 1630 in Germany. But he also had two major problems. One was the relative poverty of Sweden itself, especially in the face of the cost of mercenaries. Starting with about 40,000 men late in 1630, Gustav doubled that number within a year, and had 150,000 by the time of the Battle of Lützen in 1632. However, of this last number, at least four-fifths were mercenary. By 1631, in spite of various devices to maximise domestic revenue (including the alienation of crown lands, especially in the conquered Baltic provinces), there was no alternative to shifting the burden on to Germany itself, by imposing 'contributions' (war taxes) on East Prussia and other lands as they were occupied, and by imposing tolls on the Baltic ports. Both techniques had been adopted sporadically from 1627, but became a regular and fully-organised feature once the German campaign proper was under way. This approach, however, tended to lead inescapably to escalation because of the need for new annexations as the number of regiments grew, and the tolls for their part caused considerable hostility from the main traders in the Baltic, notably the Dutch and the English.

Gustav's second problem was his lack of allies: in one way he could regard that with relief, given Christian's experiences, but it placed an even heavier burden on Sweden. Initial contacts with France from 1629 had been unsuccessful, since Gustav was not willing to become an agent of Richelieu's specific policies. The French negotiators at Regensburg in 1630, however, mishandled contacts with the imperial side to such an extent that Louis XIII repudiated the terms of agreement, and therefore had to reconsider his relations with the Protestant powers. The resulting treaty of Bärwalde between France and Sweden in January 1631 was indicative of Gustav's diplomatic skill: France agreed to pay subsidies of 1 million *livres tournois* per annum to Sweden in return for nothing specific except a commitment to maintain an army of 30,000 foot-soldiers and 6000 cavalry in Germany, and a promise not to interfere with Catholicism where that already existed. Within the Empire, however, Gustav failed to win the support that he had hoped for. The two north-German electors, Johann Georg of Saxony and the ill-prepared Georg Wilhelm of Brandenburg, were attempting to adopt a neutralist stand in the hope of avoiding war within their own territories. Johann Georg, at least, also genuinely desired to preserve the old imperial constitution intact and prevent foreign intervention. But in February and March 1631, at a potentially very significant meeting of Protestant princes in Leipzig, he failed to give any clear lead in spite of his dominant position in the Empire. There were even indications that he might accept an understanding with the Emperor if the Edict of Restitution was modified. A concluding manifesto at Leipzig called for the formation of a defensive alliance of Protestants within the Empire, but Johann Georg evidently remained reluctant to abandon his conservative constitutionalist stance. He had made his position clear to the Swedes from the start, and was equally consistent with Vienna. Internal differences amongst the Catholic leaders might have suggested that a compromise really was possible – Maximilian of Bavaria even went as far as accepting an alliance with France in May 1631 to cover all eventualities. But in practice Johann Georg had little to hope for in terms of the Edict of Restitution as long as a hard line prevailed in the entourage of Emperor Ferdinand.

Habsburg intransigence, however, made the Swedish position no stronger, especially since most of the lesser north-German principalities were hesitant to exchange imperial pressure for Swedish occupation. Gustav's seizure and pillage of the Protestant Frankfurt-am-Oder in April 1631 hardly allayed these fears, and his failure to come to the relief of his first ally, the city of Magdeburg, besieged by Tilly, was even more damaging. There, however, the blame lay to a considerable degree on the two Protestant electors, who had perhaps understandably procrastinated and prevaricated over the co-ordination of an anti-Habsburg front. The sudden fall of Magdeburg on 10 May 1631 – its total destruction by pillaging and arson at enemy hands, with the loss of perhaps two-thirds of its population of 30,000 – made a neutralist stand more difficult to justify.[12] By August, Landgrave Wilhelm V of Hessen-Kassel and some other lesser north-German princes were willing to make firmer alliances with the Swedes, and Tilly's entry into Saxon territory forced even Johann Georg to follow suit early in September. The reluctant and mutually distrustful partnership between him and the impatient Gustav never became satisfactory to either side. The evaporation of the Saxon contingent at the Battle of Breitenfeld on 7 September 1631 would have turned it into a Protestant disaster, had not Swedish tactical flexibility filled the gap and ensured that Tilly suffered his first major defeat. The consequences of this battle for the course of the whole war were in the end inescapable: imperial ambitions in the Baltic were destroyed, Tilly was forced south with the remnants of his army, and much of central Germany lay exposed to Swedish occupation.

The sudden reversal of roles did not improve relations between Gustav and the German princes: they did not convert to enthusiasm for the new foreign power overnight, and had even less reason to do so as Gustav occupied vast areas in the west during the autumn. He extorted ransoms, loans and protection money from a number of cities, including by the spring of 1632 even Nuremberg and Munich, and these sums usefully supplemented the Saxon subsidies, the still small French contribution and the derisory Dutch one. With a tactlessness worthy of Wallenstein, he could also impose growing exactions in the form of quartering and supplies for his now huge forces: Nuremberg alone supplied bread in one summer month of 1632 to a value greater than Richelieu's annual subsidy. The total cost of the Swedish occupations is immeasurable because of the many concealed levies, but it is certain that Germany itself bore virtually the entire burden. The contribution of Sweden and Finland to the campaign in the Empire proper had by 1633 fallen to nearly one-twentieth of what it had been in 1630,[13] and although this favourable position for Sweden did not last, it justifies the hesitations of many of the German princes. '*Bellum se ipsum alet*' ('War will feed itself') was Gustav's principle in 1628, and remained the aim of his successors.

By the beginning of 1632, the Germans had little chance of protesting, for Gustav and his chancellor, Oxenstierna, at their headquarters in Mainz and Frankfurt respectively, had control over half the Empire. Admittedly the Saxon army had also reoccupied Bohemia, bringing back a number of émigrés led by Matthias Thurn (who proceeded to set up a new directory in Prague), but already by May 1632 Wallenstein and his newly re-established army had expelled them. Not only was Bohemia thereby exposed to a second dose of confiscations and repression, but Johann Georg's reputation was again tarnished.

Gustav therefore naturally became the centre of far-flung international diplomatic manoeuvres. He had important contacts with Russia to avoid any renewed Polish threat, and Richelieu, whose simultaneous approaches to Maximilian and Gustav were now becoming embarrassingly self-contradictory, found to his alarm that he could make little headway in persuading Gustav of the validity of French aims. Nevertheless, long-term Swedish prospects did not make a great deal of sense. Gustav had gone far beyond his original intentions and Sweden's defensive interests, and the possibility of an outright victory against the Emperor raised as many questions as it solved. How much would Sweden keep as a permanent base for security and as material compensation for the war effort? What was to be the constitutional position of the German princes in relation to the Swedish Crown? In terms of the laws of war, Gustav made undisguised and blunt claims on all but his active allies, and this hardly created a sound basis for genuine co-operation, even when the idea of a more positive, permanent Protestant military and civilian alliance under Swedish leadership began to take shape in the autumn of 1632. What to Gustav and his chancellor, Oxenstierna, seemed military sense was regarded by most German princes as a potential destruction of their constitutional rights or indeed of the very substance of the Empire. Johann Georg, in particular, was as always opposed to anything which might go beyond limited reform of the imperial institutions, and his rather too independent but able commander, von Arnim (who had resigned from Wallenstein's army in protest against the Edict of Restitution), made the most of the ever murkier political jungle to conduct secret negotiations with, amongst others, his former principal. The Swedes could never be quite sure of the reliability of any but their most dependent allies.

The Battle of Lützen on 16 November 1632 brought all the grand designs of Swedish overlordship down to earth. Gustav himself was killed, which made what could otherwise be described as an imperial defeat seem like victory to the Habsburgs (even if it did little to restore the increasingly tarnished reputation of Wallenstein). The Swedish army held together, but was soon weakened by shortage of pay. Although Oxenstierna was able to consolidate the Swedish position and bring the alliance of Protestant princes in the four south-western circles of the Empire to fruition in the League of Heilbronn of 13 April 1633, the two Protestant electors again refused to join, making the League only a limited success. It all but died with the defeat of the Swedish forces led by Gustav Horn and their ally Bernhard of Saxe-Weimar at Nördlingen in September 1634 – a battle which inaugurated the long-drawn-out and more deliberately destructive second phase of the war, faster moving and very wide-ranging, but rarely politically decisive and certainly devoid of any grand design.

Swedish intervention had clearly saved German Protestantism. The Empire, however, could never be the same again. The imperial plans of 1628 and 1629, and Gustav's of 1632 – equally unrealistic in their own ways – had destroyed some of the basic compromises of a century or more of imperial development. No participant could forget how close the German lands had come to constitutional reorganisation and centralisation under either Habsburg or Swedish auspices, and the lesson was well learnt in time for the peace negotiations of the 1640s.

The elusiveness of peace (1634–48)

The main participants up to 1632 had already demonstrated the timeless tendency for military momentum to lead to ever more monstrous schemes for final victory. The Battle of Nördlingen of 1634, however, by removing the direct Swedish and allied threat in southern Germany, especially in Bavaria, created the opportunity for a compromise, which was made all the more urgent by the exhaustion of much of the countryside in the south from military exactions, and by the fears that an imperial recovery might occur with fresh Spanish assistance on the Rhine. Johann Georg still adhered to his entrenched constitutionalist position, and it was thus natural that he should welcome the negotiations from November 1634 that led to the Peace of Prague of 30 May 1635 between him and the Emperor. More remarkable was the fact that Ferdinand should have come to appreciate the advantages of a compromise. Imperial privy councillors such as Eggenberg and Stralenberg had all along been in no doubt that implementation of the Edict would make peace unattainable, especially when earlier promises of security to the loyal Protestant princes such as Johann Georg were not honoured. But Ferdinand's Jesuit advisors had in 1630 rejected suggestions of political compromise of this kind and had rejected Johann Georg's call for at least a fair hearing for both sides in disputed ecclesiastical dominions. Instead, they had advocated as total an enforcement as possible in the name of divine justice, and delays with regard to Electoral Saxony were to be tactical and temporary only. Inevitably, Johann Georg had been pushed into the arms of the Swedes, but Ferdinand and his Jesuit confessor, Lamormaini, had retained their faith in the feasibility of the Edict. More practical men, perhaps even Tilly and Maximilian, might have moments of doubt about the wisdom of such an approach, for example after the reduction to ashes of Magdeburg (one of the archbishoprics affected by the Edict), and yet elsewhere, for example in Augsburg, a full re-Catholicisation was successfully and quite peaceably imposed against the will of the city council and the great majority of the inhabitants, thereby apparently vindicating the extremists in Vienna. It took years of increasingly indecisive but destructive fighting, culminating in 1635 in assurances from the imperial privy councillors and even from Maximilian that there were really no resources left for the continuation of war, before imperial resolution was weakened. Even then, Ferdinand would not abandon his crusading mentality in favour of political realities until he was reassured by the Empress's confessor, the Capuchin Quiroga (speaking for the Spanish party at court) and by a conference of theologians that he would not endanger his own salvation by doing so.

In fact the Peace of Prague was clearly in the end favourable to the Emperor's interests in a number of ways, for Johann Georg had been sufficiently anxious for peace to make significant concessions. The Edict of Restitution was 'suspended' for 40 years (tantamount to cancellation in the eyes of the Protestants), but ecclesiastical land was to be returned to (or left with) the possessors of 1627, and the *Reichskammergericht* consisting half of Catholics and half of

Protestants was to handle disputes. Although Johann Georg's son, August, was appointed administrator of Magdeburg, Protestant ecclesiastical administrators were to be denied a say in the imperial assembly. Maximilian of Bavaria would retain his palatine electoral title and lands, but no prince was to maintain a separate army. The Peace was open to others for acceptance, and a majority of princes in northern Germany soon agreed to it, including Georg Wilhelm of Brandenburg, who was evidently more concerned about Swedish claims than he was about the fact that the Peace contained no recognition of Calvinism. No concern was shown, either, for the strong Lutheran groups in southern Germany and for those imperial cities there which had Protestant minorities or majorities; their interests were abandoned virtually completely. But at least there was a practical and real prospect of peace in the torn Empire.

The settlement, however, had two crucial weaknesses in that neither France nor Sweden was given grounds for acceptance. On the contrary, the Peace of Prague was intended by both principals as a means of achieving German unity against foreign intervention itself. Richelieu's fear of a Habsburg revival therefore led him not only to declare war on Spain in 1635 and draw up a treaty with the United Provinces but also to back Bernhard of Saxe-Weimar and Wilhelm of Hessen-Kassel in their refusal to sign the Peace. Although Ferdinand at long last had his son duly elected King of the Romans at Regensburg in 1636, paving the way for the undisputed succession of the next Habsburg as Ferdinand III shortly afterwards, the Empire could still not be regarded as stabilised.

In the north, Swedish forces under Johann Banér had already revived in 1636 and could now treat the two Protestant electorates as outright enemies. Battles at Wittstock in Brandenburg in 1636 and at Chemnitz just south of the electoral Saxon capital of Dresden in 1639 restored the Swedish military reputation. Banér's destructive campaigns were also extended over much of Bohemia, and under his successor, Lennart Torstensson, Leipzig itself was taken from Johann Georg in 1642 after a second Battle of Breitenfeld. The resilience of the Swedish military machine was further underlined when Christian IV risked another intervention, only to be defeated by Torstensson in a rapid series of campaigns during 1643–5. Soon back in the Empire, Torstensson pressurised Johann Georg into a separate peace in 1645, defeated the imperial army again and threatened Vienna itself by 1646, while in 1647 his successor as Swedish commander, Carl Gustav Wrangel, joined up with French forces under Marshal Turenne in the south. Bavaria was again devastated, this time for two years running, while Prague was in the midst of another Swedish onslaught when the final peace treaties were signed in Münster and Osnabrück in Westphalia in November 1648.

Although the essentials of the Peace of Prague had been confirmed at the imperial assembly at Regensburg in 1640, Ferdinand's reliance on Spanish assistance had undermined his stature within the Empire. In 1640 the new Elector of Brandenburg, Frederick William (sometimes known as 'the Great Elector'), withdrew from the Prague arrangement, and the subsequent widely-flung Swedish and French campaigns made it inevitable that the Emperor could not recreate the 1635 situation. The drawn-out negotiations in Westphalia from 1645 themselves reflected the enormous complexity of what was at stake. Interminable squabbling over rank and precedence were not merely matters of protocol but also highly symbolic reflections of shifting political assumptions: as in all such multi-sided negotiations, agreements had to be reached regarding who was entitled to speak for whom. Equally, the number of foreign powers claiming interest in the outcome ensured long delays, as the rapidly growing delegations from 1645 onwards had not only to find suitable accommodation in one of the two fairly small towns where the negotiations were held (Münster and Osnabrück), but also had to secure effective communication with each other and with their home governments. Spain was too distracted elsewhere (see chapter 7) to lend substantial support either to the papacy or to their central European allies, but the Austrian Habsburg, French and Swedish government, were all deeply involved. Although Richelieu had died in 1642, his policies were continued by his successor, Mazarin, on behalf of the boy king Louis XIV. In Sweden, Chancellor Oxenstierna still influenced foreign policy, and although Queen Christina increasingly leant towards the more compromise-orientated Johann Adler Salvius in these matters, the Swedish delegation at Osnabrück remained at the centre of Protestant negotiations. The Dutch were less involved, since they achieved their essential aim of independence from and peace with Spain through separate negotiations which came to fruition on 30 January 1648.

The consequences of war and peace

The two treaties that made up the peace of Westphalia (reached at Münster for the Catholic parties including France, and at Osnabrück 30 miles away for the Swedes and the domestic issues relating to the Protestant princes) recognised the real outcome of the Thirty Years War in a number of respects. It confirmed that the Empire as a whole would not undergo consolidation of the kind experienced by other European states; instead, the legal basis was created for unchallenged princely or territorial absolutism, in that each prince was given territorial sovereignty (*Landeshoheit*) even over foreign policy, although this was not to be used against the Emperor. The imperial office became representative head of what was in effect a loose confederation, while the imperial assembly would meet permanently and act as arbiter of the Emperor's authority (Treaty of Osnabrück, article 8). Since majority interests were safeguarded in the new imperial assembly, to the extent of allowing a minority veto in all matters where the assembly could not be considered a united body – not just in religion, that is, but also in all the political and fiscal matters somehow attributable to it[14] – the imperial assembly came to resemble a permanent ambassadorial conference rather than a parliament.

The Edict of Restitution and Peace of Prague were both cancelled, and the basis for ecclesiastical territorial settlements and compensations was fixed at 1 January 1624. The Ecclesiastical Reservation of 1555 was made applicable to Catholic and Protestant church lands alike, and Protestant prince-administrators were now allowed representation at the imperial assembly. The *jus reformandi* (right of reform) was modified so that each prince would retain power to control public and private church life in his own territory as it had been in 1624, and not necessarily as his own beliefs dictated. Calvinists were recognised not as a third party but as Reformed adherents of a version of the Protestant Augsburg Confession. All other religious groups were thereby excluded from recognition: Anabaptists, Unitarians, Bohemian and Moravian Brethren, and others. Ferdinand's principal gain from the Peace was the exclusion of the Habsburg hereditary lands from its terms, especially its religious guarantees, thereby retrospectively confirming the confessional absolutism which had already destroyed the Protestant majorities existing in many of his lands at the beginning of the century. Although the Protestant delegates at Osnabrück had demanded certain safeguards for religious minorities not covered by the 1624 date, no agreement could be reached on this, beyond a general exhortation to 'toleration' and a confirmation for a limited period of the right of compensation for minorities expelled for religious reasons. Ferdinand himself reluctantly accepted some toleration for Protestants in Silesia only, and for Protestant nobles in Lower Austria, but otherwise insisted on complete religious conformity in his own lands. In the rest of the Empire, however, the geographic mosaic of religious affiliations was made permanent and some rulers even began to move in the direction of more genuine toleration – notably Elector Frederick William of Brandenburg and Karl Ludwig of the Rhenish Palatinate (son of Frederick V, and incumbent of a newly created eighth electorate in lieu of the title which Maximilian of Bavaria was allowed to keep).

At the international level, both France and Sweden gained a firm position as guarantors of the Peace. The territorial provisions for French control of the Emperor's lands in Alsace and for other positions on the upper Rhine were later to cause further difficulties (see p. 399); but in essence the Spanish land-bridges to the Netherlands and to the Austrian Habsburg territories were cut. Sweden was awarded a cash payment of 5 million Reichsthaler, retained a dominant position on the Oder, Elbe and Weser rivers, and kept a number of bishoprics, including Bremen and Verden (later of great significance in its relations with Denmark). Oxenstierna and the Elector of Brandenburg split Pomerania between them, with the vital part of Stettin remaining under Swedish control, but the administration of the archbishopric of Magdeburg was also to come to Brandenburg on the death of the holder, Prince August of Saxony. Johann Georg himself was confirmed in his possession of Lusatia, for which he had originally joined the Emperor at the beginning of the war. In addition, a number of other territorial and legal provisions were made, confirming for example the independence of the Swiss confederation. Articles 59, 69 and 70 of the Treaty of Münster also sought to re-establish free trade, notably on the Rhine, but these provisions were not readily implemented in practice.

Politically and dynastically, the Peace could be regarded as a sound compromise. No doubt it lacked clarity regarding the Rhine frontier – intentionally so, since Richelieu and Mazarin had long-term designs against the Spanish Habsburgs – but its internal provisions, while appearing to block development of any form of state institutions at imperial level, encouraged them at territorial level. A nightmare for political theorists, a paradise for the legal profession, the Empire safeguarded a multitude of different administrative systems and political eccentricities for another century and a half.[15]

In a sense, however, the war had not done much in terms of the Empire beyond making permanent a political compromise just about reached in 1555. Why so much human suffering and material damage merely for that? One could not now accept the view held by contemporaries that war was divine punishment for sin, or the deductions made accordingly by earlier historians regarding the importance of religious motives alone as fuel in the conflagration. But while it is absurd to emphasise religious beliefs out of political context at a time when the two were so inextricably intertwined at all levels, it is equally unsatisfactory to dismiss religion merely as an excuse for political aims. The pervasive religious-orientated writings of the time, with their acceptance of belief in omens and supernatural manifestations (not to mention the contemporary acceptance of witchcraft even by learned and rational men), remind us of the strength of such feelings, and their effect in producing the same kinds of blind prejudice and mutual misconceptions which crudely categorised ideologies and zealous confessional divides create today.

Cardinal Richelieu and Christian IV may have conceived their policies largely in pragmatic terms, with crown interests clearly prevailing, just as Maurits of Orange-Nassau and Johann Georg were essentially politicians, and Wallenstein even more so. Whatever sense of political direction they may have had did not always fit easily with inflexible religious agendas. But even the most cynical statesman or leader needed to pay lip-service to religious justifications in order to win broader ideological support amongst subjects and allies. And if the war aims of some participants were essentially secular – which in no way implies that their exponents were not devout and sincere Christian believers in their own ways – those of others are less readily classified. Until 1635, as we have seen, Ferdinand II clearly had no doubts about the Old Testament sanctity of his mission, and was encouraged in this attitude to politics by his even more militant confessor, Lamormaini. These two, more than the politically subtler Maximilian, must consequently bear much of the responsibility for the prolongation of the war after 1629; right until the last weeks before the conclusion of the Peace of Prague, Lamormaini remained adamantly against any compromise over the Edict of Restitution. The Jesuits, like the papacy, certainly wanted to recover church land for its own sake (once again demonstrating the indivisibility of material and ideological motives), but Lamormaini cannot be said to have subordinated the dictates of his conscience to worldly practicalities. He saw everything in religious terms, even refusing to believe that Richelieu and Louis XIII would not themselves join in a Catholic alliance with the Emperor against Protestantism – a hope which appears slightly less unrealistic only if we remember that the *dévot* party at the French court was not finally deprived of political influence until the Day of Dupes on 11 November 1630 (see p. 45).

The instinctive assumption of divine guidance (which later generations might regard as bigotry or wilful ignorance) was not a Catholic monopoly. It is in the nature of most forms of Protestantism that clerics in practice had fewer opportunities for independent political intervention, unless they were actual court preachers. In any case Protestantism was sufficiently threatened and internally divided during much of the war for it to remain without any serious plans for total victory. This, however, did not necessarily in itself create a more flexible religious atmosphere: the government-in-exile of Frederick of the Palatinate, while dominated by his advisor Christian of Anhalt, even in defeat remained hostile to the idea of toleration of either Lutherans or Catholics; and the Dresden court hardly welcomed Calvinists as long as someone like the aggressive Hoé von Hoënegg (d. 1645) was first preacher.

Of the major statesmen on the anti-Habsburg side, however, it was probably Gustav who initially came nearest to perceiving himself (and being heralded) as defender of the faith. In this capacity he too, like Ferdinand, must take a considerable share of the responsibility for prolonging the war, since it is difficult to conceive Richelieu achieving that on his own in the early 1630s. But, unlike Ferdinand, Gustav was a commander and a pragmatic ruler, and his objectives were far more complex as a result. In addition to Swedish interests in limiting imperial inroads in the Baltic and its trade, in preventing Polish-Habsburg collaboration in the military field, and in keeping warfare away from Sweden itself, Gustav had also already emphasised religious motives in 1628 when he consulted his *råd* (aristocratic council) and obtained its support for his foreign policy. Clearly an imperial Counter-Reformation victory in the Empire could prejudice hard-earned Swedish religious stability (see p. 60). Like Tilly, Gustav and his officers insisted on at least the principle of religious unity and motivation in his army, and no disciplinary and propaganda efforts were spared to approach this ideal of a godly army, even when the growth in the proportion of mercenaries made realisation more difficult. No doubt both Tilly and Gustav found that army chaplains were useful for generating ideological motivation, but it would be a distortion of seventeenth-century reality to regard this with too much cynicism. The contrast with Wallenstein's far more worldly approach is certainly indisputable.

This brings us back to a problem outlined at the beginning: what relevance did the beliefs of Jesuit-educated generals and orthodox Lutheran kings have for the ordinary civilians and troops who were the real victims of the war? Dynastic ambitions, territorial greed and political gambles were not likely to be of much interest to them, beyond being inescapable parts of the unequal and exploitative system with which they had to live. The historian finds only indirect evidence of popular mentalities in the German lands – even less for the Slavonic areas further east – and it is fair to say that a great deal of research remains to be done on this subject. Broadsheets and pamphlets intended for popular consumption were mostly written by individuals whose social position was liable to have made them unreliable spokesmen for the common people. In any case we cannot assume that those who could read, or could afford to buy visual prints, both believed what they saw and also were in a position to convinced the illiterate majority.[16] The pulpit, too, was a major influence on popular opinion, but was it as authoritative as the clergy might like to believe?

We cannot answer these questions with any degree of conviction. But we can underline with certainty one common characteristic of ordinary life during the period: the desire for security and for the preservation of the local community and its interests from war. If religion could give comfort in adversity and confidence in times of success, the realities of daily life were nevertheless almost everywhere overwhelmingly threatening for the traditional community existence which most people regarded as the real object of their loyalty. Some local officials, military entrepreneurs and suppliers profited from the presence of armies, but in wartime conditions this merely emphasised the insecurity and iniquities of life. The uncontrollable accidents of harvest failure and infectious diseases (including notably typhus and the virulent outbreaks of plague of the 1630s) were manifestly transmitted and multiplied through the presence of troops. Most armies lived off the land, Tilly's and Gustav's as well as Wallenstein's, but while Wallenstein, for example, had been careful to avoid totally ruining those occupied territories on which his army could live, such considerations were increasingly abandoned from the 1630s when troop movements ranged more widely and long-term designs became impracticable. As demobilisation finally neared completion in 1650, after lengthy further multilateral negotiations in Nuremberg over the paying-off of mercenaries and the removal of garrisons, the picture was very bleak in some parts of the Empire.

Worst affected, inevitably, were the provinces most exposed to recurrent army movements, from the northern territories of Mecklenburg and Pomerania, through Brandenburg, Silesia and Thuringia to parts of the Palatinate, Württemberg, Bavaria and the south. Historians now generally accept that the effects of pillage and random destruction were significantly worse in many parts of the Empire than, for example, in the Netherlands – partly because the ever-shifting front lines exposed large areas to an apparently endless succession of destruction by opposing sides, partly because the armies were so large and the pay and discipline so poor in the German lands that the downward spiral of violence and vindictiveness increased significantly as the war became more chaotic in the 1630s. Estimates of overall population losses through migration and death are very uncertain, but examples from specific localities can give some indication of both human and material losses. When Olmütz (Olomouc) in Moravia was finally evacuated by Swedish and allied troops in 1650, a commissar reported to Vienna that only 23 out of 77 houses of nobles and clergy were habitable, and 145 out of 623 burgher houses, the rest being either severely damaged or destroyed. In addition, all 656 houses outside the city boundary were in ruins and the population had been reduced from 30,000 to less than 1700 in the previous decade. In a rather wider context, an inventory of 1651 itemising the debts of 19 free boroughs (excluding Prague) indicated that 11½ million florins were owed, mostly to the military (and half of it to the imperial army itself, rather than to enemy forces). Such debts continued to weigh on the urban economies for the rest of the century. Rural conditions were just as grim. The indiscriminate plundering of friend and foe, and the fact that armies had to live off the land, could make conditions intolerable. The English diplomat William Crowne in 1636 reported one village as having suffered pillage 28 times during the previous two years, and twice in one day. One can hardly blame the inhabitants of such areas either for violent self-defence against any army in sight or for eventually abandoning their homes altogether to seek refuge elsewhere. Deaths and migration combined accounted for population losses of 50 per cent or more in many parts of Bohemia and Moravia, and the resulting shortage of manpower for unoccupied peasant holdings was in the long run more serious than the fairly readily replaceable material losses of rudimentary implements and seed grain. More insidious, perhaps, were the different expectations of landowners and magnates who had taken over sequestrated property since 1620 or ended up with de facto possession because of the major upheavals of the war. Even Wallenstein's well-administered Duchy of Friedland fell into destructively exploitative hands after 1634, and agrarian conditions all over Bohemia regressed under growing seigneurial oppression and state demands until the outbreak of peasant rebellions from 1680 onwards. Added to the destruction of provincial self-government and the undermining of Bohemian religious and cultural traditions by the Habsburgs, the whole process amounted to a disaster for this and other parts of the Empire.[17]

Examples and evidence are readily found to substantiate similar conclusions for other parts of the Empire, and there can be no doubt that the war really was immensely destructive. But the historian must nevertheless not be blinded to the fact that much contemporary written evidence was intended specifically to create an overwhelming impression in the reader, whether it was propaganda or petition material. Anyone who has worked with seventeenth-century sources will be only too aware that the language used for complaints, petitions and requests was highly rhetorical and formalised even to the point of stereotype. Recent work, in particular, has confirmed that for some communities the Thirty Years War was no worse than other wars (notably, for example, those of Louis XIV in the Rhine area in the last decades of the century), and recovery was often remarkably rapid. Magdeburg itself only had a few hundred surviving households at the time of the Peace of Prague, but was well on the way to recovering its former position a decade later. Leipzig was besieged recurrently in the early 1640s and occupied by the Swedes from 1642 to 1650, but its trade was not destroyed and it emerged from the war as a flourishing commercial and cultural centre. Lübeck and Hamburg were hardly affected at all and could benefit from accelerated wartime demand and market turnover. The towns of Lippe and the north-west, though damaged in parts, were able to turn war contributions into an economic catalyst if their officials succeeded in ensuring that impositions were mostly spent locally. Even migration itself, apart from the indisputable human suffering caused by displacement, could also have a beneficial effect, frequently under-recorded in the sources. The initial wave of refugees from Bohemia, settling in Pima, Dresden, Zittau and other Saxon towns, contributed to the printing industry and other fine crafts there. Alsace and the north-western parts of the Empire including Holstein also benefited in the long run from the losses recorded in severely hit areas of the centre. The Thirty Years War certainly contributed to, and sometimes accelerated, shifts in the central European economy, for example by cutting trade routes in the south. However, as we shall see in chapter 4, some of these changes were part of a much broader European pattern already taking shape before the beginning of the war.

If one's perception of the war thus varies with the area examined, most historians agree that the war is of decisive importance in the seventeenth century for two main reasons. First, it caused dislocation and human misery on a scale which was not soon forgotten. William Crowne, travelling in Germany in 1636, wrote how his party:

> came to a poor little Village called Neunkirchen, where we found one house a burning when we came and not any body in the Village, here we were constrained to tarry all night, for it grew very late, and no Towne neere by 4 English miles, spending the night walking up and downe in feare, with Carrabines in our hands, because we heard Peeces [guns] discharg'd off in Woods about us, and with part of the coles of the consumed house his Excellency had his meat rosted for supper, the next morning early, his Excellency went to view the Church, which we found rifled with the pictures and Altars abused, in the Church-yard, we saw a dead body scraped out of the grave, in another place out of the Church-yard, there lay another dead body, into many of the houses wee entered, and found them all empty. From this miserable place we departed, and heard after, that they in the Village fled by reason of the sicknesse, and set that house on fire at their departure, that passengers might not be infected.[18]

Such a picture of war, fear, plague and disorientation, giving rise also to the mercenary cynicism and escapism portrayed in Grimmelshausen's novel *Simplicius Simplicissimus*, would soon be familiar not just to those in the war zones of Germany but also (if usually for shorter periods) to the inhabitants of Poland or Catalonia, Naples or Jutland, Bohemia or Ireland. Since only the last of these conflicts was not causally related to the Thirty Years War, the meaning of 'general war' becomes clearer. In the German lands there was the additional bitterness of recognising that from 1635 the conflict was being prolonged primarily by foreign powers.

While direct damage to the economic and social fabric of the many war zones is evident, it is, secondly, also clear that the period had long-term consequences for civilians outside the main war zones. The Thirty Years War led to virtual bankruptcy in many of the participating states and principalities, in effect paving the way, as we shall see in the next chapter, for domestic revolt and internal violence. While the war was in progress few governments had any option but to strengthen the military and, in the process, attempt to control unrest by any authoritarian and often ruthlessly arbitrary means at their disposal. Subjects in all but the remotest communities were liable to feel this in some way. At the lower end of the social spectrum, enlistment or impressment became a real possibility (or threat) in the 1630s as the size of armies expanded dramatically and as losses from disease and in battle increased. Inevitably, social relations also changed under the strain of supporting an increasingly intolerable war effort. In France, as we shall see, tax revolts by the 1630s often led to some degree of collusion between different social orders against central authority. The use made of the traditional entitlement of nobles to keep their own private armies or to garrison their manors, while rarely generating anything quite as uncontrollable as the enterprising autonomy of Wallenstein, nevertheless demonstrated to the Crown just how dangerous such local resistance could become, not just for tax collectors themselves but for the very foundation of royal authority. The traditional allegiances of the Renaissance state alone were no longer sufficient to sustain the huge new burdens created by protracted European conflict.

2 Government in wartime Europe

The Thirty Years War has to be regarded as a composite European conflict (see chapter 1), and although much of the worst fighting was on German soil, the direct repercussions in northern Italy, France, part of the Netherlands and Denmark were very serious. Military and fiscal burdens caused devastating local or provincial revolts in Spain and France, and contributed to irreversible social and political change in the Scandinavian monarchies. Sweden and Poland linked east and west, even though the Baltic conflicts and the upheavals in Russia and the Ukraine (not to mention changes in the Ottoman Empire, to which we shall return in chapter 7) sprang from tensions unconnected with the German conflict. The Stuart monarchy, initially implicated in various ways in the continental struggles, later became totally absorbed in its own troubles, yet parallels between English and continental experiences at least at the general level remain discernible until the 1640s, and some contemporaries were keenly conscious of the implications for other monarchies of the English civil war.

The early seventeenth century used to be described as a period leading towards the consolidation of 'absolute' (unlimited) monarchy in much of Europe, culminating after the mid-century disruptions in the final stage of institutionalised *ancien-régime* monarchy which lasted more or less until the French Revolution. Contemporary reality, however, is likely to have been quite different: centralisation was not an altogether deliberate policy, as it was later for Joseph II or for the Hohenzollerns, nor could it have been in the actual conditions of early seventeenth-century governmental practice. Rudimentary, unprofessional and venal administrations of very small size worked in the name of idiosyncratic and mostly untrained princes, attempting, with a mixture of pragmatism and desperation, to deal with day-to-day crises caused by revenue shortfalls and recurrent insolvency, military overextension, over-mighty subjects, centrifugal provincialism, deeply engrained social and intellectual conservatism, religious fears and the inertia of ineffective and inflexibly self-conscious institutions. One needs to recall that no state was a coherent whole. Although geographically one country, France was in practice in 1600 not much more of a political unit than the Spanish peninsula: not only was there a long tradition of autonomy in Brittany and in the southern *pays d'états* (provinces with their own assembly of Estates), but the scale of revolts in most parts of the kingdom until 1675 – and perhaps even the

Camisard wars in the south at the end of the reign of Louis XIV – demonstrated the fragility and limitations of Bourbon royal power in remoter areas. Perhaps it is not entirely far-fetched to regard Brittany and Catalonia at the beginning of the century as comparable in their fierce independence from their respective Crowns, or to see their position paralleled in some respects in the German lands, in provinces such as the Lusatias, which retained their identity and separate political life after being handed over to the Elector of Saxony as part of a high-level political trade-off in the early stages of the Thirty Years War. Recent work has in fact amply confirmed that early seventeenth-century monarchy, in theory based on grand (even divinely sanctioned) assertions, was very limited in practice because of largely insuperable geographic and administrative obstacles. This explains why local loyalties were so much stronger than 'national' ones (where such existed), and why the seigneur, the urban patrician or merchant, or the church dignitary could exercise a much more immediate influence on community life than the solitary and sometimes alien local royal official. As we shall see, these limitations, combined with the continuation of factional strife especially amongst the not yet fully tamed nobility, and compounded by the economic instability affecting much of the continent from the 1620s (chapters 3 and 4), made the history of government everywhere in Europe a very uncertain struggle, the political outcome of which was anything but predictable.

In most European states – monarchies and republics – there was some tradition of provincial and national assemblies of Estates, representing the upper orders in various ways and sometimes limiting the freedom of action of the head of state. The continental assemblies have been overshadowed by the English parliament, which was indisputably far more significant in the long run and underwent spectacular development in the middle decades of the seventeenth century. Nevertheless, some of the continental assemblies were not without significance. The most influential of these, the Swedish *riksdag* (Estates General), although reaching political maturity relatively late by Western standards, was arguably also more broadly representative than most, and certainly more than the English parliament, since it continued to have four Estates, the fourth consisting of regional representatives of the wealthier peasantry. No Estates, however, could be described as 'democratically elected' in a modern sense, for their delegates were invariably chosen from narrow elites within the respective social groups. The Dutch States General, for example, represented only the narrow urban patrician oligarchies and a few inland noble families.

The structure of the various national assemblies varied enormously, from the bicameral English system through the continental three-tier French or Danish Estates General (with their Estates of clergy, nobility and commoners[1]) to the more unusual variants such as the German imperial assembly (see pp. 4–5) or the Polish diet consisting solely of king and nobles. A similar diversity was apparent at provincial level, ranging from the conventional three-tiered provincial Estates in France (such as continued to operate in Burgundy, Brittany and Provence) to the Estates of Holland with 18 town votes and one noble vote, or the various forms of *Landtage* in central Europe, some with strong peasant representation (in East Friesland and the Swiss cantons), some even without a noble presence (for example in Württemberg, where most of the nobility were free imperial knights represented directly in the imperial assembly).

Composition was only one of several factors determining the political effectiveness of these assemblies. All institutions were aware of the importance of control over at least some taxation as a basis for exerting influence on the ruler. Although no assembly on the continent made as much headway in financial terms as the English parliament, some of the German Estates, for example those of Electoral Saxony and of Württemberg, could exercise restraint on the expenditure (especially the military extravagance) of their princes by making grants for limited periods only. Few assemblies, however, were as systematic as the Hungarian diet in exploiting tax negotiations to ensure that other grievances were recorded and remedied, and there was little occasion anywhere (except in the Polish elective monarchy) to develop other prerogatives. The Estates of Aragon and the Polish *sejm* (diet) were unusual in being entitled to act as a high court of justice, even over officers of state and the King, but Aragon hesitated to use these powers after the unsuccessful revolt of 1592. The *zemsky sobor* in Muscovy, whose composition and powers are unclear, only exercised decisive power in 1613 when it chose a new dynasty of tsars, the Romanovs. In some areas, including, as we have seen, the Habsburg lands, rulers deliberately undermined the autonomy of their Estates and flouted promises made in return for support and taxation. Some assemblies succumbed in wartime emergencies: the Cortes of Castile, although briefly achieving some control over the *millones* tax in the early seventeenth century, was pushed into political oblivion from the 1630s onwards because of its exclusively urban composition and the hostility of Philip IV and his minister, Olivares. The French Estates General had already during the later sixteenth-century civil wars been turned into a political tool, and exercised no serious independent discretion at its last meeting in 1614. Some provincial Estates, such as those in Dauphiné and Normandy, were allowed to fade out because they restricted the tax powers of the Crown. The major exception to the general trend was the increasingly important and regularly called Swedish *riksdag*, but even it could readily be manipulated by a determined adult monarch, and owed much of its strength to the recurrent minorities and uncertain successions in the century after Gustav Adolf. Estates were evidently often regarded by princes as an obstacle to be reduced or removed, and at least in France and Spain only the remoter or less significant provincial assemblies were allowed to keep a measure of control over taxation and perhaps some influence on local legislation.

The States General in the United Provinces were in an altogether different position. The Dutch were inveterate defenders of extreme provincialism, with each of the seven provinces ostensibly endowed with equal influence through ambassadors at the States General meeting at The Hague. Although Holland (and especially the city of Amsterdam) in practice wielded much power because it contributed a large part of the entire revenue of the Republic, its delegation, led by the *Landsadvokaat* or *Raadspensionaris* (normally known in English as the Grand Pensionary) of Holland, could not dominate proceedings at the States General. On the contrary, at moments of important decision, not only the provincial Estates and the States General but also the literate public became involved in lengthy and detailed debate, which could severely delay major matters. This happened notably over negotiations with Spain in the years 1606–9, 1629–30 and 1646–51, when public controversy and a lively pamphlet war revealed the range and relative maturity of Dutch public opinion. The States General had powers of persuasion only: the law was not standardised, and even when it came to taxes for war, each province was responsible for its own collection. The Prince of Orange, commander (captain-general) of the Dutch forces, usually held the ill-defined but potentially powerful office of *stadholder* in many of the provinces, but never during the seventeenth century in all seven provinces simultaneously. Apart from the army and the exchequer, there were no institutions of significance covering the whole Republic, so in effect the States General was the loose embodiment of Dutch sovereignty.

Many national and provincial assemblies were left behind in the political developments of the early seventeenth century, especially since they represented only very narrow social groups. This decline of the Estates did not, however, lead directly to change in the 'political nation' or in the conditions within which government operated; indeed, no monarch could afford (or contemplate) doing without the support of the established orders in conformity with the principles of immutable natural law. Nowhere is this more clearly illustrated than in the role of the Parlement of Paris. Originally a superior law court with competence over parts of central and northern France, staffed by the upper magistracy that came to be known as the *noblesse de robe* (black-gowned nobility), the Parlement of Paris made recurrent extravagant claims to protect tradition and its perception of legality even beyond its own judicial boundaries, and ultimately in the 1640s and during the later eighteenth century adopted a populist role as a 'representative' body in the absence of any Estates General. At any stage the Parlement could create difficulties for the Crown through its right of judicial review: it could present remonstrances as a precondition for the registration of royal legislation, and although the crown could override such reservations by means of orders (*lettres de jussion*) or forced registration in the presence of royalty (*lit de justice*), legislation registered under such conditions was difficult to enforce. Even so, the Parlement never went beyond the defence of tradition and self-interest, and never created new political perspectives, not even when it had precipitated a major confrontation with the regency government in 1648.

Tax collection and the costs of war

Western European monarchies functioned not only within the limitations of tradition, representational norms and the law. On the more practical side, its scope was also restricted by financial shortcomings, clearly apparent in nearly every government during the early seventeenth century. Ordinary state revenues, typically customs receipts, income from crown land, and other permanent or regalian revenues, were increasingly inadequate, especially as war spread after 1618. Political opposition, however, could easily form around new demands for extraordinary taxation, and the nobility in particular often clung tenaciously to the theory that each prince should normally be able to run the machinery of state solely on the basis of the ordinary income. With no clear system of state budgeting, and with actual standards of administrative probity well below ideal, the early modern prince was not well-placed to substantiate and justify demands for new taxes, especially if (as was usual) he had to extract authorisation from some established institution before he could proceed. Worse still, no central government controlled the actual machinery whereby revenue could in practice be collected, and consequently had to rely at least partially on private contractors. Both France and England farmed out some of their existing indirect revenues to financial consortia, in return for an ostensibly fixed annual rent. In England, the 'great farm' of the customs revenues and various lesser contracts survived until the 1670s and 1680s, except for an interruption during the interregnum years, when parliamentary commissioners were put in charge. France had more indirect taxes and came to rely to a far greater extent on tax farming: the *gabelles* (salt taxes, varying grossly from region to region), the *aides* (excises on goods entering towns, especially beverages), and various other internal and external tolls were all contracted out.[2] Not only did the farmers expect to make a profit by collecting more than the payable rent, but the whole system was open to a range of abuses associated with the assigning of contracts at 'auctions', and the cancellation of existing contracts in favour of more generous bidders. The French tax farms allowed the state to obtain large loans from contractors on the security of forthcoming collections (a form of revenue anticipation), and the system was ostensibly meant to give a predictable income for the Crown, but in practice it rarely did because of the need for remissions or compensation to tax farmers in bad years. Moreover, because of the insatiable loan requirements of the state, reform was virtually impossible, even when the glaringly inequitable distribution of burdens between provinces and the counter-productive economic effects of escalating indirect taxation were obvious to all. It is interesting to note that, while the Long Parliament temporarily ended tax farming, the Parlement of Paris and the other courts forming the Chambre Saint Louis at the start of the Fronde in 1648 only went as far as banning anticipatory loans on tax-farming contracts. Colbert eventually consolidated the French farms into the *ferme générale* in 1681, and the system endured until the Revolution.

The Spanish monarchy went even further towards losing control. Tax farming was used there for customs and various indirect taxes including those on wool, and the contractors were often foreign bankers, notably Portuguese Jews. Impositions such as the onerous *alcabala* (a 10-per-cent sales tax), the *millones* (food tax) and other *servicios* (grants) allocated by the Cortes of Castile, which were collected by agents in each locality concerned, did not involve farming at central government level. But much of the revenue was transferred directly to *juristas* (those who had bought *juros* or state bonds) or to the bankers who had a government *asiento* (contract to pay crown expenditure, especially its military expenditure, in return for the allocation with interest of specific expected revenue). Already in 1621 revenues up to those of 1625 were allocated in this way. The combined effect of the reliance on *juros* and *asientos* from the late sixteenth century onwards, and especially in the war years from 1618, was thus also to deprive the Crown of control over most of its expenditure. As the requirements of war escalated over the next decades, monetary taxes also sometimes had to be replaced by payments in kind, which were even more vulnerable to private profiteering or evasion. In I. A. A. Thompson's words, 'every major . . . campaign was as much a financial confidence trick as a military exercise',[3] and the greater the revenue anticipations, the more expensive and difficult it became for the Crown to retain any real freedom for manoeuvre. Part of the problem, as in France, was that the crown was not particularly concerned about this state of affairs; finance was regarded merely as an irritating obstacle to be overcome by any means at hand, whether through contracting out, revenue anticipation, borrowing, forced loans (and potential default on such debts) or even by manipulation or reminting of the coinage. The consequences were serious: a systematic weakening of the efficiency of actual tax collection, with typically diminishing returns by the later 1630s and 1640s; and a fragmentation of political authority in favour of local magnates, courts of law, and local administators – making the Crown liable to appear distant and weak.

The contrast in this respect with the United Provinces is striking. There, reliance on indirect taxes was notoriously heavy by European standards, and tax farmers were again used, for example, to collect the excise. But assessment and collection were generally supervised by each municipal authority, and state accounts were subject to proper auditing, so that the Dutch Republic maintained uninterrupted financial credibility and access to loans throughout the seventeenth century. This helps to explain how the Dutch could support a huge long-term military burden, which already in 1607 (with the army at 60,000) stood at 9 million guilders annually for a population of only 1½ million – a cost which fell only marginally during the Twelve Years Truce (1609–21), and then increased further. Such financial stability was most unusual in Europe. It was certainly not attained in the Scandinavian monarchies, still relying quite heavily on crown domain revenues early in the century and on special sources of income such as the Sound Tolls (tariffs imposed by the Danish Crown on most foreign shipping to and from the Baltic). But even if the financial structures of these states, like those of much of the rest of Europe, were in some ways underdeveloped, permanent dependence on tax farming was at least avoided, and in Sweden great efforts were eventually made to simplify overall control of the Crown's finances in order to improve credit facilities.

The role of private contractors in state finance in the western monarchies meant that the effective cost of collecting taxes was high: the substantial cuts taken by contractors or by local officials, their salaries and the costs of enforcement, the losses that might nowadays be described as corruption or embezzlement, and simple inefficiency, all took a heavy toll. In addition, however, governments had to face the difficulties created by either the inability or the refusal of subjects to pay, together with losses from evasion and tax fraud by the payees. The overall effect of these cannot be quantified, but arrears and direct or indirect opposition to taxes were indisputably endemic in Europe in the early seventeenth century, varying according to the type of tax, the region, and the political or economic context. Increases in taxation easily became counter-productive, not only in terms of damage to the economy but also ultimately in precipitating violence and making collection impossible. In France, for example, the expected yield from direct taxes, including the *taille*, increased from 10 million livres tournois in 1610 to 36 million in 1635, but the real yield reaching the treasury actually fell, amounting in 1635 to only one-sixth of the nominal yield, once costs had been deducted. Arrears mounted rapidly, and by the late 1640s some of the indirect tax farms in France had no takers. By that stage fiscal burdens in Spain and in many other parts of Europe had become equally unacceptable (see chapter 7).

Clearly, one of the principal causes of the growing need for state revenue was the escalating cost of warfare. The later sixteenth century had already witnessed considerable troop concentrations in France and the Netherlands, with the chief military power, Spain, committing resources for around 60,000 men in Flanders in the 1580s. In the early seventeenth century, the reforms which Maurits of Orange-Nassau introduced as commander of the Dutch forces against Spain, involving greater flexibility and improved drilling, hinged on regular and adequate pay to secure reasonable levels of discipline amongst the native and mercenary troops used. By the second decade of the war in Germany, Gustav Adolf and Wallenstein operated on an even larger scale, with the Swedish forces alone exceeding 100,000 men early in 1632. Growing organisational and technological sophistication (which historians at one stage considered sufficiently significant to form part of what was called a 'military revolution' in early modern Europe[4]) no doubt improved the effectiveness of these forces, but also added to the costs. All the commanders in the Empire to some extent exploited local political conditions to make their campaigns as self-financing as possible. Living off the land was bound to generate huge resentments, yet even when the Swedes from 1634 found it politically expedient to resume some of the burden in order not to alienate the north Germans completely, they could do so only on a modest scale. By contrast, some of the other belligerents never had the opportunity of living off alien territory on a large scale: thus the Dutch had to fight a static and defensive war which was exceptionally expensive for themselves.

For France and Spain, after they opened hostilities on each other in 1635, the nature of mercenary warfare ensured that the conflict was as much a test of financial as of military capability. The French army, amounting to at most 20,000 at the approach of war in 1610, grew rapidly to 150,000 during the 1630s. Spain was by then responsible for the maintenance of twice that number, mostly raised, as elsewhere in Europe, by private military entrepreneurs and profit-seeking subcontractors. The increasingly complex training required for tactical efficiency was not only intrinsically costly but also gradually began to induce governments to consider rudimentary health and welfare provisions for the troops to reduce losses through disease, demoralisation and desertion. This, added to the cost of large-scale food supplies, weaponry not available from private contractors, and escalating expenditure on road and bridge building, imposed an enormous continuous financial burden. Governments always had to give priority to the army during wartime: a serious shortfall there could lead not only to the sudden collapse of a campaign (as happened to the French in the Valtellina in 1637) or to mutinies and near-mutinies (as in the Spanish army in Flanders in 1607 or the Swedish army in Germany in 1634) but also to indiscriminate pillaging and plunder of friend and foe.

In the case of France, the very rapidity of military development in the 1630s and 1640s made it impossible to develop adequate centralised state control, despite the organisational skills of Sublet de Noyer (secretary of state for war after 1636). It was partly to come to grips with problems of corruption and profiteering that the Crown made growing use of independent royal commissioners, the *intendants*, whose functions were both military and civilian (see p. 48). Spain, on the other hand, had a much longer tradition of large-scale military organisation over greater distances, and this counted in her favour in the 1630s, but the Army of Flanders alone, in the two decades before the Spanish defeat by the French at Rocroi in 1643, usually cost between 6 and 10 million florins per annum.[5] It is clear that the Thirty Years War imposed unprecedented strains on all belligerent governments – a strain which, if the administrative machinery failed and financial credibility collapsed, could lead both to foreign defeat and to domestic revolt on a major scale.

The restored monarchy and the Huguenots in France

The period from the domestic settlement and the conclusion of peace with Spain in 1598 to the assassination of Henry IV in 1610 came to be regarded retrospectively in France as a golden age, partly because of the charisma and good luck of the King, partly no doubt because of the fortunate coincidence of economic prosperity after the disasters of the 1590s. Henry IV, while undoubtedly a vivacious and effective leader in marked contrast to his predecessors, nevertheless succeeded more in disguising the weaknesses of the Crown than in durably reforming its administrative and financial machinery. His achievement lay essentially in giving new prestige to a badly damaged image of monarchy – primarily by reuniting the kingdom through the pacification of the worst of those trying to perpetuate the civil wars of the later sixteenth century, but also, through his finance minister, the Baron (later Duke) of Sully, by regaining some degree of financial credibility for the Crown.

The financial dimension was central to everything else, initially simply because of Henry's reliance on mercenary troops. He also needed to grant substantial payments and pensions to pacify those civil war leaders open to such forms of persuasion; it has been estimated that 24 million livres tournois were spent on members of the

Catholic League, and the annual drain of this kind of secret crown expenditure remained high. In 1597, as the war drew to a close, the financial plight had been so desperate that Henry, getting no useful ideas from his council of finance, had had to beg the Parlement of Paris for help. Sully and Chancellor Bellièvre were both fully aware of the political dangers of such weakness, but it was primarily Sully's combination of bullying tactics and dour tight-fistedness that eventually freed the King in this respect. Sully's methodical concern for detail in all aspects of domestic policy, and his rather ruthless and unapproachable personality, were useful assets for the King, and although the inherited debt problem was far from solved, royal finances were brought under control. An undeclared bankruptcy was effectively worked out, so that debts could either be written off or, in the case of important foreign debts, reduced and rescheduled depending on political expediency. The Swiss, for example, had claims of nearly 36 million livres tournois in 1598, equivalent to about twice the total annual expenditure of the Crown: for political reasons and because of French reliance on Swiss mercenaries, Henry staged an ostentatious reception for the 42 Swiss ambassadors in 1602 to mark the conclusion of a long-term agreement over repayment. A quarter of the debts to the Grand-Duke of Tuscany were written off as part of the dowry payable on Henry's marriage to Marie de Medici, and the remainder was simply postponed indefinitely. German princely creditors and private foreign bankers were mostly ignored, while assignations and *rentes* to domestic creditors were revised or stopped altogether. These measures, together with an increase in indirect taxation and a consolidation of revenues obtainable from the sale of offices (see pp. 163–5), enabled Sully to accumulate a surplus fund in cash in the Bastille amounting by 1607 to 7 million livres tournois. By giving office-holders a direct interest in the maintenance of solvency and by allowing a slight easing of the direct taxes such as the *taille*, these measures also contributed directly to political stability, at least in the short run. In addition, some political capital could be made out of the cancellation of hopeless arrears of taxation, out of Sully's enquiries into aspects of provincial financial self-administration, and out of the special courts (*chambres de justice*) set up to deal with the financiers and officials who could not be tackled in any other way. The purpose was political rather than a matter of objective justice: one of the *chambres de justice*, that of 1607, went rather further than Sully had intended and started raising questions about the probity of his own clients. Sully was indeed not a poor man by this stage, and the court's inquiries had to be promptly cut short by the King to avoid embarrassment.

No less important for the survival of the monarchy was the attempt to tame the aristocracy. In spite of reservations about aspects of the

Henrician religious compromise, many of the great Leaguers of the previous decades sooner or later submitted to the King in return for pensions and other favours. Princes of the blood such as Condé, however, presented permanent threats to Henry's position (in this instance complicated by the King's characteristically uncontrollable infatuation with Condé's fiancée and later bride). Revolts were attempted by several other magnates, including the Dukes of Biron and of Bouillon, one ending in trial and execution, the other in surrender and pardon. Amongst the lesser nobility, feuding was also very common, almost endemic, so that even an edict against duelling (1602) was unenforceable. Habits of violence were not readily changed, and the Crown primarily sought to ensure that feuding did not take on larger political dimensions. In one very basic sense this policy was in luck, for a time: Henry parried more than twenty attempts on his own life before Ravaillac's final one in 1610.

One of several current justifications for violence, and the one most commonly used by anti-royal conspirators, was religious belief. Henry's abjuration of Protestantism in 1593 had clearly been a move of political necessity, but his uncompromising treatment of even the moderates at the Huguenot assembly later that year at Mantes cost him the support of a number of Protestant leaders. The pacification of Nantes of 1598 (consisting of the Edict and some further agreements of detail) was a political compromise which the Huguenots were not in a position to resist now that the royal army was no longer needed against Spain. Toleration as a general principle was not contemplated, and the division between Catholics and Protestants was explicitly regarded as temporary. The Edict of Nantes was intended primarily to end sectarian conflict in matters of processions and church feasts, religious buildings and property, education, and access to offices. The Huguenots, who probably constituted no more than 7 per cent of the population as a whole, were granted some 900 places of worship, with rights to hold services on the estates of Protestant noblemen and in places where Huguenot worship had occurred in 1596 and 1597. They were debarred from holding general assemblies and hence from gaining any political coherence, but were allowed to garrison over fifty strongholds under nominal royal control. Special courts with equal Protestant and Catholic representation were established to deal with disputes. The compromise immediately aroused grave misgivings on the Catholic side: the Parlement of Paris violently opposed the Edict until Henry applied direct pressure through a *lit de justice* (formal session presided over by the King in person), and other parlements in the provinces dragged their heels even longer. Ultimately a precarious balance was achieved only through royal intervention and through Henry's deliberate policy of flexibility and appeasement towards both sides. While individual Huguenots came to establish a distinguished tradition of service to the King which survived even the Revocation of the Edict in 1685, Protestantism as such continued to depend directly on royal goodwill to survive in peace.

No major sectarian incidents occurred in the next decade, and the value of the Henrician compromise was recognised even by the ultra-Catholic Marie de Medici, who headed the regency for Louis XIII after 1610. The Edict was confirmed immediately, and reiterated without qualification over the next few years. Nevertheless, a true equilibrium had not been attained: partisans on both sides adopted an aggressive and inflexible stand whenever possible, and with the fall of Sully in 1611 the Protestants lost their last major protector at court. The regency government was in any case in a very delicate position because its interests abroad were not compatible with a Catholic orientation, especially with regard to the Habsburgs along the Rhine and in northern Italy. By 1614 Condé, dissatisfied with his exclusion from power despite his proximity to the royal succession, started fomenting trouble in league with other magnates; he clearly lacked political ability but the Huguenots approached him for support, thereby contributing to a new civil war. The secretary of state for foreign affairs, Villeroy, managed (notably by means of a double royal marriage contract with the Habsburgs) to prevent possible foreign meddling, while on the domestic front the regency tried to keep various magnate factions sufficiently divided by accepting Condé's demand for the calling of the Estates General. By the time it met in October 1614 Louis XIII had been declared of age (13 years old), and with the minority thus technically at an end the Estates could be handled more firmly. Apart from discussions regarding relations with the papacy, and the question of acceptance of the decrees of the Council of Trent, much time at the Estates was spent arguing over financial policy and venality in the administration – delicate issues dividing the Third Estate from the others. In the end, the assembly was wound up without receiving any real satisfaction from the Crown; this, the last Estates General in France before 1789, had been little more than a means of buying time for the fragile government. Condé, disappointed, tried to organise another revolt in 1616 with Huguenot participation, attracting even Bouillon and Sully himself, but little came of it. A further year of dangerous factional squabbles around Marie de Medici and her favourite, Concini, came to a sudden head when Louis XIII himself, with the aid of a confidant, Luynes, had his mother exiled from court and Concini murdered. But this still did not bring effective leadership; on the contrary, the danger that sectarian conflict and war in Europe in 1618 (see chapter 1) might at any time spread into France, ensured that the very basis for effective government remained in doubt. For another decade, at least, the French

Crown had to keep a very low profile in Europe simply in order to avoid a relapse into the conditions of civil war of the later sixteenth century.

Louis XIII was restrained from following his devoutly Catholic instincts and intervening directly in Germany on the side of the Emperor but, after ending another magnate rebellion in 1620, he did lead an army against the Huguenots in the province of Béarn. This was in one sense a natural move, given the undisguised disloyalty and armed strength of some Huguenot communities and the strong Counter-Reforming leanings of the French court. But while the campaign in Béarn was a complete military success, it immediately aroused far more widespread and dangerous Huguenot resistance all over the kingdom, drowning out counsels of moderation on both sides. Continued agitation from certain Huguenot leaders, notably the grandees Rohan and Soubise, together with the confrontational line followed by Condé (temporarily back in the royal council with the queen mother on a fundamentalist Catholic line), ensured that the Reformed (Huguenot) community as a whole could not be left alone at a time when the German war appeared to raise prospects of an international Protestant alliance. A series of royal military campaigns in 1621 and 1622 ended with the Treaty of Montpellier, whereby some of the Huguenot strongholds were reduced but the most important ones, notably La Rochelle, were preserved. In fact, the Huguenots were deeply divided amongst themselves, with considerable resistance from some quarters to any further attempt at open rebellion. At court, however, the potential threat was exaggerated by the *dévot* party and by others favouring an all-Catholic alliance with the Habsburgs. When the Huguenots in La Rochelle were offered English assistance in a half-hearted Anglo-French war inexpertly launched by Buckingham and Charles I, it was another clear warning to the Crown that domestic pacification was urgently needed. Three decades of unease came to a head at the siege and fall of La Rochelle (1627–9), which enabled the Crown to reduce all the Huguenot strongholds and impose a revised settlement. The Peace of Alais of 1629 confirmed the liberty of conscience enshrined in the Edict of Nantes, but deprived the Huguenots of any further possibility of armed resistance. In the long run, the Protestants were increasingly on the defensive, their numerical strength already well below that of the later sixteenth century, and exposed to recurrent harassment from the Catholic Church and some local officials and institutions. Yet in the circumstances of 1629, and given continuing Counter-Reforming zeal in the French Church coupled with explicit government refusal to contemplate official toleration of two religions on a permanent basis, the Peace was a generous compromise. As a piece of practical statesmanship it worked in that the Crown never again faced the combined threat of religious and magnate insurrection.

The indispensable first minister: Richelieu and Louis XIII

Much of the credit for this solution of the Huguenot question belonged to the Bishop of Luçon, since 1622 better known as Cardinal Richelieu. A protégé of Marie de' Medici, and secretary of state briefly in 1617 under Concini, Richelieu had, after the death of Luynes in 1622, developed contacts with the King. After 1624 he gradually became Louis XIII's chief advisor, impressing him with his capacity for hard work and with his highly pragmatic approach to the great issues of domestic and European policy. Richelieu was a committed bishop and cardinal, and, after 1629, also a reforming abbot, but he never regarded his clerical status as incompatible with his political ambitions of securing the reputation and power of the French monarchy in Europe. Indeed, he used the prestige of high ecclesiastical office for political ends, even in influencing the King, and with the help of his extraordinary adviser, the Capuchin Father Joseph, he worked out a pragmatic moral and political view which stood in marked contrast to that prevailing at the Habsburg court. He was also shrewd enough to handle Louis XIII with great tact, trying not to appear to dominate and always careful to consult with the King, while at the same time magnifying the public and spiritual image of the monarch through deliberate royalist propaganda and pamphleteering. In spite of Louis XIII's occasional resentment at this ministerial tutelage, a valuable political partnership evolved which survived several attempts to oust the Cardinal, and lasted until his death in December 1642, shortly before the end of the reign itself. During this period noble feuding and factional strife were not eliminated, but Richelieu's luck and skill in surviving such challenges, coupled with his deliberate use of relatives and political clients (known as *créatures*) in the administration, eventually ensured greater stability at the top than France had known since 1610.

This was particularly noticeable after 1630. Until then French commitment to Europe was hesitant, and Richelieu, because of his refusal to adopt a favourable attitude towards Habsburg ambitions in the Empire, faced severe criticism from the *dévot* party, including the Queen Mother, Marie de' Medici, and Louis's brother, Gaston d'Orléans. French attempts to challenge Spain in the Valtellina in northern Italy, and their confrontation over the Mantuan succession dispute, led to increases in taxation at home and hence to a serious wave of provincial anti-fiscal revolts in the years 1629–30, which the *dévots* could readily exploit. In addition, Richelieu's contacts with Protestant princes in Germany could be regarded as religious treason. In November 1630 Marie de Medici and the Keeper of the Seals, Marillac, nearly persuaded the King to dismiss the Cardinal; their failure, and the arrest of Marillac on the Day of Dupes (11 November

1630) was a clear indication of the King's sense of priorities. It also paved the way for a more determined European policy over the next decade, committing the Crown to ever-increasing international responsibilities and financial overburdening.

The Day of the Dupes did not bring peace within the high nobility. On the contrary, Marie de' Medici was now permanently alienated from the court and, like Gaston d'Orléans (who was heir to the still childless King), could foment recurrent and serious trouble with relative impunity. Their primary target remained Richelieu, and some of their criticisms of rash, costly foreign entanglements and financial mismanagement had enough substance to be dangerous. Open revolts centring on Gaston and the Duke of Montmorency in the early 1630s, or on the Count of Soissons, Gaston, Bouillon and the Marquis of Cinq Mars later in the reign, all involved Habsburg support. Montmorency and Cinq Mars were eventually charged with treason and executed in 1632 and 1642, respectively. When war was at last declared on Spain in 1635, the issues in one way became simpler and the restlessness of some of the nobility could be channelled in that direction. But war also rapidly turned financial instability and anti-fiscal revolts into an even greater threat to the Crown.

The French economy undoubtedly had much potential, even during the years of depression in the second quarter of the century. The Crown, however, failed to tap it efficiently and arguably did a great deal of damage to the economy. Richelieu had initially had plans for the revival of the programme for road- and canal-building, industrial sponsorship and overseas development contemplated by Sully and Laffemas in the first decade of the century, and had submitted ideas to an assembly of notables in 1626. They had been more concerned to cut crown expenditure, however, and nothing substantial came out of the meeting in the end. Over the next few years most attention was concentrated on a closer scrutiny of crown finances and a reduction of gifts and pensions, to which the *surintendant* of finance chosen by Richelieu, the marquis d'Effiat, devoted himself until his death in 1632. Thereafter two *surintendants* were appointed, one of whom was so blatantly corrupt that he was explicitly cautioned by the King. The complexity and deliberate obfuscation of accounting procedures enabled financiers and ministers (including Richelieu himself) to acquire vast fortunes. But, as military commitments grew, the financial credit of the Crown itself was shored up by increasingly devious and ultimately ruinous means.

Tension and revolt in France in the 1630s

The shift from indirect diversionary war against the Habsburgs to direct war in 1635 greatly increased the financial burden in France itself. In addition to maintaining several mercenary armies on different fronts at a cost rarely below 30 million livres annually after 1635 (in fact reaching a peak of 48.5 million in 1643), Louis was also committed to subsidising the Dutch (2.3 million annually), the Swedes (1 million in 1631, continuing with interruptions to 1648), and Bernhard of Saxe-Weimar (4 million annually from 1634 to 1639). To meet these and recurrent administrative costs, the *taille* was nominally doubled between 1635 and 1643, and indirect taxes such as the hated *gabelle* were also increased. But because this was a time of economic depression and hence of growing difficulty in actually gathering the revenues, the expedient was adopted in 1634 of selling *rentes* (bonds) on the *taille* and the *gabelle*. Richard Bonney has emphasised that the yields from this kind of operation began to fall significantly as early as 1638 because of market saturation, scepticism and heavy speculation, so that the Crown was in effect mortgaging its future at the cost of growing popular hostility and without even making a reasonable short-term financial gain – a policy that was not definitively reversed until 1664.[6] The whole war strategy came to depend on a juggling of paper transactions and accumulating state debts, only partly offset by income from contracts for new or augmented extraordinary taxes and from forced loans and other extras squeezed from hapless incumbents of venal offices. By 1643 the combined effect of *rentes*, sale of offices, tax-farming and anticipation of tax revenue, and straight loans, could easily have amounted to immediate state bankruptcy. As it happened, such a collapse was warded off for another five years.

There was more to the struggle, however, than keeping creditors off. Social and political repercussions are clearly revealed in the deteriorating relations between the Crown and its own office-holders. The Crown had attempted to abolish the sale of offices in 1618 but had agreed to renew the *paulette* in 1621 for the usual nine-year period (see p. 163). In 1630 an attempt was made to divide the office-holders by allowing financial officials a renewal in return for a forced loan while refusing it to the parlementary magistrates. The Parlement of Paris retaliated by stalling new legislation, including tax edicts, and eventually the Crown gave in. During the 1630s, proceeds from the venality system usually accounted for more than 20 million livres or around a quarter of the total revenue. The renewal of the *paulette* in 1638 was accompanied by another round of political haggling which was so acrimonious that the system was severely strained. Strategies such as office-subdivision, annulment and resale by the Crown, withholding of wages, and other of the more usual abuses associated with French venality, were acceptable only within certain limits, and by 1640 a slump in the market in offices showed that the Crown had gone too far. This was one of the factors which lay behind the total disenchantment of the 'robe' nobility which came out in 1648 (see chapter 7).

Those purchasing offices were also directly affected by the one significant administrative development of the period: the introduction of special royal commissioners, *intendants,* as a regular and permanent feature in most parts of the kingdom. Usually of robe-nobility background but non-venal himself, the *intendant* was seen as a means of circumventing provincial venal office-holders and their local allegiances. He was usually entrusted with the supervision of recruitment, military supplies, quartering and taxation, and was expected also to keep an eye on the judicial machinery and the maintenance of law and order. The vast range of duties clearly imposed its own limitations, but the *intendants* seem to have been sufficiently effective in the 1630s and 1640s to cause friction with other officials and with the parlements. These tensions, like those caused by the over-exploitation of the venality system itself, eventually came to a head in 1648.

If the *noblesse de robe,* and especially the more exposed office-holders amongst them, had grounds for complaint against the Crown, so did virtually every other group in France by the 1630s, as the state's expenses reached up to four times the earlier norm. The clergy were repeatedly pressurised into making larger so-called *dons gratuits* ('free gifts' – that is, lump sums voted by assemblies of the clergy in lieu of taxation). Even the old nobility were faced with government enquiries into their entitlements in various parts of France after 1634, with a specific view to curtailing noble exemptions from the *taille.* The failure of the summons of the nobility for active military service in 1635 persuaded the Crown that the ancient noble obligation could more usefully be commuted into a money payment, but this levy caused considerable additional resentment amongst those members of the older nobility who already felt socially and financially threatened. Although most of the nobility was by this stage in principle loyal to the monarchy, old habits of violence and lack of effective central control made it easier for them to resist fiscal agents as intruders distorting the traditional balance of the kingdom. Noble connivance at and encouragement of peasant grievances against tax collectors was particularly evident in Normandy and in south-western France.

Against this background, the veritable epidemic of popular urban and peasant revolts, especially after 1629, takes on a quite different dimension. Marillac clearly had a point, before his fall, in pleading with Richelieu for a less belligerent policy abroad so that hardship at home would not become overwhelming. Economic conditions did not fluctuate uniformly over France as a whole, and there is some indication that the southern Languedoc area, for example, was much less severely affected from the late 1620s than the north in terms of harvest failures, reduction in subsidiary employment and outbreaks of infectious disease (which will be discussed more fully in chapter 3). Where such disasters occurred on a serious scale, they did not necessarily lead to anything more than the usual bread riots or short spontaneous outbursts of fear. Occasionally, however, animosity towards specific individuals, or the latent tensions in a whole community, erupted. It was in such contexts that the burden of state demands, the unpopularity of tax officials and especially tax farmers or their agents, the rumour of troop movements or the fear of new impositions could trigger more complex revolts. Several social groups could then become involved, including disgruntled town notables, local venal office-holders and seigneurs. At such times it was in everyone's interest to identify a common external scapegoat, such as a tax collector. It might then be possible to frighten the central government into conceding political objectives, while distracting attention away from local differences of interest. Otherwise a riot could turn poor against rich, as happened in Bordeaux in 1635, and that was far worse. Rural riots and revolts during this period, interestingly, lost virtually all trace of explicit anti-seigneurial grievances: attention was turned entirely to the outsider, whilst many landowners fraternised with peasant rebels. Perhaps the most important, and potentially dangerous, element in the popular grievances of the 1630s and 1640s was precisely this tendency for particular animosities between different social groups to become submerged in a common front against the tax-collector. Even urban and peasant grievances could in some contexts converge, as in the Cascavéoux revolt in Aix-en-Provence in 1630. Although proper co-ordination across such disparate groups proved difficult, the mix was very explosive. This happened for example in Agen in 1635, when the fury of the urban crowd against the '*gabelleurs*' (in reality against a threatened hike in wine taxes) had the active support of peasants around the city. Very quickly a series of violent incidents led to systematic attacks on anyone associated with the new tax – including both local municipal officials and royal office-holders deemed to have responsibility for fiscal administration or for the new financial courts in the city. Not only were their houses attacked and pillaged, but whole buildings were set on fire to force the inmates out. Altogether 24 people were killed in the ensuing violence – all of them connected directly or by implication to the actual grievance at hand. Their bodies were ritually mutilated (sometimes including castration), dragged round the streets, or left to be eaten by dogs or to rot. Even a church official was killed because he had hired labourers and deducted one-sixth from the promised pay to cover the new tax – he tried to jump off the city walls, but was lynched by the peasants waiting below, who proceeded to mutilate his body, whilst pointedly sparing his right hand because it had served in religious services to consecrate the host. Other groups of peasants attacked the rural property of those targeted in the city riots, ensuring that there was no easy escape. It took a series of solemn religious processions, complete with sacred symbols carried to various barricades in the city, and several weeks of carefully managed public appeals by respected churchmen unconnected with the '*gabelleurs*', before a precarious calm was restored to the city and its hinterland.[7] Although this rioting in Agen had turned unusually violent, it very forcibly illustrated the extent to which popular opinion regarded any new tax as part of the same exploitative machinery, and how dangerous it was for anyone to become associated with such demands. The peasant may above all have been concerned about the *taille*, and the urban worker mostly about indirect taxes such as the *aides*, but if a common cause was established, local office-holders and other representatives of the state were in a very dangerous predicament.

As local unrest increasingly directed itself solely against taxation, the challenge to government policy was clear. The Crown at first followed a pragmatic policy of trying to contain revolts by means of local concessions, by a more lenient approach to the peripheral and potentially separatist provinces (especially the *pays d'états*, which had their own assemblies of Estates), and by direct repression in cases where the army could be redirected and where insurrections did not die out spontaneously from loss of momentum. Rebels often declared their explicit loyalty to the King, and even addressed petitions to him against fiscal abuses; such rebellions readily subsided if arrears were cancelled or new tax demands abandoned, as happened in Burgundy and Provence during 1629–30. The resulting uneven distribution of taxation was nothing new, and taxation became simply a kind of political bluff on both sides. Nevertheless, some of the later revolts presented a major threat to the Crown. The biggest was the Croquant revolt of 1636–7, centring on several different areas at once and engulfing up to one-quarter of the kingdom. Essentially objecting to the *gabelle* and the dramatic increases in the *taille*, the Croquants generated a rhetoric and an organisation of their own. Those in Périgord chose as commander a local seigneur, La Mothe-La Forest, whilst their brethren in Poitou had to use threats to force the gentry to join. Another overwhelming revolt of this period, that of the Nu-Pieds in Normandy in 1639, resulted in a substantial rebel army being formed under the leadership of a local priest, Jean Morel. Here even local office-holders became sufficiently involved to make Louis XIII curtail the privileges of the Parlement of Rouen by way of punishment. At such a level, the political overtones of revolt could be considerable, and even if popular urban and rural commotion was very largely for conservative or reactionarily defensive ends, the refusal to pay new or greater taxes could, in the context of the later 1630s and 1640s, itself be very dangerous for the state. Even the protestations of loyalty to the King's person could seem menacing if accompanied, as in the Croquant demand of 1636, with demands for the calling of the Estates General and for cuts in unnecessary crown expenditure, while no attempt was made to disguise the violent hatred of tax officials and 'Parisian agents' – the latter evidently risking gruesome butchery if they were rash enough to turn up.[8]

There is no doubt that the French monarchy did eventually gain some consistency of purpose during Richelieu's ministry, compared with the regency that had preceded it. But the genuine threat of military disaster, culminating in 1636 when the Army of Flanders penetrated as far as Corbie, and Paris itself seemed exposed, ensured that the government more often relied on improvised emergency solutions (sometimes implemented with ruthless determination) than on any real long-term state-building programme.[9] Richelieu was a formidable politician and manipulator, but it would be a mistake to read too much of a grand strategy into a period which was all too often dominated by crises, insurgence and political factionalism. It will also be apparent that the cost of the European commitments was enormous, and that the Crown was generating such widespread and dangerous resentments amongst its own subjects that the whole gamble could have failed. The administrative structure could not really carry the load imposed on it, and the increasingly autocratic style of government, complete with rigged political trials and unforgiving harassment of critics of the Cardinal, was little more than a desperate attempt by Richelieu to keep a few steps ahead of financial disaster and uncontrollable social insubordination.

Castile and the Spanish system

France and Spain at the beginning of the seventeenth century were not in obviously comparable situations: the one, although geographically (if not administratively) coherent and with considerable human and material potential, had barely survived a debilitating series of civil wars that had produced administrative collapse and financial disaster; the other was the centre of a vast European and colonial empire, had a long tradition of strong (if cumbersome) government, was by far the most dominant military power in the world, and commanded considerable resources, if not at home then at least in its various dominions. And yet by the second quarter of the century the central council of each of these two monarchies was in effect headed by a royal 'favourite' or first minister of boundless energy and ambition, who could with justification regard the future of their dominions with despondency often verging on despair. Richelieu and Olivares, nearly exact contemporaries in the political life of Europe, were both haunted by visions of decline and disintegration in their respective kingdoms, and each ultimately saw the other as one of the main causes of their difficulties. Straight comparison between the two societies and systems encounters a variety of obstacles, but it is now clear that the outcome of their collision was anything but a foregone conclusion until at least 1640. One needs to ask not so much why France ultimately came off better, but how each could keep going for so long in the face of extreme financial overextension, administrative inadequacy and growing domestic opposition at all levels. The very continuation of the Franco-Spanish war until 1659 emphasises the remarkable resilience of the Spanish system and the tenacity of Bourbon dynastic ambitions at a time when neither meant very much to the great majority of their subjects.

The Spanish (or more correctly Castilian) monarchy rested on an elaborate conciliar form of government which was already ponderously ineffectual because of Philip II's attentiveness to every detail, but which became even more deeply restrictive with the noble-dominated bureaucratic control which flourished under the much weaker Philip III (1598–1621). He allowed himself to be dominated by self-seeking favourites (*validos*) such as the Duke of Lerma (disgraced in 1618) and then his son the Duke of Uceda, both of whom were more interested in the exploitation of patronage to secure their family interests than in the detailed running of government. Even so, cumbersome council routines ensured that Spanish policy as a whole remained fairly consistent, guided by a well-established diplomatic service. The negotiations leading to the truce with the United Provinces in 1609, for example, may have been unsatisfactory for Spain in that sovereignty was virtually conceded to the Dutch without effective guarantees against colonial and overseas competition from them, but this was probably the most sensible approach in the wake of mutiny and exhaustion in the legendary Army of Flanders. In addition, the Crown was now free to turn to a domestic issue which seemed to offer compensation: the expulsion of the Morisco (Arab) population from the eastern and south-eastern provinces of Spain, especially Valencia and Aragon. This operation, carried out with great military efficiency and ruthlessness in the years 1609–14, may seem as unacceptable nowadays as Louis XIV's expulsion of the Huguenots three generations later, but to a few powerful advisors in Madrid, influenced by some notoriously bigoted clerics such as the Archbishop of Valencia, de Ribera, it seemed necessary and desirable in order to remove the constant threat of heresy and political subversion from an 'alien' and possibly unassimilable minority with strong connections across the Mediterranean. More than nine-tenths of the original 315,000 Moriscos were pushed out or deported, causing noticeable but only local problems of depopulation and labour shortage.

Even within the Iberian peninsula itself, the Spanish monarchy presided over a hugely diverse and historically distinctive conglomeration of independent kingdoms, principalities and provinces conscious of their legal rights and substantive autonomy. At the centre was Castile, the extensive but quite docile heartlands of the Spanish possessions. It had no recent history of revolt, noble feuding, religious dissent or even precarious regency government comparable to that of France at the turn of the century.[10] The peripheral kingdoms and provinces were more volatile, with remoter areas reputedly beset by banditry and violence, but such problems were amenable to containment if the local authorities made an effort – as they did for instance in the north-eastern province of Catalonia under the viceroy, Albuquerque, for a few years after 1616. Generally, the peripheral kingdoms caused little trouble as long as the Castilian-dominated royal government respected their autonomy and traditional rights. Philip III even encouraged seigneurial consolidation and financial decentralisation by alienating large tracts of crown land to favourites and creditors of noble status, a policy continued by Philip IV in spite of the obstacles it put in the way of effective administrative and tax reform. The Spanish crown never tried to introduce an official equivalent to the French *intendant*: the nearest equivalent, the *corregidor*, was posted permanently and thus able to develop the strong local and family connections which made him unsuitable for the kind of supervisory and fiscal tasks required by a government engaged in protracted war.

The extensive imperial commitments of the Spanish monarchy in northern Italy and Flanders, as well as overseas in America and the Far East, entailed continuous expenditure on a military machine which could not readily be wound down in peacetime or even during the winter months because of the scale of defensive requirements. Although there were some 16 million Europeans under the Spanish Crown, their share of the burden was extremely uneven: two-thirds of them were largely free even of conscription. Most taxation was carried by Castile (amounting to three-quarters of total imperial costs in 1616), whilst the peripheral provinces even within the Iberian peninsula itself, thanks to traditional privileges preserved by their assemblies of Estates, contributed little or nothing. The Cortes (Estates) of Aragon, the Basque provinces and the annexed but separate kingdom of Portugal voted no subsidies for Philip III, and the Cortes of Valencia only one, in 1604. The Catalonian Cortes and its standing committee invariably resisted any kind of contributions for the monarchy as a whole. The Italian possessions, especially Milan, Naples and Sicily, by contrast contributed far more, and Milan was also a military training ground and crossroads. The American colonies sent their massive shipments of silver from the mines at Potosí and elsewhere, but this bullion had ambivalent effects on the native Iberian economy, encouraged parasitism and financial irresponsibility within the governing elite, and was in any case never (owing to losses at sea, fraud and foreign encroachment) sufficiently steady and predictable during the seventeenth century to encourage skilful management.

Philip III, who had inherited substantial debts from his father incurred especially in the war in the Netherlands, attempted to overcome immediate cash shortfalls by means of debasements of coinage. The issues of copper vellon in 1602–3 and again in 1617 and 1621 compounded the monetary instability already created by an irregular downward trend in silver bullion shipments from South America. In 1607 there occurred one of the recurrent more or less explicit bankruptcies of the Crown when tax farmers and *asiento* entrepreneurs had their high-interest contracts payable from allocated revenue converted into low-interest state bonds (*juros*) in order to free incoming revenue. Although no further bankruptcies occurred until 1627, the Crown had already by the beginning of the war in 1618 assigned nearly all of its income once more to contractors and *juros*-holders, giving itself very little room for manoeuvre.

Olivares: integration or disintegration?

Although financial problems and the resulting unavoidably hasty demobilisation in Flanders had helped persuade Madrid of the need for a truce with the Dutch after 1607, the question of resources was not prominent in the deliberations surrounding Spanish policy at the outbreak of the Thirty Years War. No great effort was made to prolong the truce or settle differences, especially since critics of the truce were gaining the upper hand both in the United Provinces and at the Spanish court after the fall of Lerma in 1618. The decision to intervene in central Europe and to consolidate the military route from Italy to Flanders was a deliberate one, and continuity was maintained after the premature death of Philip III in 1621 thanks to the prominence of the experienced ambassador and hard-liner Baltasar de Zúñiga in the Council of State. Zúñiga's nephew, Gaspar de Guzman, Count of Olivares, had already as head of the Crown Prince's household gained nearly total domination over the reasonably intelligent but totally inexperienced Philip IV, who was only 16 years old on succession. On Zúñiga's death in 1622, Olivares gradually emerged as the most determined, perceptive and ambitious minister at court, with qualities of pragmatic leadership and defects of personality which in some respects invite comparison with those of Richelieu. Both exploited the hold they had over the King they served, manipulating and hectoring, or threatening to resign if all else seemed to fail. But Olivares was less self-assured and perhaps less clear-minded than his rival. In the words of John Elliott, Olivares's letters and state papers reinforce the image conveyed by contemporaries of an extravagant, out-sized personality with a gift for endless self-dramatisation. His inflated and tortuous prose wanders down interminable labyrinths. He digresses, he repeats himself, he consumes an enormous quantity of words to make a relatively simple point. He blames himself before God and the king, and in general seems to use the device of the state paper as a mixture of advocate's brief and confessional.[11]

Like his counterpart, Olivares saw his primary function in terms of shoring up an apparently threatened international position, and regarded most domestic matters as ultimately a means to that end. But he could also call on a long tradition of officially tolerated public opinion amongst the political elite and amongst intellectual commentators such as the *arbitristas*. These latter (who can be described as political–economic theorists and moralists producing a variable range and quality of written recommendations or *arbitrios* for government reform and social regeneration) helped to create a wider awareness of the need for change in economic policy, trade, poor relief and religious outlook. Some *arbitristas*, notably Sancho de Moncada (in 1619) and Jeronimo Zeballos (in 1621) even advocated a rational restructuring of government as a means to more effective use of royal power, suggestions which Olivares could use to make state intervention more acceptable.

One obvious and already well-tried means of invigorating the cumbersome council government in Madrid, and increase speed, was to use smaller committees or *juntas*. Olivares adopted this approach extensively in the 1620s to achieve better administration of revenues and even, through the *junta de estado*, to circumvent the Council of State itself in the handling of crucial foreign policy decisions. A stricter control was also imposed on the King's use of crown revenue for special royal favours (*mercedes*), on royal household expenditure and on some of the other financial abuses that had accrued in the large and parasitic court of Philip III. An earlier *junta de la reformación* was revived in 1622 to check on a wide range of degenerative abuses including peculation in the bureaucracy itself, but this, like Olivares's typically unrealistic sumptuary laws, seems to have generated more hostility than actual economies. As in France, the tax system itself was grossly unfair both geographically and socially, and in 1622 Olivares compiled plans for a replacement in Castile of the harsh *millones* food tax by a more equitable military contribution. This scheme, like various ideas for economic development to try to compete with the Dutch on their own terms, came to grief because of Cortes resistance and governmental clumsiness. Most important, however, were Olivares's far-sighted plans to integrate the diverse parts of the Spanish system more closely for mutual security. First formulated as a 'Union of

Arms' in 1624, involving set quotas of troops to be provided by each province and territory, the scheme was intended ultimately to curb provincial autonomy, reduce tariffs and political barriers, and produce some uniformity, particularly in the Iberian peninsula itself. It was hoped that this would reduce the disproportionate strain on Castile and create positive opportunities for the nobility of Aragon, Valencia and Catalonia, who habitually complained of discrimination in honours and appointments. Not surprisingly, the scheme met considerable hostility in the peripheral kingdoms, but in theory the basic military contribution system of the Union was eventually accepted not only in most of the Iberian provinces (including even Portugal), but also in Flanders and Italy. The Cortes of Catalonia, however, greatly weakened the scheme by refusing to co-operate or even to vote any war subsidy at all. In the 1630s Olivares was forced to supplement recruitment by hiring mercenaries from as far afield as Catholic Ireland and by compelling seigneurs to raise troops on their own estates by means of 'feudal' levies. This last measure caused offence because of Olivares's increasingly autocratic and arrogant attitude at court. His refusal to allow the grandees a meaningful role in conciliar government, and his growing reliance on his own appointees in small committees such as the *junta de ejecución* of 1634, ultimately contributed to deep resentment and alienation amongst the high nobility.

It is clear that most early seventeenth-century monarchies could disregard the financial realities of government to a remarkable degree, but the vitality of the entire economy was a different matter. Both the Iberian peninsula and Italy were from the early 1620s experiencing what can probably be described as a period of long-term economic depression and gradual depopulation, which led to severe contraction in traditionally important cities such as Valladolid and Toledo and impoverished some of the very high and barren rural inland areas. Antiquated agrarian techniques, growing peasant debt, unchecked seigneurial encroachment and the difficult conditions on the arid central plateau ensured that Castile was one of the areas most severely affected by the grain failures that hit all of Europe in the 1620s and again in the late 1640s. In spite of this trend, the burden on the Castilian taxpayer increased dramatically, effectively doubling during Olivares's ministry. In the peripheral provinces some recovery and agrarian diversification can be detected from mid-century, but for Castile the process of economic collapse seemed irreversible, and even large-scale sheep-farming organised by the old *mesta* (sheep-farmers' guild) stagnated in spite of the reputation which Spanish wool still enjoyed on the European market. Textile production, measured in terms of the number of operational looms, dwindled in the half-century from the 1590s, as did some other manufacturing industries and the dependent trade fairs of Medina and Burgos. The consequent growing reliance on foreign (even Dutch and English) suppliers for a widening range of commodities, including many types of war material, benefited ports like Bilbao but did not help the balance of payments. There was at the same time a gradual long-term change of relationship between Spain and its American possessions, during which (partly thanks to Dutch, French and English encroachment) the colonies acquired far greater economic self-sufficiency and commercial autonomy, while Spain itself seemed incapable of compensating for the loss of this preferential relationship by developing new sectors of the economy. The Crown aggravated the precipitous downward trend in the Atlantic trade in the second quarter of the century by resorting to an increasingly desperate and short-sighted taxation policy which merely encouraged fraud or business failure. In the 1630s the Crown's deficit was so serious that the government repeatedly resorted to outright confiscation of private silver shipments in return for depreciating vellon or *juros* compensation. One must avoid overestimating the extent to which seventeenth-century government could influence the overall state of the economy, but there can be little doubt that these crude and violently criticised policies contributed noticeably to the difficulties of the merchant communities in Seville and Cadiz at a time when the rest of the Spanish economy was also suffering from mismanaged taxation policies and lack of foresight.

These indications that all was not well in the Iberian economy did not go unnoticed: not only did the *arbitristas* list them all, but the Crown itself could hardly fail to notice the shortfalls in its tax revenue. As long as Spanish policies seemed to work satisfactorily in Europe, however, few statesmen abroad would dare make any easy assumptions about Spanish 'decline'. The capture of Breda in 1625 raised hopes in Madrid of at least limited success in Flanders, and encouraged the authorities to strengthen the economic blockade of the Dutch which, together with Dunkirk-based privateering, was making some impression on shipping even though restrictions were difficult to maintain for certain types of strategic materials for which Amsterdam was the main supplier. More serious was Spain's intervention in 1628 in the dispute over the Mantuan succession which, although understandable in terms of French, Savoyard and Venetian threats to the Spanish military centre in Milan, nevertheless turned into one of Olivares's most serious and expensive mistakes, nearly costing him his own ministerial position.[12] By then the Dutch had returned to the offensive in Flanders and in Brazil, establishing a valuable base in Pernambuco at the expense of the Portuguese. In 1635 the long-delayed declaration of war by France added a major new dimension to Spanish commitments, while the cutting of the Milan to Brussels land route in 1638 and the failure of the two large-scale naval expeditions against the Dutch in the north and in Brazil in 1639 began to indicate the scale of Spanish difficulties.

Throughout the 1620s the fiscal and hence military survival of the Spanish system had not seemed in doubt. The state bankruptcy of 1627 was deliberately precipitated by Olivares in order to free the crown of some of its expensive Genoese bankers and replace them with more amenable Portuguese Jewish and *converso* (Jewish-turned-Christian) financiers. Yet this move, coming shortly before the spectacular loss of the entire American treasure fleet to the Dutch in 1628, damaged the Crown's credit sufficiently to reduce the scope for the staggering level of deficit-financing which had kept the system going before 1627. Immediate shortfalls were made up by means of increased sales taxes and another issue of degraded vellon coinage, but by the early 1630s the situation had taken a decided turn for the worse. A wide range of additional and highly unpopular fiscal measures was attempted: payments due to holders of *juros* were confiscated, more vellon was issued in 1636, and extensive sales of crown lands were authorised, in addition to the desperate attempts noted earlier to squeeze more out of the Atlantic trade. A serious anti-fiscal riot occurred in Portugal in 1637, socially divisive and therefore readily suppressed but nevertheless indicative of the resentments building up. The Portuguese were increasingly dissatisfied with what they regarded as the Habsburg failure to prevent Dutch colonial encroachment and accused Olivares of leniency towards Jewish financiers (including the many who had emigrated to Amsterdam). In 1640 Portugal went into open revolt when Madrid asked for help to suppress disorder in Catalonia.

Trouble in Catalonia had occurred periodically: the Catalans had consistently refused to contribute to anything outside their own frontiers and were reluctant to face up to French border violations. Olivares, in any case increasingly short-tempered and harassed, decided to force Catalonia to accept the principle of the Union of Arms by making this region the base for military action against the French. A billeting of the Castilian army on Catalonia during the winter of 1639 to 1640, however, provoked open resistance and revolt (see chapter 7). Olivares hung on to power in despair until 1643, in the teeth of aristocratic revolt and ill-will, but the Spanish system had effectively given in. Olivares's nephew and successor, Don Luis de Haro, soon definitively abandoned all the aspirations of the previous decades. In May 1643 a Spanish force invading France from Flanders was crushed at Rocroi, and only the domestic weakness of France prevented any follow-up.

Sweden and the challenge of empire

Sweden can hardly be regarded as a naturally expansionist state in the early seventeenth century. Its slight human resources, amounting to a total of perhaps 1½ million in Sweden and Finland, were not favoured by any major economic advantages – except perhaps the Falun copper mines, the Bergslagen iron mines and the resultant manufacturing enterprises which supplemented the potential of an otherwise over-whelmingly agrarian northern society. By European standards, the Swedish economy was underdeveloped and beset by enormous limita-tions, not least of which were difficulties of transport and the over-whelming reliance on barter or payments in kind for all types of transactions, even within the state's own offices and agencies. The Crown itself, separated from Denmark–Norway in 1523, had been weakened after the death of Gustav Vasa in 1560, when political rivalry and extreme religious differences between his sons destabilised an otherwise successful ruling dynasty. The Augsburg Confession and other fundamental Lutheran dogma was only formally accepted in 1593, a year after the succession fell by hereditary right to a grandson, Sigismund, already Catholic King of Poland. Resistance and usurpa-tion eventually enabled Sigismund's uncle, Charles (youngest son of Gustav Vasa), to have himself proclaimed King in 1604, but in so doing he brutally exploited religious and factional animosities, raised new sectarian spectres through his Calvinist sympathies, and created a long-term nominal constitutional threat to the Swedish throne from the older branch of the family in Poland. Religious controversy in fact never became serious, but Sweden remained one of the most staunchly inflexible Lutheran states in Europe, giving it an ideological stability which most other powers lacked in the Thirty Years War. The usurpation itself, however, was an issue which Sigismund could use in the emerging power struggle around the eastern Baltic provinces and which (after his death in 1632) even his sons continued to exploit.

The area from the eastern end of the Gulf of Finland to Lithuania, including the major ports of Narva, Reval and Riga, was the main outlet for a lucrative trade in naval supplies, furs and other raw mate-rials for the West. Denmark, Sweden and Poland–Lithuania all sought to control and profit from this trade, while Muscovy attempted to gain a permanent maritime outlet of its own. Sweden's direct involvement began in 1560 when Reval asked for protection against the other powers. Economic prospects, as well as political and strategic consid-erations, led to Swedish expansion through Estonia and (in 1600) even Livonia. The death of Boris Godunov in 1605, which plunged Muscovy into anarchy (the Time of Troubles) and temporarily ended its role in the Baltic, also enticed Sigismund to attempt an invasion of Russia. Although this moved the centre of conflict eastwards, the potential threat to the Finnish border remained considerable, and the Vasas felt obliged to intervene in Muscovy against the Polish claimant. In 1611, however, Christian IV of Denmark launched a direct attack on Sweden which presented Gustav Adolf, on his succession later that year at the age of barely 17, with an enormous military task on two fronts. The Danish war, ending with the Peace of Knäröd in 1613, was not fully decisive, but Christian secured various concessions including a five-year hold on Älvsborg, Sweden's only North Sea port, subject to a redemption fee of one million riksdalers. This part of the settlement emphasised the degree to which Swedish overseas trade was intentionally hemmed in by the Danish Crown: all shipping now had to pass through Danish territorial waters and most of it would go through the narrow straights off Helsingør (Elsinore) where the Danes checked on all vessels including Swedish ones, despite their exemption from the usual toll payments. It is not surprising, therefore, that the Swedish *riksdag* (Estates General) accepted the imposition of a huge extraordinary tax which, together with Dutch loans, just paid off the redemption fee in time. The recovery of Älvsborg, however, did not entirely remove Swedish fears of encirclement, and effective co-operation between Christian and Gustav Adolf in the European war consequently remained out of the question. War between the two monarchies was avoided until 1643, yet the Swedish Crown could never be sure whether Christian would exploit an awkward moment of diplomatic friction (as in 1624) to attempt to redress the balance.

On the eastern front, Sweden achieved a more decisive settlement. A peace with the still-weak Romanov dynasty in Muscovy was signed at Stolbova in 1617, granting Sweden control of the rest of the area around the Gulf of Finland, which was mostly wasteland but of strategic significance in further debarring Muscovy from access to the sea. Relations with Poland, however, remained very tense, especially as Sigismund tried to secure wider Habsburg and Counter-Reformation assistance against Sweden. Gustav responded by pushing through draconian legislation designed to reduce domestic contacts with Catholicism (the Statute of Örebro, 1617), so that the war against Poland, continuous except for reluctant periods of truce, acquired a more explicit confessional dimension. The capture of Riga in 1621, however, also underlined the substantial economic aspects of the conflict in that it gave Sweden control over another large segment of the eastern Baltic trade, including some of the grain exports. Originally intended as a bargaining counter, Riga in fact remained in Swedish hands, and by 1626 most of Livonia was secured. Gustav then moved westwards to the mouth of the Vistula, establishing a strong base in this economically prosperous area, but he failed to secure Danzig itself in time for Tilly's and Wallenstein's sweep towards the Baltic (1627–9). The alteration in the German balance, and the threat that it posed to Swedish religious and political interests once Danish resistance to imperial forces collapsed, not only facilitated the short-lived co-operation between Christian and Gustav over Stralsund in 1628 but also hastened the signing of the Polish Truce of Altmark of 1629, mediated by the French envoy Charnacé in order to clear the last obstacle to direct Swedish involvement in the Empire.

That Sweden was gradually sucked into the European conflict in this way is not surprising, given the long-standing threat from Sigismund, the lack of political stability in the eastern Baltic, the value of the trade through that area and the escalation of the war in Germany itself. What *was* extraordinary was Sweden's ability to sustain such a rapidly growing role in European affairs, despite its recent political troubles and still only limited resources. Royal charisma and a handful of effective administrative and military advisors account for part of this achievement; rapid development of industrial resources and a successful naval deployment and army reorganisation in the 1620s clearly also helped. The unusual emphasis on nationally conscripted foot-soldiers made army discipline easier to achieve, and was indispensable at first because it imposed less of a direct financial burden on the state. The loss of native manpower, however, was considerable, for upwards of half the 10,000 annual conscripts from Sweden and Finland in the years 1626 to 1631 did not survive their first year of service, particularly because of epidemics in the war zones. The effects of such a drastic loss of young men on a thinly populated country were clearly observable by the 1630s and have left unmistakable evidence in parish records. The Crown eventually tried to minimise the damage by concentrating its nationals on garrison and domestic duty, but in any case the proportion of conscripts to mercenaries dwindled as the total size of Swedish forces increased from about 18,000 men in 1621 to over twice that number in 1630, followed by an even more pronounced growth over the next two years. The shift towards expensive hired troops, however, created a far more urgent problem of finance, for which the Crown was not well prepared.

Gustav Adolf had taken over some of his father's debts in 1611 and quickly incurred new ones, not least over Älvsborg. This produced a sharp rise in the rate of interest payable when new loans were needed in the 1620s, sometimes approaching 20 per cent. The demands of war had made the wholesale adoption of tax farming unavoidable in 1621 in order to convert the predominant payments in kind (especially in agrarian produce, tar, copper and other local commodities) into money that could be used abroad. As elsewhere in Europe, however, revenue farming created its own problems, and was gradually abandoned in the early 1630s. The sale of offices and titles by the Crown was avoided altogether. But amongst the expedients that were definitively adopted was the alienation of crown land for cash (mostly at first in the new Baltic provinces), and the gradual imposition of new or augmented extraordinary taxes affecting all subjects. The *boskapshjälp* of 1620, for example, was a tax payable in cash on both arable land and domestic animals, granted by the Estates and gradually extended fully even to the hitherto privileged tenants living within a Swedish mile of a noble manor. Various indirect taxes and poll taxes were also attempted, including ones without concessions to noble interests, but none of these domestic expedients made sufficient impression in terms of the huge expenditure of war. The real breakthrough in this respect came with the extension of the Baltic campaigns westwards in 1626–7. Naval control or occupation of most of the Prussian and Livonian ports gave Sweden ready access to customs and toll revenues from Baltic shipping, and in this respect the Polish truce of 1629 was preferable to a proper peace since occupied areas were not relinquished meantime. Tolls were not always reliable, and fell during 1630 because of a slump in trade and harvests. But by that stage a sophisticated and carefully managed system of contributions, impositions or ransoms, partly payable in money and partly in supplies and quartering, was being imposed on all available areas in Germany. This rapidly brought down the share which Sweden itself had to pay towards the costs of the war in the Empire itself, but (as we have seen in chapter 1) made territorial expansion and deepening political involvement unavoidable, and hence soon generated friction with the north-German allies.

Remarkably, domestic friction was relatively limited, despite the inexorably growing demands of the Crown and the well-established precedents for civil disobedience generated by several of Gustav's predecessors on the throne. Sweden had in fact become a kind of elective–hereditary monarchy in the later sixteenth century, in that two legitimate rulers had been deposed (Erik XIV in 1568 because of aristocratic hostility and his own increasing insanity; Sigismund in 1599 because of his Catholicism and the ambitions of his uncle), and in their place a suitable senior member of the Vasa family had been 'elected' by an assembly of Estates. In the second instance, however, this election had occurred only after an interval during which Charles (IX) was at first made regent for life of a 'monarchy in abeyance'.[13] His insistence on various constitutional niceties before being crowned in 1604 could not disguise the breach of the hereditary principle, and his ruthlessness towards hostile factions within the aristocracy and amongst Polish émigrés had hardly induced forgiveness amongst his political enemies. The succession of Charles's son, Gustav, had been accepted by the Estates in 1604, but the charter which Gustav had to sign in 1611 amounted to an ominous condemnation by the aristocracy of the excesses of his father. It also imposed stricter limitations on the constitutional authority of the King, who was to some extent bound to listen to the advice of the *riksråd* (council) of magnates.

In practice, potential conflict between Crown and aristocracy was quickly defused thanks to the exceptional abilities of the man who was appointed chancellor, Axel Oxenstierna – himself a leader of the aristocracy but willing to form a fruitful working relationship with the King lasting for the entire reign. Even so, the early years were still characterised by failures to assert royal authority against individual overmighty subjects and by the difficulties of creating anything that could remotely be regarded as an effective local administrative system loyal to the Crown alone. The establishment of a supreme court in 1614 was intended to help restore royal judicial control, but reform of the local courts was beset with problems. The substantial reorganisation of the antiquated central administration, and the gradual emergence of five major departments or colleges (including the wide-ranging chancellery and the crucial treasury) undoubtedly helped to secure effectiveness at the centre, but even then intercollegiate rivalries and the shortage of trained staff continued to cause difficulties.

At the local level, new burdens were placed especially on the clergy, who were made to help compile conscription lists and were expected to back the all-pervading war effort from the pulpit – partly to maintain domestic ideological cohesion, partly to broadcast the basic moral justification for what contemporaries regarded as a 'just war', a war of legitimate self-defence. Most of the Swedish clergy accepted this role, and there can be no doubt that for Gustav Adolf and most of his subjects the moral and religious case was incontrovertible.[14] The weight of such argument, combined with a policy of divide and rule towards the Estates as a whole (and towards the nobility in particular after the new ranking system imposed on them in 1626), helped to contain incipient resistance to the war. In the 1620s, indeed, local opposition focused mostly on the recruiting agents and tax farmers, particularly if a local seigneur was one or both of these, or if he had acquired inadequately defined authority as a recipient of lands and revenues alienated by the impecunious Crown. Sometimes, as in 1627 in the notoriously restless area north-west of the capital known as Dalarna, open revolts did occur, but they were poorly organised, geographically isolated and (in contrast to some French revolts) lacking in effective leadership.

The years after Gustav's death in 1632 brought territorial setbacks and hence new financial difficulties in Germany. In Sweden itself the war began to appear distant and pointless, and there was a belated reaction against the overwhelming burdens and the autocratic style of government which Gustav's policies had entailed. In 1635 the anxious and despondent *råd* in Stockholm accepted an extension of the truce with Poland on unfavourable terms, involving the relinquishment of

Prussia and its valuable tolls, while at the same time it recognised that Sweden would have to reduce its exactions in Germany in order to arrest growing disenchantment with its presence there. This was undoubtedly the most difficult period for Sweden, for its aims of security and financial compensation seemed to recede beyond reach, and its resources became so inadequate that Oxenstierna himself was kept hostage in Magdeburg in 1635 by his unpaid troops.[15] His definitive return to Sweden the following year, however, restored firmness to the regency government, while the military revival in Germany and renewed subsidies from France after 1637 once again reduced overseas costs. A more lenient conscription policy and greater flexibility in the imposition of extraordinary taxes on the politically sensitive tenancies in noble domains eased the strain by the end of the decade.

Another reason for the preservation of a frail domestic tranquillity was perhaps the growing effectiveness of the *riksdag,* which consolidated its influence in the period after agreement had been reached on the Form of Government in 1634 (a kind of constitutional document outlining the regency system but also permanently defining key structural elements in the Swedish government). The aristocratic council had initially hoped to consolidate its constitutional position permanently after Gustav Adolf's death, but in practice the Form of Government was not recognised by the Estates as an immutable fundamental law binding also on an adult monarch. The Estates had even gone so far as to claim sovereign authority for the duration of the minority, the right to confirm appointments to high offices of state and the right to form its own resolutions, and although such powers were not conceded by the regency, the claims give some indication of growing political maturity in which even the Fourth Estate (the peasantry) had some share. After the end of the regency in 1644, however, latent grievances re-emerged: the political dominance of the high aristocracy did not end, and Oxenstierna himself provoked considerable resentment, not least with Queen Christina herself. In addition, Christina was irresponsibly generous with crown lands and revenues, which she alienated and donated to favourites and supporters on an unprecedented scale, stretching Swedish finances at the very time when the generous terms secured at Westphalia in 1648 should have made some relaxation of wartime austerity possible. It was on this, in particular, that the Estates of 1650 focused their attention, revealing in the process some of the deeper divisions that had formed in Swedish society over the previous decades (see chapter 7).

Christian IV and 'elective monarchy' in Denmark

At the beginning of the seventeenth century, Denmark was regarded as the dominant Baltic power. It had a well-established role as an entrepot in the northern European trade network, could export cattle and some grain to Germany and the west, and, because of its possession of Scania and other parts of what is now southern Sweden, it stood astride all the waterways connecting the Baltic with the open sea. Its dynastic union with Norway, although entailing some drain of manpower and leadership away from the less developed region, provided the basis for uninterrupted trade links in northern Europe beneficial to both. The dual monarchy had neither the decisive mineral resources of Sweden nor the vast potential for competitive grain production of Poland, but it was in closer commercial, cultural and political contact with the rest of Europe.

Not unlike the Holy Roman Empire, the Danish–Norwegian states were ruled by a nominally elective but in effect virtually hereditary dynasty. The elective principle, even when the succession was not in fact in doubt, nevertheless enabled the high nobility to impose electoral capitulations or charters on each succeeding monarch. This practice, formalised from 1282, had after many successions resulted in the fairly restrictive charters of the early modern period, including that signed by Christian IV at the end of his minority in 1596. According to these charters, sovereignty was held jointly by the King and the aristocratic council of state (*rigsråd*), and the consent of the latter was required notably for declarations of war and for the imposition of extraordinary taxes. The council usually also had some influence on appointments to high offices of state and was customarily consulted over other central issues. But the King had considerable room for initiative simply by virtue of controlling daily administration and by constituting the central executive power at all times, especially when the council was not in session. It is interesting to note that although the council held sole sovereignty during the minority for Christian IV from 1588 to 1596 and was clearly represented at the church service which constituted the centrepiece of the coronation in 1596, the Bishop of Zealand, Peder Vinstrup, nevertheless on that occasion also referred explicitly to the ideas of divine right monarchy current in Europe at the time: that the King was a reflection of God on earth, and his agent there, endowed with special qualities raising him above ordinary mortals, and ultimately responsible to Him alone for the way he carried out his duties as prince.[16]

In practice, the balance between the circumscribed monarchy sought by the aristocratic council and the more personalised form visualised by the dynamic and colourful Christian was a precarious one. The King evidently co-operated with the high officers of state, but never worked in close harness with any particular ones in the way that Gustav Adolf did with Oxenstierna in Sweden. On the contrary, the King deliberately delayed making new appointments both to the council and to the offices of state when vacancies occurred, and sought to split the council by encouraging individualism behind its corporately united facade. Although he consulted the council over matters of legislation and aspects of domestic policy, including his various mercantilistic schemes for economic development, he regarded especially financial policy and foreign relations as his particular responsibility. He pressurised the council into backing his war with Sweden in 1611 and, although his resources were insufficient to gain a decisive advantage in this conflict, the mercenary army made enough impact on the still relatively unsophisticated and otherwise committed Swedish conscript army to achieve the moderately advantageous peace of 1613, which reinforced the King's position. As mentioned earlier (p. 13), Christian's policies in northern Germany over the next decade made sense in terms of his own reading of Danish–Swedish rivalry in northern European trade and in the Baltic balance of power, but his precipitous direct intervention in the Thirty Years War in 1625 had an immediately destabilising effect on domestic politics.

A central aspect of Christian's growing independence of the council until the later 1620s was his financial strength. During the later sixteenth century and the early years of the reign the Crown had achieved a financial surplus by means of some reorganisation of crown-land revenues and by tightening the terms on which nobles were made governors of the *len* or royal fiefs. (This policy, incidentally, also caused some resentment amongst both the new governors and those members of the lesser nobility who felt they were being discriminated against in the choice for vacancies.) In addition, income was also increased from the tolls imposed on international shipping to and from the Baltic passing through the Sound. Any resulting surplus was, in accordance with tradition, regarded as being at the direct disposal of the King's own chamber (royal treasury) without reference to the council. By 1623 Christian had a surplus of around one and a half million thalers, a position of strength unusual amongst the monarchs of the day. As Christian became increasingly impatient with what he regarded as the restrictive myopia of the council in the early 1620s, he used his financial reserves to take certain liberties with constitutional restraints and aristocratic advice. The council, for its part, had by 1624 come to regard his German policies with alarm, fearing an involvement which they could not actually prevent as long as the King could manage without the grant of additional taxes. They were correct in assuming that even if Christian entered the war in his capacity as Duke of Holstein, the whole kingdom would soon be involved. But they were probably also more uncooperative than necessary because of their fear of royal autocratic tendencies and their failure to adapt their own individual and collective role to the changing circumstances of the early seventeenth-century state.

Christian's intervention in the Thirty Years War proved, as noted, a serious miscalculation. Military defeat led to the destructive occupation of Jutland by Wallenstein's forces from 1627 to 1629, which reduced the Crown's ordinary revenue by a substantial amount. In addition, the cost of hiring mercenaries quickly exhausted the King's accumulated financial surplus. He was compelled hastily to recall significant loans made over the previous decades to individual noble families, thereby generating considerable resentment amongst those debtors who could not readily find other credit because of wartime disruption. Ultimately he was also forced to fall back on emergency taxation, which had to have council approval.

The scale of the damage to Jutland by Wallenstein's occupying forces was aggravated immediately by poor harvests in 1629 and 1630 and by the havoc of a concurrent plague epidemic. A complaint from merchant interests of the towns in Jutland in 1629 pleaded for a conscript national army to replace the rapacious mercenary forces. It also specifically attacked noble privileges which might damage urban trading interests and were liable to shift most of the real costs of national defence on to the towns and peasants of the Crown. The King allowed these grievances to be formulated more strongly at a meeting of town representatives in Ry later that year, where the tone clearly turned very hostile to the nobility generally. But since the King was not prepared to take up burgher complaints at such a critical juncture, nothing came of this first attempt by commoners to take collective action against noble privilege in Denmark.[17]

Although the terms of the Peace of Lübeck of 1629 were very lenient for Denmark, the conduct of the war and the scale of expenditure led to mutual recriminations and deep resentment focusing on the constitutional balance between king and council. Already in 1628 Christian demanded extraordinary taxation to.compensate him retrospectively for his war expenditure, and refused to ratify the Lübeck terms until the council had promised a large sum repayable over a period of years. This might have enabled the King to restore his own financial surplus, had it not been for the continuing costs of the army and navy which the precarious international situation after 1629 dictated. Sweden's successes in Germany made this even more necessary after 1631, so that the King was unable to restore his financial autonomy. The council did authorise the imposition of more extraordinary taxes, the overall burden of which amounted in the years 1629–43 to twice that of the equivalent pre-war period. But once the council's compensatory grant of one million thalers had been paid in 1637, the King was in effect put under council administration as far as tax revenues were concerned. Control was exercised by means of a *generalkrigskommissariat* staffed by the aristocracy, and its scope was sufficient to deprive the Crown of any flexibility in terms of its other revenues and commitments. The King considered reforming the royal fiefs once more, but since most of the provincial governors were members of the upper aristocracy this approach had to be abandoned for fear of further council opposition. A fundamental shift in the basis of state funding was beginning to take place, with profound consequences for crown and council alike. The records do not allow us to ascertain what the council in fact expected the King to do, but they may have clung to outdated financial assumptions of the past, expecting the Crown to meet costs, at least in peacetime, out of its normal income. The creation of a standing army in 1637 made this impossible. In the circumstances Christian had to resort to other expedients, including new loans and, in 1638, a drastic increase in the Sound Tolls. This worked in the short term but soon raised international protests, notably from the Dutch. The council was aware of this danger but seems to have offered no alternative.[18]

By the end of the 1630s, therefore, the growing commitments of the Crown had resulted in a deadlock between king and council which amounted to something not far short of a constitutional crisis. The King had clearly not made co-operation easy, thanks to his obstinacy and the extravagance of court life in the 1630s (including the spectacular wedding festivities for a son and a daughter in 1634). On the other hand, even the council had to recognise the legitimacy of national defence interests, which were brought emphatically into relief during the short but disastrous confrontation with Swedish forces under Torstensson (1643–5). Denmark was thereby demonstrably reduced to a second-rate power in the Baltic by comparison with Sweden and was eliminated from any significant role in the final negotiations leading to the Peace of Westphalia in 1648. But the burden of debts on the Crown was also increased once more, making the need for additional extraordinary taxes acute in 1645. In fact, demands were now, at five times the level of 1601–5, near the limit of what a disrupted economy could support, and by 1646 refusal or inability to pay taxes produced a major gap between anticipated and real revenue for the state. More heavy-handed collection procedures led to the first signs since 1629 of dissatisfaction amongst commoners over the unequal distribution of taxation and over the continuing if now incomplete exemption of the nobility.

Christian IV, characteristically, had attempted to divide the council into opposing factions, notably via two of his aristocratic sons-in-law, Corfitz Ulfeldt and Hannibal Sehested. While the latter remained loyal to the King and acquired much influence as Viceroy of Norway, Ulfeldt freed himself from the King by 1645 and became a leader of the opposition. The council's control over taxation was radically strengthened in 1645 and the procedure for election of new council members was clarified so as to fix membership at 22 and reduce the

King's freedom in the choice of new candidates. At the same time, however, the burden of taxation had led many of the lesser provincial nobility to question the desirability of the council's exclusive and domineering influence on policy and to demand a more effective say in government by means of standing provincial commissions of nobles known as *landkommissariater*. These commissions had been set up at the Estates General of 1638 but became much more influential in the last years of the reign. Detailed studies of membership of the council and the *landkommissariater*[19] have shown that this development did not correspond directly to a confrontation between the higher aristocracy and the lesser nobility; on the contrary, social backgrounds, careers and education within these groups were very similar and a number of those serving as commissioners in fact became councillors in due course. Nevertheless, the commissioners did to some extent provide an alternative focus to the exclusive council, especially for those who had failed to gain high office and who did not have family contacts with the high aristocracy. The commissioners even gained some collective influence on the choice of new council members and had a say in the imposition and use of extraordinary taxes for the armed forces. By the time of the death of Christian IV early in 1648, therefore, the political situation was quite unstable: on the one hand, the balance between crown and council had led to deadlock over a number of key aspects of government, with neither king nor council providing a fully satisfactory kind of leadership in the context of the later war years; on the other hand, there was at least some basis for the formation of a stronger power-base for the nobility as a whole, perhaps in connection with the Estates structure, along lines similar to those emerging in Sweden during the regencies. Additional immediate uncertainty was created by the fact that the intended crown prince, Christian, had died before his father (in 1647), so that the succession fell to a younger prince, Frederick, who had not been trained for kingship and who was a withdrawn and awkward person.

Crown and Parliament in England

By tradition and, until fairly recently, common consent amongst historians, the history of early seventeenth-century England (more than Scotland or Ireland) appeared to offer so many contrasts with that of other European countries that comparative treatment seemed pointless. The Whig tradition in English historical writing, with its vision of early Stuart history as a protracted and irreversible trend towards the constitutional confrontations of the civil war and ultimately towards the 'liberation' of the Revolution of 1688, contrasted sharply with developments on the continent towards dynastic and supposedly centralising absolutism. No other major power was able to isolate itself sufficiently to avoid foreign war from the 1630s into the 1650s, no other society experienced as rapid and pervasive a political apprenticeship as England in that period and no other European country had a parliament strong enough to resist and then fight its own monarch successfully. Although England formed an essential part of the debate over 'the crisis of the seventeenth century', to which we shall return, its deep-reaching civil war, and much of the constitutional development preceding it, seemed unique.

This distinctiveness has in many ways been emphasised by the enormous amount of research done not only on early seventeenth-century parliaments and some of the leading political figures but also on the development of individual localities, making us far more familiar with England than with any other part of Europe in these decades. Yet, in the process, certain doubts also emerged concerning the traditional framework of parliamentary history: the polarisation into 'government' and 'opposition', into court versus country. In 1975 H. G. Koenigsberger suggested that the survival of the English parliament was due not in the first instance to its long-assumed institutional or procedural strengths but to unpredictable external factors, notably the Scottish intervention of 1640 and the Irish rebellion the following year. The challenge was taken up by Conrad Russell in a compelling revisionist article published in the following year. Subsequent reinterpretation and debate, although not always as constructively cautious as that of Russell, has at the very least led to an acceptance amongst historians that English parliamentary history is less linear or 'progressive' than it once appeared, and that the 1630s in particular can be seen from a number of different perspectives.[20]

The Tudor and Stuart monarchy was different from many of its continental counterparts in that national sovereignty was embodied jointly in King and Parliament (and not just in King and aristocratic council as in France or the Scandinavian monarchies). The English Crown was subject, just as on the continent, to accepted if ill-defined norms of law, but was also expected to abide by parliamentary statute in order to retain the co-operation of the political nation. Elizabeth, despite growing tensions towards the end of her reign, had basically preserved this consensus. The substantial costs of the war against Spain (1585–1604) and the Irish rebellion were met at least in part out of those local taxation and parliamentary grants for defence which were customary in times of extraordinary need. Elizabeth's legendary niggardliness meant that the ordinary revenue of the Crown (from crown land and regalian rights) appeared sufficient for the rest. In fact neither the outright sale of crown lands nor her way of rewarding servants in kind (for example with grants of monopoly rights) prevented her from accumulating debt, and her legacy to James in this respect soon became obvious. Not only was he expected to compensate the servants of the Crown with greater generosity, but the size of his royal family, coupled with his financial insouciance and personal extravagance, soon made crown solvency a chimera. Robert Cecil (later Earl of Salisbury) attempted to increase crown revenues by farming out the customs in 1604 and, as Lord Treasurer after 1608, proposed a major reform of state finances (the Great Contract) which was seriously considered by Parliament in 1610 but ultimately abandoned. A decade later Lionel Cranfield (Lord Treasurer 1621–4) belatedly tackled the costliness of the wardrobe and the royal household itself, but the fact that he was a protégé of the Duke of Buckingham did not save him from the inescapable unpopularity of such reformers and he was impeached in 1624. As in the continental monarchies, therefore, no restructuring of the state's financial system was achieved. The crown continued to muddle along by means of ad hoc expedients: for example, the sale of baronetcies yielded altogether £420,000, not far short of the total sums granted by Parliament over the first 14 years of the English reign, while the revenue from customs could readily be increased from the £70,000 a year cited in 1614. Indeed, there was already a clear case to be made, from purely financial standpoints, for preferring the kind of autocratic fiscal expedients characteristic of continental monarchy to the inevitable limitations of income based on parliamentary consent. Both approaches were in fact tried and neither worked.

Co-operation between Crown and Parliament had always been based on a rough consensus over aims. Under the Tudors, the House of Commons had assumed something like political parity with the hereditary House of Lords and, for all its weaknesses, the system of elections to the Commons did ensure representation for the gentry and a considerable part of the better-off adult male population.[21] As a result, no one questioned the absolute validity of parliamentary legislation on secular matters and its decisions were binding. This was convenient for the Crown, as long as it could achieve a reasonable part of its aims by carefully managing parliamentary sessions, and the political nation as a whole also stood to gain, for their delegates could rely on tradition and precedent to voice local grievances and could sometimes even gain remedies by means of a private parliamentary bill. By comparison with continental assemblies, these were clear points of strength.[22]

The history of the English parliament, however, is not a simple success story. In 1610 James told Parliament:

Kings are justly called gods for that they exercise a manner or resemblance of divine power upon earth . . . Kings . . . make and unmake their subjects; they have power of raising, and casting down; of life, and of death, judges over all their subjects, and in all causes, and yet accountable to none but

God only. They have power to . . . make of their subjects like men at the
chess . . . and cry up or down any of their subjects, as they do their
money.[23]

Later in that speech James qualified this by emphasising his respect
for the natural law of the kingdom. And in practice he was both too
lazy and too disorganised to exercise anything remotely resembling
this kind of autocratic control either in England or in Scotland. Like
most of his continental counterparts, however, James could and did
veto legislation, did appoint his officials and advisors unhampered,
did have an obvious advantage in being the central part of a continuously operating executive and, not least, had the right to adjourn or
dissolve parliament (or not call it at all) if he felt that that would best
serve his own interests. It is a central argument amongst the revisionist historians that these powers have been underrated and that in fact
Parliament was a much more precarious institution than hitherto
assumed. Conrad Russell emphasises that Parliament before 1640
usually failed to link the redress of grievances effectively to the voting
of subsidies. Although the Commons recognised the importance of
such a bargaining power all along, they only once used it against
James, in 1614 over the issue of impositions (customs levied by the
Crown without parliamentary consent), and the result was immediate
dissolution. The parliament of 1621, by contrast, voted supply with
alacrity, in the hope that James would be well disposed towards the
calling of Parliament in future. However, the subsidy bill was in fact
the only legislation passed by that parliament.

From this one can only draw the conclusion that James maintained
at least the spirit of consensus between Crown and Parliament. He
clearly had his faults, including his inefficiency, his awkwardness and
his inability in his ailing later years to provide his English subjects
with convincing leadership. Chronically short of funds, James and his
entourage were particularly susceptible to venality and to persuasion
accompanied by money. Such was, for example, his acceptance of
Alderman Cockayne's project of 1614, an unsuccessful speculative
project seeking to channel all cloth exports through the still very
underdeveloped English dyeing and finishing industries, in the event
contributing to a slump in the whole industry. More damaging to his
public reputation was his failure to tackle the large-scale corruption at
court, aggravated as it was by his homosexual penchant for male
favourites and his inability to ward off their predatory families, most
notably the Howards and the kin of George Villiers, Duke of
Buckingham. Yet, for all the tensions and misunderstandings with the
Commons and the growing hostility of the public, James was not
fundamentally out of step with the interests of his subjects. His ability, for example, to keep religious extremism at bay was respected by

the majority. His pacific foreign policy also had obvious advantages for English and Scottish taxpayers and merchants, but was less widely appreciated after 1618 owing to popular sympathy for the Protestant cause and for Princess Elizabeth in the Palatinate.

Charles I and the abandonment of consensus politics

Charles aroused more genuine antipathy as soon as he succeeded in 1625. He avoided some of the 'Scottish' idiosyncrasies of his father's style of kingship so noticed by the English, but instead appeared aloof, arrogant and cold. An almost Spanish formality at court was imposed immediately and access to the King was severely curtailed. Charles liked to work alone and did not tolerate as much outspoken independence from his councillors as James had done. The Duke of Buckingham achieved the remarkable feat of remaining at the centre of the court after the succession but his abuse of the patronage system and the enormous gains of his family made him a growing liability for the Crown. Charles characteristically refused to let himself be influenced by outside pressures, so by the time the Commons in 1626 initiated impeachment procedures against Buckingham they had broad support in the Lords and even in the privy council itself. They also made more subtle use of their bargaining powers by approving subsidies in principle but delaying the bill in committee pending the impeachment – at a time when the Crown was particularly short of funds because of the war against Spain (1625–30). But even in these circumstances, as revisionist historians have emphasised, Charles eventually simply dissolved Parliament and replaced the lost subsidies with a forced loan which, although unpopular, was successfully collected. He also continued to collect Tonnage and Poundage, although its customary approval by Parliament in 1625 had not gone through.

The strains of war showed clearly in the parliament of 1628, for even though England was at the periphery of the Thirty Years War, Buckingham and Charles had mishandled their foreign policies so remarkably that they had provoked a war with France (1627–9) while that with Spain was still in progress. Significantly, the Commons did not resume immediate criticism of Buckingham – the problem disappeared when he was assassinated later that year. Instead they voted five subsidies and again delayed them in committee while submitting the Petition of Right. Chief amongst its grievances were the burdens of martial law, billeting of troops, arbitrary taxation (including impositions again, not to mention the forced loan) and imprisonment of those who refused to pay. Charles accepted the Petition but later made it clear that he had done so subject to his own interpretation of its terms, in practice invalidating it. By the second session of that parliament

(January–March 1629) this was clear to many members, and yet, as the revisionist school has stressed, the Commons did not try to make a constitutional issue out of it. A point had already been made and it was recognised that, since the sums being offered in the subsidy bills were in fact too small to be worth the effort, the Crown could terminate discussion at any time. Charles was well aware of his ability to raise funds by extra-parliamentary means, and the redress of grievances would often have involved the loss of significant crown resources anyway.

Had Parliament by 1629 gone beyond being a traditional vehicle for government by consent, a useful guarantor of fiscal legality? There is no doubt that political consciousness developed rapidly in England as a result of the major conflicts in the parliaments of 1626 and 1628–9 and that a parochial and limited outlook characteristic of, say, the French Estates of 1614 no longer predominated. There was one exception to this, namely matters of foreign policy: the Commons remained – perhaps owing to an incurable insularity of English public opinion – unrealistic and irresponsible in this respect. MPs were under pressure from their constituencies, where understanding of the European conflict was so minimal that Charles's and Buckingham's diplomatic incompetence was not fully grasped, but where the threat posed by wartime policies to the traditional system of autonomous local self-government was all too clear. In the long run, the Crown was forfeiting the full co-operation of its local officials – members of the gentry who were not paid but who expected rewards in terms of local influence, patronage and advantages in, for example, tax assessments. Many MPs responded to, or exploited, the mounting provincial resentments and increasingly in the later 1620s emphasised issues of principle. Opinions differed over how to react to the Crown's demand for very large war taxes: some MPs refused to assist until the manifest corruption around Buckingham had been reduced, while others advocated giving the Crown a reasonable financial footing in return for a measure of power for Parliament and a guarantee against dissolution. But there was also a deeper dilemma for individual members as the demands of constituents and the Crown became more incompatible: it was becoming impossible to get through the private bills which might help to iron out local grievances and would give each member standing in his home community. At the same time MPs realised that their own careers and possible preferment to royal office, at a time when the Crown still employed men of all persuasions, might no longer be a social asset in the country. Impeachment procedures, even when unsuccessful, were becoming a highly effective propaganda tool against the Crown, but such tactics also widened the gap between court and country and reduced the possibility of compromise or reconciliation. In 1627 Charles's arbitrary and provocative imprisonment of some gentry who refused to contribute to his forced loan created prominent political martyrs and forced moderates in Parliament to reconsider their stand.

The most divisive issue, however, was religion. Fears grew concerning the high-church tendencies of Charles's entourage, and his own sympathy for Arminianism (with its modification of Calvinist belief in predestination and its greater emphasis on ritual and formality at the expense of the sermon). Given the disruptive power and all-dominating significance of strong religious convictions in early seventeenth-century Germany, France and Sweden, its significance in England and Scotland will come as no surprise. Arminianism threatened the peace within the Church, so painfully constructed in both countries since the later sixteenth century, and carefully preserved by James. When the Commons forcibly raised the question of Arminianism in 1629 they also fuelled fears of crypto-Catholicism at court (and not just around the French queen, Henrietta Maria). However, it is important not to exaggerate these problems: even Arminianism was more of a tendency than a consolidated deviance from established norms. The lack of clear division between government and 'opposition' was apparent in the ambivalence of many individual MPs; many were deeply worried by scenes such as the tumultuous vote on three protesting resolutions in March 1629, when the Speaker of the House had to be held in his chair by force to prevent adjournment. But if the resulting dissolution of Parliament seemed superficially to restore calm and put an end to any nascent corporate identity forming in the Commons, the authority of the Crown had not gone unchallenged.

By 1629, then, government by consensus had broken down, but not in a very clear-cut way. The personal rule of Charles, despite his manifestly unpopular church policies and disregard of fiscal conventions, did not cause serious trouble for almost a decade, and one may wonder whether a monarch less politically inept than Charles might not have steered England permanently towards a continental pattern of monarchy at this stage. Already, back in 1625, a prominent member of the Commons, Robert Phelips, had warned that Parliament might not be immune to the threats of encroaching princely power of the kind already visible on the continent. After 1630, when England withdrew from war and avoided the costs of standing armies which were so crippling for the French and Spanish monarchies, it did seem as if Parliament was a dispensable and troublesome luxury. Perhaps, as critics of the revisionist tendency have argued, the calm was only superficial: the speed with which Parliament evolved as an institution in the early 1640s suggests that the collective memory of the role of the Commons in the 1620s was still powerful. But whether we regard the 1630s as an unfinished experiment in English 'absolutism' or merely a lull before the storm, there is no doubt that the relative success of the

Crown's financial centralisation was crucial, not least in the context of continental efforts in that direction.

Ever since Bate's case in 1606 (a constitutional test case regarding customs) the Crown had been entitled to impose customs duties on foreign trade without reference to Parliament, and by the 1630s the combination of additional impositions and a growth in trade had raised the income from this source to £218,000 a year. It was thus not difficult to make up for the loss of the direct taxes authorised by Parliament. Ship money, traditionally an emergency tax for the navy in times of national danger, was imposed in 1634 and turned into an annual tax worth £200,000. Revenues from wardships, fines for knighthood and income from the sale of monopolies brought the total to nearly £1 million a year by the later 1630s, or twice that available to James three decades earlier. Only some of these measures generated resistance: the sale of monopolies, for example, did because of the cost to the consumer in terms of high prices and because important mercantile interests were affected. Yet even the trial of John Hampden in 1637 for refusal to pay ship money, in which five out of twelve judges voted against the Crown, did not produce immediate large-scale opposition. As late as 1638 nearly all ship money was still being paid, and resistance showed itself mostly in an administrative rather than a constitutional context in the form of complaints about ratings and valuations.

Given the overall increase in crown revenue, what causes most surprise is in fact the failure to balance income against expenditure even in these years of peace. Lord Treasurer Weston's efforts to reduce the deficit in the early 1630s had had no permanent effect, and royal household expenditure in particular remained very high. The Crown, very much like its continental counterparts, had to resort to anticipation of revenue, which by 1637 already amounted to the equivalent of one-third of annual income. Other expedients were contemplated, but an accumulating crown debt showed that, even at a time of low military spending, the situation was not durable.

More ominous was the fact that the Crown was now finding it surprisingly difficult to raise loans amongst the merchant interests of the City of London. Robert Ashton ascribed this to the fact that although monopolistic privileges and special concessions granted by the Crown were highly prized by London merchant interests, Buckingham's policies had damaged overseas trading in a number of significant ways, at the very time that the Commons (especially in 1626 and 1628) moderated their criticisms of corporate monopolies. The result was a split amongst the concessionaires: those involved in the unpopular domestic concessions continued to depend to some extent on crown protection but those in overseas trade – the most powerful in the municipal government – turned increasingly against the Crown. To make matters worse, there were confrontations between the City and the Crown in the 1630s over various issues, including the management of the Londonderry plantation in Ireland (which the City forfeited with a fine in 1635). A majority of the aldermen were therefore sufficiently critical of crown policies by the late 1630s to deprive Charles of an obvious source of credit, and their support for the moderate parliamentary cause in 1640 was crucial.[24]

London had also experienced Arminian church policies at first hand, since William Laud was Bishop of London from 1628, before he became Archbishop of Canterbury in 1633 and hence the most influential churchman at court. As unreceptive to public fears and resentment as Charles himself, Laud not only caused unnecessary offence in the 1630s by the way he implemented relatively harmless and well-meant policies designed to improve reverence and ritual dignity in church (for example, by moving and railing off communion tables), he also alienated much of the middle ground in Calvinist England through his more deep-reaching Arminian teaching, and the range of his influence could be alarming. Through the Court of High Commission Laud could exert a decisive influence on the censorship of books, and his views on subservience to established authority brought him well into the political arena in this respect, as in others. His desire to improve the position of the clergy led him to challenge the rights of recipients of those church tithes alienated after the Henrician reformation, potentially undermining a central part of the property system so sacred to the gentry. In short, Laud's policies were a double affront even to the respectable and conservative middle ground in English society, and pushed much moderate Calvinist opinion into the arms of the more fundamentalist Puritan wing.[25] This was particularly unfortunate given that the strengthening of the Church was an aim in fact shared by Puritans and Laud. The methods adopted by the Arminians – including the savage punishment meted out to three anti-episcopal pamphleteers in 1637 – seemed to push England back into an earlier age of violent intolerance which some of the Puritan extremists themselves were adept at exploiting. Between the two of them, Laud and Charles (who must be regarded as personally responsible for many of these developments) succeeded in alienating virtually every conceivable interest group by stirring up religious, economic and political resentments simultaneously. Historians have long since abandoned a crude categorisation of court against country interests, but there is no doubt that there were plenty of grievances and resentments building up, many relating to issues where there seemed little scope for pragmatic compromise.

Scotland and the Long Parliament

The tensions that came to a head in Scotland after 1638 were of a different nature from those in England, although provoked by the same monarch. Scottish kingship had historically tended towards much greater informality and had for centuries relied on a divided aristocracy to keep its balance. After decades of political uncertainty fuelled by the Reformation of 1560, Scotland had welcomed the return of order and effective government when James VI's minority ended in the mid-1580s. His political and intellectual abilities, even if at times bordering on pedantry in later life, had enabled him to restore the prestige and security of the Crown surprisingly quickly, and, as Jenny Wormald has shown, his style clearly worked better in Scotland than it did later in England.[26] His political conservatism no doubt created strains at a time of rapid bureaucratisation and growing lay participation in local and kirk affairs, but the King's active involvement until 1603 in council and Parliament secured effective leadership at the general (if not the detailed, day-to-day) level. After his departure for England, the pattern was to some extent maintained through the Crown's parliamentary steering committee, the Lords of the Articles, and through his regular and detailed instructions by post. One measure of his success is perhaps the fact that his fiscal demands, unprecedentedly large by Scottish standards, did not produce serious trouble until 1612.

The long-expected succession to the English throne, however, dramatically altered the nature of government and royal authority as perceived in Scotland. Its accessibility, for better or for worse, was lost, and James acquired a new style of entourage. Despite his best intentions, and those efforts to unite the two kingdoms which the English parliament rejected so scornfully in 1607, Scotland soon suffered unmistakably from absentee monarchy: its institutions, apart from the zealous kirk, were still insufficiently developed to work effectively. Not only did the Scottish court as such disappear – and with it the successful patronage of cultural life in the kingdom – but James came to depend for daily administration on a growing 'service nobility', consisting of lesser or younger members of the nobility promoted by the Crown but frequently lacking the natural authority needed to deal with the great nobles and heads of families. Certain policies regarded as important by James came to be viewed with suspicion and resistance because, being products of the King's English experience, they appeared alien. Such was the reaction to his introduction of justices of the peace in Scotland in 1609 and to his imposition of the church reforms known as the Five Articles of Perth on a reluctant general assembly (1617) and Parliament (1621).

James knew Scotland well, but neither Charles nor his ostensibly

Scottish advisers did and, after 1625, there were no adequate means of communication between Crown and Scottish subjects. The Scottish parliament, composed of three Estates like many of its continental counterparts, was vulnerable to manipulation by the Lords of the Articles, and in any case had much less scope for initiative than the English parliament. The other important collective forum, the general assembly of the church, was not called after 1618 because it was too rigid for the Crown's liking. Misunderstandings consequently occurred regularly and were apparent already in the reactions to the Act of Revocation of 1625, where Charles called into doubt all grants of crown and church land over the past one or, in some cases, several generations. The purpose was at least in part to secure better material support for ministers of the church, but the act also challenged important privileges of lordship, alienating some of the most power- ful members of the aristocracy on a very doubtful basis of law. Charles's reluctance to use and trust his father's service nobility, combined with his failure to give the Scottish privy council a full role in government, and his reliance on the small Scottish episcopate for advisors, deepened the gulf between monarch and subject which his first visit to Edinburgh in 1633 failed to bridge.

Most ominous was the growing fear of Charles's Arminianism, at least as unacceptable to the Scots and their kirk as to the English. A petition against royal church policies led to a show trial and narrow conviction for treason of Lord Balmerino in 1635. But it was the Book of Canons of 1636 and the Prayer Book of 1637, both produced with- out any Scottish consultation outside the dependent episcopate, that brought open and widespread resistance in Scotland. The Prayer Book was not outright Laudian, but its deliberate disregard for Scottish tradition, and the way it was imposed by royal prerogative alone, ensured rioting in St Giles in Edinburgh at its first reading. Further disturbances followed elsewhere, encouraged by the kirk. A protest movement led to the drawing up of the National Covenant in February 1638, which soon gained widespread support as a statement of opposition to Caroline church policies. A general assembly met later that year in Glasgow in such a loaded atmosphere that some moderates stayed away: it asserted its independence of the Crown and took some decisions (including the abolition of bishops) designed to safeguard the presbyterian form of church government. Mutual distrust and intransigence soon ruled out any prospect of compro- mise, so the Covenanters raised an army, financing it in part with appropriated customs revenues. The first Bishops' War (1639) did not involve much actual fighting against Charles, but the second (1640) did and resulted in the occupation of parts of northern England by the Covenanter army. This precipitated an immediate financial crisis for the Crown not only because of the costs of the military operations but also because of a taxpayers' strike which had begun to gain momentum in England from 1639.

This predicament could have been avoided. The Scots were in many respects reluctant rebels – ultimately they did not declare a republic even after the execution of Charles – but government policies appeared manifestly alien and unyielding. Indeed, rather than making comparisons with England, it may make more sense to suggest parallels between Scotland and Catalonia at this time. Both were nations with long traditions, resentful of absentee kingship and of a government dominated by 'foreign' influence; both were pressurised by fiscal demands and were reacting in self-defence against what were regarded as unlawful crown policies undermining native institutions and traditions. In Catalonia an army of occupation caused the final outburst, but in Scotland (as a contemporary observer remarked) an even more dangerous religious dimension was added. Neither Charles nor Olivares realised the extent of the opposition until it was too late, and by then they already faced financial disaster. Here, perhaps, the analogy ends: the Scottish rebellion was even more striking in that alienation was of much more recent date, and the outburst was directed against a king who had, after all, been born in Scotland.

The Short Parliament which met in London in April and May 1640 achieved nothing beyond pitting the Crown's needs for subsidies against the demand for the redress of accumulated grievances. By the end of August the Covenanter army had occupied enough of northern England to extract a truce costing Charles £850 a day. The implications were clear to a number of the King's councillors but, in insisting as usual on making up his own mind, Charles moved too little too late. Resistance to the use of the English militia against the Scots built up, and the Crown's failure to raise further loans on its own credit forced Charles to call another English parliament for November 1640, the Long Parliament.

The expectations raised by this development were considerable. It was clear that Parliament did now have fiscal bargaining power, which could be used to control abuses of royal prerogative. Some also hoped for a more radical restructuring of Church and State. The new parliament at first concentrated its efforts on the removal of the King's most dangerous and resented men, and in this there was broad agreement between Lords and Commons. Thomas Wentworth, Earl of Strafford, who as Lord-Deputy of Ireland from 1633 had acquired a reputation of ruthless efficiency, especially in fiscal and military matters, was arrested immediately. Prosecution charges were pressed vigorously, but Strafford conducted his defence so well that Charles was instead pressed into signing a Bill of Attainder in May 1641 whereby Strafford could be executed without trial. Laud and some lesser crown agents were treated more leisurely but also removed.

It was the need to consolidate the power of Parliament itself, however, which raised new questions. Within eight months Parliament had passed legislation asserting its sole right to dissolve itself and insisting on a maximum of three years between parliaments, dispensing if necessary with royal summons. Parliament also abolished the fiscal expedients of the 1630s together with the prerogative courts used to impose royal control. Dismantling autocracy, however, was easier than putting something in its place. There had been plans around the Earl of Bedford and John Pym (in the Commons) for a moderate scheme to gain control of the existing framework of royal government, but these collapsed in May 1641. By that stage, differences between moderates and radicals within both Houses were beginning to show. Popular demonstrations demanding a complete restructuring of church government and the abolition of bishops 'root and branch' aroused misgivings among more moderate MPs, some of whom feared the kind of extremism within and outside the Commons which had already led to the judicial murder of Strafford. The King succeeded in exploiting such differences in order to form a royalist group in both Houses, in turn provoking more radical suggestions from Pym and his sympathisers for the protection of the constitutional reforms already achieved and even for the personal safety of MPs themselves. In June the Lords and Commons passed a series of propositions suggesting some degree of parliamentary influence over the command of the army and over the appointment of officers of state. Such proposals, though moderately worded and quite understandable in the circumstances, clearly indicated that the parliamentary leaders were moving beyond the traditional ground of constitutional conservatism prevalent in nearly all the continental rebellions at this time. Their aim remained the preservation of a balanced monarchy – but, given what they regarded as the King's betrayal of his office, that aim could no longer be secured by conventional means. Charles's departure for Scotland in August 1641 therefore also raised immediate fears and led Parliament to appoint commissioners to keep an eye on his movements.

The Scottish parliament of 1640, meeting in defiance of a royal prorogation, had already gone a long way in a similar direction, notably by abolishing crown-controlled committees (including the Lords of the Articles) and passing a triennial act. As we have seen, there was little sympathy for Charles in Scotland, and the royal visit, complete with a minor and unsuccessful royalist conspiracy, did nothing to change this. Yet the Covenanters were also experiencing internal differences, not least over the way in which the Covenant itself was being forcibly imposed and over the legality of defying royal authority in the way in which it was being done. In September 1641 an agreement between the Crown and the Scots was finally ratified whereby Charles, in return for a withdrawal of the Scots and their army, made considerably greater concessions than he had so far done in England, thus avoiding confrontation for the time being.

This might have jeopardised the position of the English parliament had it not been for the major violent revolt of Ireland in October 1641. Tensions had been building up there both over religious issues and over the plantation policy in Ulster initiated by James whereby native Catholic Irishmen and older settlers had been displaced by Scottish and English Protestant landowners. Strafford had been able to contain the situation in the 1630s but his departure quickly resulted in a collapse of law and order. Aggravated by an economic recession, the revolt and the reports of atrocities led to anti-Catholic scares in England and Scotland. Normally, armed English intervention would have followed, but there was a marked reluctance to trust Charles with any military force at this stage. By December Pym and others in the Commons demanded parliamentary control of such an army, a concession Charles utterly refused to make. The atmosphere in London was already tense following the narrow decision by the Commons in late November to have its Grand Remonstrance against the King printed and circulated. Such a deliberately inflammatory move, and the intimidation that went with it, strengthened the royalist party. On 4 January 1642, however, Charles ruined his carefully rebuilt moderate image by attempting – and failing – to arrest five parliamentary leaders (including Pym) on charges of treason. Compromise between Crown and Parliament was henceforth very difficult and, as Charles hurriedly left London, the Commons took measures to protect itself physically. With the implementation of a new parliamentary tax and, uniquely in the European context, the issue of a militia ordinance without royal signature in the spring, Parliament unambiguously assumed powers traditionally held solely by the King. A flood of increasingly angry pamphlets and declarations from each side, playing on prejudices and fears, made any position of neutrality ever more difficult. Petitions and demonstrations both in London and in the provinces were encouraged, and although many grievances were of a local or economic nature outside government control, they did nothing to allay the fears of those opposed to constitutional innovation on such a scale. There was by this time enough support for each side for civil war to become unavoidable.

England had gradually, perhaps since the summer of 1641 or the beginning of the second session of the Long Parliament that autumn, been sucked into what we might now regard as a classic (and for most participants unintended) escalation towards serious political confrontation, towards revolution. Each side was guilty of provocation or extremism in its struggle for influence over the still uncommitted middle ground: on the one hand, a small group of radicals demanding ever more changes to forestall backsliding, and using crowds and inflammatory tactics to achieve this; on the other hand, an unrealistic king at times playing on fears of threats to the social order and of crowd violence in order to gain support from those who were genuinely moderate, yet at the same time displaying his true autocratic instincts and lack of understanding in occasional lurches towards the crude use of force.

It is here that the contrast between England and the continental experience of the later 1630s and 1640s becomes striking. For although all the continental monarchies discussed in this chapter went well beyond constitutional precedent and tradition – in Sweden this was cloaked in law, but the German intervention was itself a radical departure from the past in every way – nevertheless, opposition everywhere was conservative, and (as we shall see in chapter 7) never acquired a full-scale revolutionary momentum of its own. The continental monarchies were floundering from one desperate financial and administrative expedient to another under the stress of war, but everywhere it was assumed that the return of peace and a restoration of the old structure would suffice. Everywhere, too, there were compelling reasons why the elite of wealth and influence should work towards such a settlement in order to prevent economic and social disruption from getting out of hand. In England, however, confrontation centred on a city experiencing exceptional economic development and on a parliament capable both of reinforcing its unique traditions and of winning genuine support amongst the politically aware. This was what put England on a decisively different course from the rest of Europe (and from Scotland). England shared some of the difficulties of continental royal governments in the decades before the early 1640s: resistance to fiscal overburdening, serious religious disunity, regionalism and disruptive popular rioting. Like most of its counterparts, the English Crown failed to achieve any durable restructuring of government to help with rapidly growing administrative tasks. But it had no scope for (or probably even taste for) military reorganisation of the kind organised by Richelieu and Oxenstierna and attempted by Christian IV and Olivares. Even so, the wars of the 1620s were expensive enough to cause trouble even in England, and by the late 1630s Charles's financial position was so weak that a minor border skirmish forced him to take notice of public opinion. More significant, the 'political nation' in England differed from that in the rest of Europe, including that in Scotland: the attitude of Charles I to his role as King was so uncompromising, and the political traditions so strong that support emerged for parliamentary initiatives which by 1641 or 1642 could no longer be justified convincingly on historical precedent alone.

In the conclusion to this book we shall return to the question of how far the institutions and structures of the early modern state evolved during the seventeenth century as a whole, and in what precise directions. At this stage, however, it is worth asking how far the process of 'state formation' up to around 1640 was undermined (even negated) by the difficulties of the 1620s and 1630s, and whether there were convincing signs of what later generations, from the eighteenth century onwards, came to regard as 'absolute monarchy'. Most historians now accept that the growth of the state in early modern Europe was a very gradual and hesitant process, driven on more by political accident and short-term crisis management than by long-term strategic planning. If 'absolutism' (absolute monarchy) is defined as a system where the King believed himself to have essentially unlimited power, often (as in Divine Right monarchy) in his capacity as God's representative on earth, then James VI/I and Gustav Adolf would seem to qualify, judging from their own statements, and probably the French and Spanish monarchies would too. But if we define absolute monarchy in terms of the reality of political authority – the extent to which monarchs could genuinely exercise absolute (unqualified) power over their subject populations – we reach a rather different conclusion. As demonstrated in the huge fiscal resistance faced by the French and Spanish governments, or the obstructions limiting most other princes, no ruler had the practical means of imposing his will with any real degree of success. Rather, political power had to be exercised through carefully maintained clientage networks, through nobles and influential churchmen who opted for loyalty to the Crown as the best way of serving their own interests and through careful use of persuasion, bribery or (in the last resort) confrontation to win over those who mattered. It is difficult to make a persuasive case that any monarch substantially changed either the fundamental structures of his dominions or the basic political realities that he had inherited from his predecessors during this period – Gustav Adolf perhaps came closest to creating a new political context, but even that did not last for long. Looking across Europe, we notice some new or consolidated mechanisms for control, such as the *intendants* in France or the Swedish administrative colleges which became embryonic government departments. But rarely were any of the older structures removed – not even those representative parliaments and law-courts which could limit royal authority. The ineffectual French Estates General was in abeyance from 1614, but no-one considered abolishing it altogether; the Swedish *riksdag* rarely restricted the scope of an adult male monarch but commonly recovered its decisive role whenever minorities or other dynastic problems temporarily weakened royal authority. On the other hand, attempts in Denmark to create a powerful and personalised dynamic around the (still elective) king also foundered in disaster in the 1640s. As we shall see in chapter 7, contemporaries were deeply alarmed by the prospect of instability and social disorder, and rulers could to some extent exploit such fears to strengthen their own position. But there were few signs of any durable strengthening of royal authority of the kind associated with absolute monarchy after 1660 – indeed no monarch in Europe could in 1640 have had much reason to believe that the stability or coherence of his dominions was at all secure.

3   The framework of life

Throughout the seventeenth century neither government officials nor interested laymen had any comprehensive quantitative idea of what was happening in the economic life of their own region, let alone of Europe as a whole. Some Italian cities had already compiled censuses in the sixteenth century, but that was exceptional. There was no shortage of commentators and politicos, such as the *arbitristas*[1] in Spain who wrote on a variety of contemporary social and economic problems, but most of their output was generalised and rhetorical, often trying to promote particular political interests. The disadvantages of lacking recorded information and statistics on many aspects of material life were gradually recognised towards the end of the century when the fiscal needs of governments, together with improvements in scientific and statistical methods, began to provide the incentives and means for steps in this direction. But only during the eighteenth century did the study of political economy and the training of administrative officials catch up with practical realities to such an extent that long-term government policies might take hold and become more than just piecemeal and often ineffectual application of sometimes self-contradictory measures advocated by particular pressure groups to shift financial burdens, to affect the balance of trade, to protect infant or ailing industries or to secure commercial monopolies overseas.

The corollary to this, from the point of view of the economic historian, is that answers to a number of basic questions about material conditions in the seventeenth century can only be conjectural and perhaps unrepresentative because the source material is inadequate or unsuitable for our purposes. Nevertheless, there is fairly broad agreement that possibly in the 1590s, and certainly by the early seventeenth century, much of Europe was leaving a period of relative prosperity, and entering a period of economic stagnation of a severity perhaps comparable to that of the fourteenth century. In some respects this depression can be said to have lasted until at least the second decade of the eighteenth century, but a great deal of argument has arisen regarding its exact symptoms, chronology and effects, which of course varied regionally. The seventeenth century has often been described in terms of a cessation of population growth, particularly in much of central, eastern and southern Europe, coupled with agricultural depression over most of the continent, monetary and financial instability, and commercial retrenchment in the Mediterranean. A fairly small area in the north-west of Europe escaped lightly and the Dutch maritime provinces were able to ward off a depression alto-gether, at least until the last decades of the century, because of their highly developed Baltic and overseas trade, but for the rest of Europe material life was uncertain. The seventeenth century is therefore of considerable interest to economic historians, since it marked the height of the last (and therefore best-documented) major secular depression in pre-industrial Europe.

Population and food supply

Estimates of population density and distribution in this period are necessarily approximate, based as they are on extrapolations from the first censuses (compiled at least a century later), a range of specialised demographic analysis techniques, and reconstitutions from parish registers, tax rolls and other indirect sources from the period itself. A few cities had already begun to compile fairly convincing surveys (the most notable being Venice and Rome, whose example was followed in some other towns in Italy by the early seventeenth century) but in most parts of Europe the low level of literacy and the lack of a suffi-ciently trained bureaucracy made accurate counts impossible. Attempts were made in France under the supervision of Colbert and again in the 1690s, but the results were clearly defective. The esti-mates by Gregory King in his *Natural and Political Observations* of 1696 were uniquely sophisticated for their period but still relied at the local level on assumptions whose accuracy cannot be taken for granted. Much greater problems arise for central and eastern Europe, the Balkans and Russia, where very little information is available.

Even if precise figures cannot be obtained, and even if the margin of error is particularly large for the earlier half of our period, some features can nevertheless be emphasised. It is clear that two of the more densely populated regions, namely France with a population of around 21 million by 1700 and the Low Countries with about 3½ million, together with the British Isles (totalling over 9 million by 1700 if we include Scotland and Ireland), experienced some demographic growth over the century as a whole, amounting in some regions to as much as 20 per cent, but varying substantially both geographically and chronologically across notably France. The growth in Scandinavia was much less, the total population of nearly 3 million by 1700 concealing heavy losses in the wars of the middle decades of the century, espe-cially in Denmark. The very dense population of the Italian peninsula declined in the early part of the century and no more than recovered its previous level of 13 million by 1700, while the Iberian peninsula also experienced net population losses in mid-century, probably falling well below 9 million. The Thirty Years War and the resulting migrations cut deeply into the population of parts of the German lands and, since recovery there was remarkably slow, the estimates for the end of the century, ranging from 12 to 15 million, are considerably lower than those for 1600. Switzerland and the Habsburg lands outside the Empire probably remained at a fairly constant level in spite of temporary fluctuations, but what evidence there is for Poland again points to demographic decline. This may also be true of other parts of eastern Europe and the Balkans, although we do not know with any degree of certainty.[2]

Significantly, although there was some population growth in the north-west, this may only just have offset the serious losses suffered especially in the early half of the century in central Europe, the Mediterranean area and perhaps in the east. The north-west thus supported a proportionately larger part of the total European population (totalling at most 110 million in 1700, if we include the 10.5 million in Russia) than it had done at the end of the sixteenth-century growth period. This, as one would expect, corresponds with changes in other sectors of the economy.

One of the most direct factors in demographic change was the quality and quantity of food supplies. Attempts have been made to distinguish different types of food-related mortality crises: those, on the one hand, which were in effect Malthusian readjustments of population to finite food supplies; and, on the other, those which were 'accidental', produced for example by climatic aberrations (like the unusually harsh winter of 1659–60), where demographic recovery would be much quicker once food supplies returned to normal. In practice, however, this distinction is difficult to maintain, not so much because of statistical uncertainties but because mortality crises were nearly always composite. The classic example often cited to illustrate this problem was the catastrophic famine which hit most of Europe just after the end of our period, in 1709–10: it appeared at first to be 'accidental' – the result of an exceptionally long winter and two poor growing seasons – but the slowness of the return to demographic equilibrium in, for example, France (although complicated by a series of debilitating dysentery and typhoid epidemics in the years 1706–12) suggests that it was also a long-term readjustment of population in relation to an insufficient food supply. Here, as in many of the seventeenth-century subsistence crises, food shortages reduced resistance to infectious diseases (and caused digestive ones),[3] while at the same time depressing the economy as a whole by lowering demand for other goods and hence for labour. Harvest failures could thus produce a terrifying range of side-effects, especially in areas of predominant monoculture and if the crop failed two years in succession.

Nutritional 'norms' for the seventeenth century (as for later periods) can only be conjectural, and chronic malnutrition may have been a problem for certain social groups even in average years, at least in some parts of Europe. But severe periods of outright famine are easy to identify simply because grain prices rose very rapidly over a period of a few months, out of all proportion to wages. This happened on an extensive scale increasingly frequently in the last two decades of the sixteenth century, most severely around 1596–7. The early decades of the seventeenth century were comparatively stable in Europe as a whole, until the violent economic upheaval of 1620–2. Evidence from Vienna, for example, indicates that in the period 1621–3 the staple bread cereal, rye, reached a price more than twenty times its lowest level between 1611 and 1615, and that wages, although increasing because of inflation, nowhere near kept up. In England the good harvest of 1620 was followed by two poor ones and Scotland faced a severe famine in 1623; the grain exports from the main Baltic port, Danzig, dropped very substantially after 1621, whilst similar evidence points to a simultaneous food crisis in France and parts of the Mediterranean. Admittedly, international trade and the mercantile capital market were gradually becoming so developed that economic fluctuations (and especially variations in grain prices) tended to move in parallel over increasingly wide areas: a price rise in the Baltic, and hence on the Amsterdam market, could quickly affect prices in, for example, Paris, even if local harvests themselves did not dictate as much of a fluctuation. Nevertheless, evidence from many parts of Europe suggests that 1621 marked the start of genuine instability over most of the continent. Acute inflation hit especially those areas affected by the Thirty Years War, but there were indications of much wider dislocation even in those branches of overseas trade not connected with the war, such as the Atlantic trade from Seville. This has led a number of historians to see 1622 not merely as a food crisis but also as an obvious turning point in the European economy, heralding a century-long depression.

Harsh winters in 1624 and 1625, coupled with poor summers in many parts of Europe, aggravated the price rise experienced in the previous two years. The outbreak of war between Sweden and Poland in 1621 widened the serious dislocation caused by the Thirty Years War in central Europe, and in 1627 the crucial grain exports from Danzig stopped. The effective Swedish blockade of several Baltic ports in the next few years contributed to a violent price increase in most of the European grain trade by 1630, when the harvests were again poor. Sweden exploited this situation by imposing on the Baltic ports a levy designed to help finance its war effort in Germany and this kept grain prices high not only in Amsterdam but also, for example, in Paris as late as 1631. Grain prices then fell rapidly to about half on the Amsterdam market, and the recovery of the Baltic trade helped to stabilise the price of rye at around 60 g of silver per 100 kg for over a decade. In the Empire and the Rhine area, however, wartime conditions were such that even very local harvest failures could create acute food shortages, as in Würzburg in 1634 or in Leipzig four years later; in Augsburg even the prices of the meat of dogs and cats were recorded in 1634. Cases of cannibalism may have occurred.

The middle decades of the century brought renewed fluctuations on the European markets. The exceptionally good harvests occurring around 1645 and in the mid-1650s were both followed by acute shortages, culminating in the years 1648–52 and 1659–62 respectively, varying slightly between different parts of the continent but remarkably consistent overall. Administrative measures, such as the provision of municipal grain stores for emergency use or the public financing of long-distance grain transport to badly affected areas, had become routine in many states but were not always sufficient to cope with the sharpest fluctuations. Prohibitions on the export of grain were common throughout the period in years of serious shortage, primarily in order to calm popular unrest; in 1656 the Elector of Saxony took the more unusual step of prohibiting the import of grain in order to protect rural interests in a year of abundance.

Wheat and rye prices in Berlin, different parts of northern France, Lombardy and Denmark in the last four decades of the century make it quite clear, however, that even if administrative measures could take the edge off acute shortfalls and attempt to mitigate slumps that might endanger the peasant economy, the overall pattern (caused primarily by natural fluctuations) was virtually the same everywhere: moderate shortfalls in a number of regions around 1675 and 1684, followed by the acute double famine in the last decade of the century in the years 1693–4 and 1696–1700. Evidence even from Finland makes it clear that this last crisis had exceptionally serious demographic consequences, causing the death of between a quarter and a third of the Finnish population in 1696–7 and that the Baltic area was as badly hit as western Europe. Only England largely escaped famine in the 1690s, probably because both winter and spring grains were grown in adequate quantities to make up the difference if one crop failed. Scotland shared the continental experience.[4]

Some historians have suggested that agricultural productivity between 1645 and 1715 may have been affected by a temporary but significant overall climatic deterioration, related perhaps to a drop in sunspot activity and producing an overall drop in temperature of possibly 1°C, which significantly shortened the growing season. Certainly this so-called little ice age of Louis XIV was marked by some extraordinarily severe winters, such as those during 1658–60 or in 1709, and by spells of poor weather all year round, as in the later

1690s. We are now acutely aware of the potential damage caused by small but permanent changes in overall climatic conditions, and this explanatory framework (although focused on natural phenomena rather than human irresponsibility) has led to closer study of environmental evidence. But more research is needed on other geographic regions before this explanation for the agrarian depression of the later seventeenth century can be confirmed.[5]

Grain prices may seem a rather crude barometer of material conditions in early modern Europe but remain the most convincing. The cereals, especially rye and wheat, were the staple foods of most of Europe during the seventeenth century, to such an extent that demand for them was quite inflexible. Natural fluctuations in grain yields might perhaps be levelled out if they were specific to areas accessible to maritime trade, but on a wider scale they produced price fluctuations which were greatly magnified by comparison with those caused by other less fundamental foods. It is interesting to note, for example, that in Vienna in 1622 the price of meat products did not rise nearly as sharply as that of rye, and that the price of the less commonly used and more expensive wheat only increased slightly faster than the wages of building workers. The price curves of individual cereals may arguably therefore need to be set in some context in order to serve as reliable indicators of food shortages, and attempts have been made to construct more complex indices of living standards, based on a range of common necessities. But the sparseness of statistical information, and in particular the difficulty of assessing real wages, makes it inevitable that such indices can have only limited validity. Ultimately, in view of the unavoidable dietary conservatism of all but the wealthiest social groups, the essential characteristic of a food crisis could really only be a rapid increase in the price of bread, and this fact was universally recognised by contemporaries. Moreover, although in theory wide price fluctuations should have affected consumers and producers in opposite ways, with grain growers benefiting from periods of high prices, in practice this was rarely so: the majority of the rural population became buyers rather than sellers when harvests were even moderately poor and prices therefore higher. Only the urban population, perhaps representing something like a tenth of the total numbers in western Europe, could benefit from plentiful harvests and low prices, since wages tended to lag behind price movements. But such benefit, of course, depended on a number of other factors in the urban economy.

Existing evidence on land utilisation points unequivocally in the direction of a heavy emphasis on the cultivation of rye and barley in northern and central Europe, and wheat in the south and west. But other specialisations did develop, particularly where trade conditions were favourable. Denmark had developed an extensive cattle-export trade for the north German and Dutch meat markets in the sixteenth century and, although the overland drove routes were affected by the Thirty Years War, the trade declined only quite gradually. Hungary also took advantage of the demand for meat in southern Germany and Italy. Sheep-rearing was common in many of the less fertile or more mountainous areas, in central Spain the spread of large-scale monopolised sheep-farming may even have restricted grain production, but international demand for the high-quality Castilian wool declined in the later seventeenth century. The southern and western areas of France relied heavily on viticulture, a form of farming which was sufficiently labour-intensive to support a relatively high density of population on the basis of a dynamic international wine trade. In some parts of Europe 'new' crops also came into more extensive use, such as the high-protein buckwheat increasingly widely used on poor and marginal lands, valued because it was not subject to the same climatic aberrations as the cereals. Rice was grown in certain parts of the Mediterranean, especially in the lower reaches of the Po, where, at least after the introduction of the even higher-yielding maize, agricultural intensification helped Venice, for example, to survive in the less hospitable economic climate of the seventeenth century. The potato was introduced into Spain and Italy from South America at the end of the sixteenth century, and in England and Ireland around the same time, but it was mostly treated as a garden vegetable and did not, outside Ireland, become a major part of the diet until the eighteenth century. Pulses (particularly important quantitatively in southern Europe), vegetables and dairy products provided at least some potential for dietary variation and, where distribution was adequate, could make meat dispensable by providing a good nutritional balance. This was achieved in normal years in areas of reasonable soil and rainfall, for example in some of the coastal areas of Spain and Italy, and of course much more so where agrarian development was taking place, as in the coastal provinces of the Netherlands. Market gardening developed in the vicinity of many bigger cities, within the limitations of the transport system, and sometimes with deliberate state assistance as in the case of the *hollænderier* favoured by Christian IV around Copenhagen.

European agricultural techniques were thus not without scope for development. Indeed an extensive literature and especially Dutch expertise could be applied to improve land through drainage schemes or to develop more sophisticated rotation schemes than the simple two- or three-field rotations common in much of Europe. In the long run this did have a noticeable effect on the productivity of agriculture, particularly in much of western Europe by the later eighteenth century, but during the period covered here progress was significant only in a few exceptional areas in the north-west. Source material on agricultural yields is difficult to interpret, but it is safe to say that in areas of traditional farming methods grain harvests would in normal years, depending on the area, give between three and six times the amount sown (that is, a threefold to sixfold yield). Because of the lack of defensive measures against crop diseases, pests and other accidental factors including the weather, however, the 'normal' year might at times appear more like an ideal. A number of other factors also conspired to keep the yield low, including the open-field or strip-field system itself, the proverbial conservatism of the rural population (including land-owners, as one can see from French lease contracts, for example, which forced tenants to pursue short-term interests) and, just as limiting, the shortage of manure, the tendency in some areas to sow quite densely and the lack of capital for productive agrarian investment. In the fertile Parisian plain, in parts of Flanders and the United Provinces and, at least by the later part of the century, in England, yields of eightfold or tenfold could be attained with reasonable regularity; elsewhere in the west, in Denmark and even in the major grain-growing northern parts of Poland a fourfold harvest would be considered good, and a twofold yield or less not very unusual. Research on the extensive estates of the archbishopric of Gniezno in Poland suggests that grain yields actually declined, from an average of 5:1 in the later sixteenth century to around 3.8:1 by the later eighteenth century, and that most of this drop occurred during our period. Similarly, yields from Hungarian demesne land were on average between threefold and fourfold during this period, but do not appear to have deteriorated. Given that the seed for the next growing season would have to be subtracted from each harvest, and that seigneurial demands together with mounting fiscal burdens imposed by the state absorbed a good proportion of the rest,[6] it becomes apparent why the rural economy was so exiguous and why debt, default and starvation were so real a threat in the life of the European peasantry (see chapter 8).

Amongst the exceptions to this generally gloomy picture was the outstanding example of the first and most rapid agricultural revolution: that which occurred in the north-western half of the United Provinces. The development there in both the rural and mercantile sectors of the economy, culminating in the period between the later sixteenth century and the middle of the seventeenth century, has been analysed in detail by Jan de Vries. The weakness of seigneurial interests in the provinces of Holland, Friesland, Groningen and the western half of Utrecht, and the strengths of urban markets and capital investment, were clearly important in creating the best climate for development. But the unsuitability of the soil for corn-growing, coupled with the availability of large quantities of cheap grain from the Baltic, made agricultural diversification particularly attractive. A high urban population density could be tolerated because of alternative food supplies derived not only from trade but also from fishing and whaling. This in turn led to greater specialisation and commercialisation in both the urban and rural sectors, and in the intermediary zone of village crafts and intensive rural industries closely linked to the wider market. The agricultural revolution itself was achieved through a combination of livestock husbandry using special fodder crops, large-scale dairying for export and the extensive cultivation of pulses, root vegetables and various industrial crops which improved soil balance, together with the adoption of complex crop rotations and convertible husbandry sustained through heavier manuring using industrial by-products and urban waste. Agrarian production, freed from the constraints of cereal predominance, could become much more flexible, and could make the best of a basically fairly poor soil: milk yields were twice as high as elsewhere, regularly exceeding 1200 litres per annum per head of cattle on Friesian farms throughout this period, and even where corn was grown the yield was much better. Until the middle of the seventeenth century a sustained investment in land reclamation and drainage, coupled with the development of heavy barge transport (especially for peat and manure), tied the urban and rural sectors closely in what amounted to a rapid economic growth not paralleled anywhere before the industrial revolution. Although profits dwindled after the 1670s, the United Provinces remained essentially free of the food-crisis syndrome experienced by nearly all its neighbours.

England also underwent substantial agrarian development during the century, making it a net exporter of grain from the later 1660s onwards. But the change was less dramatic and more protracted than that in the United Provinces, stretching from perhaps the sixteenth century through at least the eighteenth, and the final result was different in one essential respect, in that large-scale tenancies became more common in many parts of the country at the expense of smallholdings. During the seventeenth century this consolidation was still slow, but the reduction of crown influence after 1640, including the abolition of the Court of Wards and the Prerogative Courts, marked the beginning of a new phase of uninhibited enclosure, which accelerated over the next century and was accentuated by the concentration of land in the hands of a numerically declining English aristocracy. More important, changes in demand, coupled with the pressure of price stagnation from the mid-seventeenth century, encouraged the implementation of technical improvements along lines similar to those of the Dutch. In fact, many changes in England were directly inspired by the Dutch, as shown by the interest in reports from travellers in the region and by the success of such works as Sir Richard Weston's *Discours on the Husbandry used in Brabant and Flanders*, published in

1645, reissued three times in the next decade and extensively plagiarised in a flood of literature on the subject.[7] The practical effects were visible in new crops, especially coleseed and turnips, and in more complex rotations, which were particularly fruitful in the fairly flat areas of Norfolk and the south, while thousands of acres of excellent arable were reclaimed in East Anglia through Dutch engineering expertise (aided by rising rents for some types of land). The geographic spread of these new techniques was both slow and very uneven, but the fact that net exports of grain from England, starting from a trickle in the 1660s, became very substantial by the end of the century in spite of a growing population, gives at least some indication of success. By then, however, the public debate had become thoroughly mixed up with the argument over enclosure and over the virtues of new non-feudal land-tenure practices. Changes in land tenure were often associated with heavier capitalisation, regional specialisation and especially with livestock farming. In fact, improvement and enclosure by no means had to (or invariably did) go hand in hand, but the two together made English agrarian structures depart radically in the eighteenth century from those prevalent in the rest of Europe, producing a major shift in rural social conditions and eventually a surplus of labour resources.[8]

The demographic effects of disease

We can be fairly certain that dearth had a significant impact on mortality patterns – very visibly so, for example, during the late 1640s and in the 1690s, but probably also at other times, even if parish records are not always of sufficient quality to provide convincing evidence. By contrast, the impact of epidemic diseases was more clearly, and sometimes dramatically, documented. Medical knowledge at the time was too rudimentary to permit what we would regard as accurate distinctions, but descriptions of symptoms are occasionally sufficiently detailed to permit some classification beyond the loosely used terms such as 'plague' and 'fever', even in cases where the diseases have since changed character. The most feared was the plague, which first ravaged Europe in 1347–52 with such devastating effect that it became known as the Black Death and which returned (but with slightly diminishing severity) at intervals thereafter, gradually receding from western Europe in the seventeenth century and disappearing in the late eighteenth. In addition, there were a number of common infectious diseases, notably influenza, typhoid fever, typhus, smallpox, infantile diarrhoea and dysentery, which were not as lethal and frightening as the plague proper but which were nevertheless of great demographic significance because of their more regular (or, in the case of smallpox, continuous) occurrence. The seventeenth century makes a virtually uninterrupted list of outbreaks of various kinds, spreading over greater or lesser areas, with population losses ranging from a few per cent to as much as 90 per cent in very severely hit localities. Even allowing for the fact that contemporaries could not always distinguish between losses caused by death and those caused by flight, and that a single epidemic could vary enormously in intensity even over a fairly small area, the impact could be disastrous. During the 1630 plague epidemic in northern Italy, for example, Mantua lost 25,000 through death and flight out of a total population of 32,000, but Bologna lost only a quarter of its population of 62,000, and a few cities were not touched at all. The actual plague mortality rates appear to have been lower in northern Europe, commonly around 10–15 per cent if one can judge from the estimates for London in the 1625 and 1665 epidemics, or for Amsterdam in 1636 and 1664. This must have been either because of lower infection rates or because actual counter-measures (to which we shall return) were becoming more effective.

Cities were generally more susceptible to epidemics than rural areas, primarily because of poor sanitation in the overcrowded districts and because of impure water supplies. Although only a dozen cities had more than 100,000 inhabitants in 1600, the population density was extremely high, especially in the cores of southern European cities. Estimates suggest that the densest areas could often have 500 inhabitants per hectare, and that Naples, for example, may have had double that in its worst areas. However, taking the built-up area as a whole, most cities had a much lower density, normally below 200 inhabitants per hectare in northern Europe.[9] Most demographic historians have hitherto assumed that cities had higher mortality rates than the countryside and therefore drained away a slight overall rural population surplus, but the real situation was more complex. Some cities, like Copenhagen in the later seventeenth century, appear to have grown not just because of immigration from the countryside but also because of an internal birth rate generally higher than the death rate. Moreover, Allan Sharlin has argued, persuasively, that it is necessary to distinguish between permanently resident citizens and transient or migratory labour in towns, since there is evidence to suggest that only the latter group had a higher mortality rate.[10] If this is so, we can no longer assume that urban population growth was wholly dependent on immigration, even if it is true that the urban economy would have suffered without cheap unskilled labour. What is certainly clear is the fact that mortality rates amongst citizens, particularly in the better quarters, were normally significantly lower than in the urban districts inhabited by the transient and poorer social groups. The London Bills of Mortality and evidence from other cities also indicate that epidemics regularly began in the poorest quarters, where overcrowding was similar to that in developing countries today. This, combined with the ability of the wealthiest groups to move out of town to avoid the plague, could cause considerable social tensions and hatreds during epidemics, especially since the poorer groups rarely had significant food reserves to last them through the period of economic dislocation caused by an epidemic and a quarantine. When the plague or some other very serious epidemic hit a particular locality several times over a relatively short span, the consequences could easily go beyond short-term economic ones, contributing to a long-term decline or stagnation like that experienced by some Italian cities in the seventeenth century.

Medicine had a negligible effect on mortality rates before the late eighteenth century. Although drugs such as quinine were known in the seventeenth century, and significant progress was made, for example, in the critical empirical reassessment of old medical orthodoxy (especially Galen), there were nevertheless no effective cures for any of the common infectious diseases. Indeed, it is disputable whether medical advice and treatment (for the few who could afford it) was beneficial or harmful. The medical history of, for example, Louis XIV is above all proof of an extraordinarily robust constitution combined with good luck.[11]

At a more general level, however, the need for administrative measures to improve public health was increasingly clearly recognised, especially in the struggle against the plague. Already in the fifteenth century most Italian cities had well-organised health boards (either temporary or permanent), whose primary function was to attempt to control this disease. The boards gradually acquired extensive powers over urban sanitation, food and water supplies, epizootics, medical and pharmaceutical organisation, hospital administration and the control of vagrancy. By the end of the seventeenth century the Venetian health board, for example, had on its normal pay roll not only a physician and a surgeon, but also 18 food controllers, 7 footmen and 60 guardians. When an outbreak of plague was suspected, extra staff were employed to try to enforce, through emergency powers, the common protective measures such as the closure and quarantine of cities, the prohibition of public gatherings and church services, the burning or fumigation of suspect goods and the locking up of infected houses, with the inmates either maintained in isolation at public expense or transferred to a special pesthouse. Given the enormous cost of these measures (not only in terms of direct expenditure but also in terms of unemployment, the total cessation of trade and the loss of raw materials including those for domestic industry), it is not surprising that the health officers faced enormous practical problems and personal dilemmas when the plague appeared. Equally naturally, there was, at least initially, the danger of substantial popular resistance to (and fear of) all restrictive measures, making the task of the officers even less palatable. Studies of the plague in northern Italy have nevertheless revealed an impressive and often remarkably efficient machinery, exemplary in Europe at the time and studied by specialists from abroad.[12] The keeping of detailed records, such as the bills of mortality normal in Italian cities since the early sixteenth century, and the provision wherever possible of medical staff in the pesthouses themselves meant that city authorities could rely on a considerable fund of practical knowledge and experience, even if there was no margin for experimentation. *Cordons sanitaires*, isolating whole areas and cutting off the main trade and military routes along which the plague travelled, were obviously sensible and effective, but health officials at the time, and epidemiologists since then, have wondered whether any of the other measures had any effect once the plague had arrived. Ignorance of the means of transmission of plague made the process of civic regulation a hit-and-miss exercise, and certain measures may have had the wrong effect. Total quarantine was no doubt effective when enforced, and the insistence on at least 22 days of quarantine in lazarettos or convalescent homes (sometimes even 40 days or more) may well have slowed down the spread of infection. The burning of household belongings may also have worked, but whether fumigation was of any practical use depends on what precise disease the plague really was.

It is now apparent that the plague which so traumatised Europe for centuries may not have been the bubonic plague as assumed by earlier historians, and on which much of the historical explanatory framework has been built. As Sam Cohn has demonstrated, neither the aetiology nor the epidemiology of the late medieval and early-modern disease matches that of the rat-based bubonic plague identified by medical science in the later nineteenth century. Contemporary descriptions of actual symptoms, of contextual medical information, of the conditions in which the disease spread and of the severity of its demographic impact (including both its initially catastrophic fatality rate and the gradual appearance of natural human resistance to the disease after some generations) are at variance with what a knowledge of the modern disease would lead us to believe. Even the buboes (swellings or boils) in the groin associated with the modern disease (though not unique to it) are not consistently prominent in early descriptions. The modern variant, pneumonic plague which is spread through the respiratory tract, also does not help to bridge the gap.

If the plague of the early modern period is roughly the same as (or at least an evolving variant of) the Black Death of the fourteenth century, then historians will need to revise some of their explanations for its disappearance. The plague began to recede from western

Europe in the later seventeenth century, with only minor and sporadic outbreaks in Scotland after the 1640s, in England after the London epidemic of 1665–6, in Spain after the 1680s and in Italy (except for Sicily) after the 1650s. The violent outbreak in Marseilles in 1720 was exceptional, and by that time the disease had also receded from Scandinavia, the Netherlands and central Europe, including the Austrian lands, but not yet from Russia. The reasons for its disappearance are difficult to identify as long as we cannot be sure what kind of a disease it may have been. However, traditional historical explanations centring on the species of flea responsible for the transmission of bubonic plague, or on the displacement of primary hosts in the form of the black and brown rats, clearly do not now help. Explanations centring on nutritional or sanitary improvements are equally implausible given the nearly simultaneous disappearance of the plague from such widely dissimilar societies as, for example, Scotland and northern Italy. The more general conclusions reached by Biraben in his major study, indicating that there is a clear correlation between certain types of administrative measures (especially quarantines) and the containment of bubonic plague, are broad enough to offer a more plausible hypothesis, especially given what we know of the infectiousness of the mediaeval and early modern disease. Quarantine measures were initially adopted in individual communities sufficiently well-organised to enforce them, but from the later seventeenth century onwards were often applied on a larger scale under the auspices of national governments. According to Biraben, only a nationwide approach could be fully effective, so the consolidation of stable and more centralised governments in the later seventeenth century was a crucial factor in the elimination of the plague from the west. The *cordon sanitaire* established by the Austrian Habsburgs after 1728 along more than a thousand miles of Turkish border, with elaborate quarantine and disinfection centres which were maintained until 1873, adds weight to this argument because of its indisputable effectiveness.[13]

Once the risk of plague had receded from most of Europe in the later eighteenth century, however, many of the health boards succumbed to popular resistance and were abolished. The experience gained during the early modern period in combating the plague was thus not applied consistently to the other less lethal infectious diseases: they caused less fear because they seemed less virulent, and in any case quarantine measures had been hugely costly and controversial. The most cataclysmic threat to public health had disappeared and the wide range of other epidemic diseases, though very significant for the individual, seemed to have less collective and psychological impact.

The impact of war

It has often been suggested that seventeenth-century armies caused more deaths through the transmission of disease than they did on the battlefield. This is, of course, unverifiable, but there is no doubt that the presence of troops in encampments, or their mere passing in transit, could have disastrous consequences, particularly where political authority had broken down, such as in the Paris region during the Fronde (1648–53) or the more severely disrupted parts of the Empire during the Thirty Years War. A vivid and powerful description of the latter is found in the best-known work of German literature of the period, Grimmelshausen's *Der Abentheurliche Simplicissimus* (1669). The earlier parts of this novel are to some extent autobiographical and, although satirical and influenced by Spanish picaresque examples, give the most immediate (if in parts implausibly colourful) picture that we have of the opportunism and savagery of privately organised mercenary warfare in the later 1630s and 1640s. Other contemporary reports on catastrophes such as the sack of Magdeburg in 1631 make it clear that the consequences could be overwhelming. But Germany was not the only part of Europe to suffer such extremes: although it was the battleground for arguably the first protracted general European war, involving a wide and shifting spectrum of belligerents and freebooters, lesser conflicts, at least until the first signs of greater army discipline towards the end of the century, could be as savage. The brutality of Cromwell in Ireland in 1649–50, for example, was no less appalling, pitching a vindictive and well-organised army against strongly motivated but incoherent rebel forces.

Parish records sometimes supplement the literary material. Registers from parts of Schleswig in the 1650s thus poignantly illustrate the extent to which a typhus epidemic was intensified by the presence of foreign (allied) troops in 1659, creating devastating mortality rates of up to 90 per cent in some of the parishes of transit and encampment. The fact that contemporaries clearly recognised that undisciplined troops not only caused violence and material damage but also vastly increased the risk of epidemic disease may help to explain why seventeenth-century armies, whether friend or foe (or even government troops), were commonly the object of fear and sometimes of violent attack from peasant communities.

Nevertheless, evidence on the human and material damages caused by war cannot always be taken at face value. Since governments and administrators lacked precise statistical information, there was nothing to prevent individual communities or towns from requesting compensations or concessions on the basis of exorbitant claims for damage which appear implausible even on the basis of the limited evidence that has survived. This technique was one of many used in

the Lippe area in north-western Germany, where local civilian administrators in some towns managed to keep their posts during the war
years from the 1620s onwards and were thereby also able to mitigate
the effects of troop quarterings by a judicious policy of compromise
and delay, which worked well as long as open fighting was kept to a
minimum. If this failed, maurauding troops could be bought off with
protection money or 'contributions', a system which became highly
developed in Germany during the Thirty Years War and could give
mercenary commanders such as Wallenstein considerable income.
Such material incentives were effective even on conscripted troops,
since their period of service was often long, forcing them to sever their
civilian roots and become part of a military caste where regular pay
was usually inadequate.

It is not surprising, therefore, that there has been substantial
controversy over the real economic and demographic effects of this
particular war in Germany. Clearly, participants would tend to drama-
tise personal experiences, so that an overall assessment is difficult to
reach. Historians now agree, however, that population displacements
and losses in the Empire varied enormously, with Hamburg going
unscathed and much of the Austrian duchies and the north-western
parts of Germany only marginally affected, whilst a central belt from
Swabia and the Palatinate to Mecklenburg and Pomerania was very
seriously hit, as were parts of Bohemia. In the central belt, where both
material destruction and the effects of disease and violence were at
their worst, overall population losses through death and displacement
were commonly 30–50 per cent, or more in certain districts.
Generalisations on this scale mean little, but the Thirty Years War
period probably imposed on the German lands (and especially the
countryside) an average population loss of such overall dimension and
duration as to be the most serious anywhere in seventeenth-century
Europe (see chapter 1). Comparable estimates are not available for
other belligerents at this time but neither Spain nor France is likely to
have suffered anything on this scale.

The long-term economic consequences of warfare during the
seventeenth century are also difficult to measure with any accuracy.
The timeless argument emphasising technical spin-off from warfare,
though not untenable in this period in relation to specific areas of the
economy such as mining or finance, pales when balanced against the
costs. The fate of Bohemia's previously flourishing economy once the
Battle of the White Mountain in 1620 had exposed the country to
Habsburg centralisation, or the difficulties experienced by many south
German cities after 1648, leave no doubt that the cutting of trade
routes, the disruption of existing social and political balances and the
impact of war on local markets could upset the economic life of a
region for a long period. The Thirty Years War, however, was arguably

the last major conflict dominated by private enterprise in mercenary warfare, and in the later part of the century a need emerged for stricter state control and disciplining of troops, producing a clearer separation of soldier from civilian which should in theory have reduced the most unpredictably disruptive side-effects of warfare and which certainly spread its growing fiscal cost. As troops became better trained and more expensively equipped, it seemed expedient to protect them (and thereby also the civilian population) against avoidable health hazards. In this respect the Spaniards had set an example, notably in the Army of Flanders in the last decades of the sixteenth century, with extensive and remarkably effective medical treatment provided in military hospitals. In the later seventeenth century the extension of state control over recruitment and supplies also made it easier to implement both military and civilian health measures centrally. After mid-century, it has been argued, there are also the first signs of a trend towards the more formal, almost ritualised, war of the eighteenth century: campaigns became longer not because of the kind of crippling and uncontrollable momentum of the Thirty Years War but because of the increasing need for extensive siege work and its attendant protracted manoeuvres, which rarely resulted in pitched battle.

The temptation to overstate this tendency towards more 'civilised' war needs, however, to be resisted. Pillaging, for example, was very difficult to control, as shown when the French troops invaded the Palatinate in 1689 and caused destruction with an undiscriminating savagery which only Louvois seemed to think necessary. Gradually, if governments found stricter discipline convenient and necessary, the plundering adventurer turned instead to overseas opportunities. But, as we shall observe in chapter 12, state-orchestrated violence was hardly more attractive than that perpetrated in the name of private interests. Europe remained a continent almost chronically beset by warfare, and habits of violence naturally spilled over into local and family contexts.

Prices and wages

Any assessment of the material quality of life in seventeenth-century Europe must take into account the irregular and unpredictable movement of prices and wages. Since, however, the underlying economic variables were mostly beyond the reach of governments, and usually beyond their comprehension, the evidence which has survived is very difficult to handle and not at all readily converted into quantitative generalisations. Accuracy is unattainable when it comes to questions of the size of the labour force, normal working hours and wages, demand and output, or profits and their distribution. Not just geographic but also especially cultural variations make generalisations even more difficult with regard to such fundamental factors as the value of labour itself (and the huge gender discriminations which contemporaries took completely for granted), attitudes to investment and 'usury', or the potential clash between traditions of relatively constant market transactions and more commercially-oriented expectations of profitability. The development of a wider consumer market was fairly slow and was significant primarily in the more prosperous parts of urbanised Europe from the second half of the seventeenth century onwards, but luxury commodities and a market orientation, especially amongst the skilled trades, were of course not new.[14]

The most basic structural price fluctuations were, of course, those of the main cereals, already discussed because of their immediate social and demographic consequences. The price range for a broader selection of ordinary commodities was not quite so changeable, even though demand from the less wealthy groups of society could fluctuate considerably in inverse ratio to basic food prices. A complete list of monthly prices for individual commodities in the main market towns of Europe would be an ideal material for our purposes, but at present the mosaic is still very incomplete. The profusion of different coinage systems even within a single area adds another complication, especially since the wildly fluctuating cereal prices cannot be used as a basic standard. Nevertheless, in the fourth volume of the *Cambridge Economic History of Europe*, Braudel and Spooner analysed European price movements on various terms, including money of account and silver, which still create a useful overall framework: they found that the rapid inflation of the sixteenth century came to an end in the first half of the seventeenth century, and that, in spite of severe disruptions during the Thirty Years War period and in the 1690s, the later seventeenth century was a period of relative price stability.

Unfortunately, information on wages is much less reliable. Governments often attempted to control wage increases by legislative means, just as they wished to reduce the mobility of labour and discourage short-term service. But, mostly lacking even the rough kind of information which could be collected regarding price fluctuations, administrative officials had no chance of ensuring that wage legislation had any tangible effect. Further complexity is created by the fact that nominal wage payments might be supplemented by payments in kind, such as meals, accommodation or other benefits. In the countryside, in particular, wages were usually composite: the Danish government, for example, struggled in vain to prevent peasants from offering payments in kind or allowing their labourers to sow part of the land on their own account. These bonus systems were, of course, not always in the interest of the wage-earners, but they should warn us against treating at face value those nominal wage payments which appear to remain constant for decades at a time, regardless of price fluctuations.

In 1956 Henry Phelps Brown and Sheila Hopkins published a well-known index of real wages based on material from southern England (one of the best-documented areas for the period). Their price index for a selection of household goods, weighted throughout at 80 per cent for ordinary foods, 7.5 per cent for fuel and light and 12.5 per cent for textiles, was plotted against the wages earned in various trades connected with building work in the same area. The wage-ingredient in this estimate suffered from some of the weaknesses just mentioned, so that the result may not be very reliable even for its limited area and social group. Nevertheless, it indicates that wages lagged behind prices during the early decades of the century but began to catch up marginally after 1640, although never attaining the apparent favourable ratio of the beginning of the inflationary sixteenth century. Similar estimates for Vienna and Geneva point in the same direction, except for a renewed divergence at the end of the seventeenth century, while in Augsburg builders seem to have been able to redress the balance rather more substantially in the period after 1650, only to lose ground again in the 1690s. Detailed work by Goubert on the Beauvaisis suggests broadly similar conclusions (derived from different methods) and the same appears to be true also for parts of Italy. Venice, however, may (if these generalisations are roughly correct) be a partial exception in that Pullan has shown that the relationship between certain builders' wages and prices remained comparatively stable at least until 1630; the United Provinces, too, do not seem to fit the general picture.[15] The building trades are comparatively well-documented for this period and, even though there are big question marks over the price of non-food items such as housing and over effective average working hours per week, it does seem reasonably likely that at least some groups of wage-earners did become slightly better off during the second half of the seventeenth century compared with the first half. The virtual cessation of population growth in much of Europe no doubt contributed both to a steadying of food prices and to a shortage of manpower which would be conducive to wage increases. Some economic historians have suggested that this may be one of the reasons for the rising demand for non-essentials, including, for example, porcelain, tobacco and coffee, creating the basis for such new phenomena as recognisable retail shops and even for public entertainments such as opera, which became established during the century (see chapter 10). Clearly this development should not be overemphasised, but it may have been noticeable in the urban communities of north-western Europe with their more complex economies. In the countryside any change of this kind is likely to have been negligible, given that the rural population would have had difficulty enough in most parts of the continent in attaining the most basic material security. The only exception in this respect, predictably, was the peasant population in those parts of the Netherlands where the agricultural revolution took place and where inventories and notarial records reveal a substantial acquisition of non-essential items.

Occupations and wealth distribution

Gregory King's *Observations* of 1696 includes a well-known 'Scheme of the Income and Expenses of the Several Families of England . . . 1688', a tabulation of social categories and incomes. According to this table, just over half of his estimated total English population of 5½ million is classified as labouring people, out-servants, common seamen and soldiers, cottagers and paupers, whose income per family averaged from £20 p.a. downwards and who were consequently deemed by King to be 'decreasing the wealth of the kingdom' – a term which may denote those earning no surplus from their labour and thus living, without savings, around or below subsistence level. The types of families classified as 'contributing to the wealth of the kingdom' ranged from those of artisans and craftsmen with a yearly income averaging £40, together with shopkeepers, tradesmen, small farmers and members of the lower clergy earning about the same, through freeholders, military and naval officers, the middle clergy and the professions with higher educational qualifications (including the law) to merchants and office-holders with a yearly income of several hundred pounds. At the top of the hierarchy King placed what he called 'gentlemen' and the higher titled ranks of the leisured elite, whose income came largely from landed wealth. If one uses these figures for further calculations, it would appear that this leisured upper class consisted of slightly more than 1 per cent of the total number of families, or (including their large household staff) just under 3 per cent of the total number of persons, but accounted for 14.5 per cent of the total yearly income. Those whom King classed as 'decreasing the wealth of the kingdom' constituted over 62 per cent of the total number of families or (since their households and families were on average smaller) over 51 per cent of the total population, whilst their annual income represented less than 21 per cent of the national total. In fact, as Geoffrey Holmes and others have argued, King's tabulation is very much less reliable than his demographic estimates elsewhere in that work; in particular, the income of the higher groups is very seriously underestimated (perhaps because of King's own political views and his purpose in writing), so that if these numbers in fact mean anything, they almost certainly understate the inequality of income distribution at least by the last decade of the century.[16]

The proportion of people at or below subsistence level (however that may be defined for our period) was undoubtedly horrifyingly high in western Europe, with estimates during stable times ranging from a few per cent to a third or half of the total population, depending on the time, place and criteria. King suggested that in England 25 per cent were what he called 'cottagers and paupers' and vagrants. Hearth tax records from English towns in the 1660s and 1670s indicate that a quarter or more of the population were often exempt on grounds of poverty. According to Vauban, writing in the 1690s, the French population consisted of 10 per cent beggars, 50 per cent near-beggars, and another 30 per cent *fort malaisés* (very badly off)[17] – perhaps a pessimistic estimate, given the economic uncertainty of that decade, but even if Vauban did not attempt elaborate political arithmetic and surveys the way King did, he wrote on the basis of years of experience and observation in most parts of France, and was well informed by the standards of the time. In New Castile over half the rural population in the 1570s were day-labourers and, as such, near or below subsistence level, a situation which had not changed significantly by the eighteenth century, but in the more fertile parts of Spain this proportion was normally somewhat lower.[18] Similar reckonings exist for other parts of western and central Europe and although statistics on poverty clearly cannot be other than subjective (since there was no way contemporaries could actually measure the problem over any period of time), recent research nevertheless confirms the overwhelming and grim reality of wealth inequality and threatening poverty in the seventeenth century (see chapter 6).

The nature of the pre-industrial economy also emphasised other social characteristics of the period. The low average productivity of labour in virtually all sectors of the economy meant that an adult male could not necessarily support a family alone. Compared with industrialised society, a high proportion of dependants in the seventeenth century were children, but in the absence of generally available schooling the majority could make a substantial contribution to family income by means of seasonal labour in agriculture or manual work in domestic industries such as textile production, or by other means. Female labour also took a variety of forms, from domestic service (a very significant sector in early modern society), household and agricultural work and wet-nursing or other traditional roles to many kinds of manufacturing work in textiles, sailmaking, mirror-making or even the metallurgical industries. In spite of male predominance and prejudice in most guilds, women could clearly play a major and even top-level role in certain sectors of the urban economy especially, but did so exceptionally rather than generally. Guild regulations and practices as a rule allowed widows to continue their husband's craft for as long as they remained single, and even to take on apprentices in the usual way. Many guilds, especially in the textile sector, also seem to have accepted women as members in their own right, no doubt on differential terms but at least with some participatory rights and some of the protection afforded to men. In Paris around 1600 a woman 'town plumber' had a contract with the municipality for the maintenance of the city fountains. Venice also had women whose occupation was unambiguously listed as 'sailor' or 'chimney sweep'. Much more exceptional were the corporations primarily or exclusively intended for women. There were three such guilds in seventeenth-century Paris, including flower sellers and linen- and hemp-producers. The linen-women's guild obtained a decree from the Parlement against any interference by husbands, who were entitled to serve solely in a subordinate capacity as assistants. But this was probably unique; in England there were only two female guilds, the wool-packers of Southampton and the silk-women of London.[19]

Nearly everywhere in Europe a large majority of the population had agriculture as their primary occupation. Probably 70–90 per cent of the working population over the continent as a whole came into this category, although the proportion may have been higher still in eastern Europe, and slightly lower in exceptional areas such as the coastal strip of the United Provinces or in some of the Italian city-states where alternative occupations were more highly developed. Agricultural work, however, was not continuous, and (as detailed studies of regional economies have amply demonstrated in the last few decades) the rural population provided a readily tapped supply of cheap labour for the entrepreneur capable of organising an effective putting-out system in, for example, textile production. In the countryside, therefore, occupational labels such as may be found in some parish registers or in notarial records were normative, inconsistently subjective or even directly misleading.

In the urban economy, the occupational structure during the pre-industrial period is better documented. Often textile production together with the food-processing and food-marketing sectors were the most substantial (see chapters 4 and 6). The clothing and building trades absorbed a large part of the remaining skilled and unskilled labour market, but demand in the building sector in particular was variable. Higher up the social scale, the legal and medical professions may not have been very significant numerically but, like the public sector, they were influential because of their role in society, their corporate strengths, their relative influence and their higher level of education.

Social and geographic mobility

In spite of the conventional formal social stratification (which will be discussed in later chapters), there was a much greater degree of both social and physical mobility in certain parts of Europe than historians used to recognise. Precisely what proportion of the common rural population could be deemed static (in either sense) is no longer open to generalisation, since surprising regional differences have been discovered through parish registers, tax rolls and other sources. Physical mobility may not have been characteristic of more than a small minority in the remoter and less developed agricultural areas of Europe, beyond what was unavoidable to relieve overpopulation (notably in parts of the Mediterranean region, in Switzerland and later in Scotland), but larger towns and ports could exert considerable positive attraction over great distances in north-western, central and northern Europe, partly through expectation of the social mobility that might come from such movement. English evidence suggests that in some parts of the country inter-parish mobility was the norm rather than the exception – much of it, naturally, amongst the young seeking service or occupational training, some of it seasonal, but by no means all. On the continent there was substantial seasonal migration of labour in, for example, southern France and other mountainous areas where agricultural resources were insufficient to sustain the male population. Military operations or religious persecution also caused substantial forced mobility, for example in the German lands during the Thirty Years War or in France when Louis XIV allowed official persecution of the Huguenots to be implemented (see chapter 11).[20]

Mobility appears to have been particularly common at either end of the social spectrum: on the one hand amongst vagrants and the poor struggling for survival and on the other amongst the better-off seeking opportunities elsewhere (including merchants, English yeomen, professionals and, of course, the landed elite) – 'subsistence' and 'betterment' migration respectively, in the terms of Peter Clark.[21] The former was common all over Europe in times of economic hardship and is impossible to measure with any degree of accuracy. Historians have made greater progress in terms of the latter since the source material is more diverse, but much still needs to be done. With regard to status-mobility one can point to striking individual examples, such as that of Samuel Pepys, rising from household service to quite prominent public service and rarely, during the period covered by his diary, hesitating to feather his own nest by whatever means were available to him as an office-holder. In January 1661 he considered himself 'worth' £300, but during the Dutch wars he could exploit his central position as clerk of the acts at the Navy Office (with an official salary of £350 p.a.) to augment his personal fortune in the course of 1665 alone from £1300 to £4400. In 1663 he could spend £55 on 'a velvet cloak, two new cloth-suits, black, plain both – a new shag-gown, trimmed with gold buttons and twist; with a new hat and silk tops for my legs, and many other things, being resolved henceforward to go like myself', whilst he rather more grudgingly spent £12 on clothes for his wife. By 1666 he had portraits done of himself and his wife at £14 each, and the purchase of a carriage in 1668 was a major event in his quest for visible social status.[22] London undoubtedly provided a unique range of opportunities and possibilities at the time: probate records reveal a considerable range of wealth within the business community, where freemen not uncommonly acquired fortunes of £10,000, and some went well beyond that. With such fortunes often came the acquisition of landed estates, still the primary status symbol.[23]

The cities in the province of Holland were also renowned for the range of opportunities for social mobility, at least until the later seventeenth century. Holland was essentially an urban area, with one of the greatest concentrations of population in Europe, but it also acquired a reputation for freedom. The nobility had only a very minor role to play politically and socially, and government (or what there was of it within this loose republican structure) was thoroughly dominated by the magistracies of the major towns and especially of Amsterdam. Although patrician families (the 'regents') narrowly controlled urban politics and secured continuity for themselves by means of co-option to offices and nepotism, these urban oligarchies were open to renewal from outside – at least until after the political crisis of 1672, when dissociation from active trade gradually began to make regent families socially and culturally distinct from the rest of the better-off citizenry. During most of this period the very rapid growth of Amsterdam and of other cities in the area also guaranteed a certain degree of skill- or wealth–determined mobility right down the social scale. But, as elsewhere in Europe, the greater the urban attractions the greater also the risks of extreme poverty and deprivation.

If trade and the urban economy (particularly in the north-west) provided one possible means of social mobility, other chances of breaking out of the traditional social hierarchy might in some instances be provided by the state bureaucracies, the professions and the churches. Much work still needs to be done but it appears that, during the seventeenth century at least, these alternatives were not as significant as they became later. Education was available only to a small minority, and the network of connection, wealth and patronage was a limiting factor in all sectors. The official churches were far from egalitarian (in contrast to dissenting groups, which often lacked material assets anyway). Here again one can only suggest tentative generalisations, given the relative sparseness of research on the social history of the seventeenth-century clergy, but it seems that in Protestant countries ecclesiastical offices had only limited status value and so went mostly to a narrow group of trained applicants, often running in families, while in Catholic countries, where the Church had far greater endowments but lacked familial continuity owing to celibacy, benefices predominantly went to members of corresponding social groups. Of the early graduates from the new seminary in Beauvais, for example, those of urban family were mostly the sons of merchants and office-holders, while some were from prosperous shopkeeper and artisan backgrounds. Textile workers and labourers never got their sons into the priesthood. A similar tendency is evident amongst the rural contingent, and this is not surprising given that priesthoods were rarely worth less than 300 livres per annum in the Beauvaisis.[24] Oversimplification of a complex problem is an obvious risk, but church institutions, like the professions, were essentially bastions of the existing social order, especially in Catholic and Lutheran Europe, and (exceptions apart) are not likely to have provided major opportunities for social mobility.

Family and household

The early modern household was fundamentally different from the kind that became common in industrialised Europe some centuries later. It was to a considerable extent determined by the physical and material circumstances already described – especially the high but unpredictable mortality rates common all over Europe, which in turn disturbed both inheritance patterns and the duration of a large proportion of marriages. Inheritance rules themselves, as well as other economic pressures, produced additional variations, whilst religious and local cultural expectations imposed certain restraints. But we should remind ourselves that the early modern household is not readily fitted into simple patterns: there were extraordinary variations even within particular localities, just as the shape of a particular household varied enormously over time according to the life-cycle of the main family unit itself. The early modern economic system itself, relying as it did on labour-intensive processes both in agriculture and in the crafts and manufacturing, often turned households into economic units of production where sometimes more than two generations of a family co-habited with 'servants' (manual or domestic workers), apprentices and journeymen, all eating together and sharing what space the building might provide. If we add in contemporary expectations regarding power relations and discipline within the household, it is easy to understand why the early modern experience of 'family' differed so fundamentally from more recent norms.

In early modern Europe historians have also discerned some unique patterns in marriage and child-bearing which fit neither simple biological assumptions nor the norms observed in other societies. Evidence from the non-Mediterranean parts of western and

central Europe suggests that marriage tended to take place significantly later in life than one might have assumed: for men the mean age
at first marriage was around 27 years, for women between 24 and 25.
Given that female fertility rises to its full level around the age of 20
and declines by the late 30s, it is apparent that the child-bearing
potential was very significantly curtailed, even in those communities
where co-habitation was customary between betrothal and marriage.
The reasons for this delay are not altogether clear but may include
shortage of housing (in those regions where extended families were
not the norm) or, more commonly, the custom of saving up for some
years for basic household goods before marrying. It was decidedly the
norm for widows to remarry but the delay in doing so varied enormously, partly according to custom, partly of course according to age
and personal circumstances, again limiting natural fertility. In addition, permanent female celibacy was considerable, averaging perhaps
10–20 per cent in western Europe, especially in societies and classes
where the nunnery was regarded as a desirable or expedient means for
families to economise on dowries. All told, it is not unreasonable to
suggest that upwards of two-fifths of the entire female reproductive
potential was unavailable in Europe at any one time. These restrictions
probably applied less in eastern Europe, where people married much
younger.

Even for married women, however, the average frequency of preg-
nancies was not as great as might be expected. French research has
shown that there was on average an interval of 25–30 months between
each child in most areas and social classes, and an average of only 4 or
5 births per family. Contraception, especially coitus interruptus, was
not unknown, although very emphatically (if euphemistically)
condemned by the Church as a male vice. More important in reducing natural fertility may have been the practice of extended suckling
and the effects of malnutrition or ill health. Epidemics certainly
produced dramatic fluctuations in average birth rates over the short
term, while food shortages, apart from reducing fertility, also led to an
increase in the number of children who were abandoned at institutions or put out to a wet-nurse, in either case giving only a minimal
chance of survival in the vast majority of cases.

Overall, these various factors were of striking cumulative significance. In addition, infant mortality was high: it has been estimated
that in France during the seventeenth century one-quarter of all children died before their first birthday and that another quarter failed to
reach the age of 20. This appallingly low life-expectancy, averaging
around 23–26 years at birth, taken in conjunction with delayed
marriage and restricted fertility, explains why the overall population
of Europe was virtually stagnant, each generation only just succeeding in reproducing itself. To modern eyes the most striking reflection

of this – confirmed in the paintings of the period – would have been the higher proportion of children in any normal community, with consequently high dependency ratios even if we allow for the fact that children were expected to contribute to the family income at an early age.

Delayed marriage unavoidably entailed a problem of illegitimacy, limited though it was in this period by comparison with the less puritan and morally strict eighteenth century. According to French research, there was a very low rate of illegitimate births in the countryside (perhaps around 1 per cent), and even in cities, where pregnant unmarried women might seek refuge from religious and moral stigma, the rate was quite modest, perhaps 4–5 per cent in Paris. By contrast, premarital conceptions were very common, accounting for as much as a quarter of all first births in those parts of Europe, including England, where folk custom sanctioned or tolerated co-habitation after some kind of engagement and before actual marriage.

Seasonal demographic patterns were also noticeable: Advent and Lent had noticeably fewer conceptions in some parts of Catholic Europe, whilst in England and Scandinavia the conviviality of Christmas appears to have had the opposite effect. The rest of spring on average had the highest number of conceptions, perhaps in rural society out of tacit recognition that child-bearing was best avoided in the busy summer season. Death rates also fluctuated seasonally, reaching a peak for infants during the summer and autumn because of sanitary factors, while old people were most at risk in winter because of inadequate nutrition and heating.

As already noted, the family and its ties of kinship were stronger than they are in modern society and at all levels, except perhaps the poorest, provided a network of assistance and obligation. Amongst the better-off, kinship was crucial, together with patronage, in determining social and promotional opportunities: Cardinal Richelieu's network of *créatures*, consisting both of clients and of actual kinsfolk or in-laws placed in positions of influence, is a well-known example. It is more difficult to determine the strength of kinship ties further down the social scale or assess the extent to which they were undermined by social mobility as well as by the normal strains of human proximity. But it is clear that collective responsibility within kinship circles, as well as concern for family property and inheritance, were widely accepted and respected.

At a physical and practical level, the 'family' was also often more complex than modern stereotypes would suggest. If we define 'family' as a co-residential group of relatives eating together and sharing the use of a house and property, then it is apparent that a wide range of main types of family structure co-existed all over Europe. We should perhaps also remind ourselves that, even if certain patterns tended to be more common in specific regions than in others, in the course of a life-cycle a family would move from one main type to a substantially different one. Most basic was the surprisingly common solitary house-holder, including not just clergymen in Catholic Europe and confirmed spinsters and bachelors but also the numerous if only temporary widowers and widows, and the old, sometimes with a servant or lodger and sometimes completely alone. The nuclear-family household, consisting (apart from unrelated servants, appren-tices and others) solely of parents and unmarried children, may have been the norm in north-western Europe but elsewhere it is misleading to regard it as standard.

Stem-family households (involving more than two generations in direct line), extended families (with non-linear relatives) and multi-ple-family households (with children living-in after marriage or older relatives remaining as subhouseholds in a dependent position) were still common at all social levels in southern France, northern Italy, parts of central Europe and Scandinavia, appearing in even more pronounced forms in Russia, the Baltic provinces and the Balkans. When a *pater familiae* died, several couples of married children might, especially in times of hardship or war, decide to remain together in the family home as a kind of *frérèche* (sibling household), or the oldest son might take over as head of the household and manager of the property and marriage-interests of the house. In the countryside such family patterns were particularly associated with regions of non-partible inheritance customs, where a holding would pass to one heir undi-vided, the land itself being a crucially decisive factor. In small and remote villages such complexities also help to explain the concern of church authorities with biological or spiritual consanguinity and its attendant impediments to marriage, special dispensations being required for what were regarded as endogamous unions.

A single example from England underlines the extraordinary range in the size of households: in a Kent village in 1676, the average size of family was a normal 4.5, but the inadequacy of such a statistic is revealed by breaking it down. Amongst the poor the average size of family was less (3.2 amongst labourers and a mere 2.1 amongst paupers), whilst 12 out of the 26 yeoman households accommodated 100 people between them, and one gentry household included 23 persons. In other words, nearly half the village population lived in households that were at least twice the average size. It is not surpris-ing, given the mortality factors described earlier, that pauper families were small, incidentally disproving the common prejudice that poverty reinforced itself by breeding. But the size of household at the other end of the scale helps to explain the significance attached to notions of kinship and lineage.[25]

Noble households tended everywhere to be complex and very large, and might often be described as polynuclear if there were married relatives or servants living in. Urban society, however, also appears to have encouraged non-nuclear formations, even in north-western Europe, particularly in artisan and craftsman households where more distant relatives lived in, as well as unrelated and unmarried apprentices or servants. The latter, however, seem by far the most common: demographic studies suggest that a large proportion of town-dwellers had direct experience at some stage in life of large households with one or more unrelated members living in on a long-term basis.

Gender and power

Closely connected to the question of family structure was that of the legal and *de facto* position of women, children and servants. Multiple-family households were often, where they existed, based on equality between the family, as in the Franche Comté and the Massif Central, but within a single conjugal unit there was always a clear theoretical hierarchy of authority up to the head of the household. All the literature of the period emphasises the need for this hierarchical authority, often in terms which compare the head of the household with the head of state and which seek justification in scriptural and historical assumptions of patriarchal authority and subordination. In law, the status of women was by the seventeenth century ambiguous and seemingly deteriorating. Marriage was a union celebrated in church but was also a contractual arrangement between two families, usually with clear implications in terms of property and money. The higher the social status of the two families involved, the more a marriage involved carefully negotiated settlements and financial investment fixed by parents to secure the long-term interests of the clan. Women were not regarded as legally autonomous but were assumed to need the guardianship first of a father and then of a husband. Use of their property was transferred in law from father to husband, with little or no scope for independent decisions or ultimate control by the woman herself. The law offered virtually no protection against financially irresponsible husbands and no complementarity: whilst a husband held the lifetime right of use of his wife's property, the reverse was not the case. Ironically, therefore, widowhood might often have seemed the only true liberation.

Diaries and other contemporary material naturally reveal a broad range of real relationships, depending on personality, affection, distribution of work, fear caused by drink and brutality, and other aspects about which it is impossible to generalise because of the inadequacy of reporting mechanisms. Although the husband traditionally had extensive rights of discipline over other members of the household, including the right to inflict corporal punishment, in theory this was no longer unqualified. The Danish law code of 1683, for example, stressed that if the head of a household, in the process of imposing discipline, seriously hurt or damaged the health of those living in his house, he could be prosecuted as if he were a stranger, while husbands treating their wives 'tyrannically or in unchristian fashion' could be sent to forced labour. Interestingly, if women were themselves heads of household they were explicitly given the same powers as a man would have had. Double standards persisted, in this as in matters of sexual licence, but it is perhaps significant that writers also began to question the husband's responsibility for his wife's morals. In practice, however, these matters tended to be regulated by communal action, including the kind of public humiliations and harassments that were regularly inflicted during charivaris on cuckolded or hen-pecked husbands, wayward wives, masters taking advantage of female servants, domineering women or others regarded as upsetting the natural order of things.[26] Clearly marriage was regarded as an extension of the public order system where fathers (like rulers) had extensive powers of discipline and chastisement over the other members of the household.

Both legal concerns about paternity with respect to the inheritance of property, and the very traditional sexual (double) standards of all the Churches, dictated absolute insistence on female chastity before and within marriage. The various wordings used in the religious marriage vow itself tended to emphasise this, and both the law and common usage regarded female fornication or adultery as much more reprehensible than that of males. For most individuals the only escape from marriage was through the death of one of the partners: divorce was extremely difficult to obtain (especially for women) in Protestant Europe and all but impossible in Catholic areas (except in cases of non-consummation or if the marriage was discovered to be non-valid because of consanguinity). Only a few brave (and isolated) voices spoke out critically about contemporary marriage norms – amongst them the great English poet and intellectual John Milton and, a generation later, John Locke – and they had no apparent influence on contemporary expectations. For women, the only alternative to marriage was admission to a religious order or nunnery; permanent spinsterhood was difficult and likely to carry significant social stigma. An unmarried woman who became pregnant was usually subjected to enormous social and moral pressure to reveal the paternity of her child and, if possible to marry before delivery. Single women who were visibly pregnant suffered huge penalties in terms of loss of reputation, loss of work (for example, eviction from a household in which she had been a servant) and loss of future expectations. As a result, infanticide was quite common – the only means by which an unmarried woman might preserve some hope for the future, but at great personal risk, since discovery meant immediate prosecution for one of the most serious of all crimes. Infanticide invariably carried the death penalty, though the authorities often did commute such a sentence to forced labour, the workhouse or other extreme long-term punishment.[27] Significantly, there are no recorded instances of parents prosecuted for the physical abuse of children, whose death (except in the case of new-born infants) was invariably recorded as accidental.

Religion itself offered only limited consolation. A rather forbidding reliance on patristic and patriarchal traditions in both the Christian and Jewish Churches ensured official attitudes which seem little short of misogynistic. Suppression of some of the more liberal Apocrypha, and use of symbols of female purity and passivity within most of the Christian Churches, gave only limited scope for active participation by women except within extreme radical groups such as the Quakers. The ritual of purification and ceremonial reintroduction into the church (the so-called churching ceremony) after childbirth and lying-in clearly reflected the double standards imposed in the name of religious belief. All of these cultural accretions and traditions were used by contemporary writers to justify relegating women to an inferior status which went virtually unchallenged during the seventeenth century. In the Ottoman Empire, under Islamic law, women suffered additional discrimination: whilst a Muslim man could in theory have up to four wives as well as sexual partners amongst his slaves (if he could afford them) and could legitimise any resulting offspring by recognising them as his own, a woman could marry only one man at a time and was confined to a largely domestic life concealed from public view. Although sufficient research has not yet been done on this period, it is possible that under Islam there were compensations for women in respect of, for example, better access to divorce and clearer recognition (at least in law) of separate property rights, provided the woman was herself Muslim. But everywhere in Europe, it seems, religious belief and religious institutions had an ambivalent impact on the status of women, on the one hand providing a network and a spiritual community in which women could take an active if subsidiary part, on the other lending moral authority to a whole array of contemporary discriminatory attitudes which locked women into a perpetually inferior position with regard to personal rights, property, the law, education, active participation in society, control over family strategies, courtship and marriage itself, and conformity to contemporary moral and sexual expectations.

In the context of the discussion in this chapter as a whole, however, we should be cautious in ascribing this solely to cultural and religious discrimination against women. Early modern society was in many respects built on brutality, exploitation and abuses of power across a wide range of social contexts – sometimes motivated by and frequently aggravated by fear that the social order and its traditional values really were vulnerable. Gender stereotyping was inflexible, hypocritical, obsessed with potential threats that might undermine patriarchal norms and totally unforgiving towards deviations of any kind. This extreme intolerance is even more apparent with respect to attitudes towards lesbianism and homosexuality – the former barely even recognisable in contemporary writings and evidence, the latter utterly condemned as an unnatural crime. But unattractive though such prejudices are to modern observers, it must be recognised that they were part of a larger set of cultural and social attitudes which to varying degrees downgraded and demeaned the life of everyone who was not in a privileged position: men of lesser social status as well as women, non-whites, religious nonconformists and the huge array of 'outsiders' (gypsies, migrants, vagrants, decommissioned soldiers, beggars, prostitutes) whose lifestyle did not match that of the moral majority. If the precariousness of life created an environment which was so inward-looking and inhospitable to the great majority, it is understandable why women themselves did not articulate their griev-ances very clearly: they were only one group amongst many victimised by fear and intolerance during this period.

4 Enterprise and profit

The Danish port of Ribe in south-western Jutland, with a population of 3500 in the early seventeenth century, was quite small by European standards but remained an important centre of Danish trade with Hamburg, Amsterdam and other northern European ports. One of the most prominent citizens of Ribe was the merchant Hans Friis, whose account-books for the years 1630–50 give an interesting illustration of what constituted a successful merchant business at the time. He owned substantial property in the town, served as mayor of the city and, like many of his kind, acted in a number of capacities, as retail, mail-order and wholesale trader, shopkeeper, moneylender, agent and middleman for the cattle exports of Danish noblemen, and local employer. The stock of merchandise listed in the inventory after his death in 1650 included some of the nearly two hundred different qualities and types of textiles that he normally carried, various hardware ranging from scythes to sewing needles, wine, salt, grain, building materials (including timber), various luxury articles, glass and paper, altogether valued at 3000 slettedaler (approximately £500 at the time) or the equivalent of about one year's turnover. His accounts reveal that he also traded in iron, lead, fish and spices, although the local apothecary specialised in the last. His customers, numbering a total of 234 during the year 1640, ranged widely in terms of income and social status; although the better-off were predictably well-represented, two-thirds of the total number were peasants from the surrounding countryside, accounting for one-tenth of the total turnover. That Ribe was anything but a consumer society is underlined by the fact that Friis, although probably the biggest merchant in town, appears to have averaged merely three retail sales per day in his shop (where most transactions took place), with none at all on some days, and only sixteen on one of his record days, Christmas Eve 1640. Many transactions were barter rather than purchase for cash, and Hans Friis, like most of his contemporaries, did not produce balance sheets to indicate his overall profits. Nevertheless, for some of the agricultural products where values were indicated and the mark-up not actually disguised by means of his cryptic signs, his profit ranged from 13 to 69 per cent, averaging around 34 per cent. Against this he had to bear substantial transport costs and trading risks, as well as allow long-term credit (with or without interest) to some of his regular customers. His diverse business, spreading itself over a sufficient range to give reasonable security and continuity, was probably quite typical of the period: successful enough to support Friis's family and his staff in comfort in the 26-room townhouse that he inhabited and where he kept most of his stores, and yet with a turnover small enough to emphasise the limitations of the consumer market at a time when most people everywhere in Europe had to be largely self-sufficient, and when disposable income was low.[1] Neither the human nor the physical environment was conducive to significant change in this respect during the pre-industrial period.

The most immediate obstacle to trade in the early modern period was the level of communications and transport. The supply of all but the most local raw materials was erratic and costly, whilst planning decisions were difficult to make without up-to-date information on the market at which the merchant aimed his products. The publication of weekly price quotations became customary in the big cities during the seventeenth century, following the example of Amsterdam (from 1585), but beyond that a merchant had to rely on personal contacts, correspondents or agents to gauge markets for him. Overland travel was slow, averaging perhaps 50–60 km per day in normal conditions where horse-drawn transport was feasible, and every travel diary of the period confirms that it was fraught with hazards ranging from breakdown to highway robbery. Postal services could in theory be at least as fast, but in practice seldom were (particularly between smaller towns where there were no direct connections). In England in the 1660s letters travelled at an estimated 3–4 miles an hour, and on the continent only some main connections between principal cities were specifically organised to ensure maximum speed, such as the 56-hour courier between Amsterdam and Hamburg organised in 1660. Goods travelled slower still, essentially at walking pace, averaging at best 30–40 km per day in satisfactory conditions, and because of the extremely rudimentary nature of most roads the effort and cost involved were enormous. Mules remained the characteristic form of goods transport in southern Europe, most notably in Sicily and in central Spain (even to and from Madrid itself), and this effectively crippled the economy by making inland development impracticable. The cost of genuine road-building was formidable, but military planning in the stronger states eventually made this a central aspect of government enterprise, particularly in the second half of the century. In England the turnpike act of 1663 provided a basis for private road-building in return for the right to collect tolls from users.[2]

Transport by domestic waterways was an obvious alternative, especially for bulk trade, but the investment needed to make rivers navigable meant that progress in this direction was slow. The Duke of Sully had ambitious schemes for developing the French waterways early in the seventeenth century, but it was only by the time of Colbert that the Loire was finally made serviceable and its connection with the Seine undertaken (completed 1692). Colbert's scheme for the Canal des Deux Mers connecting the Mediterranean with the Garonne and hence the Atlantic was also beset by problems, and proved a disappointment once it had been completed in 1681. More important was the building of the Oder-Spree Canal in 1662–9, linking Breslau to Hamburg by water. In the coastal regions of the United Provinces, extensive canal-building proved economically viable, leading to the construction of some 500 km of canals before the boom ended in the 1670s. But for the rest of Europe trade over moderate or longer distances was confined to luxury goods with a high value-to-weight ratio, while trade in bulk goods over greater distances was viable only by sea.

Entrepreneurial initiatives beyond a narrow geographic radius were hampered by obstacles other than those of transport and communications. The relative ineffectiveness of central government meant that local interest groups such as landowners and town oligarchies had been able to establish myriad toll barriers and customs monopolies which slowed down trade in most parts of Europe and greatly increased its cost. On the 100 km stretch of the river Saône between Lyon and Chalon, for example, there were 12 toll points. Although these negative effects were recognised, the system yielded its beneficiaries too much immediate revenue to make government schemes for substantial reform realisable: Colbert's tariff ordinance of 1664, for example, was typical in attempting to simplify and organise the patchwork, in securing some revenue increase for the state itself and in failing to overcome the strong provincialism which survived for another century or more. In Europe as a whole, tariff structures, monopolies, legislative restrictions on the practice of urban trades, and the already rather antiquated guild structures were all left largely unaltered, or even in some cases extended, particularly in those areas (like the Holy Roman Empire after 1648) where the political situation reinforced economic conservatism and local autonomy.

The scope for government intervention in national or regional economic development (or even in colonial and overseas trade) was limited more by the lack of effective control than by any lack of ideas and theoretical advice. Various schools of economic interventionists flourished during the early seventeenth century, often lumped together by historians under the term 'mercantilists'. In England, where legislation during the Tudor period had already brought together the interests of Crown and merchants to a considerable degree, there was a long tradition for writers in this vein, culminating notably in Thomas Mun's book entitled *England's Treasury by Fforraign Trade*, written in the 1620s and published in 1664 at the height of the trade conflict with the Dutch. Across the Channel, Hugo

Grotius and later Pieter de la Court proclaimed principles of free trade, which the Dutch trading interests generally followed as long as it suited them to do so. In France mercantilism had a number of exponents, including Henry IV's controller of commerce in the first decade of the century, Laffemas, and the tendentious writer Antoine de Montchrétien. Unlike Mun, Laffemas at least did not concentrate solely on overseas trade, but made a number of suggestions for the domestic economy, a few of which were actually tried. On the whole, however, it seems that intervention in the economy could best be done on municipal initiative and on a not too ambitious scale, whilst central government could not yet hope to go much beyond the kind of vague and pious generalisations expressed in, for example, Richelieu's *Testament politique*. After the upheavals of mid-century new attempts were made out of recognition that a sound domestic economy was important for revenue and for generating employment, but (as we shall see in chapter 11) the results were uneven.

Finance

Developments in the financial sector were more tangible. By the seventeenth century, banking families were no longer so closely tied to the personal fortunes of bankruptcy-prone ruling dynasties, and the banking facilities available in northern Italy, Antwerp and Amsterdam helped to integrate the international financial network. Nevertheless, the major monies of account (i.e. the monetary units used for official government accounting) fluctuated considerably during the political upheavals of the period. Extra uncertainty was being created by the now increasingly erratic silver imports from America, by the growing use of copper coins (such as the Spanish *vellón*) which caused a rapid rise in the value of silver and in the opportunities for speculation and reminting (for example in Bohemia, as noted in chapter 1), and by other government coinage manipulations such as the drastic Spanish devaluations of 1680 and 1686. The pound sterling was the only money of account which virtually kept its value in silver terms throughout the period, remaining equivalent to just over 100 g of silver. The German lands had various monies of account, but all suffered during the crisis which culminated in the early 1620s; the silver Reichsthaler, however, remained a fairly stable and widely accepted standard coin, often being used as a multiple of the money of account and fixed originally at around 26 g of silver. The Dutch florin (guilder) was equivalent to just over 10 g of silver until it slipped slightly in the last third of the century, but the French livre tournois, nearly equivalent to the florin in the 1630s, suffered during the period of Louis XIV and had fallen to 7 g of silver by 1700. The Venetian lira (2/13 of a ducat) fell slightly to below 3 g of silver in the course of the century. Actual coined units (species) were, of course, rather less stable than these monies of account and existed in such a multiplicity of forms, even within a single territory, that major speculation and fraud were regular occurrences.[3]

In spite of the shortage of silver on which to base currencies, it is unlikely that the business community overall suffered any real shortage of capital during the period (even though there is some divergence of opinion on this). Interest rates on the Amsterdam money market declined steadily and a similar trend was observable in other banking centres. Even governments could raise substantial loans on a generally fairly stable basis provided that there was no extraordinary element of risk: in the early seventeenth century the Republic of Genoa could raise loans by offering a mere 1.5 per cent interest, and in Venice a funded system of state obligations was the basis for the success of the Banco del Giro established in 1619. The government of the United Provinces became so renowned for its public finances and the reliability of its accounting procedures that it could offer permanent negotiable government bonds and annuities as a form of investment to the general public and, since interest payments were guaranteed by budgetary allowance, the scheme was so popular that interest rates fell below 5 per cent by the 1640s. England established a long-term national debt in 1693, with parliament as guarantor, and this again proved so successful (despite temporary problems) that the government could raise far bigger loans at smaller cost than could its main international adversary, France – the Bourbon monarchy continued to rely on private financiers for its increasingly exorbitant and security-deficient borrowing requirements, paying very heavily when its credibility was low (especially from the 1690s onwards).

Other possibilities for investment also developed during this period, the most notable being the opportunities offered in joint-stock companies. A system of permanent joint-stock funding emerged gradually in connection with the privileged Dutch and English colonial trading companies early in the century. Shares in these companies became freely negotiable in practice, and the publication of regular share-price quotations in London and Amsterdam effectively created a recognisable stock market, whose success could be gauged by the rapid rise in share prices above their face value. The market for joint-stock company shares and fixed redeemable bonds not only created capital resources for the companies themselves (and indeed gave handsome returns as long as speculation was kept under control) but also encouraged greater flexibility in the market for short-term and smaller loans. For most forms of credit, private entrepreneurs had until the sixteenth century largely relied on their personal contacts in their family or business community (a fact which helps to account for the business success of the strongly cohesive religious minorities such as the Jews or the Huguenots). Promissory credit notes or letters obligatory were, however, increasingly often assigned to successive bearers as acceptable payment for debts and legislative steps taken to protect the beneficiary when he no longer personally knew the original creditor. During the seventeenth century the use of written cheques as payment spread from Italy to the rest of western Europe, but these were not always negotiable. On the international financial market, too, credit transfers by means of bills of exchange had been known for some time, and by the end of the sixteenth century Antwerp (in contrast to some Italian cities) had fully adopted the practices of endorsing and discounting these bills, creating a practice of 'bill-broking' which rapidly spread to other financial centres such as Hamburg. A sophisticated system of credit transfers was thus coming into regular use which did not rely on actual cash and which greatly increased the flexibility of the money market. Further steps were taken towards the integration of the international financial market with the establishment of public exchange banks, notably the Venetian Banco della Piazza di Rialto of 1587, the Amsterdam Exchange Bank of 1609 and the Hamburg Girobank of 1619. The latter two, set up for the local business community to help reduce monetary confusion, soon served as major European clearing banks and as models for similar banks elsewhere in the north-west. Although the public banking world itself remained very cautious, the United Provinces in 1651 officially sanctioned the system of endorsing and discounting bills, thus formalising existing practices of negotiability and removing any lingering hesitations concerning the use of bills in lieu of cash in complex trading operations. It took some decades for the governments of France and England to take similar final steps, but the practice had already become generally acceptable amongst exchange brokers in the main commercial centres. The establishment of the Bank of England in 1694, although more important for public finance than for commercial life, marked a further stage towards greater capital fluidity, since the bank was authorised by charter of incorporation not only to handle the newly established consolidated national debt (whence came the promissory banknotes that were eventually accepted in the city as paper money in the early eighteenth century) but also to accept bills of exchange and to borrow money or lend it on security.

The seventeenth century thus saw an increasing use at least in western and central Europe of more flexible techniques in the financial world, supported by more sophisticated public banks. Private banking, of course, survived, and was still often preferred by those who could offer land as security for a cash loan repayable by means of traditional annuities (*rentes* or *censos*). But for the urban business community these comparatively new practices (and the more tolerant attitude towards what had once been thought of as 'usury') made capital more readily available and, at the same time, created new opportunities for speculation. Even for the poorer social groups credit at reasonable terms was available in those Italian towns which had established *Monti di Pietà* (charitable pawnshops) under public supervision. This example was followed in the United Provinces with the creation of the Bank van Leening in Amsterdam in 1614 and the establishment of public lending banks elsewhere, operating on essentially commercial lines.

Industry and trade

The growth of more complex trading patterns, encouraged by this 'financial revolution' (to use a rather overdramatic term for a fairly protracted and still very exclusive development), was already obvious in parts of Italy and Antwerp in the sixteenth century, and in the ports of the United Provinces and in southern England in the seventeenth. In other parts of the continent the effects took longer to materialise, and growth was often faltering, especially in the years 1630–50, although our knowledge of this is very patchy; but the main seaports such as Hamburg and Lübeck, and inland commercial centres such as Leipzig later in the century, paved the way. Nevertheless, although a great variety of local industries had developed over much of central and western Europe since the Middle Ages, with concomitant trade routes, most of these still depended ultimately on the agrarian sector, and consequently changed only very slowly. Industrial technology, in spite of significant improvements in, for example, mining, did not begin its dramatic growth until the late eighteenth century. Even the most complex processes in, for example, the textile industry continued during the early modern period to be operated by very basic equipment powered by wind or water, or by human and animal effort. According to workshop inventories from different trades in Venice, capital investment in equipment was small compared with the costs of raw materials and the value of finished unsold goods, even in as sophisticated an industry as printing. Concentration in bigger workshops was reserved exclusively for the few enterprises, such as glassmaking, mining and metallurgy, and sometimes soapmaking, where scale could cancel out those disadvantages of centralisation created by labour and transport problems. By far the greatest part of industrial production took place in small family-based workshops (if necessary organised in a putting-out system), where skilled labour was indispensable. Not only weaving, but also leather work, the manufacture of nails and clocks, paper-making, pottery, knitting and small-scale metalwork were all perfectly suited to this type of village industry.

Apart from the building sector, the tangible legacy of which is still occasionally visible in urban Europe, the most important source of non-agrarian employment was the clothing industry. Textile production for a wider market existed in some form in most parts of the continent: Italy and Flanders had led the way but faced serious competition from France, the United Provinces (especially Leiden) and England, where the most important production centres could now be found. With the rise in popularity of the 'new draperies' (worsted fabrics and mixtures first developed in the sixteenth century) and various non-woollens including cotton mixtures, the United Provinces and England in particular secured a major export market for their textiles, and during the seventeenth century developed the alum mines which were essential for dyeing the lighter cloths destined for the luxury market. The silk industry had previously been restricted primarily to a few specialised regions such as Bologna (which had a complex power-driven silk mill, for long considered a vital and tantalising industrial secret), but now also spread over much of lowland northern Italy and eventually also rooted itself firmly in southern France and in Valencia.

Urban growth not only placed greater demands on the agricultural sector in the surrounding countryside but also served as a stimulus for more sophisticated building and planning techniques and for developments in the production of commodities such as glassware, ceramics and furniture to suit the tastes of wealthier groups (in the developing economies, at least). A gradually growing demand for education, printing and book-production also became apparent, although the most impressive upturn in this respect only came in the following century in western and central Europe.

Mining had benefited from large-scale enterprise in certain regions for a long time but underwent some interesting changes during the seventeenth century. The yearly production of coal in England, for example, may have passed 3 million tons by the late seventeenth century (possibly a tenfold increase over a century, but the figures are very uncertain), and this in turn paved the way for emancipation from timber as the main fuel and created considerable technological challenges. As far as metal extraction is concerned, the most spectacular development occurred in Sweden, whose iron and copper output came to occupy a key position in the European market thanks to a mixture of government interest, Dutch expertise coupled with corporate financing techniques, and technological improvements in the ore-milling machinery designed by German and Walloon workers. This allowed Sweden to become a major producer of iron utensils and arms, and helped Gustav Adolf and his successors to play their substantial role in European politics. All mining operations, however, were affected by technical problems (notably drainage difficulties) which often gradually reduced the profit level on particular sites until work was abandoned. Overall, Swedish copper production fell at the end of the seventeenth century, just as south German silver-mining had become uncompetitive a century earlier when Spanish silver imports from America approached their highest levels.

Significant growth in the overseas colonial and far-eastern trade[4] also had substantial domestic repercussions. The Spanish trade system began to crumble in the 1620s when both silver imports from America and commodity exports in return became erratic and when French and Dutch infiltration encouraged the colonial economies to become more diversified and self-sufficient. The silver crisis itself created difficulties in the Asian trade, which was notoriously costly since European demand for pepper and spices far exceeded the value of goods which could be sold there in return, a factor which soon forced the Europeans to develop their carrying trade to make the most of price differences between overseas markets. With the economic instability of the second quarter of the seventeenth century, and a glut of pepper by 1650, competition between the big joint-stock companies became so severe that the Dutch faced trade wars with the English and French in Europe itself. The resulting protection costs for overseas and international trade not only contributed to the end of Dutch trade dominance in favour particularly of England, but also encouraged a fruitful diversification in long-distance trade. Certain types of textiles, costly raw materials, exotic foods, coffee, tea and sugar came to play a much greater role from the later seventeenth century onwards, giving new scope on internal European trade routes and, above all, providing opportunities for the few industries capable of responding to the challenge of limited overseas demand (notably for English cotton-based textiles, Silesian linen and armaments), such that the bullion drain to the east could be reduced. The domestic demand for oriental goods also generated European-made imitations, notably in porcelain and the oriental-style furniture designs which became so popular by the eighteenth century. The economic benefits of colonial trade were unevenly spread within Europe, and the impact both on Europe and on other continents was (as we shall see in chapter 12) very mixed. Particularly degrading were parts of the Atlantic trades, which came to rely on the rapidly growing slave trade in order to provide manual labour for plantations in the Caribbean and North America. But for Europeans at home, overseas trade seemed to open new horizons, and created huge opportunities for the imaginative entrepreneur.

Regions in the European economy: the Mediterranean recession

It will already be apparent that changes in various aspects of material life during the seventeenth century were far more significant in north-western Europe, notably in the coastal region of the Netherlands, in southern England and in a few other areas, than elsewhere on the continent. The United Provinces achieved a remarkable degree of agricultural specialisation, industrial development, financial maturity and commercial competitiveness over a period of less than a century, from around the 1580s or slightly earlier. England, although experiencing the economic crisis which affected most of Europe except the Netherlands from the 1620s to the 1650s, was able to proceed to a more durable economic growth after the Commonwealth period. By contrast, France, despite vast economic potential, was slightly disadvantaged by social attitudes hampering the growth of an active and independent entrepreneurial class comparable to that existing in its northern neighbours (a problem which will be examined in chapter 5). The Spanish peninsula, on the other hand, signally failed to achieve anything durable from its sixteenth-century economic opportunities, and seems to have allowed what entrepreneurial talents it had to all but disappear. Clearly the factors conducive to economic development were complex, and improvements in transport, in credit facilities or in agrarian productivity were not the only crucial variables. The role of government could be significant in creating either conditions of security or aggressive strength for entrepreneurial development, and perhaps even in providing capital for certain sectors such as mining and heavy industry. Public demand (especially in the form of taxation) could itself become an economic stimulant by forcing taxpayers to produce for profit. But while few statesmen denied that prosperous manufacturing and trading interests were essential, a wide range of extraneous political, social and religious factors also came into account. Clearly the minimalist approach of the Dutch and later the English governments, basically sympathetic to and influenced by the interests of the business community, was economically more successful than, for example, the Bourbon monarchy, with its extravagant foreign policy and its inflexible attitude to the business-minded Huguenots during the reign of Louis XIV (see chapter 11). The problems experienced by the Mediterranean economies, however, warn us against an oversimplified explanation of economic change, and suggest that a comparison of what can be regarded as the three main trading zones of Europe – the Mediterranean, the Atlantic north-west and the Baltic – may give some indication of the real complexity of the factors which produced such striking economic divergences during the seventeenth century.

The Mediterranean, and especially the great Italian cities such as Venice, Genoa, Florence and Milan, had been at the focus of sixteenth-century economic life. It connected the Levant (particularly the ports of Constantinople and Cairo) to the central and south German trade routes serving the Rhine. Further west the development of Marseilles and the Rhône valley relied on similar market potential, as did Barcelona and Andalusia in the west. The years between 1580 and 1621, however, saw first an agricultural downturn (against which no measures of agricultural reform were attempted) and then a period of both commercial and financial uncertainty, marked by a drop in urban industry (and even in total population), so that much of the Mediterranean area began its regression from sophisticated production and high-quality services to a structure relying mainly on the production of primary materials for use elsewhere in Europe. Even the Italian financial market lost its strength, since Genoese bankers in particular had become deeply involved in the ever-deteriorating finances of the Spanish monarchy and suffered the consequences when silver imports to Spain from the new world could no longer be relied upon after 1620 to sustain the overextended imperial commitments of the Spanish Crown. There is no doubt that Spain's littoral economy suffered economic problems similar in some respects to those of Italy, but in addition it suffered from silver-induced coinage instabilities and especially from erratic and excessively uneven fiscal policies. The records of the Casa de Contratación (a government trade council) in Seville do not indicate more than a moderate decline in the volume of the Spanish–American trade in the period 1620–50, but the nature, value and place of origin of the commodities altered significantly in favour of other European countries (especially the French) at the expense of the domestic Spanish economy. What limited economic potential Spain may intrinsically have had was further damaged by the political deterioration visible from the later 1630s. As a result, the Iberian peninsula was no longer strong enough to affect the overall European economic balance. The overseas western and eastern trades (the latter symbolically breached by the Dutch rounding the Cape in 1595) were still quantitatively relatively minor, but here shifts again influenced the domestic European balance.

The real challenge occurred in the centre of the Mediterranean itself, when competition from outside seriously cut into the trade and manufactures of the Italian cities. This process has been studied in greatest detail in the case of Venice, whose prosperity was seriously and visibly threatened by the early 1600s. The growth of piracy and renewed Ottoman turbulence in the previous decades had raised defence costs for the city, but the strengths of its sophisticated economy and the quality of its luxury manufactures, cloths and glass products had enabled it to retain a crucial position in the competitive Levant trade. Around the turn of the century, however, Dutch and English commercial undercutting and market infiltration became serious. A shortage of timber for shipbuilding forced Venice to import substitutes from northern Europe, and the seriousness of the situation became clearly apparent in 1602 when the Senate passed legislation which discriminated against foreign merchants trading in Venice, and imposed restrictions on the hire of foreign ships by Venetian merchants themselves. The effects of this were predictably negative in that English and Dutch merchants merely used other ports, such as Leghorn. When the Thirty Years War cut the overland trade routes through Germany, Venice's geographic position at the head of the Adriatic lost some of its natural advantages. This proved a permanent change, since the south German trade never regained its former levels even after the return of peace in 1648.

By the second quarter of the seventeenth century, cheaper English textiles were flooding traditional Venetian markets, while Dutch low-cost shipping was cutting into the western Mediterranean by virtue of its control over grain and naval products from the Baltic. The Venetian economy carried heavy overheads, including the cost of the much respected and elaborate (but rather rigid) quality-control mechanisms on all its main products. The reputation for quality, however, merely invited Dutch and English merchants to use smuggling, fraudulent trade marks and deliberate imitation in order to infiltrate the Venetian trade routes, a process which was all the more advantageous in that labour costs in the north-west were much lower than in Venice. Soon French, English and Dutch business interests (sometimes with government backing) encouraged technological spying and attracted immigration of skilled craftsmen from the south. They were able to create imitations (or derivations) of the high-quality glass and mirror industries, luxury soap production, printing and paper-making, and sophisticated cloth manufactures for which Venice had been famous, but in environments which were freer both from indirect taxes and from guild or state restrictions. Undercutting became unavoidable, and Venetian textile production was particularly badly hit: the fivefold increase in the production of draperies in England between 1600 and 1640 seriously damaged the Venetian counterpart.

The government in Venice recognised the dilemma but at first stuck to its protectionist policies in the hope that the reputation of its goods would eventually make the difference. Anchorage receipts dropped repeatedly after 1602, and by 1625 the spice trade had also been lost to the new trade routes operated by the north-western merchants. The Cretan war after 1645 damaged Venetian local interests in the eastern Mediterranean. Unlike other Italian cities, however, Venice managed to adapt remarkably successfully to these changes of circumstance, achieving the first signs of real recovery after its new tariff policy of 1626. Development of the terraferma (the Venetian mainland), with emphasis on large-scale production of rice and silk, was combined with redeployment in more local eastern-Mediterranean trade routes specialising in dried fruits, oil and other products of the region, so that anchorage receipts in Venice again rose substantially after the end of the Cretan War of 1669. The work of historians including R. T. Rapp has indicated that it is in fact misleading to talk of 'decline' in the Venetian economy at all: Venice may have been unable to stand up to competition from the north Atlantic maritime powers, but it maintained its prosperity, employment rates and living standards in absolute terms through the seventeenth century by virtue of a successful adaptation away from manufacturing and international long-distance trade towards a more local function. Since the population of the city did not decline in the long term (in spite of temporary ravages such as the plague of 1630), workers gradually transferred from those sectors which were no longer competitive towards more secure areas, and guilds such as those in the textile industries reduced their intake of apprentices. Employment statistics compiled by Rapp for the period 1539–1690 indicate that the food industry took up an increasing share of the labour market after 1603 (rising from 14 to 19 per cent over the century), as did retail trade (from 9 to 15 per cent) and construction work (from 4 to 6 per cent), whilst the share based in manufacturing declined from 37 to 29 per cent (not, however, without important exceptions in the printing industry, in glass and jewellery, in tailoring and in other high-skill manufactures which grew during this period). Over the century from 1595 employment in export-related sectors fell from 44 to 33 per cent in favour of the domestic sector. Rapp interestingly points out that by the end of the seventeenth century the Venetian economy was in many respects similar to what it had been in 1539, before its great boom period: prosperous but not spectacular.[5]

Venice, however, seems to have been an exception as far as the Mediterranean is concerned, and historians of seventeenth-century Italy agree that in most other regions there was a serious economic decline, produced by factors similar to those besetting Venice (especially the collapse of textile production) but without enough of the constructive response. Italy was relatively poor in raw materials, and the independent city states (like those in the German lands after 1648) tended to protect a conservative guild structure and an economic framework which could not compete with the newer Dutch, English and French manufactures. Wages in many urban areas of Italy had also kept up rather better with food prices than in much of the north-west, further reducing the profit margin of manufacturing enterprises. In many regions, textile production was moving out of the cities into the countryside, whilst the divide between north and south deepened as the south failed to benefit from the significant agrarian development experienced by the north. By the end of the seventeenth century, Italy was seriously lagging behind in the European economy, becoming an exporter even of some primary goods such as wine, oil, silk, dyestuffs and fruit and an importer of manufactured goods from the north-west (increasingly carried in foreign shipping).[6]

The growth of the north-west

The coastal provinces of the Netherlands had already by the sixteenth century attained a high level of prosperity based on the Baltic and northern trade, on fishing and whaling, and (especially in the southern part) on trade via the Rhine and the Atlantic coast to the Mediterranean. But the revolt by the northern provinces against Spain and the intensification of Spanish repressive measures (especially when the political situation hardened in the 1580s) severely damaged the trade and the essential textile industries of the southern part. Antwerp was sacked in 1585 and a very significant number of skilled workers and craftsmen (often called Walloons) migrated to the northern provinces, to England, Germany and Scandinavia, where the scale of their involvement in economic life was a clear testimony to what the Flemish economy had lost. The newly formed United Provinces in the north not only escaped much of the actual war damage, but emphasised the shift by blockading the south and taking over much of the long-distance trade, making Amsterdam the natural successor and substitute for Antwerp because of its geographic position and its productive hinterland. The increasing prosperity of the United Provinces would not have come about without the striking agrarian and structural diversification already noted (see chapter 3), but maritime trade also played a key part. No less important were a number of other factors working in the same direction: gradual relaxation of religious battle fronts culminating in an unusual degree of religious toleration once the perceived political dangers of such relaxation were seen to be unfounded; a loose administrative and political framework which retained many of its distinctive local features until the external threat to the United Provinces became too great in 1672; less ostentatious or elitist attitudes amongst the leaders, remarked upon by foreign visitors, although also ultimately undermined; and of course an intellectual freedom which helped to make the province of Holland a legend in Europe at the time. These factors will be examined more closely in different contexts, but taken together they help to explain the economic successes of the Dutch.

Most relevant at this juncture was the combination of industrial, financial and commercial assets which made the Dutch the dominant economic power in the early seventeenth century. Bulk production of certain types of textiles, ceramics, books and high-quality maps, fine instruments and other items gave Dutch traders a domestic input to supplement their growing carrying trade between the Baltic and the Atlantic. Even though no new financial techniques were developed, Amsterdam provided an ideal climate for the full and uninhibited integration of existing techniques, so that the city became in effect the world financial centre, a position it kept, despite mounting competition from London, through most of the next century. And, not least significant, the Dutch developed an acute sense of business efficiency outwardly symbolised in the cost-cutting *fluit*, a large-capacity cargo ship designed by them specifically for easy handling and reduced crew requirements, and built cheaply using wind-powered sawmills and standardised shipyard techniques. Capital resources and competitive commercial and managerial skills were applied wherever the prospect of profits seemed reasonable: not only in overseas colonial development, notably through the innovative structure and monopoly powers of the Dutch East India Company as it was restructured in 1602, but also in northern Europe itself, in the Scandinavian countries and the Baltic.

The Baltic involvement has probably been the most controversial, since Dutch grain purchases from Poland, Livonia, Pomerania and East Prussia reached such enormous proportions that it created a long-term imbalance in the local economies. A very detailed impression of the Baltic trade can be obtained from the Sound Toll registers, recording the dues imposed by the Danish Crown on shipping to and from the Baltic, through the narrow sound between northern Zealand and Scania. These registers do not give a totally reliable picture – complications arise over temporary exemptions (especially for Sweden in the later seventeenth century), over fraud and smuggling (both there and via the lesser waterways between the Danish islands) and over the allowance that needs to be made for other trade routes which went overland through Schleswig or further south, or (on a much smaller scale) by sea via Archangel – but nonetheless the registers are outstandingly rich in statistical material whose potential has been far from exhausted.[7] It is clear that Baltic grain played a vital part not only in alleviating specific harvest shortfalls in crisis years in the west but also in overcoming a substantial permanent grain shortage in the United Provinces themselves and in other western European markets. Particularly large quantities of rye and wheat were shipped westwards in the years around 1618 (over 100,000 lasts per annum) and again in the 1640s and 1680s, most of it coming from Danzig and to a lesser extent from Königsberg, Riga, Reval, Stettin and other ports. Throughout the seventeenth century, cereals remained the most important product going west, even if timber, iron, copper, coarser textiles, skins, potash, hemp, flax, pitch and tar played a growing part in the cargoes, and substantially affected trade patterns by the early eighteenth century. The eastbound cargoes included salt, textiles, herring, wine and colonial products, with the deficit made up in bullion when necessary. Of the total number of ships passing through the Sound, the Dutch at their peak owned well over half, but their share gradually decreased relative to that of other trading nations as the total tonnage sailing in the Baltic expanded from the end of the seventeenth century. The Dutch trade in the Baltic was not merely of northern European significance, since cargo ships often followed complicated routes, taking in salt from Portugal or wine from France to maximise effective usage of ships and crews. It is not surprising, therefore, that the United Provinces should be constant advocates of free trade in order to preserve their lucrative carrying and entrepôt activities, nor indeed is it surprising that their role was the object of envy and enmity amongst other nationalities with commercial aspirations, so that the Dutch were forced to take a major part in the political and international relations of the area, particularly to keep Denmark and Sweden fairly evenly balanced so as to limit the kind of disruptions of trade which occurred in the later 1620s and in the 1650s.

For the Baltic countries themselves, this trade had important long-term consequences. The huge western demand for grain encouraged landowners in the corn-growing plains from Pomerania to Lithuania to develop large-scale farming for marketing, using serf labour and enclosing land in order to overcome labour shortages (which were particularly severe in the first half of our period because of wartime losses and destruction). The revenues from grain sales, however, were very unevenly distributed, with the landowning nobility becoming accustomed to such comfortable profits that no investments in agrarian reform or in land improvements were contemplated. Not only was the serf economy thus emphasised, but the size of the price differential between the Baltic and Amsterdam grain markets (estimated by Bogucka at an average of 521 g of silver per last for the early seventeenth century) ensured substantial trading profits for western merchants, even if they offered western goods at cheap prices or indulged in tactical dumping to retain control of the trade. Some historians have argued that these factors, combined with the constant trade surplus in favour of the Baltic grain-exporting areas during the later sixteenth and early seventeenth centuries, damaged local manufactures there by destroying any incentive to develop a better-balanced and diversified economy. The magnates, who took most of the grain profits, tended to indulge in extravagant luxury-spending which could only be satisfied by means of foreign goods (or through purchases made while on foreign tours) which did not help the local economy. In addition, the unequal economic relationship made the Baltic countries vulnerable to western crises. The financial crisis of 1621 was very clearly felt in Poland and was aggravated by the sharp decline in exports to the west during the following years. This in turn greatly reduced Polish purchasing power for manufactured and luxury goods, and produced an outcry amongst the Polish nobility – without leading to any initiatives which might have stabilised export demands. The severe repercussions of the mid-century wars created another monetary crisis (late 1650s and 1660s) which was exacerbated by coinage devaluations authorised by the weak Polish Crown. Danzig wage-earners, whose income was already depressed, certainly felt both of these crises very clearly, and there is evidence that wealthier merchants and patricians there and in, for example, Königsberg also suffered from the imbalance created by the dependence on western markets. Tightness of credit and banking instability encouraged a significant amount of hoarding, which of course removed capital from productive use in the local economy. The efforts of landowners to circumvent urban middlemen in order to reduce their own periodic profit losses affected even the bigger Baltic ports by the later seventeenth century, especially since the nobility could often exert a controlling influence directly by virtue of the exploitation of their right to own property within town boundaries. Recent work suggests that the explanation for these problems lies not just in relations with the west, but it is clear that the Baltic economies were in disequilibrium during this period in spite of a foreign trade potential, and that social divides were widening.[8]

The role played by Amsterdam in the Scandinavian economies was more constructive in the long run. Sweden was already in the sixteenth century exploiting its silver, iron and copper resources successfully with German technical assistance, but by the turn of the century several Walloon families also became interested. Gustav Adolf, with his ambitious plans for Swedish development, used a Walloon contact already working in the Swedish mining industry, Willem de Besch, to attract further financial and technical assistance. Several Walloon and Dutch families, such as the Trips and the de Geers, became leading figures in the Falun copper mines and the ironworks of Bergslagen. Louis de Geer acquired control of gun-founding in Sweden between 1627 and 1648, winning contracts with most European belligerents regardless of religious or political implications. (Only a few decades later Dutch interests in the arms trade had become so lucrative that Louis XIV could buy what he needed in Amsterdam immediately prior to launching his war against the Dutch themselves in 1672!) The Swedish Crown, however, kept an important stake in the mining activities, and established a College of Mines in 1637 in order to retain some degree of overall supervision. Major entrepreneurs like de Geer himself had to accept naturalisation, which in fact gave him an opportunity to obtain further privileges (and a patent of nobility) and to spread his interests into virtually every major area of development, including Swedish overseas trade organised through his Africa Company. When he died in 1652 he was the richest man in Sweden and, like other Netherlanders, had received major land settlements in return for his claims on the Crown.

Gustav Adolf made copper the basis for Sweden's coinage in 1625, but this measure was a mixed blessing because of the impractical weight of the larger coins. He also used the virtual Swedish monopoly on European copper production to finance his intervention in the Thirty Years War, in spite of the fact that Dutch firms controlled the handling of much of Swedish output. Sweden's foreign trade did increase substantially, notably benefiting Stockholm and the newly established outlet to the west at Gothenburg. When the Falun copper mines approached exhaustion in the last quarter of the seventeenth century, iron exports (especially from the Värmland works) developed rapidly, facilitating continued Swedish contacts with Europe as a whole, and especially with its most important customer for iron, England.

In Denmark–Norway Dutch capital did not have such obvious objectives, even if Christian IV was as concerned as Gustav to foster a diversified domestic economy. The main contact came slightly later, and was dominated above all by the Marselis family (also of Walloon origin, now based in Hamburg). Celio Marselis became a major entrepreneur, government advisor and state contractor for Christian IV, and as such provided substantial support for the Danish fleet, for example, in its 1645 confrontation with the Swedish fleet (which on its side had partly been chartered by Louis de Geer). The Marselis family became invaluable to Christian's successor Frederick III, especially during the Swedish wars from 1657 to 1660 when much of Denmark was overrun. The resulting crown debts were so large that Celio and his brother Gabriel Marcelis had to accept major land settlements after 1660, both in Denmark and Norway, and often on unfavourable terms. The Irgens family, who had acquired major financial stakes in the Norwegian copper mines in Trondheim, also became substantial landowners in this way.

It is clear that capital from Amsterdam was attracted into the Scandinavian economies at a price and that the political consequences could be considerable. Nevertheless, Dutch and Walloon involvement produced significant economic developments in mining, shipbuilding, land drainage (for which the Dutch were appreciated in many parts of Europe), manufactures and timber exploitation. Their enterprises might remain under monopolistic family control for a time but tended to produce competition from other Dutch businessmen and even in some cases from the Danes and the Swedes themselves. The presence of reasonably decisive crown interests helped to create a better balance, even if the size of royal debts both in Sweden and in Denmark–Norway was a drawback. In the long run Amsterdam capital helped to lay commercial and industrial foundations whose potential was more fully realised in the eighteenth century. A comparison of the Scandinavian kingdoms with Poland warns us against treating Dutch involvement in the latter area as purely 'colonial' or exploitative. No doubt the aim of the Dutch entrepreneurs was profit, but given reasonably mature political development in the host country the result could be beneficial: Poland, lacking political strength or coherence, was in no position to control the domestic consequences of a developing Baltic trade.

Dutch commercial predominance in northern and western Europe, however, was relatively short-lived. Their trade-generated prosperity, backed by comparatively little military or political strength, made them an obvious target for both French and English ambitions. The challenge from France became explicit after 1660, when the huge French potential in terms of military ambitions, manpower and resources was pitched directly against the much smaller Dutch republic (see chapter 12). More difficult to explain, on the face of it, is the emergence of England as no less serious a competitor. Relatively small in terms of population, still well behind the Dutch in terms of shipbuilding, and latterly dependent on the London–Antwerp axis for its international trade, early Stuart England might not have seemed particularly promising. Its industries and productive techniques were less advanced than those of some of its continental competitors, as indicated by the import of quality goods and expertise from Italy, the Netherlands, Germany and elsewhere. In the words of D. C. Coleman (discussing the Tudor and early Stuart period): 'English demand for manufactured wares was limited largely because levels of wealth and income, as of culture, sophistication and urban achievement, were inferior to those of the great towns of Europe.'[9] Clearly this inferiority disappeared very rapidly from mid-century onwards, for reasons which are only partially understood: the economic perspective is one side of the story but in the present context other aspects stand out. England, like the United Provinces, evidently offered a favourable climate for productive adaptation and for the application of skills brought notably by Protestant refugees from abroad. The cloth industry is an obvious example of this after the severe setback in woollen exports in the decade from 1614 (partly caused by the misconceived Cockayne Project of that year, restricting the export of unfinished cloth) the shift to the 'new draperies' secured a more competitive and durable export sector which increased in absolute terms during the century, such that woollens still represented over two-thirds of all domestic exports by 1700. To this was added a still small but significant development in non-woollen textiles, including cotton in imitation of Indian imports, as well as rapid progress in other types of production in the later seventeenth century, notably sugar-processing, metalwork (especially in the West Midlands) and more sophisticated manufacturing industries, reducing the need for continental imports. London was ideally placed to compete with Amsterdam for the European and overseas carrying trade, especially once the control in London of much of this trade by a variety of privileged trading companies was beginning to give way in the middle decades of the century to independent *ad hoc* trade partnerships (where specific expeditions were financed by sharing the cost of vessel and crew, as in the Dutch *rederijen*). The west European and Mediterranean trade had been easily the most important for English merchants before the civil war and had flourished because of English non-participation in the Thirty Years War, but after the Restoration the American colonial sector expanded rapidly as the colonies themselves grew and as the potential for re-export trade in Europe was realised. English involvement in the slave trade, too, was consolidated in the 1670s. The eastern trade also showed greater promise: the East India Company (founded in 1600 but not particularly successful in the first half of the century) was, by 1700, importing goods worth £1.5 million on the London market.[10]

The full potential of the English economy took much longer to realise, but by the turn of the century there was no doubt that the north-west harboured more than one expanding commercial power. The peace of 1648 with Spain enabled the Dutch to consolidate their Atlantic and Mediterranean presence, and cross-channel rivalry became intense during the middle decades of the century. Although this was smoothed over as a result of French aggression and the succession of William of Orange and Mary to the English throne in 1689, the Dutch were in the long run less well-placed than the English for long-term commercial expansion. Dutch economic growth was levelling off before the end of the century, its domestic sector less buoyant after the 1670s (as shown in declining investment returns in land-drainage schemes, for example). Similarly, its role in the Baltic trade was decreasing relative to that of other states. But we should be careful not to see this as an absolute 'decline', which it was not. Rather like the Venetian Republic, the Dutch were adapting to a rapidly changing political and economic environment. Amsterdam remained the financial centre of the European economy for decades, even if it lost the enormous domestic growth potential and natural resources which London and the by now thriving provincial English towns could tap. In the long run the United Provinces also had difficulties matching the political, military and naval strength required to exploit the dynastic and expansionist rivalries which became the sport of eighteenth-century rulers. But Dutch prosperity remained legendary throughout the period covered here, and well into the Enlightenment.

The frontier in the east

Muscovy was until the end of the seventeenth century largely an unknown quantity in western European eyes, isolated as it was by geography, climate, culture and socio-political structure – to such an extent that contacts were still characterised more by adventure and surprise than by predictability. Although an important trade route had been established by the English via the White Sea (Archangel was founded in 1584 and rapidly became the most important port of access of Russia), weather conditions there ensured that efforts would still be concentrated in the Baltic. Sweden realised early on how significant this trade could be: its seizure of crucial areas on the eastern coast of the Baltic and its conflicts with Poland in the later sixteenth and early seventeenth centuries were at least in part motivated by such factors. Starting in Estonia (the port of Reval was taken in 1561), Sweden gradually over the next century acquired a band of Baltic provinces from Kexholm in Karelia in the north to Riga further south. Given the growing weakness of Poland (and the Swedish acquisition of parts of Pomerania, Wismar and Stralsund following Gustav Adolf's intervention in the Thirty Years War), Sweden secured dominance in the Baltic and control of the Russian trade there until Charles XII was defeated by Peter I in the Northern War after 1700. The consequent lack of direct access to warm-water maritime trade limited urban development in Russia: Moscow, Novgorod, Pskov, Kiev and a number of smaller towns relied on artisan trades and the market for basic commodities and raw materials for their material survival, and much of their development was a product of administrative and military functions rather than purely economic development.

The main exports to the west via Archangel and the Baltic included furs, leather, grain, flax, hemp and other natural products such as isinglass (a type of gelatine) and caviar, but Europeans also became interested in Russian trade routes south to Persia and elsewhere (especially through the port of Astrakhan on the Caspian Sea), which became the exclusive preserve of Russian traders thanks to tsarist monopoly regulation. Ironworking, tanning, salt production and other activities developed during the early modern period, but did not have any real flexibility to respond to domestic or foreign demand, neither did they provide a sufficient economic basis for the growing military and diplomatic ambitions of the government. That was why Russian tsars were recurrently interested in importing 'high technology' from the west and thereby developing the more sophisticated large-scale manufactures which the local economy was not yet mature enough to create by itself.

Recruitment of western skilled craftsmen, engineers, doctors, scholars and teachers had been attempted in the fifteenth century but faced obstacles, especially in the form of attempts by Polish–Lithuanian authorities (later also by the Swedes and Germans) to hinder the military growth of their eastern neighbour. The success of late sixteenth-century English traders, followed by the Dutch and French, led to formal protests to their respective governments on this account, but the growth potential was so great (and so clearly realised by Muscovite rulers from Ivan IV onwards) that the 'westernisation' of the Russian economy could not be blocked. In any case, the dependency was mutual in that the Dutch and the English soon came to rely on rope and other naval products from Russian manufactories established by western experts. The Time of Troubles in the first decade of the seventeenth century interrupted this growth but it was revived immediately by the new Romanov dynasty, especially thanks to a Dutch approach in 1618 and subsequent sales of military equipment to the Tsar by Netherlanders such as Elias Trip and Paul de Willem in the next decade. English investment declined over the years leading up to 1649 when Tsar Alexis used the execution of Charles I as an excuse for the revocation of the duty exemptions which the English Muscovy Company had obtained in the 1550s. As a result, the development of larger manufactories in Russia in the second half of the seventeenth century was dominated by Dutchmen, Walloons, Swedes and Germans, many of whom settled fairly permanently in Moscow's foreign quarter. Fuhrmann has shown that entrepreneurs such as Andries Vinius, Thielemann Akema and Peter Marselis (brother of Celio and Gabriel Marselis, already noted for their involvement in Denmark) took leading roles in mining, iron-smelting (notably at Tula), arms and gunpowder production, using imported foreign skilled craftsmen and local Russian adscript labour but gradually also training some native apprentices in order to secure a stable and permanent workforce. The extent of this training is uncertain, since western entrepreneurs and their foreign skilled workers were evidently anxious to remain indispensable, but it did occur to some extent, eventually allowing Russian landowners such as Boris Morozov (a friend and for some years a partner of Vinius) to develop independent iron manufactories. Foreign involvement in the foundries, in glass-making or in the paper and textile industries in fact never became entirely secure: entrepreneurs naturally sought maximum profit and control, but political complications and the desire of the Muscovite government to secure a say in the industries generated tensions which could make the career of men like Peter Marselis very uneven. Marselis suffered a temporary setback in 1662 when found guilty of complicity in a major minting fraud, and his property was confiscated, but thanks to his wide diplomatic and family contacts he secured a comeback in 1667, albeit on more closely circumscribed terms. Entrepreneurs had to contend with considerable bureaucratic control over development, production and especially export, and political influence at court remained indispensable to secure stable profits. Initial concessions on tax and duties were granted for limited periods to new enterprises but, like state loans, could lead to very complex financial tangles after the initial tsarist enthusiasm and goodwill had worn off or been eroded by foreign exploitation. This problem was not effectively sorted out with the Commercial Code of 1667, which imposed restrictions and extra dues on foreign activity. Additional tensions emerged locally, often consisting of hostility both towards the harsh conditions at the enterprises and towards the intruders who operated them in the midst of backward peasant societies. This could lead to protracted riots, as at the Olonets ironworks during 1684–94.[11]

There are major gaps in our knowledge of the seventeenth-century Russian economy, but certain features seem to stand out. Russia by no means lacked native trade or even basic industries, yet its capital–earning potential, especially in foreign trade, was limited, there was little urban demand, and any enterprise showing economic promise was, in any case, liable to come under direct and often deliberately imposed autocratic state control. Imports and exports, particularly in luxury goods, were closely supervised, and the Tsar had no compunction about exercising monopoly rights whenever the gain could be significant. In these circumstances it was perhaps natural that the state, recognising that the native economy was not yet ready for substantial development by itself, should impose an accelerated (imported) development in accordance with its political purposes, however unclearly these may at times have been formulated. But there were a number of consequences. First, native traders and craftsmen were at a disadvantage unless they could secure association with state interests, and this may be one of the reasons why Russian towns failed to develop any corporate autonomy, distinctiveness or economic initiative, unlike their western counterparts. Secondly, since Dutch, English, Scottish, German and Scandinavian adventurers undoubtedly went with a wide variety of motives and inclinations, they brought to Russia new approaches and outlooks not only in industrial management but also in a wide variety of fields from military strategy, shipbuilding and architecture to books and entertainment. 'Westernisation' was thus well under way for at least a century before the accession of Peter I, and with it came tensions. On the one hand, the programme of forced development produced a deepening social divide – aggravated both by the inaccessibility of the new goods to the less privileged in Russian society and, more especially, by the increasing tendency to secure unskilled labour not on the open market but by means of adscription or other forms of compulsion (institutionalised in the early eighteenth century when serfdom was extended fully to industrial enterprises). On the other hand, 'westernisation' also produced an ambivalent attitude towards the foreigners themselves, including reactions of deep hostility which remained characteristic of some elements in Russia well beyond our period. Whilst wanting technological experience from the west, the Russian government and church authorities constantly struggled to limit the impact of western cultural values on Russian society, except perhaps for a period during Alexis's reign when a cultural relaxation occurred. Specified residential quarters were prescribed for foreigners in certain towns, and Moscow's own foreign quarter was reorganised in 1652. But cross-fertilisation could not be prevented. Some foreigners (such as Akema) converted to orthodoxy and became naturalised, and some Russian nobles adopted western habits, starting with Morozov himself, who as tutor had greatly influenced Alexis, and continuing with members of the high aristocracy such as Prince Golitsyn. The process, however, was very selective and merely aggravated the social divide in Russia between the privileged elite and the vast majority, a divide which was clearly distasteful to eighteenth-century observers such as Diderot.

Western involvement in Russia thus produced a kind of economic growth which was far more politically sensitive than anything seen in the west or even in Scandinavia, and which had significantly different results in terms of social and cultural development. The process may not have been as immediately traumatic in Muscovy as Dutch and Swedish interference was in Poland, but the long-term consequences were at least as significant. And while Poland had long-standing links to northern Germany and Sweden, the gradual transition in the east from an apparently wild and strange Muscovite principality into the major Russian military power of Peter the Great came as a surprise to many westerners. In terms of social and economic structures, in particular, the graft joins and new growth remained clearly distinctive for rather longer in Russia than elsewhere.

The pre-industrial economy

The timescale of most of what has been discussed in this chapter was extremely long by the standards of seventeenth-century lifespans. What we now regard as the 'pre-industrial system' had little potential for visible change. It was based on an invariably labour-intensive agrarian sector with minimal marketable surplus, on small-scale enterprise relying heavily on skilled artisan labour, and on rudimentary (and mostly traditional) industrial machinery built primarily of wood and powered by wind, water, animals or human effort. To contemporaries, the unpredictably cyclical fluctuations of harvests, disease, violent disruption and underemployment were so much more in evidence, so intrusively emphatic, that everyday assumptions about long-term material unchangeability are understandable. Indeed, one might argue that the changes we have noted were quantitative rather than qualitative and that even Amsterdam, for all its capitalist and commercial success, was merely a sophisticated but terminal overgrowth of the pre-industrial system, unable after the late seventeenth century to free itself further from the restraints inherent in that system. One might look to the English economy for more truly proto-industrial ingredients, but whether there was much irrefutable indication of such, even by the last decade of our period, has been questioned in recent years.

Nevertheless, it will be apparent that 'pre-industrial' does not mean totally static. Those parts of Europe accessible to water-borne trade, in particular, were taking increasing advantage of greater capital fluidity and of the opportunities of international markets – in spite of (or perhaps because of the challenge of) long-term price stagnation in many basic commodities, at least from mid-century onwards. Business partnerships outside family circles were becoming common, although still mostly on a temporary basis. Yet the more permanent chartered joint-stock companies themselves achieved unprecedented development in size: by the end of the century the Dutch United East India Company directly employed some 12,000 men over astounding distances.

Less immediately impressive, but of considerable social significance, was the growth in the putting-out network (*Verlagssystem* or domestic system), where a merchant, operating over a fairly substantial local district as a kind of peripatetic manager or *Verleger*, provided materials for village industries, marketed the finished products and secured his own profits by tapping a seasonally underemployed labour force outside guild control. Such arrangements had been used for centuries all over Europe, especially in the textile industries; but rural networks developed on an unprecedented scale as guild structures weakened and as long-distance maritime trade expanded the opportunities in international markets in the seventeenth century. The putting-out system may also have been particularly well suited as an alternative for those poorer groups in the rural population who could no longer (perhaps because of rising tax burdens) support themselves solely from agriculture. Some urban industries, such as the Haarlem linen industry, consequently came to face very severe competition from the surrounding countryside, and this challenge could only be overcome by specialisation in more sophisticated products or by technical development. Such further development happened in the

Leiden textile industries, assisted by the ready availability of relatively cheap labour resources. Towns such as Nördlingen even underwent internal economic reorganisation in the direction of a putting-out system in order to compete with the cheap production in the hinterland (p. 185). We do not quite have the quantitative evidence to be able to estimate the scale of these changes, but there is no doubt that in some areas the shift over a few generations could involve quite significant proportions of the total population.

The impact on the groups who were directly involved with the putting-out system was even greater. First, opportunities to take part in domestic industry generated enough alternative rural employment (insecure and unpredictable though it was for the workforce) to encourage a gradual split in rural social stratification: those retaining their primary interest in traditional agriculture continued to adhere to more traditional household strategies, whilst those who specialised in market production could make do with less agricultural land under their own control (even if they doubled as farm labourers in the harvest season). A 'rural proletariat' with distinctive lifestyles and different demographic patterns became discernible during the seventeenth century, for example around Zurich, where the textile industry allowed couples to break away from a closed and static agrarian framework, marry younger and gradually form separate communities of their own. This trend may have eased economic strains temporarily but could also lead to an inescapable dependency on the *Verleger*. Evidence of such developments can be found in many parts of Europe, including Flanders and parts of the Netherlands, Norfolk and Electoral Saxony. The putting-out system could thus be conducive to a break with the relatively static pre-industrial patterns of rural social structure, and greatly increased the size of the cottager population surviving on a tenuous economic base.[12]

Secondly, from the point of view of the merchant too, the system had significant repercussions. Reliance on rural labour was in one sense easy and profitable, allowing the merchant to cut back quickly or adapt easily to changing demand. But it did involve considerable capital tied up in raw materials and products for longer periods than might otherwise be necessary. Even if the cottagers themselves had to provide the tools (including the loom, hand-tools for nail-making or whatever), this drawback, combined with the fact that the merchants could not impose productivity rates, fraud control or even much of a check on quality of workmanship, might in the long run lead to attempts to centralise rural industry or even set up actual manufactories outside urban confines. Such a development is discernible in our period only for the mining and metallurgical industries, and to some extent in glass-making; it does seem to indicate that the putting-out system was genuinely proto-industrial.

The Ottoman economy

It is apparent even from the still quite limited amount of research done so far on the subject[13] that the Ottoman economy was based on assumptions which were different from those in the rest of Europe. Basic to the Ottoman outlook was a belief in the static immutability of the social order, a belief confirmed by the Muslim faith itself. Economic management was therefore also seen in relatively static terms, based on the expectation of constant rather than dynamic relationships – assumptions only gradually undermined as a result of economic recession both at the beginning and the end of the century, and as a result of growing encroachment by western maritime powers in the eastern Mediterranean itself. American-induced silver inflation, western trade infiltration and the decline in importance of the eastern Mediterranean trade routes met with only limited responses. As elsewhere in Europe, measures such as belated and counter-productive currency manipulations (for example, the issue of new silver coinage in the 1620s and 1680s), import and export restrictions (for instance, against grain exports from 1604) and attempted price regulations merely encouraged smuggling and contraband whilst inhibiting capital accumulation and entrepreneurial investment. Growing military needs also failed to produce the kinds of structural changes needed, for example, in the landholding system on which army supplies depended (see p. 175). The Ottoman government had understandably become so accustomed to military success against the Europeans that when, after mid-century, the technological and organisational edge of the European states began to be felt, the response was limited. As with the rest of its educational system, Ottoman traditions of military training were slow even to recognise the need for adaptation, let alone implement actual change. Equally, the challenges of war did not seem either to stimulate the economy or to lead to any substantive fiscal and political reforms of the kind crucial to the western European powers in this period.

That said, it would be misleading to see the Ottoman economy of the seventeenth century as heading towards irreversible decline. As in many other parts of the Mediterranean, the problems were relative and the competition new and unexpected. The regulations determining the activities of foreign merchants trading through, for example, Izmir were interpreted loosely, with enough flexibility to allow mutual benefit. It is also clear that local crafts, manufacturing and trade, both amongst Muslims and permanently settled non-Muslims, remained strong in spite of restrictions on profit margins and the official regulation of prices. The guild structures which prevailed all over the Ottoman Empire were predictably traditionalist (as they were in the west) but the division of some city guilds into Muslim and non-Muslim branches in the later part of the century need not be seen as a negative response in economic terms, even if it may have weakened the principle of co-existence and religious toleration. Increasingly, however, guilds in some parts of the Ottoman Empire became subject to stronger administrative (even military) controls, a process no doubt driven by the needs of the state but liable to have a damaging effect on merchant interests. Although the wealthier large-scale merchants escaped close regulation, and were even in a position to organise a kind of putting-out system, we lack detailed under-standing of just how far the economy could adapt to the wider regional and long-distance needs.

As in western Europe, small traders and pedlars were essentially unregulated, as was domestic service and other low-level economic activity. Contemporary travellers often commented on the ease with which good relationships could be established and services obtained. We lack detailed information on many aspects of the economic infra-structure, including food production and demographic change, private finance (as opposed to the well-documented state financial structures), internal trade patterns and aspects of manufacturing, but there are strong indications that, despite some problems during the seventeenth century, there was enough vitality to produce a significant recovery during the eighteenth century. So, on the basis of our present knowledge of the Ottoman economy, there are strengths and weak-nesses of the kind that we would expect in most other regions and, although we lack specific quantitative evidence on a number of key aspects, the Ottoman economy seems not out of line with that of the rest of the Mediterranean. Above all, we should remind ourselves that the Ottoman state was more genuinely multicultural than most west-ern societies, and avoided such damaging short-sightedness as the persecution of religious minorities implemented, for example, by the French state against its economically productive Huguenot commu-nity in 1685.

Perhaps historians tend to overemphasise change at the expense of continuity; in a discussion of European economic enterprise this may be a particular danger. Nevertheless, it is tempting to see seventeenth-century Europe in terms of a patchwork of differently governed regions with economic strengths and weaknesses of their own coming into increasing (and in some respects profitable) contact through trade, migration and outright competition. The economic relation-ships between the long-established northern Italian towns, the more recently developing north-western communities, the relatively depen-dent Scandinavian kingdoms, the relatively backward Baltic provinces and the exotically different Ottoman south-east reveal in this perspec-tive the characteristic tensions between older, established economic centres and traditions on the one hand and newer perhaps more dynamic centres of economic enterprise on the other. As this and the previous chapter have made clear, many parts of Europe experienced very serious economic difficulties during the seventeenth century, in the face of which most governments were powerless. But it is also worth observing that these economic difficulties were liable to exacerbate social inequalities – most clearly observable in the domestic putting-out system but also visible (as we shall see later) in the sometimes frighteningly high levels of underemployment or unemployment and in the precariousness and squalor of life endured by the large majority who were irretrievably stuck at the lower end of society. Looking at the century as a whole, there were no grounds for real optimism: the economic crisis of the 1690s merely confirmed an apparently cyclical pattern of distress which had returned, seemingly unrelentingly, to plague both towns and countryside at fairly regular intervals over the century.

5 The structure of society: nobility, office-holders and the rich

Seventeenth-century society was seen by contemporaries as essentially static and hierarchic, endowed with a natural order which most of the writers of the time found both necessary and generally acceptable. This is not to say that there were no protests of a deeper kind, for although many revolts and riots were sparked primarily by immediate (often material) factors such as dearth or increases in taxation, a number were genuinely revolutionary in terms of underlying motives. We do not need to look very far to find strikingly subversive dimensions in some of the larger French peasant revolts, let alone the radical popular movements in civil-war England. But on the whole the structure of society was assumed to be unchanging except in detail. Contemporary writers, being themselves members of the elite, liked to divide it into ranks or orders according to status, wealth, influence and (in particular) the social estimation and dignity attached by society to each group. Although there were, of course, interesting differences of approach between individual writers, there was also a great deal of common ground. Amongst the frequently cited authorities, Charles Loyseau's *Traité des ordres et simples dignités*, published in 1613 when its author was nearly 50 years old, is typical of much of this kind of literature.[1] Loyseau assumes a divinely ordained 'great chain of being' throughout nature, with human society above the rest of the material world but itself clearly divided into regulated orders which, although not immutable because of man's free will, nevertheless form an indispensable framework for civilised life. At the most general level there were traditionally said to be three formal orders or Estates: a comparatively well-educated first Estate of church functionaries and members of the holy orders; a second Estate of families with hereditary noble status, claiming precedence on the grounds of military distinction and *virtu*; and a third Estate comprising all the rest. Only in Sweden was the peasantry formally and constitutionally recognised as a fourth Estate, distinct from seigneur or burgher. Each of these orders could be subdivided into ranks and degrees: Loyseau divided the nobility, for example, into princes of the blood, more distant relatives of the King, the high nobility (including dukes, marquises, counts, barons and châtelains) and the simple gentlemen by birth whose principal traditional function was military. In a similar vein, the third Estate was headed by the highest officers of state who were not noble by birth (even though their office might carry a noble title); they were followed by the professions, the financiers, merchants and traders, and, further down the scale, craftsmen, *laboureurs* (wealthier peasant tenants), manual workers and others entitled to live off trade and production. Each group had its distinctive dress, titles and corporate privileges, but the lower end of the spectrum was indistinct.

Loyseau, himself a lawyer whose family came from a relatively humble background as recently as in his father's generation, reflects a growing ambiguity in seventeenth-century French society by suggesting that those serving the King as office-holders were in fact the first order, politically as opposed to socially: they were extensions of the King's arm, entitled to precedence in terms of power. This question of precedence – differentiating status by birth from status acquired through office (service) or even personal ability – was a key issue in France for the rest of the century; indeed it had become so already in the later sixteenth century as a result not only of increasing social fluidity but also of a rapid growth in the sale of offices. The same issue emerged in other European countries to some extent at least, but did not until later become sufficiently controversial to encourage as detailed a discussion as it did in France. Even there, conservatism remained strong, represented at the end of Louis XIV's reign by Saint-Simon who, as a typical exponent of the old nobility, railed (in vain, of course) against the growth of a class of professional bureaucrats with more long-term power than even the princes of the blood. In Spain and in the German lands conservative opinion on the whole prevailed, although the picaresque novel could make fun of traditional noble values gone wrong. In the Scandinavian kingdoms the strengthening of royal government produced practical challenges to traditional social values, but again the issues were not always clearly voiced except in times of confrontation, and real change was at most times slow. Even in England, where shifts in the traditional social structure during the seventeenth century probably exceeded anything seen on the continent, writers were slow to reflect it. At the beginning of the seventeenth century, writers such as Thomas Wilson saw English society in terms of nobles, burgesses, yeomen, artisans and rural labourers, but although, for example, the literature of the period contains much evidence of social mobility, at the end of the century someone of Gregory King's conservative bent could still minimise the striking growth in urban upper-level incomes amongst the professional groups and could bypass opportunities for analysing functional subtleties in the middle and lower levels of society as well. With similar brevity, Robert Molesworth, William III's special envoy to the Danish court in

1689, wrote in his entertaining if less than impartial *Account of Denmark as it was in the Year 1692* (London, 1694):

> in [the] disposal of offices [in Denmark] it is remarkable, that such as are of ordinary Birth and Fortunes, are much sooner preferred than those of contrary qualities: so that there may be found several in the most profitable and honourable Employments who have formerly been Serving men, and such like; and these prove the best Executors of the Will and Pleasure of Arbitrary Power, and therefore are caressed accordingly.

He added that such men were also more readily disposed of as scapegoats when convenient, but beyond that he too offered little further comment on this phenomenon and its social significance.[2]

Seventeenth-century society was clearly still bound by a legacy of ritualised relationships originating in feudal times, but the practical realities were changing more than contemporary observers expected. Wealth generated by the kinds of economic enterprise discussed in the previous chapter became increasingly potent as a solvent of traditional social structures everywhere in Europe. At the same time, the major conflicts of the early half of the period played into the hands of monarchs with overextended military ambitions, and militarisation in turn led to far greater demands for administrative co-ordination as well as fiscal extension. Government centralisation made new demands on the administrative staff and also at a deeper level encouraged functional shifts from which non-nobles and newcomers could benefit, especially if they had the skills required in the critical sectors of public administration, had good social contacts and influence and had enough surplus wealth to sustain their social aspirations. In the west, the shift towards wealth as the clearest practical determinant of social mobility and status was arguably more dramatic during the seventeenth century than in the sixteenth or eighteenth, largely because of the effects of social disturbance and the rapid growth in bureaucratic government. But it needs to be emphasised that the weakening of birth and lineage as determinants of status, and the upward mobility of commoners, did not result in any overall levelling throughout society. In fact, the contrary is true for the seventeenth century: different (or in some respects more pronounced) social divides appeared between rich and poor, between archbishop and the impoverished provincial vicar or between the greatest ennobled officials of commoner ancestry and the unskilled urban day-labourer. The acquisition of wealth by an individual or family was rarely a signal of the slackening of social barriers: on the contrary, the influx of new wealth (suitably presented) was necessary for the preservation of existing social differentiations. Society, at least in the more prosperous parts of western Europe, became more complicated and less stereotyped, and traditional social relationships were overtaken by new, equally potent but subtly different distinctions of power and influence. We are still, in this period, nowhere near a society that can be described in 'class' terms, yet the old framework of three or four 'Orders' or 'Estates' no longer fitted perfectly either.

Tradition and noble status

In most of Europe, and more particularly in the west, the nobility was already in fact anything but a clearly definable and distinct group. Most privileges could be bought or acquired by adoption or usurpation, and in the west, with its growing economic diversification, hereditary privileges were blurred by material factors which could leave the income of provincial nobles far behind that of merchants and office-holders. Titles of address, coats of arms, ostentatious dress, lifestyle, hunting rights and other outward signs became an unreliable guide to true status in France, Spain, England and the German lands, since there was no simple way of checking the validity of fraudulent claims made to secure 'respect' from social inferiors. Sumptuary legislation was commonplace throughout Europe (including England) but was never enforceable and was frequently more of a challenge than a restraint. Certain honorific privileges, including the right to carry a sword and the entitlement to trial by peers (with distinctive punishments), were perhaps not so readily usurped by commoners, for they symbolised position in more precise military or judicial hierarchies which were already at the higher levels the preserve of nobles of one kind or another. The same had applied to those honorific court positions where proven or accepted noble lineage might be a prerequisite, but the standards varied from one court or ruling system to another (particularly in the politically divided German and Italian lands) and were by the early seventeenth century highly susceptible to devaluation through court favouritism and the more or less disguised forms of venality of offices or sale of honours which became endemic at the imperial court in Vienna, at the French and the papal courts and in the entourage of Philip III and of James VI/I (especially after 1603). This development, in particular, established an even closer assimilation of the hierarchy of material wealth and that of political influence. More exclusive were the higher ecclesiastical offices, at least in the Catholic countries where the Church was well-endowed. There, proven lineage was often a necessary qualification for the highest ranks, but even so in a country such as France (where the Concordat of 1516 had given the King control over nominations to church vacancies) and in the Austrian Habsburg lands (where church, nobility and state worked in closer partnership) ecclesiastical appointments were political and subject to careful patronage. All in all, appearance, titular status or formal office were no longer a sufficient or reliable guide to hereditary status, at least not in those parts of western and central Europe where social structure was becoming more diversified.

It follows that estimates of the numerical size of the nobility in Europe can only be very approximate. Gregory King's table would suggest that in England the privileged aristocracy (the peerage) together with the gentry (baronets, knights, esquires and mere gentlemen) constituted just under 3 per cent of the total population, and local studies suggest a figure around 2 per cent. Estimates for France are slightly lower, between 1 and 2 per cent, depending on the area, but are rather higher for parts of Spain, perhaps well above 5 per cent because of widespread usurpation. Polish estimates are higher still, perhaps around 8 per cent for the seventeenth century. Estimates (or guesses) for other parts of Europe are in a similar range, but should not be considered as anything other than the crudest of guidelines.

The most fundamental historic prerequisite for acceptance as a nobleman was paternal lineage. Descent from noble ancestry through, say, three or more generations (or perhaps even since time immemorial) was seen as a guarantee of noble 'virtue' or purity of blood. In Spain, where such concerns became mixed up with the desire for protection against suspicions of heretical Jewish or Muslim blood in the family, a veritable legal–genealogical industry was created to furnish documentary 'proof' of ancestral purity for those desiring entry into the public service or the Church, or seeking admission to one of the exclusive *Colegios Mayores* which by the seventeenth century were the formal stepping-stone to office or benefice. Proof of lineage or other documentary evidence of nobility might also be necessary in most of Europe in order to avoid the quartering of royal troops, or to avoid certain specific obligations like the *corvée* in France, and certain types of personal taxation from which the nobility had traditionally been exempted, such as the *servicio* in Spain or the *taille personnelle* in France. But the most important of these entitlements, tax exemption, was itself no real indicator of status since at least in the west it could be bought by commoners. In any case, the seventeenth century saw recurrent government encroachment on tax exemptions in most of Europe, affecting even those of recognised noble status, so that it is not possible without qualification to talk of tax exemption as being a privilege of the nobility. In short, lineage and attendant privileges, if important in some respects, were open like all status symbols to usurpation and false claims, especially during the periods of civil unrest and of weakened central government which naturally gave more scope. Some of these claims might subsequently be challenged: after the Fronde in France in the middle of the century, for example, the Crown authorised inquiries into the validity of noble titles in various parts of the kingdom, resulting in a major *recherche* (inquiry) over the whole kingdom from 1664 to 1665. From a political point of view this was important in that the Crown's agents, the *intendants*, now became the effective judge of nobility, at least in those cases where documentary evidence was tenuous. But although such searches created a great deal of stir (and brought the proceeds of confiscations or of rehabilitation fees and dispensations into the Crown's coffers) the basic concepts of nobility and lineage were not redefined or clarified. The increasingly common practice of royal grants and sales of new titles to wealthy or deserving commoners meant in any case that an ever-dwindling proportion of nobles could genuinely trace their ancestry back for many generations.

Nobility was commonly associated with landownership and the exercise of seigneurial powers, but it must be remembered that the two were legally quite distinct. Needless to say, the nobility was in fact the most important private landowning group, together with the Church, and possession of land was for both of these supposed to be static and durable, a status symbol and a means of support rather than an object of investment or speculation. But in much of Europe commoners, too, could acquire land by purchase or through the default of noble debtors, and they could take over many of the seigneurial privileges attached to landed estates. This was not the case in Castile, where noble landownership was protected by a strict system of entail known as *mayorazgo*, which in the long run not only hampered economic development but also tied Crown and nobility more closely together.[3] In central and eastern Europe, notably in the eastern parts of the Empire and the Austrian Habsburg hereditary lands, in Poland and ultimately in Russia (confirmed *de jure* in the eighteenth century) the nobility was sufficiently dominant, politically, to secure sole legal entitlement to ownership of seigneurial land, alongside the Crown, the Church and certain institutions. Although this did not entirely prevent commoners from possessing agricultural land of a less privileged kind (especially in the vicinity of towns, where ownership might be corporate), in practice their involvement with landed estates was normally as leaseholders or as creditors of noblemen. Further west, however, where the nobility was less powerful by comparison with urban interests (notably in some western parts of the German lands, in parts of France and in Switzerland), commoners could invest more directly in land. Around Paris or Dijon, and in Alsace or in the Beauvaisis, for example, townsmen acquired a major stake in agricultural land, while in the United Provinces and England there was no obstacle to or prejudice against commoner landownership at all. Although simple investment interests might be predominant in these areas, social aspirations were never far below the surface, as illustrated most clearly in the continuing popularity of land purchase in the United Provinces in the last decades of the seventeenth century and beyond, when financial returns diminished.

In Scandinavia, by contrast, it was direct crown action that reversed the growing exclusiveness of landownership. In Sweden crown estates were granted to favourites with decreasing social discrimination at least from the 1630s, but the process was reversed in the later seventeenth century, especially by Charles XI in the 1680s (see p. 382). The finances of the Danish–Norwegian monarchy were so unsound by 1660 that more drastic expedients had to be adopted. Crown creditors, including a number of Netherlanders and other commoners, were forced to accept repayment in crown land on unfavourable terms. Some objected, including, for example, the Marselis family, who so resented the settlement (and the inconvenience of having funds tied up in doubtful assets in a foreign country) that they tried to surrender their estates in return for at least some of their original claims in cash. Others, such as the merchant's son Henrik Müller, who had risen through large-scale private enterprise and state service to become a leading figure in the Exchequer by the 1660s, made the most of his acquired status and influence, and earned a reputation as a hard seigneur.[4] The scope for commoners to rise into the upper ranks of society was still not very great, but Denmark experienced substantial shifts in landowning patterns and social structure which the newly-established absolute monarchy reinforced (see p. 171).

In France and the Iberian peninsula noble status traditionally required avoidance of involvement in retail trade and production (or indeed in any kind of work, according to some). Manual ('mechanical') work and ordinary profit-making, in particular, were supposed in accordance with Roman Law to be degrading and contrary to noble *virtu*, and could ultimately result in derogation, that is, loss of noble status. The French monarchy, from the time of Henry IV through Marillac's Code Michau of 1629 to Colbert's commercial policies and legislation of the 1660s, had hoped to limit derogation and to make at least large-scale business compatible with noble status, but the antiquated sense of honour and social conservatism amongst provincial nobles was not readily overcome, not even when promises of royal rehabilitation grants were made, in accordance with existing legal practices, for those established noble families who might suffer actual derogation. The Council of Trade called in 1700 clearly recognised that attitudes in this respect were not changing much. In practice, the greater nobility and those families with financier and merchant connections continued to take part in business, if necessary through agents, but it seems that the lesser provincial nobles, who most needed additional income, remained hesitant even about the traditionally accepted activities such as glass-making, mining and ironfounding. No doubt they feared derogation because it entailed loss of *taille* exemption (and tax-collectors did initiate derogation procedures), but they may also have been concerned to preserve what appeared to be one of the remaining defences against commoner infiltration, one of their last proofs of status in the face of a new political elite which included venal office-holders and financiers. A similar attitude (despite regional variations) seems to have survived also amongst the Spanish lesser nobility in the seventeenth century, possibly contributing to the economic backwardness of much of that kingdom. There, too, legislation by the Crown failed to reduce the fear of derogation.

Outside France, Spain, Portugal and parts of Italy the concept of derogation had little or no practical significance. No doubt many types of occupation were deemed menial and therefore degrading, and nobility was reputedly incompatible with 'mean profit' in England, Italy and parts of central Europe. But in practice these prejudices were social conventions rather than legal standards, and there is plenty of evidence to suggest that Scottish, English, German, Venetian and eastern European nobles and landowners often took an entrepreneurial or even managerial role in trade or market production, based on resources on their own estates and the use of cheap labour. Innumerable examples can be cited, ranging from the collieries and lead-mines of Scotland to the fish-farms of Bohemia, or from the cattle-export trade of Danish landowners to iron-smelting in Silesia and to property development around London, all with substantial (if not exclusive) noble involvement. Many historians have seen the nobility of the early modern period in the role of risk-taking large-scale investors who could provide the economic stimulus for which others might not have sufficient resources. This was probably the case in some of the less urbanised parts of Europe and, even if such adventurousness does not necessarily indicate great economic foresight, there can be no doubt that direct profit was a primary objective. Nobles serving as crown officials and administrators also had immediate opportunities of becoming involved in (and interested parties to) entrepreneurial and mercantilist schemes launched in the name of the state. The Sinzendorf family in Austria, for example, did just that, while one of them, Georg Ludvig, could indulge in large-scale embezzlement and fraud in his capacity as treasury president in 1656–80. Alternatively, nobles could concentrate on the kind of military entrepreneurship which had existed for a long time and which could yield enormous profits in the hands of men such as Wallenstein. In areas lacking a strong centralising authority providing state sponsorship the nobility still did not hesitate to make the most of the economic potential within their reach: some of the trading and industrial initiative of those in Holstein such as the Rantzau family survived into the seventeenth century, and even affected urban life in those ports (such as Kiel) which failed explicitly to exclude nobles. In the Baltic, too, noble encroachment damaged the economic life of the great ports such as

Danzig: as in Hungary and Russia, there were in effect no restrictions on noble participation in business and there was no government strong enough to pass legislation to protect urban crafts and occupations.

Whatever the economic viability and social consequences of this diversity of noble entrepreneurial effort in most of Europe, it is clear that derogation was a problem only in a few states and that nowhere was it as effective as some theorists and some impoverished French provincial nobles liked to think. In practice, nobles could and did take an active part in most forms of business, wholesale trade and industrial production, not to mention overseas colonial development, even if discretion, conservatism or possibly growing snobbery might dictate the use of agents and managers. In this respect, as in others, practical reality was considerably more complex and fluent than simple literary and social convention would admit.

A 'crisis of the aristocracy'?

The role and identity of the traditional nobility was clearly not static in the later sixteenth century and the seventeenth century, and for a while historians argued whether the shift within the social elite in Europe was on a scale sufficient to merit the term 'crisis'. The debate centred particularly on the old nobility exposed to the challenges of growing absolutism and venal office-holding, including both the upper ranks (the aristocracy in the narrow sense of the term) and the poorer end of the older gentry and provincial nobility (the impoverished *noblesse d'épée* in France known as the *hobereaux*, the *hidalgos* in Spain, and their equivalents in central and northern Europe). Although most historians have now abandoned the 'crisis' framework as too restrictive, it did help raise a number of general propositions useful for comparative purposes. *First,* an erosion of income may have been experienced by noble landowners as a result of inflation in the later sixteenth century, agrarian uncertainty in the early seventeenth century, wartime damage, military costs and state demands for service. This may have been aggravated by rising expenditure caused by greater expectations and more ostentatious lifestyles, visible notably in the continental tours and in extravagant indulgence in the building of country houses. Owing to a failure to adapt to changing economic circumstances or to supervise estate management effectively, this often led to substantial debts. Aristocratic indebtedness was acceptable (or even normal) up to a point, but could lead to the sale of lands. *Secondly,* the local network of loyalty and patronage which had been the real basis of power for the nobility in the sixteenth century was increasingly the object of crown interference: attempts to eliminate private armies of retainers and clients, to reduce feuding and to establish crown control over jurisdiction and administration in the provinces inevitably produced open confrontation between noble factional interests and the centralising government. By the early seventeenth century this confrontation had taken on many different forms: from the 'court versus country' opposition in Stuart England to the anxiety over provincial *fueros* (privileges) in the Spanish peripheral kingdoms, or from the resentment against tax officials and *intendants* in France to the rebellion of the Bohemian seigneurs which sparked the Thirty Years War in 1618. By this stage the aristocracy (in the sense of upper nobility or peerage) were only part of a wide-ranging confrontation involving lesser nobles and many other social groups, but the long-term political consequences were particularly important for them, in that they were arguably deprived in most of Europe of their status as an uncontrollable political force (notable exceptions being Hungary and Poland). *Thirdly*, and partly as a result, the old nobility experienced a functional crisis in the west, in that their role in government was challenged: they failed (except ultimately in England) to meet the demand for better trained jurists and administrators, and indeed in some regions openly resisted any attempt at adaptation, perhaps in protest against the spread of venal office-holding. They also, in some parts of the west, resisted changes in military organisation and techniques, thereby making themselves increasingly unfit for their most ancient function, that of military leadership: in France, for example, the old feudal levy, the *arrière-ban*, was increasingly often commuted by the Crown in the early seventeenth century, and under Louis XIV the nobility's military role remained doubtful in spite of the revival of noble military orders such as that of St Louis (1693). In western Europe, it was argued, the aristocracy and much of the rest of the conservative old nobility were consequently left with merely an empty role as a court entourage or leisured elite, a role which ultimately became increasingly difficult to justify, especially once the inflation in honours had had its effect.

The debate on the 'crisis of the aristocracy' and on the related problems facing the lesser nobility and gentry was valuable in challenging historians to re-examine a range of evidence from particular areas of Europe in the light of overall trends. We will not explore all of these here, particularly since part of the controversy has centred on the later sixteenth century and is outside the scope of this study. But it is worth emphasising that the debate over the English peerage and gentry, which generated a major confrontation between leading historians in the 1950s and 1960s, highlighted crucial methodological issues. The 'storm over the gentry', in particular, by pitching one senior historian diametrically against another, discredited attempts to prove general points by reference to individual descriptive examples chosen without systematic sampling techniques.[5] Lawrence Stone's major study of the Elizabethan and early Stuart aristocracy, published in 1965, raised the debate to a new plane by introducing a wide range of sociological techniques to supplement a comprehensive statistical treatment of the evidence available on the peerage as a whole. Although some of his conclusions and methods have been challenged, his attempt 'to describe the total environment of an elite, material and economic, ideological and cultural, educational and moral'[6] set aims which changed the way we study historical elites.

That said, the comparative framework does not apply equally well everywhere. In the Empire and in the Habsburg hereditary lands the Thirty Years War was so disruptive of both economic and social developments that Europe-wide comparisons are not very helpful. What evidence we have suggests that economic difficulties did set in before 1618 in the seigneurial economy in, for example, Bohemia, and the war itself cannot be made to sustain the crisis theory in any meaningful way because of the massive changes imposed politically on landowners and tenants alike. In much of central Europe, indeed, old as well as newer nobility ultimately came to be linked with princely authority in an active and mutually stabilising partnership which lasted well beyond our period. In the Habsburg hereditary lands (including Bohemia from the 1620s onwards) this partnership was built on increasingly strict religious conformity, often at the expense of Protestant nobles not only in Bohemia and Austria but also ultimately in the separate kingdom of Hungary during the reconquest in the later seventeenth century. Conversion to Catholicism brought political acceptance into the *Herrenstand* of landowning seigneurs (with a substantial role in government) or into the *Ritterstand* of lesser nobles and nobility of the sword (not entirely inaccessible to commoners through service). In this way durable state backing for noble power and privileges in the Habsburg lands was ensured. In the rest of the Empire the religious factor was much less significant, single noble families in Germany often having members belonging to different Churches. In some areas there was a sufficiently strong urban element to avoid an excessively close alliance between ruler and nobility, but there was no question of any weakening of the nobility. The same could be said of Sweden during the reign of Gustav Adolf, for he and his chancellor, Axel Oxenstierna, fostered a fruitful partnership between Crown and aristocracy which was formalised in the *Riddarhusordning* of 1626, an ordinance which made a royal patent the sole qualification for nobility and specified the hierarchy to be observed in the entire noble estate. The privileged political position of the aristocracy was not challenged until later in the century, and then under circumstances which were unique in Europe (see p. 382). There is no real evidence so far to suggest that the Swedish nobility experienced any major economic setbacks unique to their social position. In regard to southern Europe, too, the economic difficulties may have been exaggerated: the nobility in Piedmont and in many Italian city-states seem to have escaped the economic squeeze quite lightly for the time being.[7] Rents and income from landed estates appear not to have fallen on a long-term basis in much of Europe until the later seventeenth century.

In the more conventional monarchies, however, there are signs of genuine difficulties for the nobility. It is hardly surprising that the Danish nobility, with its highly exclusive status and conservative outlook, or the Castilian nobility, hindered by a restrictive entail system and by the inability of many of them to improve their financial credibility, should suffer serious revenue shortfalls and obtrusive debts during the decades of wartime stress, monetary instability and mounting state demands from the 1620s through the 1650s. Their impoverishment may often have been less than acute by comparison with that of the commoners who bore the real burden of material insecurity in those years, but economic strains aggravated divisions within the nobility in each country between the magnates or politically active nobles on the one hand and the poorer, lesser nobility on the other. In Denmark this division was very marked by the 1640s when the recession in cattle exports had precipitated a growing indebtedness of the lesser to the upper nobility (and even to commoners), a process which the Crown directly exploited in the events of 1660. In Castile the result was different in that those who flocked to the court of Philip III were able to exploit royal generosity, in the form of concessions in the entail system or sinecure offices, to cushion their lifestyle, whilst the rest suffered diminutions of available wealth even when their landed family estate endured. In Castile a 'crisis' never fully matured, since the fall of Olivares in 1643 brought about a sudden relaxation of tension within the court and a renewal of crown favours on a lavish scale, allowing the nobility to maintain their local powers and political influence unaltered. By contrast, in Denmark the coup of 1660 and the consequent elimination of the old aristocratic council from political influence gave the new established absolute monarchy an opportunity to reorganise the bureaucracy and set about creating a formal service nobility (see p. 171). In a sense, therefore, Denmark experienced something akin to all three stages in the 'crisis' pattern outlined above.[8]

The French nobility and the Crown

The French nobility would appear at first sight to fit the general pattern quite well, too. Social tensions and even anti-seigneurial resentments had been prominent in the later sixteenth-century wars of religion, and were only partially dampened after the peace of 1598.

By the early seventeenth century, at least, some noble families experienced economic difficulties and had to rely on royal handouts (as in Spain) to maintain their lifestyle. The early Bourbon years, from 1598 until the 1670s, were marked by seemingly interminable and destabilising factional intrigues involving various aristocratic families. In response to these, Louis XIII's first minister, Richelieu, sought to reduce feuding and weaken rival political networks. Equally essential for the survival of an effective monarchy was the marginalisation of noble military autonomy and, where necessary, actual destruction of noble fortifications – forms of crown consolidation which were bound to be interpreted by opponents as a challenge to local noble autonomy. The magnates claimed to have a natural function as advisers to the King in council, as provincial governors and as generals or admirals, and this too was being thrown into doubt with the rise of new men in royal service. The old nobility lacked judicial training and therefore appeared ambivalent about active government service, especially since the now consolidated system of venality (see the next section) gave the third Estate opportunities for durable social promotion by wealth into the upper administration. Nevertheless, the old nobility did not surrender its notions of honour and independence readily: the continuing and only very gradually effective campaign by the Crown against feuding and duelling was merely one aspect, and far more serious for Louis XIII and Richelieu were the waves of local rebellions and noble conspiracies, especially in the years 1626–32 and from the 1640s onwards (see chapter 7). Louis XIV, exploiting the widespread reaction against the violence of the Fronde, appeared to succeed in restoring a more harmonious and mutually advantageous relationship between Crown and elite at Versailles.

This view of strains and changes within different sections of the French nobility, the gradual pacification of the old 'feudal' nobility (including the magnates, the princes of the blood, the *noblesse de race* and the *noblesse d'épée*) and its partial displacement by the lawyers and bureaucrats of the *noblesse de robe* (those who had acquired noble title through judicial office) has to a considerable extent become the accepted view of this period of French history, at least at the general level. But detailed work has indicated that a single overarching interpretation of this kind may not suffice. The question of economic difficulties experienced by the nobility is (as we have noted in the context of other countries) still very much an open one, and selective impressionistic approaches are no substitute for comprehensive statistical work, especially given the very wide divergence of fortunes between families and regions at this time. In particular, the sixteenth-century inflation cannot be blamed for everything, especially not when many seigneurial dues (in spite of some commutation to money rents in France, as in England) were payable in kind rather than in a fixed cash sum; more likely, poor estate management, in a time of economic insecurity for everyone, may have been the real problem. Much more fundamental, however, are the serious objections raised against treating different groups within the nobility as distinct and identifiable, and of suggesting the displacement of one by another. Many of the crown officials, including a large proportion of the higher executive officers of state, as well as the higher judicial officials in the sovereign courts who were of clear *robe* status, had as respectable a lineage as some of the 'feudal' noble families and cannot be regarded as anything other than part of the *noblesse de race* (nobility with ancestral status). There were, no doubt, differences of lifestyle and mentality between the traditional *épée* squire and the black-gowned *robe* official in and around Paris, but these were professional rather than social differences, of doubtful significance in terms of family interconnections. Recent research has indicated that there was also far too much geographic variation to allow us to make valid generalisations. In the *élection* of Bayeux, for example, there was such widespread intermarriage and assimilation between old and new nobles that *robe–épée* distinctions are meaningless. Office-holding was admittedly more common amongst the recently ennobled families than amongst the old nobility there, but military service was the preferred career of the new nobility, and the two functions were often mixed in one family or even in one person. Moreover, in Bayeux it was the new nobility who were most prone to indebtedness, often with the old nobility as creditors. Similar signs of social blurring have not invariably been found in the few other areas where such detailed work has been done, neither is it possible to foresee whether the later seventeenth century will come to be regarded as a transitional stage in the development towards the socially more heterogeneous elite of the eighteenth century. But it is likely that future studies will reinforce the existing warnings against too simple a sociological categorisation of generalised types of older and newer families in France.[9]

The political trend, on the other hand, has been confirmed by recent work, indicating that the French Crown did, in the course of the seventeenth century, to some extent whittle away the local autonomy and patronage-based power of the old aristocracy, particularly by means of the centrally-appointed *intendants*. This process was interrupted only very briefly during the Fronde, and was resumed from 1652, so that the type of powerless old aristocracy represented by Saint-Simon became more common than the proudly independent tradition represented by someone like Eugene of Savoy, who joined Louis XIV's enemies for the sake of honour. Saint-Simon claimed, with a great deal of spiteful bitterness, that real power was by his time exercised by 'the most utter and abject commonalty'. That this assertion was technically false has long since been demonstrated – many of

Louis XIV's secretaries of state, controllers-general and other high officials were of distinguished robe nobility, their families having risen to nobility over several generations, often through the purchase of ennobling offices or through intermarriage with older noble families – but it is apparent that the 'new' men of the top ranks nonetheless achieved far higher status by virtue of their office than they would have had without it. They also achieved enormous landed and material wealth for themselves, and thanks to the venality system and their access to the King, had as great a chance of dynasty-building as the old aristocracy. In other words, what matters is not the replacement of one type of (ancient) noble in high politics with another (of supposedly newer and less august lineage); rather, it is the development of stronger concepts of service and loyalty. Service to the King became a means of rapid upward social mobility, whilst grandeur in terms of lineage was no guarantee of power. The change was not sudden: most of the institutional framework for elite networks (such as the provincial Estates, or the parlements and other special law-courts) remained intact even during the reign of Louis XIV. But the Crown actively sought the loyalty of the provincial elite by appealing to their self-interest and by integrating them into a socially and politically more stable system. As a result, noble-led rebellion became intrinsically much more difficult, and increasingly rare.

The changes in the elite in France outlined here suggest a pattern of gradual evolution and adaptation which may well have resonances in other parts of Europe. In order accurately to observe change in a social system which was fundamentally conservative and traditionalist, the historian needs a broad perspective – in the case of France, reaching at least from the great disturbances of the later sixteenth century, through the revolts, the Fronde and the post-1660 stabilisation to the abortive attempts by the French peerage to stage a political comeback in 1715 and beyond. In the process, traditional concepts of nobility were gradually eroded by economic forces, sudden conjunctural crises in agriculture for which the traditional landowning nobility were rarely well-prepared, wartime disruption, huge fiscal demands and monarchical consolidation. Being a nobleman in fact meant different things in different parts of Europe. Some form of alienation, of 'court versus country', was at least a factor in England and, in a quite different way, in Spain, but is not readily applicable in Denmark, or really in France. The displacement of lineage by royal service as a means of attaining highest status may apply in France and Denmark, but hardly in England. Above all, one cannot ignore the fact that the peerage and court gentry in England returned with the Restoration, and that a nobility (if not quite the old one) was as entrenched as ever in the later years of *ancien-régime* France, in Spain after 1643, in Denmark once the new absolute monarchy had got under way, and even in Sweden at least by 1719 – not to mention in the rest of Europe, where the nobility was never challenged. Rather than a 'crisis of the aristocracy', we see a less dramatic but highly successful and dynamic process of adaptation by the elite (where necessary) to a changing social and political environment, an adaptation which, in a much longer historical perspective stretching from the late medieval period to 1789, ensured the preservation of their social, political and materially privileged position.

Ennoblement and the sale of offices in the west

One of the crucial factors in the 'taming' of the nobility in much of Europe, apart from the obvious one of the expanding machinery of state, was the increasing sale of titles, honours and offices, not merely as a convenient source of crown revenue but also as a means of tying the material interests of the wealthy groups in society to those of the state and of taxing an otherwise largely exempt or undertaxed elite. The bestowing of favours and honours by a monarch in response to material considerations, rather than according to ideals of distinction, loyalty or service, was, of course, nothing new in the seventeenth century. The very nature of monarchy depended on an inner circle of privileged nobles which could not, in a developing society with high mortality rates, be entirely exclusive, and to which admission would consequently be controlled by the monarch as one of the forms of patronage at his disposal. The secrecy surrounding the sale of higher ennobling offices or titles, and the concoction of a suitable genealogy to support the candidature of someone of non-noble origins whose wealth or services the Crown wanted to use, were discreet methods of making the elite appear to remain exclusive and of preserving the fiction of noble virtue complete with its status value in social and monetary terms. Operated with care, such a strategy was bound to be a success: the short-term interests of the state (at least) coincided with that universal vanity and status-consciousness which guaranteed a nearly unfailing supply of customers. Salaries for offices might be inadequate or nominal, but could always be supplemented with fees, gifts and other forms of gain, which might even make the office a reasonable financial investment. It was only when discretion was thrown to the winds that problems arose, and this was what happened under James VI/I in Scotland and England after 1603, and in France in the 1630s and the middle years of Louis XIV's reign – in both cases because the Crown was desperately short of revenue. An excessive or ill-disguised sale of titles or offices, apart from the public resentment it caused, and the disrepute into which it brought the Crown, was also counterproductive, since it brought devaluation and ultimately a market glut. More serious, perhaps, was the fact that venal offices (except in the papal states) were customarily regarded as private hereditary property, and while at first this might help to create new dynasties of families independent of the traditional clientage system operated by the aristocracy, ultimately the security of the property rights of the purchaser could overshadow the public nature of the function with which he had been entrusted. In theory at least, the sale of offices could thus become an obstacle to change: the Crown might not be able to afford the financial outlay required to recover control of particular groups of venal offices and the power-relations that went with them. Moreover, in some areas functional (judicial) qualifications for office were often considered of secondary importance compared with the wealth and status of the candidate, and as the standards set for admission became perfunctory the dangers of a top-heavy and incompetent bureaucracy increased. These dangers were explicitly recognised early on, but the revenue requirements of the state, combined with the vested interests of existing office-holders, invariably aborted any schemes for reform.

The classic example of this in early modern Europe is France. There the origins of the system of venality can be traced clearly back at least to the fourteenth century, when certain office-holders were allowed to buy the right to resign their office in favour of a person of their own choice. By the early sixteenth century, more direct forms of sale had become common on a large scale, and various expedients had been adopted to increase revenues, notably the splitting of existing offices into two or more parts (with the purchasers holding in rotation), or the creation of *offices imaginaires* and of new institutions rivalling existing ones. Not only did the Crown itself take direct part but it also donated blocks of offices to favourites for them to dispose of for their own gain or influence. The weakness of the monarchy in the later sixteenth century enabled stronger nobles and crown favourites to develop extensive clientage networks by means of the venality system, and by 1598 the requirement that new incumbents swear that they had not paid for their office was ignored. One remaining means of crown control, the rule according to which a resignation was invalid if the holder died within 40 days, had ensured that an unpredictable number of offices reverted to the patronage of the Crown from time to time. But even this rule had been circumvented by means of sales of dispensations allowing *survivance*, whereby the incumbent could nominate his heir in advance and complete the formalities (including paying a transfer tax to the Crown) but retain the office nominally until his death, while the beneficiary would, to a mutually agreed extent, take over the practical functions until he obtained full possession. Henry IV considered prohibiting this *survivance* arrangement in the interest of restoring royal control, but at Sully's suggestion (and against the advice of Chancellor Bellièvre and others) instead allowed the institutionalisation of venality through the *paulette* decree of 1604. This allowed certain types of office-holders, once they had paid an annual *paulette* tax amounting to one-sixtieth of the royal council's valuation of the office, to be exempt from the 40-day rule while retaining customary hereditary possession of the office for their family.

The annual *paulette* was so called after the first person to farm the new tax, Charles Paulet, secretary to the King's Chamber and head of a consortium of financiers who paid nearly one million livres tournois for the farm for its first year. The revenue of the *Bureau des Parties Casuelles* which handled the venality system was thereby very substantially increased on a regular basis, and this explains why the *paulette*, although in theory open to cancellation at any time (and in fact not renewed in the period 1618–21 when due for renegotiation), in effect became a durable part of the *ancien régime* in France. Criticisms of the system were certainly voiced, notably at the Estates General of 1614 and in the Fronde, and both Richelieu and later Colbert seriously considered abolition of the *paulette* and perhaps even of venality of offices. But vested interests were so strong, and the financial needs of the Crown rose so dramatically (especially from the 1630s), that these prohibitively costly plans could not be realised. Instead, the *paulette* was extended to include more and more offices, especially judicial and financial ones, new layers were added to the bureaucracy, and increasingly dubious expedients of extra taxes, confiscations and resale of existing offices became common. The average annual revenues to the Crown from all this exceeded an estimated 20 million livres tournois during the war period in the 1620s and 1630s, but ultimately at the cost of saturating the market and making the public increasingly aware of the 'prolonged confidence trick' (as Robin Briggs describes the system) which was being played on them. Not only did the income from the *paulette* slump by 1639, but by then the obstructive or even directly insurrectional potential of key groups of venal office-holders had become clear. The build-up of riots and provincial revolts in France during these war years, culminating in the civil war (the Fronde) in 1648, are discussed elsewhere (see chapter 7), but the role of the robe nobility of the Parlement of Paris and other venal office-holders in this breakdown emphasised the extent to which venality could exert a stranglehold on the political aspirations of the French Crown at a critical juncture.

In the early years of Louis XIV's personal reign, revenue from the trade in offices was relatively low, thanks to Colbert's attempts to reform the system. But the demands of war from the 1670s onwards induced the Crown to repeat the escalation that had occurred under Richelieu, complete with the usual array of extortionate measures: recurrent 'loans' payable by office-holders, annulment followed by resale of blocks of offices, and even the sale of dispensations from Colbert's new regulations governing minimum age of incumbents and plurality within families. The lesser office-holders, in particular, had little defence against such measures, and even the Parlement of Paris found it more difficult to exert a strong influence after its right of remonstrance had been curtailed in 1673. By the late 1690s, as in the late 1630s, trade in offices had slumped badly, contributing to a period of financial chaos which lasted until the end of the reign.

For the Crown, the trade in offices had clearly become just a financial expedient to be exploited when necessary. For prospective buyers, however, the venality system, except when overdone, created opportunities for upward social mobility which might not otherwise have existed. Direct ennoblement by royal letter did occur, but was a comparatively exclusive privilege until Louis XIV tried to sell blank patents of nobility at 6000 livres each in the 1690s. Straight purchase of a noble title was nothing new, but its suspect status-value ensured that it was normally a last resort. It was more practical to buy, or to get the promise of a resignation of, an ennobling office. The most expensive offices, some of them selling at prices in the range of 100,000 livres or more in the later seventeenth century, were those conferring outright hereditary nobility either immediately or (if held for a minimum of 20 years) for life. By the mid-seventeenth century most of the robe serving in the sovereign courts were in this category. Lesser offices, such as those in the financial courts, were suitable for those content with a more measured social rise over several generations, for such positions conferred only personal nobility, and hereditary status could not be achieved until after several generations of linear succession. The real dividing line in French society may in fact have been at this point, between those in possession of hereditary nobility and those with merely personal status: only hereditary nobles had 'made it' in social terms, whilst the rest were still often regarded as commoners. Further down the scale were the municipal offices which conferred *noblesse de cloche*, but their status was badly damaged by the Crown's abuse of venality, particularly in the later years of Louis XIV.

The gradations imposed for the *capitation* of 1695 (a poll tax designed to include the privileged orders) give some indication of the extent to which these social developments were officially recognised. The first class of taxpayers (assessed at 2000 livres) included princes of the blood, ministers and tax-farmers in general, all interestingly juxtaposed at the same wealth level; the second class (at 1500 livres) included the first member of the robe nobility, namely the President of the Parlement of Paris, in addition to much of the peerage, the great officers and *intendants*; the third class (at 1000 livres) included the high military and robe nobility side by side, whilst the next three classes (down to 300 livres) consisted mostly of high robe officials. Only in the seventh class (at 250 livres) did the ordinary non-robe nobility appear in substantial numbers, and the last *hobereaux* (impoverished old noble families) were placed in the nineteenth class (at a mere 6 livres), only three classes above the bottom rung of day-workers.[10] Obviously a tax scale gives no indication of the extent of social change, and even approximate estimates of numbers have proved highly conjectural because of technical difficulties. Nevertheless, the trend is unmistakable, and is confirmed by eighteenth-century developments: there were opportunities for social mobility at many different levels, and the elite in France was open to parvenu wealth. There were evident political drawbacks to the system of venality, but it clearly also acted as a useful social leavening.

Titles and venality in Castile and England

In Castile similar practices of sales of offices had developed, and probably as early as in France. Owing to the financial needs of Philip II the abuses escalated during the later sixteenth century, rising from municipal and notarial level into the upper reaches of the central administration. By the early seventeenth century Olivares could express good intentions of reform with as little effect as Richelieu's. Yet although the system continued to grow from then onwards, and was firmly engrained in Spanish America as well, its long-term social and political significance was much less than in France. This was partly because ordinary noble (*hidalgo*) status was more common in Spain to begin with, and far more easily usurped because of the lack of legal barriers and the decentralised nature of local government. As a result, although an official career might still be desirable, there was less incentive to buy an office solely for its ennobling characteristics. More important, however, was the fact that higher judicial posts (not officially sellable, although this was now disregarded) did not secure admission to any institution with as significant a role as the parlements and other sovereign courts in France. Venal office-holders in Castile, in other words, lacked the power-base for the kind of independent and potentially oppositional role which their ownership of office might otherwise have enabled them to fulfil. Criticisms of venality by the moribund Cortes (Estates General) of Castile may also have discouraged the monarchy from letting the system become anything other than an abuse like many others. Its most striking result was merely its contribution to the ever more top-heavy and supernumerary officialdom for which later seventeenth-century Spain was a byword.

The direct sale of noble titles was of only marginal significance in Castile, both numerically and in social terms. Fewer than 200 patents were sold during the seventeenth century, most of them during the

1630s, and trade was remarkably sluggish, partly because the Crown was ambivalent about the actual policy, pricing the titles accordingly high, and partly because there was little to be gained from purchase in practical terms in many provinces. *Hidalguía* did not secure exemption from the rapidly escalating *alcabala* or *millones* purchase taxes, and venal titles were considered inferior in terms of status. Most of those who did buy a patent in fact had already laid claim to noble status, and were of the same social groups as existing nobles, so no change in social composition occurred as a result.[11] Clearly venality of offices and titles in Castile did not generate political and social fluidity in the same way as it did in France, and this may help to explain the unadaptable rigidity of late Habsburg Spain.

Sale of both offices and titles occurred in England during the seventeenth century, but it was particularly the latter that caused controversy during the years 1603–27. Reacting against Elizabeth's extreme parsimony over the grant of titles, James VI/I went to the opposite extreme, virtually trebling the number of knighthoods within two years of his succession. James did not sell these titles for direct crown profit, but rather rewarded or paid courtiers by granting them the right of creating knights, and these rights soon found their way on to the open market. A shortage of crown revenue led in 1611 to the establishment of a new order, the baronetcy, available for £1095 to those ostensibly of suitable background fulfilling substantial property qualifications. The order was to be restricted to a total of 200 members (a restriction which Charles I did not respect), but James had already by 1618 lost control over who should be admitted when he began to use this title as a form of payment to courtiers. The resulting open sales, grossly exploited by the King's favourite, George Villiers, Duke of Buckingham, meant that by 1622 the right to create a baronetcy had fallen in value to a mere £220. Even peerages were put on the market from 1615, with a resulting drop in value from the initial £10,000 to about half by 1627, and here too James and his son allowed crown control over the quality of purchasers to become nominal. It was perhaps not so much the number of new admissions that rankled (serious though that seemed to older title-holders facing endless challenges over precedence) as the fact that the indiscreetly corrupt influence of the Howard and Villiers families paid scant regard to the old order. Moreover, the saturation of the market with hereditary titles undoubtedly deprived the monarchy of a useful form of political patronage, and aroused cynicism about the substance of royal authority itself. The assassination of Buckingham in 1628 led to a sudden termination of the sale of titles, but the attempted reforms of the next decade did not have as much effect on the prestige of the monarchy as they might, owing to Charles's inability to put himself across. In 1641 the sale of titles was briefly revived as a desperate financial expedient and as an attempt to gain royalist support, but it soon became a prime target of parliamentary reform plans. The abandonment of a proposal of 1638–9 to institutionalise the sale of titles through an annual payment (like the French *paulette*) meant that existing purchasers did not acquire a vested interest in the survival of the system; on the contrary, resentments and bitterness amongst the gentry families not benefiting from court favour became a destabilising force, especially since no one outside the peerage had any tangible corporate privileges comparable to those of the continental nobility.

If the sale of titles was almost too successful in increasing apparent mobility within the gentry (adding to tensions within a social group which, because of the indeterminate status of younger sons in English gentry families, was already traditionally less clearly separated from trade and the professions than in other countries), the sale of offices on the other hand was less significant than in France. Various reasons have been suggested to explain this difference. It appears that the English Crown never became financially dependent on such revenue and, as with titles, never institutionalised the system. Although the statute of 1552 restricting the sales of crown offices had not been effective, and sales did grow from the 1590s through to a climax around the years 1615–23, Buckingham's fate appears to have made some impression on Charles also in this respect, especially since one of the earlier impeachment charges against Buckingham had been precisely the sale of offices and the concomitant abuses. Consequently the practice was virtually abandoned in the 1630s. In any case, G. E. Aylmer's work indicates that the sales by the Crown, even during the peak period, had no discernible practical effects on the type of incumbents and their qualities, distinct from the kind of results which the extensive reliance on patronage and patrimony in all branches of the administration was having. Since there were so few paid offices in English local administration that any venality there would be insignificant by comparison with, for instance, France, it is natural to conclude that the sale of offices by the Crown was of only marginal significance in terms of English social mobility and was unimportant relative to the sale of titles.

More important was the element of private venality in the central bureaucracy in England, ranging from simple sales to complex reversion arrangements which tied some offices for generations, often in close linkage with patronage and family influence. This gave considerable power to heads of departments and superiors in the administrative hierarchy (who had a decisive and hence lucrative say in those non-heritable offices which were not directly within the Crown's gift, especially middle- and lower-ranking ones), and profits were considered part of the 'pay', alongside the fees and gratuities which made up for defective salaries. These private practices, however, whilst contributing to some redistribution of resources within the political nation, do not appear to have encouraged any major shifts in social structure. Private venality revived after the genuine attempts at reform during the interregnum, but did not lead to the emergence of a distinct bureaucratic 'class'. The political nation of Restoration England was not very different from that of the early seventeenth century.[12]

The sale of offices in western Europe, if carried to excess, could evidently have drawbacks both for the Crown and for the purchaser. Intrinsically, however, there are no grounds for assuming that it led to any lowering of standards. For most offices there were no professional requirements of a type recognisable today (the exception being the law, where some sort of training was necessary for entry into the more exclusive parts of the profession). The combination of patronage, family connection and venality often meant that access to the public services was via private service in the household of someone of influence, and this might give at least some experience and (more important) establish those bonds of obligation and duty which kept the machinery oiled. No doubt there was plenty of scope for abuses, not least in the form of pluralism and absenteeism: many entrants may have been looking primarily for pensions, sinecures or (perhaps especially) status without gain, but it is unlikely that any practicable alternative would have worked any better. It could even be argued that the convention of making profits from fees and other prerequisites of office was, in the circumstances and within limits, not altogether unreasonable, given that the alternative would have been even heavier taxation demands. The danger, of course, was that the Crown might lose control over its own office-holders and that the administration would in part be 'farmed out' to private individuals, creating a situation in some respects analogous to that produced by the practice of tax-farming.

Nobility and government service in central and northern Europe

Venality was not exclusive to western Europe but appears to have been less controversial elsewhere, even in the Austrian Habsburg lands. The major social impact of the Bohemian war and of the beginning of Habsburg centralisation in the period after 1620, combined as it was with religious repression not only in Bohemia but also in Upper and Lower Austria itself, and later in Hungary, reduced the scope for autonomy amongst the elite. Whilst some older magnate families and other provincial nobles tried to continue maintaining the strong territorial particularism represented corporately through the provincial Estates, others withdrew from state service because they refused to accept Catholic conformity for one reason or another, or went into exile from Bohemia or Austria as a result of the developments of the 1620s.[13] At the same time, it is apparent that those who were Catholics, or were willing to adopt that faith, had great scope for advancement through service, as in the case of the Lobkovic, Dietrichstein and Eggenberg families. They could exploit the opportunities of the early seventeenth century to consolidate larger estates, and protect them by means of *Fideikommisse* (entails) similar to the Spanish *mayorazgo*. The developing court nobility (*Hofadel*) was remarkably cosmopolitan in ethnic composition. During the first quarter of the seventeenth century, the Habsburgs encouraged social mobility by employing men of foreign or commoner extraction, and nobility was often acquired (or foreign titles confirmed) through actual service, particularly in the army, as happened to the two generals Piccolomini and Montecuccoli. Perhaps owing to the strains of war, however, the court nobility became increasingly closed and exclusive from the 1620s onwards, making the ennoblement of commoners much rarer. The table of ranks of 1671, issued by Leopold I, shows that a substantial group of ennobled men, with or without landed property, had to be accommodated in the official upper hierarchy, but they were now placed in a category below that of the old nobility of the *Herren-* and *Ritterstand*.

The Habsburgs rewarded and patronised by means of a measured grant of titles of either domestic territorial (Austrian, Bohemian, Hungarian) or imperial type, the latter having immediate status in the Holy Roman Empire (*Reichsunmittelbarkeit*) so that the bearer was a direct subject of the Emperor with a voice in the imperial diet. Venality was an ingredient in some of these patents, and it is clear that the craze for titles and social status was at least as highly developed in central Europe as elsewhere. Imperial noble titles (and a host of privileges, legitimations and other grants) were sold by the Habsburgs either directly or through the imperial chancellery, or via the so-called *Hofpfalzgrafen* (nobles, local dignitaries and minor princes who had acquired – after 1659 perhaps bought – the right to sell letters-patent and coats of arms on behalf of the Emperor). Ennoblement by the chancellery cost between 60 and 100 florins in the mid-seventeenth century, less from one of the *Hofpfalzgrafen*, while a title in the high nobility, starting with a countship, might cost 4000 florins according to the official tariff of 1659. The proceeds were shared by the Emperor and the Arch-chancellor in Mainz.

Venality of offices at the Habsburg court, however, was disguised by means of the expedients of advance loans and donations to the Emperor. All prospective financial office-holders had, reasonably enough, customarily made an obligatory tariffed loan as security before taking up office (this loan was known as an *Amtsdarlehen*), but a growing number of office-holders were expected to provide additional loans as a matter of course. Interest payments of 5–6 per cent were supposed to be made on these during tenure, but in practice neither this nor a refund on completion of service could be counted on. Jean Bérenger concludes that these loans became so closely linked to the taking up of offices, and became so universal at least after 1690, that they were equivalent to state-controlled venality. Admittedly neither hereditary claims nor reversions were institutionalised, but expectations to offices not yet vacant (including ennobling ones) could be formalised by venal means as in the west.[14]

The question of access into the territorial nobility in the Habsburg lands and elsewhere in the Empire has not yet been studied in any detail. Substantial differences of ranking and status existed in the numerous territories of the Empire – Württemberg scarcely had a territorial nobility at all, only imperial nobles, and in much of the south-west many nobles had both imperial status (as *Reichsritter* of a small territory), and territorial status (as lord over estates under another *Landesherr* or prince). But it is clear that in the northern and eastern parts of the empire noble landowners were able to exploit political conditions after 1648 in their own favour, not only in terms of seigneurial power (see chapter 8), but also in terms of securing dominant administrative and judicial roles in those principalities where centralisation was occurring. This development came to fruition only during the eighteenth century, but even in the later seventeenth century clear signs are visible, for example, in the Hohenzollern lands under Elector Frederick William. His compromise settlement of 1653 with a committee of the Brandenburg Estates concerning army taxation was an important step towards the power-alliance between prince and nobility which became a cornerstone in eighteenth-century Brandenburg–Prussia. Historians generally accept that it is doubtful whether there was much genuine social mobility amongst German propertied classes in the later seventeenth century: a simple explanation of this, which may also account for the apparent absence of controversy about venality of offices, may lie in the relative weakness or in some areas near-absence of a competitive non-noble challenge from below. The elite in Germany was sufficiently buttressed by tradition, intellectual attitudes, crown protection and economic inertia to restrict mobility within narrower confines than was the norm in the north-west.

The Danish nobility was very exclusive before 1660, protected by social barriers which were reinforced by privileges and landownership rights spelt out in law and government practice. Even within the nobility there were clear distinctions of landed wealth and status, with a mere handful of the 282 noble families during the period 1536–1660 occupying nearly half the high offices of state as well as a large share of the landed wealth. Although service in the central administration became an increasingly important criterion of advancement in the early seventeenth century, benefiting members of the lesser nobility, the exclusiveness was only really broken after 1660, when the establishment of absolutism led to an explicit annulment of hereditary political privilege by royal edict. The Crown intended to make merit the prime qualification for office, and although the social and seigneurial privileges of landowners were not affected, the Danish elite underwent a profound change in composition and to some extent in outlook over the next decades. The effective bankruptcy of the Crown, and the resulting alienation of about half its land to creditors and private landowners, resulted in a drastic transfer of property ultimately affecting well over one-third of all land in the kingdom (around 7 million rigsdalers' worth) by 1680. Since the new higher servants of the Crown, including commoners, were granted official status equivalent to or higher than that of the old nobility (an arrangement which was confirmed on a hereditary basis in 1693) and were given access to the ownership of landed estates, and since new aristocratic titles were offered (in accordance with the 1671 decree on rank) in return for services to the Crown, substantial opportunities for social advancement were created both for natives and for foreigners. The numerical displacement of the old aristocracy in the administration in fact took place fairly rapidly over the next decades, but apart from a short-lived experiment in 1701 there was no state-sponsored sale of offices in Denmark. It is clear, however, that the old nobility who had dominated the land market before 1660 were now reduced to the possession of less than half the total number of private estates by 1700, while the new service nobility by then had acquired a sixth of the total number of estates, and non-nobles (especially office-holders, but also some burghers) two-fifths. Although such figures, like any manor-counting exercise, do not indicate the actual nature or importance of the transfer of land, it does confirm that a major status displacement of the old aristocracy by the servants of the Crown was taking place. Many of the latter became the social and political elite of eighteenth-century Denmark.[15]

In Sweden, admission to the nobility, and precedence within it, was directly controlled by the Crown after the promulgation of the *Riddarhusordning* of 1626. Gustav Adolf initiated substantial changes in the composition of the order as new members were admitted through wealth, talent and royal favour, including a number of foreign financiers, entrepreneurs and soldiers. Michael Roberts has pointed out that between 1611 and 1680 over half the new ennoblements (360 out of 670) went to foreigners, whilst commoners and civil servants each represented more than a quarter (180 and 190 respectively, with, of course, some overlap between all three categories, since promotion either in the army or in the civil service resulted in ennoblement at a certain stage). By mid-century this had created sufficiently strong antagonisms and tensions within the noble estate to become a politically important issue, as it did again around 1680 (see p. 382). But the process of ennoblement for service was accentuated even further by Charles XI, who admitted sons of commoners or even of peasants to the highest rank of the nobility in the later 1680s and the 1690s. Of the 67 new counts and barons that he created, 36 were of immediate commoner background and hence founders of the titled status of their family. Given that membership of the upper ranks of the aristocracy provided access to the highest offices of state, it is apparent that Sweden's social and political elite became remarkably open during the later seventeenth century, partly as a result of the impact and influx resulting from Sweden's imperial role in the Baltic and Germany and partly as a result of Charles XI's personal form of absolutism.[16]

The Polish and Russian elites

In eastern Europe, the picture was entirely different in that social mobility was carefully restricted because of the nature of the relationship between Crown and nobility. In Poland and Hungary, in marked contrast to Russia, the monarchies were too weak to influence the composition of the elite, and in any case the gap between the leisured and the peasantry was not bridged by any significant social group from which upward mobility might have occurred. In Poland, indeed, the magnates acquired such a stranglehold on the elective monarchy that central authority all but disintegrated, and they could thereby maintain the traditional values and privileges of their class. *Szlachta* (noble) privileges, mostly consolidated in the sixteenth century, included the exclusive right to land, offices, local administrative posts and higher church offices; full control over the peasantry through serfdom and jurisdictional powers; a considerable influence on towns through noble entitlement to own town property; and exemption from duty on commercial dealings from their estates or via Jewish agents: in short, a position described by a historian of Poland, Norman Davies, as 'the nobleman's paradise', at least for those who were not at the impoverished bottom end of the scale. From 1601 the *sejm* (diet) acquired explicit control over ennoblement itself, leaving the King the right to make grants of nobility within strict limits only. Mobility at the upper end of the social scale was not totally stopped, but the *szlachta* could reinforce its exclusiveness.

The social structure in Muscovy was so different that it is difficult to make meaningful comparisons with the west. The Russian noble service class, consisting of the old landed aristocracy (*boyars*) and the formerly distinct middle-ranking servitors or gentry (*dvoriane*), had real material privileges, especially regarding landholding and the right to use serfs. Some two dozen *boyar* families formed an inner circle amongst the servitors in the early seventeenth century, with exclusive rights of access to the highest offices. But the servitors had none of the security of the western nobility in political or in personal terms, and their service obligations (especially military) could be very onerous. Rank throughout the service class had traditionally been regulated according to the *mestnichestvo* (placement) code, which was based on complex and studiously preserved genealogical claims, honorific status and family traditions of precedence. Although the *mestnichestvo* system became increasingly unworkable during the seventeenth century, leading to endless disputes of the most trivial kind and seriously obstructing effective government, its formal abolition in 1682 did not solve the problem. Lineage and family rivalry remained significant, in spite of the establishment of the principle of status through service to the Tsar.

Alodial lay possession of land, however, had been all but destroyed by Ivan IV in the 1560s and 1570s, and replaced at least in principle by a system of tenure of often deliberately widely scattered estates normally held (in spite of growing acceptance of hereditary claims) on a fairly short-term basis. A high turnover rate meant that the *dvoriane* lost any local territorial base of the kind absolutely crucial to the political power of the nobility further west. This, combined with the unimpressive financial returns that could be expected by the provincial *dvoriane*, greatly emphasised their dependence on the Tsar. The law itself, notably the code of 1649, confirmed this dependence, making Peter I's reforms of the ranking and service system early in the eighteenth century the culmination of a gradual reduction of the collective political power of the elite to the point where they had no means of durably limiting tsarist autocracy.

Quite different was the kind of power exercised by the mostly non-aristocratic lesser servitors of the administrative class, the *prikaznye liudi*. They were not entitled to own serfs or hold service land, but they compensated for this by gaining a fairly durable hold on the day-to-day working of the state. Although family connection was the simplest means of initial access to this group, neither venality of offices nor inheritability was known; patronage, ability and subservience were apparently the basic prerequisites for promotion within this very hierarchic salaried bureaucracy. Some nobles, although often lacking certain qualifications, did seek chancery service because of its relative security and convenience, but the detailed formal regulation of the *prikazy* (chanceries), and the fairly heavy work routine, ensured that the nobility restricted itself to a largely decorative role in the pre-Petrine administration. This functional separation may have been peculiarly Russian; indeed, it has been argued that a long-term effect of Peter I's Table of Ranks of 1722 was to water down the professional efficiency of the bureaucracy by forcing the nobility to take a greater part. But there is some indication that the underlying social distinctions may already have been fading well before Peter's reign, owing to the practice of rewarding distinguished service with a noble title.[17]

Landholding and service in the Ottoman Empire

Ottoman governmental structures had developed to a high level of efficiency and co-ordination earlier than in central and western Europe. In order to secure the military needs of the state, land through much of the Empire was often held by cavalry servicemen (*timarli*), whose obligations to the state originally had been well-defined and standardised. After the death of Sultan Suleyman the Magnificent in 1566, however, central control became less consistent, and there were intermittent periods of apparent weakness from which those with local power could benefit: the *timar* (land held in return for service) became more prone to de facto hereditary claims, or was converted into a form of tax-farming similar to that coming into use in France, allowing the individual interests of subcontractors to grow more pronounced. The very large military machinery itself became prone to factionalism, where local leaders and provincial governors acquired an increasingly prominent and autonomous role. Consequently, land came to be regarded more as personal estates, with property rights – even though such claims were not recognised in law. As in eastern and central Europe at this time, surrender of local authority to increasingly well-ensconced landholders was liable to have a damaging impact on the peasant population who worked the land, especially since labour was scarce. In practice, restrictions on peasant mobility were implemented, similar to those in areas of serfdom elsewhere in Europe but possibly driven more by fiscal necessity than because of demands from the timar-holders themselves.

The consolidation of landholding privileges amongst the upper levels of Ottoman social structure was a slow process which did not become irreversible until the eighteenth century. But it was encouraged by two trends: the changing military needs of the Ottoman state itself, resulting from technical developments amongst the other European military powers; and the increasing reliance on local initiative and the entrepreneurial inclinations of local officialdom in order to meet the growing fiscal needs of a state whose viable geographic limits had long since been reached. The *chiftlik* (consolidated estate aimed at market production) was thus a natural response to attrition within the system, made possible by the more variable quality of central leadership offered by successive sultans and their advisers in Constantinople. This trend was facilitated by a long-established tradition whereby educational and other community-based activities were funded through a notionally 'charitable' foundation (*vakif*) – in practice often landed estates managed privately to provide annual rents for the beneficiary – which could serve as a front for private landowning interests. As in the west, those who worked the land could be brought into a more pronounced dependency-relationship through increased obligations and the accumulation of arrears and debts – abuses which the central Ottoman government did not control effectively, even though it had a clear interest in protecting the tax-paying status of the original holdings.[18]

It is too early to know precisely how the Ottoman elite exploited these potential advantages. But what is clear is that this trend did gradually facilitate the emergence of wealthy landowners whose lifestyle and interests converged with those of the nobility in western and central Europe. As the sultan's own position and status changed, so did the role of the elite both in terms of the actual exercise of power and in terms of the system of clientage and patronage operating within the Ottoman Empire. Travellers' descriptions are not always a reliable source of historical evidence, but by the late seventeenth century there was a growing interchange between the elites of Christian and Muslim Europe, based partly on curiosity and the search for novelty on both sides and partly on some actual similarities of lifestyle and socio-political status. Given persistent cultural differences, this trend should not be overstated, but during the eighteenth century mutual interest between the Ottoman and Christian elites became fashionable, and with it came better understanding and some relaxation of traditional prejudices.

For the social historian, nobility may not be the most difficult term to come to grips with in the early modern period, given the relative ease of identification and the substantial amount of documentary evidence on the subject. Nevertheless, no overall description of a group as heterogeneous as the European nobility can hope to do justice to the complexities and variants in societies at such unequal stages of economic and political development. In eastern Europe the relationship between Crown and nobility was clearly crucial, but Poland and Muscovy constitute highly contrasting examples. In central Europe, because of prevailing political conditions, the nobility in some areas managed to preserve a more secure and traditional role both as privileged landowners and as an unchallenged elite to whom local power and authority came with birth. In western Europe the picture seems more complicated, for if the nobility was an estate in political theory, it was certainly not a socio-economic class in any meaningful sense. It is abundantly clear that the criteria of noble status used by contemporaries were not only divergent from one area or writer to the next, and in some cases incompatible, but were also perhaps increasingly remote from the realities of the time. Nowhere in later seventeenth-century Europe west of the Elbe could the nobility be regarded as closed or exclusive, and its supposed distinctiveness of lineage, quality and function was little more than a convenient fiction. Even the Venetian patrician nobility opened its ranks in 1646 to those willing to offer 100,000 ducats for a title.

In both east and west, rulers with sufficient power tried to make service a determinant of status, but wherever they had at least partial success the elite adapted successfully to changing circumstances. Although concepts of nobility centred on the preservation of important traditions, individual families showed considerable initiative not only in adapting to the relevant power structures but ultimately also in exploiting the commercial and economic opportunities that appeared in ways that were sufficiently dynamic to preserve or even enhance their social position. All over Europe, from France to the Ottoman Empire, service to the state in practice could provide privileges and opportunities from which individuals and family networks could gain immeasurably. Accordingly, the seventeenth century was not a period where the gap between the rich and the poor narrowed. On the contrary, as we shall see in the following chapters, huge and persistent social inequalities at times led to bitterness and outright social confrontation across all of Europe, with neither the State nor the Church doing more than absolutely necessary to tackle underlying problems. Since the elite generally remained in control of both the top levels of political patronage and the main levers of judicial and executive power, there was little prospect of significant change. That said, in the economically sophisticated north-west, wealth gradually did supersede lineage as the real determinant of social and political influence and advancement. With it came new forms of conspicuous consumption and ostentation which provided skilled craftsmen with great market opportunities and led to the creation of some of the greatest works of art of the period (see chapter 9). Those wishing to escape the patronage of the nobility could sometimes do so in the growing and at times anarchic bustle of the western European urban environment. But seventeenth-century society remained strongly hierarchical, with wealth and power very predominantly located in the small minority of privileged families who knew how to use the system to best effect.

6 The structure of society: urban life

A major distinctive feature of western historical development in the later medieval and early modern periods was the growth and consolidation of towns not merely as conglomerations of people but as communities with a life and structure of their own. The German saying '*Stadtluft macht frei*' was a shorthand for the fact that in most of Europe towns of any size had acquired a corporate autonomy which freed them from the seigneurial control exerted over the surrounding countryside and often also gave them a large degree of independence in town government, administration, the law and taxation. The town wall (where there was one) thus not only protected the community, and enclosed the market or manufacturing which had constituted the original function of the town, but also represented administrative and jurisdictional boundaries of enormous practical significance. Although much of the community framework had emerged in the medieval period and institutional change in the early modern period was slow or virtually non-existent, the external strains of the seventeenth century could not help affecting the life and structure of even the most secure towns. Demographic factors, as we have seen, introduced an enormous element of uncertainty, whilst economic fluctuations had an obvious impact on urban food supplies, demand and secondary employment throughout the period. Even more fundamentally challenging during this century, however, were the threats posed to towns on the one hand by emerging and rapacious royal government and on the other hand by a growing aristocratisation of the upper levels of society. These were challenges which the community framework had not originally been designed to cope with, and in some parts of Europe they endangered the very coherence and corporate stability of urban society. This was particularly so since amongst town-dwellers there was little of what in more recent times might be labelled 'class-consciousness' – no 'bourgeoisie' in the modern sense of that word.[1] Compared with either the self-awareness that was commonly taken to exist within the nobility or the clear functional distinctiveness that bound together the whole clergy in spite of the large differences of background and income between upper and lower ranks, most urban communities lacked a genuinely inclusive corporate identity of the kind that might have drawn together the socially quite hierarchical and deeply divided layers. Townsmen were undoubtedly keenly conscious of belonging to their *particular* community, but they had very little regional (let alone national) corporate awareness and no sense of inclusiveness towards the unskilled labourers, servants and poor who seemed to throng the streets. Not only were there different levels of recognised citizenship, ranging down into the upper levels of artisan groups, but in French and many Mediterranean cities the patrician elite often held noble status: the Venetian nobility is the obvious example, but in France there was also the urban *noble homme* and the municipal official acquiring *noblesse de cloche*.

A legacy of medieval development, the hierarchically differentiated layers of urban society tended by the seventeenth century to give diminishing scope for political participation except for a carefully prescribed minority. Moreover, the defensive economic self-sufficiency characteristic of most medieval and early modern towns did not readily give way to genuine economic integration with the countryside, except in a few atypical cases of rapid growth. This meant that although towns relied on a carefully controlled supply network in the rural surroundings for food and other raw materials, and at the lower end of the social scale even created substantial opportunities for geographic and functional mobility, they were neither genuinely egalitarian communities within their own jurisdiction nor effectively open partners in a wider network. The town–country relationship was made unequal not only by the relative economic and commercial dominance of towns but also by their seigneurial ownership of surrounding land, by their control of capital and marketing and by their ability to shun the worst part of royal taxation through privileges and tradition. Even rural industry, sometimes a serious competitor to urban crafts (especially in textiles), was often organised and exploited by urban merchants, and had its main outlet through urban middlemen. In addition, there were other forms of domination: towns provided a social life, reinforcing the habitually condescending attitudes towards rustics. Judicial and provincial institutions were invariably urban-based, as were cultural, educational and most religious foundations, and indeed the administration of the church itself. Even parish priests tended to be of urban origins: 47 per cent of the clergy in the diocese of Reims at the end of the seventeenth century were townsmen, while in that of Bordeaux the proportion was no less than 81 per cent.

But towns cannot be lumped together as a whole without serious oversimplification, in this as in any other period. Several approaches are possible, but the most basic distinction for the early modern period is a broadly geographic one, between the towns of western and central Europe and those of the east and south-east. In the Ottoman Empire, flourishing economic life in the early modern period gave a number of cities considerable status and some autonomy, while the Islamic tradition allowed local *muftis* (scholars clarifying the law through *fatwas* or pronouncements) and local judges to operate fairly independently. However, despite the development of guilds and the prosperous autonomy of many coastal settlements, Ottoman towns do not seem to have developed a strong corporate identity in their own right, and municipal officials remained firmly subservient in the strictly controlled hierarchy of officialdom. Only Constantinople itself, with over half a million inhabitants and an old commercial tradition, was a total exception. Arguably, Russian settlements were not 'towns' in the European sense at all, since they lacked any real corporate autonomy. Muscovite settlements were mostly military and administrative centres, and even if some were sufficiently well-placed on trade routes to profit from a substantial and healthy commerce, they could never emancipate themselves from the political and fiscal control which the hierarchical structure of the tsarist state imposed. Official town life (not merely in the newer frontier settlements) was geared to the needs of the state, and this severely hampered the emergence of independent commercial enterprise and of urban services. Individual communities had little scope for securing any autonomy or communal property rights, and successful manufacturers or traders were often drawn into state service. Demands for self-government could therefore be ignored in the preparation of the *Ulozheniye* (Law Code) of 1649, and townspeople, although not serfs, were subjected to restrictions on mobility and other forms of regulation as part of the *tiaglo* (tax-paying) subject population. Since noble landowners could also freely engage in trade and manufacture, it is not surprising that there was little trace of wealthy or self-confident urban life in Russia.

East-central Europe offered more scope for the market production and commerce necessary for genuine urban development. In Poland, only Danzig (Gdansk), Elbing (Elblag) and Torun retained the right to take part in foreign trade after 1565, but the importance of the river Vistula as a grain-carrying artery ensured substantial growth for inland cities like Warzaw even into the seventeenth century. By then, however, a number of factors began significantly to retard urban development. Unstable conditions in the Baltic, and by mid-century major foreign incursions on to Polish territory (see chapter 7), damaged urban prosperity. The economy of Poland–Lithuania, like that of Hungary, was based primarily on the export of agricultural produce and some other raw materials: urban manufacturing was on a small scale and the demand for such goods was too restricted to create competitive alternatives to imports from the west. More ominous in Poland, however, was the ability of the aristocracy, through their control of parliament, to secure entitlements contrary to the interests of townsmen: the right to purchase urban property, to hold it on privileged terms with respect to town laws and taxes, and to take part in (and eventually dominate) the grain trade without going through urban market controls. As a result, by 1667 the citizens of Cracow, for example, owned merely 28 per cent of the property within the walls, the rest being held by nobles and wealthy clergy. In Bohemia and the most prosperous parts of Hungary noble domination had emerged even earlier. As far as the lesser towns are concerned, perhaps two-thirds in Poland and Bohemia, and an even greater share in Hungary, were seigneurial foundations on private land whose dependence on a single nobleman prevented the political emancipation and self-government so essential to late medieval urban development in the west. In such settlements agriculture in any case often became a dominant form of employment to compensate for market stagnation. There were, of course, important regional differences; nowhere except in Poland did the nobility secure totally unrestricted power over their subjects. But the overall trend in east-central Europe, towards relatively weakening towns, was of enormous long-term importance.

From the central parts of the German lands westwards, true urban development is quite unambiguous. What evidence there is suggests that the urban population in central and western Europe averaged perhaps 10–30 per cent of the total, but the enormous difference between areas such as Castile (with minimal urban commercial life) and the Netherlands (with some two-thirds of the population in the province of Holland being genuinely urban) makes such statistics very nearly meaningless. The biggest cities, such as Naples or Paris, with perhaps a quarter of a million or more inhabitants at the beginning of the seventeenth century (surpassed by London in the course of the period) were a world of their own, but the growing number of cities with over 100,000 people by the end of the century (including Amsterdam, Rome, Milan and Venice), were all quite extraordinary phenomena in terms of both economic infrastructure and social development. But the scale of change needs to be kept in perspective: by the end of the seventeenth century there were only just over two dozen cities with more than an estimated 60,000 inhabitants. Even the major second-rank towns of the day, such as Norwich, Strassburg or Lübeck (all with some 20,000 inhabitants in the later seventeenth century), were small in area and quite rural in terms of gardens, domestic animals and smells, and although the growth rate might be substantial they rarely produced the population densities of the very big cities (which might reach 300–800 inhabitants per hectare in the centre).

The strongest urban consolidation existed in the western part of the Holy Roman Empire and in Italy, where there was little or no political interference from any national institutions, and more generally in the north-west. There, distinctions of size and rate of growth can usefully be made a basis of classification. Major differences in kind are discernible between those cities with a growing economic and demographic potential (such as Amsterdam, Hamburg or London, and, on a lesser scale, Newcastle, Bristol, Cadiz or Bordeaux) and the relatively static (often inland) towns pursuing a more conventional role as provincial and manufacturing communities (such as Beauvais, Nuremberg or Nördlingen, to mention some which have been extensively studied). Obviously, such a generalisation may underestimate elements of change: the city of Venice could be said to move from the former to the latter group during the early seventeenth century. Such changes in the rate of development could also be produced by non-economic factors, for example if a city was the normal residence of a court or a political capital. Copenhagen is a case in point: with a population of around 25,000 after the mid-century wars, it benefited from the staple rights (exclusive commercial privileges) granted in 1660, from government protectionism and from the establishment of absolutism to such an extent that it passed 60,000 by the end of the century. Its growth was in striking contrast to the stagnation of provincial towns in Denmark and Norway during the same period. An extreme example of growth attributable almost entirely to political function was Madrid, which, with a population of 30,000, became a permanent capital in 1561 and had reached a population of 170,000 seventy years later without any economic logic.[2]

Preliminary work[3] on the whole suggests that urban demographic growth in the seventeenth and early eighteenth centuries was concentrated on larger cities, and that smaller towns (especially those lacking access to the sea) did not expand proportionally. It was particularly the capitals and ports that felt what demographic expansion there was in Europe in the second half of our period and that experienced the effects of the considerable tidal fluctuations in population caused by mobility (see chapter 3). This is not surprising, given the relatively greater opportunities available in the large cities, yet it created enormous new problems of an administrative and social kind, and further distanced these cities from the old form of closely integrated town life where 'active' citizens would know each other, and where a traditional lifestyle was both guaranteed and inescapable.

At the risk of oversimplification, it is perhaps reasonable to discern altogether three main generalised types of town in western and central Europe: first, the traditional smaller towns (of fewer than, say, 10,000–15,000 inhabitants) which on the whole did not change very rapidly and tended to be on the defensive about their economic basis and political traditions; secondly, the larger and sometimes rapidly growing commercial centres whose structures were threatened by a far greater influx of strangers, by possibly rapid social development, by more widely flung supply-lines for grain and fuel, and in some cases by important long-distance trade; and thirdly (in some respects over-lapping with the second category), the newly important political capi-tals, with a large proportion of more or less unproductive administrative personnel, court staff, hangers-on and former traders who had become rentiers by acquiring land, offices or titles. The bigger cities of the second and third types often relied on a constant influx of skilled and especially unskilled labour from outside in order to maintain a positive economic balance.

The smaller towns

The most numerous urban settlements in central and western Europe were of the type which may be described as relatively small and fairly static towns, and whose size tended to be in the order of a few thou-sand inhabitants. Mack Walker has suggested that a total population of around 10,000 might have been near the upper limit within which the 'active' citizens (heads of burgher households, numbering perhaps one in five of the total population) might still be personally acquainted with each other's interests to a degree sufficient to preserve the community feeling. The lower limit in terms of size is difficult to determine, since a settlement of, say, 600 might be a market town if it had specialised non-agrarian functions, but would be a village if it was merely a concentrated extension of the countryside. Towns, in contrast to villages, also had rather more complex social and political structures, especially if they had effectively escaped from seigneurial control and achieved formal corporate status. Those of several thou-sand inhabitants might have considerable economic vitality because of manufactures or port facilities or might be enlivened by university or church institutions – such factors often resulted in a more heteroge-neous and complex social composition, and stimulated a greater range of trades to satisfy internal demand for books, paper, cloths, house-hold possessions, specialised craftwork and luxury goods. On the whole, however, towns of modest size experienced difficulties or at least stagnation during the seventeenth century, either because of wartime strain and damage or, for example in England, because of competition from the more viable bigger towns and ports. The threat created by new towns could also be significant: dockyard centres developing as part of naval state planning, with special privileges or concessions to help their growth (such as Chatham, Plymouth, Karlskrona, Fredericia, Brest and Rochefort), and the less regulated emerging industrial centres such as Leeds could drain labour resources and market opportunities away from older conservative towns.[4]

It is perhaps misleading to generalise about the social and political structures of the smaller towns in central and western Europe during the early modern period: evidently no two towns were alike in terms of economic patterns, and their institutional idiosyncrasies were often deliberately preserved for the sake of independence. In the German lands, in particular, the rivalry between the Emperor and local princes created ideal conditions for the survival of constitutional distinctions, not merely in the 51 independent imperial cities subject only to the Emperor but also in the innumerable smaller towns which might use the imperial machinery or the mutual suspicions of neighbouring princes to safeguard traditions of autonomy. This was certainly possible in the south-western part of the Empire, with its very fragmented map; in the north and east, towns had fewer traditions and were after 1648 constrained by the existence of bigger territorial units such as Brandenburg–Prussia.

Urban society was invariably highly hierarchical. Unequal status values were attached to different occupations and to different levels of material attainment within any given occupation. The most fundamental social distinction in any urban community was an essentially economic one, between citizens (freemen) and non-citizens; that is, between on the one hand those who were permanently resident, property-owning and independent members of the urban community (merchants, craftsmen, shopkeepers, professionals and the like), and those on the other hand who were subservient or economically dependent by virtue of being labourers, apprentices and servants, or were genuine outsiders (in the geographic sense) without any right to protection. Even amongst the citizens themselves there were rankings according to the relative prestige of the guilds or the functions and offices held within any one guild. Such ranking was meticulously displayed in formal and processional dress, in church seating, in the scale of family feasts, and by other means. Movement from non-citizen to citizen status was nearly automatic for sons of citizens and was relatively easy for those journeymen who married into or otherwise gained acceptance into a trade which was in demand. But for those who lacked such opportunity, and especially for those who were both poor and geographic outsiders, upward mobility might be very difficult in the economically stagnant conditions of the seventeenth century. Most towns imposed minimum wealth requirements on applications for citizenship, and further restrictions were imposed on men who might compete in a trade where demand was limited. Women, on the other hand, generally faced fewer obstacles to admission since they were not seen as economic competitors to the same extent.

It is sometimes possible, on the basis of tax rolls and similar source material, to get some impression of the rough occupational distribution in statistical terms. A tax roll of 1696 for the provincial French town of Beauvais, for example, gives a distribution in terms of the number of households within certain categories. The textile industry provided the main occupation of 745 heads of households (29 per cent of the total number liable to pay), including 99 merchants, 104 manufacturers and 542 workers (but not counting the 100 specially privileged workers at the Royal Tapestry Works); another 582 households (23 per cent) were those of craftsmen and shopkeepers, including 211 in the food industry, 204 in the clothing industry and 167 in building and other trades; 374 (15 per cent) were those of rentiers and office-holders, including 57 exempt non-noble office-holders and 22 taxed medical staff (namely 6 doctors, 5 apothecaries and 11 surgeons); another 221 (9 per cent) were semi-rural, deriving their main earnings from gardening and agrarian work; 640 households (25 per cent), including a significant number of widows and the poor, had special concessions or were taxed lightly on the basis of minor work subsidiary mostly to the textile industry. There were also 460 exempt clergymen and 350 institutionalised poor, none of whom was liable to pay (and they are therefore not included in the percentage calculation above). If, however, one accepts that the actual sums payable by each household for this 1696 tax give at least some indication, however approximate, of relative wealth or income, the inequalities become far more striking: although the tax-scale ranged from nil to 400 livres in impositions, no less than 54 per cent were to pay less than 2 livres, and over four-fifths were rated below 10 livres. Perhaps because of exemptions at the top end of the scale, a mere 1.7 per cent were rated over 50 livres. This was in a year when, in spite of the economic distress of the second quarter of the decade, the distribution was not radically different from what it had been in 1691. It seems fairly clear that a very large proportion of the urban population was overwhelmingly poor. Many of these were in the textile sector, while the craftsmen in other occupations, and especially the shopkeepers, were slightly better off (mostly paying between 2 and 20 livres). It is interesting, however, that a large proportion of those in the 'liberal professions' (the lawyers and the medical staff) were within this same bracket, in other words not as well off as one might have expected in a town of some 12,000 inhabitants. Goubert suggests that 300 families (mostly office-holders, rentiers and merchants) or one in eight of all households could be considered comfortably off.[5]

Nördlingen, in southern Germany, was a slightly smaller town, with a population of probably around 9000 at the beginning of the century. There, no fewer than half the male heads of households were employed in textile, clothing and leatherwork before the Thirty Years War, although this proportion decreased slightly after the war when fine-cloth production nearly died out and was replaced by the linen industry. Other crafts accounted for around 18 per cent throughout most of the century, but the food and drinks trades employed an increasing share of the workforce, amounting to 20 per cent by the end of the century. The rest included the learned occupations and office-holders (8–10 per cent), but there appear to have been rather fewer rentiers than in Beauvais, perhaps because the town did not have wider administrative functions and because it experienced economic hardship not just during the Thirty Years War but also later in the century during Louis XIV's wars.

The town's tax registers are sufficiently regular and reliable, according to Friedrichs, to allow a closer study of changes in the wealth of individuals in terms of their taxable property (which included both movables and immovables, regularly reassessed, but excluded any valuation of actual income). On this basis Friedrichs has demonstrated an enormous degree of wealth mobility at most income levels and in all the main professions in the first two-thirds of the century, with the poorer groups benefiting particularly from the economic recovery experienced after the worst phase of the war in the 1630s. But it is also apparent that upward mobility became more diffi-cult after around 1670, at a time when the richer groups were increas-ing their share of the total wealth of the city. The tensions generated by this tendency were aggravated by the gradual organisation by the Wörner family of an urban putting-out network (*Verlagssystem*) designed to make a large number of poor textile workers economically dependent on a single merchant house, and although this entrepre-neurial development was temporarily halted by a confrontation in 1698 and the intervention of the town council, it heralded a new age of dwindling artisan independence and encroaching large-scale market control. Such change was indeed already well under way in the seven-teenth century in other towns, notably in Nuremberg. Nevertheless Nördlingen was still an open society of fairly equal opportunities, and even if the median wealth of the textile workers was well below that of certain other trades (notably the very prosperous innkeeping trade and the relatively secure butchers' and bakers' trades), the tax registers also reveal that there were no occupationally determined barriers to indi-vidual upward mobility in terms of wealth. Since craftsmen of any trade could (and did) rise even into the wealthy elite of the city, it is clear that status cannot be determined by means of any one simple classification: rank, property ownership and occupation need to be considered as complementary criteria. Moreover, given that the over-all inequality of wealth in Nördlingen was as extreme as it appeared to be in Beauvais in the 1690s, with the top 2 per cent of the citizenry rarely owning less than one-quarter of the total wealth of the city and the bottom 50 per cent owning at various times during the century between 3 and 8 per cent of the total wealth, one is led to conclude that Nördlingen was a type of community where inequalities were at least as evident within any single occupation as between different types of occupation (except, of course, for commerce and unskilled labouring, which were inevitably at the top and the bottom of the wealth scale respectively).[6] It is too early to determine whether either Beauvais or Nördlingen can in any way be regarded as 'typical', but the latter, in particular, warns us against assuming that the inequalities of wealth in early modern towns created any clear socio-occupational class hierarchy.

The forms of government in smaller towns varied in detail but had a number of common features. One of these was the explicit or tacit exclusion of all but a propertied minority from any effective political power, an approach which had its practical uses since councillors might have to provide financial assistance to the community from their own resources. Town government was often headed by a small governing council where each member had specific responsibilities, even though the council as a whole operated on a collegiate basis under the presidency of a mayor. Membership of the inner council was usually achieved at least nominally via a less frequently called larger assembly or outer council, itself chosen from those citizens who satisfied the property qualifications. In towns where the property barrier was low a considerable and unpredictable (sometimes even seditious) popular influence could be brought to bear, but elsewhere the inner council restricted such uncontrollable factors by giving craftsmen a nominal role in government through co-opted and often docile representatives of the guild or craft associations. In some towns (in Nördlingen in 1552, for example) the proper craft guilds had been so politically independent that they had been replaced by occupational corporations or associations largely controlled by the town council. There was a danger inherent in excessive exclusiveness, however: some ties with the community as a whole had to be maintained, together with some genuine accessibility to offices; otherwise, stability could be endangered. In those towns which experienced a tendency towards the formation of a privileged patriciate[7] reserving power for themselves, corruption and other abuses often became so serious a problem that tensions were generated which could culminate either in internal rebellion or in outside intervention (or both), followed by a return to more open government. In the Holy Roman Empire, in particular, such cyclical patterns were quite common in smaller towns such as Brunswick (1613–15) or Erfurt (1648 onwards) but in the imperial cities, as in the larger towns in the western monarchies such as France, princely authority usually backed an enduring conservative patrician tendency.

Tensions in the political life of the small towns were often defused either through personal and family contacts (one of the principal advantages of limited size), through the courts or through mediation by the small administrative bureaucracy, by the clergy or by the various social, medical and occupational corporations which existed everywhere. The guilds or craft corporations in particular served a composite role as economic regulators, political bodies and social guardians: functions which might be economically restrictive but also had beneficial consequences both in terms of the protection of the economic independence of each craftsman against larger-scale merchants (as, for a time, in Nördlingen at the end of the century) and in terms of the stability and security of the community. Nevertheless, genuine self-government was increasingly undermined in central and western Europe in the early modern period by a growth in full-time professional municipal bureaucracies with a tendency to rely on a self-perpetuating group of lawyers and educated administrators. Even without the formation of a clear patriciate, therefore, the relative openness of urban politics was whittled away by the increasing complexity of public life.

Larger cities

Generalisations are much more difficult to make about the nature of cities as widely divergent as Frankfurt, Newcastle, Hamburg, Lyon, Bologna, Leiden or Seville – not to mention cities such as Venice or The Hague, which were capitals of a territorial entity without having a genuine court life of the kind surrounding the Crowns of Europe. Common to all the bigger cities was the need for more far-flung supply lines in the surrounding countryside and (if there was maritime access) overseas, creating economically dependent areas which satisfied urban demand and provided raw materials or labour for urban sectors. Such economic relationships could be beneficial in a number of ways, and might stimulate demand, regional development and transport. But they also commonly led to growing functional specialisation not only between town and country but within the urban economy itself, resulting in social divisions between the upper wealthy patriciate and the lesser citizens; between entrepreneurs, middlemen, large-scale merchants and professionals on the one hand, and the traditional craftsmen and small traders on the other. It is not surprising that bigger cities, especially those relying on more distant markets, were also particularly prone to the encroachment of an urban form of putting-out organisation (*Verlagssystem*), which increased social differentiation.

Those cities which had real growth potential during the seventeenth century were usually the ones playing a major role either in long-distance and overseas trade or in industrial production, or both. Newcastle lived primarily on its rapidly growing coal exports to London and northern Europe which amounted to over half a million tons a year at the Restoration and made the area easily the biggest coal producer in Europe. Hamburg had developed rapidly in the later sixteenth century on the basis of its excellent position near the mouth of the Elbe, whereby it could act as a major cosmopolitan centre for trade between the west and the German hinterland, especially when the Spanish–Dutch war was renewed in 1621, and could displace the more tradition-bound and closed Lübeck merchant community as the commercial leader of northern Germany. Baltic ports such as Danzig and Königsberg relied on corn exports to the west as the mainstay of a trade which included a variety of other products as well: Danzig grew to a size of some 80,000 on the strength of a dominant position in the entire economy of Poland. By contrast, cities such as Leiden or Lyon (with around 70,000 inhabitants each) were primarily textile centres and, as such, vulnerably dependent on fluctuations in that rather unsteady sector in the early seventeenth century, especially since (unlike, for example, Norwich) they had difficulty coping with rural competition and market limitations. The relationship with the hinterland and with other towns or producers in the area, commercial accessibility, the availability of food as well as raw materials and investment, and factors in international relations all affected the urban economy in different ways. But only in western- and central-European cities did a commercial elite with sufficient capital for long-distance international trade emerge: east of the Elbe and in the Austrian lands such development took much longer owing to less favourable economic and social factors.

Prosperous cities (or indeed any urban communities with potential of some kind) were of particular interest to rulers for political or fiscal reasons, and such interest perhaps represented the greatest threat of all during the seventeenth century. The growing burden of state impositions (or, in the case of German towns, protection payments) could easily become a means of political interference or a cause of internal division within a city. In France, for example, town councils throughout the early seventeenth century had to tread a careful path between the tax demands of the central government and the popular hostility which such taxation engendered once imposed on the community. At least until the end of the Fronde it was still sometimes possible for the civic authorities to play off one against the other, particularly in regions where revolts were endemic and where civic privileges or corporate tax exemptions created a protective if not impenetrable legal defence. After the restoration of order under Louis XIV, however, the *intendants* gradually extended their control over the appointment of town officials and over municipal elections, taxation, finance and even legislation for the reform of civic constitutions. This was part of Colbert's concerted reform programme and was in many ways both necessary and beneficial, especially where embezzlement and corruption amongst municipal officials had gone unchecked and where towns had accumulated long-term debts, but it strangled healthy community government and exposed the towns to direct exploitation by the Crown in the later years of Louis XIV when the financial needs of the state knew no bounds. The enforcement of guild membership for all French urban workers after 1673 was largely a measure designed to augment crown revenues. Much more damaging were the successive creations and suppressions of large numbers of more or less imaginary venal municipal offices from the 1690s onwards, generating considerable resentment and disillusionment, especially since many towns were reluctant to opt out for fear of losing control of at least the significant appointments. The cost of block purchase of these offices often forced towns to borrow from wealthy citizens, and the venality system itself naturally also emphasised the exclusivist trend amongst urban oligarchic elites by the end of the century. From the Crown's point of view, however, this was an easier procedure than to try to devise and implement a fairer system of urban taxation, a task which few *ancien-régime* governments could contemplate.

If few rulers went as far as Louis XIV in cynically exploiting town prosperity, the tendency towards greater legislative and administrative intervention was nevertheless universal. Even English towns, which had initially developed fairly freely within a decentralised provincial structure, succumbed to change during the Restoration period. This was partly because of the explicit political aims of the Restoration monarchy, most clearly revealed in the extensive revisions of town charters by the Crown during the years 1681–6 and especially by James after 1687. The city of Königsberg in East Prussia suffered a far more deliberate and heavy-handed subjection at the hands of Elector Frederick William in 1662, when he imposed control over the city council and the estates of Prussia by means of a show of force, imprisoning the active and independent president of the City Court, Hieronymus Roth, on a doubtful charge of treason. Magdeburg, within the Empire, lost its free status to Frederick William in 1680 as part of his continuing efforts at centralisation. Other imperial towns were more fortunate in exploiting local political rivalries amongst neighbouring princes, or using imperial institutions for their protection. There were other threats however: less immediate, but potentially as damaging to long-term economic prospects, were the tolls, excises and restrictions by means of which many German princes after the Treaty of Westphalia in 1648 tried to increase their own revenues and extend their sovereignty. Such obstacles, together with the fact that foreign powers controlled the mouths of the major waterways after 1648, further reduced prospects of economic recovery for a number of German cities, and hence their political stature.

Larger cities were also more prone than their smaller neighbours to the formation of exclusive ruling oligarchies of patricians who had withdrawn from active enterprise altogether in favour of a more aristocratic style of life. The city of Nuremberg, a thriving centre in the sixteenth century, stagnated thereafter, primarily owing to a negative and restrictive attitude amongst the patriciate. At times such elites exposed themselves to challenge from below by those whom they had excluded from effective influence on community politics. Conflicts between patrician councils and at least the upper ranks of townsmen were common during the seventeenth century, especially over allegations of the misuse of judicial and administrative powers of corruption or of the imposition and misapplication of levies. The city of Frankfurt, for example, which had escaped from the Thirty Years War relatively lightly (with only limited physical damage in the 1630s), and had made a good recovery after the war to become the leading commercial and banking centre in the Empire together with Hamburg and Leipzig, had one of the most conservative constitutions. The powerful city council controlled its own membership and had, by the late sixteenth century, come to consist predominantly of patricians and lawyers who lived as noble rentiers. Although a nominal representation of wholesale commerce was tolerated on the council, it had been whittled down to such an extent that the merchant community became increasingly resentful of its second-class status. A movement for constitutional reform succeeded in securing imperial arbitration in 1612, but the resulting constitutional compromise-agreement was scuppered by the more radical (and also violently anti-Jewish) Fettmilch uprising. External intervention in 1614 and the execution of the riot leaders in 1616 enabled the council not only to ignore the 1612 agreement but also to get imperial backing for the abolition of the independent artisan guilds and their replacement with innocuous, nominated craft corporations. As a result, when the latent conflict finally erupted in the period 1705–32, the patrician power monopoly was reduced in favour of the upper citizenry and the burgher militia officers, but the lesser townsmen could now only play a supportive role with little political benefit for themselves.

Such confrontations between patricians and burghers were common all over Europe (including England), and could in some cases lead to violence. The French port of Bordeaux experienced growing social tensions in the 1630s and 1640s, culminating in the Ormée revolt of 1652 at the end of the Fronde (see chapter 7). In Hamburg, where an exclusive patriciate had never established itself as fully as in Frankfurt because of the risks inherent in long-distance trade and because of the prohibition against nobles owning town property, conflicts over taxation, foreign policy and especially the nature and extent of burgher participation still brought city government to the brink of anarchy in the second half of the seventeenth century (especially the 1680s and

1690s) – so much so that the Emperor had occasion to intervene to impose a compromise in 1712.[8] Patrician government, however, did not invariably encourage political challenge from below: the Venetian nobility, one of the most exclusive patrician groups in Europe at the time, avoided serious conflict by means of the careful use of patronage, political propaganda and public display, by granting the old high-ranking burgher families (the *cittadini originari*) a secure role in the bureaucracy and by lending an expediently sensitive ear to the highly developed and politically effective guilds when necessary, as in the difficult years 1611–12.[9]

Capital cities

The political map, particularly of central Europe and Italy, warns us against making distinctions between capital cities, in the modern sense, and other large cities serving as regional administrative centres, the seat of provincial Estates or of regional law-courts and parlements. Such cities attracted a substantial number of resident noble families, and hence a large service sector: Aix-en-Provence in the 1690s, for example, had a domestic service sector amounting to around 22 per cent of the total population. Nevertheless, steps towards centralisation in the consolidated monarchies did give certain cities distinctive features. Those cities which were (or became) capitals for a court of significant size were less prone to the internal tensions of other large towns simply because of the presence of the organs of government and the consequent efforts to regulate city life. But capitals were exposed in acute form to the urban problem of supply, compounded by a social imbalance created by the presence of a rapidly growing number of individuals attached to the court rather than to the city *per se*. Court and commercial growth usually went in tandem to some extent, as in The Hague, in Stockholm or, most strikingly, in the solid commercial basis behind London's prodigious expansion. But this was not always so. More artificial, at first, was the growth of Berlin from 10,000 to 60,000 during the century up to 1710. In Saxony, both Dresden and Leipzig grew by about 50 per cent during the later seventeenth century, from their 1648 population of around 15,000 each, but in the former case it was largely thanks to the presence of a court, in the latter because of commercial development. The sixfold expansion of Madrid, already mentioned, was entirely court-related: not only did the city lack any economic basis but it also severely disrupted what economic balance the region had previously had, directly contributing to the decline of Toledo after 1609 (see note 2). Even capitals with a solid economic foundation were tangibly affected by the impact of growing governmental bureaucracies in the early modern period: in Munich, for example, an estimated 13 per cent of the households in 1500 had been those of clergy, courtiers and bureaucrats, but by the end of the seventeenth century these groups represented 26 per cent of a population which by then had reached some 20,000. In Copenhagen in the early years of absolutism after 1660, the households of civilian, military and naval employees of the Crown constituted an estimated 40 per cent of the total. The presence of a princely court with growing ambitions for political control and centralisation deprived citizens of any real say in the government of their community, and the disruptive effect of such an imbalance in the urban hierarchy continued to increase into the eighteenth century.

The most extreme illustration of court-related growth was the village of Versailles during the reign of Louis XIV. Originally housing about 400 inhabitants in 1660, it grew rapidly, first because of the enormous influx of building workers as the royal palace began to take shape and then because of the removal of the court there in 1682, with all the attendant services and specialised trades. By the end of the reign Versailles was a major city of between 25,000 and 32,000 inhabitants, but it clearly did not have a normal balanced economy, as shown by the fact that over a third of all marriages and deaths recorded were of servants. Even then, much of the royal administrative personnel had remained behind in Paris, so that these figures represent only part of the total number of individuals attached to or surrounding the monarchy.[10]

The French monarchy fostered what was undoubtedly an extreme example of court opulence and size, but the wider repercussions of the growth of the state were felt in many of the political centres of Europe. The demand for entertainment, cultural and educational facilities, luxury goods and colonial imports increased with the number of professional, administrative and court-related inhabitants (or noble and gentry visitors), as did the demand for services of all kinds, from domestics or temporary accommodation to legal, business or medical services at all levels. Capital cities thus became major centres of social life for the better-off, thereby also attracting large numbers of skilled or unskilled workers who had found provincial opportunities too restrictive. The prime example of this is, of course, Restoration London, whose rapid growth meant that by the end of the seventeenth century it housed one in every ten Englishmen. The West End was dominated by the rich and the 'political nation', the central parishes were increasingly the preserve of the commercial elite, while the East End and the periphery were full of high-density habitation for migrant labour and the poor. The slums, with their rapidly changing population mostly coming from outside London, were particularly prone to swamping the resources and competence of the city administration, making them danger zones in terms both of epidemics and of agitation.

Paris did not grow at anything like the rate of London, nor did the French court abandon its peripatetic traditions until the construction of Versailles, but the city nevertheless experienced distinctive developments and problems. In spite of the presence in France of competing commercial, cultural and social centres in the provinces, many nobles and high-ranking office-holders built their own townhouses or *hôtels* in Paris with much greater extravagance than their English counterparts. At the same time, the hazards posed by the poorer quarters were recognised to such an extent that the *Conseil de Police* of 1666–7 appointed a new executive Lieutenant of Police to head an administration which was separated from the judiciary of the city. The first incumbent of this office, Nicholas Gabriel de la Reynie, initiated strong repressive measures against the underworld, notably by raiding in 1667 the '*Cour des Miracles*', a criminal slum so named because of the instantaneous cure experienced there by 'invalid' beggars on their return home. The writer Sauval, who had seen the *Cour des Miracles* before La Reynie's onslaught, said that to get there 'one must often lose oneself in the narrow, wretched, stinking, unfrequented streets; to enter it one must descend a long, tortuous, uneven slope. I saw there a half-buried mud hut, not even four *toises* (*c.* 7 metres) square, tottering from old age and rottenness, where were nevertheless lodged more than fifty households encumbered with an infinity of children – legitimate, natural and stolen.' Clearly the area was a genuine urban slum, for all the mockery implied in its name.

La Reynie also extended and improved the night-watch system, and even took the first steps towards organising a proper street-lighting system financed by means of the 1667 *taxe des boues et lanternes* (mud and lantern tax). This tax was to provide for over 5000 lanterns lit until 2 in the morning from 20 October to 31 March, and the system, once consolidated, not only greatly increased safety in the main streets but also attracted the admiration of foreign visitors as the first of its kind in Europe (the Dutch were experimenting with their own system for Amsterdam, implemented fully in 1670). La Reynie and his no less energetic successors in office, helped by a reorganised group of 48 *commissaires*, also gained wide powers over the provisioning of the capital, market regulations, price control, urban immigration and other potential threats to the maintenance of law, stability and order: the Parisian force became the prototype 'police' organisation in Europe, in the *ancien-régime* sense of that word.[11]

The urban poor

Citizenship, guild membership and participation in the corporate life and privileges of towns were, as we have seen, invariably circumscribed by restrictions regarding wealth, property-ownership, residence, skilled qualifications and other criteria of 'respectability'. The wealthy patrician families constituted the narrow top end of the urban social scale (often merging into the nobility of one kind or another), while ordinary established craftsmen, guild members, traders, small-scale entrepreneurs, petty officials and shopkeepers made up the middle layer. Below them, every town had a very large number of inhabitants who were underprivileged and largely unprotected, in effect non-citizens even if they had lived all their life within the walls. This 'urban proletariat' of the pre-industrial era included unskilled labourers (those who had not had the opportunity, ability or persever-ance to qualify for a guild-regulated trade), domestic and personal servants, and those who, owning no significant personal property, lived in often overcrowded rented accommodation. Many journeymen also fell into this category, as did footloose ex-apprentices and others in various occasional employment or without work. Although guilds may have operated a closed-shop policy in many trades, there is evidence to suggest that some sectors used unregulated subsidiary labour for a number of initial stages in production. The textile indus-try, for example, needed a considerable amount of preparatory work which could readily be done by semi-skilled workers within an urban putting-out system. The numbers so employed are very difficult to establish, but tentative evidence from the textile industry in as well-controlled a community as Venice suggests that certain branches employed as many hands outside guild protection as within it.[12] Whereas most guilds made some provision for relief for poor members, unregulated labour was defenceless in times of market slump or personal misfortune, and could only turn to begging or to one of the public works projects which municipal authorities attempted to organise from time to time in the early modern period.

At the lowest end of the scale were the genuinely marginal groups: casual labourers, prostitutes, minstrels, the disabled poor, pilgrims, soldiers and deserters, genuine or fraudulent beggars, and various types of criminal poor – all to some extent rejected by society (the disabled and pilgrims too, if a community was under stress), all victims of discrimination, repression and bad luck, and for the most part unlikely to achieve significant upward social mobility. Because of their marginal position, they have left only occasional and one-sided marks in the records, most commonly if they were arrested for vagrancy or for some other offence. Such evidence is necessarily insufficient either for numerical analysis or for any real appreciation of the subculture of the poor (if such a subculture existed).[13] All that we can say with some degree of certainty is that the marginal elements in western European society were difficult to control and geographically surprisingly mobile. Many congregated in towns: the population of a quiet provincial town such as Beauvais included 10 per cent outsiders, and in a major new port such as Brest more than half the population in the later half of the seventeenth century were immigrants, though not all poor.

Given the absence of reliable statistical material and the arbitrary nature of contemporary estimates, it is not possible to measure either urban or rural poverty at any time during the seventeenth century in any meaningful way. But all the evidence, be it tax rolls (like that of Beauvais in 1696 or the English Hearth Tax assessments from the 1660s), church records, the observations of King and Vauban, or those of Italian city health officials, point broadly in the same direction: towards a chronic and unsurmountably overwhelming social problem. Serious enough in the countryside, where the poor might at least have the advantage of access to a bit of land or to the commons and might be reasonably well integrated into a local community, poverty and begging in towns more often went with uprooting, loneliness, real destitution and disease. The poor quarter of many cities, such as the East End of London and its extra-mural outgrowths, might perhaps have some community identity, albeit a grim one. The so-called *Cour de Miracles* in Paris even had a certain mystique, until La Reynie launched his police on it in 1667. But for the majority of the poor, urban life is likely to have been a fairly hopeless struggle for survival, their prospects and security varying with bread prices and the state of the labour market, their control over events virtually nil.

Provided not too great an expectation of accuracy is raised, it is possible to compile certain crude estimates of subsistence standards. If one assumes a minimal daily food requirement of 2000 kilocalories for one not very tall, moderately active adult (modern recommendations suggest slightly more for sedentary women and between 2500 and 3500 or more for men, depending on the type of work, body size and other factors) and if one assumes that wholemeal bread, containing as it does a good proportion of protein as well as carbohydrate and a little fat, could provide a staple (if not very balanced) diet sufficient for survival for those not able to afford more expensive nutrients, then each adult would need the equivalent of just over 220 kg of wheat per year, or 0.6 kg of wheat per day, making just under 1 kg of daily bread when baked. At average London wholesale prices of wheat in the later seventeenth century, the cost of feeding one adult on wheat bread alone for one year would cost around £2 in stable periods, £3 on average in bad years such as 1693–7, and perhaps £5 at such times if the person were doing heavy manual work in the building trades or similar, and consuming 3000 kilocalories per day at the very least. No doubt this calorific intake could be achieved more cheaply using other cereals for gruel and barley for beer, but allowance also needs to be made in the opposite direction for retail mark-up and the cost of baking or brewing. All additional foods, including the relatively scarce milk, vegetables, butter and pulses, were normally more expensive on the urban market compared with their calorific value. Thus we can suggest that a labouring family of four with growing children might, if relying primarily on wheat bread, be able to survive on a cereal expenditure of some £9 when prices were stable or £14 when prices were high. Such averages do not, of course, reveal the short-term hardship caused by more considerable fluctuations in the price of cereals on a week-to-week basis. Nor could the cost of fuel, clothing and rent be altogether avoided if destitution were to be kept at bay, and these items may (according to Brown and Hopkins, or according to Abel for the end of the early modern period) have added 20–25 per cent to the basic cost of subsistence at any time during the pre-industrial period. Keith Wrightson and David Levine, working on the English village of Terling at the end of the century, found that the total hypothetical expenditure for a family of five, according to the overseers of the poor there, would be £13 4s. including food, clothing and a little fuel and rent – rural evidence, of course, but some indication that these estimates may not be totally out of proportion.[14]

Wages for urban labourers naturally varied considerably, but the nominal builders' wage in southern England cited by Brown and Hopkins, namely around 1s. per day in the later seventeenth century for an ordinary labourer, is not inconsistent with other evidence. If such a labourer could work for 200 days during the year, that would make £10. If he was more skilled, earning 1s. 6d. a day, and managing to find work for 250 days in one year (probably as much as was normally possible when seasonal slack was largely avoided), he could reach £19. Even allowing women and children some earning capacity, it is clear that a labouring family was dangerously close to the basic bread subsistence costs suggested above. Interestingly, these figures are not incompatible with Gregory King's assumption that an annual family income of £20 marked a low threshold below which was poverty, while an income of £40 was needed to 'increase the wealth of the kingdom' or give some surplus for saving.

If we turn to France, we can cite Vauban's contemporary estimate made on similar premises. In the *Dîme Royale*, Vauban cites the typical income and outgoings of a weaver and his family. The weaver may earn 12 sous per working day, but will lose Sundays, holidays and other time when he needs to go to the market, plus some days of illness perhaps, leaving him only 180 real working days per year (a rather pessimistic estimate by comparison with other trades, it seems, but Vauban may have allowed for the substantial fluctuations in demand in the textile sector, equivalent to the 'fallow' periods in, for example, the building trades). Vauban does not give the full outlay of a weaver family, but cites those for an unskilled rural labourer earning 9 sous a day or just under 90 livres per annum for the same number of working days. From this would be deducted 3 to 6 livres in war tax (we are dealing with the 1690s) and nearly 9 livres for the obligatory salt purchases for a family of four, leaving 75 livres. The bread cereal for such a family, which Vauban describes as being half wheat and half rye, would amount to 10 Paris *setiers* (15½ hectolitres) costing 60 livres. (This volume of grain, 43 bushels, would weigh approximately 1300 kg and feed four people, suggesting once more that the initial estimates above were absolute minima; 6 livres per *setier*, on the other hand, must be regarded as an optimistic low price appropriate for years with good harvests.) The 15 livres left over would have to be supplemented by earnings on the side and by his wife's earnings (not readily quantified) to cover all other family expenditure, including rent, clothing and the few household goods that he could afford.[15]

We are evidently dealing with very rough, almost impressionistic, estimates with a large margin of possible error and subject to significant regional and individual variation. Nevertheless, it is clearly apparent that bread cereal alone could absorb an overwhelming part of the disposable income of families at the lower end of the earnings scale, even before taking account of accident or illness. If one adopts the most basic criterion of poverty for the pre-industrial period, namely the food-purchasing power of daily or weekly wages earned by a labourer with his family, it is readily apparent that statistical quantification of the underemployed and unemployed 'conjunctural' poor (as opposed to the permanent structural poor such as the old, invalids and abandoned children) would need to be done on a weekly or similarly short-term basis: if the threshold of poverty is, say, at the point where a family of four spends four-fifths or more of its disposable income on bread (as Gutton suggests), then the number below this line will vary enormously in line with short-term price fluctuations as well as over the medium term, and will fluctuate quite considerably even from year to year, creating psychological stresses and fears as potent as poverty itself. Even price increases of 30–50 per cent, moderate by the standards of crisis years, could have devastating effects on the type of family budget suggested above, and, by extension, could endanger law and order. During severe crises, the predicament of the poor was far worse: in the Halles market in Paris, the price of good wheat, normally between 10 and 14 livres tournois per *setier*, and priced at 13½ l.t. at the beginning of January 1649, tripled in price by the end of the month and quadrupled by March, whilst the slightly cheaper poorer qualities of wheat, and the rye normally priced between 5 and 8 l.t., experienced fully comparable increases over the same period. March prices for wheat and rye were in fact two and a half times the average for that already bad agricultural year as a whole (August 1648 to July 1649), emphasising the extent to which such averages conceal the worst short-term crises.

Rioting and crime

Food riots were endemic all over the continent in the seventeenth century. Not many have been analysed in great detail, but some that have indicate the complex interplay of practical, psychological and local political factors in the short-term perspective. The sequence of grain riots in Maldon in Essex in 1629, studied by J. Walter and K. Wrightson, is a clear example of the kind of moderate direct action taken by the poorer inhabitants of a small town and its environs during a spring of anxiety when trade had slumped, grain prices were rising after an inadequate harvest, and unemployment was becoming critical, especially amongst textile workers. Initial popular protests against the export of grain from Maldon, deliberately underscored by the local authorities in their report to the central government, led to some half-hearted Privy Council directives. By March, however, it was apparent that no effective measures were being taken, so over a hundred women (including some from surrounding villages) boarded a Flemish grain ship and demanded the surrender of token amounts of rye from the cargo which had been loaded there. The subsequent belated arrests of the ringleaders resulted in no serious action: instead the local authorities in effect recognised the legitimacy of the women's protest by purchasing the cargo for distribution and by stressing the severity of the economic situation to the central government. As the economic situation deteriorated, and the Crown did nothing beyond pointing to a hopelessly inadequate poor-law system, rioting escalated in May, still led by women but this time including male participation. The response was swift: eight leaders were tried and three soon hanged, and heavy ideological pressure was applied via the pulpit and the judicial system. Clearly the threat to property and to law and order had become too much for the better-off. Nevertheless, the rioters had scored some success in that restrictions on grain exports were now actually enforced (with merchant middlemen conveniently blamed for the trouble), and special care was taken the following year to secure satisfactory grain supplies to the area. As Walter and Wrightson emphasise, limited once-off rioting was considered legitimate if the authorities manifestly needed prompting, and it was only the repetition of unrest on a more threatening scale that brought severe reprisals. Despite the executions, the social order was in the end reaffirmed. Even the Crown had been forced into action, and indeed, after the worst was over in Maldon and elsewhere, a codified and extended series of regulations on food marketing, disease and poverty for the whole of England was drawn up and published in 1630–1 in the form of Books of Orders.

Supply- or price-fixing riots were most likely to occur in towns and where substantial movement of grain occurred, or when rumours and perhaps administrative actions generated fears of shortage. At their simplest, such confrontations could consist merely of a direct attack on a grain conveyance and an on-the-spot deal between the transporter and the attackers, or the ransacking of a flour mill or of a baker's shop by hungry and aggrieved locals, often with some form of 'fair price' imposed on the victim. Women were frequently prominent, perhaps because of their responsibility for children, perhaps because of their ambiguous position in law which meant that they were more leniently treated by the authorities. Only when individual incidents got out of hand, and random thefts, pillaging or other forms of crowd action occurred, were authorities forced to act; and then, especially in an urban environment, the outcome was very unpredictable.[16]

The period from the 1620s through the 1650s was a disturbed one in much of Europe. France alone experienced over 100 urban revolts of varying degrees of severity in the quarter century before the outbreak of the Fronde in 1648 (see chapter 2) but most of these were caused by more complex factors and grievances than just food prices. Political factors were particularly prominent in the major urban revolts in many parts of Europe in the 1640s, such as those in Barcelona in 1640, Palermo and Naples in 1647 and Bordeaux in 1648–53, which will be discussed in the context of the mid-century crisis (see chapter 7). But even where there were major grievances such as the burden of taxation, governments never forgot that a food crisis could easily spark off rioting which might otherwise have been contained. Repressive political measures were thus naturally combined with attempts to prevent sudden and drastic increases in the price of basic commodities. The control of grain supplies to cities was the most obvious first step, and cities like Venice had long since set up public granaries to help stabilise market prices in the case of short-term emergencies. This method was also adopted in Geneva, parts of the Netherlands and elsewhere, although effectiveness was inevitably proportional to actual reserves available per head of population. The existence of such a grain reserve could, however, itself add to the risk of panic-buying and hoarding, and this was one of the reasons why Paris, for example, did not attempt to establish public reserves until the eighteenth century, and then only furtively. Even so, the French government watched the grain trade with great vigilance, and was prepared to (and was indeed expected to) act in the case of serious shortfall, commonly during the critical period in spring and early summer when the new harvest was not yet ready and when price riots were most likely to occur. Louis XIV thus ordered costly long-distance grain purchases from Danzig and elsewhere in 1662 to relieve public anxiety when the price of the standard loaf rose to 8 sous. The Crown even arranged for special baking, and proceeded to sell the King's Bread at 2½ sous, an action which could also conveniently be

used to magnify the popular image of the monarch. A similar operation was undertaken briefly in 1693.

From the point of view of authority, such panics about food prices
were of major and continuing concern. But for the poor, and especially the urban poor, less dramatic times of hardship could in some
ways be as bad, because there might be no alternative to begging or
petty theft (or a combination of the two). Obviously, many forms of
crime were quite unrelated to material circumstances, and criminal
records themselves present a number of pitfalls for the historian in
terms of contemporary definitions and concepts, inconsistencies in
the implementation of the law and of punishments, and the implicit
social selectiveness of the cases themselves. It is quite difficult to get
an overall impression of how petty crime was spread out across seventeenth-century society: the records are not representative, in part
because rural communities could deal with certain types of unorganised crime at minimal cost and disruption by avoiding recourse to the
law altogether, whilst in urban society it often went unreported.
Overall, however, small-scale theft in urban communities probably
fluctuated to some extent in accordance with the price of food, the
level of wages and the availability of work – that is, in relation to material hardship.[17] The relationship is not a simple one: certain external
circumstances, such as wartime recruitment or demobilisation, could
have a dramatic impact on crime rates, and towns whose size and
importance created greater opportunities and greater actual inequalities of wealth probably also experienced a disproportionately high
theft rate. Urban poverty- and deprivation-motivated crime, perhaps
slightly more so than rural variants, could look like an act of defiance,
and this in turn helps to explain the growing anxiety amongst the
better-off about crime in general, and larceny in particular. The severity of punishments – for example, hanging for theft – inflicted for
what we would now regard as minor offences reflects the determination of the better-off to use deterrence to protect their property, but
it needs to be added that courts often avoided rigorous interpretation
of individual cases in order to mitigate the law.

Leaving aside cases of morality and witchcraft, cases of theft
(alongside lesser property offences such as trespass) were easily those
most commonly tried in seventeenth-century law-courts. In Essex
between 1620 and 1680 property offences appear five times as often in
the records as assault. In the countryside most theft was opportunis-
tic, commonly perpetrated by the resident poor, by migrants or by
vagrants, and rarely involved either much violence or (except in
remote and forest areas prone to highway robbery) any recognisable
conspiratorial underworld. Small towns may not have been very
different, but it is reasonable to expect to find a greater element of
violent robbery and gang organisation in larger cities and capitals. In

Madrid in the later seventeenth century the total of recorded assaults and murders far outnumbered that of ordinary thefts, and although these incidents were by no means all caused by the lower social orders, vagrants and soldiers certainly played a large part.[18] Given the greater opportunities and lesser risks of committing theft in bigger towns, and the tendency of migrants and the unemployed to congregate there in the early modern period, it is clear why urban authorities regarded vagrancy as a problem of growing urgency.

All over Europe, the vagrant was habitually assumed to be idle out of choice, and was seen as a threat to society and a rebel against its values. Cyclical economic explanations of poverty were not clearly understood, and the equally devastating impact of warfare was most commonly regarded as an inevitable fact of life. Contemporary writers therefore tended to adopt a strident and moralistic, but rarely analytical, approach to the problem, whilst the typically repressive responses adopted by local authorities show little sign of any effort to understand the problem. Charges of vagrancy were easy to make because of the intrinsic weakness of the defendant. The unending attempts at legislation on vagrancy across Europe, from at least the sixteenth century onwards, testify to the growing concern at municipal and national level. Amongst the most extreme policies adopted in the west was the Scottish Act of 1606 and the sequence of degrading parliamentary statutes there up to 1672, giving employers the right to seize vagabonds and enserf them for life to work coal-mines, lead-mines, salt pans and other enterprises. But everywhere there were attempts forcibly to eliminate idleness and especially to immobilise unskilled labour through attempted enforcement of the use of testimonials and passports even for local travel. Specific legislation was regularly renewed: the Vagrancy Act of 1657 in England, elaborating and repeating Elizabethan legislation on the registration of vagrants; the decrees of 1666 and the late 1680s issued by Louis XIV's government to define vagrancy and its penalties; the very severe Swedish statutes of labourers of 1664 and 1686; and the innumerable other examples from just about every administration in Europe, with more to follow during the eighteenth century. Draconian though much of this vagrancy legislation was on paper, practical implementation was quite different. Attempts were sometimes made by means of sudden campaigns of arrests, such as that in England in the 1630s ostensibly involving 26,000 vagrants in 37 counties, where punishments could range from flogging to transportation or impressment. But, on the whole, geographic mobility amongst the migrant and vagrant population was far too great to allow effective local control, particularly with regard to the bigger towns and their wider catchment area. Of the vagrants recorded in Colchester in 1630–64, 14 per cent claimed places of origin more than 200 miles away. There was already a significant emigration of Irish to

England and the continent, just as the Netherlands attracted labour from poorer agricultural areas such as the west of Jutland. Paul Slack's study of vagrants in England in the early seventeenth century reveals that the opportunities to exploit urban and suburban conditions to evade settlement regulations ensured that towns (and especially London) were an important stage on the road from the temporary unemployment of runaway servants or the underemployment of unskilled labourers, minstrels and pedlars, to the permanent long-distance pauper vagrancy from which there was little chance of rehabilitation. It was this latter group that was the real object of attempted repression – in contrast to the probably larger number of genuine economic migrants who had some chance of betterment and who could be welcomed by urban communities. It is still too early to say whether contemporaries were greatly exaggerating the problem in order to provide an excuse for administrative ineffectiveness. The 651 vagrants (including 51 children) recorded in Salisbury in 1598–1638, the 237 in Colchester in 1630–64, and the 161 expelled from Norwich in 1630–5 (at a time when the former two cities had around 7000 inhabitants each and Norwich twice that) are evidently only the tip of the iceberg of urban poverty.[19]

Charitable responses to urban poverty

The traditional Christian responses to the needs of the poor, namely individual acts of charity, donations and legacies to charitable foundations, and various forms of philanthropic work, were still the principal forms of assistance during the seventeenth century. Very broadly speaking, giving to the poor was for Protestants primarily a social and Christian responsibility, and the intention was often to provide practical help for all those in extreme need. For Catholics, charity was also a means of salvation for the donor, so it is natural to assume that a greater respect for unorganised alms-giving and for the mendicant poor might prevail in southern Catholic Europe. But in practice there was general agreement both in Catholic and Protestant states that the structural or 'deserving' poor, that is, those unable to work because of old age, disability, disease or other accidental factors, together with orphaned and abandoned children, should be given more helpful and charitable treatment than the 'unworthy' poor, those who were deemed capable of work but were unemployed or 'idle' in a socially unacceptable way. Contemporaries wrote and thought about ways of handling both these categories – institutionalising the 'deserving' poor in hospitals or looking after them by means of outdoors or home relief, sometimes identifying them by means of a special mark or pauper's tag; protecting especially single women and children to prevent their falling into crime and prostitution; providing protected work or forced labour for those who needed it; somehow sending strangers and vagrants 'home' to their parish of birth so as to concentrate relief resources on the resident poor only – with, in some instances, the ultimate aim of removing beggars from the streets. But lacking accurate information either on the poor themselves or on the economic framework of the time, no writer or reformer before the economic crises of the 1690s seriously tackled the underlying causes of conjunctural poverty or even identified what they were. Perhaps all attempts at solving the problem of poverty were in any case bound to fail: both the social conventions and the economic limitations of the period militated against substantial reform.

Private charity and even institutional work during the seventeenth century is once again difficult to quantify. The pioneering attempt for England by W. K. Jordan met with substantial criticism, particularly regarding his ideological insistence on the positive impact of 'puritanism', and his faith in the supposedly growing significance of merchant and gentry contributions during the sixteenth and early seventeenth centuries relative to those of the old noble and clerical elite. His statistical work, purporting to show an absolute growth in charitable bequests, particularly during the early Stuart period, has also been challenged in several fundamental respects. Inflation, the growth in population and the probably disproportionate increase in urban poverty during the later sixteenth and early seventeenth centuries is likely to have outweighed increases in the nominal value of bequests, even if their actual yield may have increased by accumulation. There does, however, appear to have been a detectable swing towards secular aims amongst donors, with greater interest shown in independent education, orphan care, loan funds for poor craftsmen, aid for prisoner rehabilitation, and similar developments. But these private bequests, even at the best times, never exceeded perhaps ½ per cent of national income; in other words, they were derisory by comparison with the scale of the problem of poverty itself.[20]

Private charity and independent institutional relief via religious orders and confraternities played an old and well-established role in Catholic Mediterranean countries. In Spain, although the desirability of state intervention and public administration of poor relief was recognised in theory by writers such as Juan de Mariana (1599), earlier practical attempts had been thwarted by jurisdictional disputes and other obstacles, and little was done in practice during the seventeenth century. Only in the second half of the eighteenth century were public poorhouses established in Madrid, and in the meantime the Crown restricted itself to a few orphanages and hospitals, together with the usual ineffective legislation against vagrancy and criminality. The power and resources of the many religious orders, the massive charitable handouts of the Church, and the growth in corporate charity ensured that there was little scope for public or secular initiative, or indeed for rationalisation. Outdoor relief, as far as we can judge from the work done on the subject, remained a very prominent part of urban life in the Iberian peninsula, so much so that vagrants and the poor from southern France and other parts of Europe apparently went to Spain in considerable numbers (no doubt in the process adding to the area's reputation for brigandage so vividly portrayed in the typically Spanish literary form, the picaresque novels of Mateo Alemán, Quevedo and Cervantes). Administrative ineffectiveness, remoteness and economic hardship all aggravated lawlessness not only in Spain but also in similar conditions elsewhere in the Mediterranean, in wartorn Germany and the Rhineland; it even made contemporaries see gypsies and gangs as evidence of the existence of an international brotherhood of beggars. Descriptions of the brotherhood's organisation, special language and elaborate tricks were literary commonplaces in the sixteenth century, and could still be found in works by the Dominican friar Nobili (*Il vagabondo*, 1627), by Frianoro (same title, 1621, published in French in 1644) and many others. But whether such a brotherhood existed outside the imagination of contemporaries increasingly conscious of the failure of society to deal with the social consequences of poverty is open to doubt.

Spain was probably exceptional for the administrative abdication of its secular authorities in the face of poverty. Venice, by contrast, gives a clear indication that a Catholic government could be as functional and practical as any in the handling of charity and relief in the early modern period. As Brian Pullan and others have shown, the wealthy Venetian *Scuole Grandi* had during the sixteenth century taken on a wide range of organised relief, including hospital work, provision of medicine, and payment of dowries for poor girls to secure respectable marriage. They also reinforced the political status quo by means of their formal and processional functions. Although continuing to emphasise charity for religious motives, the state imposed an increasingly discriminating and pragmatic approach towards the poor, encouraging the careful administration of private funds by means of corporate institutions and boards. This combination of motives also dominated the *monti di pietà* (charitable pawnshops) to which the respectable poor in the mainland provinces of the Republic of Venice (as in other north Italian city-states) could turn when they needed a loan to tide them over a difficult period. In addition, the state had a large requirement for spare manpower in the navy, to which the poor could either be attracted via the Scuole on a relatively voluntary basis or be consigned forcibly as vagrants. Venice clearly recognised the need for state intervention in matters of health and poor relief in order to maintain law and order, and had even levied compulsory poor rates in periods of crisis as early as 1528 and 1576. There can be no doubt that all these developments helped the state to weather the trading and financial difficulties which hit the Mediterranean in the early seventeenth century.

France relied very largely on private charity which, during our period, was mostly channelled through a proliferation of foundations and special institutions which dominated the urban scene until the 1760s, when financial problems and more secular attitudes brought change. Amongst these institutions were the old town hospitals, some dating from the leprosy epidemics of the Middle Ages and traditionally expected to care for the ill in general. By the seventeenth century they were often able to organise additional charitable work thanks to specific earmarked donations and bequests. Other forms of charitable activity also grew during the period, aimed at reducing the need for simple begging. Aix-en-Provence, for example, benefited from a spate of new foundations in the 1630s and 1680s, which, as Cissie Fairchilds emphasises, were mostly secular and entirely private non-governmental initiatives. Contemporaries were no doubt acutely aware of the dire need for more relief during the disruptive second quarter of the century, prompted as they were by the mood of the later Counter-Reformation and by the work of various new confraternities and societies. An austere and unofficial association of vigilante moral reformers known as the Company of the Holy Sacrament was developed in the 1630s specifically to ensure a greater emphasis on the religious message in charitable work, rather than its material aspects. But the Jesuits took a more practical line in their encouragement of local initiatives to set up *bureaux de charité* (charity distribution centres) to pool alms and redistribute food and clothing. Added to the religious motivation, however, was also a growing concern over the frequent breakdown of order and stability from the 1620s onwards in France (as elsewhere), producing not only additions to the flow of legislation on vagrancy already discussed but also a search for more effective institutions to control the poor. A regulative and disciplinarian approach clearly, according to French evidence, met with support not just amongst the wealthy urban minority but also amongst the substantial number of ordinary craftsmen, shopkeepers and even journeymen or servants (including a large number of women) who subscribed modest but significant sums to all the varieties of institutionalised poor relief being developed, or who deposited savings in the popular charity *rentes* (perpetual loans to an institution in return for a low rate of interest). These contributors were clearly satisfied that an institutional administration of charitable resources allowed a more discriminating and functional approach to aid. Given the absence of any clear recognition of the economic and social causes of unemployment, it is not surprising that benefactors and donors accepted and strengthened the emphasis on helping the structural 'deserving' poor, especially women and children, whilst the rest, the able-bodied who were merely out of work, would be lucky to get much significant assistance beyond what they could extract by begging or by other means.

Official urban poor relief

Public poor relief throughout Europe was tackled very much on these basic premises. Contemporary attitudes to relief measures for the poor varied, as one would expect, over a wide spectrum. Traditional and medieval notions of Christian charity were still voiced during this period. Some writers added that, while equal sharing of property was in practice out of the question, everyone had a duty to ensure that no member of a community lacked the basic essentials of life. At the other end of the scale, Sir Francis Brewster voiced an all too familiar attitude in the 1690s when, speaking of the Elizabethan poor law, he noted:

> There is no Nation I ever read of, who by a Compulsory Law, raiseth so much money for the Poor as *England* doth: That of *Holland* is Voluntary ... but our Charity is become a Nusance, and may be the greatest Mistake of that Blessed Reign, in which that Law was passed, which is the Idle and Improvident Mans Charter.

The practical solutions worked out in different parts of Europe suggest wide recognition of at least the symptoms, but there were major practical obstacles.

The English poor-law system is of special interest because of two unusual ingredients: the early appearance of a compulsory poor levy or rate and the substantial degree of government direction already apparent during the Elizabethan period. Neither was a total success but they did set precedents for other European countries in their efforts to rationalise relief operations and control the perceived social threat from the underprivileged. The English poor rate had emerged gradually over the sixteenth century, with an element of compulsion in some towns from at least 1552. Casual alms-giving was discouraged and restrictions reaffirmed on wandering paupers, the intention being to make each parish responsible for its own resident poor. These principles were codified and elaborated in the Acts of 1597 and 1601, but none of the legislation was very specific regarding the actual assessment and collection of the compulsory levy. It appears, however, that the system did become established in many parishes by the time of Charles I (who, thanks to Laud and Wentworth, took some interest in its implementation in the 1630s), with county and borough magistrates supervising local arrangements, appointing overseers of the poor, and auditing the accounts of the funds handled. Various systems of assessment appear to have been tried, usually based on the value of property in the parish and the means of its occupants but evidently leading to much controversy over claimed imbalances and omissions. Nevertheless, it is clear that when funds were collected by this means (the rate was in many areas levied only in times of need) they far outweighed those derived from charity and bequests, giving England a much more substantial relief system than any other major European state.[21] The needs of the poor were assessed, and those considered eligible were given aid in the form of food, clothing, money or rent rebates, together with assistance for children where appropriate, the levy being scaled according to the amounts needed rather than the other way round. There were of course problems, especially because the system relied on reasonably efficient local overseers, but its decentralisation could also be a virtue in that organised relief seems to have continued functioning even through the interregnum. The need for houses of correction for the able-bodied unemployed was also recognised early on, and provisions made in the Act of 1610. But just as the Elizabethan local works projects and the municipal houses of correction (such as the London Bridewell founded in 1553) had achieved uncertain results, so it proved difficult to find effective solutions in the second quarter of the seventeenth century for those already unemployed because of the depression in certain sectors of the economy. The London Corporation of the Poor did set up an orphanage in 1649, which appears to have worked well, but it was closed at the Restoration in 1660. Only at the end of the century were permanent workhouses established, starting with that in Bristol founded in 1696. In practice, many able-bodied poor were consequently given relief like other parish poor, making the simple distinction between deserving and idle poor difficult to maintain. This compounded the problems associated with determining the residential qualification imposed on the poor: the law discouraged mobility of labour and, following the legislation on settlement of 1662, migrant workers had to carry a certificate from their home parish guaranteeing their eligibility for relief there if it became necessary. These certificate regulations, which clearly underscored the reluctance of any parish to take on more than the minimum number of resident poor, were elaborated between 1685 and 1697 because of the number of disputes and the amount of litigation they caused. Mobility gradually became easier, but relief for the able-bodied remained controversial.

The Scottish poor law was quite similar in legislative origins, but developed along pragmatic lines significantly different from those in England. Poor relief was central to the kirk's functions, while lay authority was generally reluctant to impose compulsory poor-rating or to build workhouses for the unemployed. Short periods of assessment did occur to deal with specific emergencies, but otherwise church and charitable funds continued to provide what relief was available, generally on a much more Spartan level than south of the border, to take into account the relative poverty of most Scottish parishes. Most of the Scottish poor law remained a pipedream typical of the limitations of seventeenth-century government.

Although no direct taxation for the poor was adopted nationally in *ancien-régime* France, most townsmen who had any means were expected to contribute to relief, if not before their death then at least in their wills. Following shifts in emphasis and incipient laicisation during the sixteenth century, the tendency was now towards more carefully organised and institution-centred poor relief designed to make the most of resources. Prominent amongst the experiments of the period was the *hôpital général* (a blanket term used for institutions whose principal function was as a poorhouse, as distinct from the traditional hospitals or hospices for the sick, often known as *hôtels Dieu*). Following the Dutch example and some abortive earlier attempts in Paris and elsewhere, Lyons set up one of the first relatively successful *hôpitaux généraux* in 1614, financed in part through a cumulative funding of most private alms and bequests, in part through the grant of certain privileges or revenues (a wine tax in Lyon). The Lyon institution, characteristically for this type of foundation, combined almost monastic Christian indoctrination of the inmates with a work routine either imposed within the hospital precincts or in special workshops and projects set up for the purpose. Similar attempts were made in other French cities during the 1630s and 1640s, and after the Fronde the Crown took up the idea in the hope of securing sufficient local and municipal involvement to remove all types of beggars from the streets without direct state involvement or expenditure. Under pressure from the Company of the Holy Sacrament, and contrary to the specific intentions of the religious reformer St Vincent de Paul, the Parisian *hôpital général* planned in the 1650s and formally created by edict in 1656 was granted powers of compulsory internment for all beggars. This Paris institution, formed through the amalgamation of several earlier foundations of different types and in part financed by a compulsory poor rate in the city, was to be governed by 26 directors with policing and punitive powers, and the intention was to cover both 'deserving' and 'idle' poor by providing simple work to keep the fit occupied. The edict and its legislative sequels over the next decades in fact emphasised the desire to eradicate vagrancy, criminality and prostitution, and postulated harsh penalties for those who were fit but remained without work. In special circumstances, for example during the economic crisis of 1693–4, the *hôpital général* even co-operated with the Parlement of Paris to provide public work-projects for 3000 or more able-bodied beggars, but such initiatives were invariably only temporary because of shortage of funds.[22]

Repression, mercantilist insistence on productive labour, and Christian charity were conveniently rolled into one. Illusions about the Paris *hôpital général*, however, were soon dispelled, as resistance to the archers who were supposed to round up the poor increased and as rumours even spread that some of the inmates were being deported to America. Colbert appears to have been ambivalent about such deportations, but they did occur fairly regularly until 1720. By the end of the seventeenth century, of the 10,000 or so inmates that the various sections of the Paris institution housed, the great majority were unfit through age, disease, mental disturbance or because they were too young to work: the workhouse had become a prison, a dump for misfits or the superfluous.

In 1662, a few years after the opening of the Paris institution, the French Crown issued an ordinance designed to encourage every city in the kingdom to set up its own *hôpital général*. The aim was primarily the 'deserving' poor and orphans, and exclusively those who were long-term residents (not rural immigrants), but no clear formal distinctions were made regarding the conjunctural 'idle' poor. The Crown evidently again hoped that such institutions, endowed with a royal charter and certain privileges, would attract enough funds and donations to work without state support. The Jesuits helped to encourage local initiatives, and nursing staff was usually quite readily available at low cost from the rapidly growing female religious orders such as the Sisters of Charity. But there were enough practical difficulties over buildings and funding to make realisation of this plan very slow and halting: the second major exhortative royal ordinance of 1686 merely demonstrated how little progress had been made.

The intended institutionalisation of all types of urban poor in France, however, had the important consequence of making most beggars liable to criminal prosecution under vagrancy legislation. Although in no way enforceable in practice, this approach had the effect of lumping all beggars, 'deserving' or otherwise, more or less in one category at the margin of society. Internment, where attempted, caused tensions and strong feelings of solidarity or religious sympathy amongst the labouring and underprivileged groups in many towns, and even led to occasional attacks on clumsy or unlucky hospital archers. The riot in Lyon in 1675 involved not only artisans and workers but also two noblemen, and a subsequent incident there in 1692 led to the death of one archer.

There was also considerable resistance to the degradation of the old image of Christ as a beggar, but although monastic and other forms of private charity continued into the eighteenth century (especially amongst the many religious orders and confraternities, and in the countryside), the problems of urban poverty were clearly becoming too great for uncoordinated alms–giving and casual relief. Whether even those new urban poorhouses that were actually able to function by the end of the seventeenth century made significant inroads into the problems, however, is open to doubt: some improvement in the distribution and use of resources was achieved in some French towns, but the refusal of the Crown to become involved except in a very indirect way, and the particular reluctance of the royal government to provide any funds, meant that only a minority of the poor could be given assistance of any significance.

If France with its relatively sophisticated administrative system could only begin to touch on urban poverty, it is hardly surprising that other European countries made even less real progress. No one could rival the apparently well-administered institutions for women, orphans, the sick and the unemployed which so impressed visitors to Amsterdam in the seventeenth century and which were financed partly from charity and partly from taxes (including one on the profits of the East India Company). Even the Dutch, however, while being well ahead of their time, had difficulties: there are indications that other towns were less well provided for and that in any case the influx of labour from outside was such that demand for help could never fully be met. Elsewhere in Europe, results were far more meagre. There was no shortage of urban poor laws and legislative efforts, such as the detailed 1683 ordinance on urban poverty in Denmark, with its characteristic call for registration of all claimants, the expulsion of strangers, the creation of work projects, and the appointment of official collectors to avoid the unseemly disorder of street begging. In Brandenburg–Prussia similar legislation from 1687 onwards sought to establish a workhouse where the inmates would contribute to their upkeep by making crude textiles. In addition to the old distinction between so-called 'worthy' beggars and those regarded as wilfully idle, there was also growing recognition that permanent compulsory poor rates such as those in England were becoming indispensable. Some French municipal authorities considered such an approach in the hope of raising more revenue, and in Copenhagen a quarterly levy for the poor was tried in 1630 and discussed again by the reform commission of 1691 (eventually bearing fruit in the Copenhagen poor law of 1708, although it was not properly implemented). Always, however, there was a yawning abyss between legislative intentions and actual practice: funding initiatives invariably met resistance and bureaucratic impediments, and one may at times be forgiven for concluding that the primary intention was to enforce law and order rather than to alleviate the problems of the poor. But, given that reliable information was available neither to contemporary administrators nor to social reformers, it is likely that poverty was simply ignored as long as it did not reach dangerous levels. Ultimately, no one may have been in a position to offer constructive alternatives, for while the severe conjunctural poverty of the decades up to 1650 fortunately did not last, underemployment was still a fundamental barrier to improved living standards at the lower levels of society all over Europe.

7 Provincial revolts, civil war and crises in mid-century Europe

In 1647 the price of wheat in England rose to an unprecedented level, and the yearly average did not fall significantly until 1650. During previous dearths in 1630 and 1637, the price of a secondary staple such as oats had echoed the price of wheat, but only over relatively short periods; now it remained at one and a half times its normal level for much longer. In the grain market in Les Halles in Paris, the price of the best wheat (averaged over an August–July agricultural year) was more than 50 per cent above its normal harvest level for two seasons running in the periods 1625–7, 1630–1 and 1642–4, but this was mild by comparison with a run of six years from 1648 to 1654 when prices were higher than ever before and when the annual average twice reached a level three times the norm for settled years.[1] Here again, oats followed suit, if on a marginally less dramatic scale. As already indicated (see chapter 3), the years 1648–51 were times of widespread food shortages over much of Europe, including not only the north-west and parts of the Mediterranean but also – because of the scale of the shortages – pushing up prices on the markets of east-central Europe. It is no coincidence that one of the major sequences of urban and rural unrest occurred precisely then.

But food shortages and bread riots, although frequently producing unrest, were hardly rare events. More is required to explain the scale of disruption, social as well as political, in many different parts of Europe in the 1640s and 1650s. Major upheavals occurred in Scotland, Ireland and England, as well as in Catalonia and in Portugal, from around 1640; in Naples and Sicily in 1647; in Denmark in 1648 and again in 1660; in France from 1648 through into the early 1650s; in Poland and Muscovy after 1648; in Sweden around 1652; and in many parts of the German lands at the end of the bitter and destructive Thirty Years War. Since the 1950s a vigorous debate has taken place among historians about the precise causes, nature and consequences of what at one stage became known as 'the general crisis of the seventeenth century', in the process producing a considerable range of not always compatible chronological and substantive definitions, and some outright denials of the value of the crisis concept itself.[2] More recently, the debate has overflowed on to neighbouring periods that might be treated as 'general crises', such as the 1680s and, most interestingly, the 1590s.[3]

We should, of course, not expect distinct European states or regions to experience revolts that were more than superficially similar: given differences of development and social structure which were far greater than those prevailing in Europe today, comparison in depth is very difficult. But the debate has also caused disagreement as to whether the words 'crisis', 'revolution' and even the milder 'revolt' are perhaps being used too freely and enthusiastically to retain much meaning. It was only the last of these terms, together with words such as 'rebellion', 'unrest' and 'sedition', that were used in this kind of context by contemporaries.

Perhaps the clearest and most helpful way of using the term 'crisis' is that adopted by T. K. Rabb a generation ago, using medical analogies: a short and sharp phase of deterioration, following on from but distinctly worse than an earlier condition and necessarily leading to a resolution (collapse or recovery).[4] From a political perspective, various forms of deterioration are clearly visible in much of Europe during the 1630s (see chapter 2), and, as we shall see, some of these did culminate in quite unprecedented challenges to established authority in the years around 1648–60. But historians have extended the 'crisis' concept more widely, using it to emphasise the scale of economic difficulties culminating in the 1640s and 1650s, and (perhaps less conclusively) to underline the uncertainties in intellectual and social life brought on by the challenges to authority of every kind experienced in much of western and central Europe.

The terms 'revolt' and 'rebellion' can be regarded as roughly synonymous, and most will agree that such terms apply to a level of protest more serious than 'demonstration' or possibly 'collective resistance'. In the early modern period, revolts often explicitly challenged the way authority was being used or the motives and role of those officials exercising it, and the purpose was to restore an idealised concept of how the community had functioned in the past. In the rarer circumstances where the social and political order itself was violently challenged and where immediate and deliberate change was sought in the hierarchy of authority or in the structure of government, we could legitimately speak of genuine revolutionary potential – and if any such conscious change was implemented (even if only for a short time) the term 'revolution' is appropriate. But it is necessary to avoid imposing twentieth-century concepts of 'revolution' on an age where the desirability of preserving or restoring the past was universally taken for granted: the inherent conservatism of the early modern period in fact makes events such as those in England in the 1640s even more remarkable. Although there were legitimising notions underlying many revolts, there was no revolutionary ideology as such, except perhaps in chiliastic Christianity (the expectation of a second coming). Even radical ideas were invariably held by only small minorities; the actual triggers of unrest in the 1640s were nearly always much more prosaic.

Harvest failures, routinely commonplace though they were on a small scale, could in certain circumstances have significant political overtones, at least within the community itself. Given the increasing interdependence of European markets, such stresses were readily transmitted elsewhere, tending to iron out local differences in basic prices in years of serious shortage. It is significant that although the United Provinces probably experienced little of the stagnation in agricultural output apparently affecting much of the rest of Europe from around the 1620s onwards (see chapter 3) and avoided the worst of the mid-century slumps because of its diversified farming practices, the Amsterdam grain market was nevertheless badly affected in the late 1640s by the harvest failures elsewhere and by disruption in the Baltic. Consequently, Holland had its share of urban popular unrest, culminating in 1650, and some of the other sectors of its economy suffered from the decline in demand usually accompanying times of high food prices. Even if this does not point to a universality of the 'crisis' experience, it does confirm that no part of Europe could entirely escape the scourge of urban poverty, underemployment, vagrancy and mobility of despair so characteristic of most of the seventeenth century and so difficult for municipal authorities to cope with (see chapter 6). The case-studies in this chapter confirm that it was the potential confrontations between the haves and the have-nots that were politically dangerous, rather than simple and regularly recurring harvest failures or demographic crises in themselves.

The short-term vagaries of food prices and grain supplies, extreme though they were in the 1640s and 1650s, need to be examined in the context of two other trends contributing to a climate of uncertainty over a slightly longer period: an apparent stagnation in at least some other sectors of the early modern economy, and the cumulative effect of war impositions. Economic stagnation is visible not only in the rarely measurable domestic industries closely dependent on the agrarian sector, but also in long-distance overseas trade. Chaunu demonstrated that the total value of the trade between Seville and Spanish America began to fall in the third decade of the seventeenth century, but this decline may have been largely the product of Dutch and English infiltration in the Atlantic trade, damaging only to Spain itself. As far as the Baltic trade is concerned, the massive archive resulting from the collection of Sound Tolls by the Danish Crown at Elsinore also presents the historian with difficulties of interpretation but, even allowing for these, there is a steep decline in the total number and tonnage of ships passing through the Sound in the decade after 1618. This may, however, be attributable to short-term production crises in grain and to the severe disruptions of war rather than to the kind of genuine long-term depression in all branches of the Baltic trade noticeable after a brief boom in 1650.[5] But whatever the cause, there is no doubt that some major long-distance trade routes were marked by instability during the second quarter of the century.

To this evidence we can add indications that there was a substantial fall in textile output in some of the established production centres in Europe around the same time, or at any rate between the early seventeenth and early eighteenth centuries. Leiden was affected (except perhaps for its output of *laken* – high-quality broadcloth), as were Lille, Augsburg, Venice and Beauvais. In some instances this was primarily caused not just by the disruption of war but also by a rapid growth of more competitive forms of domestic industrial production in the surrounding countryside; such relocation and reorganisation had a major disturbing effect on the labour market and, in the Mediterranean region at any rate, it was accentuated by a loss of overall economic competitiveness (see chapter 4). Both in trade and in textile production, however, the 'crisis' is a prolonged one, affecting different parts at different times and often anticipating the political crisis of the 1640s by two decades or more. A direct causal link between economic depression and the unrest of the 1640s, therefore, does not seem very convincing.

The other long-term cause of tension and uncertainty was the sequence of wars from the 1620s to 1659. In the first two chapters we observed the degree of monetary disruption and gross fiscal overloading which the Thirty Years War brought in much of the Empire, France, Spain, Denmark and elsewhere. In all the western and central European states there were protests, riots and ultimately in some cases revolts against the fiscal excesses of the state and against related aspects of perceived misgovernment or autocratic high-handedness. As this chapter will show, the most serious challenge to the authority of the state came for most of the belligerents in the west at the very time when war was coming to an end, coinciding not only with the worst food prices for generations but also with expectations of rapid improvement once hostilities were ended. The worst confrontation on the continent, the Fronde in France, went out of control because the Crown failed to make peace with one of its principal enemies, forcing its subjects to sustain another decade of fighting against Spanish forces both in Flanders and in the south.

There was also, however, a fundamental issue of legitimacy. In contrast to the anti-fiscal revolts of the 1620s and 1630s, those of the 1640s often confronted monarchies in transitional weakness. France and Sweden were ruled on behalf of minors, by regencies whose own lack of experience was noticed by contemporaries. Denmark, reaching the end of a very long and increasingly unpopular reign, was bound to experience a sharp reaction. Spain and England were ruled by kings whose gross political incompetence was becoming increasingly obvious. In the German lands there was less of a sharp down-turn in central authority beyond the protracted and painful political restructuring caused by the Thirty Years War itself. But, further east, Poland, under very different circumstances and over a longer period, reached a political deadlock only resolved in 1668 with the abdication of the King himself. No system of government exposed to the unpredictability of dynastic accident or hereditary eccentricity could expect to enjoy permanent stability, and these were not the worst personal cases in our period: the Empire at the turn of the century had survived under Rudolph II, a recluse suffering progressive insanity, and Spain had to suffer even more pathetic results of Habsburg genetic degeneration after the death of Philip IV in 1665. But an already dangerous coincidence of destabilising factors in the 1640s was clearly in many cases aggravated by the absence of indisputable authority which might have been able to stop or contain the escalation of popular unrest and noble discontent of that decade. If this analysis stands, then the crises of the mid-seventeenth century were not in the first instance economic or, in a straightforward sense, social, but political. Desperate and truly unprecedented fiscal policies, adopted for the sake of even more desperate and ultimately destructive military schemes, provoked consistent resentment in every major state, and the resulting reactionary crises often coincided with particular weaknesses at the centre of power in each state. It was this combination of factors that made the unrest of the 1640s more serious than anything seen for generations – more serious also than that of the 1590s, when the catalyst of famine and insecurity had been as serious for the common people as it was in the 1640s.

Liberty, anarchy or tyranny: Poland, the east and the Ottoman troubles

Before looking at the obvious examples of mid-century 'crises' in western and central Europe, it may be helpful to look at an interesting variant, perhaps even exception, to the general trend: the Polish–Lithuanian commonwealth. After the extinction of the Jagiellon dynasty in 1572 the elective basis of the monarchy had become strengthened and voting rights in crown elections had been extended to the entire nobility. Until then, it has been argued, the Polish Crown had had a considerable amount of authority, notably in the appointment of high officers of state, but, from the royal election of 1573 onwards, increasing restraints were imposed by the gentry through electoral charters. The credibility of some candidates was also undermined by the extravagance of electoral promises.

Sigismund III (1587–1632) was no exception, but he did subsequently attempt to reverse the trend by means of a series of reform proposals (1605–6) designed to limit the gentry right of veto in the *sejm* (diet), increase crown revenues from taxation and strengthen the King's control over the army (especially against the grand *hetman*, commander for life of the Polish army if the King was absent). In response, the nobility exercised their constitutionalised right of rebellion against the Crown, forcing Sigismund to abandon all his proposals. In 1607 a commission of the senate, the upper house of the diet, secured a permanent check on crown policy. This might still have given scope for a development similar to that in the electoral kingdom of Denmark–Norway (see chapter 2), had the Polish Crown had anything like the financial resources of Christian IV. In fact Poland–Lithuania was an underdeveloped domain state where the yield from crown land was not only intrinsically low but also increasingly often alienated in the Crown's attempts to buy support amongst the gentry and the magnates. It has been estimated that by the early seventeenth century the King had only half the domain revenues of his Danish colleague, despite a population ten times that of Denmark, and lacked the additional income, such as the Sound Tolls, so crucial for Christian IV. Sigismund was consequently in no position to try to reverse the trend towards ever more restraints on royal authority and towards comprehensive privileges for especially the upper nobility who dominated the *sejm* (parliament). The magnates became almost independent territorial princelings, with their own patronage network and with considerable local authority (from the 1640s even over taxation and local defence). The Crown's bureaucracy appears to have failed to develop, and the principle of social advancement through royal service, so important in western monarchies, had little or no relevance.[6] Sigismund's attempts to compensate by gaining military prestige against Sweden and Muscovy met with only half-hearted support amongst the nobility. Once Smolensk had been captured in 1611, for example, the Polish diet resisted plans for further campaigning in the face of mounting Russian national and religious resistance. There was even less enthusiasm in the *sejm* for Sigismund's long-standing dynastic claims against Sweden. Only in 1626, when Gustav Adolf threatened the Baltic coast of Poland itself, did the diet vote substantial taxes, and these did not secure effective defence against Sweden. Although its cavalry still enjoyed a high reputation, and commanders such as Koniecpolski presented considerable obstacles to Gustav Adolf in the 1620s, Poland was beginning to fall behind the European powers in terms of resources and the central authority required for effective military development.

This became apparent only gradually, however. During the later stages of the Thirty Years War the Polish magnates and gentry could regard their constitution as a model of liberty: most of their western frontier was safe in the hands of their Habsburg allies, Sweden after 1632 was on the defensive and the Ottoman Empire in the south after 1621 was temporarily static. One recurrent problem lay in the south-eastern reaches of the Ukraine and along the Dnieper below Kiev, an area dominated by frontier tribes of Cossacks. Some of these had come formally under Polish sovereignty, in return for complete recognition of their privileges, while others were in effect bands of robbers exploiting the uncertainty of the Christian–Ottoman borderlands. Sigismund's aggressive Counter-Reformation policies and his encouragement of Jesuit activity in the area, however, generated opposition amongst the largely Orthodox Cossacks. The attempts by Wladyslaw IV (1632–48) to adopt a more flexible religious approach, notably at the Colloquy of Torun of 1644, seem to have come too late to reduce bitterness against Poland, and there was also resentment against the failure of the *sejm* to back Wladyslaw's planned military expedition against the Turks. Ultimately the Cossacks turned to Muscovy for assistance against Poland.

The authority claimed by the Tsars of Muscovy, and fully exploited by Ivan IV (the Terrible) in the later sixteenth century, was a complete antithesis of the Polish model. It was truly autocratic, unlimited by any institutional practices or unalterable legal traditions, and bolstered by more widely believed divine attributes than anything in the west. Consequently, the murder by Ivan of his own son and heir, and the absence of any clear successor, produced a critical power vacuum only temporarily filled by Ivan's councillor, the able if ruthless magnate Boris Godunov. His death in 1605, at a time of growing popular unrest triggered by the horrific consecutive harvest failures from 1601, produced a delayed reaction against the tyranny of Ivan IV. Conspiracies amongst leading magnates, distrust between these and the service gentry whom Ivan had used to displace the old aristocracy (the *boyars*), and provincial revolts such as the one in the south-west led by the former slave Bolotnikov in 1606–7 (and numerous other disturbances organised at different stages in the name of at least twenty tsarist pretenders) combined with popular revolts of despair and deprivation to destroy central authority in Muscovy virtually completely. Sigismund of Poland, who had already encouraged several pretenders, invaded Muscovy on a full scale in 1609 to counter Swedish moves and to promote first his son and then himself as candidate against a Swedish contender. A rejection of foreign intervention finally led in 1613 to the election as tsar of Michael Romanov, an indirect relative of Ivan. This superficially ended the Time of Troubles, but the Swedes ultimately had to be bought off with territorial concessions at Stolbova (1617), and the Polish army, after another attack on Moscow in 1618, withdrew only when a treaty was signed in

1619. Michael Romanov's father, Fedor, known under his monastic name of Filaret, was freed from Polish captivity and returned to become patriarch and the main political power in the Kremlin. Michael himself appears to have had little ability in the face of enormous tasks of reconstruction; Filaret, not interested in the west, saw the best hopes of recovery in isolation, and made no attempts to rationalise the byzantine intricacies of government in Moscow. Apart from its trade with the west via Sweden and Poland, Muscovy therefore remained cut off and backward. Only in 1631 was a permanent foreign diplomatic mission established in Moscow – that of Sweden, a potential ally against Poland.

The Polish interregnum and elections of 1632 had tempted the Russians into a brief war against Poland (1632–4), but it was only with the outbreak of large-scale revolt in the Ukraine in 1648 that both the Polish and the Muscovite governments were really put to the test. A Cossack officer, Bogdan Khmelnytsky (or Chmielnicki), gained wide support amongst the Ukrainian peasants objecting to the repressive Catholic policies and seigneurial regime operated by the Poles. The rebels lost ground by 1651 owing to the withdrawal of Tartar aid, and Khmelnytsky, with increasing urgency, pressed Muscovy for help. Tsar Alexis (1645–76) had held back because of a domestic crisis in 1648 (to which we shall shortly return) but eventually agreed on condition that the Cossacks submit to Russian sovereignty. This brought on a new and much more prolonged Russo-Polish war.

The Muscovite army recovered Smolensk in 1654 and inevitably presented a potential challenge both to the East Prussia of Frederick William of Brandenburg–Prussia, and to the recently consolidated large estates of a number of Swedish magnate families in the Baltic provinces. Charles X of Sweden, Christina's successor on her abdication in 1654, decided to anticipate the Russians by declaring war against Poland in 1655. Charles rapidly occupied large central tracts of Poland, including Warsaw and Cracow. The ruling Rákóczi family in Transylvania, exploiting the internal turmoil and financial weakness in the Ottoman Empire to which they were nominally subject, joined what they hoped would be a Protestant crusade, and the Elector of Brandenburg was forced into an alliance with the Swedes in 1656. The Poles themselves, however, reacted in a remarkable nationalist outburst which not only made the Swedish position precarious but turned against minorities in Poland itself, especially the Jews and all kinds of non-Catholics. Moreover, the scale of Swedish operations, and the danger of a new Protestant onslaught in the Holy Roman Empire, frightened the Habsburgs and rekindled the Russian war effort. Even the Dutch became anxious about their Baltic trade routes, and in 1657 Frederick III of Denmark launched an attack on Sweden in the hope of reversing the setback the Danes had suffered in 1645.

In other words, the whole of northern and east-central Europe was at war, and this probably saved Poland from partition. Although Denmark was rapidly defeated in 1658 and again in 1660, the Swedish position in Poland did not improve. The Transylvanian army allied to Sweden disintegrated, and Transylvania (together with Moldavia, Wallachia and parts of the Ukraine) was brought back under the control of the now resurgent Ottoman Empire led by Mehmed Köprülü, grand vizir from 1656 to 1661, and his son Ahmed Köprülü. The Treaty of Oliva of 1660 resulted in no territorial losses for Poland to Sweden, but did confirm Elector Frederick William's autonomous possession of the duchy of East Prussia, hitherto under Polish sovereignty. The Polish settlement with Muscovy at Andrusovo in 1667 confirmed the loss of Smolensk and Kiev to Alexis, while much of the Ukraine remained unstable for decades.

Not even these warnings, however, convinced the magnates and gentry of Poland–Lithuania that reform was necessary. The Vistula area had been heavily devastated, the Polish currency thoroughly destabilised by copper debasement, and the vital grain trade itself disrupted. The response of landowners, however, was to increase demand on the serf labour force, rapidly depressing rural conditions. On top of this came an increasingly intractable political confrontation which deprived the country of effective leadership. King Jan Kazimierz, brother and successor of Wladyslaw, had since his election in 1648 attempted to exploit his powers of patronage to strengthen crown control over the chief officers of state. In Poland, however, offices, once granted, could not readily be revoked, and a royalist party was in any case difficult to preserve in a period of military setbacks and challenges to centralised government. Predictably, the King provoked magnate resistance when he attempted to adopt more doubtful expedients to strengthen his hand, and in 1658 he failed to carry a moderate constitutional reform programme through the obstinately tradition-bound *sejm*. Even the war effort against Muscovy was undermined by factional squabbles and feuds amongst the magnates, and by fears that royal military success might be used to establish hereditary or centralising monarchy. In the 1660s the King's efforts to secure the election of a successor while still in power, in breach of conventions which deferred elections until after the throne had actually become vacant, forced some members of the nobility to resort to the wrecking tactics of the free veto in the *sejm* and later to open military confrontation. Finally, in 1668, Jan Kazimierz abdicated in disgust, warning the assembly as he left that Poland faced a real threat of dismemberment by its neighbours.[7]

By this stage, Poland was the only remaining genuinely elective monarchy, and its constitution was clearly too finely balanced to allow the kind of political adaptation that its neighbours were going through. Comparisons with other European monarchies is not at all helpful – exceptionally, in Poland, a piecemeal erosion of the authority of adult and active monarchs was taking place in times of potential or actual foreign threat. A terminal crisis was averted for the time being thanks to resilient Polish nationalism and a considerable military tradition, but the failure of attempts to reform the *sejm* during the lives of Sigismund and his two sons not only created constitutional deadlock but probably also made the gradual emasculation of central authority an irreversible trend. Significantly, not even John III Sobieski (1674–96), despite his military ability proven at the siege of Vienna in 1683, could use his position to arrest the increasing domestic political anarchy.

The Ottoman Empire offers a rather different perspective on political power. Despite a long tradition of centralised authority, often based on the personal military strength and reputation of the reigning sultan, central leadership had become more unpredictable early in the century. A turning point may be identified with the death of Mehmet III in 1603 – the last sultan to have trained as a military commander and governor in the provinces before taking over central authority. More frequent succession struggles from 1617 failed to produce political stability, and a sequence of very young, inexperienced or even totally incapacitated sultans changed the realities of power in the Topkapi palace in Istanbul – graphically illustrated by the number of reigns that ended in forced depositions or other violently premature terminations, or by the instances of fratricide and imprisonment ordered in the name of claimants who were themselves manipulated by factions within the palace. The unprecedented lack of actual military experience displayed by this sequence of sultans inevitably encouraged recurrent revolts amongst the janissary elite bodyguards, including one in 1648 which deposed the mentally unstable Ibrahim. Although the mothers of some of these sultans could at times exercise significant moderating and stabilising political power through the machinery of the inner palace (the harem)[8] and the support of senior officials, this was not an effective long-term alternative to the traditional role of the sultan. Islam did not sanction for the sultan anything resembling the kinds of divine-right status claimed by some rulers in Christian Europe during this period, and so it was more difficult to gloss over serious defects in a particular incumbent. Eventually, stability was recovered after 1656 through the efforts of the Grand Vizier Mehmet Köprülü and his son Ahmed Köprülü from 1661 (with consequences for the Habsburg lands to which we shall return in chapter 11). But it will be obvious from the problems described here that the instability experienced by the Ottoman state in the early half of the century was specific to that cultural and political context, and could never be made to fit convincingly into a common European framework. The absence in Muslim thinking of any concept of change, and the extraordinary dependence of the Ottoman structure on despotic power exercised by or for the sultan within strict Koranic guidelines, made the unrest in the 1640s and early 1650s totally unlike anything found in Christian Europe.

The unrest in Muscovy between 1648 and 1650 is much more recognisable for the western historian, even though some aspects remain unclear. A wave of riots swept Moscow itself from 1 June 1648, the primary target being some particularly corrupt salt-tax and land officials, as well as the 19-year-old Tsar Alexis's tutor and close advisor, Boris Morozov. Underneath this, however, were deep factional divisions within the Kremlin itself, and long-standing grievances amongst the lesser *pomeshchiki* (military service-nobility), dissatisfied with the terms of their *pomestiya* (landholdings allocated in the provinces during the period of service) and concerned by shortages of peasant labour. Alexis repeatedly had to try to calm the crowds himself, but order in the streets was restored relatively quickly by means of the sacrifice of some officials (who were lynched by the crowd) and the temporary exile of Morozov. To confirm his good intentions, and consolidate his own potentially very great authority, Alexis called a *zemsky sobor* (assembly) for September 1648. It approved a new law code (*Ulozheniye*) already in January 1649, whereby the nobility were given even more formal powers over their serfs (see chapter 8), and the overawed representatives of some towns gained minor concessions regarding urban tax burdens. But further revolts occurred in 1650 in Pskov and Novgorod, caused by allegedly oppressive officialdom and by food exports at a time of rising prices. The Pskov rising took three months to repress, but punishments for the rebels were mild. What resemblance, if any, these conflicts had to those in the west is difficult to judge. Only in the Moscow riots can one detect familiar themes – riots caused by severe urban food shortages, combined with criticism targeted at hated advisers who misled the Tsar. As in the French peasant revolts of the 1630s, the sanctity of the ruler himself was respected.

Urban revolt and provincial secession: Spain and its territories in the 1640s

Deprivation and hunger – the rising price of bread or, more commonly, the dwindling weight and increasing adulteration of a fixed-price loaf – were the most common precipitant of popular unrest in the early modern period, and (as we noted in chapter 6) in the eyes of some authorities such protests were almost a legitimate aspect of community life. But bigger revolts, of the kind likely to make some political impact, were often more complex phenomena.

Religious or even millenarian motivations commonly emerged by way of justification, especially in Catholic countries, where images of saints, relics and other symbols were carried in peaceful processions or were used on either side in more violent confrontations. In cases where food – and those obviously trading in it, such as merchants or millers – was not the sole focus of attention, wider social and political grievances could acquire tangible form. Attacks on tax officials, for example, were frequently accompanied by collective symbolic actions closely related to, and often coinciding with, traditional popular festivals. The mocking imitation of the rituals of authority itself, the use of false emblems of authority, the caricature of roles and even the language of protest could convey messages of considerable complexity.

A typical instance of this was the Masaniello revolt in Naples in 1647. The kingdoms of Naples and Sicily were both under the Spanish Habsburgs, governed by wealthy local aristocracies whose plundering of the impoverished peasantry depended on continuous repression backed by the authority of the Crown. The urgency of tax requirements in Madrid forced the Crown to rely heavily on private financiers and tax farmers, who were obvious targets of popular hostility. Major cities such as Naples and Palermo attracted an unusually large proportion of poor trying to escape rural deprivation but, since municipal government was also essentially aristocratic, this created ideal conditions for revolt. Naples, with 300,000 inhabitants, would at the best of times stretch municipal administration to its limits, but the sequence of revolts in 1647 was the most serious in that city since the late sixteenth century. An impression was made in Naples by the news of revolt in Palermo shortly before, caused by deprivation and tax impositions, and resulting in the destruction of government buildings, the opening of prisons and a temporary loss of control over much of the city to a popular leader, La Pilosa, who was an escaped convict. In Naples a major religious festival on 7 July, an attack on a tax office handling a new fruit tax, and a march on a flour store coalesced into a riot in one of the poorest districts of the city. While formal respect and deference were shown towards the Habsburg dynasty itself, the viceroy's palace was sacked and its movable property either destroyed or given to the poor. A few days later a fisherman, Masaniello, called out the local militia and assumed leadership with the support of several advisers, including the experienced reformer Giulio Genoino. Strict orders were given against looting and theft, and violence was directed against 'traitors to the people', including officials, tax farmers and others. In the hope of defusing tension, the viceroy conferred official authority on Masaniello, who was heralded as a 'king' by some of the rebels. On 16 July, however, he was assassinated, and his reputation rapidly metamorphosed through different forms. Whereas, after an earlier attempt on his life, the would-be assassins were lynched by the crowd amidst rituals of popular justice, this time Masaniello's own body was at first ridiculed and abused. But when the authorities attempted to reduce the weight of the standard loaf, the dead leader was given hero status, complete with a ritualised funeral, and his memory almost sanctified. In contrast to Palermo, where internal division amongst the rebels had allowed Spanish troops to occupy the city by September 1647, the Neapolitan revolt did not break up at this point. Instead, it gained new impetus from the impoverished silk-workers, whilst waves of unrest swept the countryside, resulting in attacks on the estates of a number of landowners. In October a Spanish fleet failed to gain control, and a republic was declared in Naples on 24 October, with nominal support from France. Although the new regime appears to have been shallow and lacking in effective power, it was not until April 1648 that Spain recovered its hold on this essential part of its supply network for the European war.[9]

The Spanish peninsula itself experienced revolts which were more substantial and which for political reasons were triggered earlier than in most other parts of Europe (see chapter 2). The coup of 1 December 1640 which marked the secession of Portugal was caused in large part by growing instability in the Atlantic trade (culminating in 1638–41) and by grievances regarding the failure of Spain to take decisive action against Dutch infiltration of Portuguese overseas possessions. Once it had broken free, Portugal, allied to France and later to England, created a new military problem for Spain, and actual war lasted from 1657 until the formal recognition of Portuguese independence in 1668. But the bloodless secession itself, breaking a union formed only just over two generations earlier (1580), had apparently no social implications and was not accompanied by any of the popular disturbances that precipitated the governmental crises elsewhere.

The Catalan uprising, by contrast, was much more than just an outburst against years of reluctant subordination to Castile, precipitated by the fiscal pressures of the Spanish system. As already noted (p. 58), Catalonia had been forced into closer military co-operation with Castile during the winter of 1639–40, but owing to the weakness of the viceroy, Santa Coloma, and the genuine impoverishment of the province, Olivares's uncompromising tactics over army billeting generated an unusually fierce resentment which was not fully understood in Madrid until it was already too late to make concessions. In May 1640, well-organised bands of peasants and poorer townsmen formed in many parts of the province, making life difficult and dangerous for the regular soldiers. The army's presence could be justified on the grounds that Catalonia had to be defended against French incursions, and yet the troops were regarded with hostility and resentment by the inhabitants. Provocation and violence on both sides increased and, in the second half of May, insurgent bands began to destroy the property of wealthy citizens and of anyone who might be regarded as a 'traitor' because of connections with the royal administration. Initially, in the towns, some of those in authority connived with the rebels, exploited the violence for their own ends, or were simply afraid of becoming targets themselves if they did not join the rebels. But, after the murder of the viceroy on 7 June and the period of five days of anarchy in Barcelona that followed, the insurgents increasingly turned against anyone of wealth anywhere in the province. The ruling classes were losing control of a movement they had initially hoped to harness, and the revolt turned into a struggle of the poor against the rich, of peasants and the landless against seigneurs, and of the urban underprivileged against municipal oligarchies. Since the Catalan elite would merely have fuelled popular hostility if they had called on Madrid to help against the social revolution, they were gradually persuaded by Pau Claris, president of the *diputació* (commission) of the Catalan Cortes, to seek contacts with France. The outcome was quite extraordinary: a complete transfer of sovereignty over the whole principality from the Habsburgs to the Bourbons in January 1641. This bold move contributed to the final collapse of the whole concept that Olivares had been striving for, but did little to help the province of Catalonia itself. Characteristically, Aragon and Valencia did not join the Catalans in revolt, partly because of habitual parochialism and partly out of fear amongst the elite that social revolution itself might spread. French interest in the province dwindled even before the outbreak of the Fronde in 1648, and the plague epidemics of 1650–4 reduced Catalonia to extreme poverty. When the province accepted renewed submission to the Habsburgs in 1652 its traditional notoriously autonomous constitutions were confirmed, but the economic and social damage took much longer to repair.

The Catalan revolt, whose origins in terms of Spanish government policy and local sensibilities have been so brilliantly analysed by J. H. Elliott, does not appear to have realised much of its social revolutionary potential. The two main driving forces behind the movement – the lower orders with long-standing social grievances, and the ruling elite – had aims which were ultimately incompatible once the Spanish yoke had been thrown off. As elsewhere in Europe, no effective challenge to noble–seigneurial domination could be maintained, least of all in a period of economic instability. Significantly, the loyalty of the already crippled Castile, the heart of Philip IV's dominions, was not shaken by Portuguese or Catalan protests, and there were consequently no major changes in the Spanish system of government. The revolts in Palermo and Naples in 1647 merely confirmed amongst other things that the fiscal, administrative and military resources of a major warring power were dangerously inadequate. In fact, a state bankruptcy was declared shortly afterwards, ruining many Portuguese and Genoese *asiento*-holders, and driving up the cost of future loans even further. But the Spanish giant wobbled on, pursuing the war against France to a stalemate in 1659 and surviving the unexpected attack of Cromwell in 1655. While accepting that there was a real revolutionary 'crisis' in Catalonia itself, we may therefore agree with R. A. Stradling that the Spanish system as a whole experienced no such sudden jolt. Instead, it underwent piecemeal loss of possessions, colonial resources and military reputation through a series of costly and futile conflicts, starting with the Dutch war of independence in the later sixteenth century and not ending until 1715. Escaping real challenge at the centre, the actual power-structure of the monarchy did not react to the gradual erosion at the periphery, merely becoming increasingly out of date and inadequate.[10]

The Frondes: challenge from a divided elite?

Following the death of Louis XIII in 1643, the period of regency by Anne of Austria and Cardinal Mazarin in France was a precarious one. Decades of provincial urban and peasant revolts, forcibly resisting the growing wartime exactions of the Crown, its desperate fiscal expedients and its greater political ambitions (see chapter 2), had been serious enough for an adult monarch. Under a minority regency, however, provincial rebellion and protest movements across social barriers became much more dangerous. Although most rebel leaders still justified their actions defensively in terms of legal, religious and political traditions, the absence of an adult king enormously increased the scope for criticism of the Crown. Thus Mazarin's determination to continue Richelieu's confrontation with Spain in the Spanish Netherlands, Italy and Catalonia made the cardinal extremely unpopular. There was widespread unrest in France between 1643 and 1645, including some effective popular revolts such as that in Bordeaux in 1643. But the situation became more serious after French military setbacks in 1646 and especially after it became apparent that the Spanish war would go on despite negotiations to bring peace in the German lands. The resulting series of revolts, the Fronde (1648–53), revealed all the weaknesses of the French monarchy and yet came nowhere near providing any real political alternatives.

For the first time for over half a century it was in Paris itself that the revolt started. Popular desperation over fiscal extortion by the tax farmers, excruciating food prices and disease created a dangerous mood in the capital, and in January 1648 rioting occurred against new taxes on the citizenry which breached ancient privileges. The venerable *noblesse de robe* (lawyers) of the Parlement of Paris then began to exercise their considerable powers, exploiting latent opposition to the regency's autocratic manoeuvres by challenging the fiscal edicts of 15 January (which could consequently be passed only by means of royal orders in a *lit de justice*). By April the regency caused further resentment by casting doubt on the renewal of the *paulette* (see pp. 164) for certain categories of lesser robe office-holders. The Parlement called for a session of the Chambre St Louis, consisting of representatives of the Parlement and of the other sovereign courts, and this duly took place from 30 June to 29 July. A reform programme of 29 articles was drawn up, including demands for the abolition of the *intendants*, control of *taille* farming (and a reduction in the tax itself by one-quarter), enquiries into the fiscal system as a whole, a freeze on the creation by the Crown of new offices for sale, and a freeing of political prisoners (that is, primarily members of the robe nobility itself who had been penalised for earlier criticisms of the regency). The Parlement assumed legislative initiative in passing some of these and sought to make its role as constitutional arbiter more explicit. Some of the demands, especially those regarding judicial, financial and fiscal abuses, were couched in terms deliberately designed to generate wider public support. When the regency responded by means of a combination of selective concessions (notably on the *paulette*) and threats (including the arrest of some parlementaire leaders) riots again broke out on 26 August. Barricades were built in the capital to prevent the Crown using armed force, and a flood of pamphlets (the first 'Mazarinades') lampooned the Cardinal. The regency had to give way, mindful of the situation in England at this time and weakened by tax strikes and by the bankruptcy that occurred in July. Anne of Austria, the King and Mazarin left Paris in September and soon officially accepted all the demands of the Chambre St Louis. When this later turned out to be an insincere tactical manoeuvre, open civil war broke out between Paris and the regency, accompanied by a vitriolic pamphlet war which raised broader constitutional issues. After a few months, and partly because of the shock of the news from England of the execution of Charles I in January 1649, a compromise was reached whereby the regency ostensibly confirmed many of the concessions already made (11 March). Significantly, however, the Parlement, despite its popularity in the city, did not exploit this opportunity to go beyond its original purely conservative demands. Afraid of rousing too much popular enthusiasm and perhaps endangering their own interests, the parlementaires held back from any institutional or administrative reforms of a genuinely innovatory kind. Nevertheless, their stand, if consolidated by means of political and institutional alliances, could have amounted to a permanent check on the aggressive fiscal authority of the Crown and hence its ability to conduct an independent foreign policy or continue the existing war effort.

Food shortages persisted, however, and violent unrest spread also in the provinces. For the high nobility and princes of the blood, many of whom sided with the Parlement, the settlement was unsatisfactory. Not only the opportunists among them including Paul de Gondi (later Cardinal de Retz) but also the initially loyalist Gaston d'Orléans (brother of Louis XIII) and Louis, Prince of Condé (a royal cousin) resented political trends which undermined their own influence – in particular the encroaching bureaucratisation of the inner workings of the state and the growing influence of lower-born war-mongering advisors such as Richelieu and Mazarin. Many nobles also wanted the original demands of the robe implemented more effectively and forcibly, together with a quick Franco–Spanish peace settlement in accordance with a long tradition of noble resistance to the Spanish war. Since the regency was so weak, these grievances now resurfaced in a more complex Fronde of the Princes (1649–52), a period of political confusion where primary goals and coherent leadership were overshadowed by personal ambitions and the desire to settle old scores. Many magnates sought to recover a more direct influence in the King's council, and as long as the King himself was a minor the oppositional role of princes of royal blood such as Condé against an unpopular outsider such as Mazarin could be decisive. An attempt by Anne of Austria and Mazarin to have Condé and some other princes of the blood imprisoned in 1650 provoked renewed revolts as well as Spanish intervention, and Mazarin himself was exiled from France early the following year. Again, however, no constitutional renovation occurred and, with Louis XIV declared of age at 13 in September 1651, the uncoordinated violence of the aristocratic factions formally took on a more directly treasonable character. Condé himself concluded a new agreement with Spain late that year, at a time when the French Crown had few resources left to continue the war. Attempts were even made by the Frondeurs to have the Estates-General called, amidst demands from some quarters for a return to earlier forms of more restricted monarchical government. The Parlement, however, attempted to follow a more moderate line, especially in the face of the mounting anarchy and destructiveness of the civil war around Paris (1651–2), and the high-handed approach of Condé and the Duke of Orléans in the city itself during the summer of 1652. Many of the nobles left Paris, and when Mazarin was dismissed a second time the magnates lost any sense of purpose. Condé fled and the King returned to Paris in October 1652.

Some pockets of resistance survived in the provinces, notably in Aix and in the radical anti-robe revolt of Bordeaux to which we shall shortly return. On the whole, however, co-operation between provincial robe nobles and the high nobility was rarely durable, and the Crown ultimately succeeded in dividing the conservative interests sufficiently to clear the way for forcible repression of the popular urban or rural disorder. Most of the magnates settled up with the Crown, although Condé went into Spanish service until 1659. Mazarin, who had once more returned to power early in 1653, ensured that the *intendants* were quietly restored in the provinces. The Parlement of Paris itself submitted to a formal curtailment of its authority, and many of the reforms of 1648–9 were quietly abandoned. In return for confirmation of the *paulette* system, a new set of fiscal edicts was pushed through in 1653. Implementation of these, like the collection of arrears, proved difficult in many parts of France and caused further sporadic revolts in the south-west in the later 1650s, but no substantial co-ordinated resistance occurred. Despite the bankruptcy of 1648, the Crown was able to return to many of its earlier extortionate financial and fiscal expedients and hence resume a determined foreign and military policy. Only in 1661 did the financial administration finally give way under the weight of corruption and revenue-anticipation, and by that stage the main political dangers had been averted.[11]

The Fronde was very much part of the sequence of French revolts from the 1620s onwards, in so far as it was provoked by dearth, by the fiscal pressure of the Crown, by the vested interests of office-holders and robe nobility and by aristocratic and old noble grievances over their gradual displacement at the centre of power around the King. Each of these issues had caused conflict before, but the Fronde was unusual in that all the factors converged nearly simultaneously in Paris itself, at a time when a regency government was pursuing a controversial and dangerously extended foreign policy. Rebellion at this stage was particularly damaging for the Crown. As Mazarin himself expressly warned, Spain would exploit the situation directly by raising its own conditions for peace while at the same time subsidising notably Condé, thereby making the rapid settlement demanded by the Frondeurs themselves unattainable. As in the 1630s, domestic unrest also directly weakened French defences and military operations, but whereas the Norman revolt of 1639 had led to the diversion of 4000 foot-soldiers and 1200 cavalry from the front, the civil war of 1649–52 produced a virtual military collapse. The monarchy survived only because of Spain's inability to take advantage of the opportunity.

From this perspective, the disintegration of the Frondeur cause and the rapid resilience of the monarchy are sufficiently surprising to require further explanation. David Parker has argued that the Fronde in fact never had much potential: it merely revealed the depth of divergences of interest within French society, and the minimal amount of constructive co-operation attainable amongst the Crown's critics compared with what had occurred in the civil wars of the later sixteenth century. Significantly, the princes of the blood and the magnates now had great difficulty in raising both reliable support in the localities and adequate financial credit. Not even Condé was unanimously welcomed in Bordeaux in 1651 when he decided to use his connections there as a centre for resistance. Antipathy between the high aristocracy and the lesser nobility, already visible in the Estates General of 1614–15, was effectively exploited by the Crown from 1649 through assemblies of the lesser nobles. The princes themselves were easily divided, Mazarin, for example, buying off Turenne to head the royal forces against Condé in 1652. Similarly, within the robe nobility, although their grievances were to some extent corporate, institutional rivalry over jurisdictions and entitlements was more often in evidence than co-operation; deferential conservatism was in any case universal. Similar patterns were apparent further down, for example amongst the towns, whose administrations were frequently run by venal office-holders. There was often deep rural resentment against urban privilege and property rights, and no conceivable basis for the kind of commoner participation visible in England in, for example, the New Model Army. Finally, in the absence of any real ideas for constructive reform, the threat of popular disorder and the fear of the uncontrollable fury of the politically powerless *menu peuple* deterred respectable citizens and landowners from going too far.[12]

That said, one of the French provincial revolts did achieve some development of democratic ideas and social levelling: the Ormée revolt in the city of Bordeaux. It had taken shape in the summer of 1651 as a popular movement consisting largely of lesser citizens opposed to the exclusiveness of the robe and the city notables, and it backed (but was hardly controlled by) the Condé faction based there. In June 1652 the movement succeeded in forcibly ousting the Parlement of Bordeaux from power, running the city by means of a central assembly of 500 under a committee of 30. Although continuing (until its defeat in July 1653) to operate on the basis of decisions reached in its open assembly, the Ormée was not egalitarian in an innovatory sense nor was it remotely republican: it looked back to an earlier mythical golden age of guild community-government under a 'just' crown. The Ormée did not become truly republican until, in the last months, it was past its peak and was facing a unified front of parlementaire, crown and merchant opposition – only then, too, did agents from Cromwellian England, led by the Leveller officer Sexby, make any substantial impression. By that stage the Condé faction was abandoning the Ormée because popular and aristocratic differences had become too obvious. Factional squabbles and attempts at subversion from within soon destroyed the power of the rebel organisation, and the Ormée went the way of the rest of the Frondeurs, its crumbling front leaving it exposed to crown repression without compromise.[13]

The English civil wars and Scotland

The events in London during 1641, the initiatives of the Long Parliament during that year and the forced departure of Charles I from London after his failure to arrest five parliamentary leaders in January 1642 (see chapter 2), would in themselves have qualified for discussion in terms of a 'crisis of authority' in at least the political (if not the social) sense. By then, as we have noted, parliament had already assumed a role unique amongst the institutions of monarchical Europe: Pym and his associates, for all their assertions of protecting the traditional constitutional structure of the kingdom, were in fact taking initiatives that Charles could justifiably claim, as he did with some skill and moderation in 1642, to be unprecedented attacks on the royal prerogative and on the traditions of the past.

By the time the first civil war (1642–6) broke out, the confrontation unavoidably if gradually took a much harder line. It is no longer possible to talk of 'parties' on either the parliamentary or the royalist side in the early 1640s, for the vast majority clearly still hoped for moderation and an early compromise. Although the King had most support in the north, the south-west and Wales, with the populous south and east and (most important of all) much of London tending to back parliament, the division was hardly clear-cut, much less was it constant. At times there were indications of socio-economic determinants in the choice of sides: areas in Yorkshire and Lancashire dependent on textile production, for example, leant towards the parliamentary side. No simple conclusions can be drawn along such lines, however, and communities or even individual families were split in their allegiances. The actual armed forces were small and largely conscripted, each side claiming the other was raising troops unconstitutionally. The parliamentarian soldiers were mostly inexperienced, poorly supplied and largely ineffective until 1644, but even if royalist forces, especially those commanded by prince Rupert, were more impressive, parliament had the backing of the navy and controlled the main ports and many of the economically important larger towns. Nevertheless, loyalties were still primarily to the locality, and choices were made on the basis of pragmatic self-interest which often dictated neutralism or even occasional support for both sides. Rebellion did not seem to come easily in a country that had avoided large-scale popular revolt for decades: indeed, resistance to war was widespread from 1643, and by 1645 became more clearly organised with the 'clubmen' and other groups seeking pacification and a return to the status quo of 1640.

Within parliament itself in the early 1640s, most historians discern a peace group at one end of the spectrum, including men like Denzil Holles, whom the king had wanted to arrest in January 1642, but who was now anxious to end the conflict on nearly any terms in order to avoid social destabilisation, and at the other end radicals including the younger Henry Vane, seeking change on a scale that few of the gentry would welcome. The middle ground, however, is more difficult to define, for the relatively moderate policies of men such as Pym (until his death in December 1643) and Oliver St John unavoidably entailed the development of a parliamentary administrative system to sustain the quest for a permanent constitutional balance which would prove immune to the kind of royal duplicity displayed for neither the first nor the last time in January 1642. While recurrent peace negotiations were attempted up until the spring of 1643, neither side became particularly entrenched. The King, indeed, quickly backed down in one respect, namely church policy, and both Laud and what he stood for were abandoned. But when Charles's negotiations for Irish support became common knowledge that summer, parliamentary resolve strengthened. The committees controlling administration became more authoritarian in nature, the sequestration of royalist property was stepped up and a new system of taxation developed, including a substantial excise (purchase tax) on a wide range of common goods, and the notorious assessment (direct tax on property) designed to tap especially wealthier social groups who had hitherto escaped lightly.

One of the issues of constant if rarely decisive[14] importance was that of a church settlement. Charles's high-church and Arminian outlook had been widely feared and resented for years, and in 1642 parliament excluded all clergymen from government. In 1643 the diocesan administration was to be replaced by a presbyterian structure more in line with that in Scotland, and an assembly at Westminster was instructed to devise a church settlement. Scottish representation there helped pave the way for the Solemn League and Covenant of 1644 which secured a military alliance between the two parliaments. Although the English remained deeply suspicious of kirk dominance in state politics, the terms of the agreement were sufficiently vague to allow co-operation for the time being, and Scottish reinforcements contributed to the first major parliamentary victory over Charles at Marston Moor in 1644. Co-operation across the border, however, remained frail because of basic differences of outlook. The English Church ordinances of 1645 and 1646, although abolishing bishops and confirming the presbyterian ecclesiastical structure in England, did not go far enough for the rigid Covenanting Scots in freeing the English Church from parliamentary control. Parliament, to the Scots, meant something very different from what it was in England. In short, there was little mutual understanding of the priorities and aims of each side. By the time a rapprochement between the Scots and Charles became conceivable late in 1644, attitudes in the Westminster parliament on religious matters had in any case already hardened at the expense of the moderate middle ground. Many MPs were becoming concerned at the spread of religious dissent and radicalism, which often took the form of demands for greater religious toleration and for wide practical autonomy for each congregation. Independents and Congregationalists (each term carrying both political and spiritual connotations) came to be regarded as a threat to the established order – especially to the State Church which was so central a part of that order and which had hitherto had a claim on everyone's allegiance, willing or otherwise. The Presbyterians and those afraid of wider upheaval might well see the Scots and Charles as the lesser of two evils. MPs concerned to defend what had so far been achieved, on the other hand, had to turn towards the minority political Independents for support.

This fundamental divide within the parliamentarian side remained crucial throughout the civil war and interregnum period. Indeed, since 1642 royalist propagandists had made the most of gentry fears of social upheaval and radicalism in their pamphlets. Equally, they could challenge the constitutional propriety of parliamentary attitudes and authoritarian policies: while admitting that the Crown itself had posed a threat to traditional liberties in the 1630s, they now argued that the threat came from parliamentary activists. In fact most MPs and office-holders were no different from their predecessors: conservative gentry, motivated by a mixture of local and wider interests, seeking constitutional safeguards without upsetting the social hierarchy. The war itself, however, inevitably worked against compromise.

Local support for either King or Parliament remained uncertain, especially as each copied the authoritarian methods of the other, and as war contributions and the burden of quartering and supplying troops made ship money and pre-war taxation pale into relative insignificance.[15] Especially on the parliamentary side, wartime policies were deeply contentious and divisive. Local organisations, such as the county commissions that appeared in many areas, were orientated towards local needs, and were usually reluctant participants on either side. The regional associations encouraged by Parliament, on the other hand, were generally not very effective, with the exception of the eastern association. It was there that the basis emerged for the parliamentarian military reorganisation demanded by the political Independents which culminated in the New Model Army of 1645. This force, commanded by Fairfax, Skippon and later Oliver Cromwell, tipped the balance in the field (for example, at Naseby) and helped to secure royal defeat and surrender to the Scots at Nottingham the following year. In July 1646 Parliament presented the Newcastle Propositions as a basis for settlement with the King, insisting on a confirmation of the presbyterian structure for the Church of England and on parliamentary control of the militia for 20 years.

The period from the end of the first civil war to the start of the second in 1648 proved how difficult it was to achieve a lasting political settlement acceptable both to a reasonable proportion of the parliamentarians and to the ambivalent or devious royalist leadership. Outside the poorer parts of London and the parliamentarian armies, there was wide support for a political Presbyterian compromise with Charles, made more urgent by the deteriorating economic conditions from 1647 and by recurrent plague in London and around Westminster. The armies themselves became a major problem as arrears of pay (probably surpassing £2 million) undermined discipline and caused a succession of damaging mutinies. The Presbyterians naturally pressed for demobilisation, but were opposed by the political Independents and by the unpaid troops themselves. Even the New Model Army, though better paid than the other parliamentary forces, became a threat because of the subversive religious and political views flourishing in its ranks, open as it was to those of very humble background. Some of the New Model Army commanders, notably Cromwell, encouraged religious toleration and dissent amongst the soldiers as part of a quest for a 'godly army'. In addition, the rapidly developing London artisans' movement, the Levellers, won adherents in the ranks from early 1647: their demands for wider and more democratic franchise together with the abolition of the House of Lords and the monarchy were explicit and well formulated. Initially, soldier demands had been restrained and basically apolitical, but this link between city and army created the basis for a new radical political force which proved totally unacceptable both to traditionalist parliamentarians and to the establishment generally.

Those still claiming to be defending the King against his evil advisers, and exploring possible compromise with Charles in 1646–7, thus found themselves looking anxiously over their shoulders at the growing political awareness in the army, while their attempts to reduce and control it without trying to understand soldier grievances had the opposite effect. Late in May 1647 this came to a head when there was hope of negotiations with Charles on the basis of Presbyterianism for three years and parliamentary control of the militia for ten. The Commons voted to disband the New Model infantry without paying much of their arrears: the troops responded by seizing the King's person from his parliamentary captivity, drawing up a Humble Remonstrance, and establishing an army council consisting of an equal number of officers and representatives of the privates. By mid-June 1647 Cromwell and Ireton confirmed officer acceptance of a limited politicisation of the army in a programme calling for a purge of parliament and for confirmation of liberty of conscience.

This development in itself was unique in European terms, a product of the unusual structure of the New Model Army and of its contacts with the precocious London radicals. The Levellers, although appearing at a time of growing economic and material insecurity, were much more than a passing artisan movement of the kind common in this period. The Leveller leaders and publicists, John Lilburne (himself an army officer until 1645), Richard Overton and William Walwyn, had a sophisticated long-term programme involving comprehensive religious individualism, substantial political democratisation, drastic legal and fiscal reforms, and a broadening of educational opportunity. Although rejecting the monarchy and the Lords, most of their demands were in effect directed against parliamentary government and were regarded by the Commons as thoroughly subversive. Lilburne and Overton were both imprisoned for their political and religious views (1646–7), and Walwyn, though more retiring, was regarded as equally dangerous because of the power of his writing. In this tense atmosphere, attempts by the Presbyterians at Westminster to mobilise violent counter-revolution[16] in favour of a quick settlement with the King provoked army retaliation in the form of an occupation of Westminster on 6 August and the removal of the 11 MPs who had led the call for peremptory demobilisation. The Commons bowed to the inevitable: the army was in effect in charge of the radical revolution, and remained so until 1649.

Yet the political struggle was far from over, for even the army command was concerned about Leveller radicalism. Cromwell, like other officers, was still seriously interested in a settlement involving the restoration of the King, and adhered to the principle of monarchy until as late as December 1648. At a series of debates held in Putney from 28 October to 1 November 1647, Ireton and Cromwell also confirmed their refusal to countenance some of the other political demands of the Levellers' *Agreement of the People*. Colonel Thomas Rainsborough, who demonstrated his commitment to democratic principles during the debates, was pushed out of the army to the navy, in order to limit his influence on the troops.

A deeper rift was avoided because of the escape of Charles from captivity on 11 November, and his acceptance of the generous Engagement with the Scots involving recognition of a Presbyterian Church in return for military assistance to secure a restoration in England. Since 1645 there had been growing dismay in Scotland at the failure of the Presbyterians in England to secure a 'pure' church settlement. But the Scottish political nation, like the English, was in fact deeply divided between moderate conservatives seeking a quick and peaceful settlement, and radicals who, in the case of Scotland, were primarily interested in a true Covenanter church settlement rather than in political reforms or guarantees. At this juncture, it might have appeared that both interests could to some extent be served by another armed invasion of England, but both kirk and nobility were too deeply divided, and the faction around the Duke of Hamilton (who undertook such a solution) failed to carry conviction. South of the border, civil war had already erupted early in 1648 in the form of widespread provincial revolts against the impositions and stresses of renewed army demands, and against the prospect of continuing arbitrary government. But the New Model Army, abandoning its divisive debates, was able to deal with these poorly-timed revolts before the Scots arrived; the Scots in turn were defeated at Preston in August.

Although this episode was further proof that Charles would never change his ways and could never be trusted, the Presbyterians still had sufficient support in the more conservative provinces to secure a Commons vote on 5 December in favour of continuing negotiations. During the following days part of the army under Colonel Pride therefore retaliated by purging parliament (preventing a quarter of its 507 members from entering, and making many more absent themselves). The remaining Rump of at most 70 members then debated and eventually approved a procedure for the trial of Charles.[17] To the consternation and open horror of moderate opinion in England, Scotland and abroad, the King was executed for treason, tyranny and bloodshed on 30 January 1649.

Revolution and the search for stability in England

Historians have agreed that the revolution of December 1648 to March 1649 – the trial and execution of the King, the establishment of a republic and the abolition of the House of Lords – was carried through by a small minority and amounted virtually to a military coup against moderate majority opinion in Parliament and amongst the gentry. Pride's Purge was an overhasty move, indisputably in flagrant breach of contemporary notions of law and tradition. It ignored widespread revulsion against the excesses of both royalist and parliamentarian autocratic government and perpetuated a military prominence which most Englishmen resented and feared. The coup also scuppered the kind of compromise settlement (on the basis of the gains of 1641) which the vast majority of the gentry had consistently hoped for.

Nevertheless, as Robert Ashton and others have warned, we should not immediately assume that England had acquired, even temporarily, a hard revolutionary dictatorship in the style of 1793–4 or 1917, at least not without trying to understand what options were open to those who were not prepared to sacrifice all principles for the sake of elusive compromise.[18] The Presbyterians had failed, as did leaders elsewhere in Europe at this disturbing economic juncture, to comprehend the legitimate grievances of the underprivileged either in the army or in the streets of London and elsewhere; more seriously, they fatally misjudged the mood of the common soldiers. The Scots, resented as aliens when they moved across the border, had had no help from uncoordinated provincial revolts and merely succeeded in reuniting the New Model Army; in any case the Scots were themselves divided, and their religious aims had little in common with those of the Presbyterians in England. Even more fundamental was the fact that the genuine alternatives were fewer and far more stark than moderates were willing to recognise openly. Charles had never given solid grounds for trust, and his track record of respecting negotiated limitations on his authority had been consistently appalling since 1628. Peace with the King on the terms of 1648 would almost certainly have been followed by substantial demobilisation, whereupon nothing would have stood in the way of forcible counter-revolution. Given that a violent London-based counter-revolution had been a real prospect as late as the summer of 1648, the refusal of the Presbyterians to abandon persistently abortive negotiations could only be regarded as disingenuous or at best naïve. There may in fact have been no safe ground between total surrender, including loss of the limited but important gains of 1641, and effective elimination of Charles from all political influence. If the Purge was a crude shortcut to that end, the fact that the execution of Charles was anything but taken for granted during the trial does some credit to those who agreed to sit in judgement.

One other aspect deserves at least brief mention, not least given continental experiences. While the gentry and the observing crowd in Westminster were clearly horrified at the execution, fearing a complete collapse of order, we should not forget that there was still substantial support for the deeper institutional and administrative reform which had continuously been put off. How substantial such support was remains unclear, and more research is needed on attitudes amongst those below the gentry. The Levellers notoriously failed to convince outside the army and London, and had little grasp either of practical politics or of the problems of other groups (such as rural labourers or the really poor and destitute) worst hit by the agrarian crisis of 1647–50. But what we know of the proliferating religious sects and pamphlet outpourings suggests that there was now some hope of real reform and change. Even the Levellers, although losing support in the army by early 1649, still had to be treated seriously by those officers who had recently given the movement half-hearted support in the hope of controlling it. Lilburne and Walwyn recognised that the political revolution that had taken place was of extremely limited use in terms of their long-term grievances against the system as a whole, and said as much in their *England's New Chains Discovered*. They also satirised the hypocrisy of the army grandees, including Cromwell. The typical reactions of a fearful establishment – the arrest of four Leveller leaders on 28 March and the efficient repression of another Leveller mutiny in the army in May 1649, coupled with the imposition of new censorship regulations – suggest that the threat of a second and deeper revolution involving social change could not yet be dismissed.

The first, and crucial, measure to prevent the revolution from going any further was to remove the parliamentary armies from the political arena by means of improvements in pay, refunds of arrears through the sale of lands, and, more especially, expeditions to Ireland and Scotland. During the summer of 1649 Cromwell took 12,000 men to reduce royalist strongholds in Ireland: his slaughter of civilians and garrisons at Drogheda and Wexford became legendary for its brutality, but raised hardly a murmur of disapproval in England. Complete pacification was achieved in a few years, but little impression was made on Catholicism by Protestant pressures. A mass transfer of land and tenants to English landowners reduced the proportion of land held by Catholics in Ireland from about 60 per cent in 1641 to 20 per cent in 1656, easing public debts in England at the cost of enormous resentment. The Irish economy was left to make a slow recovery from devastation.

Despite direct, if ambivalent, contacts with the son of the last king, Charles Stuart, the Scots were treated very differently. Cromwell defeated one large but faction-rent army at Dunbar in September 1650 and another at Worcester a year later, but the repressive and confiscatory policies of Ireland were not repeated. The union of the kingdoms in 1653 formally ended Scottish independence, and the abolition of the general assembly beneficially reduced kirk influence on secular government. After a royalist uprising led by Glencairn in the Highlands (1653–5), however, Scotland settled under the moderate and efficient supervision of General Monck and Lord Broghill. This eased the republic's international position, making it possible for Cromwell to consolidate a settlement with the Dutch in 1654, after a short maritime conflict, and to engage in the Baltic and against Spain from a position of strength.

Keeping the armies and navy occupied, however, did not improve the image of the Rump. Preoccupied with practical matters and in any case disinclined to radical policies, Parliament achieved very little substantial reform beyond some tightening of administrative practices and plans for simplification of the legal system. Church reform was as ever hampered by the persistence of old habits and Anglican traditions; puritan moral legislation, such as the Act against adultery which notably confirmed engrained discriminatory double standards by providing for the death penalty for women alone, was unenforceable. The regicides themselves were clearly conservative in social and most other respects, and by the time Cromwell and others had persuaded some dozen absentees to return to Parliament, any lingering radicalism was even further diluted. Only one substantial group of religious fundamentalists was directly represented, the Fifth Monarchy Men – exponents of an extreme theocratic version of the common millenarian expectations of Christ's forthcoming rule on earth. In contrast to many of the radical sects, the Fifth Monarchists wanted to impose a draconian Old Testament faith on the nation, complete with the use of Mosaic Law for moral offences. Cromwell himself appears to have accepted some of their priorities for a while after the dissolution of the Rump in 1653 and its replacement with the army-nominated 'Parliament of Saints' (Barebones Parliament). This understanding did not last, however, and at the end of the year an Instrument of Government created a new constitution with Oliver Cromwell as Lord Protector and a new parliament elected from all three kingdoms on the basis of substantially reformed constituencies.

The regime tried to justify itself through the government paper *Mercurius Politicus* (from June 1650); it also won some support from intellectuals such as the republican James Harrington and the great advocate of authoritarian government, Thomas Hobbes (see pp. 320–1). Even so, many of the radicals of the 1640s were disillusioned with the results. Leveller ideas found fertile ground amongst the religious sectarians, whose search for a deeper truth could threaten the social order in far more fundamental ways. Although the first civil war had strengthened demands for comprehensive religious toleration, dissent had not initially been synonymous with individualism and subversion: the century-old Baptists, the predestinarian Particulars and the less austere but minority General Baptists all formed quite structured regional associations in the 1640s and, despite their critics, maintained considerable control over their members' attitudes and activities, even in the disturbed 1650s. By then, however, far more radical sects were gaining support. One such group, formed by Gerrard Winstanley in 1649, was known as the Diggers or (quite appropriately) True Levellers, because of their attempt to establish a peaceful communist settlement by digging up the commons at St George's Hill in Surrey on 1 April 1649. Winstanley rejected all forms of church organisation – and in particular university-trained clergymen – as a barrier to salvation, and interpreted the Bible remarkably figuratively by the standards of the age. Equally, since his fifty or so followers were drawn largely from the poorest in society, it is sad if hardly surprising that the local inhabitants (including a parson) systematically harassed the commune until the experiment was abandoned at Easter 1650.

Even more outrage was generated by some of the other minor sects, such as the Ranters – advocating free love, denying the relevance of sin for 'saints' and, in disregarding all moral conventions, laying themselves open to a variety of extravagant accusations of sexual licence – but few of these groups had any permanence or even identifiable coherence.

Quite different in scale and long-term significance, amongst those seeking the guidance of inner light to escape Puritan predestination, was the Quaker movement. Organised by George Fox and some other itinerant preachers in northern England from 1652, it became a nationwide separatist religious organisation whose followers came from both urban and rural society, rising to perhaps 50,000 members within a decade. Like the Levellers, the Quakers had political and social as well as religious aims, but their approach was much more radical. The Quakers of the 1650s were more provocative than their later followers: they refused to acknowledge social rank in any way, they rejected the physical church totally (including 'steeple houses') and worshipped anywhere in silence until someone – the priesthood of all believers, man or woman – should be moved to speak. The Quaker movement became heir to much of the earlier radicalism, especially amongst those at the lower end of the literate part of society: both Lilburne and Winstanley joined, attracted by the lack of explicit theological uniformity and the genuine feeling of equality amongst members. Pacifism became a central Quaker belief only in the 1660s, but extensive support in the New Model Army, including many in its garrisons in Ireland and Scotland, had already caused problems of discipline. The Quaker habit of interrupting clergymen during established services soon fuelled the repressive hostility which developed around them. When an extreme Quaker leader with Ranter tendencies, James Nayler, in 1656 entered Bristol on a donkey to represent Christ's second coming, a parliamentary committee, although steering clear of martyring him, condemned him to be branded and bored through the tongue. The Vagrancy Acts and a Blasphemy Act of 1650 were also invoked in attempts to suppress the movement and, from 1657, Quakers could be prosecuted for not attending an established church service each Sunday. As Barry Reay and others have argued, the Quakers had become the most obvious bearers of the social revolutionary tradition in England, and even the republican government was responding with alarm. Fear of the Quakers may ultimately have contributed in 1659 to the search for stronger government and the restoration of monarchy.[19]

Amongst many, therefore, the return of domestic peace and stability did not generate much enthusiastic loyalty towards the unimaginative Commonwealth and Protectorate. At a practical level, too, the army, which amounted to 70,000 men at its peak in 1652, continued to place great fiscal strain on the nation. As we noted in connection with the Thirty Years War in Europe, the response to fiscal burdens depended very much on precedent, on administrative effectiveness, and on a convincing show of strength by the state. Given growing economic prosperity, both England and Scotland had probably faced quite light fiscal burdens in the decades before 1640, even counting monopolies and other hidden burdens, or allowing for the unavoidable corruption, fees and costs payable to officials and private agents alike. This changed drastically with the war. The excise of 1643, though less wasteful than the monopolies of the Stuarts, created a persistently heavier and regressive fiscal burden on the less well-off. The parliamentarian assessments, on the other hand, were designed to reach the landed income especially of wealthier men, and at one stage yielded £120,000 per month, or one and a half times the total monthly revenues of the Crown in the 1630s. This tax in particular, and the total burden of all state revenues amounting to an estimated £1.7 million a year in the early 1650s (upwards of twice the effective load of Charles's later years),[20] ensured the growing unpopularity amongst the gentry of a war-orientated and army-based regime. Financiers and creditors were even less enthusiastic, for the sudden release of risky confiscated land on to the market, and the forced loans expected of existing creditors, merely confirmed the precariousness of the state's financial survival.

The Protectorate was in many ways a promising alternative to monarchy. Although there are a number of still unresolved questions surrounding its establishment and operation, it is clear that Cromwell's powers were constitutionally limited in crucial ways: in terms of the army, in terms of the central executive (operating through a predominantly civilian council) and in terms of the legislature (a reformed parliamentary system with important powers). The Protectorate ensured that a church settlement was reached, acceptable to moderate opinion, and Cromwell was willing to countenance minorities (including both Catholics and Jews) provided there was no threat to order as he conceived it. He was more sympathetic to the Quakers, too, than many local magistrates. The first elected parliament (September 1654 to January 1655), however, was hostile and problematic, and was dissolved before any bills were passed. Soon afterwards a short-lived royalist rebellion, Penruddock's Rising, led to the establishment of 11 'cantons', each under a major-general, which generated further political resistance and exposed the regime to charges of military dictatorship. A second parliament was purged by the council even before it met in 1656. Nevertheless, steps such as the end of the canton system, Cromwell's efforts to consolidate moderate civilian support for his regime, and the acceptance by parliament of a new constitution presented in the Humble Petition and Advice of 1657, ensured some degree of political 'normality'.

The Protectorate had two weaknesses, however. One was the mutual suspicion of army and civilian government, dramatically illustrated in Cromwell's reluctant decision to refuse a crown for fear of officer retaliation. The other was the problem of succession, and when Oliver died in September 1658 his son Richard, broadly welcomed by conservative public opinion but lacking army backing, could hardly hope to continue his father's balancing role. Renewed radical agitation, a conspiracy between sections of the army and extreme republicans, the recall of an unhelpful Rump, and Richard's abdication produced a gradual slide into confusion. With the return of General Monck and his army from Scotland, and a rapid shift in public opinion towards a restoration of the monarchy, the end of the republican experiment in England became unavoidable early in 1660.

As with subsequent major revolutions in European history, each observer will have subjective as well as objective views about these extraordinary years in England – the most drastic of all upheavals in the early modern period. Most may well agree that the radical and social second revolution in England was never likely to come off, partly because its contributors were too divided amongst themselves and too lacking in political strategy and partly because the vested interests of the better-off were still too strong and pervasive. But the moderate first revolution achieved something: a reversal of the Crown's church policy; the removal of one of the most stubbornly and wilfully inept rulers; the consolidation of a republic (if only temporarily because of the problems associated with the transmission of power and with the stabilisation of the military ingredient in revolution); and the strengthening of a parliamentary tradition which, although unstable over the next decades, was quite exceptional in Europe. And if the social contract and constitutional experimentation proved too difficult even for one of the most developed societies in the seventeenth century, the attempt itself revealed hidden potential and resources which were not easily forgotten – or erased from record – on either side of the social and political confrontational lines.

Non-violent 'crises' in the Scandinavian kingdoms

In contrast to English, Scottish, French and Spanish experiences, the crises of authority in Denmark and Sweden involved no actual violence. The death of Christian IV in February 1648 produced an immediate shift of power within the Danish monarchy. After a long and idiosyncratic reign this was inevitable, especially given the unexpected twist in the line of succession resulting from the death of the 'crown-prince' elect, the accumulated resentments against royal autocracy within the *rigsråd* (aristocratic council of state), and the more recent establishment of regional commissions (*landkommissariater*) through which the non-conciliar nobility could exercise some political influence (see chapter 2). These commissions had already, since 1645, gained control of most military revenue, thereby not only restricting the King's scope for hiring mercenaries under his own control but also in the process paving the way for a demand for greater legislative influence for the nobility as a whole. This development, however, was not sustained at the decisive meeting of the Estates General in April 1648. The election of Frederick III as heir to the throne was a formality, and the addition of new clauses to the electoral charter to limit the scope for autocratic tendencies was predictable. But the attempt by the non-conciliar nobility to act as spokesmen for all three Estates against the aristocratic council was foiled by the council's simple tactic of promoting some of the leading regional commissioners to the council itself. Demands for annual meetings of the Estates to give formal consent to taxation and legislation were ignored, and the noble Estate for its part was easily won over by offers such as explicit tax exemption for noble demesnes. The regional commissioners lost all political initiative, and the traditional joint sovereignty of king and council was heavily weighted in favour of the latter. Above all, the council aimed at restricting the financial independence of the Crown, which was in any case damaged by a legacy of debts. Symbolically, the coronation could only take place after the actual crown had been recovered from the Hamburg banker with whom it had been lodged as security for loans.

The codification of conciliar monarchy achieved in the charter of 1648, however, provided no solution for the many practical problems that had caused friction between Christian IV and his council. The latter had never adopted a fully realistic approach to the international situation, especially with regard to military organisation in the face of growing Swedish power in the Baltic. Increasing administrative burdens likewise required expertise and commitment which the magnates were in the long run unable to provide. Rivalry amongst the leading members of the *rigsråd*, and the increasingly blatant corruption of one or two (notably the king's brother-in-law, Corfits Ulfeldt), reduced its political credibility. More seriously, the council was rarely in full attendance in Copenhagen and therefore had little of the political continuity that the new power balance required. A committee of four councillors and two of the highest officers of state was set up in 1655 to try to overcome this difficulty, but apparently with only limited success. Although the burden of taxation fell somewhat in the 1650s from the record height of the previous decade, the international situation did not permit complete relaxation: the renewal of war against Sweden in 1657, for which the King was largely responsible, led to new conflict between king and council over control of the troops. Defeat did not, however, end the political stalemate in the central administration in 1658, and it took the second attack by Charles X and the occupation of most of the kingdom except the besieged city of Copenhagen (1658–60) to precipitate what amounted to a state bankruptcy. It was clear that aristocratic constitutionalism was not viable under such circumstances.

The Estates General called for September 1660, only months after the end of the war, was the last and most interesting in Danish history. The aristocratic council, down to half strength because the King had stopped filling vacancies, was blamed by the lower orders for mishandling the war. As a reward for holding out against the Swedes, Copenhagen had been granted a number of privileges of status and trade. Its patricians now took a lead within the Third Estate, together with the clergy, and demanded drastic reform of the fiscal and financial system. Proposals were put forward for salvaging the Crown's credit by means of the sale of lands and by abolishing noble tax privileges; effective reform could best be achieved, they emphasised, if all officers of state were turned into salaried staff. Despite concessions from the nobility, deadlock was unavoidable. In October the First and Third Estates, no doubt with discreet royal encouragement, suggested freeing the King from the electoral charter, and this was eventually accepted by the nobility under duress. Frederick was acclaimed hereditary monarch in return for nothing more than vague promises to draw up a new charter for the kingdom – an opportunity of which the King made far more radical use than anyone had foreseen. Once the Estates had gradually petered out, its members returning home, the Crown circulated an act for signature by the notables, giving the King absolute (unlimited) and hereditary authority.[21] Over the next few years one of the most extreme charters of royal absolutism was drawn up, and steps initiated to reorganise the whole central administration, tax structure and ranking system. This was not what Christian IV had aspired to achieve: he had been interested solely in the practical power of a Renaissance prince, not its constitutional or even administrative form. Nevertheless the twelve-year experiment in aristocratic government from 1648 to 1660, in effect an attempt to reverse the trend of the previous decades, had on the contrary demonstrated that structural changes were needed. Even without the additional threat of major popular revolt, the military catastrophe had a traumatic impact on political perceptions. The apparent failure of the council to provide an adequate structural substitute for royal authority was entirely consistent with the wider European experience.

Sweden, however, fits the European pattern less well, despite its major involvement in the Thirty Years War and the acute strains which that produced in the years 1630–7 (see chapter 2). As Michael Roberts pointed out,[22] the Swedish *riksråd* (aristocratic council) around Axel Oxenstierna was fully conscious of the epidemic of unrest sweeping Europe in the late 1640s, and expected similar outbursts in Sweden when the harvest of 1649 failed as badly there as elsewhere. At the meeting of the Estates General in July 1650 the consequences of the massive alienation and sale of crown lands, resumed with increased urgency after 1638, became a focus of argument. The clergy and burgher estates took an unprecedented initiative on 9 October in submitting a petition against the alienation process, on the grounds that it reduced the demesne revenues of the Crown and forced the government to turn wartime taxes into permanent ones. Churches and schools were deprived of income, they argued, while those freehold peasants who had their tax payments alienated to private hands could find their security and welfare seriously threatened by determined landowners, and their position in law weakened. The clergy and burghers also demanded access to offices on the basis of competence rather than status, and universal equality before the law. These demands amounted to a major attack on the privileges of the nobility and, although couched in terms of respect for ancient custom and law (especially for Magnus Erikson's Land Law of 1350), there is no doubt that in Sweden such arguments were particularly strong because of a well-developed historical consciousness across all four Estates.

Queen Christina had in fact encouraged the lower Estates for reasons of her own: namely, to have her cousin Karl Gustav declared heir against noble opposition. As soon as this strategy had achieved its aim, the demands of the lower Estates were deferred except for a statute of 1652 regarding the amount of extraordinary labour services that could be demanded from alienated peasant freeholders.[23] The alienations, however, far from being rescinded, were continued at the extravagant level promoted by Christina in the late 1640s. In some cases this was done to pay mercenaries from Germany or to free the Crown from awkward *in natura* dues and to acquire ready cash, but more often Christina was simply handing donations to favourites, not always even in return for good service. Royal revenues were as a result nearly halved between 1644 and 1653, with direct consequences for the lesser nobility who were salaried office-holders. The alienation of tax-paying peasants unavoidably led to an increase in the burden on those who remained, and since freeholders and crown tenants were the ones represented in the peasant Estate itself, it is not surprising that the whole issue reappeared at subsequent meetings of the Estates General.

The Swedish *riksdag* (Estates General), in contrast to most of its counterparts elsewhere in Europe, had been strengthening its constitutional position. Since 1632 the principle of redress before supply had become firmly established, and all legislation now had to have the approval of a plenary session rather than just a committee. The 1650 petition by the non-noble orders amounted to an assertion of the right of legislative initiative, and during that session they even postponed consideration of the Crown's Proposition while debating their own stand. Christina's abdication in 1654 (and departure from Sweden to join the Catholic Church) raised further constitutional problems. With that background, one would have expected subsequent meetings of the Estates to have been stormy. In some respects they were: the *riksdag* of 1655 approved a *reduktion* (resumption by the Crown) of a quarter of all land and revenues alienated since 1632, but only after acrimonious confrontations between the lesser nobility and the council aristocracy and after determined tactical pressure from the new king, Charles X. Yet in this struggle, and in its sequel of 1660 following the premature death of the King, the lower orders played a relatively minor role, and the power of the *riksdag* as an institution was not strengthened.[24] It was a striking characteristic of all the sessions of the assembly that loyalty to the Crown was total, and indeed an integral part of the strategy of the lower Estates then as in the crucial session of 1680 (see chapter 11). This was so even when the Crown was manifestly dependent on the Estates for financial survival. The Swedish *riksdag*, in other words, was not a vehicle for limiting the Crown's authority, the way the English parliament was and the French parlements occasionally regarded themselves, but rather a means of strengthening the Crown. Unlike her successor three decades later, Christina in 1650 discarded her populist alliance as soon as it had secured her dynastic interest, and the peasant cause, while continuing to simmer, did not acquire as much momentum as some of the rhetoric had suggested.

If there was a Swedish 'crisis' in mid-century, therefore, it must be regarded as hinging on a divergence within the nobility itself, with the Crown exploiting the traditional loyalties and fiscal self-interest of the lesser nobles and the other estates against an exclusive and domineering (but not irresponsible) council aristocracy. There were undoubtedly some parallels with the situation in Denmark, but the Swedish council was better equipped to lead than its Danish counterpart and less tainted by the recent past. Significantly, Charles X had no intention of provoking a confrontation with the magnates; rather, the aim was to restore equilibrium between greater and lesser nobles, and between the four Estates, so as to ensure stability. So, whereas 1660 marked a clear break with constitutional tradition and governmental practice in Denmark, and placed that state firmly within the European pattern of tax-based monarchies with substantial military expenditure and bureaucratic growth, in Sweden the balance between crown and council was not yet so unstable that major change was necessary. Ultimately, as we shall see in chapter 11, Sweden opted for resumption of crown land rather than major fiscal and bureaucratic growth.

The ebb and flow of republicanism in the United Provinces

A persistent exception to most generalisations about political life in seventeenth-century Europe is the United Provinces. Lacking central authority except for the loose confederal framework provided by the States General and the ill-defined rival authority of the *stadholder* in each province (see pp. 35), the republic experienced recurrent crises of authority during the seventeenth century. The truce with Spain from 1609 to 1621, for example, generated much controversy between, on the one hand, the Amsterdam patricians led by the *Landsadvokaat* (Grand Pensionary), Oldenbarnevelt, who favoured a permanent settlement with Spain, and, on the other, the militants led by Prince Maurits of Orange, supported by some of the provincial nobility and even by some of the great merchants who wanted to dismember the Spanish–Portuguese colonial empire. The province of Holland, and Amsterdam in particular, contributed so large a share of the republic's revenues that its influence especially on military matters was decisive, but there was considerable resentment and jealousy over this amongst the other provinces, especially those inland. Maurits could rely on their backing for any challenge to Holland's dominance amongst the seven provinces in terms of control of foreign policy, not least when his strategy was presented as a move to strengthen the central institutions of the republic against the provincial separatism which Amsterdam's stance in effect amounted to. A particularly contentious issue was the status and control of troops raised by individual towns in Holland to stem growing urban unrest. Deep religious differences sharpened the potential for conflict: a majority of the Calvinist preachers tended towards an aggressive fundamentalist stance opposed to any settlement with Catholic Spain, while the more moderate Arminian minority, the Remonstrants, who favoured a secularised state and some degree of genuine religious toleration, were largely confined to Holland. Oldenbarnevelt and the Amsterdam regents succeeded in deferring until 1618 the general synod demanded by the fundamentalists to impose religious uniformity. Maurits, for reasons of political expediency and self-interest, then placed his army behind a coup which resulted in the arrest of Oldenbarnevelt and the ousting of his Remonstrant supporters from power in Holland. Oldenbarnevelt was tried for treason in the name of a divided and uncertain States General and, unable or unwilling to recognise the dangerous political motives of Maurits and the prosecutors, was convicted and executed in 1619. The church synod of Dordrecht predictably confirmed the

Counter-Remonstrant (fundamentalist Calvinist) line which suited Maurits's intentions. In the long run, however, the consequences were less severe than one might have expected: Maurits, although now in complete control of military affairs and able to exercise considerable political patronage, carried through no major political reforms.

Holland remained the centre of latent opposition against the House of Orange during the second stage of the war against Spain, and its regents were instrumental in achieving the early peace settlement of January 1648. By that stage the House of Orange, headed by Frederik Hendrik until 1647 and then by the brash Willem II (son-in-law of Charles I of England), had pursued dynastic and crypto-royalist policies so far as to turn the office of *stadholder* into a threat to the republic's interests. Willem tried to subvert the peace and involve the republic in a campaign of territorial annexation in the southern Netherlands in alliance with France. The province of Holland was concerned not only about the fiscal implications of renewed war, and the potential damage to trade at a time of exceptionally high grain prices and a slump in the textile industry: relations with England were also delicate, and Holland feared an involvement by Willem on the royalist side in England. When the patricians demanded a reduction of the army, a political stalemate followed. This was in effect a replay of the 1609–19 struggle for power between the Holland regents and the House of Orange, but with stronger republican–royalist overtones. A crisis was precipitated in May 1650 when Holland, already encumbered with a war debt of 120 million guilder, announced that it was ceasing to pay a proportion of the army still standing. A deputation by Willem on behalf of the States General failed to sway a sufficient number of towns in Holland, and ultimately Willem unilaterally ordered the arrest of six leading Holland deputies. He failed, however, in his plan to have Amsterdam itself occupied, and shortly afterwards had to accept a compromise with the province, settling none of the outstanding differences except the number of troops.

Whether further confrontations, or even civil war, would have occurred is uncertain, but both sides were clearly aware of English precedents. In November 1650, however, Willem suddenly died from smallpox, paving the way for the triumph of the Holland regents once more. Most of the other provinces followed Amsterdam's lead in refusing to appoint a *stadholder*, and the Grand Pensionary of Holland became in effect the head of state. For 22 years the United Provinces remained in balance under a fully mature republican government, most of that time under the leadership of Johan de Witt, who was Grand Pensionary from 1653.

The final stage in this struggle for power came in 1672, as a direct result of the collapse of the ill-prepared Dutch defences against the French attack of 1672. By then the Orange party had recovered popular prestige, and the still young son of Willem II, Prince Willem (William) had gained a seat in the Council of State. The traumatic military emergency, combined with renewed resentments against the regents, mounting street violence, and inflammatory activity amongst some fundamentalist preachers, forced Holland to appoint William *stadholder*. This did not allay mob violence, however, and in August Johan de Witt and his brother Cornelis were hacked to death in The Hague. Prince William became effective head of state, but, like Maurits in 1619, did not introduce formal constitutional change. Concerned primarily with his military position, and from 1689 frequently absent as co-ruler of the British kingdoms, he concentrated on the struggle against Louis XIV. On his death without issue in 1702, the United Provinces once again reverted to a purely republican model of government without a *stadholder*.

The Dutch political crises of 1618, 1650 and 1672 logically belong in a sequence which cannot easily be fitted into the pattern of the rest of Europe. Although England and Sweden also experienced a delayed follow-up to their mid-century search for stability some decades later, the Dutch pendulum-swing was arguably integral to the republican system itself, unavoidable for a state attempting to find an alternative political route in an age of rampant dynastic and militarist monarchy. At each change-over there were refreshing displacements amongst the regent families and the incumbents of town and local government offices, and a great deal of public political debate. The coup of 1650 involved threats of violence but no actual bloodshed, in contrast to the upheavals of 1618 and 1672, and if economic uncertainty, as we have noted, contributed to the unrest of 1650, acute economic deprivation was less obvious as a catalyst of popular violence in the United Provinces than in most other parts of Europe. If the events of 1650 in Holland have any reasonably close parallels, it must be with the narrow power struggles in the political elites of Denmark and Sweden between 1648 and 1660. But neither of the latter had anything like the political maturity and complexity of Holland, or its economic strength, and neither could have forced their ruling dynasties into as impressive a compromise as Amsterdam had done with the house of Orange even before the death of Willem.

The debate about 'the crisis of the seventeenth century', then, has provided no straightforward framework for the analysis of particular confrontations. Detailed research, especially on particular localities, has revealed exceptions to, and divergences from, all the general explanatory frameworks that contributed to the original debate – hardly a surprising conclusion if we remind ourselves that we are dealing with a period where unrest, starvation, rebellion, war and economic dislocation were more common than peace and stability, and where local and regional loyalties were stronger than embryonic 'national' ones. There was never any significant causal connection between the revolts of the 1640s and 1650s, except in the case of the obvious clusters that shared a particular set of grievances, such as Catalonia–Portugal, Palermo–Naples, or Scotland–Ireland–England. At most, elsewhere, there were shared economic experiences, perhaps some awareness of general unrest, and at times willingness (if not always ability) to exploit the weakness of political rivals, be it across the Pyrenees, in the factions of Poland, or within individual provincial or urban power structures. Indeed no 'crisis' anywhere was a simple two-sided conflict, nor would anyone familiar with the evidence seriously sum up the confrontations in terms of a struggle between two 'classes' in any meaningful sense. European society was far too composite for that, too torn by faction and narrow rivalries of interest within what we have called 'the elite', too lacking in common popular consciousness – so much so that, as we have noted in particular in connection with the French and English upheavals, there were often several different confrontations running in parallel or in sequence.

What then is left of the 'general crisis'? At a detailed level, not much. Yet with all these qualifications made, the 1640s and 1650s are still exceptional. This chapter has confined discussion essentially to the failure of the state and of local authority to fulfil the functions expected of them, and the resulting collapse of normal concepts of order, deference and resignation. Glimpses of such failures are discernible earlier, for example in the Austro–Bohemian peasant revolts of the 1620s or in the tax revolts in France, particularly in the 1630s. In the 1640s, however, the combination of war-induced fiscal disintegration with either loss of nerve or outright incompetence at the centre of power produced resistance across society on an unprecedented scale. The expectations of long-overdue peace and the timing of the bitter Europe-wide harvest failures of the late 1640s meant that popular impatience and frustration often erupted in different places at roughly the same time: a few years earlier in Spain because of Catalonia and the enormity of Spanish commitments; earlier in England, too, because of the Scots and the Irish and because theirs was a war unrelated to the continental conflicts; but elsewhere mostly within the period 1648–53, with resulting shock-waves until 1660. During these years rebellion, although essentially conservative and tradition-bound, acquired legitimacy because of the degree of provocation and the degree of government failure. In England above all, but briefly and on a much more restricted scale also in the Ormée in France, the challenge took on a distinctively independent and innovative form which could temporarily link different social groups and seek a new basis for government by consent. The threat that such a development might pose to the established orders everywhere was decisive in producing the political reactions and restorations that swept much of Europe around 1660 – inaugurating a period where the state eventually came to exercise an unchallenged monopoly of power and 'protection' in the exclusive interest of those with status and wealth.

8 The structure of society: peasant and seigneur

The historian may attempt to make some generalisations about the structure of seventeenth-century elites and of urban communities in different parts of Europe, and may even conclude that gradual changes can be perceived, particularly in north-western society, in some of the functions and attitudes of those groups who regarded themselves as 'the middling sort' or as persons of 'quality' and rank. But the 70–90 per cent of the population who were non-noble country-dwellers really do defy all generalisation. Ranging from a normally small minority of well-off peasants (most clearly visible in the few prosperous areas of Europe), through smallholders, craftsmen, cottagers, fishermen or foresters, to migrant labourers, transhumant mountain communities, vagrants and the destitute, their conditions of survival depended on a wide range of variables. It is worth emphasising that the term 'peasantry', especially in western and central Europe, is liable to give a misleading impression of a vast and diversified rural population, often hierarchic and distinctly layered, and lacking any social coherence or cultural unity even within particular regions – so much so that some historians have opted not to use the term at all, preferring instead terms such as 'villager' or 'village farmer' to describe the non-noble rural population generally, and the term 'subject' to reflect their status in relation to the rights of lordship exercised by landowners and the Crown. Such terminology, however, can itself cause confusion, and in the absence of better alternatives the generic term 'peasant' will be used here – albeit with the proviso that in Europe as a whole generalisations about, and comparisons of, historical trends in rural society necessarily have to be treated with great caution.

The most basic variables were undoubtedly climate and geography. Southern European climates were relatively hospitable if the land held moisture and was low-lying and fairly flat – conditions which many parts of Italy and Spain did not meet. At the other extreme, tillage of permanent holdings was difficult in the Scottish Highlands and impossible in the northern parts of Scandinavia and of Muscovy, regardless of altitude above sea level. Iceland could grow neither grain nor timber for its own use, and its income from fishing was limited by the tariff policies of the Danish government which held sovereignty there. The climatic deterioration culminating in the later seventeenth century affected all of Europe to some extent, but in the north, even if weather conditions had been stable, the shortness of the growing season, the harshness and darkness of winter conditions and the physical inaccessibility of many areas would have militated against any material security. The more fertile parts of central and southern Europe, on the other hand, often had to support a higher density of population; no less importantly, these areas, if not too remote, were also of far greater interest to landowners and state officials trying to cream off agricultural surplus either directly in cash or kind or indirectly through demands for labour services. In most of Europe, however, there is evidence that the last third of the seventeenth century was a period of agricultural stagnation or depression, with unstable or declining market prices. For most of the rural population this entailed economic difficulty, disappointing productivity and income, a decline in the value of land itself and perhaps social tension.

Apart from the uncontrollable factors of geography and the aberrations of climate, the consequences of which we have already noted (see chapter 3), rural conditions were determined by a number of man-made factors. The most obvious was what we might regard as a failure to adapt the intensive husbandry of the Netherlands and England to conditions elsewhere in Europe – a failure probably best explained in terms of a fear of novelty and a lack of either the market incentives or the extra resources needed for experimentation. In the vast belt of lowland open-field (strip-field) farming which stretched from south-western England and northern France through southern Scandinavia and northern Germany to central Russia, the land was suitable for cereal cultivation. It was common to grow two types of grain: rye was the most widespread, in France and England sometimes in a mixture with some variety of wheat (maslin), but oats were also popular because they required less fertiliser, while barley (or the Scottish variant, bere) was hardier against the cold in the north. Millet, buckwheat and other cereals were common further south and in poorer soils both in and out of the grain belt.

Whatever the combination, land in the grain belt was mostly tilled according to the customary triple-rotation system, with one year under each of two cereals, and a third year fallow.[1] Strictly speaking, therefore, most land was not dependent on the vagaries of a single crop as in monoculture, but the result frequently amounted to something nearly as insecure, partly because the common reliance on two closely-related crops increased the relative potential damage from bad weather or blights and partly because there was a shortage of fertiliser. Seaweed, lime and other additives were available only in some areas and were not always exploited, while domestic animals were too small and too few to secure enough manure for generous yields from rye or from the more demanding wheat.

Domestic animals were underfed and underdeveloped even by eighteenth-century standards: peasant horses, for example, although used for ploughing in Denmark and northern Germany in preference to oxen, were commonly too small to pass muster for cavalry use. Similarly, the milk yield from cows (except in the dairy lands of the north-western Netherlands) was rarely even a quarter of the modern equivalent, and the live weight of domestic animals on average well below half. Owing to shortages of fodder, flocks had to be severely reduced during each winter, and the surviving animals were not always able to walk into their pastures by themselves in the spring. There might have been readier scope for development of the basic tools used, but in this respect as in others it was rare to see significant change from one generation to another. Thus the heavy and unmanoeuvrable wheeled plough, which might require three or more pairs of animals and two men, was not superseded in many lowland areas despite the existence of alternatives. Nor, despite its obvious speed and convenience, did the scythe supplant the sickle for harvesting.

Outside the grain belt, a vast variety of farming patterns existed, often creating a more varied landscape with forests, hedgerows, fruit-tree plantations, vineyards and olives (especially in western France and the Mediterranean), and a greater range of major crops. In higher moorlands south of the cereal belt, or in regions where the quality of soil was manifestly inadequate for grains, animal husbandry was given much attention. In Jutland and Schleswig-Holstein, and in the upland and inland areas of Poland and Hungary, cattle were reared for live export to the meat markets of the cities of central and western Europe, grazing on the way. Over 50,000 head of cattle passed through customs in Gottorp in the peak year of 1612, going south from Denmark and Schleswig. Yet such specialisation failed to foster much awareness of the need for selective breeding or careful husbandry to reduce the risk of epizootics: agricultural science had not developed far enough for that. The cattle route through the duchies, however, did encourage the spread of a variant of convertible husbandry known in northern Germany as *Koppelwirtschaft*, whereby enclosed fields were worked in a 10–12-year cycle, half under various cereals, half under pasture for the cattle. The results were good on both counts, the pasturing phase being sufficiently intensive to fertilise the fields effectively. *Koppelwirtschaft* became the basis for agricultural improvement over a wider area during the eighteenth century.

In the open-field system of land usage, where each villager would till unfenced strips within the bigger plots shared by the community, considerable co-ordination amongst participants was essential to ensure consistency and compatibility. Such co-ordination was even closer where several peasants shared one farmstead, a normal practice all over Europe but particularly common both amongst freeholders in Norway and amongst tenants in the ferme touns (farm settlements) of Scotland. In Russia and more rarely in Poland and Hungary, some villages even operated through fully communal regulation, with individual householders controlling only a small house-plot for their own exclusive use. By contrast, in the upland regions of central and southern Europe, peasant holdings were commonly enclosed and autonomous, yet even there there was little evidence of the adoption of rotations other than those customary in open-field regions. Clearly, soil conditions and altitude in themselves imposed important variations, but generally the European peasant remained true to long-established traditions geared towards self-sufficiency and subsistence survival. Poverty and unfavourable tenure conditions emphasised the worst features, leading, as in Brittany or Burgundy, to more intensive cropping and even continuous cultivation, which the soil could not bear. Continuous cultivation could only work in the type of infield-outfield (often runrig) systems used for example in upland parts of Britain (particularly in Scotland), where the infield was subjected to careful manuring from the outfield and where the outfield itself was tilled in complex rotations.

Crucial in terms of land utilisation and peasant standards of living were two other particular factors. One was the availability or otherwise of additional employment, particularly during slack winter months, in textile production or other domestic industry. Where this was present – often in the catchment area of larger markets, notably in Flanders and in northern Italy – the economic and social consequences could be very significant (see chapter 4). Not unrelated to this was the second factor, namely the customary practices and constraints which determined whether a peasant holding would remain undivided or not. Where peasants were predominantly tenants of one kind or another on land owned by a seigneur, the landowner would naturally as part of his lordship rights insist on having a say in the transmission process. That holdings should be passed on undivided was commonly required by seigneurs in eastern Denmark and northern Germany, for instance, while in the areas of east-central and eastern Europe where seigneurial authority was often stronger still, the peasant generally had little or no control over succession to his holding. Even those who, in various parts of Europe, had freehold status of some kind found their rights of disposition undermined by seigneurial claims, except if they were living in remote areas or had a rare written title to their land.

Inheritance and succession patterns, however, were also affected by legal norms and community traditions which were sometimes contrary to seigneurial interests. In the west of France and in Normandy, for instance, partible (divisible) inheritance in principle favoured an equal division amongst heirs, even if this could at times result in portions too small to be reasonably viable. In the Midi and the Pyrenees, on the other hand, although seigneurial influence was much less direct, impartible inheritance ensured the preservation of a family holding, so that extended- and stem-family patterns were far more common there than the simple nuclear family prevalent in areas where holdings were readily divided. In areas of tradition-bound impartible inheritance, the non-favoured siblings were never totally excluded: they would have some claim either on employment or on the movable property and yield of the family holding (for example, to cover dowries for girls). In contrast to the stricter primogeniture favoured within noble families, impartible inheritance patterns could favour a younger child, including a daughter if there were no sons present. It could also, notably in Scandinavia, involve formal contractual provision for the maintenance of a widowed parent, or even of both parents if they surrendered the holding to a successor before death. The distinction between partible and impartible systems, in fact, is not always easy for the historian to observe because of the various compromise solutions – often designed to steer a course between the severe loss of status or opportunity for less-favoured heirs on the one hand and excessive subdivision of land damaging to the family's core holding on the other. Notably in western Germany (north and south), where partible inheritance had originally been the norm, there were as many interesting juxtapositions of contrasting patterns as there were actual autonomous political units.

Whatever the particular local variant – and every part of Europe seems to have had its own 'norms' – inheritance patterns had decisive effects on the viability of the resulting holdings and on the location of potential labour resources. Areas of partible inheritance were more likely, as in Switzerland or northern and western highland England, to produce a scattered and marginalised labour market suitable for domestic industry, or, as in Normandy, to create a potential breeding ground for revolt amongst impoverished peasants. By contrast, in areas of impartible inheritance, siblings might at least potentially, as they did in southern and eastern England, move elsewhere and leave the land less heavily populated.[2]

Of all the factors governing peasant conditions in Europe, however, the one most susceptible to change in a period of economic stagnation or strain was the actual peasant–seigneur relationship itself. It used to be common to divide Europe in this respect into an eastern half, where serfdom was of decisive importance, and the west, where peasants at least formally remained free agents. West of the Elbe and the Alps the prevailing pattern was that known as *Grundherrschaft* (lordship over land), where landowners did not generally have large demesnes (land worked directly from the manor): an estate of 100 hectares (250 acres) would be regarded as large for the purposes of direct farming, and might in any case be administered by a leaseholder. Because of the relatively high density of population in the west, there was sufficient cheap labour to satisfy the limited needs of the demesnes. The great bulk of the land was worked in smaller peasant holdings, held on some form of contractual basis in return for rents and relatively moderate labour services. In the west, serfdom was fairly rare, and the peasant was in theory free to end his contract, to act in his own interests and to go to law if necessary.

East of the Elbe, by contrast, much of the land, at least in the grain-growing belt, was worked as part of large manorial estates, in what is known as *Gutsherrschaft*, where lordship rights were exercised more extensively for the benefit of the demesne. In Mecklenburg the average size of demesnes in the early seventeenth century was around 150 hectares, and a significant number were over 300 hectares; even more strikingly, estates of at least 100 hectares (250 acres) constituted over 50 per cent of the total arable area of the province. In Brandenburg, part of Saxony, Silesia, Pomerania and the Prussian provinces large-scale demesnes accounted for at least 30 per cent of the total arable.[3] A landowner might well be absentee, as in the west, but instead of being content with the predictable and small returns of the rentier he would, it is argued, operate with a clear eye to the market wherever possible. Fieldwork was done at minimal cost by peasants subject to far greater and more arbitrary compulsory labour services than in the west, and they would be required to bring their own tools and draught animals – the only way profits in the decisive export market could be maintained. Peasants would have only a relatively small holding for their own use, held without any security or inheritance rights in law; they would have little independence from their seigneur and would commonly have no legal personality (that is, they would not be entitled to plead in law-courts in their own right). In addition to the prohibitions against peasant mobility which, because of fears of a shortage of manpower, were at the core of the system, serfdom proper also involved restrictions of personal freedom with regard to marriage and children. In the German lands, children were required to perform prescribed domestic service for the seigneur (*Gesindedienst*), often for a year but sometimes (as in Prussia from the late sixteenth century onwards) for an unspecified period on demand.

The relative absence of developed urban life in eastern Europe made it difficult for a fugitive to seek an alternative livelihood, and the unrivalled role of noble landowners in local and central administration ensured that state legislation and policies were designed to preserve peasant subservience. In most areas nobles alone were entitled to own landed estates, so that social divisions were sharpened. At the same time, and especially during the early seventeenth-century wars, urban life was sufficiently disrupted to reduce demand for agricultural and other produce, and this in turn forced landowners to adopt more restrictive practices in the hope of maintaining profits.

Outlined in this way, the *Grundherrschaft* of the west and the *Gutsherrschaft* of the east were substantially different systems of land usage and of rural social relations.[4] As we shall see in the next sections, such a simplified polarity is liable to misrepresent a far more complex reality on the ground, where patterns of land usage, and the social relations that went with them, created a wonderfully complicated mosaic. In addition, we need to remember the very substantial differences between northern and southern Europe, both in terms of the kinds of agriculture possible and in terms of the widely divergent patterns of market development possible during the unstable years of the early seventeenth century. Just where the rural conditions in the Ottoman Empire might fit in, in this more complex picture, is still not clear, but research so far suggests that a decline in central control allowed large-scale landholders (originally military servitors: see p. 175) to acquire powers over the peasantry not unlike those of feudal-type landholders in the areas of serfdom. Ottoman peasant rights and obligations were not identical to those of serfs – vestigial personal freedom was retained, combined with some security of possession, but the obligation to remain on the registered land was strengthened through detailed fiscal record-keeping. Nevertheless, some comparisons with peasant conditions both in east-central Europe and in some parts of the Mediterranean seems plausible.[5]

Serfdom in Muscovy

Serfdom, when fully developed in eastern Europe in the eighteenth century, amounted to very comprehensive seigneurial domination over the peasantry. By then, serfs on private estates could in practice be bought, sold or transferred, with or without their land, and their services were customarily reckoned as part of the capital assets of the estate. There were no real limitations on the exercise of seigneurial authority, except that of paternalistic self-interest. In contrast to peasants bound to the land in France or Denmark, serfs in the east were tied to the particular landowner by social practices and legal restrictions that were clearly demeaning and utterly one-sided – and which also directly affected the status of women. Serf–seigneur relations were not contractual but part of an institutional and social framework unconditionally backed by the law and the state.

The legal framework for serfdom was only gradually worked out, but there is good reason to assume that the realities of the system had become well ingrained in practice before formal legislation was complete. In Muscovy the peasantry, originally free, had by the later fifteenth century been subjected to substantial restrictions on their entitlement to move from one estate to another, and in the period 1581–92 these were tightened with the help of new tax registers. It is not clear who was behind this, but landowners and servitors were concerned about severe manpower losses in central Muscovy caused by peasant migration, flight and war. According to Hellie, the middle-ranking servitors in particular were anxious to secure the labour resources on their service lands, and could exploit the state's dependence on their military service to secure this before they themselves became militarily obsolete in the later seventeenth century.[6]

Peasants had traditionally been entitled to give notice around St George's day (26 November) if they wanted to leave their tenancy, but individual landowners were able to obtain dispensations from this practice: from the 1590s the so-called 'forbidden years', when peasants were not allowed to move at all, became continuous. By the second quarter of the seventeenth century, after the disruption of the Time of Troubles, the Tsar had further consolidated the position of his servitors with generous grants of land, so much so that within a couple of generations an estimated four-fifths of all *tiaglo* (tax- and service-yielding) subjects were in private ownership, including around a tenth under church ownership. It was in the interests of the state not only to protect these landed servitors in order to ensure satisfactory operation of the whole machinery of state, but also to prevent tiaglo-subjects from roving to remote or newly acquired lands. At first, if a peasant broke the restrictions of the 1590s by flight there was a time-limit on pursuit by the landowner, but in the 1630s and 1640s this limit was extended to ten or fifteen years. It was apparently the lesser servitors who wanted this, for many magnates, and most landowners in the south, had benefited from the limitation on pursuit to acquire manpower from elsewhere. Finally in 1649 the *Ulozhenie* (Law Code) adopted by Tsar Alexis and the *zemsky sobor* removed all restrictions on the duration of pursuit, not only with regard to heads of households but for all members of the peasant community. The Code also formally ended the right to give notice of intention to leave an estate, so that the Russian peasantry was conclusively enserfed.

The Code of 1649 curiously omitted to specify penalties for peasants who adopted the only available solution of running away illegally – that only came in 1658, and punishments for flight were occasionally suspended (as in the years 1684–98) to facilitate army recruitment. But the Code did confirm total seigneurial control over the family arrangements and property of the peasantry; both the property and the family of the peasantry had long been seen as qualifiable assets which the landowner could sell. As a further concession to the lesser servitors who could ill afford to take action to recover peasants 'poached' by more enterprising magnates, the Code also obliged landowners to verify the condition of any person seeking employment on their estates. The assumption throughout was that the seigneur's interest in maintaining his labour force was the sole issue at stake: the serf was subject in all respects to the sole will of the landowner, and deprived of all defence in law or in livelihood. The Code ostensibly restricted the sale of serfs without their land, but this was universally disregarded. Only if the seigneur was guilty of crimes against the Tsar's interest was a serf entitled to petition. Harsh though this seems, however, it was entirely in accordance with the overall trend in Russian society: the Code, after all, bound townsmen in similar ways, and while servitors became the intermediary between state and peasant, they themselves were expected to serve the Tsar unconditionally and without any right, for example, to emigrate. Muscovy after 1649 was approaching the rigid stratification of a caste society.

The clauses of the 1649 Code which so completely bound the Muscovite peasantry were adopted, it seems, only under pressure. In 1648 the servitors had appeared to be the main bulwark against the spread of further popular revolt in Moscow and elsewhere, and Alexis had after some delay given in to their demands. The nature of the rigid social hierarchy in Muscovy and the heavy obligations on each class, however, would have made any other development unlikely. There was a constant drain of manpower away from the central regions of Muscovy towards emptier lands, and the presence of nomadic or semi-nomadic tribes in the Cossack south and the Tatar south-east made control difficult. Many servitors already had inadequate income, being in some cases little more than peasants themselves, with just a few *tiaglo* homesteads under their control, or even none at all. The soil and climate in central Muscovy rarely produced much surplus, and the frequency of crop failures meant that there was little material security except for the magnates. Peasants had for long been at great risk of falling into debt, and those who did were in effect already tied to their seigneur.

The actual burdens on the peasantry in Muscovy varied enormously, especially in remoter areas. On the whole, however, the load seems to have been increasing noticeably during the seventeenth century, along with taxes payable to the state. Rents (*obrok*) were often converted into money to ease collection, and increases here may only just have exceeded the rate of inflation. In the central and western regions, however, labour services (*barshchina*) were augmented substantially after 1613, especially when servitors there, holding the more generous allocations of land alienated by the Romanovs, became aware of the marketing potential for agricultural produce. The proportion of arable used as demesne is not quantifiable in this period, but was probably fairly high in the areas of new colonisation in the Kama basin, south of the Oka river and in the east. It was also increasing in the central provinces, making labour services crucially important. The landowner Boris Morozov, who by mid-century held over 6000 home-steads and as chief adviser to Tsar Alexis was amongst the wealthiest magnates in Muscovy, usually demanded around two or three days *barshchina* per homestead weekly in those areas where such services were usable.

The Code of 1649 removed the only bargaining power available to the peasantry: the ability to exploit the shortage of labour to obtain better conditions of tenure. Seigneurs naturally continued to try to increase their manpower, but henceforth did so (despite severe penal-ties in law) by kidnapping peasants from other estates or by using other tactics available at least to the more powerful. The peasant himself now stood to gain little from such change: he would invariably be classed as a runaway, and many seigneurs in any case terminated the few concessions and incentives they had offered before 1649. Only the small minority (perhaps 10 per cent) of peasants on unalienated state land retained some measure of traditional status. Peasants on church land (perhaps another 10 per cent) also had some advantages of secure tenure, but labour services there were generally very heavy. For the rest, collective hatred of the seigneur could occasionally burst out in harsh and bloody revolts such as that led by Stenka Razin in the Volga and Don basin in 1670, but these only united the elite and the state in acts of repression which made the reform of peasant conditions unthinkable.

A peculiar feature of Russian society, clearly indicative of the pres-ence of empty land and harsh economic conditions, was the impor-tance of slavery. A tenth of the population is estimated to have been slaves (16 per cent of the male adult population of Moscow itself in 1638), the great majority of them native Russians who had sold them-selves for the sake of some security.[7] Slave labour was used by servitors of the upper and middle ranks, and also by the Church and a few wealthy merchants. More than a tenth of the homesteads in some regions were held by slaves, although the average was normally lower. It is clear that some peasants voluntarily accepted slave status, perhaps for a limited duration, in return for the cancellation of debts or (until 1679) in order to escape taxation by the state. Such drastic steps were commonly taken in the 1580s and in the Time of Troubles, but the process was naturally closely related to the trend towards total enserf-ment of the peasantry generally. One of the reasons, indeed, why the lesser servitors were particularly concerned to restrict the mobility of their tenants may have been that they could ill afford to buy slaves outright. Slavery, however, extended well beyond the peasant popula-tion, and there was even a slave elite serving in the cavalry whose primary function was initially in fact to ward off Tatar raids and prevent the enslavement of native Russians captured by the nomads. Higher up the social scale, instances have also been noted of townsmen, soldiers and even lesser servitors offering themselves into slavery in order to escape destitution or heavy service obligations to the state.

The German lands and east-central Europe

In Muscovy, the formalisation of serfdom came late and was a by-product of the obligations imposed on the *dvorianstvo* (service nobility) by the state – the servitors were granted control over their peasantry to ensure an adequate economic basis for state service. Elsewhere in eastern and east-central Europe, state authority was generally weaker; instead, varieties of serfdom developed as part of the manorial economy (*Gutswirtschaft*) in response to economic factors, particularly the demand for agrarian produce (notably grain) in urban and overseas markets. Access to such markets was a necessary precondition for the development of the large Polish Crown or magnate demesne (*folwark*) and its equivalents in the plains stretching from Holstein, Mecklenburg and western Pomerania to the Baltic provinces and parts of the Ukraine. Estate management here is usually described in terms of its dependence on cheap labour provided by the peasant population: in those areas of the north-east where the demographic and material consequences of the Thirty Years War were most serious, the personal and economic autonomy of the peasantry could be undermined by various means. Peasant land was enclosed in the demesnes, tenants sometimes being moved to remoter farms or transferred to smallholdings with relatively heavier labour services. The ruling authorities (mostly princes who were themselves landowners) accepted the demands of landowners. Peasants in northern Germany and Poland had already in the sixteenth century been deprived of any access they might have had to royal or princely courts of justice, and this loss of legal protection lasted until emancipation in the eighteenth century or later. The Polish diet regularly passed laws against runaways, and prescribed penalties (as in 1632) on cities housing fugitives. In Prussia, too, cities were expected to turn away fugitive peasants, and few municipalities had the courage and conviction of Königsberg, which in 1634 openly denied the validity of seigneurial claims and refused to countenance serfdom as a system. Generally the peasantry had little defence, and in Pomerania, for example, the authorities by 1616 assumed that all peasants were serfs subject to the full range of restrictions. Taken in conjunction with seigneurial monopolies on milling, brewing and sometimes marketing, and with dues payable to the landowner in kind, conditions were often unfavourable for the preservation of peasant independence in either economic or social terms.

Serfdom appeared to guarantee the availability of labour, and landowners sometimes held village communities jointly responsible for the fulfilment of obligations in order to facilitate control. Since serfs were given the use of smallholdings rather than actual payment for their services, the grain crop of the demesne could be sold at very competitive prices compared with the produce of estates using wage labour. Peasants themselves were only in a position to compete if they were situated in the immediate vicinity of major export centres such as Danzig and Elblag where transport costs were minimal and conditions of tenure from urban owners more flexible. Further inland, both peasant producers and even lesser-gentry landowners were badly affected when grain prices became highly unstable after 1620. The large-scale landowners (the Church, the magnates and in Poland the Crown itself) could take advantage of this and accelerate the concentration of land in fewer and bigger estate conglomerations.

The complexity of serf–seigneur relations in the east-European grain belt makes it practically impossible to measure the real productivity of demesnes relative to that of peasant holdings. Although many estates were large and consolidated, there was little interest in experimentation either with crops or with managerial systems, and little active investment in land. This, combined with the lack of incentive for peasants yielding labour services on the demesne, ensured that demesne productivity was poor. Some historians have even suggested that it was poorer than that of peasant holdings in comparable conditions, but the evidence is very incomplete. Analysis of yield ratios for Polish and Hungarian estates certainly suggests that seigneurial land had a low and perhaps even intrinsically declining output during the seventeenth century – admittedly, though, at a time when agrarian conditions everywhere were stagnant. This is also reflected in the low market value of noble land east of the Elbe after the Thirty Years War, compared with the later sixteenth century. Most landowners appear to have responded to this trend by demanding more restrictive legislation and by attempting to increase their consolidated demesne, for example by reducing the size of peasant holdings or by removing peasants to those chronically vacant holdings which could not conveniently be enclosed in the demesne itself. In short, the profitability of manorial *Gutswirtschaft* farming hinged not on improved efficiency or productivity, but on the ability of landowners to press more labour out of their serfs (at minimal cost) for use on large estates. This applied in accentuated form also to the Polish Crown estates, often managed by agents and officials indifferent to possible long-term consequences.[8]

Nowhere in Europe, however, did either complete *Grundherrschaft* (land leased to peasant tenants in return for reasonably fixed rents payable to the landowner in kind, cash and labour) or complete *Gutswirtschaft* (land managed directly by or for the – usually noble – landowner through unrestricted compulsory labour services) exist in pure forms. Similarly, neither a free contractual agreement between landowner and peasant tenant, nor a comprehensive and universal serfdom, existed anywhere in reality. Much of Pomerania came close to the latter after the Thirty Years War, when seigneurial interests became totally dominant in the Estates and administration of the province, and over half the total land area was demesne. But neither in Brandenburg nor in Prussia, although part of the grain belt, was serfdom ever universal. A recent study of the east-Elbian region of Prignitz in Brandenburg has graphically illustrated just how remote some areas were from the conventional image of oppressive serf-based agriculture managed by authoritarian and conservative noble landowners.[9] We also know that at the end of the century at least 12 per cent of the peasantry of East Prussia were free *Kölmer* or yeomen, and as we have already noted there was scope for an economically autonomous peasantry and relatively free wage-labour in the environs of powerful cities like Königsberg. There were other variations: in Lithuania, although serfdom developed early, large-scale demesnes remained relatively few in number, while a small number of wealthy peasants actually increased their holdings in the course of the seventeenth century.

Further south, especially in the more hilly parts of Silesia, southern Poland, Bohemia and Moravia, where grain was not so readily grown for bulk export, the development was very different. In Bohemia, for instance, the nobility had not traditionally demanded very large labour services because the seigneurial economy was orientated towards fish-farming, livestock-breeding, brewing and other specialised industries which were not so labour-intensive. During the sixteenth century, however, the growth of towns not only under royal protection but also on private noble land made market production more attractive. Even so, the consolidation of enclosed estates and demands for compulsory peasant labour services remained for a time limited by comparison with northern Germany, and the legal and personal restraints of serfdom were not exploited very fully. It was the military defeat of the Thirty Years War, and the changes in landownership from the 1620s onwards, that seem to have brought the most marked deterioration in peasant conditions in Bohemia. Seigneurs assumed stronger repressive powers to deal with the consequences of wartime devastation, and emphasised restrictions on peasant mobility to compensate for population losses. The peasant revolts of the later 1620s (see chapter 1) were repressed with brutality, and the constitutional changes wrought by the Habsburgs destroyed the vestigial legal and personal rights of the peasantry. Labour services (*robota*) apparently increased rapidly after 1620, often rising to more than half the total available number of work days for one man per holding. Prominent nobles such as Prince Eggenberg were able to acquire more than 5000 land-holding serfs; noble- and church-owned land in general amounted to four-fifths of the total by mid-century, and so the Crown, even if it had wished to, was in no position to counterbalance seigneurial pressure on the peasantry. The petitions from, and subsequent revolts on, 129 estates in Bohemia in 1680, directed against labour services and the seigneurial system, did result in a regulative decree, but the Crown essentially backed seigneurial demands and used troops to repress the unrest and execute a number of its leaders.

Generally in central and east-central Europe, although the evidence is scattered and far from consistent, the burden of labour services probably tended to increase during the seventeenth century, albeit from a lower starting-point in the south than along the Baltic. In Silesia, where labour services at the end of the sixteenth century may have averaged no more than 50–70 days per annum, serfs were used in industrial enterprises, including mining, and the economically difficult years from the outbreak of the Thirty Years War are unlikely to have eased the burden. In Hungary too, all aspects of serf–seigneur relations were from 1608 formally removed from central government and Estates to the magnate-controlled provincial governments. Nevertheless, reconquest of the Danubian basin from the Turks at the end of the century resulted in special incentives offered to peasants willing to settle there, including easy commutation of labour services. Already in the last years of Leopold's reign this seems to have produced some relaxation of conditions for the peasantry, lasting into the eighteenth century.

Entrepreneurial land usage in central and western Europe

Assumptions that both peasant and seigneur in seventeenth-century Europe were by and large traditionalists do need to be qualified. A particularly interesting area, especially given the overall bleak economic situation in Italy by this stage (see chapter 4), is the Lombardy region examined by Domenico Sella. He emphasises that, despite falling land values and severe military and fiscal oppression, convertible husbandry continued to flourish there in the 1640s and 1650s, involving stock-raising, cereals, artificial grasses and important industrial crops such as hemp and flax. A pronounced awareness of market opportunities helped to ensure not just a variety of food crops, including some maize and (in marshier, flat areas) an expanding rice crop, but also encouraged subsidiary employment in the silk industry, other textile production, metalwork and paper production. On some of the bigger ecclesiastical estates the effects of careful management are discernible not merely in the provisions for post-war reconstructive relief but also in more sophisticated long-term tenancy contracts with elements of sharecropping and more meticulous supervision of crop management by agents of the landlord. What evidence there is for the province as a whole, however, suggests that the impetus came from various directions: significantly, from generation-old landlord families themselves, but also from merchants and tax officials with capital available for investment in rural development. Not least, the peasantry itself seems to have been willing to adapt and even to accept, for example, the loss of freehold status to urban buyers in order to raise cash to continue as tenants on the same land. Elsewhere in Italy a variety of patterns have emerged: clearly there were areas of prosperity and market development, but in the poorer areas historians have debated whether the instabilities of the seventeenth century brought a kind of 'refeudalisation' – that is, revival of old seigneurial demands and return of seigneurial privileges, abuses or oppressive burdens on the peasantry.[10]

North of the Alps, there are certainly signs of more systematic exploitation of seigneurial rights and market opportunities by noble landowners. As noted earlier (see chapter 5), nobles were in practice not particularly bound by notions of derogation when it came to metallurgy, textile production or trade. In the western German lands it was not difficult to find counterparts, at least on a smaller scale, to substantial east-Elbian entrepreneurs including General Wallenstein in Bohemia. In parts of Saxony west of the recognisable *Gutsherrschaft* regions, in Bavaria and in Upper Austria there emerged what some have identified as an intermediary type of peasant–seigneur relationship, known as *Wirtschaftsherrschaft* ('feudal capitalism' or 'entrepreneurial lordship'). With less scope for commercial involvement by townsmen and outsiders in the overall rural economy than in say Lombardy, *Wirtschaftsherrschaft* was a combination of the deliberate seigneurial market orientation of east-European demesne farming with a western style of tenant–rentier relationship. Because of the relative abundance of manpower and the limited size of the actual demesnes, serfdom was not necessary: indeed, depending on the type of crops and other products, traditional labour services themselves were sometimes commuted into cash, enabling landlords to rely primarily on hired cheap seasonal labour as required.

In Upper Austria the trend towards this kind of devolved entrepreneurial landownership was accelerated by the mortgaging of Habsburg crown estates in lien administration (*Pfandherrschaft*). This was done as security for loans provided by the service nobility and some other financial groups, but the result was a growing network of seigneurs who all had connections with the central administration. By the seventeenth century, although a quarter of the 45,000 peasant household-units accounted for tax purposes in Upper Austria were immediate subjects to the Crown, nearly all of these were in fact coming under the actual administration and control of magnates (prelates and the high nobility). Because of the financial weakness of

the Habsburgs, *Pfandherrschaft* was in effect tantamount to a permanent alienation – the recipients of the land often acquired judicial,
regalian and tax-collecting rights over the tenant population, and had
to ensure police and order as well. According to Hermann Rebel, peasant tenure was commonly standardised within a bureaucratic system
of estate management over much of the province. Personal serfdom
had by the sixteenth century virtually disappeared, but instead the
whole tenant population came to be regarded as uniformly hereditary
'subjects' (*Erbuntertanen*): free in person but quite distinct in terms of
rights and status from the more privileged social ranks, and increasingly under seigneurial tutelage in terms of the law. Impartible hereditary tenure became firmly established, but by the end of the sixteenth
century the practice of formal seigneurial valuation of peasant property transfers had become standard both on lands under lien administration and on lands owned outright by the nobility. Tithes, dues and
labour services were often commuted into money rents for ease and
flexibility of administration, maximising seigneurial market adapt-
ability while making it more difficult for tenants to cling to specific
traditional precedents.

Nevertheless, the valleys and pastures of Upper Austria were sufficiently fertile to provide for a flourishing and diversified rural economy where the more enterprising peasantry, benefiting from the
hereditary principle and sometimes from specific seigneurial authori-
sations or privileges, could attain considerable prosperity.
Participation in the innkeeping and transport sector, in linen production, in other domestic industry and even in financial operations was
common through all social groups and was not always directly regulated. The officially-required inventories taken on the death of a
householder reveal that although, as one would expect, the majority of
holdings had limited resources, there was a fluid gradation up to the
well-off. Inheritances worth 750 florins or more were not uncommon.
The Khaislinger peasant estate in the Hausruck area valued in 1613 at
1300 florins, including a good horse with harness and four oxen
totalling 97 florins, 19 other larger farm animals, three iron harrows
and three ploughs (at 5 florins), plus considerable stocks of food and
textile materials, was highly exceptional but gives some impression of
the scale of peasant enterprise possible in this kind of environment. It
was a socially diverse (and hence disunited) peasantry which had to
face the repressive policies of the Austrian Counter-Reformation in
1626 after the collapse of Bohemian Protestantism (see chapter 1); this
may explain why a second attempt at revolt after 1632, by the poor
alone, was even more rapidly crushed.[11]

It is clear that conditions in different parts of central and western
Europe varied so much that typological classification of
peasant–seigneur relationships may conceal as much as it clarifies.

The term *Wirtschaftsherrschaft* has normally been applied only to some German lands, but entrepreneurial initiative may have been more common in rural communities than historians of seventeenth-century Europe are wont to recognise. In areas with accessible urban markets and relatively high population density, market production was natural: notably in parts of the southern (Spanish) Netherlands and north-eastern France. There are signs of hesitant agrarian development even in Catalonia in the later half of the period.

One area where the combination of market-orientated estate management and traditional peasant tenure was clearly visible was eastern Denmark, especially within the extending catchment area of the capital, Copenhagen. In the Danish kingdom as a whole, only 9 per cent of the total arable land was under demesne cultivation (most of it operated separately from the common cultivation of peasant holdings, but rarely enclosed in the English sense). On Zealand, where market production for Copenhagen was secure, some demesnes were comparatively large: the average demesne area there, according to the 1688 land register, was 94 hectares (230 acres), but demesnes of this size or more in fact covered only 5 per cent of the region's total arable area. Most noble estates probably had effective overlordship over an equivalent of the 25 full peasant tenancies required to qualify for tax exemption for the demesne itself under the new land registration of 1682, and labour services were thus taken care of. But, in addition, peasants on Zealand, although not serfs, were subject to restrictions on their mobility: since the fifteenth century, every male peasant born there was a *vorned*, and as such was not entitled to leave the estate of his birth without seigneurial permission. Judging from the substantial fees paid for emancipation even on crown estates, and the trouble some private landowners took to pursue runaways, this bond on the tenant population must have been regarded as of importance either to ensure sufficient labour services or, more likely, to protect against a shortage of tenants for holdings under the estate.[12] From the point of view of landowners (including the Crown itself, whose estates were amongst the largest), this combination of demesne and peasant agriculture worked well: substantial payments in cash and kind were received from tenants, but access to labour services also made grain-growing and large-scale dairying attractive. Copenhagen itself provided an obvious market for the latter, but grain was also exported in substantial quantities to Norway (in return for fish and timber), to Lübeck and further afield. For the peasantry, however, conditions were not so attractive. Labour services were unregulated and in this context liable to increase (as they did drastically in the eighteenth century). Moreover, peasant participation in the market economy was limited partly by official regulations designed to help the towns, partly by the absence of significant domestic industry and partly by the relative poverty of the underfertilised soil.

Commercial farming in the Netherlands and England

It has already been noted how economic necessity and opportunity combined to encourage dramatic technical change in the methods and priorities of farming in the north-western United Provinces and, more gradually, in parts of England (see chapter 3). The north-western Netherlands had to a large extent escaped manorial development; instead there was what Jan de Vries describes as a 'free peasantry living in a relatively autonomous society'. Even where there were substantial noble landholdings, seigneurial privileges were much less extensive and often more of a formality than elsewhere in western Europe. In some provinces, notably Holland, burgher landowners exercised considerable economic influence over surrounding land, but this never produced the level of peasant dependence that we have observed elsewhere.

Peasant freehold ownership was well-established, and even those who were tenants customarily owned their farm buildings, a tradition which in itself encouraged long-term or even hereditary tenure. Even by contemporary standards the United Provinces were not spared the problems of poverty, particularly in areas of high population density and extensive labour migration, and a pronounced social stratification in the countryside was unavoidable, ranging from substantial farmers to cottagers dependent on specialised crafts, domestic industry or casual labour. But the range of employment opportunities was wider because of the developed transport, shipping, fishing, fuel-supplying and service sectors. Within the agrarian sector itself, the demand for a number of industrial crops added a diversity particularly important for the fairly poor soils of the north. Demand clearly hinged on the prosperity of other sectors in the economy, but at least until the 1670s remained fairly buoyant, encouraging high levels of specialisation and capital investment in agriculture.

Notarial records relating to farm households – though clearly a self-selecting source – suggest that during the seventeenth century various signs of comfortable affluence became more widespread: oak chests, curtains and floor rugs, clocks, porcelain and outright luxury ornaments such as silver buttons and gold ornaments were no longer very rare. The Oudshoorn farmer, Jan Cornelis Schenckerck, who died in 1700 leaving not only a herd of 17 milk cows but also 3 books, 8 paintings, 7 tablecloths, a suit with silver buttons, 11 shirts of his own (his wife had 14), 29 bedsheets and 10 woollen blankets, was clearly extraordinary by European standards, but in the United Provinces similar consumption patterns on a lesser scale were not unknown amongst even more middle-ranking peasants.[13] The prosperity of much of the coastal region from Friesland north-east to Ditmarsken in Schleswig is evident in the magnificent farm buildings that have survived: a striking example is the one from Ejdersted, now at Frilandsmuseet (Sorgenfri), its single vast pyramid-shaped roof enclosing barns, stables and a threshing area as well as the substantial living quarters which in part are older than the frontispiece date of 1653.

In England, the commercialisation of agriculture in roughly the southern and eastern half of the country was less advanced and slower during the seventeenth century. Cereal cultivation was still predominant in the arable lowlands, although often mixed with dairy farming and other forms of animal husbandry. Accordingly, various forms of land usage existed, dependent on local traditions as well as economic conditions: much enclosure happened piecemeal over centuries and did not in itself necessarily lead to agrarian improvement. Consolidated holdings had existed for a long time not just in the sparsely populated hilly pasture land of the north-west, where one would expect it, but also in parts of the deep south-east; nonetheless, open- or strip-field farming remained normal in the grain belt. It seems that late medieval and Tudor enclosures had been concentrated in the Midlands, and had often been applied to more marginal land which could do as well when turned into pasture to exploit the growing demand for wool. Where enclosure and 'engrossing' (the absorption of lesser holdings into one larger farm) did occur, it could cause considerable controversy, culminating for instance in the 1607 Midland revolt in protest against depopulation, hardship and the loss of common rights. In practice, however, not that much land was affected: perhaps only 10 per cent of the open-field arable land had in reality been enclosed in Leicestershire, where the 1607 revolt was centred. A commission of enquiry was set up to examine the scale and consequences of enclosure in the worst affected counties, but it was the last one on this scale.[14] For the next century, enclosure was not a major issue: grain prices stagnated, and those most at risk from what seigneurial encroachments there were, the smallholders of the grain lands, found themselves in an increasingly weak position in terms of organised resistance. By the 1630s the Crown was itself half-hearted in its efforts to enforce protective legislation against enclosure, engrossing and the conversion of arable land to pasture, and the civil war brought an end to the last vestiges of governmental protection of the peasantry. When economic conditions on smaller arable holdings became uncertain from the 1660s, much enclosure could now normally be done by 'agreement'. But Parliament was in any case predictably reluctant to place any obstacles in the way of the landowning interest, as was clear in the rejection in 1656 of a bill regulating enclosures. From 1677 the security of smaller freeholders and copyholders was further undermined by stricter requirements for irrefutable documentary evidence of their terms of tenure.

Because England was well behind many continental states in terms of bureaucratic and fiscal development, we do not have reliable information on landholding patterns across the country. It is generally agreed that most of the wealthier established English peasantry[15] traditionally had considerable security in terms of their land: this applied not just to the 25 per cent or so who were freeholders, but also in lesser measure to the copyholders (tenants with long-term or even hereditary tenures governed by custom), who constituted probably around two-thirds of the rest. In contrast to France, English freeholders were not predominantly smallholders. In moorland and higher pasture areas seigneurial interests were generally relatively slight, and even in those parts of the north and the west of England where arable land was good the gulf between rich and poor seems to have been less pronounced than further south. There was possibly also some provision for the poor in these regions, reducing the risk of unrest involving several social groups. In the vicinity of towns, although rents could be very high, the scope for intensive market gardening ensured the continuing prosperity of smallholders. In contrast to continental European experiences, labour services in England were by this time largely symbolic and vestigial, amounting to perhaps a few days per year.

The main change in peasant–seigneur relations, where it occurred at all, centred on the socially more polarised grain-growing areas. As everywhere else in Europe, those most at risk were the poorer peasants and those whose holdings, subject to partible inheritance patterns, had to be supplemented by other land. Tenants-at-will had only limited means of resisting seigneurial pressure, but some copyholders, depending on their terms, could also be vulnerable. Tension was most likely to occur over the interpretation of customary terms, over efforts to enclose more land with the demesne, or, not least, over moves to restrict access to common and forest rights. Leasing the demesne or other holdings as a unit to more substantial commercially-orientated tenants, on terms decided by the state of the market rather than tradition, ensured maximum revenue for the landowner and a greater degree of flexibility than with customary tenancy arrangements. Leases in England, in contrast to those common in France, usually ran for one or more generations, encouraging investment and long-term improvements by the lessee. This became particularly important once land rents, which had increased substantially since the sixteenth century, levelled off or even declined from around the 1670s. However, large-scale farming per se was not usually the most profitable in areas where crops other than grain were of some importance. There were not, therefore, substantial increases in the proportion of land held on these commercial leases until the eighteenth century, and we should probably regard the English countryside as fairly static during the seventeenth century.

Experimentation in farming techniques did, however, produce significant results during this period, both in enclosed and in open-field systems. The apparent stagnation of agricultural prices from mid-century onwards, surprisingly, seems in the long run to have served as an incentive to increase productivity. Some landowners had to cover large debts after the disruption of the civil-war period – even if permanent transfers of land were relatively slight – and the increasing use of strict family entail on landed estates may also have necessitated and perhaps encouraged more efficient use of resources. Similarly, some newcomers to the land market wanting safe placement for commercial profits may have helped to reinforce a 'modern' image of the enterprising landowner. Leasehold tenant-farmers on economic rents no doubt had strong incentives, too. But even freeholders and substantial copyholders seem to have sought to cover rents, fees and rapidly growing tax burdens (the Hearth Tax of 1662 and the Land Tax of the 1690s) by means of better productivity. It is generally agreed that, although major progress in agricultural techniques only came later, there were signs of change in the last decades of the seventeenth century. In areas of lighter, drained soils, and even hitherto fairly marginal, sandy soils, various types of root and forage crops grown in complex Dutch-style rotations – particularly when combined with animal husbandry for manure – gave dramatic increases in profits comparable to or greater than those from land reclamation and drainage. Estimates suggest that a return of 10–25 per cent was possible on investments in land in parts of England from the later seventeenth century onwards, compared with perhaps at best 5 per cent in France. It was clear to contemporaries that certain types of land merited more than just passive investment of capital and traditional methods – just as had been the case in parts of the United Provinces earlier.[16]

Peasant, bondsman and labourer in western Europe

Serfdom west of the Elbe was not widespread, but was far from extinct in parts of the Empire such as Hanover, Baden and elsewhere in the Rhineland region. In the late eighteenth century nearly half the peasant population of Franche-Comté were still serfs (*mainmortables*) because of conditions adhering to the land they occupied and the communities of which they were part. Similar forms of bonded tenure were common in the Savoy and in the far west in Brittany. In practice, however, serfdom in the west was more akin to its central European counterpart of *Erbuntertänigkeit* (hereditary subjection) than to the servile conditions of Mecklenburg or Muscovy. Peasants were normally bought and sold with their land rather than as movable chattels, and they could hold other land on legally independent terms.

Their property in theory still belonged to their seigneur, but in practice this was enforced only in Franche-Comté and some other areas. In some parts of Germany where enserfed and free holdings existed in the same village, the best and oldest holdings were often those carrying serfdom.

Even where serfdom did not exist, however, the peasantry in the west could hardly be regarded as free agents. Peasants and cottagers who held land from a seigneur would be required not only to keep the holding in satisfactory condition but also to pay considerable fees of various kinds. A new tenant would pay a succession fee, which in the case of the French *lods et ventes* could be between 12 and 33 per cent of the value of the tenancy, unless the holding had been vacant or special terms were offered for other reasons. Recurrent rents usually included a traditional sum in cash or kind, such as the French *cens*, the German *Grundzins* or the Danish *skyld* or *landgilde*, representing the hire of the 'dominium utile' (use of the land) at anything from notional to fairly substantial rates, payable annually. In addition, tenants would be required to 'recognise' seigneurial overlordship in a great variety of additional ways, sometimes with symbolic peppercorn rents, sometimes with more substantial payments in cash or kind such as the French *champarts* (a due on crops), and frequently by acknowledging seigneurial *banalités* like his monopoly on milling, the distilling of spirits, baking, wine-pressing or other services. Seigneurial hunting rights, too, not only required peasant assistance but could also entail severe damage to crops. Last but not least, tenants would be expected to yield labour services, including variants such as the carting service or the hospitality service customary in remoter parts of, for instance, Norway. Usually a large part of the labour services, like the ariage on Scottish estates, was on the demesne (mains) itself, often concentrated in the periods of most intense activity, for instance at harvest time. Even freeholders, though owners of their land or at least of the right of its usage, were expected to recognise feudal overlordship through some kind of payments or services. In Denmark, for example, although freeholders had hereditary rights over their land, they had to pay recognition fines and heavier taxes than tenants, and they could, according to the law code of 1683, be required to yield up to one-quarter of the labour services expected of tenants, assuming, that is, that they had enough documentation confirming their freehold status to avoid worse. Only in Norway and Iceland was peasant ownership of land absolute in the sense that their rights were comparable in law to those of landowners of higher rank and were free of 'feudal' burdens.

Labour services, though less onerous than in the *Gutswirtschaft* economy, were generally judged in terms of local seigneurial requirements, unrestrained by custom or by effective legislation. As in the case of other impositions, there were enormous differences over western

Europe. In France, for example, labour services on the whole appear to have been slight, perhaps just a few days per year for each full holding, usually in the busy summer period. In northern Germany and the more fertile parts of Denmark and southern Sweden 50 days a year may well have been normal by the later seventeenth century for holdings that may not even have counted as full-size 'whole' farms. Whilst this was well below, for instance, the maximum of 3 days per week specified in the 1680 ordinance on labour services in Bohemia, or the even heavier loads common in Mecklenburg, it still added significantly to the overheads on peasant farming, especially if concentrated in the busy season and if equipment and draught animals also had to be brought when reporting for work. Unpaid services, though sometimes well-regulated and broken by meals provided by the host, could also easily generate humiliating discipline or peasant ill-will, particularly if – as was usually the case – the seigneur acted through a bailiff, factor or other official. For some peasants, for instance in late seventeenth- and eighteenth-century Scotland, an alternative commutation or quit-rent was possible, but that was rarely feasible for smallholders.

The peasantry in all but the Orthodox and Muslim parts of Europe also had to pay tithes (tenths) to the church. In practice this could vary in size, in France generally from 3 to 12 per cent, but was usually measured gross at source, consequently representing a substantial burden. In Protestant countries the tithe was shared between crown and other institutions, and sometimes leased out to landowners, but was no less onerous for that. In Catholic areas, too, it was often managed or leased by noble members of the upper clergy, so that it regularly figured in peasant grievances along with seigneurial impositions. Tithes were a particular obstacle to land development in France, since changes in patterns of usage often entailed the end of tithe-exemption. Added to military service obligations and taxes payable (often via the landlord) to the state, tithes ensured that the peasant in western Europe was far too heavily encumbered in cash and kind to be financially and materially a free agent. Seigneurs in western Europe, already advantaged because of the higher overall population density compared with the east, in effect rarely needed to secure full legal restrictions on rural mobility in order to safeguard their labour: accumulating peasant debts provided alternative means of restraint. Arrears on dues or actual outstanding loans effectively tied peasants to the land or the seigneur, giving the latter the means, if he so wished, of gaining concessions over common rights or of imposing less secure tenancy terms.

In the long run, peasant impoverishment could create the basis for very unequal tenancy relationships, like some types of sharecropping in Brittany, where the peasant with typically 5 hectares (12 acres) of land had little hope of avoiding a downward poverty spiral during the seventeenth century. Nearly everywhere there was indeed a wide divergence of wealth within the peasantry itself. The few substantial peasants holding full-size farm units were greatly outnumbered by gradients of smallholders, who themselves were well above the utterly dependent cottagers and landless labourers. In Beauvaisis the *laboureurs* (substantial tenants) at the top may have amounted to about one in twenty. Pierre Goubert has estimated that a normal family of six would require, in the triennial system of rotation there, between 6 and 13.5 hectares of land to produce enough grain just for their consumption, in good and poor years respectively. With tithes, taxes and dues payable, and seed to be bought for the following year, the required areas would be doubled. Less than a tenth of the peasantry there towards the end of the century met that requirement for years of poor harvests, and at least three-quarters had less even than the 12 hectares required for economic viability in good years.[17] For the majority, therefore, dependence on subsidiary sources of income and on the work of women and children was unavoidable. The resulting polarisation of peasant society into widely divergent wealth- and income-levels was most common in the grain belt of northern France, but can be seen in different forms elsewhere. In western France the vine, with its requirement for skilled and intensive labour, provided reasonable incomes for owners of just a few hectares of land. Only in the higher pastural regions of southern France, where all cultivation was marginal, did the rural population depend on seasonal migration of their male adults for survival. The conditions of peasants in the poorer areas of Spain or on the large market-orientated estates of southern Italy, where seigneurial interests were utterly paramount, were even more precarious.

On the whole, however, rampant peasant impoverishment was hardly in the landowner's long-term interest, especially since it could lead to peasant flight and a chronic problem of vacant or derelict holdings. In Denmark after the destructive wars of the middle decades of the century, dereliction was such a problem that major concessions had to be offered, but in the 1680s at least 5 per cent of all peasant holdings in the kingdom were still unoccupied or uncultivated. Since most land in Denmark was taxed, irrespective of its current status, it is not surprising to find a landowner in northern Jutland petitioning the exchequer in 1687 to be allowed to relinquish formal title to six holdings which had been vacant for 20 years and for which he could not afford to pay taxes. An ordinance of 1691 suggests that derelict land was to be valued at merely one-fifth of the going rate for demesne land.

The rural economy of the west, then, involved a delicate balance which required sense and moderation on both sides of the peasant–seigneur divide. But for the peasant, debts, combined with the requirement that a holding must be left in as good a condition as when it had been taken on, no doubt seriously limited the extent to which all but the most fortunate peasants could make use of their entitlement to give due notice of intent to leave a tenancy. More likely, they would slide into the omnipresent groups of smallholders and landless labourers that testify so graphically to rural poverty all over Europe.

In contrast, those who actually had freehold rights over their land must have had an overwhelming incentive to stay, even when conditions were less than ideal. Peasant ownership of land in practice meant different things in different parts of Europe, and figures on landownership can never be fully satisfactory. In Scotland and in Denmark the proportion of peasant owners was probably very small, but in France perhaps nearly half the land was owned by peasants, although commonly (80 per cent by area in the Beauvaisis) in small holdings of 10 hectares (25 acres) or less. Supplementing such small plots with fields leased on varying but often short-term contracts was standard practice, producing a rural population closely tied to their community of birth. A few gained better material conditions as lessees of medium-sized holdings which might be in the order of 30 hectares (75 acres) but were commonly rather less in the south, rather more in the Paris region. These were the men best placed to rise above the normal level by becoming, as *fermiers* or well-off *laboureurs*, money-lenders and agents for absentee owners. Even at that level, however, leases were customarily only for six or nine years, creating less incentive for investment and improvement than the generation-long leases favoured in England, for instance.

The access of urban commoners to the ownership of land probably on the whole did not change economic or social relationships very greatly, but it could have important repercussions in other respects. In the period from the late sixteenth to the early eighteenth century, lawyers, office-holders, merchants and even city-based noblemen in France exploited their means of obtaining reductions in *taille* and *aides* (commodity taxes) to augment their ownership of farm land at prices against which peasants themselves could not compete. Per capita taxation received by the Crown at least trebled in real terms between 1600 and the 1640s, and, after a slight easing in the 1660s, increased further by the 1680s. The real burden, adding the costs of collection, undoubtedly rose substantially faster, and rested as we know largely on the peasantry. A transfer of land was thus inevitable away from the peasantry towards those social groups whose property was less affected by the growing fiscal demands of the French Crown. This shift in landownership patterns, like the threat of chronic revolts from the 1620s through to the early 1650s, forced the Crown, through the local *intendant*, to take some interest in land transfers, debt relations and the overall nature of the taxation system.[18]

Rural conditions in western Europe in general and peasant–seigneur relations in particular, therefore, hinged on a number of factors. Whether a peasant owned the land he used may have affected his endurance, but not his options to any great extent. More important was the range and kind of contacts he had with members of other social classes. Every village of any size, in addition to 'outsiders' like the often notorious miller, usually had a tavern-keeper, a vicar and perhaps one or several agents for landowners and perhaps for townsmen with rights in the area. When it came to increases in taxation, to military conscription or to straightforward disputes of one kind or another, these contacts, and the conflict of interests at stake in the village, were crucial. Here again the state could not avoid becoming involved, either as a landowner, a guarantor of law and order, or as the ultimate loser if local tax farmers or collectors faced difficulties.

Peasant protest and state involvement

In the late 1690s Vauban, in his project for the Dîme Royale, wrote that it seemed to him that not enough attention had been paid to the plight of the ordinary people: 'the most ruined and most miserable section of the kingdom, although they are the greatest part both in terms of numbers and in terms of the real and effective services they yield, for they carry all the burdens, have always suffered most, and still do suffer the most'. His sentiments are far from unusual for the period, but as always there was a long way from good intentions to effective policy implementation.

The rural population all over Europe had a number of ways of responding if they felt that they were being unfairly treated or that conditions were intolerable. An individual might seek to enlist the help of local influential persons, including the village priest or minister; he might resort to magic or gang up with other villagers to make life difficult for whoever was deemed responsible, even attacking anyone sent to impose discipline; or he might simply refuse to co-operate, or obey with as little grace or enthusiasm as he could muster. Such reactions were probably quite common, but are impossible to gauge simply because they did not, unless the problem got out of hand, create any reliable evidence accessible to the historian.

More visible to later generations, and certainly also more impressive to contemporaries, was formal opposition using a specific institutional or ideological framework – a lawsuit instigated by the person who felt wronged, a formal petition by an individual or a group appealing to the supposed fairness of the prince, a demonstration caricaturing or confronting those in authority, or, usually in the last instance, a protest containing more or less explicit hints of insubordination, violence and revolt. These four types of reaction were not as distinct as they may seem to us nowadays: with no clear separation of 'public' from 'private', either in terms of office-holders or in terms of responsibilities, petitions and lawsuits, for instance, might well be combined in the hope of attracting the attention of someone higher up the social scale who might help. Similarly, a demonstration, an organised refusal to work or even a parade could easily turn into a revolt.

For the peasant the most difficult and probably the least satisfactory course of action would be to attempt legal proceedings. As we noted with criminal cases (see chapter 6), there was no system of public prosecution, and a plantiff would always have to cover the costs himself. That in effect ruled out a large proportion of the rural population. More seriously, the courts of first instance in many parts of Europe were so much under seigneurial control that there was little chance of success against an overlord. In Scotland until 1747 most landowners were entitled to hold their own baron court, chaired by their appointee, the baillie. Its powers were only gradually reined in by central government, and could be used to serve various purposes, both exploitative (the landowner usually pocketed the fines) and potentially beneficial (settling disputes between tenants, or protecting the still very limited agrarian improvement attempted by parliamentary legislation in Scotland after 1661). In France, landowners were usually entitled to exercise some local justice at least for minor cases and sometimes also, subject to confirmation by a royal court, for matters of high justice (involving capital offences). The kind of small-scale seigneurial courts which divided the kingdom into tens of thousands of separate jurisdictions could deal with disputes over grazing and commons rights, land boundaries, inheritances, the allocation of work and the seasonal timetable within common-field farming. Meeting in the local manor house or the tavern, staffed by a 'procurator fiscal' acquainted with local customs and laws as seen from seigneurial eyes, and presided over by a judge appointed by the owner of the jurisdiction, such courts could work well enough in disputes between villagers but were of little help if the grievance was directed against any superior, least of all if against the seigneur himself. These courts were also often responsible for the enforcement of royal edicts and of taxation, again on the same premisses. Appeals to higher courts could be made, but the route to a royal court often went through several layers of local jurisdiction, each requiring considerable funds and determination on the part of the plaintiff and, at some early stage, probably also the literate assistance of a lawyer.

A great deal of work remains to be done on this subject, but it seems unlikely that the peasant would experience anything more encouraging in southern or central Europe during this period. Further east, as we have already noted, serfdom involved severe restrictions on the right to plead at all in a court of law. This discouraging picture may not be quite appropriate for those areas with the strong autonomous peasant communities and traditions of self-government found in parts of southern Germany and in the Swiss cantons. But even these were under threat. The entitlement for instance in Bavaria to make a formal appeal against the decisions of summary seigneurial justice, embodied in the *Landes-* and *Polizeiordnung* of 1616, may not in practice have been of much value, even if, as seems clear, the peasantry were aware of the long-term effects which economic and social changes might well have on their status and security. Similarly, the legendary (perhaps mythological) 'Swiss freedom' was clearly being whittled down by town and landowner control in the early modern period: the peasant revolt which started in Luzern in 1653 and led to the creation of a peasant league covering several cantons aimed to restore traditional legal privileges and rights of self-government. It, too, ended in defeat and collapse, as a result of which the compromise solutions reached during the conflict were abrogated by the authorities, 35 leaders were executed and many others (also predominantly from the better-off peasantry) blacklisted. With the destruction of the peasant league and its charters went many of the political and juridical rights of the village communities.

More distinctive legal institutions existed in Scandinavia. The northern and remoter parts of Norway, Sweden and Iceland necessarily had to settle their own disputes locally, in practice without seigneurial intervention. The ancient *ting* (court) continued to function well in this capacity during the early modern period. In central and southern Sweden and in most of Denmark there was a much stronger seigneurial presence, but even so the network of law-courts (quite similar in the two kingdoms) was relatively simple and efficient. In Denmark and parts of Sweden some substantial seigneurs acquired what the Danes called *birkeret* over their immediate tenants, whereby they were entitled to appoint the judge presiding over the hearings, and perhaps to some extent influence the selection of the local jury-members or formal witnesses normally present at the weekly meetings of the court. Everywhere else, however, the peasantry had access to a local *herredsting* presided over by a permanent official chosen by the royal governor of the region and assisted by a similar group of respected residents. In Denmark decisions of the court could be made the subject of appeals to a middle-level court and from there straight to the King's high court (or from the *birketing* direct to the high court). There was still ample and occasionally provable scope for blackmail or insolvency for those who chose this route, but examination of samples of these court records shows that persistency could be rewarded, particularly if the interests of the Crown itself or of influential magnates were not directly at stake. A not insignificant number of freeholders pleaded before the high court in Copenhagen in the last decades of the century, as their status (and especially their entitlement to perform fewer labour services) came under threat because of alienation to private landowners: they did not invariably fail in law, and regularly achieved at least a full-scale crown enquiry.[19]

Greater faith was generally placed in petitions and other forms of direct appeal to the Crown. In the Empire complaints could exceptionally lead to hearings at the Reichstag itself, as at Regensburg in 1658, but more usually resulted in commissions of enquiry similar to those sent to mediate in city conflicts (see p. 191). In 1666 some Kempten subjects even asked jurists at the University of Ingolstadt for an expert opinion on complex new impositions, and had a very helpful reply.[20] Whilst appeals direct to the Crown could be regarded simply as an extension of traditional relations between poor and rich, peasant and landlord, they were in fact qualitatively different for two main reasons. One was the implicit faith in the absolute justice of the ruler, always referred to in suitably deferential terms at the beginning of every peasant complaint, regardless of cause or grievance. In the case of appeals over the fiscal burden imposed by the government of Louis XIII (see pp. 50), the distinction between just prince and wicked advisers may have seemed threadbare to insiders. But the only alternative compatible with religious faith would have been that adopted by Russian rebels both before and after Bolotnikov (see p. 215), namely to argue that the ruler was in fact a usurper and that the true prince was the leader they themselves were following. The Catalonian approach, claiming that the Crown had forfeited its sovereignty by abusing its rights and failing to offer protection (see p. 58) was inconceivable without instigation and leadership from other social groups.

The second and in this context more crucial distinctiveness of peasant appeals direct to the crown lay in the response: because of the growing requirements for fiscal revenue and military strength, the state in seventeenth-century western and central Europe was increasingly sensitive to any overburdening of the peasant population that might jeopardise tax payments or devalue rural and demographic resources. This may even have applied in those states east of the Elbe where the ruler had virtually capitulated to the demands of noble landowners, as in Brandenburg and later also in Prussia. It is no exaggeration to say that all government attempts at rural reform were primarily inspired by these basic considerations, or at worst by fears of unrest that might easily follow if seigneurial and state interests were not kept within bearable limits. Ultimately, however, the Crown was itself a landowner and could not do without the support of its magnates: hence the ambivalence of Colbert in the 1660s, or the distinctly double-edged rural legislation of the Danish Crown during the following decades. A typical example of the latter is the 1682 prohibition against the enclosure of peasant holdings within a demesne: in theory helping tenants, the edict in fact sought to prevent a growth of tax-exempt land, and was in any case balanced by a reiteration of the disciplinary and managerial rights of the landowner.

The fear of seigneurial disciplinary powers and of reprisals was clearly a potent factor in any kind of petitioning movement. Peasants sometimes signed petitions radially round a central point on the page in order to avoid giving any clues as to leadership or instigation. But in any case they could not be sure of the outcome. Quite characteristic of the period is the hearing conducted at Herlufsholm south of Copenhagen in 1696. No fewer than 80 peasants on the estate supporting a school there had submitted a petition against the manager, complaining of unfair tax burdens, harsh treatment in connection with debts, and misappropriation of funds. Two royal commissioners called in by the rector conducted a public hearing in the presence of the persons against whom the peasants had complained, and each signatory was required to confirm his complaints and identify the person who had actually written the petition. Over three days of hearings the peasant case fell completely apart, an increasing number claiming that, being unable to read, they had not known what was in the text, had certainly not meant to cause offence and were in any case quite ignorant of what had or had not been occurring on the estate.

In Norway the peasantry had traditionally been more prominent in the national assembly than their counterparts in Denmark, but the burdens of war had generated considerable friction and complaints during the 1620s, leading to attempts at fuller regulation of rural conditions by law (1632–3). No further meetings of the Estates occurred after the establishment of absolutism in 1661, but it is interesting to note that the peasantry were still strong enough to exercise some influence on government policy over the following decades. According to registers from 1661, 31 per cent of all *landskyld* (land rent) in Norway was owned by peasants themselves, against just 9 per cent by townsmen and 8 per cent by nobles – a remarkable distribution, for even in Denmark (under the same Crown, albeit in different legal contexts that make such comparisons problematic) freeholders probably held no more than 5 per cent and nobles 40 per cent at this stage. When the Crown tried to improve its financial position over the next decades by disposing of its own estates, some attempts were made by recipients such as Gabriel Marselis (acquiring land to the value of 200,000 rigsdaler) to maximise revenues by imposing heavier dues and services on the peasants. This resulted in unrest, so that the statholder Ulrik Gyldenlöve (viceroy in Norway from 1664 to 1699) in

1684 secured a confirmation of life-tenure for tenants together with a more detailed regulation of peasant–seigneur relations generally, all of which was confirmed in the new law code (*Norske Lov*) of 1687. In the long run, however, the real advantage for the Norwegian peasantry lay in the difficulty of generating substantial profits from larger estates: market factors in many parts of the country produced a gradual shift of ownership towards the peasantry itself, which became very pronounced by the early eighteenth century.

Most fortunate were those peasant communities that retained some form of effective political representation at a higher level. Territorial assemblies with peasant representation continued to function in the Alps (the Tirol, Voralberg), in a few German states and in East Friesland. But the only major state where such representation was more than just symbolic was Sweden. Those in possession of substantial holdings there, being directly represented as a separate Estate in the *riksdag* (national assembly), could take advantage of moments of political uncertainty to make appeals. A considerable amount of crown land had been alienated to crown creditors, magnates and favourites, especially but not solely since the beginning of the regency for Queen Christina in 1632. It has been estimated that by the 1650s or within the next few decades private landowners had doubled the number of peasant holdings under their control to around two-thirds of the total for the whole kingdom. Crown tenants complained because if they were alienated they might come under landlords seeking to maximise services or dues, while if they were not they would have to bear a proportionately bigger share of crown burdens as the number of crown peasants dwindled. Included amongst the alienated was also a large number of so-called *skattebönder* (tax peasants), who had free-hold rights over their plots and whose representatives at the *riksdag* (diet) of 1650 made common cause with the other Estates to appeal against the effects of crown land alienation. The peasant Estate declared, 'We know that in other lands the Commonalty are slaves, and we fear that the like may happen to us, who are yet born a free people.'[21] As noted (see chapter 7), this effort was not particularly successful, merely resulting in a limited edict of 1652 restricting the labour services that could be expected of alienated peasants to 18 days per year. The whole question of the *reduktion* (resumption) of alienated crown land remained open from 1654 until the special commission set up in 1680 (see chapter 11), but at that point the peasant Estate were able to make a significant contribution to a major change of direction in Swedish public finance and landownership, in the course of which the proportion of peasants on private estates was once more reduced to probably around a third of the total.

Some recent Swedish research has suggested that the peasant grievances presented at the 1650 and later diets may have been considerable exaggerations. Except in Finland, there is little evidence in the records from individual estates to suggest that noble landowners who acquired *skattebönder* tried to overburden them sufficiently to produce the three years' tax arrears required for the loss of ownership rights; nor is there much evidence from mainland Sweden of any serious oppression beyond the kind of exploitation of seigneurial rights common to landowners all over Europe in this economically difficult period. Swedish landowners may have tried in some instances to rationalise holdings in order to make the most of the tax- and conscription–exemptions available for land within a certain distance of, and subject to, a noble demesne, but that is hardly surprising in the context of the rapidly escalating demands for the war effort. Probably no more than around 8 per cent of the total arable land in Sweden was ever demesne land, and labour or transport services are on the whole not likely to have increased dramatically on private estates except where new enterprise (such as mining and forestry) was being developed. Although it seems unlikely that there were no good grounds at all for the numerous complaints, they may have been in part the result of an overall deterioration in economic conditions – after all, the Crown itself was looking for increasing income and especially transport services from the peasants over whom it retained control. Ultimately, however, the peasant Estate need only have looked to Swedish Pomerania to see some of the worst forms of east-Elbian seigneurial exploitation – and they were clearly aware of how much they could lose.[22]

It will already be apparent (see chapters 2 and 7) that outright peasant revolt was endemic in many parts of Europe, especially from the 1620s through to the 1650s, and particularly in France, the Spanish peninsula, the Habsburg lands and elsewhere in war-torn central Europe. It is clear that these revolts were often highly politicised: the Croquants in France (see p. 50f) were conscious both of their rightful relationship with the Crown itself, and the questionable legality of the tax-farming systems which so distorted the actual fiscal demands. How far these more sophisticated peasant grievances were actually new is not yet clear, and recent work on late medieval peasant unrest may lead to new insights for the early-modern period.[23] What is apparent, however, is the extent to which the peasantry were capable of becoming active participants in, and conscious of, the struggles not just against change but also in support of certain ideals of fairness and freedom from oppression, some of which were expressed sufficiently clearly (as in France) to win support amongst other groups in society. In that sense, the escalation of demands from petitions (or in some areas lawsuits) through demonstrations and protests to outright rebellion was a logical escalation when satisfaction was not received by traditional means.

In the light of the great regional contrasts illustrated in this chapter, it will also be clear why it is always necessary to qualify generalised explanations for Europe as a whole. There are obvious reasons why only certain parts of rural Europe were beset by recurrent conflicts pitching villagers against those trying to exercise lordship rights over them, or endeavouring to increase fiscal and military demands. Nevertheless, certain common themes of resistance recur during the seventeenth century in addition to the particular political–fiscal grievances: a worsening economic climate clearly took a deep toll and was often the reason why seigneurs themselves tried to extract more than was customary from their land; intrusive armed conflict too, as we noted particularly in the first two chapters, affected the rural population both directly and indirectly. Peasant–seigneur relations, however, were influenced by many other factors. Despite the hundreds of revolts that can be cited during the seventeenth century, many areas remained quiet simply because traditional relations were not upset or because the peasantry had sufficient peaceful outlet through the law, petitions or assemblies to avoid recourse to more direct action. The strength of traditional community self-government evidently helped to protect some areas in central Europe against full-scale serfdom. However, if in theory the ruler might also be expected to have made an effort to intervene, in order to balance the interest of tax-paying peasants against pressures from the landowning elite to which he himself belonged, in practice this was rarely possible. Even in Sweden, the success of the Fourth Estate in bringing attention to its problems in the early 1650s was probably contingent on the precarious political balance leading up to the abdication of Queen Christina, rather than an illustration of access to real political influence. There is no need to ascribe 'humanitarian' motives to what little protective state legislation there actually was: the treatment meted out to the last peasant revolts in France in the 1660s and 1670s (see chapter 12) confirms that revenue and the protection of the traditional social order were the sole aims.

This may help to explain why rural rebels so rarely seem to have achieved outright success. Sometimes, as in the Swiss cantons in 1653, the temporary reconciliation of divergent demands within the peasant community itself, between those with substantial holdings and those with little or no land, did not last long enough, even against a common threat from outside. Sometimes, as in Upper Austria in 1626 or in Sweden in 1650, action was based on the interests of only the better-off. Not only social but also geographic fragmentation of settlements might make co-ordination more difficult, particularly if the target was a powerful local seigneur rather than a more distant state government. In any case, the repressive resources available to the nobility and the state were far more powerful than the endurance of peasants deeply dependent on seasonal work and incomes. As in other respects, however, early modern government, local and central, was less than a complete success. The complaints at the heart of popular revolts were often sufficiently justified to be recognised by the authorities, and some limited change might result after the violence itself had been repressed, as was the case in Switzerland in 1653, in Bohemia in 1680 over labour services, and in many other instances. Persistence and obstinacy could bring a stalemate, or might even, as in France, succeed in nullifying at least new taxes; failing that, migration was possible. The peasantry in much of northern, central and western Europe did also have some scope for making use of the contacts and opportunities created by urban markets and by the social diversification of some regions, and in England and the Netherlands they could even take a leading role in innovative practices. In short, the European continent covered a wide gamut of peasant conditions, from fairly free and economically self-sustaining systems in those relatively rare areas that were prosperous and stable to far more confrontational and impoverished systems in those parts of Europe where the rapidly increasing fiscal and military demands of the state, seigneurial oppression or market forces made rural relations highly volatile and dangerous.

9 Beliefs, *mentalités*, knowledge and the printed text

Religion provided a universal mode of thinking and of expression which pervaded all aspects of life in seventeenth-century Europe. There were an ever-growing number of belligerent variants within the Christian world, and some significant differences between Christian Europe and the Muslim south-east, but such differences almost invariably led to dogmatic entrenchment and intolerance. For the great majority, strict conformity was both natural and unquestioned. Yet historians agree that the period also marked a crucial stage in the emancipation of the human mind from the blindly accepted dogma and intellectual traditions of the past. Such emancipation, as we would expect, does not occur suddenly, and it would be misleading to portray what has been called the 'intellectual revolution' and the 'scientific revolution' of the seventeenth century as a compact and easily definable phenomenon. Its roots clearly stretched back into the early Renaissance or before, and the Reformation (as we shall see) provided a crucial impetus; similarly, its effects are not altogether clear before the high enlightenment of the eighteenth century. But it can be argued that several crucial milestones in the emancipatory process were passed during the seventeenth century: if so, what were they?

Many aspects of seventeenth-century history may seem unfamiliar to the modern eye, but the mental world of the ordinary townsman or peasant during that period is undoubtedly the most remote of all. If any generalisations in this area are valid at all – and the account of the perceptions of the late sixteenth-century miller Menocchio suggests caution[1] – one might say that astrology, divination, animism and the fear of nature, alchemy, sorcery, demonic possession, witchcraft and belief in magical healing were all part of the normal outlook of the early seventeenth century, accepted by the majority of the educated and the illiterate alike. We face, however, not just a conceptual barrier in trying to understand something which is generally regarded as alien to modern scientific experience but also a practical one, in that large elements in society left little or no spontaneous evidence of how they actually felt about these matters. Censorship, combined with the fear of non-conformity, ensure that the inner mental world of the great majority remains largely hidden from view.

At the time, information itself was often unreliable or irretrievably garbled by rumour. Geographic distance was of great physical and psychological importance, and while each community held no secrets from its members, it was often isolated from the wider world to a degree unthinkable today. Newspapers were until the end of our period mostly state-sponsored media for official commentary rather than for information as such, and, like journals and books, were primarily intended for the literate and wealthy minority. Transmission both of news and of value judgements was therefore very largely done by word of mouth, through ordinary gossip or the reports of travellers, through rhymes and formulaic parodies recited by itinerant entertainers, or through songs, dances and plays performed on market-days, on Shrove Tuesday (carnival), May Day, Midsummer (eve of St John the Baptist) or during other recurrent festivities of one kind or another. The imagery of these forms of entertainment could be crudely stereotyped but could also be powerfully influential through criticism and ridicule. 'Rough music', mockery, the parody of local authority through popular processions deliberately turning the world upside-down, charivaris, publicly staged (often sexual) insults, defamation and other forms of communal action were an important part of the mechanism of social order, giving release to tensions and frustrations; equally, however, they could easily boil over into actual rioting, or at least make individuals think seriously about the hierarchy within which they were living. In these circumstances, where the pulpit and the local administrator's office were the main contacts with the outside world, the incumbent of either might well be regarded as an outsider, albeit with a grudging acceptance that was not always extended to real strangers.

There has been much discussion recently about the validity of reconstructing the mental world of the past from records largely compiled by members of the literate minority – by inquisitors or authors of popular fiction, diarists and antiquarians, parish priests and government or judicial officials conducting formal enquiries. It has been argued that the period from the Reformation to the early eighteenth century marks a crucial stage in the imposition on the uneducated of some degree of cultural uniformity, and that in doing so church and government officials rechannelled or even destroyed some parts of the popular tradition. To what extent this so-called 'acculturation' was at all successful over the shorter term is of course open to doubt. The survival of folk traditions and superstition into a much later age may not in itself be a satisfactory indication of failure, but reformers regularly found that common people were hardly as malleable as they might have hoped: there were already too many different mediators at work for that to happen. When, after 1660, cultural conformity was promoted by the elite in order to strengthen order and stability after the mid-century upheavals, it was only superficially successful. There are many aspects of popular culture beyond our reach, but arguments that it was somehow filtered and ultimately suppressed by churchmen, lawyers, government officials and upper-class writers do not constitute a full explanation of the seventeenth-century experience.

More fundamentally, however, it is far from obvious whether the historian can in fact validly differentiate between popular and elite cultures at all in the sixteenth and much of the seventeenth century. There was naturally a wide variety of cultural forms, to some extent related to wealth and geography, yet, as will be clear from this and the following chapter, also in important respects shared by different social groups within one locality. Strong oral cultures, as far as we can judge, linked the imagination across apparent social barriers, but so did the popular literary culture reflected in a vast quantity of chapbooks and pamphlets sold by pedlars and printers. The spread of literacy and education, combined with the desire of those in authority in the seventeenth century for better moral and social discipline, no doubt had some repercussions on popular attitudes in matters of religious belief. One might, for example, point to the visible effects of both Reformation and early Counter-Reformation activism in reducing what contemporaries regarded as superstition, idolatry and disguised paganism in the uneducated laity (in contrast to which, it might be noted, historians have had less success in identifying patterns of observance amongst the elite itself). Nevertheless, there is, as we shall see, a large question-mark over why people of all sorts went to church, and what they thought once they were there. It would be rash to assume that the physical hierarchy in the seating plan of every church reflected a genuine mental reality in terms of religious acculturation. In respect of other beliefs and attitudes, interactions between different social groups are even less amenable to simple categorisation.[2]

If we accept that the spiritual and mental world was heterogeneous, and that no clear divide separated 'popular' from 'elite', we can also agree that there were certain nearly universal ingredients in the outlook of the period. One understandable one was fear. The recurrence of virulent epidemics such as the plague, which contemporaries had no means of understanding, created a fatalism which only began to be dispelled during the later part of the period. Other diseases then took over, with only slightly less horrendous results. Equally unpredictable were the vital factors producing climatic aberrations and crop failures. To these disasters may be added that of war, whose destructive potential (despite its rudimentary technology) is amply testified. Better understood by everyone, but nearly as difficult to prevent in an age of timber frames and thatched roofs, were the frequent house fires which in villages and towns alike could totally ruin the richest man in minutes. The density of habitation in bigger cities ensured that the rudimentary buckets and ladders of the fire service were utterly without effect in impeding disasters such as the huge conflagration which made an estimated 100,000 people homeless in London in 1666. In an age generally without fire insurance, the personal losses were total and irreversible.

No wonder that the theme of the 'wheel of fortune', of the proud reduced to dust, of panic or of resignation in the face of adversity, was such a commonplace in both the religious and the secular literature of Christian Europe. Disasters of one kind or another were readily interpreted as divine punishment rather than as possibly remediable accident. If we can judge by the literary evidence, the later sixteenth and early seventeenth century was an age riddled with feelings of guilt and sinfulness. Religion may have offered some escape from the 'vale of tears' that many saw around them: asceticism, prayer or self-flagellation were the natural corollary to an overwhelming awareness of the temptations of moral sin and the guilt of original sin. The day of last judgement was sensed as imminent: imagery of the macabre, of death and of corruption, was consequently still obsessively present in the more pessimistic writings of the period, at least until the uneventful passing of 1666 – the year when the predicted Second Coming of Christ would have ended the struggle of good and evil in a new Kingdom of God.[3] Equally, the debate over predestination, over the invulnerability of the 'elect' and over the efficacy of grace and good works, were matters of spiritual life or death that split both Protestants and Roman Catholics internally, as well as pitting them against each other. In these circumstances, religious intolerance, the utter inflexibility of the orthodox mind and the refusal to compromise is unsurprising. With it came a dogged determination to combat deviance of any kind, not just because it might endanger individual salvation but because it was deemed to put the whole community or even nation at risk.

Witchcraft prosecutions

Belief in magic, sorcery and other forms of supernatural action or power is common in varying degrees to all civilisations. It takes several forms, including belief in the powers of black magic or *maleficium* (doing evil), of white or benevolent magic (for example, to cure disease by invocation) and of sorcery proper, where potions, incantations or paraphernalia of some kind are normally involved. The actual line separating white magic from practical religion (for example, the Christian belief in transubstantiation) was and is blurred or subjective, even if the theoretical ideological distinction (not within the historian's brief) may be clear enough. Similarly, there is no obvious dividing line between science, as practised at least until mid-century, and the 'high magic' of the educated (such as alchemy and divination, as opposed to the 'low magic' of simple spells practised empirically by the uneducated witch). Astrology, in particular, was highly rational and intellectual, and its practitioners included prominent scientists such as Johannes Kepler.

If witchcraft, therefore, was a recognised and unremarkable part of life, it did in the early modern period evolve an additional and distinctive ingredient not prominent in other civilisations: the idea that witches had an explicit pact with the Devil, often sealed at the witches' sabbath by the ritual performance of inverted Christian rites and by means of sterile sexual intercourse, and perhaps involving a mark on a hidden part of the witch's body. It has been argued that it was this Satanism, the deliberate abandonment of God in favour of a demonic pact with the Devil, that came to be regarded – with or without actual *maleficium* – as the real threat to society, meriting the elaboration of new criminal procedures and grounds for prosecution and conviction, and producing the mass executions characteristic of the early modern witch hunt. Satanism was the most explicit form of heresy, and if a Christian turned to the Devil he was also guilty of apostasy. Charges of lesser heresy might arguably have been made against magicians and the simple practitioners of *maleficium*, but the authorities naturally did not regard such individual practices as a significant threat to the established religious and social order. By contrast, the witches' sabbath implied a collective flouting of all accepted standards by reputedly large numbers of witches flying to night-time rendezvous. It is significant that the mass prosecutions that erupted in the later sixteenth and early seventeenth centuries, though triggered by individual accusations of *maleficium*, were commonly handled as diabolical conspiracies by the prosecuting authorities, whose main interest appears to have been the compilation of lists of fellow devil-worshippers extracted from convicted witches by means of torture or the threat of torture. Needless to say, no convincing evidence of conspiratorial pacts, let alone of the kind of collective organisation implied or expected by the prosecutors, was ever found. Understandably in a period of deprivation and insecurity, ordinary people were in any case more concerned with *maleficium* as such (as an alternative explanation for misfortunes which could otherwise only be regarded as divine punishments or tests) than they were in the theological and conspiratorial niceties of Satanism. This divergence between popular perceptions of witchcraft and the aims of the authorities is crucial.

Amongst the upper-class protagonists of witchcraft allegations were first and foremost the religious orders and the papacy. Pope Innocent VIII's Bull of 1484 had sanctioned the witch-hunting organised by two Dominicans, Heinrich Kramer and Jakob Sprenger, who drew up what became the first influential textbook on the subject, the *Malleus Maleficarum* (1486). Yet the witch hunt and the attendant surge of publications and collective fantasy did not gain real momentum until the 1560s and 1570s. By then secular authorities were deeply committed. Except in Spain and Italy (where the Inquisitions remained in charge), and notwithstanding the fact that the crime was essentially spiritual, secular courts took over the major part of the administrative and formal work of prosecution on the basis of legislation newly enacted in many parts of Europe in the last years of the sixteenth century. This secularisation, particularly where local courts (as in the German lands) were relatively autonomous, helped to accelerate the rate of prosecution. Amongst the uneducated such increase was made acceptable by long traditions of magic, by the feelings of guilt and sin so carefully instilled by churchmen into their parishioners and by the suggestive or auto-suggestive atmosphere which the investigators themselves created during the actual outbursts of hysteria. Popular pressures regularly fuelled the process, especially since those initially accused, commonly older women and outsiders of one kind or another, could be treated as scapegoats for disasters of various kinds. Many victims confessed more or less spontaneously in the knowledge that, once accused, defence or resistance could mean an endless ordeal, and even acquittal was no guarantee of acceptance back into society.

Extensive research over the last few decades, often concentrating on particular localities, has brought to light significant evidence regarding the number of individuals accused of witchcraft, and the proportion that were actually executed during the climactic century from 1570. Because of the nature of the trials and the surviving descriptions, there is still a large element of conjecture, but historians have recently tended to revise overall figures in a downward direction. It is now commonly accepted that the number of those formally accused is unlikely to have been much above 70,000, and that the resulting executions probably amounted to around 40,000 in total. Execution rates varied, from nearly 90 per cent of the accused in those parts of Switzerland, such as Vaud, where hysteria reached very high levels, down to 25 per cent or less in some parts of Europe, such as Muscovy, where Satanism was not fully recognised. Generally, in England, much of France, the Netherlands and most of Scandinavia (except Denmark) execution rates were quite low, sometimes because the authorities took a less proactive role or were inclined towards more lenient sentences. Significantly, in those countries where there were restrictions on the use of torture before sentencing, fanciful denunciations of Satanic conspiracies were less likely to emerge from amidst the welter of *maleficium* allegations typically associated with local communities in panic. But exceptional circumstances could push traditionally fairly quiet regions towards full-scale witch crazes with mass accusations, as happened in England under the zealot Matthew

Hopkins (1645–6) and in Sweden from 1668 to 1676. By contrast, the apparently low execution figures for Italy and Spain suggest that the Inquisitions in both regions, having developed quite sophisticated judicial procedures early on, were able to unravel the unconvincing nature of the testimony of those who came forward to confess. The Inquisitors exercised sufficient influence to dampen popular frenzy, enabling them to concentrate instead on individual cases of *maleficium* (alongside other forms of superstition and heresy) for which the formal punishment might be less severe. In Portugal there were hardly any executions at all.

By contrast, the obvious centre of witchcraft prosecutions was the Holy Roman Empire, especially its southern and western regions: already torn by deep – one might say paranoic – confessional rifts, it lacked any stabilising central judicial control. As Catholic and Protestant authorities vied with each other to prove their zeal, and fought out their confessional disagreements with extraordinary bigotry, the shifting front lines in the German-speaking lands alone resulted in at least 20,000 executions. This enthusiasm affected neighbouring areas. A significant proportion of the 5000 or so prosecutions from what is now France originated in the eastern borderlands, but actual execution rates were kept relatively low by the growing reluctance of the Parlement of Paris to confirm such death sentences within its area of jurisdiction. The sparsely populated Switzerland suffered very badly, with perhaps as many as 3000 executions (971 in the canton of Vaud alone between 1580 and 1620 – the worst single concentration in a Protestant region). Denmark is now regarded as having executed at least 1000 witches, higher than once thought. In Scotland there were also over 1000 executions, resulting from at least twice that number of clearly identifiable accusations. England generated around 500 executions, and as in Scotland these were concentrated in the troubled years around 1630 and from 1642 to 1662. Figures for Poland are relatively low, but (as in Hungary, and in contrast to the west) prosecutions there intensified after mid-century and lasted well into the eighteenth century.

These figures may not fully account for the victims of unauthorised hunts conducted by overzealous parishioners, as happened for example in the Basque country in 1610, in Burgundy in 1644–5 after a judicial ban was imposed by the Parlement of Dijon, and in England in 1665 and 1694 – usually when the authorities were reluctant to respond to popular hysteria. Nor do global figures indicate the very uneven nature of the witchcraft prosecutions both in time and space: at its height, there were usually sudden outbursts of fear, resulting in mass accusations, confessions and prosecutions in one or more successive waves within one particular locality or jurisdiction, followed by a lull of exhaustion as even enthusiasts reeled under the human and material costs, or realised the dangers of potentially unstoppable momentum. Historians have tended to assume that the majority of the victims were from amongst the lower social levels, the poor, and the marginalised. Although much of the historical evidence itself is too cursory to substantiate this claim, it is compatible with the fact that most witch hunts were ultimately rooted in community tensions, fear and personal enmities. It is rather more complicated to explain why the majority (on average three-quarters) of those executed for witch-craft were women: after all, women did not have direct access to the levers of power in early modern society, but often had no hesitation in acting as accusers. Even if many commentators and prosecutors were blatantly paternalistic and misogynistic in outlook, this does not explain the patterns adequately. Just over half of those executed in France on the authority of the Parlement of Paris were men, and in some outbursts, such as the so-called *Zaubererjackl* persecution in Salzburg in 1677–81, over two-thirds were men (mostly young, sturdy beggars). Were these merely aberrations from the norm, in a society where women were always relatively more vulnerable and where they occupied a social and domestic space particularly exposed to gossip, stress and quarrelling?[4]

There were voices of doubt about witchcraft beliefs early on, such as that of the Protestant humanist Johann Weyer in Cleves, who as early as the 1560s described witch-beliefs in rational medical terms, or Reginald Scot, who in his *Discoverie of Witchcraft* (1584) allowed for certain types of witchcraft but disputed the existence of actual pacts with the Devil. But intellectual opponents of such liberalism were at first much stronger, ranging from the French jurist and exponent of absolute monarchy Jean Bodin (1530–96) to King James VI/I, who ordered Scot's *Discoverie of witchcraft* to be burnt by the public hang-man. As late as 1635, the Saxon judge Benedict Carpzow published *Practica rerum criminalium*, giving Lutheran authorities and intellec-tuals new comprehensive guidelines on all the ramifications of witch-craft. Significantly, however, the German Jesuit Friedrich Spee produced almost simultaneously a systematic denunciation of German trial procedures in his *Cautio Criminalis* of 1631.

It is far from straightforward to explain why large-scale prosecu-tions of witches died down after mid-century. The United Provinces had characteristically led the way in first abandoning the death penalty and then in 1610 also dropping all official prosecution. At the very same time the Spanish Inquisitor Salazar y Frías rationally tested a series of confessions in Navarre and convinced his superiors that all the evidence relating to the witches' sabbath was valueless.[5] But, despite scepticism in certain other quarters such as the Parlement of Paris from 1615, the rest of Europe did not follow these examples for another half-century or more, Poland and the eastern Habsburg lands only in the early eighteenth century. It is clear that no single explanation for this gradual termination of witchcraft prosecutions can be offered. Exhaustion and some degree of political stabilisation after 1660 no doubt helped. At a technical level, the widespread tightening of the requirements of judicial proof, and stricter enforcement of the regulations regarding the use of torture (for example, in Spain in 1614 and in Scotland in 1662) made mass convictions rarer. Even more effective in changing the attitude of those in power were instances of manifest fraud, as in the Hoarstones hunt in England in 1633 when a boy admitted that his father had suggested names as part of a personal vendetta. It is also interesting to note that in some of the last big hunts many of the accused appear to have escaped actual prosecution: in the Scottish hunt of 1661–2, for example, doubts and evidence of deliberate fraud may account for the marked increase from May 1662 in the number of individuals who are mentioned before the High Court of Justiciary or the Privy Council without indication of further proceedings.[6] More frequently occurring acquittals also helped defuse some panics.

At the same time, as we shall see later in this chapter, intellectual attitudes underwent dramatic change as a result of the scientific revolution and the spread of Cartesian deductive scepticism. Although these developments probably had no impact on the popular mind for a long time, they helped to convince those in authority that many aspects of sorcery and magic were open to rational explanation.[7] There is clear historical evidence that while some witches did practise *maleficium* in the belief that it worked, officials on the other hand seem to have come to regard the whole phenomenon as individual aberration rather than as any kind of collective negation of accepted values, or genuine demonic pact. Members of the elite were no doubt further encouraged to call a halt when their own kith and kin became implicated or when they were personally accused, as happened to the Bishop of Würzburg in 1629. The central role played by children in some hunts, as in the Basque ones of 1610–14, in the northern Swedish hunt from 1668 and in that in Salem, Massachusetts, in 1692, also clearly helped to convince some that the whole process was absurd. Ultimately the state might intervene directly to end prosecutions, as did Charles XI of Sweden in 1675 on the recommendations of a commission, and Louis XIV in 1682. By 1690 the Dutch pastor Balthasar Bekker could publish a comprehensive denunciation of the entire witch craze, though he was defrocked for his pains. Instances of individual prosecution for witchcraft did not end there, and there were both executions and mob lynchings in the eighteenth century, but large-scale witch-hunts no longer occurred in the west.

In the end, it is difficult to escape the conclusion that, while witchcraft and belief in the supernatural were deeply embedded in popular culture, it was the attitude of those in authority that turned petty *maleficium* into mass executions and communal hysteria. The role of secular authorities, taking over from church courts, was decisive. In Scotland, for example, prosecutions were clearly concentrated along the coast south from Aberdeen and in the Forth-Clyde lowlands: that is, in those areas accessible from the capital, Edinburgh. As Kirsty Larner argued, the witchcraft prosecutions coincided in Europe with the period when Christianity was the exclusive political ideology, in the sense of being 'a total world-view which serves to mobilise political action or to legitimise governments'.[8] Like apostasy and heresy, witchcraft acquired sufficient prominence for governments with theocratic tendencies to feel that formal prosecution was necessary. This phase lasted roughly as long as Church and State were inseparable and mutually dependent: state-sponsored witchcraft prosecutions came to an end when the intelligentsia abandoned the kingdom of God as a realisable political objective.

The struggle for religious conformity

It is difficult to overestimate the power and influence of the Church in early modern Christian Europe. It was the interpreter of what was for most people unchallengeable spiritual and moral authority, exercised through an hierarchy of regular and secular clergy more numerous and in many respects better organised than the political administration of the state itself. The Orthodox and Roman Catholic Churches in addition had formidable landed and financial resources at their disposal. During the seventeenth century the established Church in each state also remained in very close partnership with the secular government, each on the whole serving the other's interests (see chapters 1, 11 and 12). Nearly all denominations could rely on elders and lay members whose supervisory functions in the community could be very extensive. Genuine toleration as a policy of state was rare: in areas of confessional dispute (such as central and south-western Germany) and in remoter parts of politically unstable regions (such as Hungary) where some religious latitude had developed, this was not regarded as a satisfactory or durable condition; as we shall see in chapter 11, the military power of the state could still in the later part of the century be marshalled to repress dissent. But by the later seventeenth century the main pattern of official church affiliations was beginning to stabilise. The Iberian peninsula and Italy were solidly Roman Catholic, France was mostly so and the Habsburg lands had moved substantially in that direction as dwindling Protestant minorities were being systematically pressurised and persecuted. The Holy Roman Empire and the Swiss Confederation were mixed, with a solid Roman allegiance in the south, an equally solid Lutheran one in the north, and important Calvinist (Reformed) areas scattered throughout the west. The United Provinces and Scotland were Calvinist, England was predominantly Anglican despite substantial dissent, and Ireland was still largely Roman Catholic in spite of British intolerance. Scandinavia was solidly Lutheran, while Poland, though preponderantly Catholic, was still very composite. Muscovy was split between two variants of the Orthodox Church, one slightly modernised, the other very archaic. In many parts of Europe there were also scattered Jewish communities, some still surviving in southern Europe but a large part now resettled in the north-west and especially in east-central Europe. Officially, at least half the 110 million people in Europe must have been Catholic and perhaps a quarter Orthodox, whilst most of the rest would have belonged to a variant of Protestantism, Judaism or Islam, but, as we shall see, such figures in practice do not mean very much.

The Ottoman Empire represents a quite different pattern. The absence of western-style tax-registers and early censuses, even for the eighteenth century, makes it impossible to estimate the relative significance of different religious affiliations. But what is clear from all accounts is that the Ottoman state did not regard religious nonconformism as a problem that had to be eradicated. Throughout its long history, the Ottoman Empire embraced Jewish, Greek Orthodox Christian and other minorities with ease. The Quran and Islamic law provided the formal basis for everything involving Muslims, but other religious groups were, in accordance with Islamic tradition, explicitly allowed to settle their internal affairs according to their own beliefs. Although Muslim religious life was defined quite precisely in the various commentaries that had been compiled since the eighth century, the relatively conservative nature of Islamic beliefs created greater stability and security for minorities than in Christian Europe. There were divisions between different Islamic traditions (with the sultans remaining predominantly Sunni in orientation), but no religious arguments that might serve as a seed-bed of nonconformism such as that created by the Protestant reformation. Nor, despite the need to create new frameworks to deal for example with criminal law, did the growing local powers allocated to *muftis* (Islamic scholars) and judges lead to significant victimisation of outsiders or foreigners, provided they lived peaceably.

In Christian Europe, the established Churches aimed at monolithic patterns of belief, propagated since the Reformation through sermons, church visitations, catechisms, religious education and popular missionary activity. But what this meant to the recipient is difficult to ascertain. Churchmen regularly complained of the inability of many people to distinguish between paganism and Christianity. In 1686 parishioners in the diocese of Autun in France sacrificed a heifer to the Virgin Mary to protect their flocks against plague. Religious processions, in particular, were readily experienced as rites to ward off communal physical as well as spiritual dangers: in Paris, officially sanctioned processions were thus used to call upon saints to bring rain (1615 and 1694) or to make it stop (1675). Perambulations of the parish boundaries, or the carrying of relics into vineyards, were common occurrences where the priest might not even attempt to disclaim associations of magic. Equally, exorcism was freely used and generally expected in response to natural threats, as when a whole village near Chamonix was threatened by the advance of glaciers in 1644. Exorcism was also the obvious way of dealing with individuals or whole groups affected by madness or alleged demonic possession: in 1634 the Ursuline convent at Loudun, in the throes of a hysterical seizure of Satanism, was successfully dealt with in that way. Significantly, religion and belief in various forms of the occult went hand in hand at all social levels. The diary of the comfortable merchant Samuel Jeake, a dissenter and respected lay preacher in Rye in Restoration England, is a striking example of the extent to which an educated person might then, as some still do, carefully observe the astrological context for anything from his own wedding to business deals or near-accidents.[9] An age that could endow chairs of astrology at the universities of Bologna and Salamanca, and whose greatest intellects could be addicted to the practice of alchemy in the name of science, could clearly also be expected to accept miracles and divine intervention on their particular side of all conceivable causes.

It is outside the scope of this book to examine the argument that late medieval Christianity had been merely a thin veneer over a complex world of traditional beliefs, paganism and folklore which the Reformers and Counter-Reformers sought to bring under control;[10] neither would it be appropriate to try to assess how far, as Calvinists and more radical sectarians claimed, the Roman Catholic or the Greek and Russian Orthodox Churches were still supporting an ideology which in many respects was hard to distinguish from white magic. As always, enormous differences persisted in the relative emphasis contemporaries placed on different parts of the Bible and over the interpretation of fundamental points such as transubstantiation or the Trinity. Substantive debates over theological niceties (going beyond mere diatribes) were primarily the preserve of an educated minority, as illustrated by the stand of the Jansenists, the powerful but very small group of Augustinian ascetics at the retreat of Port Royal near Paris. The Jansenist doctrinal emphasis on predestination, and refusal to accept Jesuit and Roman rulings in other matters, started a long-running battle in the French Church, just as their politically critical stand earned them the deep hostility of the French Crown from the 1630s right up to the end of Louis XIV's reign. But the moral and social implications of this famous controversy notwithstanding, such fairly esoteric issues may have been of less relevance to most Frenchmen than, for example, the broadly politicised debate over Arminianism was to Dutchmen around 1618, or practical Laudian reform to Englishmen during the following decades. Traditional beliefs and practices meant a great deal to everyone, but what we know of the mental world of the great majority, through the evidence contained in judicial and visitation records, dairies, letters and other material, suggests that even basic Christianity had some way to go before becoming a meaningful common language of the time.

In February 1648 the Württemberg vintner Hans Keil had a vision of an angel addressing him in a vineyard. The message consisted of moral condemnation of the sins of the community, and the angel warned of divine retribution unless there was a response, within six months, in the form of collective penance and the adoption of comprehensive moral reform to eradicate cursing, sexual laxity, female vanity and blasphemy. But the vision also had more specific subversive ingredients. There was explicit mention of hunting on Sundays, of the extortionate taxation imposed by the princely government and of the avaricious materialism of the clergy. The veracity of the vision was confirmed by a physical sign, the trickling of blood from grapevines in the field, adding a dimension which everyone in the village could (and did) observe. Keil's story and the vines were duly examined by the authorities and reported to the ducal government. Attempts by local officials to prevent Keil from going in person to the ducal court in Stuttgart merely made them targets of local hostility as well. A second vision three days later brought the whole village and the surrounding countryside into great alarm, especially since the local pastor vehemently backed Keil's story. It was taken for granted that God's wrath was directed not just at individuals but at the whole community: everyone was his brother's keeper, and retribution would be universal. Attempts by the authorities to defuse the tension by demonstrating that Keil's vision was in fact an intentional or unintentional fraud, based on overliteral interpretation of the pastor's own sermons and on various prophetic texts and broadsheets in Keil's possession, did little to calm what was turning into a combined religious and seditious riot whose consequences were spreading into the surrounding villages. Only Keil's own confession and punishment, combined with substantial repressive orders from the government, secured an end to the commotion.[11] Given the common stereotypes of sin, punishment and repentance to which war-weary Germans naturally were particularly susceptible, it is hardly surprising that the official explanation seemed inadequate to the villagers. In the present context, however, it is striking to observe how much power a single imagination could have on a community of believers, especially when supported by the local pastor.

As the range of secular government gradually expanded during the seventeenth century, and the efficacy of church control improved, attempts were made to channel popular festivities and communal activities into what it was hoped would be innocuous directions. In many parts of Europe, bonfires to celebrate St John the Baptist (St Jean in France, Sankt Hans in Scandinavia) were a long-established tradition of probably pagan origin. In France, efforts were made in 1665 to subject this annual event to state regulation because of the variety of superstitions associated with it but, significantly, it was not banned outright. The religious confraternities, with their strong traditions of independence and self-sufficiency, were also subjected to closer scrutiny by the Church in France and Italy, and some of the traditions associated with their public and convivial functions were repressed. The aim was to channel popular and communal piety into uniform parochial practices approved and determined by the clergy; to this effect more consistent checks on individual devotion were also attempted by means of fuller registers of births, communions, marriages and deaths. Regulating popular religious observance, however, was easier said than done: there was a real risk that enthusiasm might also be destroyed. The authorities even in Protestant Europe recognised that missionary activity of the kind long organised by the Roman Catholic orders, and since 1622 also by the Jesuit Congregation for the Propagation of the Faith, was an effective means of maintaining vitality. But few Lutheran preachers in this period had the charisma necessary to rival preaching such as that of the fiery Capuchin Marco d'Aviano who, at the siege of Vienna in 1683, rallied townsmen and peasants alike with his outspoken sermons.

Less spectacular were the methodical instructional programmes designed to ensure habitual Christian observance in many parts of Europe. In the Roman Catholic world these were organised amongst the rich and powerful especially by the Jesuits, and amongst the poor more often by the Oratorians, the Capuchins and various newer orders. As a result, by the end of the century some free primary-school provision was available in nearly all parishes in privileged cities such as Paris, and some impression was also being made on provincial towns and even on a few rural parishes. In Protestant and Catholic Europe alike, printed catechisms were extensively used as compulsory manuals of Christian guidance. In France, where many new editions appeared from the 1640s onwards in conscious imitation of Protestant practices, a commonly used set of catechisms involved one of 27 pages for small children, 93 pages for older children preparing for first communion, and 382 pages for the use of educated adults and preachers.[12] In Denmark, the fundamentalist professor of theology at Copenhagen and later Bishop of Zealand, Hans Resen, exercised enough influence over the King not only to secure a new school curriculum in 1604, for which he supplied some of the textbooks himself, but also to hound out of office any colleagues and clergymen showing signs of deviation from literal and anti-rationalist Lutheranism. Obstacles were put in the way of students wishing to study abroad, in an effort to limit their exposure to other ways of thinking. In Sweden, orthodoxy was even more strictly enforced owing to fears of Calvinist or Catholic subversion. The accession charter of 1611 had excluded all but native Lutherans from a wide range of offices, and further severe penalties were threatened in 1617 against anyone cultivating contacts with Catholics; tolerance of economically useful foreigners and even embassy staff was very closely circumscribed as late as 1671.

At parish level all over Europe, Church and State worked hand in hand to repress nonconformity or deviation of any kind. This is apparent not just in Lutheran areas with their strong Erastian traditions and in the direct influence exercised by the Roman Catholic orders on all aspects of life in southern and western Europe, it is also clear in Calvinist areas, where one might have expected a greater separation of Church and State. In Scotland, for example, the kirk session of minister and elders in each parish monitored the morality and subservience of the whole community. The elders checked on absenteeism during services and made it their business to ascertain everything that might be regarded as sinful. Culprits were heard before the session, their cases if necessary transferred to either presbytery or secular courts. Fines for moral offences helped to support the poor of the parish. Kirk-session monitoring was far more detailed and effective than anything that the laird or the secular courts could have imposed, but collaboration with lay authorities was invariably close. In rural areas ministers were mostly chosen and paid by the heritors (landowners) of the parish, and the elders were selected from the more substantial tenants. As a result, the Church in effect upheld the established order, acting as the policing and moral arm of the seigneurial system, with little effective authority over the landowners themselves.[13]

The behaviour and beliefs of the elite were in most of Europe treated with greater leniency. If we accept that witchcraft prosecutions invariably originated in accusations against those at the bottom of the social scale – even if prominent citizens might later be implicated – it is striking by comparison that alchemy and astrology, both forms of educated magic, never elicited any significant repressive measures from Church or State. In 1648 Ferdinand III, observing mercury being converted into gold in his presence, rewarded the alchemist with a noble title as Baron von Chaos.[14] The literature of the occult was widely available in monastic libraries, and many of the foremost practitioners were clergy. Arguably only the Spanish and

Italian Inquisitions, thanks to their meticulous and slow procedure, came anywhere near to disciplining the elite as thoroughly as they did ordinary parishioners. The Spanish obsession with *limpieza de sangre* (purity of blood, free especially of Moorish or Jewish taint), closely bound up with elaborate notions of honour, deeply affected the middle and higher ranks of society. By the seventeenth century, however, the Inquisition was adopting a moderating stand in this respect, being by then more concerned with superstition and sexual morality.

At the same time, the Catholic Church attempted, in the spirit of the reforms initiated at the Council of Trent, to discipline the morality and conduct of the priesthood itself. In the diocese of Paris, for example, a general prohibition of 1672 sought to exclude priests from taverns except if they were travelling more than two miles from their residence. Clerical absenteeism was also a major problem, especially in rural Europe. The French spiritual leader Saint Vincent de Paul himself employed a substitute to look after his parish from 1613 to 1626, and in the remoter parts of Spain and Italy the difficulties were acute. Greater use of financial penalties against unauthorised absenteeism seems to have reduced the number of French parishes which were completely devoid of spiritual care, but the distribution of manpower between town and countryside remained highly unsatisfactory, not least because of the inadequacy of remuneration in many rural areas. Equally persistent, it appears, was the related problem of poorly educated rural clerics whose ignorance of basic Latin and lack of books ensured that they could scarcely contribute meaningfully to their parishioners' enlightenment. Individual efforts apart, it seems that only slow progress was made in these areas until the later eighteenth century. Evidence from other parts of Europe points in the same direction: in England, for example, there were enormous differences in the degree of religious commitment in various parts of the country, but it is still surprising to come across a Yorkshire boy who did not know 'how many gods there be, nor persons in the godhead, nor who made the world nor anything about Jesus Christ, nor heaven or hell, or eternity after this life, nor for what end he came into the world'.[15]

In spite of such evidence, the seventeenth century was clearly a period of deep religious commitment. The outburst of radical and often highly original religious thinking in mid-century England is the most striking proof of the level of sophistication attainable amongst laymen when regulatory uniformity and clerical direction lapsed. Why this occurred in England and nowhere else at this time certainly has much to do with the rigidity of Charles I and the failure of Laudian reformers to understand the importance of lay participation and fellowship in religious observance. Early on, the English

Reformed Church had fostered the sense of freedom so effectively exploited by Calvinist lay preachers and the puritan critics of court elitism – separatist congregations flourished in secrecy from the early decades of the century, only coming into the open with the collapse of effective control in the 1640s. Significantly, the Quakers, the Fifth Monarchists, the Muggletonians and perhaps even fringe groups such as the Ranters relied to a considerable extent on the support of London artisans and middling commoners. The freedom of spiritual choice under the Commonwealth was, thanks to Cromwell's adamant insistence, unrivalled anywhere in Europe. As we have noted (see chapter 7), the Quakers made so much of this that they became a real threat to the state as traditionally conceived: not just in their refusal to conform to the norms of social deference, or in their subsequent uncompromising pacifism, but also in their search for subjective and personal guidance in the Scriptures without the mediation either of clergy, of systematised sacraments or even of the buildings for worship (which they demonstratively called 'steeple houses').

The Restoration of 1660 brought a return of institutionalised Anglicanism, complete with existing defects and backed once again by strident demands for conformity.[16] Roman Catholicism remained the target of particularly crude and vicious popular prejudice, most noticeably in London. But the experience of the commonwealth period, of the voluntary lay associations of spiritual seekers, could not be completely obliterated. Amongst the radical sects mentioned, only the Quakers survived as a clear alternative to established religion but, together with Baptists, Presbyterians and other groups, they ensured that nonconformity remained a characteristic feature of religious and political life in England despite the penalties of the Clarendon Code, including the Corporation Act of 1661. Many emigrated to the United Provinces or across the Atlantic in the hope of securing a more peaceful existence. The so-called Toleration Act of 1689, while recognising the permanence of the dissenting Churches, did not extend full citizenship (in the sense of access to offices or entitlement to equal civil and educational rights) to Protestant nonconformists. But there was some scope for individual choice: by 1711 perhaps one Londoner in six was a dissenter, and provided they could put up with the limitations on their legal status, they could count themselves lucky – especially by comparison with Catholics or Jews. In the English colonial possessions, conditions ranged from exemplary tolerance of all, in Rhode Island, to continuing extreme intolerance of Catholics in Ireland.

Genuine toleration, as distinct from grudging de facto concessions to minority faiths, was rare in seventeenth-century Christian Europe. There was no equivalent to Ottoman policies of explicit acceptance of different faiths. In the Holy Roman Empire, apart from the legislated toleration of Brandenburg–Prussia (see p. 395), some interesting forms of confessional co-existence had developed, as in the duchy of Cleves, where Roman Catholics and Lutheran clergymen at times shared the same building for worship. The United Provinces acquired an enviable reputation for latitudinarianism, based not in law but in the failure to enforce the strict penalties against non-Calvinists laid down by the Synod of Dordrecht of 1619. Amsterdam, alongside Hamburg, also became one of the main settlements of Iberian Jews. The Sephardim, in particular, contributed to the economic prosperity of both cities, whilst the generally more conservative and more numerous Ashkenazim, the majority of whom had been pushed eastwards into Poland–Lithuania during the Reformation, tended to remain more cut off from Christian society.

The most interesting example of – admittedly threadbare – confessional coexistence during this period may well be Poland–Lithuania. Every major European variant of Christianity was represented there at the beginning of the century, in addition to the substantial and widely scattered Jewish settlements. Importantly, the formal distinctions between beliefs were often blurred: predestination was not stressed by Calvinists, and veneration for the Virgin Mary was widespread not just amongst Catholics. During the later sixteenth century, religious diversity had become one of the hallmarks of the Polish nobility, protected even by Catholics as part of the heritage of political decentralisation. The enthusiasm of Sigismund III (1587–1632) for Counter-Reformation absolutism made Protestantism an ideology of noble independence, but the different sects utterly failed to co-operate amongst themselves or to form a defensive alliance with the more directly threatened Orthodox Church. As long as landowners extended protection for particular minorities within their own estates, there was at least some diversity, even if the enserfed peasantry did not benefit. But Sigismund, under Jesuit pressure, imposed civil disabilities on non-Catholics wherever he could and used his powers of patronage gradually to achieve the conversion of all but 5 of the 41 dissidents in the Senate. From the 1630s systematic harassment was used against some of the less well-protected sects such as the Antitrinitarians, and although religious refugees from other parts of Europe were still welcomed, the governing elite became increasingly conformist. The recurrent conflicts with Sweden, Russia and the Ottoman Empire up to mid-century made Catholicism a proof of loyalty to the state: Protestants and the Orthodox were suspected, not without justification, of wanting to place their own alien candidate on the Polish throne during the crisis of the 1650s (see chapter 7). Consequently the *sejm* sanctioned openly discriminatory policies. By 1668 conversion from Catholicism became punishable by exile, and shortly afterwards conformity became a precondition of admission to the nobility. The contraction of Protestant communities in Poland–Lithuania was by then clearly measurable, and although they never experienced persecution on a level of brutality comparable to that in, for instance, France, the cultural diversity of the state was lost.[17]

The printed word

Censorship of books, journals and other publications was intensified after the Reformation in order to restrict the dissemination of heresy and other religiously subversive opinion. Spain had one of the most rigorous systems of control, with the Inquisition naturally monitoring both imported foreign material and the output of presses operating within its jurisdiction. An index of over 500 prohibited books was compiled in the 1550s, independently from the one promulgated by Rome in 1559 and approved in a slightly modified version by the Council of Trent five years later. By the time Quiroga's index was set up in 1583, the Spanish list of illegal books had multiplied fivefold, ranging from foreign translations of the Bible to editions of Bodin's and Thomas More's political works and Servetus's medical writings. In Italy, the revised index of 1596 also systematically banned all vernacular translations of the Bible itself. France compiled its own lists, but in a somewhat less systematic or culturally inhibiting way. In the absence of any Inquisition, the faculty of theology at the Sorbonne together with the Parlement of Paris jointly controlled the licences essential for legal publishing and sale in France from 1563. This was supplemented in 1618 by stricter regulation of the whole trade through a Chancery-controlled guild of booksellers, printers and binders. The abbé de St Cyran, founder of the Jansenist community at Port Royal, was imprisoned for five years from 1638 for disseminating unacceptable ideas, and Descartes went into voluntary exile in the Netherlands from 1629 to 1644 in fear of what penalties his own writings might bring. It may not have been very difficult to evade the regulations, for example by using false imprints or even imaginary places of publication, but for those unable or unwilling to do so the machinery was clearly regarded as highly repressive. Descartes's choice was understandable in terms of the enviable reputation acquired by the United Provinces: the University of Utrecht challenged him in 1642, threatening him with arrest, but nationally no effort had been made to try to enforce censorship regulations since the religious controversies culminating at the Synod of Dordrecht of 1619 had ebbed. In France, by contrast, the reign of Louis XIV brought new measures to control the Parisian book trade, yet even the ingenuity of the police chief from 1667, La Reynie, did not prevent the number of printers in the city being twice what Colbert had authorised.

Freedom of expression in many Protestant states was meant to be as closely regulated as in Roman Catholic ones,[18] but the systematic implementation of restrictions was far less effective in practice. In the Scandinavian monarchies Calvinist and Roman Catholic influences were kept out quite effectively during the early seventeenth century by means of travel restrictions and censorship. England, like many other states, required every new publication to be licensed, and the book trade was by 1586 formally regulated through the Stationers' Company. The publishing of news-sheets, becoming popular in the 1620s because of the war, was also controlled fairly effectively until 1641, when a flood of printed material turned London into a censor's nightmare. Detailed regulations were reimposed from 1662, but political circumstances ensured that government control of the press became increasingly ineffective from the 1680s. Precensorship of the press was in effect abandoned in England in 1695.

In the German lands effective censorship was also difficult to maintain, for different reasons. Europe's most prestigious book-trading centre was Frankfurt, where several scholarly firms were based and where one of the earliest newspapers with a genuine international reputation, the *Frankfurt Zeitung,* was also published from 1615. Frankfurt, however, was an imperial city and, as such, it was exposed to monitoring by the imperial book commission and the Jesuits. They ultimately succeeded, despite the notorious weaknesses of the imperial government, in exploiting wartime insecurity sufficiently to strangle the international book trade there, pushing it north-east to Leipzig instead. The political diversity of the Empire, however, made overall censorship (and indeed copyright protection) virtually unenforceable: the peace of 1648 confirmed the autonomy of each territorial prince in this respect, ensuring a very uneven, and probably ineffective, pattern of control.

Only one state seems to have been largely unaffected by the rapid spread of printing technology: the Ottoman Empire. The Muslim faith encouraged abstract art rather than personalised representation; equally, its reverential attitude towards sacred texts may have perpetuated the long-standing tradition of reliance on a limited distribution of hand-written material, most of it provided by a large group of professionally trained scribes. The multiplicity of dialects and inflections in Arabic, across a wide-flung empire, may also have reduced the attractiveness of print as a medium. When the first printing presses were established under central Ottoman control in the early eighteenth century, texts on religion and the law were explicitly excluded; the range of printed books was restricted to military and some scientific works, and actual output remained exceptionally low by European standards.

The book trade was affected not just by state regulation. No less

important were the financial and practical limitations of so technolog-
ically complex an industry. The cost of paper was generally greater
than that of printing, even at a time when editions rarely exceeded
1000 copies. Although paper manufacturers were known to act as
financiers for printers, the latter had to rely on religious works and
pamphlets if they wanted a predictable demand or quick turnover.
Only very large-scale firms could be more adventurous, such as the
Plantin presses set up in Antwerp in the later sixteenth century, relying on a highly respected scholarly reputation to employ around a
hundred workers operating up to 24 presses. Few could rival that size,
but one of Plantin's employees, Louis Elzevir, exploited the market
for cheaper publications and for second-hand books to set up another
family business which by 1620 ran the prestigious Leiden University
Press and after 1638 also dominated the international Amsterdam
market. By then the United Provinces had become the safe haven for
the publication of controversial material, and the Elzevirs had many
leading scholars on their lists, including Descartes, Bacon, Milton and
Comenius.

Elsewhere in Europe printers and publishers experienced growing
difficulties after the outbreak of war in 1618. The Huguenot family
firm of Wechel had built its reputation in Frankfurt not just by
publishing Calvinist theological works but also by including a number
of major controversial authors on its lists, notably Kepler, Giordano
Bruno (burnt for heresy in Rome in 1600) and the English Hermetic
writer John Dee. There was a considerable demand for such writings
until the sack of the Palatinate in 1619 led to the disintegration of the
Hermetic and occult intellectual circles centred there – groups of
widely influential scholars and writers, such as Johann Valentin
Andreae, who sought inward truth through forms of mysticism
supposedly rooted in antiquity, in the process rejecting the rationalism
and the search for empirical knowledge which they saw as deceptive
ignorance. In spite of its interest in this market, the Wechel press
submitted pro forma, for the sake of its connections in Prague and
Vienna, to monitoring by the imperial book commission. To some
extent it preserved its integrity until the outbreak of the war by means
of a satellite press in the nearby town of Hanau. But in the 1620s, its
humanist ideals increasingly untenable, the Wechel firm could not
even count on its original staple, for Calvinism itself was suffering
major political setbacks.[19]

Availability of print, regulated or otherwise, was only one stage in
the communication process, however. Much more difficult to ascertain is the extent of literacy in Europe during the early modern
period. Important changes in educational methods had been
suggested by the major humanist writers of the later sixteenth
century, including the Frenchman Montaigne (1533–92). By the

seventeenth century there were various suggestions for the abandonment of rote learning in favour of more spontaneous and practical methods. Francis Bacon (1561–1626) and the widely travelled Moravian educationalist Johann Comenius (1592–1670) were particularly important in this respect, but their influence was to some extent counteracted by growing wartime disturbance and by restrictions on the 'republic of letters' (the international community of scholars communicating in the common language of Latin). Later in the century some groups, such as the Jansenists in Port-Royal, became genuinely interested in child development and psychology, while the Roman orders adopted a more systematic approach in their parish work. All told, however, no major improvements in education at any level were achieved during this period.

Yet this does not imply that basic literacy rates were essentially stagnant. Historians have had some difficulty agreeing on standards of evidence suitable for quantitative analysis, not least because basic schooling (where it existed) concentrated on religious memorisation, and because reading and writing were taught as separate skills. The ability to sign a document (a petition, a contract, a will) is not a reliable indicator of the ability to write anything else, nor does it indicate to what extent fluency in reading has been attained. There is evidence to suggest that simpler texts (including ballads and broadsheets) were accessible to a larger number of people than was once thought. If we are in reality dealing with a stepless gradient from total illiteracy, through basic reading skills of familiar religious texts or popular broadsheets to habitual reading of unseen texts, then any attempt at quantified measurement for this period is liable to mislead. The estimates reached some years ago on the basis of signature evidence alone – indicating male literacy rates in England at the time of the civil war at around 30 per cent, in lowland Scotland around 25 per cent, in France much the same – in any case conceal some significant social discrepancies. Whatever evidence we use, northern France had literacy rates twice as high as the south, whilst in England the geographic distribution seems even more complex. Consistently, however, literacy rates in towns were much higher than in the countryside, with Amsterdam, London and other prosperous cities experiencing a rapid increase in the use of print. Female literacy invariably appears lower than male, perhaps as low as half during the early seventeenth century, but this may in part reflect types of evidence which tend to magnify gender differences.[20]

Calculations based on the unusually detailed catechism-reading tests in Sweden, suggesting very high success rates of 50 per cent and more from the later seventeenth century, may be proof of learning by rote rather than ability to read (let alone understand). Nevertheless, the Protestant world optimistically emphasised literacy as a tool for

Christian betterment: contemporary writers were often wary of letting ordinary people loose on a text as complex and contradictory as the Bible, but seemed nearly unanimous that the advantages of individual reading of approved catechisms outweighed the risks of promoting popular access to unauthorised printed texts. The Roman Catholic and Orthodox Churches seemed more ambivalent about lay access to religious texts, and the continued use of Latin and church Slavonic in southern and eastern Europe respectively militated against active literary involvement by laymen. By the eighteenth and nineteenth centuries Protestant Europe undoubtedly had higher functional literacy rates than the rest of the continent but – as indeed the evidence from different parts of France suggests – this may be partly attributable to other factors, including economic development.[21]

Immediate practical reasons undoubtedly also influenced demand for education. Political flysheets conveying their message in pictorial symbols had been very important in the German lands during the Thirty Years War. Evidence on the book, almanac and pamphlet trade in London suggests an enormous increase in output during the civil-war period, with between 1000 and 2000 new titles appearing annually, some in large editions of several thousands. Much consisted of scurrilous or highly provocative ephemera, so much so that one is surprised that the Commonwealth regime allowed as much latitude as it did after 1650. The interest in news and topical information is undeniable, however, and – as in the main cities of the United Provinces during the war with Spain in the 1620s and 1630s – lends support to the conclusion that there was a rapidly growing popular political awareness amongst social groups in London who had hitherto largely been uninvolved. Apart from the Dutch cities, the nearest continental equivalent in the middle decades of the century was the surge of interest in the pamphlets against Cardinal Mazarin during the Fronde, but the restoration of control in Paris by 1660 was far more effective and durable than that in London the same year.

In the French and English provinces, as far as one can judge from the sparse evidence that has survived, flysheets, ballads, almanacs and chapbooks were much more conventional and apolitical in nature. There was apparently more demand for devotional literature, for tales of romance and for sensational stories, than for news as such. In France, pedlars of '*livrets bleus*' (small pamphlets on low-quality paper), like the chapmen in England, could make some sort of living fulfilling limited demand in market towns and, later on, also in the countryside. The price of such prints, in England a penny or two, was usually low enough to be occasionally within the range of at least skilled labourers. The surviving evidence, however, is utterly inadequate for any kind of quantification either of readership or of demand, let alone of the effect on popular consciousness.[22] We know from surviving private collections that popular prints did find their way into the libraries of men such as Samuel Pepys and his superiors, just as members of the elite still enjoyed street entertainments and popular festivities. But even amongst the more educated groups in society, from *savants* and teachers to office-holders and courtiers, the impact of more readily available print is difficult to assess. The growing number of new titles published, and the larger share appearing in the vernacular language rather than in Latin, is perhaps the best indication we have of changing demand.

Scepticism, Galileo and the expanding universe

Amongst late medieval and sixteenth-century men of learning there was no incompatibility between science and strict religious belief: the discovery of nature was also the discovery of God's creation. As long as observation and reasoning were regarded as contributors to a universal truth, where levels of knowledge, like states of being, could be organised in a perfect hierarchy down from the Creator, there was no conflict. Many of the great names in science, from Robert Grosseteste in early thirteenth-century Oxford to Nicolaus Copernicus in sixteenth-century Frauenburg in Poland, were in any case themselves respected churchmen. The fundamental elements of Aristotelian scientific method, which had remained dominant from the time of St Thomas Aquinas, could be adapted for contemporary needs – as had already been amply demonstrated, for example, at Padua, the most advanced intellectual centre in the late fifteenth and sixteenth centuries. Even later, the Englishman William Harvey (1578–1657), who had studied at Padua University, worked out essential aspects of the circulatory system (published in *De motu cordis* of 1628) without believing that he had departed from the fundamentals of Aristotelian and Galenic physiology.

The persuasiveness of the existing scientific system is clear in many of the major works of the sixteenth and early seventeenth century, and it would be misleading to impose twentieth-century standards of novelty on a period where intellectual accumulative traditions were more highly valued than individual originality. Copernicus's most important book, *De revolutionibus orbium coelestium,* had for this reason not created much controversy initially on publication in 1543. It entailed a recasting of the accepted Ptolemaic theory of the universe to allow for a stationary sun, but achieved that by traditional scholastic means and without upsetting the assumed geometric perfection of the whole – so much so, in fact, that it was at least as complex and in many respects no more convincing than the system which it was meant to replace. There is some doubt about the status of the book's cautiously worded preface which suggests that the whole work was to be regarded as an abstractly theoretical hypothesis rather than as an attempt at real explanation. In fact, the whole text is studiously unpolemical and in no way iconoclastic in the style of, for instance, Servetus, so Copernicus need not have hesitated over publication for as long as he did: *De revolutionibus* was not placed on the Index of Prohibited Books until 1616.

The delayed controversy over the heliocentric (more accurately heliostatic) theory, and over the status of science as a whole, sprang from more complex factors. One was the tension between the followers of what van Gelder called the 'minor reformation' of Luther and Calvin on the one hand, and the humanist tradition of the 'major reformation' on the other. Some of those who followed the humanist tradition came to regard the details of religious interpretational dogma (whether Protestant or Roman Catholic) as inhibiting and restrictive, preferring to see religion as a philosophy of life, as ethical principles, rather than as an exclusive prescription for salvation and theological purity. This latitudinarian approach, obviously central to the writings of Erasmus himself, later went into retreat because of the hostile climate of Counter-Reformation confessional confrontations. Some of the more radical latitudinarians, such as Giordano Bruno (1548–1600), were persecuted wherever they went and were reduced to an itinerant existence. But the tradition still found influential echoes amongst leading members of the intelligentsia in seventeenth-century Europe. The very nature of this humanist outlook precludes accurate delineation, and may have produced offshoots such as, for instance, the seventeenth-century Cambridge Neoplatonists, but one can argue that many of the greatest minds in the scientific and intellectual revolutions of this period had it in them to some extent, including Kepler and even Galileo at the turn of the century, some of the followers of Descartes soon afterwards, and men such as Boyle, Newton and Locke a generation or two later.[23]

Excessive intellectual latitude, however, was precisely what many feared, as we have already noted in connection with religion itself. Ginzburg argued some years ago that the age-old concern over the dangers of too much knowledge – over the subversive potential of 'forbidden knowledge' or over the Icarus-like pursuit of what is beyond man's proper limitations – was strongly voiced during the sixteenth and seventeenth centuries.[24] Copernicus certainly opted for caution in his published work, but Montaigne and Galileo were more outspoken. Later, Descartes, in fearful reaction to the hornet's nest that Galileo had stirred up, proclaimed his own desire to avoid what he saw as intellectual folly; the fact that his *Discourse on method* ultimately became even more subversive of cosmic, religious and scientific absolutes was not something he had foreseen. By mid-century, in effect, the traditional orthodoxy of perfection, absolute truth and cosmic order appeared threadbare to those who dared to think outside traditional norms. The roads away from certainty varied, and might involve either the abstract deductive reasoning of Descartes or something akin to Galileo's combination of structured observation and pragmatic analysis. But if the term 'revolution' can be applied in intellectual and scientific history at all, it is surely appropriate for those processes culminating in the early seventeenth century whereby individuals working in widely different ways came to the conclusion that truth was infinite, that the traditional Christian world-view did not altogether go well either with logical reasoning or with empirical observation, and that intellectual caution might be safe but also barren.

Astronomy was the first field in which tension between established authority and intellectual independence came to a head. The highly detailed and accurate observational work of the Danish astronomer Tycho Brahe passed on his death in 1601 to Johannes Kepler (1571–1630), a man widely respected for his skills in astrology but also equipped with outstanding mathematical and analytical abilities. It was his mathematical analysis of observational data, summed up in what became known as the three laws of planetary motion, that established with certainty that the planets (including the earth) moved in elliptical rather than in perfect circular orbits and that the solar system was more of an explanatory reality than Copernicus had postulated. Kepler's approach implied the wholesale rejection of the geometric Ptolemaic–Aristotelian universe, the replacement of perfection with a series of recognisably modern dynamic and open-ended scientific hypotheses resting on verification and ascertainment of relative knowledge. Acceptance of his conclusions was slow: indeed, the scale of his achievement only became fully apparent when Newton added the concepts of momentum and universal gravitation, making it all feasible as a model of reality. Kepler was typical of his time in the special mystical emphasis he placed on the sun as a central, almost divine driving force, yet the mechanisation of the universe was well on its way.

The person who brought the latent tensions into the open was Galileo Galilei (1564–1642), professor of mathematics at Padua from 1592 to 1610, then court mathematician to the Medici in Florence. His empirical studies of mechanics, motion and acceleration led him to distance himself from the Aristotelian abstractions of contemporary philosophy early in his Paduan career. But it was his use in 1610 of a much improved version of the recently invented telescope that led him to demonstrate in his *Starry Messenger* both the roughness of our moon's surface and the existence of Jupiter's moons. This persuaded him to use astronomical observation for his work on motion and, in the process, to deny the Aristotelian distinction between celestial and earthly physics. Despite considerable differences of temperament and method, Galileo and Kepler were in contact at this stage, the latter defending some of Galileo's conclusions in print against Aristotelian criticisms.

It was during the following years that the watershed in Galileo's career was reached. From 1613 he conducted a lively controversy with the Jesuit astronomer Scheiner regarding the nature and apparent cyclical pattern of sunspot activity. In the process he also for the first time spoke unequivocally in print in favour of the heliostatic theory. The Jesuits had hitherto been enthusiastic supporters of Galileo's work but, owing to a dispute over who had made the first sunspot observations, considerable friction was now generated. Historians of science have tended to emphasise Galileo's assertiveness in such controversies and his manifest gifts as a polemicist and populariser, suggesting, for instance, that he was supporting the heliostatic theory without sufficient proof. Others have argued not only that Galileo was in fact being strictly scientific (in the modern sense) in backing a theory which provided him with a better explanation of his accumulating observations but also, more importantly, that Galileo and his supporters were in fact trying to persuade the Church not to take a categorical stand at all on an issue where empirical observation might lead to conclusions in conflict with a narrowly literal reading of the Bible. The advancement of learning could best be achieved on its own merits, and the Roman Catholic Church might well risk its own credibility by making either side's argument an article of faith. In his *Letter to the Grand Duchess Christina* of 1615 he made a strong case for the need to allow metaphorical interpretation of the Bible in those few instances (such as the story of Joshua stopping the sun) where the Scriptures and science might not be in apparent accord. The papacy, however, was reluctant to open the door to a potential flood of reinterpretations and, on the advice of Cardinal Bellarmine, the matter was referred to the appropriate advisory council, the theological qualifiers. In February 1616 they declared the heliostatic theory 'foolish and absurd in Philosophy, and formally heretical inasmuch as it contradicts the express opinion of Holy Scriptures in many places'. *De revolutionibus* was placed on the Index pending emendations, and Galileo was warned that discussion of the theory would be permissible only in hypothetical terms.[25]

In his writings over the next years, Galileo steered clear of this area altogether. But after the election of Urban VIII in 1623, and with the new Pope's apparent encouragement, he returned to the subject. In 1632 he published the *Dialogue on the two principal world systems*. Although this book was given prior clearance by the church censor in Florence, its appearance resulted in an immediate summons to Galileo to appear before the Inquisition in Rome at the express demand of

Urban VIII. Historians have disagreed over the reasons for this, some suggesting that Galileo was being unnecessarily provocative in his presentation of views held by Urban himself. The Pope also appears to have been persuaded that Galileo had been given a more sweeping prohibition in 1616 than was in fact the case and that he had not been entirely frank about it during their discussions of 1624. What appeared to the Pope as deviousness was in fact the result of misleading record-keeping (as Galileo himself demonstrated at his trial) and of real disagreements (and perhaps vendettas) within the Roman Church. It is possible that the Jesuits had already for some years questioned Galileo's orthodoxy, and that publication of *The Assayer* in 1623 allowed them to accuse Galileo of a form of atomism which would make nonsense of the Eucharist itself.[26] To conceal such damaging matters, or to avoid the embarrassment of an acquittal, the trial focused on the issue of his disobedience to the 1616 injunction. Galileo may have been trapped by the prosecution into a denial that he had ever upheld the Copernican system, which in turn exposed him to simpler charges of trying to mislead the court. Although in the final sentence he managed to avoid having to confess to a deliberate perversion of the truth or of the Catholic faith, his famous involuntary recantation, like the tone of the *Dialogue* itself, made the whole issue a major sensation in Europe.

Galileo was condemned to house-arrest for the rest of his life, and publication of anything by him was prohibited. He did in due course recover sufficiently from the shock to complete new research: a Latin edition of the *Dialogue* was published from Strassburg in 1637, and other work subsequently by the Elzevir firm in the Netherlands. But public opinion was now fully conscious of the fact that the Roman version of religious orthodoxy appeared to leave little room for the advancement of science. Contrary to Galileo's intentions, the papacy had landed itself with an ultimately destructive categorical stand on its exclusive right to judge areas of knowledge outside the scope of theologians. This did not bring an end to substantive scientific research in Italy – the impressive range of microscopic physiological research done by Marcello Malpighi (1628–94) at Bologna illustrates the contrary – but it made clear who were the ultimate judges of truth. Significantly, even Malpighi remained entirely dependent on the Royal Society in London, and especially its able secretary Oldenburg, for contacts with the scholarly community at large and for dissemination and discussion of his own research.

Science and the commonwealth of learning

In 1605 Galileo had asked, 'What has philosophy got to do with measuring anything?'[27] His emphasis on applied mathematics and on observation made him fundamentally different in approach and achievement from the other seminal figure of the early intellectual revolution, the Frenchman René Descartes (1591–1650). Descartes, in his insistence on the study of causality and in his almost scholastic desire from 1619 to create a complete new system of knowledge where only details would need to be filled in, seems in some respects out of date by comparison. His methodology, however, was of enormous importance for later seventeenth-century intellectual development. As he announced in the *Discourse on method* (published in 1637 as part of a bigger work), he aimed at strict deductive and mathematical reasoning from first principles in order to attain absolute certainty. The process, later detailed in his *Meditations on first philosophy* of 1641, started from the position of a total sceptic. Denying the reliability of any sensory perception, he was left with nothing but the existence of the thinking mind; from there, he achieved the knowledge of God, who was to serve by definition as a non-deceiving guarantor for the subsequent deductive process. Empirical evidence was not excluded in the later stages of analysis, but it is fair to say that neither observation nor applied mathematics figure prominently in his published work. That is true even of a treatise which was written in 1632 as a mechanistic explanation of the origin and structure of the universe but was not published because its Copernican orientation was too controversial at the time.

Descartes made important contributions both to geometry and, for instance in his optical studies and his formulation of the concept of inertia, to physics. His science and metaphysics remained the dominant orthodoxy in much of Europe for a century, at least in its adaptations by Malebranche and Christian Huygens. But in the present context his method of doubt is more important. Taken to its logical extreme, it was devastating: if one also doubted God and the principles of deduction that Descartes took as self-evident, what certainty was left at all, what truth or tenable belief? Descartes himself denied the validity of such a conclusion, but his critics denounced him as the arch-sceptic. Neither was there in Descartes any explicable link between mind and matter, between thought and the mechanical body, including the brain; as a result, some of his own followers ended up in total materialism. Later in the century others battled with this Cartesian dualism of mind and matter: Spinoza and Leibniz both tackled it without real success, the latter veering towards atheism in the process. Even the great sceptic and advocate of total toleration, Pierre Bayle (1647–1706), backed away from its destructive potential in his highly influential *Historical and critical dictionary* of 1696.[28] By that stage the Jesuits had long since had the main Cartesian texts placed on the Index.

It is tempting and not entirely misleading to see seventeenth-century intellectual history in terms of its most original minds. But as shown in the failure of Descartes to complete his definitive *Principles of philosophy* (1644), cumulative and co-operative work was increasingly indispensable. It was normal practice for men of learning in the early seventeenth century to maintain a network of correspondence all over Europe, through which they could test new ideas and indeed establish their claims to originality. The provincial French savant Peiresc, exceptionally, had a circle of around 500 like-minded correspondents all over Europe and as far afield as Goa, while the friar Marin Mersenne was not all that unusual in acting as a kind of intellectual clearing house ('Mersenne's letterbox') until his death in 1648. In Paris the Du Puy brothers complemented their role in this respect with the upkeep of an enormous private library accessible to others of their kind. Descartes explicitly intended his *Discourse on method* not so much for active scholars as for ordinary men of learning. Many of these, as we would expect, appear to have been lawyers and office-holders, clergymen from the upper leisured ranks of the church hierarchy, the 'wits' and frequenters of the fashionable salons of aristocratic society. In such a context, Galileo's ability to present scientific argument in an accessible style was not only one of the reasons for his punishment but also a strength. In 1640 Gassendi, an ordained priest and professor of philosophy at Aix, organised an elaborate and public experiment to test Galileo's ideas on relative motion: the trajectory of stones thrown by fast horsemen, and dropped from the mast of a trireme, reaffirmed the concepts in the public mind in a spectacular way. Equally characteristic of contemporary enthusiasm for the new science was Otto von Guericke's open demonstration before Ferdinand III at Regensburg in 1654 of the failure of 16 horses to pull apart his two Magdeburg hemispheres, held together solely by a vacuum. Even some royalty progressed beyond the older fashions for astrology and alchemy: Duke August of Brunswick-Lüneburg (1579–1666) built up an astounding library through his many scholarly contacts, and Queen Christina of Sweden maintained a circle of French scholars. Her expectations of stimulating conversation from 5 o'clock in the morning is reputed to have been the cause of the habitually more leisurely Descartes catching fatal pneumonia when he stayed at her court in 1650.

A special plea for openness and co-operative progress had already been made by the English philosopher Francis Bacon (1561–1626), also lord chancellor under James VI/I until charged with corruption in 1621. Like Galileo, he argued for the separation of science from religion, since the latter was discovered through revelation and not through methods of enquiry suitable for science. He also insisted on the rejection of all scholastic and inherited tradition (the 'idols of the mind') and of veneration of authority. In their place he suggested in the *Novum Organum* of 1620 a kind of inductive experimental approach which, though imperfectly executed by Bacon himself, came by the eighteenth century to be regarded more loosely as a useful antidote to the rigours of Cartesianism. Bacon's real contribution, however, was as a publicist for utilitarian and accumulative scientific work: he saw the development of understanding not as the work of ants piling bits of knowledge together, nor of spiders spinning endless philosophical webs, but of bees making honey from flowers according to a co-ordinated programme. This may have been Utopian or at least premature, but was not entirely at variance with the ideals of the new generation of intellectuals in Europe.

More formal organisations and scholarly journals also existed through which new ideas could be presented. The Accademia dei Lincei formed in Rome in the first years of the century later sponsored some of Galileo's major publications. Its functions were subsequently revived by the Accademia del Cimento in Florence. In London, Gresham College started in 1644 as an informal gathering of savants, intended also to provide some alternative to the backward-looking attitude of the old universities. Gaining crown recognition in 1662 under the name of the Royal Society, it soon gained considerable international prestige as a forum for scholarly exchange between leading scholars, including Robert Hooke, Christopher Wren, Edmund Halley and its many foreign correspondents. In 1663 it declared with Baconian grandeur that 'its sole business [was] to cultivate knowledge of nature and useful arts by means of observation and experiment, and to promote them for the safeguarding and convenience of human life'.[29] It was able to impose a membership fee of 40 shillings to help cover the cost of regular publication in the *Philosophical Transactions*.

In France, the return of peace in 1659 led to a revival in the republic of letters, and even the appearance of a scientific review, the *Journal des savants*, from 1665. The following year the Crown set up an official Academy of Sciences to channel research into practical (especially technological and military) directions, but it was too regulated to attract the kind of independent work typical of the Royal Society in England or of some lesser equivalents in Amsterdam and other intellectual centres in Europe. The French academy nevertheless acted as a useful forum for the applied sciences, including amongst its members leading intellectuals such as Christian Huygens. Another foreign visitor to the Paris academy in the 1670s was the Dane Ole Rømer, whose interests ranged from measurement of the speed of light (which he did with surprising accuracy) to drafting the technical basis for a complete measurement and qualitative assessment of agricultural land in Denmark in the 1680s. In central Europe formal scholarly groupings were slower to appear because of the damaging effects of the Thirty Years War, but the Leipzig journal *Acta eruditorum* of 1682 is an indication of a recovery to which

Newton's great rival, Gottfried Wilhelm Leibniz (1646–1716) became the most prominent and internationally contentious contributor. Rising membership and in some instances decreasing exclusiveness of academies and learned societies all over Europe confirm the impression of growing public excitement over a variety of areas of knowledge – a mood so enthusiastically conveyed by Samuel Pepys after his admission to the Royal Society in London in February 1665.

The apparent contradictions of seventeenth-century intellectual life are summed up in Isaac Newton (1642–1727). An intermittent participant at the Royal Society from 1671, where his concept of gravity was debated eight years before its final formulation in the *Principia Mathematica* of 1687, Newton was nevertheless very much of an individualist, with a ferocious temper when it came to arguments with other scientists. Hooke's habitual accusations of plagiarism against other scholars led to Newton's unforgiving resentment against him from 1675, despite the fertile effect they had on each other's ideas. Rivalry over the invention of calculus started a hardly less bitter feud with Leibniz. Later, when he had abandoned active scientific research himself, he exercised a rather restrictive dominance in the Royal Society which no one in England could touch, even trying to use his power to force the astronomer Flamsteed to publish observations prematurely for his own convenience. On the purely scientific side, Newton's reputation was well-deserved: his work on optics, on the mathematical analysis of space, matter and time, and indeed his clarification of scientific methods of research, developed the best work of his predecessors far beyond their limitations and created a framework which was not seriously challenged until the late nineteenth century. His scientific publications were highly technical and, unlike some of Galileo's publications, utterly inaccessible to the general reader. Yet by 1693 Newton had turned away from science in favour of detailed research on chronology, prophecy, alchemy, ancient miracles and religious history, to which he devoted the rest of his life because he regarded them as more important. Whilst he had abandoned absolute certainty in favour of inductive methods in the physical sciences, as outlined in the Fourth Rule of Reasoning of the *Principia*, he still saw the function of God in absolute terms, as the regulator of the universe for all time (and, as the only explanation he could offer of the mechanically incomprehensible force of universal gravitation, capable of working unseen through empty space). The role of God in Newton's universe led in 1713 to a second confrontation, via his pupil Clarke, with Leibniz; since Newtonian science, however, in no way depended on God the way the Cartesian system did, it is hardly surprising that eighteenth-century scholars with no interest in the mystical Hermetic tradition simply ignored the later phase of Newton's work.

The history of science is thus hardly a linear development along lines that we might take for granted nowadays. Kepler's science was underpinned by mysticism, and nearly a century later Newton turned in a similar direction in search of truth. Descartes had to protest his innocence of Rosicrucian tendencies in the 1620s, while much later Leibniz was outraged at what he saw as the blasphemy of reducing God to the role of a clockmaker and repairer. Western society is prone to emphasising those aspects of its history that in the end become dominant or prove 'correct', yet it would be easy (and in its own way rewarding) to write an intellectual history of the seventeenth century where the occult sciences, mysticism and outrageously imaginative errors made up the bulk of the text. What, for example, should we make of Edward Topsell's two volumes of 1607–8, devoted to animal identification, where unicorns, dragons and the female-shaped man-eating lamia are given pride of place in order to help with references in the Bible; of Descartes's attempt in the *Treatise on Man* of 1632 to convert Harvey's circulation of the blood into a kind of distillatory apparatus; of the rejection by Bacon and others of both telescope and microscope as tools for investigation; or of the conclusion by van Helmont, following important empirical work on chemistry and on the functioning of the digestive system, that the soul was to be found in the stomach? Similarly, we should remember that the Royal Society in 1665 not only studied the (disastrous) effect of a vacuum on a live kitten, but also on 1 March attentively followed Evelyn's paper on how to make the best type of bread – French, of course.

The search for perfect government

Heresy and secret knowledge of the ancients; witchcraft and erudite international journals; the microscope and search for the philosopher's stone; catechism and the infinity of the physical universe; sectarian religious meetings and august debates in the Royal Society: no one would experience it all but, given this ferment in the mental world of so many in the seventeenth century, it is hardly surprising that the nature of government itself also became an object of even more radical inquiry than it had already been in the years of Reformation and religious civil war of the previous century. Some writers responded in a well-tried way, with Utopian tracts designed to criticise contemporary government and social norms indirectly, or simply to stimulate constructive thinking. Amongst the best-known was the Rosicrucian Johann Valentin Andreae's book *Christianopolis* (1619), Tommaso Campanella's *City of the Sun* (1626) and, not least, Francis Bacon's influential and short *New Atlantis* published in 1627. Such works were clearly didactic in intent, indicating a desire for better social discipline and harmony through controlled education and through the utilitarian application of scientific knowledge.

Others, however, preferred to adhere to more conventional authority. Aristotle and Aquinas were still used as a starting point for abstract scholarly work, coloured perhaps by the recent ideas of the French royalist theoretician Bodin. But, like Bodin, the political writers of the seventeenth century were also deeply affected by contemporary issues. The Dutch remonstrant jurist and diplomat Hugo Grotius (1583–1645), for instance, could hardly escape the reality of contemporary violence: he published *De jure belli ac pacis* in 1625 from exile in Paris, outlining his concept of the eternal and moral natural law (law of nature) which governed the relations within and between all states. Of greatest immediate relevance, given the conditions especially of the 1630s and 1640s, was the relationship between ruler and subject, notably the hypothetical contract which contemporaries often assumed to exist between ruler and subject, safeguarding the rights and obligations of each. Calvinist commentators, such as Johannes Althusius, used this contract theory to support the notion of popular representation together with the more controversial right to oppose tyranny. Ideas of this kind became particularly relevant in England from the late 1620s onwards, and were widely debated.[30] But even firm parliamentarians like Henry Parker, together with the principal exponents of republican government in the 1650s, such as John Milton and James Harrington, were concerned to limit the extent to which popular participation in the process of government might lead to disorder and further political destabilisation.

A pivotal figure adding an entirely new dimension to this debate both in the English-speaking world and on the continent was Thomas Hobbes (1588–1679). He had fled from England in 1640 and clearly based much of his political analysis on his own observations of contemporary threats to civil society. His most widely read work, *Leviathan* of 1651, a substantial development of *De cive* of 1642, was essentially a warning against the dangers inherent both in challenging and in decentralising actual sovereign power. His incisive, uncompromising and at times humorous attacks on verbal bombast and obfuscation, applied prolifically to a range of subjects from the nature of political power to the doctrine of transubstantiation, would in themselves have made him controversial. But as an enthusiastic student of contemporary scientific developments, Hobbes also drew the logical conclusion that neither God nor the soul was anything other than corporeal – that is, spirit and physical body were inseparable – a conclusion which predictably got him into serious trouble with the Anglican establishment after the Restoration, despite the protection of Charles II. Hobbes also went far further than any contemporary in applying mechanistic materialism with uncompromising brilliance to the study of man and society. Rejecting Cartesian dualism, yet using a combination of deductive reasoning and 'thought experiments' to scrutinise the human condition, he totally desentimentalised the political system, seeing it as a product of man alone.

Leviathan analyses the functioning of the state not on theoretical premises (as in most contemporary writings) but, with characteristic and unflattering frankness, as a man-made working machine. Man is to be understood in terms of passions and desires, moderated by reason and the instinct of utilitarian self-preservation rather than by any spiritual or altruistic moral standards. Hobbes consequently argues that strong government is the only way of avoiding a state of nature where life would, in his unforgettable words, be 'solitary, poor, nasty, brutish and short'. Though recognising a contract between sovereign and subject as the utilitarian framework for order, Hobbes never treated its evolution as a historical reality. Consequently, Hobbes offers no hope of escape for those who think power is being abused by the sovereign government: only if they are directly threatened are they entitled to self-defence. Political participation is not to be encouraged. Neither the Church nor the vested interests of lawyers and teachers are to have any balancing function in the state; spiritual guidance or beliefs play no practical role and, to avoid conflict religious controversies, are to be settled by the sovereign's arbitration. Liberty is 'the absence of external impediments', and Hobbes defines natural law as 'a precept or general rule, found out by reason, by which a man is forbidden to do that which is destructive of his life'. The sovereign is above the laws governing society and, as in the variants of Divine Right theory advocated by Hobbes's predecessors, the ruler is bound only by duty to God – a qualification which in the context of what many contemporaries took as Hobbes's atheism, however, is even less comforting than it was in traditional royalist theory.

With everything from the immortality of the soul to free will and moral society in shreds, and a great number of sacrosanct myths exposed, Hobbes was bound to be greeted with misrepresentation and outrage. He even found life in Paris in the company of Prince Charles uncomfortable, and returned to England in 1651 to make his peace with the Commonwealth government. His unpretentious honesty enabled him to return to favour with the King after 1660, but did not protect him from violent attacks from all sides of the establishment, including Oxford University. It is perhaps a tribute both to the utter sincerity of his analysis, voicing what others had been reluctant to admit, and to the scale of reaction against the upheavals of the 1640s and 1650s, that he lived his full 91 years without being effectively silenced.

If Hobbes is both a natural culmination of the intellectual rationalism of the age, and an extreme representative of those who feared that disorder might turn the world upside down, the other end of the political spectrum is no less interesting. The Levellers, if not the most extreme, may be regarded as the most mature spokesmen for those otherwise outside the 'political nation', those who made royalists and parliamentarians alike fear that all authority might be lost. Neither the Levellers, nor for that matter the Ormée rebels in Bordeaux, can be described as anything other than a total practical failure (see chapter 7). It is an equally well-established historical fact that the Levellers lacked internal coherence, and that many of their manifestos were in fact personal statements by one or other of the leading figures in the movement. But Leveller demands nevertheless throw unique light on what non-participants regarded as the main weaknesses of the parliamentarian order itself, and on the most essential areas of further change. In their third and last *Agreement of the People*, of 1 May 1649, they made it clear that they were very far from the irresponsible anarchists that critics had observed. Major reform of the judicial system was required, to improve fairness and accessibility for all. The legislative, executive and judicial aspects of government were to be strictly separated, the authority of the annually elected parliaments themselves carefully circumscribed, and office-holders were to be more directly responsible to the 'free people of England'. The franchise was to be extended to all men aged 21 or more, except servants and almsrecipients. But,

> having by wofull experience found the prevalence of corrupt interests powerfully inclining most men once entrusted with authority, to pervert the same to their own domination ... we therefore further agree and declare
> x. That we do not impower or entrust our said representative to continue in force, or to make any Lawes, Oaths, or Covenants, whereby to compell ... any person to any thing in or about matters of faith, Religion or Gods worship or to restrain any person from the profession of his faith ...
> xi. We doe not impower them to impress or constraint any person to serve in war by Sea or Land, every mans Conscience being to be satisfied in the justness of that cause wherein he hazards his own life, or may destroy an others.

The representative assembly is then debarred from acting in a whole range of matters, from the imposition of permanent excise duties and tithes, or the creation of trading monopolies, to the grant of legal privileges, interference with the right of parishioners to choose their own minister, or imposition of any restrictions on eligibility for office except in the case of Roman Catholics.[31] In other words, Parliament was not to be trusted with full sovereignty on behalf of all subjects.

One can see why the establishment was unwilling to countenance the implementation of such demands, yet the perceptiveness and legitimacy of many of the demands, fostered primarily by the remarkable environment of mid-century London, stand out to a modern observer. Even in the United Provinces, where the political confrontation in 1650 had been much more limited in scope, we would look in vain for a counterpart to such wide-ranging constitutional thinking. In any case, the 1660s brought a reaction which made most of the speculative political thought of the 1640s and 1650s suspect and dangerous territory. The work of Hobbes, though targeted by more conservative thinkers, nonetheless continued to be widely read on the continent[32] and influenced central European theorists such as Samuel Pufendorf (1632–94). Hobbes was also read by one of the most extraordinary intellectuals of the age, the Jewish-born Benedict Spinoza (1632–77). Trained in Amsterdam as a rabbi but excommunicated in 1656 by the Jewish community for heresy, Spinoza absorbed radical Christianity and Cartesianism in a remarkable cross-cultural synthesis. Like Hobbes, he minimised the nature and scope of those beliefs that might be regarded as essential in order to be a true Christian or a Jew; by extension, both men also advocated full toleration of anything that was harmless to society as a whole. But Spinoza went much further: he rejected all miracles as irrational and absurd, and came to regard theology both as unverifiable and as an entirely man-made construct in which supposed mysteries are merely fabrications. His *Theological–Political Treatise* (1670) was so novel in its revaluation of the Old Testament and in its call for total freedom in biblical interpretation that it caused a furore even in the relatively tolerant climate of the United Provinces. His utterly undogmatic approach to Christian values and his friendship with the Grand Pensionary Johan de Witt made Spinoza even more suspect after 1672, and his *Ethics* was not published until after his death in 1677. The following year the French Oratorian priest Richard Simon published a highly influential *Critical History of the Old Testament* which made the Bible itself the subject of detailed historical and textual scrutiny to an extent that ensured that Simon was expelled from his order. Spinoza advocated the use of the Old Testament as a general guide rather than as a text to be taken utterly literally; Simon initiated historical and textual analysis of what had hitherto been a sacrosanct book. Neither approach was remotely acceptable at the time, regardless of the spirit in which it was intended. Both exercised a profound and irreversible influence not only on Christianity itself but also on the need for rational and philosophical scrutiny of long-established texts and beliefs which had long been fundamental to the whole European culture.

Until recently it was argued that the progressive political consensus of the later decades of the century, the emphatic return of hierarchical and ordered society and the exclusion of all but the elite from political participation everywhere in Europe was most clearly summed up in the two best-known works of John Locke (1632–1704). One was the *Essay concerning Human Understanding* (published 1690), which immediately established itself as a definitive analysis of the role of experience, sensation and intuition in the formation of human knowledge. The other was the *Two Treatises of Government*, also published in 1690, after the change of government in England and Locke's return from refuge in Amsterdam. Locke had written these while deeply involved in the growing resistance to Stuart monarchy from the 1670s onwards – he was almost certainly involved in at least the Monmouth rebellion. In exile he refused any kind of compromise with James VII/II, and remained a committed exponent of the legitimacy of rebellion by subjects against monarchs exceeding their rightful authority. The *Treatises* reject divine-right monarchy, justifying in its stead a system of government similar to that which in fact came to prevail in England, and which came to be much admired in Enlightenment Europe. Locke started from a state of nature which was milder but not totally different from that of Hobbes. A social contract led to the formation of civil society, where natural law and the rights of freedom and property were to be protected by the sovereign. In contrast to the recommendations of Hobbes, government beyond basic natural rights would be determined by majority opinion amongst the political nation. It has commonly been assumed that Locke also distanced himself from the demands of the mid-century radicals – that his political nation consisted solely of those whose wealth and education could be regarded as guarantees that they would seek to preserve stability, to the exclusion of those who worked manually for their living and would therefore be too preoccupied with daily existence. Locke was generally understood by his contemporaries to have justified the kind of government by consensus of the rich which became eminently acceptable to eighteenth-century leisured liberals. But in reality he also provided substance for a more radical democratic tradition.[33]

It would be difficult and probably self-denying to narrow down the concept of intellectual revolution to particulars. Much of what has been discussed in the later sections of this chapter make it obvious that the ferment was in the first instance amongst the highly literate intellectuals and the republic of letters and that the wider implications would be recognised only slowly. Nevertheless, comparing Galileo's work with that of Copernicus, Hobbes's with that of Bodin, or Newton's with that of Bruno, one cannot help concluding that the whole framework of human intellectual endeavour had shifted. Gone was the habitual reverence for the scholastics and the great writers of antiquity. Gone, too, was the tacit acceptance of the Church's right to interpret the physical universe and to impose institutionally propagated glosses on the Bible: only a few as yet dared exercise freedom in the latter area, but the questions had been raised. Neither the clock-making

God of Descartes, nor the purely formal God of Hobbes, nor the rationalised spiritualism of Spinoza could be accommodated within anything remotely like traditional religious belief. Some, like Pascal, found salvation by abandoning scientific work in favour of religious devotion. But Galileo had demanded reinterpretation of any texts that were scientifically untenable, methodical scepticism had taken a wider hold, and both the Quakers and Newton (in their very different ways) turned inwards to discover individually the truth of revelation. The universe was no longer hierarchic, finite or perfect; mathematical, geometric and mechanistic theories suddenly seemed to go a long way not only towards explaining some of the age-old brain-teasers in the cosmos, but also towards treating scientific knowledge not as abstract metaphysics but as an approximation to actual fact. The shifts in approach, and the clearly apparent intellectual consequences, were so great that compromise seemed impossible. The prominent intellectual position not only of philosophy but above all of religion was no longer unquestionable, and, more seriously, man was undermining his certainty about his own priority, second only to God, in the great chain of being. Random purposeless atomistic individualism was not yet openly recognised by many, but there was no longer any universally accepted antidote to it.

10   The arts, the value of creativity and the cost of appearances

On 14 August 1651 the most prestigious figure in the German early baroque, the composer Henrich Schütz (1585–1672), wrote to the son of his patron (Elector Johann Georg of Saxony) in the following terms:

> Most gracious Lord, reluctant though I am to burden your princely Highness with my repeated letters and reminders, yet I am compelled thereto by . . . the exceeding great lamentation, wretchedness and moaning of all the company of poor, neglected musicians of the court, who are living in such distress as would draw tears from a stone in the ground. [Most of them have decided] to set out for elsewhere, compelled by dire necessity. . . . They have had enough of insults, no one will any longer give them a penny's credit.

Five days later, in another appeal, Schütz added:

> the expense [of maintaining a group of musicians on reasonable terms] would be a tolerable imposition, compared with what other places spend on similar court ensembles, and in sum, I find it neither praiseworthy nor Christian that in such a great and esteemed land, where before now so much officialdom and so many bleating monks and priests have been maintained, twenty musicians can or will not be supported.[1]

The electoral court at Dresden was one of the paramount musical centres of early seventeenth-century Germany but, as will become apparent, the experience of Schütz and his fellow-musicians was far from exceptional. Unless willing to put up with extreme hardships, or prepared to be itinerant entertainers living on the verge of the vagrancy laws, those with particular artistic talents had little choice. There was no reliable market for artistic creativity outside those rarefied circles of society which were sufficiently rich to maintain a cultural profile.

Confessional disputes and the Thirty Years War blighted many aspects of literary and artistic life in the German-speaking lands for a long time. There were, as always, exceptions, and recent work has confirmed that depressed and economically insecure times were not invariably inhospitable for the craftsmen of luxury goods, or destructive of inspiration for men of genius and connoisseurs alike.[2] But wartime and post-war Germany was bound to be infertile soil for the kind of artistic creativity that required continuous financial support, the way a court band or a substantial secular building-programme necessarily would. Because of the factors we noted in chapter 7, conditions before 1660 were not much better outside the main war zones. Even in the periods of relative peace during the later seventeenth century, however, there was little substantial improvement, perhaps because of the general lack of financial foresight and ability amongst most rulers of the day. Artists and musicians at many courts in Europe found themselves at the heart of rivalries for prestige, at the mercy of corrupt and chaotic financial administrators and at the beck and call of not infrequently fickle and unpredictable patrons whose motives ranged from genuine interest to empty self-glorification. Vulnerable to exploitation because of their highly specialised crafts and because their livelihood depended on non-essential commodities, musicians, sculptors and painters were rarely in a position to bargain.

The history of artistic patronage, however, is of interest not just in terms of grandiose court life and the esoteric or egocentric tastes of the few. Elite and popular culture benefited from enough cross-fertilisation to make rigid classification difficult. In an age where more than half the population of Europe was still illiterate, visual and musical imagery was of enormous significance in many contexts and at different levels of society. A perfect vehicle for such cross-cultural communication was the new artistic trend of the seventeenth century, loosely described as 'baroque' – involving (according to most commonly accepted definitions) a considerable element of the theatrical, of subjective emotional expression and of deliberate antitheses: between marble and the human body, between architecture and the freedom of fluid space, between sexual and divine ecstasy and between harmony and the dramatic musical expression of a single voice. In all of these forms, the aim of the baroque artist was to involve the observer or audience directly in what was being represented: art could imitate real life and could be emotional and personal. Artistic patronage had perhaps always to some extent been a vehicle for status- and value-orientated publicity amongst the well-off, not least in late medieval and sixteenth-century Italy. But because of its inherent qualities the baroque lent itself particularly well to a role as active and dramatic transmitter of new values – values which, it seems, were on the whole those both of patron and of artist. This chapter will therefore attempt to cast light on what is nothing less than a reflection of the consciousness of the age.

Roman Catholic, Lutheran and other churches made substantial use of all the arts as an aid to devotion – very effectively so, given the familiar connotations of certain images and melodies to even the poorest churchgoer. Many municipalities, particularly the great commercial city-states such as Venice and Hamburg, again relied on the arts to strengthen some of the civic values and ideologies they wished to promote and, more generally, to provide tangible proof of wealth and stability. Private patrons were no less concerned about their public image, conveyed most durably through the medium of architecture and sculpture but enhanced through other forms of display. And while issues of reputation and prestige no doubt mattered a great deal, the element of genuine appreciation should not be underrated either amongst wealthy patrons or amongst the enthusiasts who flocked to exhibitions, chatted in the workshops of prominent artists or battled their way into the public opera houses springing up in bigger cities. Nor should we forget the crowd gathering around market-day minstrels, mimes and actors, the growing number buying ballad-sheets, or the family paying for music at their wedding. Just what they wanted, and what they paid for, may be difficult for the historian to recover in detail, but there is no doubt that the popular market was as buoyant as economic conditions allowed. For these reasons an attempt to convey some of the feelings and relationships that developed through the medium of the arts requires no special justification.

In any period, art – whether 'popular' or 'elitist' – is difficult to analyse and contextualise effectively. The historian of the social and economic dimensions of art and patronage has to try to avoid two serious pitfalls. The most important and most difficult to avoid is that of imposing one's own expectations and possibly anachronistic models on an area where objectivity is perhaps even more remote than in other fields of early modern history. After that, there is still the problem of handling descriptive and episodic evidence which is as suspect as any in terms of reliability, real or implicit one-sidedness, and incompleteness. As in other aspects of early modern life, we need to try to guard ourselves against the normative 'sob stories' that might appear particularly poignant when coming from individuals whose creative genius we deeply respect. More difficult still, we need to try to penetrate below the level of the few who are nowadays regarded as the outstanding talents of their age, to the many whose work may from hindsight appear more ephemeral but who arguably came closer to representing and experiencing the common values of the day. After all, the painter Peter Paul Rubens (1577–1640), with his sideline in high-level international diplomacy, his growing personal collection of art and sculpture, and his workshop of assistants helping to produce a large quantity of work to which he sometimes just put the finishing touches, can hardly be regarded as typical of the ordinary painter. Neither can Schütz himself be typical of the impoverished musicians of the Thirty Years War period, since he owned town houses in Dresden, Halle and Weissenfels, was part of a family endowed with a trust fund and had relatives who went to university or who owned an inn where Landgrave Moritz of Hessen-Kassel could comfortably stay the night.

Popular culture

Frenchmen, not just those at the highest social levels, were fond of recording many of their formal decisions and relationships before a public notary. Some of the resulting documents have survived, throwing light on the role of music in the daily life of ordinary Parisians. On 20 December 1634, for example, six musicians, all qualified masters of the minstrels' guild, entered into a contractual agreement before two notaries to form a band for ten years – a contract signed by all but one, who declared he could not write. The instrument each was to play was specified, ranging from bass violin through the smaller sizes of that family; new members would be admitted, up to a maximum of fourteen, by majority vote. No member of the band was to associate with any other guild musicians except with the prior consent of the rest of the group, nor was he permitted to play alone without the rest except for minor impromptus. The contract specifies in detail what notification each member would give the others when a 'gig' had been arranged, mostly for festivities, weddings, mascarades and morning serenades, and they would all meet at a set time every Friday to share out the earnings and additional perks equitably. Fines were specified for members guilty of various misdemeanours ranging from lateness to dishonesty, though in this particular contract, unlike others, no penalties were stated for inadequate standards of musicianship, nor for misfortunes such as infection with venereal disease which would bring the group into disrepute. The contract specifies, in accordance with guild custom, that members' children – in practice usually sons only – who met the required standard would be eligible to join at the age of 18 years.[3] Significantly in the context of what will be discussed later, provision was also made to cover appointment to the King's Music either part-time or full-time: clearly the poor guild musicians of Paris had hopes of greater things, even if the evidence does not suggest that they were often rewarded.

Similar contracts of lesser or greater formality can be found covering many other aspects of street music – not just for instrumentalists doubling on the louder hautboys and cornettos but also for those specialising in marionette and juggling acts, dancing and other public entertainment. Bands of musicians might equally be hired for more serious purposes, such as religious vigils organised by guilds and confraternities. Many of the poorer Parisian musicians just cited were indeed themselves members of the guild confraternity of St Julien des Ménestriers, traceable back to at least 1321. Corporate organisation in guilds and confraternities was essential for skilled craftsmen in any sector in the early modern period, and not least for musicians, whose occupation, like that of other entertainers, had originally been socially and morally suspect.

From the thirteenth century onwards wandering minstrels had sought to avoid vagrancy penalties by accepting service either in private households or as town musicians, and by the sixteenth century most towns with any claim to status had a band of players who formed a corporation under the control and patronage of the city authorities. These players, often referred to as 'waits' even if they did not in fact function as watchmen, were used not only for ceremonial purposes but also naturally supplemented their increasingly symbolic official earnings by playing at private functions as well. The provision of dance music became the norm especially at weddings, even for poorer couples, and fees for the guild musicians present at urban weddings were accepted as part of the socially unavoidable expenditure of such an occasion. Rivalries with freelancing interlopers and with court or princely musicians were inevitable: the Worshipful Company of Musicians of 1604, protecting the London municipal musicians, very soon had to fight (sometimes literally) for their monopoly in the city against members of the King's Music. As in other sectors, guild monopolies were impossible to maintain, and municipal authorities often adopted the compromise solution of sanctioning several corporations. This explains why, for example, in many of the more substantial German towns, the old corporation of *Stadtpfeifer* (literally 'town piper') or *Stadtmusikus* came into direct conflict in the first quarter of the century with the more adaptable lower-status *Kunstgeiger* (fiddler). City authorities often tried to establish clear social or functional demarcations, coupled with standardised fees, for different musicians' corporations within a single jurisdiction, or they set up official rota (the *Rollen* common in Hansa towns, for example) to spread available work amongst the recognised musicians. But conflicts and brawls were a predictably recurrent result of finite demand. The attempt in 1653 by town musicians from various parts of Protestant Germany to form an association to protect their privileges more widely appears to have been of even less avail.

An important additional source of income for individual musicians was undoubtedly teaching. Most of this was done informally, as it always has been, but the evidence of the notarial records again occasionally allows us to glimpse what the amateur public had in mind. Most commonly, pupils wanted to pick up the essentials of dance tunes or the fundamentals of the newly fashionable (and still barely respectable) violin. The records also suggest what practical arrangements might be made for ordinary people with modest ambitions: a contract signed before a notary in 1635, for example, indicates that a master musician is arranging for his daughter to be apprenticed to a tailor for a year, to be instructed in accordance with her ability, as partial payment for which he will give the tailor and his wife daily dancing lessons covering all the steps current and fashionable at the time.[4] For those with talent, the opportunities were enormous: contacts with a broad public could lead to improved employment offers, whilst those seeking more respectable status might seek service in the church, either as the organist or as a singer. Exceptional gifts could open all doors: the commanding figure amongst musicians at the court of Louis XIV, the violinist Lully, was the son of an Italian miller and had had music lessons from a monk; whilst the much more congenial English composer John Jenkins, who spent most of his life in aristocratic households and in the service of the Crown, was the son of a carpenter.

Historians have for some time debated the extent to which the culture of the common majority has been filtered and distorted through the eyes of those elite observers on whose evidence we necessarily rely to a very great extent. Some years ago Peter Burke suggested that, where other evidence fails, one way of approaching the popular culture of the early modern period might even be to try to read backwards from the richer descriptions of the eighteenth century.[5] But while it is difficult to quantify the role of music, dance and revelry in the daily life of ordinary town inhabitants in the seventeenth century, few would deny that spontaneous amateur music-making, particularly singing, is likely to have been an everyday experience, and this may have helped to create a broad and relatively fluid base for professional musicians ranging from the respectable city waits down to the all-purpose itinerant entertainers or even to the blind, hurdy-gurdy-playing vagrant. Actual notated music from this period, with its rich cross-fertilisation of tunes, texts, ideas and practices between popular, dance and 'high-art' abstract forms, likewise warns us against imposing artificial demarcations. City records from all over western and central Europe, like the French notarial records just cited, seem to reflect a corresponding social fluidity, with the middle-ranking musicians inhabiting a world not unrecognisable to modern freelance popular and band musicians. Minstrels, singers and virtuosi could communicate across social as well as linguistic barriers. Even in Muscovy there was a thriving minstrel tradition in the form of the *skomorokhi*, who preserved and exploited popular theatre, music, poetry and dance until Alexis's attempts to suppress them in 1648.

By contrast, when it comes to painters and sculptors, let alone architects, it is probably safe to assume that the lower popular market was virtually non-existent. The highly marginal resources of ordinary people would have left little surplus for artistic consumerism. Except in the prosperous United Provinces, there is not much evidence in wills or inventories that anything other than at best home-produced decorative art could normally be expected in households below the social level of comfortable citizens. But even here we need to be cautious: there were many popular artists in this period, such as the Mariette or Jolain families in Paris, who made cheap prints and broadsheets; there were the indispensable sign-painters, or the hack artists in southern Europe who produced small cheap religious images for the devout to buy; and there were the remarkably prolific but sometimes anonymous woodcarvers and painters who decorated the small wooden village churches and houses of rural Sweden and Norway.[6] If the relationships between, and motivations behind, supply and demand of popular culture are difficult to trace, this can clearly not be regarded as evidence that the object we are trying to study was intrinsically rare.

Church music and the city public

In the wake of the Reformation both the Roman Catholic Church and some of the Protestant ones fundamentally reconsidered the role of visual art and music as an adjunct to divine service, becoming more aware of the potential for distraction from the true purpose of meetings for worship. However, after the intense theological confrontations at the height of the Counter-Reformation in the later sixteenth century, this puritanism was relaxed in many parts of central and western Europe, albeit only slowly in areas where Calvinism was strong, and not at all definitively in England or Scotland until after the interregnum. But whereas for Roman Catholics a complete removal of pictures of saints and of holy deeds would never have been seriously contemplated, the Protestants remained permanently hostile to visual representations that might be construed as idolatrous, particularly within the church buildings themselves. Only wooden carved altarpieces and a few simple decorations remained. Yet for the Lutherans, perhaps rather inconsistently, music decidedly did not fall within similar restraints: it became to them one of the most important ways of expressing the inward emotions and individualism so central in Protestantism. That music was a natural vehicle for religious devotion was taken so much for granted in all Lutheran churches that there was little hesitation in using even overtly Catholic (especially Italian) settings, sometimes (but not always) with altered texts more closely based on the Bible itself.

The astoundingly rich tradition of north-German music running from Luther himself to J. S. Bach created a wide variety of urban employment for church organists, cantors, singers and instrumentalists. Given the close connection between secular and religious authority in the German Lutheran world, it is not surprising that appointments to posts both in the town churches themselves and in the schools run by the major parish foundations were ultimately, despite varying degrees of self-government, the responsibility of the municipal authorities. The Lübeck organist Franz Tunder (1614–67) and his even more distinguished successor Dietrich Buxtehude (*c.* 1637–1707) served the Marienkirche in the customary way, playing before and during services and providing special music for the major festivals and for Communion. To supplement their already unusually generous salary (700 florins after 1646), they both held the office of *Werkmeister,* which placed them in charge not only of the written parish registers but also of the complex financial administration of parish resources, the payment of the other church officers, the maintenance of the building and, naturally enough, of the organs and other instruments in the church. The close relationship with the city fathers, however, is even more apparent from the series of special evening concerts (*Abendmusiken*) which were put on fairly regularly from the 1640s at the specific request of the merchant community and with their financial support. These concerts were soon recognised as helping to give the city a cultural profile commensurate with its mercantile status. The exact content of the *Abendmusiken* can rarely be identified, but from surviving descriptions it seems that Italian vocal and instrumental music, as well as Tunder's and his successor's own compositions and those of fellow north Germans, came to figure prominently. By 1669, under Buxtehude's direction, these concerts had grown, despite recurrent financial and practical difficulties, into a major and regular series involving large forces placed on four specially built galleries. Now held during Advent, the concerts undoubtedly included Buxtehude's cantatas and his larger oratorio-like works on religious texts. And while admission remained free, the financial basis of the concerts was improved through the sale of programmes and special seats to local dignitaries or individual patrons, and by a partial underwriting by the city council itself from 1687.[7] The regular instrumental parts were allocated to the *Ratsmusikanten* (city-employed musicians) who here as elsewhere in Germany, thanks to the subsidised and broad education of church schools, were able to take a more prominent part in the sophisticated musical culture of their towns than the English waits. Elsewhere in Germany similar ventures were launched, sometimes under the secular auspices of a collegium musicum; Hamburg set another precedent in 1678 when it created an officially sponsored public opera house.

To many, the security of city employment was ultimately preferable to the otherwise potentially more exciting and flexible forms of princely patronage. This was particularly so in the German lands but probably also applied in Italy and the Netherlands, where the city state could survive as an entity in its own right and where the absence of centralising monarchy entailed a far greater profusion of autonomous artistic centres. Even in Amsterdam, where the Calvinist Church did not allow instrumental music during church services, there was considerable scope. The organist Jan Pieterszoon Sweelinck (1562–1621) was employed in a secular capacity by the city fathers to play in the Oude Kerk before and after services. Not only was he rewarded with a salary of 300 florins (360 after 1607) and a rent-free house but he was also highly respected as a cultural asset to the city and as a teacher of international repute.

It seems, therefore, that the city fathers of larger communities such as Lübeck or Amsterdam regarded the patronage of church or secular music as worthwhile. Music on its own could evidently not convey any clear political message, and the texts for vocal works, where they can with confidence be linked to *Abendmusiken* or their equivalent, tended to be biblical or moralistic rather than of overtly contemporary significance. In this respect urban music differed somewhat from that favoured in princely households where, as we shall see, more overt political messages were conveyed allegorically in the text and trappings of the new music of the early seventeenth century. Otherwise, there was not in northern Europe a major distinction between the kind of work wanted by patrician patrons and that required by princes. The religious and the secular were never far apart in either. Just as events in princely households were duly marked at both levels, so could the burial of a prominent citizen, for instance, be the occasion for the transmission both of civic and of spiritual values. For the city fathers as for princes, this, and the favourable impression on visitors which music was meant to produce, was presumably regarded as justification enough.

An illuminating blend of civic pride and religious exaltation can be found in one of the most important musical centres in Italy, St Mark's in Venice. As the chapel for the Doge, St Mark's acquired a representative role in which the religious and political ideology of the city-state were united to an unusual degree. It had a substantial musical staff consisting of a choir of around thirty, two organists and a small group of instrumentalists on regular pay, all directed by the *maestro di cappella* and his assistant. Their duties included performances not only at ordinary church services but also at some forty special festivals, including the annual Ascension Day ceremony at which the symbol of Venice was wedded to the sea. Several unsatisfactory appointments from the 1590s onwards, however, had entailed a less than ideal administration of the musical resources, so in 1613, on the death of the incompetent *maestro di cappella* Martinengo, the procurators of St Mark's took special trouble to look for candidates further afield. In appointing the greatest musician of the age, Claudio

Monteverdi (1567–1643), they made an artistic choice which many princes might have envied, but which seemed a little surprising given the artistic and political conservatism of the Venetians themselves, and their need for conventional church music rather than innovative stage works. However, if Monteverdi probably had a reputation for being difficult and inflexible, he was also a man of considerable administrative experience and punctilious orderliness, and this may have appealed to the city fathers. The permanent musical staff was soon increased in size, and for a while the reputation of St Mark's in Europe was restored to its earlier pre-eminence both in terms of performance – at least until the plague epidemic of 1630 – and in terms of the quality of new music by Monteverdi and his assistants or pupils.

That the relationship between Monteverdi and his new employers, the procurators of St Mark's, was mutually appreciated is beyond doubt. Monteverdi was given a generous down-payment immediately on completing his audition for the post, and his salary was within three years raised from 300 to 400 ducats. He was subsequently given sufficient freedom to undertake commissions from prominent private patrons in the city, such as that from Girolamo Mocenigo for the magnificent setting of Tasso's text in *Il combattimento di Tancredi e Clorinda*, first performed in 1624. At times the procurators used Monteverdi as a kind of cultural ambassador, not just towards his former patrons the Dukes of Mantua but also, for example, in 1627–8 towards the Duke of Parma on the occasion of his marriage to a member of the Medici family. Such outside commissions were tolerated even when they led to extended leaves of absence from St Mark's. For Monteverdi the post had many marked advantages, as he himself pointed out in several letters in which he refused offers to return to Mantuan employment. To Alessandro Striggio, a friend and fellow-artist but a man who in addition rose to the highest ranks in the ducal administration in Mantua, Monteverdi firmly pointed out in 1620 that in Venice he had total control over the musical staff in St Mark's, had sufficient time to prepare musical events properly within a schedule that did not change at the whim of a patron, had security of office until death, was paid fully and promptly on pay-day every two months, and had such a reputation in the city that he could guarantee a full house for any music he put on outside St Mark's, in the process readily earning another 200 ducats a year – none of which had been the case when he had served the Gonzagas in Mantua before 1612. Most important of all, perhaps, Monteverdi felt that the city authorities treated him fairly: one of the procurators, when raising his salary, had said that he 'who wishes a servant to be honoured must deal with him honourably'.[8]

To musicians of lesser reputation – men rather than women –

Venice also had much to offer. The pay in St Mark's, as in other churches, was not outstanding, being usually in the range 60–80 ducats for rank-and-file musicians. But several posts were often held concurrently, and some of the more than a hundred other churches in the city also supported permanent musical posts. In addition, there was endless scope for freelancing in the sometimes quite lavish celebrations of patron saints organised by the numerous confraternities: one of the biggest, San Rocco, spent 1391 lire (224 ducats) on the musicians alone during its saint's day celebration in 1627. Monteverdi refers to an admittedly very able singer and priest who earned 80 ducats in St Mark's, 60 saying masses elsewhere, another 40 as chaplain to one of the procurators ('for whom he has not yet said Mass, so that you could say he is paid for doing nothing') and 100 ducats 'by singing for religious festivals in the city'. As in other towns, not everything went smoothly: in 1637 Monteverdi himself complained to the procurators of having been abusively (and unfairly) accused by one of the singers in St Mark's of misappropriating fees earned in private outside engagements.[9] But for patrons and musicians alike, Venice catered for many needs. When a public opera house opened there in 1637 the only major gap in the range of outlets was filled. For Monteverdi himself this development resulted in a new outburst of creativity, including the opera *L'incoronazione di Poppea*, completed in 1642 when he was 75 years old. That there was a real public demand for this new art form is shown both by the social range of the audience and by the fact that at the end of the century there were altogether 16 independent opera houses in the city.[10]

The visual arts and the Catholic Church in Rome

As suggested earlier, the Protestant churches were not, music apart, keen patrons of the arts. Even in Lutheran churches there was only limited scope for visual decoration,[11] and the more radical groups during the seventeenth century were often hostile to any non-functional decoration at all. Religious images were utterly alien to their whole tradition and, in any case, the financial resources of the Protestant churches were usually limited because of the secularisation of land after the Reformation. For these reasons alone the discussion of religious visual art would naturally focus primarily on the Roman Catholic Church; in any case, Italy was the undisputed source of inspiration for most artists during this period, with the widest range of study opportunities and patronage relations. Although both Spanish and Flemish artists had made, and continued to make, major contributions to religious art, they tended to be measured in the eyes of contemporary patrons by the standards of Italy – and in the first two-thirds of the century especially by the standards of Rome, to which so many of the best painters, sculptors and architects were attracted.

The Romans themselves were not particularly prominent as connoisseurs of art, but the centralised and autocratic nature of Catholic Church government ensured that much of the considerable wealth of the Church would be available around the papal court. The pontificates of Sixtus V and Clement VIII, during the two decades up to 1605, had already witnessed a substantial increase in church-building, some of it for the benefit of especially the newer Orders associated with the Counter-Reformation. The Jesuits had consecrated their Il Gesù already in 1584, and the Oratorians followed with their Chiesa Nuova in 1599; the Theatines had to wait rather longer for the completion of their S. Andrea della Valle, owing to wrangles from 1603 over payments from Cardinal Grimaldi and his heirs, and difficulties in finding a suitable new patron. But in all these instances, as with the smaller churches being constructed in these years for particular saints, completion of the main building did not mean the end of the work for those involved. The construction of facades and outbuildings, let alone decoration of the interior and of side-chapels, continued for the best part of the century, and whatever reservations one may at times have about the gradual concealment of the simpler designs originally intended, the opportunities thus offered to artists and specialised craftsmen were unrivalled. As will be noted later, these conditions also fostered a lively market for secular art of most kinds, not just amongst cardinals and the major families otherwise associated with the highest levels in the Church.

Although by the early years of the seventeenth century some of the heat was already going out of Counter-Reformation theology, significant ideological controversies within the Roman Catholic Church remained, and with them profound differences regarding devotion, the role of the laity and hence the nature of religious art. These differences were dramatically revealed in the varied reactions to the work of the most controversial painter of the period, Michelangelo Merisi da Caravaggio (1571–1610), who had come to Rome by early 1593. From 1599 the major part of his output was religious, mostly consisting of altarpieces and paintings for chapels. The highly dramatic realism and directness of his work, which has retained its power to the present day, clearly stood out against the interpretative complexity of much of the more conventional art of the period. Caravaggio's first public commission (in 1599) was for two large paintings for the Contarelli chapel in the French church in Rome, San Luigi de' Francesi, a contract worth 400 scudi and probably won through the contacts of his patron and friend, Cardinal Francesco del Monte. Of the two works, *The Calling of St Matthew* caused a particular stir. Its starkness was uniquely Caravaggio's own, but the simple clarity of the message may have owed something to the Oratorians: although no direct connection can be ascertained, del Monte (like Caravaggio's other main protector of this period, the marchese Vincenzo Giustiniani) frequented an Oratorian. Contrary to trends elsewhere in the Church, the Oratorians were particularly keen to maintain an interest in the immediacy of religious devotion and hence the directness of its imagery. It would be rash, especially given the lack of adequate written source material, to claim that this was the only or even the main factor affecting a decisive development in the work of a man as complex and eccentric as Caravaggio. But one cannot overlook the fact that the conventional timidity that apparently led the priests of San Luigi to reject Caravaggio's altarpiece, *The Inspiration of St Matthew*, was evidently not shared by Giustiniani, who may have advised the painter in the first instance and who immediately took the picture while paying Caravaggio to do a somewhat more conventional presentation to hang in the chapel.

Until his premature death in 1610, Caravaggio produced increasingly personalised – in the eyes of some observers, improper – versions of key religious scenes. One of them, *The Death of the Virgin* (1604 or 1605), was again rejected by the church authorities concerned, in this instance Carmelites, but the painting had already caused such a stir that it was exhibited for a week before shipment to its new owner, the Duke of Mantua. Celebrity naturally secured substantial fees for Caravaggio, rising as high as even 1000 scudi for one of his last paintings. But it seems improbable that he designed his work deliberately for the market: his output remained extraordinarily personal and darkly violent, and, given the Italian context, highly unconventional also in a religious sense. For example, in his second *Conversion of St Paul*, painted in 1600–1 for the Cerasi chapel,[12] he not only typically reduced the scene to its barest fundamentals but interestingly – in a spirit almost reminiscent of Protestant radicalism rather than Roman Catholicism – omitted altogether any personal reference to God other than the angular light falling on the prostrate subject.

It is generally agreed that from the pontificate of Paul V (1605–21) onwards, with the generation active in the Council of Trent no longer alive, any lingering austerity was finally thrown to the winds in most branches of church affairs. It had already become customary for each pontiff, once elected, to reward his own family and favourites with land, wealth and power. Paul V elevated his nephew Cardinal Scipione Borghese to unprecedented heights in terms of the number of venal offices he held, the scale of church income he controlled and the influence he had through control of much of the papal administration and through the attendant clientage networks. Paul's two brothers also profited substantially, and the family palaces, including the Villa

Borghese which was open to the public, came to house a vast collection of art. Scipione acquired a reputation for the utterly unscrupulous methods he used to obtain pieces that he wanted, ranging from imprisonment of the recalcitrant painter Domenichino to outright theft of a Raphael from a Perugian church. After Paul's death, Scipione's patronage was rivalled by that of the new pope's nephew, Cardinal Ludovico Ludovisi, who for two years was even more powerful and rapacious than Borghese had been. The systematic exploitation of papal resources by the incumbent family, however, culminated with the election of Maffeo Barberini as Urban VIII (1623–44). He was determined not only to exercise real control personally but also to elevate a brother and no fewer than three nephews as cardinals, one of them at the age of 19, heaping wealth and power on them in a way that, in Haskell's words, 'was universally held by his contemporaries and by his successors to have exceeded all reasonable limits'.[13]

Partly to try to counterbalance the effects of such nepotism as this partly to enhance the visual rhetoric of Roman Catholicism via monuments that also glorified the family of the reigning Pope, massive donations to churches, shrines, Orders and foundations became the norm on an unprecedented scale. Most important, perhaps, was the intensive work to finish the main fabric of St Peter's itself from 1605 onwards, especially the nave and the difficult facade: Maderno's solution to a number of practical and aesthetic difficulties did not meet with universal acclaim, but kept many hundred craftsmen at work for much of Paul's pontificate. Owing to the absence of a clear artistic policy there were until at least the 1620s opportunities for men of widely different creative instincts, sometimes even within a single church project. Maderno himself, for example, remained principal architect to St Peter's until his death in 1629, assisted by his pupil Borromini (1599–1667), arguably the architect of greatest originality at the time, but even so Bernini had from 1623 much more real influence on the interior development of the building.

Patronage networks in Rome, particularly those radiating out from the Vatican, were characterised by problems which in some respects were more pronounced than elsewhere in Europe. The exercise of the papal office was by nature highly discontinuous: in artistic terms, the death of a pope, often after a relatively short reign by the standards of secular princes, meant a complete change in the fortune of the families concerned, and hence in patronage. At least until the election of Urban VIII there was not even much internal consistency within a single Vatican pontificate. Private commissions were often dogged by delays caused by the complexity of arrangements with the sponsoring families, or even by the frequently difficult negotiations to ensure the services of artists already working for other patrons. In both these respects it was the aristocracy at the papal court, and the Pope himself, who often set the pace, and in the second respect not even personal connections (notably those of Bernini with the Jesuits) had much effect in freeing an artist from the demands of his principal patron in the Vatican.

Papal power and practical delays alike inevitably had important consequences for many major projects. This is particularly noticeable in the efforts by the new Orders to secure suitable buildings for themselves. The Jesuits and the Oratorians, guided by their founders, Ignatius Loyola and Philip Neri respectively, had originally had relatively restrained attitudes to display commensurate with their religious aims. Shortage of funds, however, had soon forced the Jesuits into a position where their simpler building intentions could largely be ignored by their main sponsor, Cardinal Alessandro Farnese. By contrast, the Oratorians at first largely avoided having a single major paymaster, thanks to their more democratic instincts and the generosity of their socially wider following, but the decision in 1606 to commission the main altarpiece from Rubens was made because of the intervention of his benefactor, the papal treasurer Giacomo Serra, who was prepared to contribute generously to its cost. Rubens was given unusually detailed instructions, but when he withdrew an ineffective first version he was granted a freer hand in negotiation with the Oratorians to produce alternative works, to everyone's satisfaction. Similarly, during the building of the oratory and the library next to the *Chiesa Nuova,* in the years after 1637, the Oratorians were again able to determine what they would get, for Borromini's architectural imagination was carefully controlled by costs and by a steering committee from within the Order itself.[14] But elsewhere the general trend towards control by one or a few wealthy patrons was clear. The embarrassment with which the Capuchins tried in 1626 to refuse an ornate tabernacle and metal candelabra offered by Urban VIII himself for the high altar in one of their churches illustrates the dilemma all too clearly: in the end the Pope imposed on them a special dispensation from their rules of austerity, and the monks succeeded merely in toning down the lavishness of the donation.[15]

For the artists themselves, getting a foothold in the Roman art world was, as Haskell has made clear, a highly competitive business. Most artists arriving from outside would need the patronage of a prominent prelate, most easily secured with someone from the same native area. He might then, like Caravaggio, take up residence in his patron's household, and (probably more rarely) even suffer restrictions regarding his freedom to work on commissions for others – a condition aptly described at the time as *servitù particolare.* Generally, however, such household positions were highly desirable: the artist had an opportunity to study and develop in a cultural environment with good connections, while the patron gained for his retinue a potentially prestigious recruit whose work he would naturally want to show off. Pietro da Cortona (1596–1669) became established in this way with his fellow-Florentine benefactor Marcello Sachetti, himself an amateur painter and host of both artists and poets. Cortona relied heavily on Sachetti both for actual suggestions and, through his patron's close friendship with Urban VIII, for a number of highly prestigious commissions both with Bernini on the Palazzo Barberini and as architect of various churches round the city.

Exactly how the financial and personal circumstances of artists worked out in practice in this kind of environment is difficult to ascertain, particularly for the lesser men or for those engaged on major projects as part of a team. Before becoming more widely recognised around 1618, Domenichino was rarely able to get more than 50 scudi for a painting, at a time when a mason working 200 days in the year would earn around 60 scudi in Rome, a tailor perhaps half that amount. According to the contemporary art critic Giulio Mancini, a good artist should easily have been able to earn 3–6 scudi a day, but it was probably only in the 1630s, towards the end of his life, that Domenichino (then working in Naples) came comfortably into that bracket.[16] Even for the well-known figures it is difficult to interpret some of the source material. It thus seems rather strange that Maderno, as architect to St Peter's, received 12 scudi per month, whilst Bernini was allocated a monthly provision of 260 scudi by Alexander VII only a generation later. One could have represented a part-time or partial allocation, the other may have included funds intended for subcontractors or other costs. And how much of the 3300 scudi which Urban VIII paid for each of the four great statues (including Bernini's *Longinus*) to go in niches in the piers of St Peter's crossing was meant to cover materials and subcontracted work? What is clear is that the outstanding artists of that generation could earn sums that placed them well above ordinary men in terms of wealth and social status.

It was inherent in the nature of Roman Catholic Church patronage in painting and sculpture that heavy emphasis was placed on the representation of the divine mystery, on beatification and on the achievements of the saints. Art was intended to persuade and involve the observer, or at least create an illusion of the fusion of belief and reality. Naturally, a close relationship therefore had to exist between, on the one hand, the artist capable of understanding spiritually what he was commissioned to paint and, on the other hand, the generally tradition-bound church authorities. That such a relationship need not be artistically restrictive is amply illustrated in the work of Gianlorenzo Bernini (1598–1680), especially for Urban VIII but also, remarkably, for successive popes. Bernini had been noticed early and had worked for Scipione Borghese, but an exceptionally strong friendship established him as the most influential artist in Rome soon after Urban's election in 1623. His huge bronze baldacchino for St Peter's, costing 200,000 scudi, and his extraordinarily powerful marble sculptures there and elsewhere, not only gave the church a new visual dimension, but also brought into existence an impressive team working under the increasingly close supervision and direction of Bernini, including his own brother as well as the French sculptor François Duquesnoy and, for 25 years, Mattia de' Rossi. Urban was himself a man of discerning taste and years of experience as a patron. Bernini had complete authority with the Pope, and hence, because of the latter's autocratic powers over the supervisory committee for St Peter's, effectively over all work on the church for 20 years, and indeed over most Barberini patronage generally. Bernini's unique ability to excel in a wide variety of forms (including architecture, drawing, theatre and, from 1632, the staging of opera) gave the papacy a universal artist who could try to compensate with real effect for the loss of prestige of the Pope in European affairs. However, because of his close relationship with Urban, even he had great difficulty at first in reshaping his career after the reaction that accompanied the death of his patron in 1644.

The election of Innocent X in 1644 inaugurated a more subdued, if hardly economical, period in terms of artistic patronage, and the whole Barberini network disintegrated as members of the family hurriedly left Rome. Bernini's position was weakened and he even had to witness the complete removal of his allegedly unsound campanile from the facade of St Peter's, while the new Pope's existing architects, Rainaldi and Borromini, took over the main papal commissions. But this was only a temporary development for, with the succession of Alexander VII in 1655, major architectural projects were undertaken to improve the visual effect of certain parts of the city, the intention being, it seems, to replace the now lost status of Rome in European diplomacy with a dazzling visual, even theatrical, effect.[17] Bernini recommenced work on St Peter's, tackling further interior work and alterations in the Vatican Palace, as well as the dramatic colonnade to embrace the piazza in front of the complex. He remained active until near the end of his life and, with his title of nobility and a fortune valued on his death at 400,000 scudi, can in this and every other respect be regarded as one of the most successful artists of the century. Bernini's position was regarded from the 1650s as unchallengeable, not least when he was in a position to undertake for the Jesuits the entire design and execution of a church like the *S. Andrea al Quirinale* (1658) without charging any fees for himself.

Increasingly, however, direct papal patronage was affected by ever-growing financial difficulties, depriving the pontifical family of the potential that it had had earlier in the century. It is of course difficult and in some respects misleading to separate the role of the Pope himself from that of other ecclesiastical (and indeed secular) patrons in Rome, but since the second quarter of the century no individual nobleman had been able to compete with the resources available to the head of the Roman Catholic Church. All the more dramatic, therefore, was the change precipitated by the catastrophic plague of 1656 and outwardly revealed to all Europe in the severe diplomatic setbacks suffered by the Vatican in its relations with France by 1662. Resources in terms of both money and prestige were visibly reduced. From this stage onwards the popes no longer set the tone artistically, and the emphasis shifted to others. This may help to explain why, for example, the Jesuits could at last resume decoration of *Il Gesù*, and their general, Gian Paolo Oliva, could recover control over the outward image of the Order. The results were once more clearly visible: Gaulli was in the 1670s commissioned to do the ceiling frescos in a style which clearly reflected the Jesuit emphasis on practical worldly involvement rather than spiritual contemplation – this at the height of the controversy over the quietist preachings of Miguel de Molinos.[18]

Papal finances, like those of most other European principalities, were essentially badly managed, at least after the death in 1590 of Pope Sixtus V (generally regarded as a highly efficient administrator and reformer, despite the unfortunate economic consequences of some of his policies). St Peter's may altogether have cost 1.5 million gold scudi, and diplomatic, military and court expenditures evidently rose rapidly in the early seventeenth century. Paul V's nepotism consumed around 4 per cent of the entire income of his pontificate, roughly equivalent to the rather less controversial sums he spent on charity. But above all it was Urban VIII who caused irreversible damage, doubling papal debts through two decades of extravagant favouritism and through far-reaching military and diplomatic ventures in Europe – ventures whose total failure fuelled the violent reaction which followed his death in 1644.[19] Little was done to tackle the underlying causes during the following decades, and the increasingly harsh economic conditions in Italy generally were clearly observed also in Rome. It was not just papal patronage itself that failed, however, but ultimately that of Rome as a whole. In Haskell's argument, a slump in the entire art market was noticeable by the late 1650s and early 1660s, after which it was largely foreigners, especially southern German princes and subsequently Englishmen, who took over as the main employers of Italian painters and even architects – either direct or through the rapidly growing dealer network. Spain continued to provide some outlet, as did France until its anti-Italian reaction of the 1670s, but with the growth of English demand, in particular, the Roman Catholic devotional ingredient in Italian art was necessarily submerged.[20]

Buildings and symbols

Abstract aesthetic considerations aside, all the arts clearly had practical potential for ideological and communicative functions in the seventeenth century – and, with the exception of literature itself, none more so than architecture. Buildings were physical symbols of status and separation: it was hard to resist the temptation at the very least to let them demonstrate the wealth of the owner, or perhaps deliberately to create an image of security, stability and power through such obvious devices as turrets and ornate gates or to suggest artistic refinement through architectural detail and allegorical decorations. There is no lack of evidence in contemporary writings, including the architectural manuals of the day, that owners, advisers and craftsmen were as aware as they are today that buildings for the rich and prestigious had to serve the functions of practical convenience and of display as well as being of high quality. Given the architectural restraints of a Renaissance imitation of classical models, pictorial art and sculpture could then be added to convey mythical and symbolic motifs, not to mention Mannerist eccentricity, the propaganda value of which princely patrons could hardly fail to exploit sooner or later if their political aspirations tended in such directions.

Right up until the outbreak of the Thirty Years War, municipal authorities also clearly exploited the possibilities in architecture: in the north we need only look at the striking facade of the Bremen town hall, added in the years 1608–12, or the varied municipal building projects undertaken in Paderborn, Münster and elsewhere, to see how conscious city fathers were of the need to impress. The actual decision-making process, however, was made more complex by the level of funds required for major projects. In Augsburg, the highly gifted and able architect Elias Holl (1573–1646), appointed city superintendent of buildings (*Stadtwerkmeister*) in 1602, acquired considerable wealth as a skilled building entrepreneur dispensing substantial funds through his team of workmen. But he also gained prestige through his successful completion of various projects fairly early in his career, including a hospital and various municipal buildings, technical projects and fortifications. As a result, he seems to have been on sufficiently close terms with the city fathers to be able to influence their decision to go ahead with, for example, the large-scale town-hall project which was started in 1615. The foundation stone proudly proclaimed that the building was meant both 'to embellish the city and to help penurious workmen' – the latter reason given not for the first time as justification for substantial municipal expenditure. Some 16 masons, 37 stonemasons and 114 day-labourers did indeed take part, in addition to other workmen, and materials were acquired from a wide area. The main building work lasted for five years and probably cost altogether 85,000–100,000 florins – at a time when the annual income of the city was around 250,000 florins. The monumental if restrained façade, the two large octagonal towers along each side (costing 6000 florins in themselves), and the magnificent Golden Hall at the centre of the building together formed – and were explicitly meant to be – a symbol of civic pride. To outsiders it represented the stature and strength of the city, while inside pictorial decorations and inscriptions reinforced the message of law and civic virtue through moralising allegories and biblical scenes.[21] This marked the culmination of Augsburg's building programme. The war soon cut deeply into available resources; Holl himself lost his job in 1635 because he refused to convert to Roman Catholicism when, on the Swedish abandonment of the city to the imperial forces, long-standing confessional co-existence came to an immediate end.

Amongst the princes of the Empire, it is easy to find even more extravagant enthusiasm for building which lasted well into the war years. Best known, perhaps, is the work of Maximilian of Bavaria on his extensive palace in Munich, or the vast Schloss in the French spirit built at Aschaffenburg between 1605 and 1625 by the Archbishop-elector of Mainz (at a cost of nearly one million florins). In the north one may cite the work of the architect Paul Francke for the Wolfenbüttel dynasty. About these projects, however, we know very little: the stylistic evidence has been clouded by subsequent destruction and extensive alterations, and – in the few cases where the research has been attempted – the extant archival material appears to be too scanty to illuminate the ideas and aspirations of either employer or employee except perhaps in the most general terms. After the war, recovery was often slow, and when building programmes were contemplated the patronage network was often severely skewed by the new obsession with Italian styles and workmen.

A better impression of the aims and limitations of princely patronage can in fact be derived from a study of the colourful and irrepressible ruler of Denmark from 1596 to 1648, Christian IV. His ideals were more clearly expressed than most. His inspiration came consistently from the Netherlands, and he employed men of Dutch or Flemish descent or training for his major works: the Steenwinckel family from Antwerp, the painters Peter Isaacsz and Karel van Mander, the Hamburg-trained Jacob van Doort and some Danes who had studied abroad. His buildings, most of which have survived with only fairly minor external alterations, are highly personal in style and atmosphere. There is clear evidence that he took an active part in both the drafting and the actual building operations – his education had been the best available to a Renaissance prince. Although we cannot always be sure of the interior details of his buildings, enough of his very extensive correspondence and of the official records have survived to allow some reconstruction of his mental world.

Several of his buildings stand out in the present context. One is the famous Round Tower, attached to the university church in central Copenhagen and built in 1637–42 – an utterly extraordinary and unique design intended partly as access to the university library housed in the attic of the church, but first and foremost as an observatory. The stepless interior spiral by which one ascends the tower is built round a central vertical cylinder, probably designed to serve as a day-time telescope and astronomical measuring tool. Like his contemporaries, Christian IV was a keen astrologer and he commissioned a series of paintings to hang in his palace of Rosenborg explaining the influences of Planets on the humours of man. The architectural features of the tower, according to the analysis by the art historian Meir Stein, confirm that it is a symbolic representation of the astrological universe: the eight turns of the spiral represent the eight heavenly spheres, the vertical lines of seven windows the seven intervals of (Pythagorean) heavenly musical harmony, and so on. Various aspects in fact suggest detailed awareness of, for example, Robert Fludd's *History of the Macrocosm and the Microcosm* of 1617–19, and of the Renaissance intellectual traditions of which that work was part. At the same time, however, the King also conveyed a clear political message, for on the front of the tower is a large-scale inscription (the original design for which also survives, in the King's unmistakable hand) conveying in Hebrew, Latin and pictorial symbols the message of God's direction of faith and justice in the heart of the King. In short, the Round Tower broadcasts the fundamental principle of the Lutheran prince: an orthodox king ruling in earthly and heavenly harmony.[22]

That this is not too fanciful a reading is confirmed by analyses of several series of paintings and sculptures also commissioned by Christian IV, including the set of figures in niches on the front of Frederiksborg Castle, and the sets of historical–allegorical paintings he hung in the large hall in Rosenborg Palace and in Kronborg Castle – intended, as far as we can judge now, as didactic pieces fitting into a carefully conceived artistic and symbolic whole. There is no explicit political message pointing towards contemporary notions that kingship itself might have a new role to play. References to Roman imperial themes, most pronounced in the buoyant early part of the reign, are entirely typical of the late sixteenth-century humanist court traditions, as are the representations of the seven ages of man and of classical mythology – even the sun-king identification, used more prominently by Louis XIV, was nothing new or unusual in the age of Christian IV. But there are few of the kind of deliberately loaded political messages common at, for example, the English court. Christian IV was not interested in changing the foundations of elective kingship which he had inherited, even if he sometimes fretted over their inadequacies (see chapter 2).

Building being one of the preferred ways of displaying wealth and status in this as in later periods, there would be no difficulty in elaborating on the theme of princely and aristocratic architectural symbolism. The case of Christian IV, however, may serve as a warning against any reductionist approach in the analysis of motives and aims. Equally important, much evidence suggests that many patrons in fact relied heavily on the discretion and skill of their workmen, developing the scheme as work progressed. Even in major building projects, detailed designs were not always compiled before work began, and the extensive use of subcontracting in practice meant that both churches and palaces were often more composite than is customary in the modern age. Countless instances of litigation and of alterations half-way, not to mention contemporary reports and advice, confirm this impression of decentralised artistic control.

It comes as a surprise to discover that this haphazardness of princely patronage applies even to Louis XIV's palace at Versailles. Work on the building itself went on from 1668 to 1711, so it was perhaps inevitable that alterations and adaptations to changing tastes or priorities occurred. Recent studies, however, make clear that planning was at times seriously deficient and that some designs were arrived at by wasteful trial and error. Thus there were several changes of plans and even of already completed work early on, before the final scheme for an *enveloppe* around Louis XIII's original building on the site was settled. Later, constant expansion and reorganisation of the central complex seems to have become a way of publicly demonstrating continuing royal strength and wealth, and in that process, too, even relatively recent work was often undone. Thus the construction from 1679 of the spectacular Hall of Mirrors designed by Jules Hardouin-Mansart drastically altered the layout and effect of the earlier Planetary Rooms, so that their appropriate celestial imagery for Louis XIV had to be adapted and reinterpreted. Years later, when money was becoming very tight, there was outright confusion around the central sections of the Trianon (the garden palace started in 1687), which was demolished and redone three times.

Already in September 1663 Colbert, a few months before he became superintendent of the King's buildings, wrote to Louis:

> Your Majesty knows that in lieu of magnificent acts of warfare, nothing betokens more the grandeur and the spirit of princes than buildings; and all of posterity measures them by the standard of these superb buildings that they have erected during their lives. O what a pity if the greatest king and the most virtuous . . . were measured by the standard of Versailles![23]

Many years later, when Versailles had been made worthy of its occupant, that was of course precisely how the King was meant to be 'measured'. Between the major festivities held there in 1664 and 1668 the park and gardens were dramatically reworked under the supervision of André le Nôtre. From 1670 to the early 1680s a great deal of effort was put into the buildings themselves, under the supervision of a board of works headed first by Colbert, then (1683–91) by the energetic Louvois. Annual expenditure on the project rose to nearly 3 million livres in 1672, exceeded 5 million in the years 1679 and 1680, and stayed above that level for some years after 1684. By then the palace had been equipped with at least some of its characteristic features, including the imposing *Escalier des Ambassadeurs* – the vast double-branched stairs at the official entrance, designed to put foreign dignitaries and visitors in the right frame of mind. Like other parts of the palace the *Escalier* was decorated with the iconographical motifs of the King, but also had paintings of royal victories from the Dutch War. Another set of such historical paintings was designed in 1679 for the Hall of Mirrors, their more explicit adulatory imagery replacing planned allegorical cycles on the deeds of Apollo and Hercules. Later, the Hall of Mirrors was on special occasions used to receive foreign dignitaries, with the King seated on a silver throne at the far end to maximise the effect. Versailles thus became, as Colbert had suggested, a counterpart to the military prowess of France – its art collections, iconography and interior layout a symbol of French divinely ordained and grandiose monarchy.

Princely and royal court environments

The image of princely or royal secular dignity largely depended on conventional aristocratic values: on influence through clientages and connections, on an ostentatious lifestyle, on building projects, on cultural attainments and on more or less formalised martial display. During the first half of the seventeenth century, however, the political environment fostered clearer ways of distinguishing ruler from magnate in the eyes of beholders: both the scale and the ideological potential of artistic display were emphasised.

   The increasing size of princely courts in itself facilitated the creation of a permanent spectacle. The most formal example of the age was the Spanish Habsburg court, which had a core household staff of around 1700 in the 1620s, over and above the 400 actual government administrative personnel. The life of those in attendance was regulated by the strictest etiquette, prescribed by the King himself – Philip IV took a personal interest in such matters with a diligence which is difficult to understand today. When the occasion arose, the public spectacle was greatly enhanced. The unexpected visit of Prince Charles of England to Madrid in 1623, for example, provided the occasion not just for theatrical and musical performances in the

Alcázar but also bullfights, masquerades, fireworks and mock battles, complete with royal participation. It was partly with this in mind that Olivares masterminded the building in the 1630s of the Buen Retiro, a new palace on the outskirts of Madrid designed to create a more flexible frame for royal entertainments and for the reception of foreign representatives. Despite its unpretentious exterior and rapid completion, no effort or expense were spared on the interior. In addition to a vast array of artefacts, it came to house some 800 new paintings, part of a vastly augmented royal collection to which Philip IV alone may have added some 2000 pictures. He evidently had a genuine interest in painting and the decorative arts, but like other princes also saw their representational value: the Buen Retiro thus had as its focus a Hall of Realms intended to convey the military power and historical glory of the monarchy.[24]

Until 1640, visitors to Whitehall found a no less impressive spectacle. On the literary side, some continuation of Elizabethan courtly conventions and hyperbolic adulation remained visible in both poetry and drama, not just in the work of writers such as Ben Jonson (1572–1637), the 'King's Poet' from 1616 and author of many of the increasingly elaborate masque 'librettos', but also in that of a wide range of other writers. Yet James VI/I broke firmly with many of the attitudes of his Tudor predecessor: not merely was he incapable of continuing her legendary parsimony but also, no less importantly, he lacked her striking ability to exploit popular loyalty and cultural traditions, and hence ultimately to avert criticism of elitism, corruption or arrogance. James was an unusually prolific expounder of his own beliefs and political theories, but his temperament, coupled with a lack both of decorum and of resources, ensured that his grand ideals would remain remote from actual fact and that traditional respect for him was diluted. In terms of patronage of the arts, the Queen, Anne of Denmark (sister of Christian IV), Prince Henry, his younger brother Charles and prominent members of the nobility, such as the Duke of Buckingham or the Earl of Arundel, were more discerning than the King. This decentralised and unsystematic set of patronage relationships had advantages not only in maintaining the great strengths of the existing literary culture but also in securing cosmopolitan influences in other fields, whose overall effect at least in educated circles was considerable.

The task of deconstructing major pieces of seventeenth-century court-commissioned art can be difficult at the best of times, and rarely more so than in the intricate multimedia events where literary, visual and musical creativity were combined. The most original and versatile contributor to the visual display of the Stuart court right up to the civil war was Inigo Jones (1573–1652), serving as architect, scholar and Italianate artistic adviser, as well as designer of stage sets, costumes and machinery. After brief service at the Danish court, Inigo Jones had entered Anne's service in 1604, and through her patronage produced with Jonson the first of a new style of lavishly elaborate court masques. Rich in classical allusions and thinly disguised compliments to current patrons, these court entertainments must have been potential minefields for the artists, but juxtaposed with the often satirical and realistic anti-masques, they came to represent both a political argument for order and a striking reflection of current values. More durable expressions of Stuart ideology were also created, most notably in the magnificent Banqueting House which Jones built after the fire of 1619. Serving as ceremonial hall, audience chamber and theatre, this building – not least after celebratory paintings by Rubens to the value of £3000 were installed on its ceiling in 1635 – was intended to be what Graham Parry recently described as 'the Temple of the Stuart Kings'.[25] It comes as no surprise that the allegory of divine monarchy on the ceiling was as remote from reality as the glorification of kingship in the masques, or that the rather formalistic celebration of love (divine, royal and human), which was a recurrent theme in the masques of the 1630s, was openly contradicted in the increasingly bitter hostility between the two foremost image-makers of the time, Inigo Jones and Ben Jonson.

No doubt, as with nearly all patronage systems at the time, contemporary observers would have drawn their own silent conclusions as to the meaning and significance of it all. No one, however, could have been in any doubt that England was enjoying a real artistic golden age under the early Stuarts, reaching new heights when Prince Charles succeeded to the throne in 1625 (his artistic older brother, Henry, having died prematurely in 1612). Inigo Jones's Italianate building projects, including the major reworking of St Paul's Cathedral, had as much impact on a hitherto unsophisticated clientele as the brilliant portraiture by van Dyck (1599–1641) of Caroline court circles in the 1630s. Less skilled artists such as Daniel Mytens were eclipsed in the process, yet it is difficult to argue that the promotion of Stuart ideology stifled the creativeness of those in the patronage of the court. Some artists naturally found court patronage and its cosmopolitan orientation less congenial than others, and we lack evidence on how they, or those not recognised by their contemporaries, coped. Yet the overall literary and artistic vitality of Stuart England can hardly be denied, and it is now widely recognised that after 1625 the court, despite its sudden decorous formality and moralism, exerted much less of a dampening effect on imaginative artistic independence than has hitherto been assumed.[26] The court masque reached new heights of complexity, and Charles seems personally to have encouraged a quite remarkable group of composers to make the most not just of this large format but also of smaller-scale chamber music. Charles was reputed to have learnt to play the viol quite well, under the tuition of one of his father's Italian-inspired musicians, John Coprario. His genuine appreciation of this versatile instrument created opportunities for a distinguished group of musicians, including the versatile Thomas Tomkins (1573–1656), several members of a family of Venetian Jews around Thomas Lupo, and, above all, the extraordinarily creative and brilliantly original William Lawes (1602–45), whose premature death in battle, at one of the sieges of the Civil War, was another example of the many political misjudgements of Charles's reign.

Artistic patronage in England (as elsewhere in Europe) did not come cheap. Both James and Charles attempted to create a court entourage that the Crown's financial resources could barely support, and for different reasons each failed to carry conviction when it came to putting themselves over to their subjects. As a result, the sophisticated cultural life at court in the end generated as much puritanical opposition to the ideology of monarchy as it did support. Charles's eye for major works of art led to the extraordinary acquisition of virtually the entire collection owned by the Gonzaga Dukes of Mantua – a large part in 1627, for the sum of £15,000, the rest shortly afterwards. The loan required for this left the Treasury so depleted that the European war had to be abandoned and peace with France secured at any cost. Politically misplaced extravagance was no less obvious in Madrid in the building of the Buen Retiro, where as many as 1500 men were employed at the end of 1633. The total cost of that not terribly well constructed palace is estimated at between 2.5 and 3 million ducats, spread over some years, at a time when the annual expenditure of the Spanish Crown was around 10 million, and when the burden of war was in danger of bringing the monarchy to its knees. There is no lack of other examples of such financial insouciance. Later in the century, with the threat from the Turks in only temporary abeyance, Emperor Leopold I staged a spectacular opera by Cesti, *Il pomo d'oro*, as part of the celebrations for Margareta of Spain after their wedding in 1666: the cost of the opera alone was estimated at 100,000 florins, and that of the subsequent equestrian ballet 60,000, not counting the enormous expense to the individual nobles who participated.

No doubt the short-term artistic opportunities created by these ventures were substantial: certainly Olivares, like the town council of Augsburg, was neither the first nor the last to justify expenditure on ostentatious building projects by referring to the amount of work generated. But for the craftsmen, artists and musicians themselves, princely financial irresponsibility could have very damaging consequences. Painters were probably used to coping with highly erratic demand – available evidence suggests that van Dyck, for example, while in London did not rely solely on a meagre and often unpaid royal pension, preferring instead to take private commissions. Rubens did the same in the last years before his return to Antwerp (1608) when, whilst studying in Rome ostensibly under Gonzaga patronage, he accepted major commissions because nothing came from the notorious Mantuan treasury. In the later part of the century, painters with a fashionable clientele easily set up independent practices, as did the Dutchman Sir Peter Lely in London from 1643. For musicians, however, the vagaries of patronage were more difficult to cope with because their reputation depended on ensemble work and they could only exceptionally make a living as single virtuosi.

The difficulties Monteverdi had with the Gonzagas have already been referred to, and after some 20 years of Mantuan service he did not leave as a wealthy man. His later years there had been marred by bitter disputes over working conditions, over the mean and corrupt practices of the treasury officials serving the dukes and over the total unpredictability of artistic policy at the Gonzaga court. For the musicians at Dresden, conditions deteriorated even further. Elector Johann Georg of Saxony (1611–56) had inherited a substantial musical ensemble which served both in the electoral chapel and at major state occasions such as the Reformation centenary in 1617. As noted in chapter 2, Saxony kept out of direct involvement in the Thirty Years War until 1630, and cultural activity appears not to have been seriously curtailed until the military occupations and plague epidemics of the 1630s.

By then, however, the incurable inertia of Johann Georg began to affect the musicians in a more direct way. Arrears of pay had been chronic in Dresden, as indicated by a memorandum from 1611 indicating that the accumulated debt to the musicians was already equivalent to one and a half times the sum allocated annually to the entire musical staff. From the 1630s, predictably, petitions and appeals became increasingly desperate as Saxony lurched into financial disaster. Schütz tried to adapt his work to the dwindling resources at his disposal, as he explained in the prefaces to both parts of the *Kleine Geistliche Concerte* (1636–9). By the 1640s it is clear not only that church and court music was no longer regularly performed but also that the whole musical tradition in Dresden was in danger of collapse because of a lack of trainees and skilled teachers. One musician was, in 1641, after 40 years of service, owed wages equivalent to eight years' normal pay, and by 1651 the group had received only three of their last sixteen quarterly payments. A series of increasingly despondent and, on occasion, emotional appeals by Schütz, either on behalf of his staff or for his own retirement, were consistently ignored, as were urgent recommendations from both the court preachers and the heir to the electoral title.

This state of affairs would not have been particularly remarkable had it ended with the war in 1648. In the early 1650s, however, whilst economic life began to recover, morale amongst the musicians appears to have continued declining, despite efforts to bring the ensemble back to numerical strength. No attempt was made, it seems, to clear off the arrears of pay and, even if any of the musicians had had the courage to pursue their claims formally, their contracts of employment were not sufficiently specific to be of much value. Their access to credit exhausted, a few attempted to find work elsewhere, notably in Hamburg, or, like Schütz's gifted pupil Christoph Bernhard, they considered retraining for other professions. It appears that the Elector, his political role in the Empire destroyed by defeat and foreign intervention, had lost any interest in the institutions that had given the court prestige and cultural lustre. Not being artistically or musically inclined himself, he took out his own sense of failure on those for whom he no longer saw any use. Not until his death in 1656, and the accession of his more genuinely artistic heir, were the musicians given any cause for optimism.[27]

Given that music was regarded as a normal ingredient of court entertainment all over Europe, the experience of the Dresden musicians, struggling under a basically unartistic employer, was not unique. A minimum of 15 or 20 musicians (singers and instrumentalists) was required for a presentable performance of the more substantial religious and secular music of the period, and the bigger courts customarily employed far more than that. Christian IV of Denmark employed 77 musicians (including 16 trumpeters) in 1618, at an annual cost of over 10,000 thalers, while Philip IV had 63 a few years later, and his cousins in Vienna two-thirds of that number. Landgrave Moritz of Hessen-Kassel, although a second-ranking prince in the Empire, patronised outstanding virtuosi and composers such as John Dowland or Hans Leo Hassler, and had a regular staff of around a dozen musicians, augmented on a substantial scale for special occasions. A list of 1661 indicates that in England Charles II, despite the hiatus of the interregnum, already had a musical staff of 48, not counting trumpeters, drummers and fifers. Although musicians were not usually paid more than middle-rank court salaries, typically £46 per annum at the Stuart court and roughly equivalent sums elsewhere in Europe, the total and necessarily recurrent outlay on music was thus considerable. At Dresden in the 1620s the musicians accounted for nearly 5 per cent of the nominal court payroll, while at the court of Louis XIV in the 1660s the three main groups of musical staff (the Chapel Royal, the Chamber Music and the Military), between them employing over 100 men, would normally account for around a quarter of a million livres annually in wages and allowances, before either the cost of liveries or the additional expenditure on great virtuosi singers and special entertainments were added.

For many types of artist, court patronage, like that of the Papal States or of private individuals, meant complete dependence on the employer in terms of both security and pay. When Christian IV died, for example, the musical staff was rapidly reduced by his successor Frederick III, and building initiatives abandoned, yet interest in painting and the decorative arts continued, to the benefit notably of Karel van Mander. Such a shift in relations was hardly surprising in the context of the age. Apart perhaps from some of the popes, it was really only Louis XIV who thought in terms of a permanent and consciously integrated programme of co-ordinated propaganda encompassing different branches of the arts, and he and his advisers were accordingly also keenly conscious of value for money, as Bernini discovered in his dealings with Colbert during his visit to Paris in 1665.[28]

More worrying was the question of how much was actually paid to artists and craftsmen within an existing patronage system. The evidence from France, where the musicians bought their offices like everyone else, suggests that at least in the early years of Louis XIV they were on the whole paid. Yet the experience of Monteverdi in Mantua or of Schütz in Dresden suggests that total arbitrariness and gross personal irresponsibility amongst rulers was not yet becoming a thing of the past. In Dresden, for instance, the young elector in power from 1656, Johann Georg II, who was both a competent composer and an insatiable enthusiast for Italian opera, again lacked the financial ability to protect his musicians from arrears: in 1666 Schütz, now (at the age of 81) in semi-retirement, still had to submit petitions for 500 thalers owed to him. The story was no different in Restoration England, where musicians were owed substantial sums in the later 1660s and where in 1671 the stop of the Exchequer (a bankruptcy in all but name) forced the entire musical staff to accept a payment of 6 per cent per annum interest in lieu of salaries.[29]

If princely patronage, then, could at times offer less than ideal conditions, it might also create considerable opportunities: a vastly widened range of national and cosmopolitan contacts, commissions on a much bigger scale and the possibility of subsidies for publications, as well as copyright and even personal protection. Monteverdi evidently valued his Gonzaga connection sufficiently to turn to them in 1627, 14 years after leaving for Venice, when his son was arrested by the Inquisition. Princely patrons, interested as they were in giving lustre to court life, were also generous with scholarships for promising young artists to study abroad: many of the musicians serving Johann Georg thus spent two or three years in Italy at his expense, just as Schütz himself had earlier been talent-spotted by Landgrave Moritz and sent to Venice to learn. There were many other benefits for those employed at court, ranging from tax exemptions and protection against lawsuits for debts to the provision for musicians of first-rate instruments such as those bought from the Amati family in Cremona for both the English and the Dresden string players. Above all, court patronage was flexible. Henry Purcell (1659–95), when puberty ended his career as a treble in the Chapel Royal, not only worked for the music publisher Playford but also served as unpaid assistant to the keeper of the royal instruments, John Hingeston, thereby in 1683 securing the succession to that office. His contacts at court not only helped him to become composer-in-ordinary for the violins, organist at Westminster Abbey and later permanent member of the Chapel Royal itself but also ensured that he kept his posts after the accession of William and Mary in 1689.

A few could make even more of their talents, as illustrated in the career of Rubens (1577–1640). Of well-to-do Flemish commoner stock, Rubens's stay in Italy proved not just a major turning-point in terms of experience and commissions but also gave him his first major diplomatic mission to the Spanish court on behalf of the Gonzagas in 1603. In addition to proving his worth as an artist and as a restorer of severely rain-damaged paintings intended as gifts to Madrid, Rubens also impressed even that formalistic court with his tact and diplomatic ability. After his return to the Spanish Netherlands in 1608 he accepted the patronage of the archdukes, and led several diplomatic missions to the United Provinces. In 1628 Philip IV was persuaded to let him lead the ultimately successful peace mission to England, where he so impressed his host that he also secured the large commission for the Banqueting Hall noted earlier. In addition, Rubens was on friendly or business terms with a number of prominent patrons and art dealers throughout Europe, and was himself a substantial collector. He ended up with a noble title, living in considerable comfort as director of a large and internationally renowned workshop whose output fetched the best prices on the European market.

Such success was unusual, but illustrates a potential for upward mobility which was not unique. The outstanding Bohemian violin virtuoso and composer Heinrich Biber (1644–1704) was ennobled by Emperor Leopold I in 1690. An even more extraordinary story of rags to riches is that of the music entrepreneur and crook, Jean-Baptiste Lully (1632–87). Son of a miller in Florence, Lully came to France in 1646 as a household servant, guitarist and violinist. Attracting the attention of the young Louis XIV through their shared interest in dancing, he was placed in charge of the small royal string band (*la petite bande*) in 1656, and became one of the two masters of music at court in 1661. Collaborating with Corneille and Molière on the major drama productions of the 1660s, Lully in 1672 acquired a monopoly on opera in France by buying out the indebted Perrin and securing his privilege for an Académie Royale de Musique. This he proceeded to enforce by means of further patents, so that Molière and the composer Marc-Antoine Charpentier, like others, were compelled to rely on smaller and private productions. Using his strong contacts with the King and his position as *secrétaire du roi* (bought in 1681 for 63,000 livres, complete with ennoblement), Lully in effect exercised an enforceable stranglehold on stage performances in France. The thematic predictability and overt royalist propaganda at which he excelled suited Louis XIV, but his influence was undermined when Mme de Maintenon from 1683 imposed an increasingly dour and puritanical atmosphere on the court.[30] Nevertheless, his death in 1687 – from gangrene in the foot, self-inflicted in the course of excessively enthusiastic time-beating with a cane during a performance – revealed a very rich estate valued at 800,000 livres and including five town houses.

Women and the creative arts

Patronage of the arts was no doubt gender-specific, but the factors behind both overall market trends and specific individual commissions are very difficult to unravel. The male-oriented assumptions underlying most of the relevant source material from this period, such as financial accounts, household inventories, church records and official state archives, make it difficult to determine where, and to what degree, women might have been involved informally in the decision-making process. There is no indication that women would normally have had any role in the detailed planning (let alone execution) of substantial building projects; by contrast, women at the higher levels of society clearly were major players with respect to interior design, paintings and musical or theatrical entertainments.[31] Some basic training in the creative arts was deemed an essential part of female education: discerning taste, as well as potentially active participation within the domestic context, was taken for granted.

Serious full-time or professional artistic creativity by women, however, was likely to be more controversial. The guilds and academies which regulated the decorative arts, painting and music were habitually reluctant to admit women, and contemporary art critics were at best patronising towards outsiders. As always, there were exceptions. One of the foremost Dutch artists of the early seventeenth century, Judith Leyster (1609–60), became a member of the artists' Guild of St Luke in Haarlem in her early twenties, even though her father was not himself a painter. She also acquired an independent workshop of her own, complete with three male pupils – all as a result of her own reputation, since at this stage she had not yet married the artist Jan Molenaer. Such success, however, was rare. In Italy, some of the early female painters who achieved widespread recognition, such as Lavinia Fontana (d. 1614), appear to have done so without straying much beyond the confines of contemporary expectations for well-educated and wealthy women. When, as in Fontana's case, the artist was trained by her own father, it becomes still more difficult to document precisely how her career developed. For one of the best painters of the period, Artemisia Gentileschi (*c*.1593–1652) – who was also taught by her father – we now have quite detailed records regarding some of the more controversial stages of her life. But even in her case it is quite difficult to document precisely why, having been able to sustain very high prices for the astonishingly original and forceful work of her early and middle years, she had to tone down her style later in life to minimise financial difficulties.[32]

Interestingly, the greatest scope for women was in music. The first music in print by a female composer had appeared already in 1566: a set of madrigals by Madalena Casulana, published (like all the finest prints) in Venice. By the early seventeenth century sacred and secular vocal music composed by women appeared quite frequently in print, including collections of sacred music written by and for nuns. Although all the churches (Catholic and Protestant) tried to restrict the participation of women in musical performances – or at least limit their role to parts with minimal scope for virtuosic display, as choral singers or performers solely on the keyboard – in practice this was difficult to maintain. In 1580 a vocal ensemble of three female singers had been formed at the court of Ferrara by Duke Alfonso d'Este, and this *concerto di donne* (consort of women) can rightly be regarded as a major breakthrough. Although the female singers had in the first instance been appointed and paid as ladies-in-waiting to the duchess (and hence were of high social standing in their own right), they were soon recognised explicitly as professional musicians, hired for the quality of their singing and paid in recognition of regular performances in the Duke's private music. With salaries at 300 scudi (more than twice that of the *maestro di cappella* serving the Duke), these women quickly gained both status and international fame. No less significantly, they were at times joined by male singers from the existing court ensemble, thereby creating an elite mixed-gender musical ensemble. Soon similar ensembles appeared at other Italian courts, and many of the women also began to be recognised in terms of their skills as instrumental performers on both stringed and wind instruments. We might also note that Claudia Cattaneo, a virtuosa singer at the court of Mantua who married Claudio Monteverdi in 1599, remained active after her marriage, both as a performer and as a music teacher.[33]

This breakthrough in the recognition of women as professional musicians created significant precedents. Barbara Strozzi (1619–*c*.1664) became, by mid-century, one of the first female musicians to work outside the favoured environment of a princely court. As the adopted or illegitimate daughter of Giulio Strozzi, one of Monteverdi's friends and librettists, Barbara Strozzi had evidently had an extensive musical education which enabled her to exploit the exceptional freelance opportunities available in Venice. However, there are a number of puzzling aspects to her career,[34] not least the fact that she never married and never seems to have secured a steady source of income other than from her publications and her performances as a singer and viola da gamba player. Becoming a freelance musician was not normally a viable means of livelihood for women. Individual male prejudices and moral strictures aside, female musicians never had the same practical freedom and opportunities as men. The most gifted amongst them now had huge earning potential as solo singers, for as long as they were young, and in the second half of the seventeenth century they were normal participants even in large-scale musical events in those countries (such as France) where the male castrato singer was not accepted. Thus the exclusive privilege to stage opera in France, formally acquired by Perrin in 1669, made it clear that women (including noblewomen) could participate in performances, and we also know that women were regularly used as soloists in performances of most kinds of church music. But for many this was a relatively short-lived (and often part-time) burst of celebrity: a permanent career as a professional composer and soloist was rare. Even in France, where the market supported a great range of musical activities, only Elisabeth-Claude Jacquet de la Guerre (*c*.1666–1729), was acknowledged as fully equal to her male contemporaries in terms of her skills as a harpsichordist and ultimately also as a composer.

Public patronage and appreciation of the arts

At the very time that a comprehensive and rather heavy-handed system of royal propaganda was being fostered around Louis XIV, visible in the state-sponsored academies of arts and sciences, in the formal unanimity of the new palace officially inaugurated at Versailles in 1682 and in the whole atmosphere at court, the prospects for freelancing were also improving. The more settled conditions in much of Europe from the 1660s undoubtedly encouraged this trend, yet it is worth emphasising that for another century or more freelancing remained risky and fraught with difficulties, especially for writers and musicians but also for others with creative imagination.

Building and interior decoration was probably, in the nature of things, the sector with the greatest scope for independent-minded talents. The risks were considerable, not least the physical hazards of the work itself: the commissioners of St Paul's Cathedral in London and the supervisors at Versailles seem exceptional in making special efforts to help severely injured workmen and their families. But it is the wider risks, created by the seasonal and unpredictable nature of the work, that are most in evidence from building records. Some prestige projects could involve massive expenditure over considerable periods of time, such as those undertaken in England by Sir John Vanbrugh and Nicholas Hawksmoor in the years from 1699, including Castle Howard and Blenheim Palace, the latter leading to well-known and increasing friction between architect and patroness. More often, however, work was sporadic or incidental, ranging from ordinary itemised building operations to specific ornamental contributions such as the woodcarvings which brought fame to Grinling Gibbons (1648–1721) or the commissions which barely kept solvent the sculptor Caius Gabriel Cibber (1630–1700).

Even the rebuilding of St Paul's Cathedral after the fire of 1666, although supervised from the start by the commissioners and by Sir Christopher Wren, was not without its pauses, its battles over design or intent, and many substantial changes of course midstream. The commissioners at first variously represented the Anglican Church, the City of London and the Crown but, as the enthusiasm of the latter two waned in the 1680s, the church hierarchy in effect came to exercise fairly complete control. Progress was erratic because of the sheer scale of expenditure (averaging £10,000 a year until 1692, rather more thereafter, and finally totalling over £800,000): despite the national appeal of 1677 and various public subscriptions, there was growing friction over the sharing of proceeds from the coal-tax allocated for this and other purposes. The diverse subcontracting used for St Paul's, as for most other buildings, emphasised the intricate collaborative nature of the project. In addition, the records indicate that the supply of materials represented a relatively large proportion of total expenditure, compared with the costs of on-site labour (much of which could be unskilled or semi-skilled), so larger building projects of this kind clearly generated employment in a range of subsidiary industries. This no doubt helped to preserve the decentralised nature of the whole sector, in spite of efforts both in France and in England to impose some overall supervision on public and crown works.

Restoration England vividly illustrates the resulting conflict of interests. Despite the opportunity for major planning in central London after the catastrophic Great Fire of 1666, with 13,000 small houses and a number of larger public buildings destroyed, the Crown was unable to impose much rationality on the hurried efforts to reconstruct, especially since it was chronically short of the funds that such control would have required. The plans of Wren, Evelyn and others for a network of wider and more rational streets were defeated by private interests and by legal complexities. Apart from the coal-tax intended for public buildings, parliament adopted planning for only a few specific quayside areas, leaving all but the regulation of flammable building materials to private initiative. The Board of Works, headed by the Surveyor General (Wren himself from 1669 right up to 1718) and a small group of permanent officials, undoubtedly exerted considerable influence on the gradual development of professionalism in the building trade, especially through the patronage network reaching downwards through the various participatory trades. But most of the actual rebuilding was done in accordance with traditional unregulated methods, and even some of the 52 parish churches rebuilt after the fire were outside Wren's real influence. The guilds and corporations financed their new halls and premises privately through subscriptions or dues, with little official interference. Here, as elsewhere in Britain and on the continent, institutional patronage independent of the Crown remained of major importance. Innumerable major buildings, from the Brewers' and Merchant Taylors' Halls built after the London fire to the great commissions for religious orders in southern Europe already discussed, testify to the continuing importance of this kind of collective patronage.

Artists and craftsmen able to operate with considerable autonomy were of course not a new phenomenon in the seventeenth century. Painters in particular had long had some scope for going their own way by means of very loose or temporary patronage relations or by relying on dealers and exhibitions. In the United Provinces there was a particularly strong public demand for small everyday paintings and other domestic ornaments, enabling guild members to live comfortably like other craftsmen. Evidence from Delft indicates that perhaps two-thirds of all households were hung with paintings by mid-century – a truly remarkable indication of the genuine popularity of art, even allowing for the fact that it was only the rich who could afford the expensive work of known artists.[35] Real genius could also bring considerable reward without direct attachment to a single patron: Rembrandt Harmensz van Rijn (1606–69), the son of a Leiden miller, was by 1639 able to buy a substantial property in Amsterdam on the basis of earnings from work done for a variety of patrician customers. Equally significant, perhaps, is the fact that as his style became more spiritually intense, introverted, sometimes disturbing and ultimately unfashionable, his already weakened financial position deteriorated further. After the upheavals and uncertainty of war, the public wanted paintings that were more conventional and uncomplicated. Rembrandt's de facto bankruptcy in 1656 in no way indicates that he had lost his powers of interpretation – a glance at his late work, even The Jewish Bride of around 1668, confirms the contrary – but he remained in fairly straitened circumstances until his death.

It seems likely that painters had less difficulty working on their own in the relatively decentralised urban communities of the north-west than they did in Italy. In Rome, at any rate, outsiders found it nearly impossible to penetrate the market without aristocratic patronage of some kind – either the support of one of the great collectors, such as the Marchese Giustiniani (owner of 640 paintings and 1800 sculptures), or of a member of the papal entourage itself, or at least of one of the many dealers. The painter Salvator Rosa (1615–73) appears to have been determined to freelance (in the sense of doing without any single main patron, relying instead on general demand). He was in Rome briefly in the 1630s, but because of his satire on Bernini he stayed in Florence until 1649 and then settled in Rome. Of querulous and unpredictable disposition, irked by public interest in his smaller landscapes at the expense of his larger canvases, Rosa made the most of exhibitions to attract attention, yet it has been suggested that his fierce defence of artistic independence and inspiration in fact concealed a desire for formal recognition and for major commissioners.[36]

In the musical sphere, the market may not have been as restrictive in the later seventeenth century as initial observations would suggest. The French penchant for using notaries gives us interesting evidence not only on the bands formed to meet public demand for musical entertainment in Paris, noted earlier, but also on the first known efforts at organising genuine public concerts. A contract of 17 October 1641 indicates that the harpsichordist Jacques Champion de Chambonnières (1602–72) established an ensemble of ten musicians known as the *Assemblée des honnêtes curieux*, with a view to putting on twice-weekly public lunch-time concerts. Each performer, including the two female singers, was to receive 150 livres per annum, with extra pay for additional concerts, and arrangements were made for the hiring of a hall.[37] We have no indication how the public was made to pay, but evidence from contemporary theatre arrangements and in connection with problems experienced by Perrin at performances at his privileged opera house in Paris some years later suggest that not everyone gracefully accepted the necessity of paying for admission. Bouncers were often needed, and the risk of violence from offended noblemen was considerable.

John Banister, who organised the first public advertised concerts in London in 1672, may well have had similar problems, judging from a licence of 1689 to one of his successors which stressed the need to maintain order. But thanks to the relatively decentralised nature of the cultural market in London, freelancing by this time clearly was possible. Music had been a more acceptable form of entertainment during the Commonwealth period than, for example, the theatre, and there was sufficient amateur interest to keep the music publisher John

Playford in business. Both public theatre and informal concert-giving are regularly mentioned in Pepys's and Evelyn's diaries from the 1660s onwards. Roger North, in his historical notes on music, wrote that Banister initially relied on 'shack-performers' and foreigners to entertain an audience who paid at the door for impromptu programmes of light music. Elsewhere, however, he suggested that 'there was very good musick, for Banister found means to procure the best hands in towne', creating the basis for virtuoso recitals.[38] Only with the decline of active court patronage of music after 1689, however, did public demand become really attractive, and even in the early eighteenth century it required men of Handel's skill to make it pay handsomely.

It will be clear from the areas covered in this chapter that the 'luxury market' was less exclusive than one might have guessed at first sight. No doubt princely and aristocratic patronage had its serious drawbacks: not least, everyone had to put up with the seemingly universal financial insouciance of high society, aggravated by noble immunity to prosecution by more humble creditors. Rich and powerful patrons could clearly also be a great nuisance if their artistic judgment conflicted with that of the more talented men who served them. But the latter, if they could accept their ranking alongside craftsmen or household servants and could live with the resulting constraints, might enjoy some significant privileges and opportunities by comparison with those who were less skilled: social contacts, additional training and perhaps a wider circle of appreciation. Most important of all in the world of elite culture, patronage created the opportunity for travel and work abroad, and the cross-fertilisation that was so striking a feature of the best music, painting and architecture of this period.

In most of Europe, state patronage remained basically that of the ruling prince. It might take different forms, depending on personal whim, historical tradition or available resources – theatrical literary work, for example, seems to have been more actively promoted (alongside the other arts) in the major royal courts of Europe than in smaller principalities, where opera became the main stage event. Yet it is also clear that, apart from scale, crown patronage was still virtually indistinguishable from private aristocratic patronage, and that for some, such as Monteverdi or the Dresden musicians, princely aristocratic patronage was clearly unsatisfactory compared, say, with the much more durable collective patronage of a substantial town like Venice or Hamburg.

Yet there are also indications of a wider public market for the arts: for theatre, for music (including opera), for religious and secular art and even for smaller artifacts retaining utilitarian functions. This, combined with the general interest in private and public building at all levels, created outlets and contacts which we can still only imperfectly discern. It is likely that artists and musicians sought inspiration both in the 'high culture' of the elite and in their own more humble social milieu, and that high and lowly audiences alike could enjoy the result. In so far as all artists have to survive somehow, there were clearly more opportunities in royal and princely patronage, even in municipal work, than in the popular market, but compartmentalisation was far from complete.

Yet if genuine artistic appreciation was as common then as it is now, we would nevertheless also need to stress that the arts had one particular attraction central to an understanding of the seventeenth century. We have already noted the argument that the popes turned Rome into a theatre, a make-believe showpiece of spiritual and worldly magnificence, which may have served as some compensation for the rapidly declining political power and influence of the papacy in Europe from the later stages of the Thirty Years War onwards. This approach, however, was not unique to Rome. 'All the world's a stage' was a thread running through every aspect of public life in Europe, visible in the elaborately staged official ceremonies and processions, with their richly ostentatious but rigid requirements of status and precedence; in the obsessive legislation on what each rank in society was entitled to wear or even to eat at family feasts; in Calderón's play *El gran teatro del mundo* of 1641; and in the intricate stage machinery considered indispensable in operatic or dramatic performances in order to blur the distinction between stage and reality. It was by means of this ambiguity that the social and political values of patrons could most obviously be conveyed. The idea of all life as theatre fitted well with the baroque fascination for appearance set against reality, love against disenchantment, truth against disguise – the creation of a world of polarities where, as in the world of the scientists and philosophers, the notion of a balanced and static world had been replaced by more subjective and dynamic contrasts.

11 Absolute monarchy and the return of order after 1660

The later seventeenth century may be regarded as the period when absolute monarchy reached its classic form – a monarchy unlimited in law, seeking to project the King as an unchallengeable (even divinely ordained) judge and prince, underpinned by an administrative machinery whereby the daily exercise of power from the centre would become an accepted fact. This became in effect the 'normal' type of government in Europe for the next century or more. Yet, perhaps because the notion of monarchy was itself meant to be something of a divine mystery, there are relatively few formal statements of constitutional law from this period which can help clarify what precisely was intended. An unambiguous text is that of the substantial law code promulgated in Denmark in 1683, *Danske Lov*, whose very first article made clear that the monarch:

> alone has supreme authority to draw up laws and ordinances according to his will and pleasure, and to elaborate, change, extend, delimit and even entirely annul laws previously promulgated by himself or his ancestors. He can likewise exempt from the letter of the law whatsoever or whomsoever he wishes. He alone has supreme power and authority to appoint or dismiss at will all officials regardless of their rank, name or title; thus offices and functions of all kinds must derive their authority from the absolute power of the King. He has sole supreme authority over the entire clergy, from the highest to the lowest, in order to regulate church functions and divine service. He orders or prohibits as he sees fit all meetings and assemblies on religious affairs, in accordance with the word of God and the Augsburg Confession. He alone has the right to arm his subjects, to conduct war, and to conclude or abrogate alliances with whomever he wishes at any time. He can impose customs dues and taxes as he wishes. In short, the King alone has the power to use all *jura majestatis* and regalian rights, whatever they may be called. For this reason all the King's subjects (of whatever status) who live in his kingdoms or own property here, together with their household and servants, must as good hereditary subjects respect the King as the highest being on earth, raised above all human law and liable to no judgment in religious or secular matters save that of God alone. All subjects must be obedient, humble and faithful to the King, their protector, and must seek to forward the King's cause, do their utmost to prevent harm or disruption, and serve the King faithfully with life and property. All subjects are bound by oath to resist anyone

(native or foreign) who may act or speak against the King's absolute and hereditary rights, on pain of forfeiting life, honour and property.

This was a summary of many of the essential points already made in the (still unpublished) Royal Law of 1665, and it remained the clearest and most concise expression of absolutist doctrine publicly available in Europe.[1]

Danish absolutism, despite the style of Christian IV, was not an organic development, and that may well have been the reason why it was felt necessary to spell it out. The Royal Law of 1665, drafted by the King's secretary and librarian, Peder Schumacher, after confidential deliberations amongst other advisers, was derived from contemporary theory of unlimited monarchy and natural law. The text was probably not directly influenced by Hobbes's writings – the Danish king acquired neither control over religious dogma nor total rights over the property of subjects, and the succession itself was not arbitrary but carefully prescribed within the royal family. However, although the Law emphasised the sanctity and uniqueness of majesty, the introduction also implied a contractual relationship between king and subject in so far as it stated that power had voluntarily been surrendered by the Estates. Schumacher had in fact travelled in the Netherlands, England and France between 1653 and 1661, and became familiar with the political writings not only of the royalists but of men such as Harrington and John Milton, from whom he soon distanced himself. The main influences on his text appear to have come above all from the French theorist of absolutism Jean Bodin (1530–96), from a number of earlier Lutheran teachers such as Henning Arnisaeus, from the writings of James VI/I (brother-in-law, it must be remembered, of Christian IV), and from the work of the Dutch jurist Hugo Grotius (1583–1645). It was thus a particularly explicit restatement of those traditions of political thought which regained favour in the restoration years from 1660.

The French Crown never spelt out in such detail what it regarded its powers to be, but left no room for doubt regarding the image it wished to convey. In Louis XIV's so-called *Mémoires for the Instruction of the Dauphin*, a set of notes mostly written before 1670, the King condemned as unsatisfactory any system involving power-sharing either with a dominant first minister or, worse still, with the subjects themselves through representative or any other restrictive institutions: all power must be seen to come solely from the monarch and must be exercised in such a way as to emphasise his grandeur. His *Reflections on Kingship*, written in 1679, were in some ways even more emphatic. Ceremony, to Louis XIV, was not empty ritual but a practical means of distancing the King from his subjects: their respect would be proportional to the visible spectacle of royal power and, since they would not understand the real system of authority behind the facade, identification of state with monarch would strengthen each. The elaborate rituals of court etiquette had the additional function of defining the hierarchy of status in the inner circles around the King, crucially important for the exercise of power and the preservation of order or dignity.

In the 1670s the religious dimension of divine-right absolutism in France was elaborated by Bishop Bossuet, a domineering court preacher and tutor to the dauphin. He made a distinction between absolute power, as practised by the Bourbons in accordance with their Christian conscience, and arbitrary power, where the ruler did not respect traditional law: but since Louis XIV was also the ultimate judicial authority in the kingdom, this distinction was not always clear in practice. In Bossuet's formulation, God alone could question royal authority and, even if a king were to issue commands contrary to God's will a subject should do no more than petition and pray. This unambiguous message was reinforced through the elaborate imagery and pageantry of official culture, from coins and heraldry to science, theatre and music, and through the architecture and layout of the palace and gardens which Louis built 20 km west of Paris at Versailles, where the court formally moved in 1682. Versailles was not only a purpose-made display cabinet for monarchy and for the full Spanish court etiquette which the King adopted, but has also been regarded as a means of distancing some of the French nobility from the turbulence of Paris and from their traditional patronage-network in the provinces.

The limitations of central government

If the claims and the style of royal absolutism after 1660 were unmistakably grander than before the mid-century upheavals, it is by no means clear that any particularly striking 'turning-point' can be perceived in terms of the practical operations and detailed achievements of government. Much of the relative stability in Europe from the early 1660s was simply the product of peace and of a temporary abeyance of economic disaster, coupled with the end of regencies, the settling of succession problems or the escape from political deadlock of one kind or another. At best, it was a period where more bureaucratic procedures were applied to old policies.

The show that Louis XIV made, for example, of taking up full authority and responsibility in March 1661, after the death of Cardinal Mazarin, was not as significant in practice as it was meant to appear. Louis XIII had taken a central if less ostentatious role in daily government, and Mazarin, who had supervised the new king's training, had ensured active royal participation in formal council work from early on. The dramatic arrest in September 1661 of Foucquet, *surintendant* of finance, paved the way for the establishment of a royal council of finance promisingly presided over by the King himself. In fact, however, Foucquet's trial was a dangerous political manoeuvre which nearly backfired but which allowed Colbert to eliminate his main rival and create a new clientage network, and allowed the Crown to confiscate important assets.[2] Although Colbert never acquired the domineering authority which the cardinals had built up earlier, he nevertheless came to control domestic policy through the royal finances and, holding a number of key offices with a diligence that soon made him indispensable, he was effectively first minister until the last years before his death in 1683. Louis XIV was a good judge of men and was indisputably conscientious in terms of what he perceived to be his duties as monarch. Genuine centralisation in the decision-making process was achieved through his use of the very select inner council, the *conseil d'en haut*, whose membership never exceeded half a dozen. But Louis's personal interests (like those of most rulers of the day) lay primarily in the fields of diplomacy, international relations and war – the protection of the royal patrimony in terms of prestige and European power – rather than in the details of internal policy. He had neither the particular intelligence nor the foresight or predisposition to perceive the need for deeper structural changes of the kind that might have averted some of the problems of later years.

Where institutional traditions were altered, it was usually for obvious and pragmatic reasons. In addition to dispensing altogether with the Estates General as his father had done in his adult years, Louis ensured the dilution of those judicial powers which the Parlement of Paris had wielded periodically from the 1620s and had used to challenge the regency directly in 1648. Confirming the status and material privileges of the higher robe, the Crown abandoned the extraordinary war taxes and other arbitrary expedients which had often been the cause of robe opposition, thus diverting the Parlement's interests to other areas. The 'sovereign courts', including the Parlement of Paris, were renamed 'superior courts' in 1665; their right of remonstrance prior to registering edicts, crucially important to their claims for political influence earlier on, was discouraged so effectively that it was not used after 1667 and was nominally removed in 1673. Only after the King's death in 1715 did the Parlement of Paris recover its controversial role and powers thanks to a deal with the regency over the King's will.[3] However, none of the courts was actually restructured at any stage until the late eighteenth century, and their judicial functions were left largely intact: here, as with the provincial Estates and other traditional bodies, the hallmark of French absolute monarchy was conservation and adaptation to gradually changing needs.

The most important social group to adjust its priorities was probably the old nobility. It could be argued that the military power and provincial autonomy of the nobility had been broken for good with the failure of the revolts of the 1630s and 1640s, and that the nervous inquiry of 1664 organised by Colbert to clarify the reliability of the ruling elite all over the country was essentially precautionary. But if Louis XIV stressed that no one could count on automatic selection to serve him as a governor, diplomat, councillor or commander, and if the King found it expedient and remunerative to encourage the upward social mobility of men of lesser birth through service and the system of venality of offices (see chapter 5), it is equally clear from recent research that he also positively cultivated the support of the ordinary provincial nobility. He did this partly by avoiding the confrontational and openly ruthless approach of his father's ministers. But he also ensured that the elite in France, those with wealth, status and power, were protected, and, on a more tangible level, he saw that they acquired a bigger share in local resources and in the allocation of taxes for local spending, so ensuring that they had an important stake in the survival of the system. He could hardly have done anything else, for with a central administrative bureaucracy amounting to perhaps a mere 1000 staff, and with the reintroduced but more carefully supervised *intendants* quickly overwhelmed with work in their large districts, government by consent of the nobility was a political necessity.[4] Significantly, the sporadic revolts after 1660 usually lacked effective noble leadership and could be crushed by direct repression (see chapter 12). But tacit resistance and lack of co-operation by local officials and dignitaries remained a problem against which the Crown was nearly powerless: as indicated by Colbert's orders, not even the *intendants* could always be relied upon. Patronage and connection remained crucial at all levels: Colbert, Le Tellier and the Phélypeaux family all set a clear example by using their ministerial powers to protect and further their own friends and relatives, just as Richelieu and Mazarin had done before.

The monarchy of Louis XIV, then, was a well-judged compromise between strong and active central government with supervisory powers on the one hand, and, on the other, concession to the elite on a sufficient scale to ensure co-operation or at least acceptance. This compromise was probably as far as traditional monarchy could go in the complex society of western Europe. Its success on its own terms is clearly apparent by comparison with France's ancient rival Spain, now a complete antithesis, a caricature of absolute monarchy, under the mentally handicapped Charles II. Even there, significantly, the system did not collapse, for his subjects mostly accepted what there was, or at least the facade which they saw. There were enough traditions of continuity to permit some cautious attempts in the 1680s by the Duke of Medinaceli and the Count of Oropesa to reform the tax structure and revitalise the flagging overseas trade network in the Spanish Americas, showing that government was not totally dependent on royal leadership. But ministers in a position such as theirs were clearly very exposed to court intrigue and utterly dependent on shifting alliances within the ruling class, and in a European context, while the conglomerate state survived, Spain completely lost its position as a major power.

Whatever form it took, monarchy in the later seventeenth century clearly had to compromise in one way or another with the nobility or the political elite. This process, which we are beginning to understand for France, has not yet been analysed in as much detail in the other main continental states, but it is likely that, given a less complex economic and social structure, a partnership between crown and nobility emerged fairly naturally, the way it did in the Habsburg territories and elsewhere in the German lands. Even in Denmark, the theoretical claims of the Royal Law notwithstanding, the Crown could not create a new bureaucracy overnight: despite significant changes in the composition of the landowning and power-wielding elite in the decades after 1660, and the deliberate creation of a new ranking system for the service nobility from 1671 (see p. 172), the Crown did not exploit its unshackled position with striking results. One of the most dramatic beneficiaries of the new criteria of status, the royal librarian and author of the Royal Law, Schumacher, attained the title of Count of Griffenfeld in 1671, but was disgraced equally dramatically five years later. In the provinces, despite more detailed and specifically wider instructions to the regional governors, centralisation was slow: as before, royal legislation and reform fell mostly on deaf ears, and only the tax-collector or the recruitment agent in charge of conscripting for the compulsory militias of the 1660s and 1670s made any real impression on the localities. The international role of the kingdom actually became more subdued by comparison with the reign of Christian IV, and his massive building programmes and cultural aspirations were largely abandoned.

Despite the obstacles and limitations, monarchical government in the later seventeenth century did gradually become more comprehensive and intricate. Everywhere, a marked growth in routine business, whether of a judicial or an administrative nature, is discernible. Even in Muscovy this was so, for although comparisons are in many respects difficult to make (see chapter 5), the Crown there was as anxious to develop its military capability as were the western monarchies, and the administrative ramifications were just as unavoidable. In order to cope, rulers and their advisers increasingly relied on functionally specialised councils supervising particular parts of the central administrative work. The use of councils or colleges of government was of course in itself not new, as the junta system of Olivares in Spain had shown. Neither should such procedures necessarily be regarded as a form of successful rationalisation: even the fairly clearly defined collegiate structures of Sweden from the 1630s or of Denmark from the 1660s were riddled with demarcation disputes and problems arising from overlapping jurisdictions. But the trend towards permanent departments within central government was fairly clear, and became more essential with the growth in paperwork. Even the conservative Habsburg rulers moved in this direction: Leopold I, emperor as well as territorial prince from 1658 until 1705, not only secured more flexibility at the centre by allowing the old and unwieldy privy council (*Geheimer Rat*) to be superseded from 1669 by a smaller committee, the *Geheimer Konferenz*, but also ensured that this new committee included, as need arose, the head of the Austrian chancery (displacing the old imperial chancery) and the presidents of the treasury (*Hofkammer*) and the war council, all directly responsible to himself. In practice, Leopold was not very interested in the details of domestic financial and economic policies, so in both the treasury and the war council reform and long-term planning were difficult to achieve. The treasury was beginning to bridge the separate jurisdictions of the still highly fragmented Habsburg lands, but typically retained a complex book-keeping system where incomes and expenditures were handled through some twenty different accounts, not only ensuring delays and confusion but also facilitating corruption such as that practised on a massive scale by the president himself, Sinzendorf (1656–80). In spite of all this, however, the administrative framework for a major power was beginning to emerge.

With the growth in the amount and range of work at the centre naturally came a distinctive demand for more regular and fuller information on which decisions could be based – a development clearly reflected in the quantity of surviving archival material preserved in the record offices in many parts of Europe. When Colbert gained control of domestic policy in France in the 1660s he demanded a continuous and impressively detailed series of reports from the *intendants* and other local commissioners, on anything from administration and justice and ecclesiastical or military affairs to stud farms, canals and the compilation of maps. The *intendants* themselves were allowed to stay longer in each area, and, in spite of Colbert's resistance to the idea of permanent local intendancy offices, these commissioners soon acquired *sub-délégués* (resident deputies) and a substantial secretariat.

Other European governments by contrast often preferred to rely on ad hoc commissions of enquiry as the need arose. Even so, these could take on impressive proportions, as in the mammoth task undertaken by the Danish Crown from 1681 to measure out and evaluate every single piece of agricultural or forested land, together with all additional rural resources, for a new land register and land tax. The surveys and calculations took six years to complete and the massive archive so generated is a testimony to the scale of the administrative and scientific achievement: Christian V's Matrikel (land register) was not definitively replaced until 1844. It is perhaps premature to talk of a 'professional' approach to government, but there was in much of Europe a growing recognition, as we shall also see later in this chapter, that all kinds of problems could and should be tackled by rational means. It is no coincidence that in England men such as John Graunt, in his *Observations on the London Bills of Mortality* of 1662, William Petty, in his *Essays in Political Arithmetic* of 1672, and later also Gregory King (see p. 105), deliberately applied current rational scientific reasoning to matters of government.

State regulation of trade and industry

Well-informed though he was, Colbert not only believed, like most of his contemporaries, that there was a fixed total amount of international trade but, judging from his report of 1670 to Louis XIV on the kingdom's finances, he also assumed that there was a fixed quantity of money in Europe, changing only through what was lost in the east or imported from America. This logic led Colbert to argue that increasing the amount of money circulating in public commerce in France would not only enable the Crown to spend more because of growing fiscal income but would also impoverish other European states proportionately: 'which creates that double rise which we have seen increase so markedly during the past several years: one increasing Your Majesty's power and grandeur, the other humbling [the grandeur] of his enemies and those who envy him'. He reckoned that at the start of the reign the Dutch carried nine-tenths of French exports, dominated all the important trades including that of essential naval supplies and even controlled most of the coastal trade within France itself. This, Colbert argued, had been remedied somewhat by means of protectionist customs, by improvements in internal transport to facilitate lucrative exports and by promoting the manufacture of textiles, metals and other goods. He claimed that most military and naval equipment was now available within France, while commerce would be boosted by means of the new North Company, 'which is destined to bring to all the northern countries all our commodities and merchandise and to carry from them all those which serve in the construction of vessels for Your Majesty's subjects, before he has everything in his realm which is needed for that'.[5]

There was nothing new in these ideas. Schemes to increase a nation's share of the fixed total of international trade, to adopt protectionist and sumptuary legislation to improve the balance of trade and encourage domestic enterprise or to increase the manufacturing super-structure over the agrarian base of the national economy had been commonplace for a century. They are apparent in the unsystematic and often very schematic writings of those in different parts of Europe whom later historians have called 'mercantilists' or (in the more meticulously developed and comprehensive German variant) 'cameralists'. Few of Colbert's worthwhile ideas were much more than direct derivatives from the plans of Sully, Richelieu and their advisers, but he undoubtedly spent more time and bureaucratic effort on such plans in the 1660s and early 1670s than had his predecessors. As noted in connection with other aspects of seventeenth-century government, the gap between idea and practice could be very great, and it is hardly surprising that the practical effectiveness of such plans for political–economic regulation has been doubted. Colbert's staff was already overburdened, and the employment of 14 inspectors (later 24) to supplement the work of the *intendants* in supervising execution of the 200 or so regulatory edicts of the years 1661–83, affecting the manufacturing and trades of a population of 20 million, would hardly make much impression. The protectionist policies of 1667 against the Dutch and English were ineffective and had to be abandoned by treaty at the end of the war in 1678. The attempt to regulate the guilds themselves in 1673 was primarily a fiscal expedient, whose consequences (where enforceable) may have been at least in part negatively restrictive. Colbert himself had few practical ideas about how to realise his aims and appears to have hoped to rely on traditional artisanal organisation rather than larger manufacturing. The trading companies had little or no success against their rivals in London and Amsterdam. Like fiscal and financial reform, 'mercantilism' in France appeared to be the well-intentioned dream of a fairly ineffective government, soon abandoned in the face of the strains of war, or watered down through privilege, special concessions or simple corruption.

Yet if the result of state intervention was disappointing in many areas, there is some indication that it was not negligible in one or two. The production of silk, lace, woollen cloths (for example in the royal manufactury at Clermont-de-Lodève) and other branches of the textile sector did undoubtedly develop, and attempts to impose quality regulations could, despite local resistance, be beneficial against foreign competition. Once protective tariffs disappeared in 1678 some textile centres undoubtedly suffered badly, especially since government subsidies, probably minimal at the best of times, were sacrificed completely to the war effort. But even the merchants who sat on the new Council of Commerce established in 1700, despite their criticisms of post-Colbertian excesses of restrictive regulation, paid indirect tribute to the achievements in the commercial and manufacturing sectors since the 1660s.[6]

Another indirect indication of French manufacturing achievements is to be found in the debates in the imperial assembly at Regensburg in the 1670s on how to curb the import of French textiles and luxury goods as part of the war policy. In 1673, on the occasion of his second marriage, Leopold had made a point of the fact that every stitch he wore had been made within his own territories. In fact, the imperial assembly's decision in 1676 to ban all French trade proved highly damaging and unpopular in some parts of the empire, and the policy collapsed completely in 1678, despite Leopold's efforts. But within his own territories Leopold followed the current trend for growing governmental interference: he had already in 1666 authorised the establishment of a Council of Commerce in accordance with suggestions by the well-known German cameralist writer Johann Joachim Becher. Becher had made a number of recommendations, including some to arrest urban decline in the Habsburg lands by encouraging manufacturing companies and by coupling them with foreign trade through the port of Trieste. Leopold's Council of Commerce, like similar institutions established in various other German principalities over the next decades, was notable primarily for its lack of effect and its rapid disappearance into bureaucratic oblivion, but, as in France, there were now some precedents for more effective eighteenth-century experiments.

After the defeat of the Turks in 1683, vast new possibilities opened up for the development of the Danube basin. Simple suggestions to this effect, made by von Schröder and especially by the influential writer Philipp Wilhelm von Hörnigk, were adopted by the Habsburg commission on Hungary established in 1688 under the chairmanship of Ferdinand Dietrichstein. Concessionary policies to encourage repopulation and basic agrarian recovery were so successful that restraints had to be imposed ten years later to avoid draining manpower resources from other Habsburg territories. We could on this basis argue that 'mercantilist' or cameralist thinking was having a causal effect on practical policy: this may be true, in so far as von Hörnigk had a substantial audience among the educated, but it is also worth bearing in mind that repopulation and economic recovery would be in the obvious self-interest of any pragmatic government seeking to minimise the unrest consequent on underemployment and to maximise revenue and military strength. As with modern government, it is usually difficult to separate theoretical from practical motivations, except amongst the most doctrinaire: suffice it to say that during the later seventeenth century many European governments became more aware of their interests and obligations in the sphere of economic and social policy. This was so even in Muscovy, although there (see chapter 4) the lack of native foundations for western-style technological development created difficulties of a special kind, compounded by Russian reluctance to admit influences from abroad alien to their own cultural, religious and ethical traditions.

Legislative and regulative efforts were not directed solely at trade, manufactures and the creation of more rural and urban employment opportunities. Central and local government also intervened restrictively or positively in a wide range of community affairs by means of printed ordinances, decrees read from pulpits and other forms of systematic broadcasting. To supplement earlier forms of simple ad hoc prohibitions dealing with specific abuses, carefully planned comprehensive ordinances became more common in the monarchies of western, central and northern Europe from the later seventeenth century onwards, aimed at securing good 'police' – that is, order and a rational functioning of society achieved by means of administrative intervention through officials. For instance, to the sixteenth-century legislation regarding church attendance, orthodoxy, religious popular festivities and obedience, common particularly in Protestant states where the prince was also head of the Church, were added more detailed prescriptions of what form church services were to take, how the clergy were to conduct themselves, the scope for lay participation, provision for basic education and episcopal visitations, and the parameters for medical relief.

In the more secular field, efforts were made to prescribe rural employment conditions, including sharecropping practices as well as the wages payable to labourers and servants. The ability of labourers, and indeed other commoners, to change employers or move to another province was of recurrent concern, and attempts were frequently made to curb migration to foreign countries. There were restrictions on what kinds of goods could be manufactured and traded in the countryside, and on the activities of pedlars. Most impracticable of all, perhaps, were the repetitive decrees on allowable consumption at family festivities within each social rank, alongside attempts to curb vanity and social pretences by stipulating the kinds of clothes and jewellery that people in different walks of life could permit themselves. For the towns in particular, grain supplies, weights and measures, municipal administration itself, open-market practices and transport came under regular review, as did urban guilds, fire regulations, water and elementary sanitation. New legislation regarding the poor, vagrants, and the destitute (see chapter 6) reflected a growing functionalist approach, a desire to preserve orderly appearances and to reduce waste of resources and labour. All these regulative objectives could be rationally justified – and often were, in the introductions to legislation in the period – but they also underscored a basic contradiction between conservatism and order on the one hand, and initiative or enterprise on the other. As noted in connection with the putting-out system (see chapter 4), economic development often occurred along lines tending to dissolve existing social conventions and customs.

In the United Provinces and England, substantial theoretical contributions to political economy were made by a number of writers, including Grotius and Thomas Mun. In practice, however, the United Provinces did not have the central governmental authority needed to adopt economic regulative practices of any significance, beyond the protection of their own overseas trading interests, and in England the direction of policy was far more piecemeal than in the continental monarchies, often being the product of particular private pressure-groups acting through parliament and the court, or the response to a short-term emergency. In both countries overseas trade, North Sea fishing and access to naval supplies from the Baltic came to figure far more prominently than other issues, spawning acute rivalry which was liable to overshadow common religious and diplomatic interests between London and Amsterdam or The Hague throughout much of our period. Demand in England for protectionist measures against the Dutch had died down when the United Provinces became actively involved in the Thirty Years War, and English merchants could usually exploit their neutral position even into the civil war period, until the Dutch were freed from Spanish harassment in 1647. Then rapid Dutch recovery of the Baltic and colonial carrying trades (including the growing slave trade) resulted in pressures on the English government to implement the Navigation Act of 1651. This excluded Dutch vessels from English trade by such drastic measures that the first Anglo-Dutch War (1652–4) became unavoidable. Relations between the two countries remained in this state of love–hate ambivalence after the Restoration, damaged by the more sophisticated revised Navigation Act of 1660 and the second trade war (1665–7), yet nurtured after the third conflict (1672–4) by growing fears of France (see p. 416).

From mid-century onwards, then, open commercial rivalry was encouraged by government initiatives aiming at formal regulation of foreign trade. But neither the Dutch nor the English governments pursued comprehensive plans for their entire economy comparable to those of Colbert's France. In the words of D. C. Coleman, 'in English history the forms which mercantilism took were the product not so much of an over-developed monarchy ruling over an under-developed economy (though it was sometimes that) as of a central executive which believed itself to be strong but in reality was often weak. It rarely possessed anything remotely describable as "economic policy", but it always had financial problems for the solution of which it had to parley with both the creators of wealth and the payers of taxes',[7] who were consequently in a position to influence policy more directly, or even to sway argument by hiring the pamphleteers and writers of the time. This lobbying was primarily done by participants in foreign trade; by contrast, domestic manufactures (except woollens) had no government-regulated protection beyond the limits of individual patents and time-limited monopolies. Even attempts to impose quality control on the textile sector in England (1638 and 1678) failed to become law. Only from the 1690s did the government begin to use customs to protect the domestic cloth industry, and even that was the result of private lobbying by the interest groups concerned. Obvious and basic measures to encourage ship-building, to secure strategically important supplies for the rapidly expanding English navy or to support the price of grain for the sake of producers (1670–3) could gain general parliamentary approval where necessary, as could the poor laws and the redevelopment of workhouses, an area of policy where England was already ahead of other governments (see chapter 6), and which writers such as Josiah Child could see as essential for the overall health of the economy. But many of these measures lacked the centralised executive backing that Colbert would have attempted to provide in France, for the English Crown continued to rely on unpaid and to a large extent unsupervised local officials such as the Justices of the Peace.

Military power and fiscal strain in the Habsburg lands and France

The two major military powers on land, Louis XIV's France and Leopold's conglomerate territories, both illustrate the strains which dynastic and security interests imposed on fragile administrations. The Habsburg monarchy, with a population probably slightly below its pre-1620 total of 7.5 million, from 1648 supported a permanent standing army usually of between 30,000 and 50,000 men until the 1680s, rising to 100,000 men from the 1690s because of the international situation (see chapter 12). The cost of these forces exceeded 5 million florins in the 1670s, and doubled again during the following decade. This burden generated constant friction with the main regional Estates, not only those representing Habsburg Hungary but even the Austrian and Bohemian ones (despite the effects of heavy-handed Habsburg policies there since the 1620s). The total income of the state did, in fact, increase substantially in the early 1670s and again with the extra taxes against the Turks in the 1680s, but in spite of this Leopold faced a rapidly increasing deficit from 1684. In the exceptional year of 1695 an income of 14 million florins covered only slightly over half the total expenditure of 24 million, all but 2 million of which was for military purposes. The historian of Habsburg finances Jean Bérenger stresses that intrinsically the fiscal load was not disastrously heavy in a period of some economic development. The treasury was restricted not so much by peasant resistance, considerable though that was in, for example, the revolts of 1680, but by administrative inefficiency and particularly by the blocking tactics of provincial Estates representing seigneurial interests.[8] It was the failure to overcome these limitations that underscores the extent to which Leopold's authority was bound by tradition and by a seigneurial intransigence which he was not in a position to challenge. Within these limitations, however, the Habsburgs coped well with wars on several fronts, and by the end of the reign the system was not particularly overstrained.

In the case of France, the ultimate limits to monarchical power were more strikingly revealed because of the scale of Louis's commitments. With a population of nearly 20 million and a national economy of considerable strength, the kingdom could support a standing army of between 50,000 and 90,000 men in the 1660s relatively easily, especially in view of the reforms introduced by the King's military advisers, Le Tellier and Louvois, which brought army supplies and pay back under more direct crown control. Despite an inherited debt which he estimated at 450 million livres tournois, and a legacy of utter fiscal confusion and corruption, Colbert succeeded in stabilising royal finances in the 1660s and early 1670s, partly by reforming court expenditure and pension allocations and partly by efforts to improve administrative standards through exemplary trials for corruption conducted before a special tribunal (1661–9). This latter approach was far from a complete success: the actual collection of the resulting fines of 156 million livres on leading financiers was itself farmed out to others who simply took their place while the system remained unchanged. Nevertheless, Colbert was able to cancel some long-standing arrears on the *taille,* and reduce this direct tax progressively by placing more emphasis on (and securing greater efficiency in) indirect taxation, a policy which helped to reduce anti-fiscal resistance and violence in the provinces. The credit of the Crown itself greatly improved, and state loans became a more attractive investment.

The war against the Dutch (1672–9), however, inaugurated a period of growing international tension – largely, as we shall see in the final chapter, provoked by the King himself – which forced up military expenditure dramatically. By 1679 total crown expenditure reached 128 million livres tournois (compared with a roughly balanced budget of 45–70 million in the 1660s), and three-quarters of this was for military purposes. More seriously, war brought increasing annual deficits which could only be covered by anticipating revenue due in future years, by taking loans at higher interest rates and by allowing the tax-farming system in 1680 to go into the hands of a major permanent consortium of around 40 financiers, the farmers general. These developments were particularly significant because they spelt the end of the period of restraints initiated by Colbert. How far the minister himself wholeheartedly backed the King's grandiose foreign policy is less clear, given the increasingly obsequious, manipulative atmosphere now prevailing at the French court.

As the anti-French alliance took form after the outbreak of war in 1689, the Crown soon adopted measures as desperate as those used on a smaller scale by the government in the 1630s. Colbert's successors as controllers general of finance, notably Pontchartrain in the 1690s and later Chamillart, had no real influence on expenditure and were given no chance to reform the system. Vauban's suggestions for fiscal innovation were ignored, and the new *capitation* (poll tax) of 1695 was not enforced equally across the social spectrum. The Crown's finances were run on a series of makeshifts, while the famines of 1693–6 and 1709–10, by reducing real income, nearly brought about the complete collapse of France's military and diplomatic position. These developments in turn reduced the credibility of the Crown, so that the financiers imposed increasingly prohibitive surcharges on all the state's transactions. Although crown expenditure was reduced to 130–170 million livres in the early years of the War of the Spanish Succession (three-quarters of it spent on land forces, another 20 million on the navy), the tax farmers were by 1707 absorbing in costs and interest nearly half the yield from taxes and other income. In 1709 no offers were made for the renewal of the tax farms, and the Crown tried to collect taxation directly for a short while. During the last years of the reign, with 350,000 men under arms, all kinds of fund-raising expedients were attempted, including royal lotteries, further sales of offices and titles, and even the issuing of a kind of paper credit-note in lieu of coins. The King left an estimated debt of 2000 million livres in 1715, and it is hardly surprising that his death brought not only private relief but also a massive reaction against his overbearing style of government.

The costs of war in terms of the Crown's financial credibility as well as in terms of fiscal oppression were thus clear for all to see in the later years of the 'Sun King'. Less apparent but at least as significant in the long run was the growing importance of financiers within the power structure of the state. The presence of bankers next to the throne was not new in Europe, of course, but it is clear that by the later seventeenth century the families who ensured the liquidity of the French government were closely connected with the robe nobility and even with the great magnates of the realm. The reasons why attempts to clear up royal finances, through the special tribunal of 1661, for example, merely succeeded in replacing one group of devious bureaucrats experienced in fraudulent manipulation with another have been clarified by a group of historians including Daniel Dessert. He stresses that operations involving state funds yielded profits to a circle wider than that of the immediate ostensible agents. Tax officials in the employ of the Crown in practice often had to make advances to the state, so blurring the line which separated them from independent financiers – the latter were in any case often also holders of both offices and titles in their own right. Colbert himself had risen to power not just because of his financial skills but also because of his connections, and was consequently not in a position to achieve genuine reform at the expense of men who were in fact his main supporters.

Above all, however, financial interests were not beneath the dignity of even the aristocracy. Dessert demonstrates that the magnates, although operating through the agency of these same financiers and office-holders to preserve the outward signs of status and distance, often supplied the massive outlays required for these deals and shared the profits of the system. The result was a network of business and family connections between all those with power in the kingdom: office-holders, tax farmers, robe nobles, purchasers of venal offices, and the greatest aristocratic names themselves. Against such shared interests the Crown clearly had no options: it had to accept their terms of operation, most of all during wartime. Anything more than superficial reform would have amounted to a fundamental challenge to the entire elite and would have required a social revolution. The sheer scale of Bourbon military commitments, having created the need for fiscal and administrative growth, also in practice imposed severe limits on the independence and real powers of the Crown.[9]

Restructuring in Brandenburg–Prussia and Sweden

If the reality of the French monarchy was rather less impressive than it was meant to appear to be, the practical problems were even greater in small states with few traditions of effective government. A group of such states constituted the Hohenzollern lands, poorly governed during the Thirty Years War, scattered, and lacking any common identity except for the person of the ruler. As a result of the Peace of Westphalia, Sweden remained in possession of western Pomerania and Bremen, with the mouths of the Oder and Elbe rivers. Because of Mazarin's desire to avoid an early Swedish–Habsburg settlement, France had mediated a compromise over Pomerania whereby Brandenburg–Prussia avoided being totally cut off from the Baltic. The Hohenzollern position remained weak, however, partly because the best coastal area was lost and partly because some of their lands had been badly damaged during the ineffectual attempts to resist Swedish aggression in the late 1630s. When Frederick William took over in 1640 as Elector and Margrave of Brandenburg, Territorial Prince of Cleves-Mark on the Rhine in the west, and Duke of East Prussia under Polish suzerainty (confirmed in 1641), he therefore adopted a necessarily ambivalent role in the struggle between the major powers of the region. Without breaking completely with the Emperor, he quickly succeeded in reaching an understanding with the Swedes so that he could demobilise his father's ill-disciplined and unreliable mercenary forces. From 1644 he began a cautious new recruitment programme designed to protect the Hohenzollern lands from the kinds of threats faced since the 1620s and to secure some independent strength in international diplomacy.

Even before the peace of 1648, this policy generated opposition in the territorial Estates, especially those of Cleves in the west. The so-called *jus indignati* (right of the native-born) gave a monopoly of offices to those born in each province, thus emphasising barriers between the disparate lands. The physical separation of the Hohenzollern territories in any case made a co-ordinated policy very difficult. Swedish reluctance to withdraw from eastern Pomerania, for example, produced no signs of concern in the other territories, and Frederick William secured his treaty entitlement in 1654 only by virtue of imperial intervention (itself a product of the Emperor's desire to secure electoral support for his son). Disunity, however, could be used to advantage, for in 1653 the Elector took the first major step in overcoming local resistance when he reached a compromise with a committee of the unwieldly Estates of Brandenburg. In return for an extensive confirmation of noble privileges, he won a grant of taxation which, although ostensibly limited to six years, was in effect permanent. This paved the way for a standing army and for the grad-ual weakening of coherent fiscal opposition in Brandenburg. In 1667 the towns accepted a permanent excise which deepened the division between urban and rural society and made town representation on the committee of Estates redundant. The nobility prevented the exten-sion of such a tax to their landholdings and retained their fiscal exemption, their trading privileges and their extensive seigneurial rights over the peasantry: in effect a policy of divide-and-rule was taking shape, whereby both geographic and social differences could be exploited for political ends.

More direct pressures were applied in the east. During the Swedish–Polish war of 1655–9, Frederick William's position was so precarious that he temporarily had to accept Swedish suzerainty in East Prussia in 1656, then change sides and join Denmark and the Emperor. His elaborate diplomatic twists and considerable military efforts won him little territorial gain at the treaty of Oliva in 1660 but did confirm his full sovereignty over East Prussia. Formal acceptance of this and of his military policies, however, was far from automatic in his eastern possessions. The Estates of East Prussia, meeting in the city of Königsberg, had already in 1661 resisted a curtailment of their right to meet without the Prince's consent. Although they were forced into submission by a show of military force, one of their leaders, Hieronymus Roth, challenged the legality of this move and was imprisoned for life. Eight years later the Estates offered resistance to a grant of military taxation, and another of their leaders, von Kalckstein, was seized from Polish exile by Frederick William's agents and ultimately executed for treason. From 1674, following another military operation against Königsberg, arbitrary fiscal demands no longer met with any open resistance in Prussia, and the permanent pliability of this relatively prosperous province was secured through the creation of a new fiscal bureaucracy partly staffed by Brandenburgers.

Similarly threatening tactics were adopted towards the smaller possessions, including the city of Magdeburg in 1666 and again on its appeal to the imperial court in 1680. Only Cleves and Mark successfully held out for a compromise solution in 1661, backed by the *Reichshofrat* in Vienna, whereby the provincial Estates were to be allowed to continue authorising taxation. The different political and social configuration of these western lands remained a thorn in the side of the disciplinarian Hohenzollern princes: in 1722 Frederick William I spitefully referred to 'the vassals [of Cleves as being] stupid oxen but malicious as the Devil, [while] the people are great intrigants, and false into the bargain, and soak like beasts, that is all they know how to do'.[10]

These minor territories apart, and geographic incoherence notwithstanding, the foundations of the Prussian military state were soon laid with a system of war commissariats collecting and allocating taxes in a fairly standardised way over all the Hohenzollern lands. The army was still modest by international standards (reaching 30,000 men, but on the basis of a population of merely 1 million) and was not yet nationally conscripted, but its organisation, training and domestic disciplinary role were already clear. The cost, however, was considerable, partly in terms of hostility in the localities and partly in terms of a hardening of the divisions within society at the expense of the towns and the peasantry, a trend which became very pronounced over the next century. A more immediate price was also paid, for the Elector's continued dependence on foreign subsidies to pay for his forces, and the resulting tortuous foreign alliances he adopted and discarded as self-interest dictated, eventually landed him in war with Sweden (1674–9). Militarily this was a success, notably at Fehrbellin in 1675 and in the capture of Stettin from the Swedes, but the costs were nevertheless high, and little was gained at the settlement reached at St Germain in 1679. The militaristic orientation of the state had been strengthened, however. Both the War Commissariat and the War Treasury (*Generalkriegskasse*) set up in 1674 gained authority over aspects of economic and commercial development, over the settlement of French Huguenot refugees and over other matters of potential economic significance. But only under Elector Frederick III (1688–1713) were more of the institutional and cultural trappings of princely authority adopted, rounded off with a royal title for ducal Prussia in 1701.

If the newly created Hohenzollern style of government was based essentially on military force, overcoming provincial reluctance by buying off the nobility with concessions or privilege, the Swedish approach, at least until the death of Charles XI in 1697, was entirely different. Both Christina and Charles X may have used the *riksdag* (Estates General) as a political tool, but they did not do so in order to weaken it; Charles X in particular actively sought to broaden support amongst the lesser nobility and to strengthen the natural ties between crown and subject. Because a new regency was required on his premature death in 1660, headed once more by the conciliar aristocracy, a solution to the accruing problems of taxation, state revenue and land distribution was deferred. The Form of Government of 1634 was revived and extended, the aristocratic council once more claimed a decisive role in government, and major new alienations of crown land were authorised. As the Florentine diplomat Count Magalotti observed when visiting Sweden as late as 1674, the council aristocracy had not only strengthened their own material and political position, but had also succeeded in keeping the young king deliberately in the dark, restricting his independence in all matters from military and fiscal ones to the appointment of new members of the council itself.[11] But as early as 1672, when Charles XI attained legal majority, the lesser nobility showed their continuing resentment of aristocratic self-interest by helping to block efforts to impose a stricter charter on him. The other Estates made renewed demands for further *reduktion* (resumption) of crown lands and for wider access to offices. Significantly, Chancellor Magnus de la Gardie's pro-French foreign policy also became increasingly controversial after Louis XIV's invasion of the United Provinces in 1672, which threatened to drag Sweden into war and to bring Dutch retaliation against Swedish trade in the Baltic. Criticisms came to a head at the *riksdag* of 1675, following Sweden's defeat at Fehrbellin and clear warnings of financial weaknesses. Charles authorised the Estates to set up a commission to investigate fully the regency's conduct of government, and the report was complete in time for the end of the war.

The tumultuous *riksdag* of 1680 suggests parallels with the Estates General of 1660 in Copenhagen. The regency, and by implication the council from which it had been drawn, was discredited, while the other Estates were encouraged to believe that a strengthening of the authority of the Crown would be desirable, particularly in the light of the King's personal contribution to the successful conclusion of the war. Leaders of the lesser noble faction, however, forced the issue much further – encouraged by promptings from the King and from some outspoken royalists. Not only was sweeping *reduktion* agreed in order to cover the costs of military reform, but the regency and some of the council aristocracy were judged guilty of abuses of authority and subjected to substantial penalties which fuelled the *reduktion* over the next ten years. At the same time, a number of constitutional points were clarified by the *riksdag* at the King's request: it was confirmed that the Form of Government of 1634 only applied during royal minorities and that the council had no more than advisory status. Above all, it was made clear that there was no restriction on royal authority save that of the fundamental laws of the kingdom.[12]

The *riksdag* of 1680, then, voluntarily confirmed 'absolute' power in the hands of Charles XI. Like Frederick III in Denmark, he and his advisers used the opportunity to consolidate control in key areas, albeit in a more cautious and gradual way than in Denmark. The appointment and ranking of office-holders was brought under closer scrutiny (with a new table of ranks in 1680 to define status and position more clearly), and detailed review of central administrative mechanisms succeeded in consolidating the framework of a centralised state. No less important, the maintenance of a permanent levy of troops was reinforced by means of the *indelningsverk* of 1682, whereby each soldier was allocated a particular district for support and was provided with a cottage for when he was not serving. While respect for the fundamental laws of the kingdom was in practice mostly maintained,[13] the right of free speech in the *riksdag* itself was curtailed by the Crown in 1682, and retrospective censorship of parliamentary records was accepted in 1689. Even the right to consent to taxation became a formality, for by 1693, despite a standing army of 65,000, Charles could present a balanced account without additional grants. Financial recovery had initially been based on economies and harsh taxation, but in the course of the 1680s greater customs revenues and especially the fines on the regency families together with the proceeds of the *reduktion* came to play a major role. Furthermore, the committee in charge of the resumption of crown land assumed more than just an executive role: with royal encouragement, the *reduktion* became a political weapon, causing much bitterness amongst the families of the great. But the support of the lesser nobility was ensured through better access to offices and reliable salary payments, and, remarkably, the magnates who suffered most did not dare form any effective alliance for self-protection, let alone attempt open protest against the sometimes doubtful legal means employed.

Despite this settling of old scores, Charles's quite spartan absolutism from the 1680s to his death in 1697 remained broadly consonant with the strong traditions of Lutheran constitutional legitimacy which were integral to Swedish political life. He presided over a reconstruction of Swedish internal stability and external strength, which is all the more remarkable because it really was driven by a king who (in the words of Tony Upton) 'lacked . . . the capacity for analytical thought . . . lacked imagination and probably never entertained an original or novel idea in his life'.[14] Unlike most of his contemporaries on the thrones of Europe, Charles adopted a realistic and cautious approach in terms of foreign relations, freeing himself not only from foreign subsidies but also ultimately from dependence on the Estates. The result was a consolidation of the kingdom which observers of the traumas of the 1630s and 1670s could scarcely have expected. As it turned out under Charles XII, this consolidation was not permanent, primarily because Sweden could not easily extricate itself from its imperial role. The *indelningsverk* was geared only to peacetime defence and could not cope well with the extensive and endless campaigning over vast distances in the east which were launched after the turn of the century; social tensions reappeared under the enormous strains of these wars, and the new king's temperament was not suited to Swedish traditions of government. That, however, was not predictable in 1697, and Charles XI clearly deserves his reputation for political caution and adherence to simple political maxims, so unusual amongst the crowns of Europe during this period.

The 'political nation' and the Stuart monarchy 1660–88

Despite initial royalist enthusiasm, the English experience from 1660 remained distinctive by continental standards. The Convention Parliament which met in April 1660 immediately invited Charles Stuart to take the crown. But if no conditions were made, even with regard to the early parliamentary gains of the 1640s, that was probably because there was no agreement about how much should be preserved in order to achieve constitutional stability. On the advice of General Monck and of Charles's chief minister in exile, Edward Hyde (originally a moderate MP, but outright royalist from 1642 and later Earl of Clarendon), Charles on 4 April issued a declaration from Breda in which he promised a general pardon, some toleration, and reference of key issues such as the question of confiscated lands to parliamentary discretion. This undoubtedly smoothed the way to the restoration of king and House of Lords, but could do nothing to help settle uncertainty over a number of central issues including religion, the scope of royal authority and the financial arrangements for the Crown. Ominously, while it was estimated that the Crown would require £1.2 million a year to cover its normal expenditures, not even this figure, let alone Charles's own liabilities and outstanding debts to the forces, was met by the parliamentary financial committee. The

Crown immediately began to accumulate new debts rather than attempt to extract more funds from Parliament.

As far as religion was concerned, all the gains of the Commonwealth period were undoubtedly lost. Despite Charles's enthusiasm for a broad church encompassing Anglicans and at least the Presbyterians, the reaction in Parliament was far more extreme. The new Prayer Book of 1662 was narrowly Anglican, and statutes known as the Clarendon Code were passed imposing strict religious conformity on office-holders, educational establishments and, of course, all agents of the established Church. Dissenting clerics were evicted from parishes by August 1662, and further penalties imposed, notably against the Quakers. The King, despite repeated requests for a limited measure of toleration over the next years, had to acquiesce, and in fact came to see advantages in a Church so unreformed that it revived notions even of divine-right monarchy. Opposition to Crown and Church alike was soon explicitly equated with sedition, and the Anglican establishment remained intransigent.

The Convention Parliament and its successor did, however, sort through much of the practical legacy of the previous two decades. In contrast to Scotland, where a new parliament annulled all legislation since 1633 and passed an act of indemnity with a large number of exceptions, the English parliaments were less sweeping. Part of the judicial legacy was validated to avoid chaos, a bill of indemnity back to 1637 was accepted, excluding only the regicides and 30 named republicans: despite much royalist vindictiveness, the complexities of land entitlements were quite successfully arbitrated. Although parliamentary elections were conducted early in 1661 in a mood of growing recriminations and royalist disappointment – raised to hysterical levels when a minor rebellion of Fifth Monarchists under Thomas Venner revived old fears of radical sedition – the resulting 'Cavalier Parliament' in fact included many MPs with enough previous political experience to prevent a complete backlash in matters other than those of the Church. It is clear that the 'political nation' was seeking not to limit the monarchy in principle but merely to prevent a recurrence of the abuse of royal powers. The Commons seems to have been in broad agreement that effective royal power was essential in order to preserve the kind of traditional balance in government that had existed before Charles I.

Accordingly, the Crown recovered its traditional nearly unrestricted rights to call and dissolve parliament itself, to appoint ministers as well as central and local office-holders, and even to control the armed forces (including a small permanent militia). But the aggressive expedients and practices of the 1630s were not authorised, and above all Charles continued to remain shackled by the financial inadequacies of the settlement. Parliament, critical of courtly extravagance and nonchalance, and probably ignorant of the true costs of government, never fully made up the recognised deficit in the income of the Crown. This became all the more serious because the King also failed to achieve consistency of purpose at the centre over matters of routine management. Charles was certainly less conscientious than either Louis XIV or Leopold, but was also too wary to delegate sufficient authority to the closest members of the privy council such as Hyde (Earl of Clarendon from 1661). Obviously he could not be blamed either for the terrible plague of 1665 or for the disastrous Great Fire of London the following year, but these increased the government's difficulties by substantially reducing its income.

Charges of incompetence did arise when the initially popular but ill-conceived war against the Dutch (1665–7) turned into a naval disaster. Parliament covered the costs of this conflict by means of grants totalling £5 million, collected through assessments similar to those of the civil war period, but from early 1666 it also accused crown officers of severe maladministration and corruption. Because the central administration was small, and court politics increasingly riddled with a cynicism and opportunism encouraged from above, part of these criticisms also rubbed off on the King himself. A scapegoat was found in the Earl of Clarendon, who, abandoned by the King, escaped into exile in France. The war brought only minor gains, including the still underdeveloped colonial possessions of New York and New Jersey, but the costs were obvious. Putting the Treasury into Commission (1667) helped to improve efficiency and overall financial control, but was not enough to avoid the suspension of crown payments to creditors on 5 January 1672. This Stop of the Exchequer, as the partial crown bankruptcy was called, emphasised the King's dependence on Parliament for money.

Historians agree that the fluctuations in relations between Crown and Parliament over the next years were in large part a product of Charles's personal policies in matters of religion and foreign relations. He clearly still favoured relaxation of the laws against dissenters, while temporarily accepting the rigid religious attitude of parliament in order to secure generous subsidy grants (1670–1). In the meantime, however, he negotiated a secret alliance with France at Dover which earned him £225,000 a year for joining in the war against the Dutch and another £150,000 to foster Roman Catholicism in England – the latter arrangement was particularly confidential and was apparently inserted at the specific insistence of Charles himself. Perhaps the King hoped to exploit widespread hostility against the Dutch in order to win support for this kind of alliance; perhaps, as some contemporaries feared when they heard of it, Charles hoped to adopt a continental style of monarchy of the kind he had become familiar with during his exile. Whatever the motives, Charles's Declaration of Indulgence

(March 1672) in favour of dissenters was a serious political misjudgement: the prospect of war against a commercial rival became totally overshadowed by another wave of anti-Catholic prejudice and by more vigorous enforcement of the laws against Catholic recusants. Charles was forced to withdraw the Declaration, but this tactical move was outweighed by his brother James openly admitting that he was a practising Roman Catholic. In the absence of a more direct heir, this led to the first moves to limit the authority of, and ultimately exclude, a Catholic successor to the throne. Thanks to Dutch propaganda, public opinion in England was also becoming aware of the dangers of French expansion itself, and a compromise peace was reached with the Dutch in February 1674.

It is by no means clear why, looking at the issues with rational detachment, anti-Catholic prejudices should have been so strong in England by this time – much stronger, for instance, than resentment against Charles's own indolence and cynical opportunism. Research has confirmed that Catholics constituted a very small percentage of the total population, perhaps between 1.5 and 4 per cent, and were in fact both poorly organised amongst themselves and socially well-integrated in the provinces. Public opinion, however, appears to have swallowed pernicious anti-papist propaganda to such an extent that Catholic responsibility for the Great Fire or for the supposed plot to assassinate the King in 1678 (the Popish Plot) was widely believed, despite the total absence of credible evidence. Even many Protestant dissenters dissociated themselves in the 1670s from Charles's efforts to increase toleration for Catholics, and perhaps their attitude became easier to understand as Louis himself increased the severity of his persecution of the Huguenots in France in anticipation of the Revocation of the Edict of Nantes (to which we shall return).

In these circumstances the efforts by Thomas Osborne, Earl of Danby and chief minister from 1674, to smooth relations with Parliament were not, even with careful management and patronage, successful. The Crown's revenues were increased when the government in 1671 took over permanent direct administration of the customs from tax farmers, followed later by the hearth tax and the excise as well. But since Danby was obviously unable to apply his treasury skills to the court itself in order to achieve economies, Parliament remained indispensable for grants. The French alliance, and the absence of any more direct heir to displace the Roman Catholic James, prevented any effective improvement in the Crown's political position, even after the announcement in 1677 of the betrothal of James's daughter and heir, Mary, to William of Orange. The Popish Plot and its sequel of some thirty executions of supposed Catholic conspirators increased the polarisation of opinion. By May 1679 a new parliament, more hostile to the Crown, gave two readings to the first bill to exclude James from the line of succession. An organised opposition movement even formed over the next two years round the Earl of Shaftesbury, formerly a member of the inner court circle. Election campaigns for two further short-lived parliaments (1680–1) generated additional political awareness. Nevertheless, the mood during this Exclusion Crisis was far removed from any substantial acts of confrontation: the opposition was weak, torn by fears of disorders and by memories of 1641, and in any case unable to propose a convincing alternative to James. Unlike his father, Charles was also capable of making concessions, when necessary, to limit the damage done by tactical mistakes.

The dissolution of Parliament in 1681, the last before the death of Charles in 1685, inaugurated a period of stronger personal government which contemporary critics with some exaggeration compared to continental absolute monarchy.[15] Crown control of the judiciary, coupled with the harsh procedures and the heavy penalties associated with treason charges, effectively silenced the opposition. From 1681 London and 57 provincial towns had their charters systematically challenged in law, enabling the Crown and its Tory supporters to gain control of appointments to municipal offices under new charters. And, most important, the King accepted sufficient court economies to secure solvency through the growing customs and excise revenues and through better treasury administration, producing an annual income in the last years of the reign averaging £1.4 million. After James's succession in 1685 – which took place without any signs of disloyalty or obstruction – a new parliament passed resolutions in defence of the State Church, but also allocated funds for the suppression of the rebellions of the Dukes of Argyll and Monmouth against a feared Roman-Catholic autocracy. The Monmouth rebellion, indeed, involved too many 'middling' sorts of people for gentry comfort, and the brutal repression which followed it, including the 'Bloody Assizes' presided over by Lord Chief Justice Jeffreys, was welcomed or at least condoned by the political nation.

Despite this relatively promising start, and the generosity of the Scots parliament as well, James soon generated criticism by virtue of his autocratic and uncompromising temperament and by his pursuit of religious policies that were guaranteed to produce opposition amongst the gentry and in Parliament. He demanded the repeal of legislation preventing dissenters and Roman Catholics from holding central or local office (the Test and Corporation Acts), and roused further suspicions when he announced to Parliament that the army used against the Monmouth rebels would not be disbanded. Co-operation with Parliament seemed increasingly unlikely but, as crown revenues approached £2 million per annum, this was of little importance to the King. From 1686 James tried to win over Protestant dissenters by issuing personal dispensations on a massive scale, and in April 1687 he announced a general Declaration of Indulgence which would in effect suspend the laws against dissenters. Whilst the dissenters initially welcomed this, many Protestants gradually became uncertain and suspicious of the real aims behind this policy, fearing that indulgence was just a cover to introduce French-style Catholic repression. James was clearly more single-minded and obstinately self-conscious than his brother, and a less expert dissimulator. Fears seemed justified when it became clear late in 1687 and early the next year that extensive efforts were being made to secure the election of a new packed parliament which might repeal the legislation against dissenters altogether. After James's second Declaration of Indulgence, issued on 27 April 1688, the failure of his tactics became clear, for Anglicans and dissenters now joined in direct opposition to the Crown's extra-parliamentary pro-Catholic policies and his wholesale interference with local and national power structures. The birth of a male heir to the throne in June, unexpected as it was because James suffered from syphilis, created new prospects of a permanent Roman-Catholic line of succession.

Civil war, however, was still inherently unlikely. The spectre of civil disobedience and disorder stalked all opposition, and critics of the Crown were not well co-ordinated. After the trial and acquittal of seven bishops challenging the legality of James's suspension of parliamentary statutes, an appeal was sent to William of Orange on 30 June, but even this text was tentative, failing to make clear whether the intention was to depose the King or merely to restore parliamentary authority. Once he saw the threat from his nephew William and his daughter Mary, James in September began to make sweeping concessions in policy. He cancelled the writs calling the long-planned parliament, but this move came too late to be regarded as anything other than cynical opportunism and the effect was to increase rather than defuse widening hostility in the political nation. When William could finally carry out the invasion by landing a small army of 12,000 at Torbay on 5 November, many defectors to his side were probably still wanting to force James to abandon his autocratic ways rather than achieve a change of ruler. It was James's total loss of nerve, attempted flight to France, capture, and successful escape on 23 December that ensured that the Jacobite cause disintegrated. Even so, those in positions of influence were careful to prevent violence and disorder, and the parliamentary elections of January 1689 passed off relatively quietly. In February, with the throne deemed 'vacant', William and Mary were declared King and Queen. The Declaration of Rights read to them on this occasion, and the version enacted as the Bill of Rights a year later, either altogether avoided the controversial issues or phrased them in such vague or brief terms that everyone could interpret the settlement as they saw fit.

This 'Glorious Revolution', which effectively handed the Crown to William and Mary unconditionally, leaving the constitution unchanged in all essentials, was an undoubted success as a pragmatic solution to a serious constitutional crisis, but in reality it solved few of the underlying problems which had accumulated during the previous decade. William was known to be authoritarian by disposition and could exploit the fact that there was no viable alternative to his succession, but he was also intelligent enough to see the need to avoid confrontation and he had a team of able advisers. Given William's primary commitment to the European war against France (see chapter 12) and the need for massive parliamentary subsidies to keep England involved, the likelihood of continental-style absolute monarchy in England, if it had ever existed, now in fact clearly disappeared. Complete dependence on parliamentary financial support was very irksome for the King, but it did gradually, despite bitter divisions in the 1690s, force many MPs to familiarise themselves with the real problems of government, encouraging a greater sense of responsibility in the process. James himself had probably had no real designs for continental-style absolute monarchy: he had done little to create the permanent core of administrators dependent on the Crown alone which such a policy would have required and had not attempted the kind of militaristic foreign policy commonly associated with continental kingship. If William's foreign policy was of such a kind, it was defensive in origin and could never have resulted in the use of a land army for domestic political purposes in the style of Louis XIV. Just as the aims of Charles and James had been limited, so in a different way, out of practical necessity, were William's. Once James's forces were finally eliminated at the Battle of the Boyne in July 1690, the domestic political situation was sufficiently stable to enable William to concentrate on the European war. For the first time, England became a major power in Europe. But in the process Parliament gained a more fully integrated role which ensured a political structure totally at variance with the European norm.

Absolute monarchy and the churches

The 'Glorious Revolution' and the decades of uncomfortable settlement since 1660 remind us that religious beliefs had not lost their political potency since the crisis years of mid-century. The difficulties faced by James II/VII in England both before and especially after his succession had much to do with his overall political temperament, judgement and motives, but clearly also had something to do with his efforts to provide a secure place for Roman Catholics in the political life of the kingdom – efforts which stirred up the interminable undercurrents of anti-Catholicism in England. In Scotland, too, much of the unrest after 1660 was fuelled by religious intolerance: the restoration in 1661 of a modified episcopacy and of the system of lay patronage rights in the appointment of ministers ensured that over one-quarter of parish incumbents, altogether 262, refused to take a new oath of allegiance. Like the dissenters in England, they were forced to leave their churches, and in the south-west of Scotland they had sufficiently numerous followings to create continuous unrest. A minor protest movement in 1666 led to partially successful attempts at reconciliation, but in 1679 rebellion broke out which later, in the form of the Cameronians in Galloway, disowned the King and sought to recreate a violent convenanting organisation against episcopacy and against any form of religious tolerance. The attempt to impose a Test Act in Scotland in 1681, based on the Confession of Faith of 1560 but involving serious inconsistencies, created further resentment, particularly in those areas such as the south-west where it was used for overtly political ends by the government. James, who had been commissioner for Scotland before becoming king in 1685, faced as much resistance to his church policies here as he did for different reasons in England, and those presbyterians who took advantage of the Declaration of Indulgence had no intention of defusing religious animosities. Not surprisingly, the Revolution of 1688, bringing as it did the abolition of episcopacy in Scotland in 1690 and a return to presbyterianism, also brought a new wave of religious violence. Far more ministers were ousted than in 1662, and William had little success in moderating the divisive feuding and bitterness that followed.

In most of the continental monarchies, too, religion remained a central element in royal policies. In the Habsburg lands of central Europe the military successes of the 1620s had provided the opportunity for an intensive Roman-Catholic counter-reforming campaign not only in reconquered Bohemia and Moravia but also amongst the formerly strong Protestant communities in Upper and Lower Austria as well (see p. 9). This was all the more readily achieved because of the pronounced territorial and local loyalties there, making concerted opposition unlikely. Leopold, although more tradition-bound in his style of government than his overtly absolutist contemporaries on the thrones of Europe, did complete the task of making Roman Catholicism a fundamental pillar of the state during the later seventeenth century. This is particularly clear in the reconquest of Hungary from the Turks, which became a major crusading issue just as pressure from Louis XIV in the west also mounted.

The Ottoman frontier, not much more than 60 miles from Vienna across a narrow strip of the residual Christian part of Hungary, had been fairly peaceful since 1606, despite some minor incidents and border raids. Renewed activity in Transylvania and in the reviving

Ottoman Empire of the Köprülüs from the late 1650s onwards, however, brought a short Turkish war (1663–4, concluded by means of the Treaty of Vasvar). Perhaps with encouragement from Ahmed Köprülü, Ottoman Grand Vizier (1661–76), restlessness spread amongst the disgruntled Hungarian–Croatian nobility, culminating in the Wesselenyi Conspiracy of Roman-Catholic magnates in 1670. After its defeat, Leopold discarded the promise of liberty of conscience which he had reluctantly made to the Hungarian diet at his election in 1655 and turned increasingly to a selective (loyally Catholic) assembly of notables in lieu of full meetings of the confessionally divided upper and lower houses of the diet. Repressive measures adopted by Vienna against the constitutional and religious privileges of the Hungarian nobility forced many Roman Catholics and Protestants into exile in the Ottoman borderlands, from where increasingly bitter and barbaric border raids in the later 1670s coalesced into the Kurucok rebellion under the leadership of the Calvinist nobleman Imre Thökölly. This, the spread of a serious plague epidemic westwards into Bohemia and Austria, the outbreak of peasant rebellion in Bohemia, and renewed French aggression in the west forced Leopold to make some concessions to the Hungarian magnates and the Protestant towns at the diet of Sopron in 1681. Two years later the whole Habsburg structure was thrown into panic by the major Ottoman attack under Kara Mustafa which led to the lengthy siege of Vienna itself (1683). Thanks to an international army headed by the Duke of Lorraine and John III Sobieski of Poland, the siege was lifted, and this provided the starting point for a massive reconquest of Ottoman Hungary by a 'Holy League' of Austria, Poland and Venice. Thököly was defeated in 1684, Buda retaken in 1686, and Belgrade two years later. The Treaty of Karlowitz (1699) did not end the Habsburg–Turkish struggle but, after another Catholic magnate rebellion led by Ferenc II Rákóczi (1703–11), the Habsburg possession of nearly all of Hungary was eventually consolidated.

Leopold, through no military prowess of his own, thus made considerable gains in territory, potential resources and power. But it was the religious dimension of this conflict which was most important to him, as it had been for his father and grandfather in the empire. Influenced by a number of clerics, including Father Emmerich Sinelli (Bishop of Vienna), Francesco Buonvisi (papal nuncio in Vienna from 1675) and the charismatic Capuchin preacher Marco d'Aviano, Leopold had placed great emphasis on a crusade against the 40 per cent or so of the Hungarian population who were Calvinists or Lutherans. Already, during the aftermath of the 1670 conspiracy, the military government in Hungary headed by Chancellor Hocher, the Hungarian primate Archbishop Szelepcsényi and Bishop Kolonitsch had persuaded Leopold to authorise not only the use of treason trials and lucrative confiscations against Protestant nobles, whether disloyal or not, but also a massive reconversion programme in the towns using 354 Jesuits. In other words, a basically constitutional and political conflict between aristocracy and crown, in which religious minorities had to some extent been used as pawns, was being turned into a simple confessional confrontation. Hundreds of Protestant ministers and teachers were brought before a tribunal headed by Szelepcsényi and accused of treason. Of the 93 refusing to convert, nearly half were sent for penal servitude in the galleys in the Mediterranean. This, and the massive confiscations of Protestant church property ordered by Kolonitsch, became a potent propaganda tool in the hands of the northern European powers. After the barbarous Kurucok conflict in 1679, doubts were eventually cast on the validity of such forced conversions, and concessions were made by Vienna. But the balance remained uneasy: the military measures of General Caraffa from 1686 would have reopened major religious violence had Leopold not made further unavoidable compromises at the diet of Pressburg in 1687.

Because of the strength of Hungarian resistance and the unfavourable international context, 'confessional absolutism' thus never quite succeeded in the 1670s and 1680s the way it had earlier in Bohemia. The underlying aim of religious uniformity, however, was not abandoned. Many Hungarian magnates found it expedient to convert to Roman Catholicism, and the missionary and educational activity of Jesuits and other orders continued both there and in the other Habsburg possessions. Moravia and Silesia had already faced renewed counter-reforming pressures from the 1660s, and hundreds of Protestant churches were closed, for example, in Upper Silesia. In the rebuilding of Vienna during the seventeenth century and especially after 1683, distinctive use was made also of high-baroque architectural and pictorial techniques to emphasise the partnership of church, ruler and nobility in the power of the state.

The attitude of Louis XIV towards the much smaller Protestant minority in France, the Huguenots, and towards church affairs in general, was less sophisticated intellectually, but equally central to the ideology and propaganda of the state. Despite years of a kind of co-existence, there was no support for toleration amongst either the Roman-Catholic clergy or the lay population. Louis regarded the Huguenots, their complete loyalty in the Frondes notwithstanding, as a blemish on the uniformity of the kingdom and from the 1660s leaned increasingly towards a restrictive interpretation of the Edict of Nantes of 1598. Protestant schools and religious ceremonies were curtailed, Huguenots were debarred from office and deprived of protection in the law-courts, mixed marriages were not recognised, and a conversion fund was established to bribe individuals to declare their adoption of Roman Catholicism. In 1679, at Louvois's suggestion, the Crown started using the notorious *dragonnades* (quartering of troops on recalcitrant Huguenot families), and emigration increased despite restrictions. Louis XIV already faced implied criticism from the Jansenists, a puritanical Roman-Catholic group centred at Port-Royal near Versailles itself, and from 1673 he had also come into open conflict with Rome over the use of fees from vacant bishoprics and over matters of protocol. When the Crown issued a rather crude declaration of the position of the French (Gallican) national church, in the form of the Four Articles of 1682, relations with the papacy deteriorated rapidly, culminating in the actual excommunication of the King from 1687 until he backed down in 1693. His attitude towards the Huguenots needs to be seen partly in this context, so embarrassingly inconvenient for a monarch whose claims as '*Rex Christianissimus*' (most Christian king) neither corresponded with any great theological insights nor seemed compatible with his initially clandestine but soon well-known interest in the Turkish challenge to the Catholic Emperor at various stages in that conflict.

Persuaded by Le Tellier and Louvois, by some church leaders and possibly by his devout and determined mistress (eventually second wife), Madame de Maintenon, that the Huguenot problem no longer existed, and hoping also that his tarnished reputation in the Roman-Catholic world would thereby benefit, Louis revoked the Edict of Nantes in 1685. The simple optimism of the actual edict of revocation from Fontainebleau was, however, soon proved erroneous. A massive exodus of an estimated quarter of a million religious refugees, who settled in the United Provinces, Brandenburg–Prussia, England, Scandinavia, the Swiss Confederation and elsewhere, gave an enormous propaganda advantage to all the neighbours of France, already concerned over Louis's territorial aggressiveness (see chapter 12). The damage done to the French economy may have been less than opponents claimed – especially since many Huguenot bankers and entrepreneurs in fact remained behind, even at court – but the émigrés did take significant skills and expertise with them to their new hosts, and became another prosperous and industrious religious minority in the increasingly complex confessional map of Europe. Those that remained behind, especially in the remote Massif Central in the south, caused great difficulties for the Crown during the Camisard guerrilla wars from 1702 onwards. Even the enthusiasm of a number of Roman-Catholic prelates in France itself cooled once the true scale of the operation had become apparent.

The monarchies of late-Stuart England, France and Habsburg Austria thus all had such emphatic religious orientations that upheaval and violence of one kind or another resulted in the 1670s and 1680s. For very different reasons, religion also became a major source of conflict in Muscovy (to which we shall return in chapter 12).

Elsewhere in Europe there was less ground for confrontation: in some cases there were signs of a gradual recognition by the state that limited toleration of religious minorities could be convenient or useful. In Brandenburg–Prussia this recognition came early, out of necessity, because of the conversion of the prince to a faith incompatible with that of his Lutheran subjects. The expulsion of the Huguenots from France gave Protestant governments a particular opportunity of attracting useful subjects by allowing families to settle in specified towns: naturally this was exploited very ostentatiously by Frederick William of Brandenburg–Prussia, and more hesitantly by other Protestant rulers. Remarkably, the Hohenzollerns from 1671 also extended toleration to the Jews, at first on a strictly limited and contractual basis favouring 50 specific families, who were allowed to settle and trade but were banned from worshipping in public. Gradually, the number of Jews settling in Brandenburg–Prussia increased significantly. Genuine toleration became a hallmark of the Hohenzollern territories, well before dogmatic orthodoxy elsewhere had softened sufficiently to enable other governments to adopt similar policies.

With the exception of the Ottoman lands, religious dogmatism was still at the end of the century an essential ingredient in the political make-up of much of Europe. Arguably, absolute monarchy itself depended on religious belief to provide an unqualified ideological justification for a system which otherwise (especially after the political upheavals of mid-century) might seem increasingly open to challenge. Bossuet's *Politics drawn from the very Words of the Holy Scripture* (written mostly in the 1670s, first published in 1709), and the shallow propaganda which shored up the political myths of French absolute monarchy in the later years of Louis XIV's reign, may have produced a satisfying ideological blend for those who wanted to believe, but was hardly likely to convince the doubters. But it also seems inescapable that, during the 1640s and 1650s, the first steps had been taken in the direction of freeing the state from narrow theocratic uniformity in the British Isles and in parts of Protestant Europe. It would be premature to talk of a 'secularisation' of affairs of state, but there were signs of change, and the French policy towards the Huguenots began to look out-of-date within a few years of the Revocation. By then, for those in the diplomatic circles of Europe who had studied Richelieu's *realpolitik*, Louis XIV's religious conventionality was in any case an anachronism. Over the following century, the monarchies of western and central Europe gradually had to construct a new political ideology, more in tune with notional political contracts, which might be used to justify the nature and purpose of government.

12 Power and state-sponsored violence in the later seventeenth century

The decades after the upheavals of the 1640s and 1650s were characterised in the last chapter as a period of at least partially successful government consolidation, assisted by a widespread reaction against the real or feared violence and social destabilisation of the mid-century revolts. Royal or princely authority, for all its dynastic and bureaucratic inadequacies, became accepted in most parts of Europe as a bulwark against social and political anarchy, and, as we have also noted, appeared to serve well the interests of those with wealth and rank. In England, although its worst affected regions had experienced less violence than, for example, the Paris region, Parliament seemed compliant and extraordinarily reluctant to use its recently acquired experience to restrict the Crown. In Sweden the representative machinery was an even more willing prop for absolute monarchy, despite recent political experiences. Elsewhere monarchs rarely had any problems with those institutions that preserved any semblance of independence. Everywhere in Europe the arts, the printed word and rhetoric were used consciously and often systematically to convey messages of order, stability and pompous, princely grandeur. For a time the economic environment, too, was more settled in many parts of Europe, helping to create an impression of relative prosperity, visible for instance in the early years of Colbert's ministry in France.

If circumstances, together with the often redecorated facade of government, appeared to suggest a new era of harmony, the reality was not quite so promising. Dynastic rivalry was a habit that was difficult to break, and monarchs continued to regard warfare as a natural sport or as their God-given duty, sometimes seemingly regardless of the physical consequences on the ground. Although religious beliefs after 1660 were becoming less prominent as the primary cause of war, neither spiritual concerns nor any noticeable sense of international justice dampened the willingness of Christians to fight each other, or to squabble even when, as in 1683, the Ottoman advance to Vienna presented an obvious and potentially overwhelming threat to the south-eastern frontier of Christendom. The bitterness of the Habsburg–Bourbon conflict of the earlier part of the century was continued by Louis XIV in the north-east, along the Rhine frontier with the Empire, and ultimately over the succession to the Spanish Crown itself – at times by methods whereby actual territorial gains were outweighed by the hatred and frustration resulting from the open bullying and completely disproportionate destruction inflicted by what was now the major military power of the west. Because the resources of France were now better marshalled, most other European states found it difficult to avoid being sucked into a succession of conflicts which, especially when severe agrarian crises returned in the 1690s, led to hardship and disasters on a scale comparable in some regions to those of the Thirty Years War. As we shall see, popular revolts and resistance proved less effective than earlier, but this was not for want of good cause. Rather, the resources available to the larger states were now such that domestic challenges could be crushed effectively by military force – all the easier now that rebels tended to be less successful in generating alliances across social barriers than they had been in the 1630s and 1640s. In the more fortunate parts of Europe, conflict could to some extent be externalised: international wars and, where applicable, conflict over trade or colonies could help to draw violence away from the civil community and ensure that others had to pay the price.

Louis XIV and international conflict in Europe after 1660

Although the reign of Louis XIV has been substantially re-evaluated by historians since the 1960s, his central role in the initiation of war throughout most of his reign is difficult to deny. Most of the west European conflicts of the last four decades of the century, apart from the trade wars between England and the United Provinces to which we shall return, hinged on dynastic or treaty claims pursued more or less on the King's personal initiative. Louis throughout was obsessively concerned about the details of diplomatic protocol and rank, and – though hardly alone in Europe in this respect – was addicted to dynastic prestige to such a degree that he could scarcely have failed to precipitate armed resistance. In the words of Robin Briggs, Louis, 'trapped within his own narrow and egoistic vision of the world . . . was almost devoid of one ability essential to a statesman, the capacity to put himself in his opponent's shoes'[1] – and it goes without saying that he was utterly deaf to complaints from his subjects. Assisted by the best diplomatic corps in Europe, Louis took more personal interest in diplomacy (and its concomitant war) than in any other aspect of government. For him it was the obvious and natural means of consolidating the prestige of the kingdom and of his own person (the two being very nearly synonymous in seventeenth-century royalist thinking). The sycophantic atmosphere developing at court, and the apparently total silencing of any effective discussion or criticism of Louis's aims even amongst his more trusted advisers, allowed the King to continue to indulge his conventional notions of honour, reputation and *'gloire'* as long as the military and fiscal machinery could take the pressure. Louis himself, whilst prepared to show personal bravery, wisely reserved actual appearances on the battlefield primarily for ceremonial occasions; he actively exploited the full propaganda potential of war even when, as happened increasingly from the 1680s onwards, campaigns did not in the eyes of less partial observers seem to justify celebration.

Actual military organisation was delegated notably to Michel le Tellier (1603–85) and his son Louvois (1641–91). Between them they achieved substantial reforms by disbanding municipal and autonomous local regiments after 1659 and, over the following years, by means of a gradual standardisation of pay, equipment, supplies and infrastructure through a centralised war office. Adopting some of the techniques of warfare developed more than a generation earlier by Gustav Adolf, the French experimented with flexible battle formations drilled according to the exacting standards of the commander of the royal guards, Martinet. Commanding officers were, in contrast to their mercenary predecessors of the Thirty Years War, put under increasingly careful central supervision in the hope of reducing malversation. On the technical side, a redesigning of French fortresses and siege tactics by Sebastien le Prestre (1633–1707), better known as the marquis de Vauban, proved its worth by the 1680s and, like other aspects of French military organisation, set standards which other European powers could not afford to ignore. While pillage of foreign territory remained customary practice, the improved supply system (when it worked) helped to reduce damage to the home territory. After 1680 the French Crown also adopted comprehensive military–civilian regulations which, together with the rudimentary hospital provisions which the state sought to provide, went some way towards turning the armed forces from a horde of brigands into something slightly more acceptable in contemporary eyes. Progress in most areas, however, was difficult. The standing peacetime army of 50,000–90,000 men in the 1660s cost around 20 million livres a year, and although the impact of undisciplined private mercenary enterprise was somewhat reduced, different problems were created by the impressment of reluctant and often unsuitable 'volunteers' whose rate of desertion before the end of their nominal six years of service was alarmingly high. The royal militia created from 1688 in accordance with conscription practices adopted in other European states was highly unpopular, even though it was intended for local defence only. It generated a village industry of substitutions, whereby beggars and criminals easily ended up in the royal service. At officer level, status and rank were often an obstacle to efficiency, and the commutation of feudal levies failed to provide a fully satisfactory alternative to actual service.

The immediate reasons for war were rarely persuasive. The War of Devolution (1667–8) was launched by Louis on the basis of local property law and the terms in his marriage contract supposedly justifying a claim to the Spanish Netherlands if dowry payments by Philip IV for his daughter were not completed. The more protracted war against the Dutch (1672–9) was prepared and launched by Louis in irate response to the defensive alliance which the United Provinces had reached with England and Sweden after the first war in 1668, and out of resentment against Dutch commercial control of much of even the coastal trade of France. England and later Sweden, bought off from their Dutch alliance, were brought in as not very effective clients of France. The prospect of massive French annexations, however, led to the formation by William of Orange of a new anti-French coalition, and the war was not the military success Louis had hoped for. It produced, at the peace of Nijmegen in 1679, some territorial gains vis-à-vis Spain (notably Franche-Comté), but at the cost both of European goodwill and of the internal financial stability achieved by Colbert. The Dutch for their part strengthened their commercial position.

During this period the international diplomatic position of France overall had been strong. The Westphalian settlement of 1648 had left France in a solid position with regard to the Rhine frontier, effectively separating the Austrian from the Spanish Habsburgs, and the peace of the Pyrenees with Spain (1659) had recognised France as probably the leading military power in Europe. The long-standing alliance with Sweden had been maintained through the negotiations which ended the northern wars of 1655–60 and, although severed in the aftermath of the War of Devolution, was revived later in the regency for Charles XI. England had been of some assistance already in 1657, and the personal contacts secured at the restoration of Charles in 1660 paved the way for the secret Treaty of Dover (1670) against the Dutch. Following Mazarin's attempts to meddle in the imperial election of 1658, France also took part, along with Sweden, Brandenburg and a number of lesser principalities, in the League of the Rhine masterminded by the Archbishop-Elector of Mainz, Johann Philip von Schönborn, to preserve west-German neutrality against Habsburg influence. All these networks cost a significant amount in pensions and bribes, as did extensive military and diplomatic intelligence work in the Rhine area. Funds were also liberally provided for shorter-term contacts with various German princes in the 1670s, and later with the opportunist Elector Frederick William of Brandenburg–Prussia and with the Turks. The point worth emphasising, however, is that France had both the resources and the contacts to exercise a paramount influence on international relations in the period, by whatever means seemed appropriate within the quite elastic contemporary standards of clientage, pressurisation or bribery.

From this perspective French foreign policy reached a watershed in the 1680s. Already the Dutch War could be regarded as a major misjudgement, in that it confirmed an irremediable breakdown of long-standing and mutually advantageous Franco-Dutch relations. William of Orange became an implacable opponent of French ambitions, and although his task was not always easy because of the inconstancy of German politics and the difficulty of maintaining support amongst the wavering Amsterdam patricians themselves, his aims remained the same. In the 1670s the United Provinces had established durable links with the Emperor and with those German princes who were appalled at French ambitions in the Rhineland. The intimidating destructiveness of campaigns such as the one in the Palatinate in 1674 did a great deal of damage – particularly regrettable given the diligent reconstruction that had taken place after 1648 under Elector Karl Ludwig (son of Frederick, the Winter King). The expansive reach of the French military and diplomatic machinery was impressive, saving, for example, Sweden from major losses in the north in 1679. But it became more threatening than ever with the French armed territorial annexations (the so-called *réunions*) in the Rhineland during the period 1679–84 and later. These were based on an imaginative rereading of deliberately vague clauses in the Peace of Westphalia of 1648, judged in the context of complex feudal claims by French courts set up for the purpose (*chambres de réunion*), and imposed against little resistance by the French army. Substantial areas from the Spanish Netherlands south to Alsace were affected. In addition, French forces extended their hold on Savoy, and in 1681 seized Strassburg, a crucial strategic position for the Rhine. It seemed that the principles of international relations established at Westphalia – by what some historians have regarded as the first ever general European peace congress – were being deliberately flouted by one of its main guarantors.

A real shift towards major resistance, however, came only after a series of developments which made compromise difficult. First, Louis notably failed to assist the Christian 'crusade' against the Ottoman onslaught which culminated in the siege of Vienna in the summer of 1683; worse, he actually made contact with the Turks to establish mutual understanding, whilst exploiting the preoccupation of other powers to seize Luxemburg. Although the truce of Regensburg in 1684 confirmed French positions on the Rhine, his contacts with the 'infidels' severely damaged Louis's standing both in Catholic and in Protestant Europe. His attempt to improve his standing in the Roman Church, by persecuting the Huguenots in France and insisting on the crude Revocation of the Edict of Nantes in 1685, not only generated outrage particularly amongst his allies in Protestant Europe but also failed to patch up the already strained relations with the papacy itself.

The pragmatic Elector Frederick William formed an alliance with the Dutch in 1685, and in 1686 the League of Augsburg marked a tentative step towards a framework for co-operation between the major German principalities (including Brandenburg, Saxony and Bavaria), the Emperor himself, Spain and Sweden. The Revocation of the Edict of Nantes also unintentionally helped to destroy James's hold on the English Crown and hence French hopes of assistance from that quarter. By 1687 Leopold, having definitively crushed Ottoman power at Mohacs, could consider turning his now much improved and experienced forces towards France.

Louis had not planned for, and was not expecting, a long conflict when he once more took the initiative for war in 1688. But the second sack of the Palatinate – carried out under orders from Louvois which were so vicious that local commanders tried to evade them – galvanised the League of Augsburg into action. By early 1689 William could, as King of England and soon of Scotland, bring greater resources to bear. Initial parliamentary reluctance for continental war was overcome when it became apparent to the English parliament that, with French protection for James, preservation of the 1688 settlement from Jacobite threats hinged on depriving Louis himself of victory. The resulting Nine Years War (War of the League of Augsburg, 1688–97) consequently had France completely isolated in Europe against seven major opponents and a number of lesser ones. Substantial standing armies were available in Germany partly because it had become fashionable to imitate France itself in this as in other respects, partly because the Ottoman conflict had enabled impecunious princes to keep their forces in order by hiring them to the main belligerents. The smaller states in the western parts of the Empire were now also able to make the most of the regional and interdenominational framework provided by some of the Imperial Circles (*Kreise*), which in 1681 had been entrusted with the organisation and maintenance of imperial armies in those parts where no major principalities were likely to play a dominant role. With the death of the brutal and powerful Louvois in 1691, and the recall of the more moderate Simon Arnauld de Pomponne, Louis may have begun to discover the extent to which his main objectives in Europe were at risk. The kingdom's tax-paying capacity in any case slumped during the famines of the 1690s, and a truce become even more urgent when the terminal decline of the last feeble Spanish Habsburg ruler indicated that a major succession problem was imminent. At the Treaty of Rijswick of 1697, Louis relinquished most of the annexations except Strassburg and opened the way for a remarkably pragmatic solution to the Spanish questions. The alliance of the maritime and the central European powers lost its momentum, but not for long. Complications arising after the death of Carlos II of Spain tempted Louis once more into a major war, that of the Spanish Succession (1701–13), fuelled once more by his interpretation of dynastic claims which could be used to flout existing pragmatic political agreements.

The later seventeenth century witnessed a major political transformation in European international relations. The trend already observed during the Thirty Years War, of lesser princes (such as Bernhard of Saxe-Weimar) losing political autonomy and being forced to 'sell' their military position to a great power, was confirmed. Elector Frederick William of Brandenburg–Prussia, as we have noted, played this game with some cynical success, and some smaller powers including Victor Amadeus of Savoy-Piedmont achieved considerable freedom. But overall, whilst Spain had fallen from the rank of a major power to that of almost a pawn, Louis XIV had not succeeded in establishing a convincing new order. The military capability of the Austrian Habsburgs seemed increasingly slender by comparison with that of France – Emperor Leopold, although basking in success against the Ottoman Empire, failed to exploit this momentum to achieve significant internal consolidation either through closer territorial reorganisation or through forcible reduction of the autonomy and local power of the landed magnates. But international conflict took on new dimensions in the last decades of the century, producing a decidedly secular and pragmatic series of struggles where the Dutch, the Austrian Habsburgs and ultimately also the British Isles came to play decisive roles. Real power was now being asserted through the enormous financial and naval resources not just of the United Provinces but also, quite suddenly revealed, of the British Isles.

Internal opposition and state repression

Wars fought abroad spared the belligerent some of the worst effects, but still cost money. Figures are not available everywhere but it is fair to assume that military and, where applicable, naval costs consumed between two-thirds and four-fifths of all government expenditure, at least in the larger states. The main exception would at first sight appear to be England: its geographic position and isolation from continental conflicts ensured that, even with relatively modest although initially poorly administered naval expenditure, no standing army was normally required – efforts to raise one (as in 1672) were regarded with suspicion and concern by the political nation because of civil war memories. In spite of its limited military commitment, the central administration in Westminster was not particularly small or inexpensive: recently reckoned at between 1000 and 1500 before the civil war, it grew to perhaps 2700 career officials by 1725. The court, with a substantial roll of around 2600 staff under Charles I, had shrunk to around 950 by the early eighteenth century.[2] But even if the cost of this bureaucracy and the court were far from insignificant in terms either of the economy of London or of English taxpayers, it was nevertheless much more predictable and light compared with the army expenditures incurred for instance by the civil war government and by the continental monarchies after 1660. The financial troubles of the first two decades of the Restoration monarchy notwithstanding (see chapter 11), the English Crown also had some protection against outright criticism of fiscal policy in that Parliament had a real say in the allocation of revenue. The effects of this were apparent when military expenditure did suddenly rise, not just during the Second Dutch War, costing over £5 million, but especially during the war against France after 1689, costing ten times as much over eight years and resulting in the imposition of a heavy land tax in 1692. In the intervening periods military and naval expenditure was much lower: the navy could even to some extent be laid up during the winter months and when hostilities were not expected.[3] The kind of opposition emerging in England against the Crown by the 1680s was therefore, as we noted in the last chapter, quite different from the continental norm, in that it arose not out of fiscal or military overburdening but out of the intrinsic nature of the administrative and religious policies of the Crown itself.

For the continental powers, the main expense remained that of defence. The financial drain on the French and Austrian Habsburg treasuries has already been illustrated (see chapter 11), and so has the extent to which the former, in particular, could avoid outright bankruptcy only by resorting to ever more exorbitant short-term borrowing and fiscal sleights of hand – more controlled yet as damaging as those of the 1630s and of the decade from 1648. In Denmark, total crown expenditure during peacetime in the 1680s averaged nearly 3 million rigsdaler, or around eleven times what it had been in the first years of the century: defence accounted for 64 per cent of this, but even court and administrative expenses had quadrupled, not least because of the rapidly growing size of the central bureaucracy itself. The sale of crown lands offered no long-term solution and, in contrast to its Swedish neighbour, the Danish Crown remained on the brink of financial collapse.[4]

In this environment, anti-fiscal protests predictably continued in those parts of Europe where they had been common earlier. In France the insurrectionary mood of the later 1650s, particularly evident in the west, from Anjou on both sides of the lower Loire to the Angoumois, spread in the wake of the poor harvests of 1661–2 further south into the Limousin. The Pyrenean province of Béarn was soon also seriously affected, and a few years later, in 1668–70, parts of the intervening Guyenne and of the Languedoc (in particular Vivarais) had their turn. The Boulonnais in the far north was in revolt against crown demands in 1662, parts of Normandy and Brittany in 1672, and Brittany and Bordeaux on a major scale in 1675. Further minor unrest occurred in the south in 1677 and in Burgundy as late as 1680. After a lull, trouble resumed in the 1690s, though not on a scale comparable to the 1620s and 1630s.

Colbert's great enquiry of 1664 had clarified some of the underlying local problems, but no substantial reforms were attempted beyond the removal of certain fiscal abuses, a significant reduction of the *taille* burden and his deliberate efforts to rely on the less tangible forms of indirect purchase taxes. Considerable evidence indeed suggests that there was little confidence amongst *intendants* in the 1660s that stability could be maintained, and this may explain the severity with which the Crown reacted to insubordination. Repression by armed force became the norm, often followed by a condemnation of large numbers of peasants to forced labour in the galleys. Some 400 of the Boulonnais peasant rebels of 1662 were sent off to Toulon in irons, and eight innocent burghers of Boulogne were ordered into exile as exemplary punishment to avoid further resistance to fiscal demands. No less traumatically, the four-month popular insurrection in Bordeaux in 1675, directed against new excise taxes on pewter household utensils and on tobacco, resulted in the quartering of 16 regiments of troops on the city for several months, and the loss of substantial fiscal privileges. The Parlement in the city was exiled, although there is little evidence that it had encouraged the rebels in any way. But most serious of all was the revolt of the Torrébens in Brittany in 1675, sparked off by events in Bordeaux and caused by similar grievances. Both Rennes and Nantes became uncontrollable, and a peasant force of 6000 men sacked a number of rural châteaux. A gruesome repression by 16,000 regular troops was launched as soon as the war in the Netherlands allowed, and the Parlement was exiled from Rennes indefinitely.

Few of the participants in these revolts were of any social rank or status: the occasional noble leader (in the Boulonnais and Béarn risings) turns out on closer inspection to be an impoverished adventurer with no conspiratorial connections, and townsmen with any property or wealth were invariably frightened by and hostile to the aims of the rebels. This applies even to events in Brittany in 1675; although there had been complaints amongst the legal profession against the introduction of stamp taxes on official documents, the real cause of rioting was the repressive and arbitrary nature of seigneurial jurisdictional rights, together with the heavy burdens of tithes, *champarts* and banalities on the peasant population. It is clearly of the greatest significance that, although the robe had resented encroachments on their venal rights as office-holders and had been explicitly disciplined by the Crown in 1666 and in 1673, they failed to make any common cause with the popular rebels of 1675. The exile of the Parlement of Brittany from Rennes, therefore, may again not have been strictly justified; it was part of the Crown's wider desire to create deterrents against local insubordination, rather than a practical punitive measure.

The revolts of the 1660s and 1670s, in remarkable contrast to those of the 1630s and 1640s, thus failed to develop a cross-class dimension. Very often royal demands merely precipitated the hostility of the poor against the better-off within a locality, and such disjointed opposition was easier to handle for the Government. Crown policies towards noble, financier and office-holding groups (see chapter 5) seemed effectively to have deprived popular rebels of backing from other social groups, and the regular troops sent in as soon as international military commitments allowed were more often than not welcomed by the local establishment. Moreover, closer examination of crown policy suggests that Colbert in a number of instances deliberately magnified the scale of opposition in order to have a freer hand to quash local privileges. It is not, therefore, so much a reduction in the number of incidents and riots that we observe after 1660 – the subsistence riots of the terrible famine years in the 1690s suggest otherwise – but a disappearance of the leadership formerly provided by members of more privileged social groups. Without that leadership, opposition proved difficult to organise and sustain. In addition, the monarchy had now reached the point where its military resources were sufficient to control any unrest caused by the fiscal burden; in other words, taxation generated more real power than it caused effective opposition.

Very similar conclusions are reached if we look at the Spanish monarchy. There anti-seigneurial grievances had never been completely supplanted by fiscal ones, as had happened in France during the ministry of Richelieu. The Valencian revolt of 1693, for instance, continued a long tradition in being primarily a confrontation between landowners and deeply impoverished peasants. More relevant in the present context, therefore, is the series of major disturbances in Catalonia in the period 1687–90. As noted earlier (see chapter 7), Catalonia had not lost its privileges after the attempt to break away from the Habsburg monarchy in 1640, and relations between the provincial capital Barcelona and Madrid had become very harmonious. In 1687, however, locusts destroyed the harvest over large parts of the province, and the peasantry began to demand concessions on military contributions together with an end to the billeting of troops stationed there as part of anticipated hostility against France. The peasantry and the lesser townsmen undoubtedly bore a disproportionate share of these military burdens. The better-off were able to secure exemptions and seemed little concerned –

indeed, three members of the *diputacio* (Estate committee) who protested on the basis of traditional Catalan privileges were regarded as troublemakers and removed. Popular resentment rose, however, and by April 1688 a force of 18,000 well-supplied *segadors* (peasant rebels) assembled outside Barcelona: having won major concessions from the frightened government they proceeded to occupy much of the province during the summer.

A good harvest defused the situation temporarily, but in April 1689 attempts to collect a 'voluntary' army contribution led to renewed resistance. A greater number of communities became involved than had been the case even in 1640. More seriously, some leaders of the *segadors* gained the support of the French authorities across the border in what could well have turned into a replay of 1640. By the autumn, crown troops were being disarmed by the rebels in the countryside, and late in November a force of 8000 rebels once again encircled Barcelona. The new viceroy, however, launched a military counteroffensive which ultimately, after several very bloody confrontations, disposed of the *segador* leadership and the demoralised, inadequately armed peasantry. Half-hearted attempts were made in 1690 to revive the movement with French support, but no further serious trouble occurred until 1705. As in France, the complete failure of the gentry to support or even sympathise with rebel demands in 1689 had proved decisive: the loyalty of the *diputats* in Barcelona was in fact so complete that they were given a special token of royal gratitude in February 1690. In such circumstances it is not surprising that even a large force of rebels, led by commoners of substance in the countryside, had had little hope of success.[5]

Apart from the urban conflicts mentioned in chapter 6, and the tensions resulting from the upheavals around Poland in the 1650s, central Europe appears to have been less prone to confrontations capable of threatening the authority of local or central government. Part of the explanation obviously lies in the decentralised nature of political authority in the Empire after the Peace of Westphalia: when additional impositions were required for military purposes the reasons were often accordingly more obvious, as in the case of those in southwest Germany against Louis XIV in the 1680s. In the Habsburg lands proper, where the Turkish threat created more continuous and extensive fiscal demands, opposition was nevertheless muted. Open resistance tended to take other forms, as in Hungary over the Crown's religious policies (see chapter 11), or, unsurprisingly, it was directed primarily against the all-powerful authority of the landowning elite. The annual meetings of the Estates both in Lower Austria and in Bohemia, and the absence of any attempts by Leopold to reduce their consultative and administrative powers, ensured fairly stable relations between the gentry and the Crown, and ensured that the gentry, who defended their collective interests through these institutions, also became the main target of commoner grievances. Thus the peasant revolt in Bohemia in 1680 (see p. 266), in contrast to the revolts in the Austrian lands in the 1620s, was not a direct challenge to the state except in so far as the Emperor had delegated most of his judicial and administrative authority to local seigneurial interests. The resulting decree on labour services was an important precedent for the future but, since its terms were contingent on effective implementation of legislation by the Bohemian Estates, it was unlikely to have immediate practical consequences. In any case, the exemplary execution of peasant leaders, which had already been carried out, left no one in any doubt about the mutual dependence of state and landowner.

The receding eastern frontier: Russia

Some years after travelling in Muscovy on official business in the later 1630s, the Holsteiner diplomat Adam Olearius published a widely read account of his observations in which amongst other things he wrote:

> But the present grand prince [Alexis], while retaining the power just as the tyrants before him to use force against his subjects and their property, does not act in this way, although others, probably on the basis of older authorities ... have written and still write of the appalling conditions which the Russians suffer under the iron sceptre of the tyrants. Much that is written in a similar vein about the Russians is no longer so nowadays, no doubt because of the general changes of the times, the regime, and of the people concerned. The present grand prince is a devout man who, like his father, would not let any of his peasants be impoverished.[6]

While the historian might question the validity of the last comment, there is no doubt that the later seventeenth century brought not only significant change in the style of government in Muscovy but also gradually more contact with the west. Peter I (Peter the Great, 1689–1725) has earned a historical reputation both as creator of the Russian Empire out of the old Muscovy and as an avid if selective 'westerniser' of Russian technology and upper-class lifestyles. But, as is so often the case, much of the groundwork had already been done before him.

Because of internal instability and the recurrent conflicts not only with Poland but also with the Tatars and Cossacks, the early years of Alexis (1645–76), like those of his father Michael, had been highly uncertain (see chapter 7). The Tsar was theoretically an unrestricted autocrat with both sacral and patrimonial authority, responsible for all appointments, the source of all law and entitled to tax and demand services without limit, in addition to being a major landowner. He was endowed with the real power of life and death over even the highest nobility, whose tradition of addressing themselves to him as 'slaves' was not just an empty formality. In contrast to western concepts of monarchy, there were no restrictions on the power of the Tsar either by virtue of legal traditions and fundamental law or by virtue of corporate rights and privileges amongst groups of subjects. Together with the patriarch the Tsar was also, by virtue of his office, an active spiritual head of the Russian Orthodox Church – far more deeply so than his western counterparts were of their State Churches. Describing the Tsar as a despot (as many of the writers of the eighteenth-century enlightenment did) was therefore an accurate way of distinguishing him from all other European rulers except perhaps the Ottoman Sultan. As always, however, practical reality was not quite so simple: the Tsar had to preside over an advisory *duma* (council) of between 20 and 60 representatives of the Moscow boyars, the appanage princes, the higher and lesser servitors and the church leadership, all of whom, while lacking any corporate autonomy, sought to exercise some influence especially on appointments, legislation and foreign affairs. While the representative body of the *zemsky sobor* lost its significance after giving its approval to the 1649 Code and recognising the annexation of part of the Ukraine in 1653, the administrative class (*prikaznye liudi*) retained a very considerable influence through the highly departmentalised bureaucracy.

The inadequacies of the routine-dominated traditional *prikazy* (chanceries), which were left untouched or even reinforced by Filaret and Michael, were sufficiently obvious to Alexis for him to attempt some restructuring. In 1654, for example, he established a Privy (or Secret) Chancery designed to function more flexibly and efficiently, and since no subject in Muscovy, not even the greatest boyar, could lay claim to any absolute rights or entitlements whatever, Alexis was freer than his western counterparts would have been to make what use he wished of this new office. The Privy Chancery remained under his personal control and, despite its small size, came to handle a wide range of matters important to the Tsar, including not only the management of a large share his resources and of his landed estates but also much of his correspondence. The office also had a pivotal role in many of the innovations whereby Alexis provided precedents for his more famous son, Peter: the import and control of foreign books, the creation of new military formations under foreign mercenary guidance, the adaptation of western technology in the mining and arms industries, and the building of a fleet on the Caspian Sea using western shipwrights.

Despite the far more emphatic claims of tsarist divine right, governmental authority was at least as seriously challenged in Muscovy as in the west: there were recurrent problems of unrest even after the repression of the 1648–50 revolts. The Copper Riots of July 1662 in Moscow, for instance, involved a range of grievances not unlike those of 1648, catalysed by attempts to cover military expenditure by means of a substantial devaluation of the currency. There was also resentment against the burden of military conscription and the attendant severity of disciplinary measures against commoners and servitors alike. Once more, however, crowd hostility was focused on specific officials who had to take the blame both for the deliberate devaluation and for the general hardship. More serious was the Cossack revolt (1667–71) led by Stenka (Stepan) Razin, bringing together a large peasant army which entrenched itself firmly in the lower Volga region. The Cossacks, with their violent but fairly free social organisation, were an antithesis to the rigidity and subservience of Muscovite society; as noted, serfdom both in Russia and in Poland was to a large extent a response to the flight of peasant manpower to the Cossack Ukraine and further east. Razin not only attracted support because of his demand for social equality and for the end of seigneurial exploitation but also had the ability to consolidate his command to such an extent that Moscow itself appeared threatened. Like others before and after, Razin provided ideological justification for his rebellion by claiming that a son of Alexis (who had in fact died) was under his protection. He was eventually cornered in Astrakhan, arrested (significantly) by Cossacks loyal to the Tsar, and taken to Moscow for execution. However, although his followers were killed in large numbers, Cossack insubordination persisted over the following decades.

The armed forces, and in particular the *streltsy* (musketeers permanently stationed in units all over Muscovy), assumed a major political role during periods of political uncertainty. The *streltsy* probably constituted between a third and a quarter of the 160,000-strong Muscovite army in 1678 (in a total population of around 9 million) but most of the rest of the armed forces had by then been 'modernised'.[7] The *streltsy*, having already taken a minor part in the unrest of 1648, became more restless as their military role was increasingly outdated. On the death of Alexis's rather weak son Feodor (1676–82), they presented grievances over pay and conditions and then engineered a coup that led to Sofya's co-regency (1682–9) for her retarded brother Ivan V and her young half-brother Peter. The regency was intrinsically an unstable arrangement because of factions behind each family, and the unsuccessful campaigns of 1689 in the Crimea emphasised the political and financial strains. It was rumours of impending *streltsy* intervention in August 1689, however, that precipitated the preventive action by Peter and his entourage, culminating in the relatively bloodless removal of Sofya's administration. The disruptive influence of the *streltsy* came to a head during Peter's visit to the west in 1698 and, although 130 ringleaders had already been hanged and the units disciplined by the time of his precipitate return, he insisted on conducting further investigations in order to implicate other elements of opposition in Moscow. Two bouts of mass executions followed, totalling around 1000 men and carried out with a display designed to maximise the deterrent effect. The rest of the *streltsy* were reassigned to often dangerous duties elsewhere, but not yet in fact disbanded, despite the substantial military reorganisation attempted by Peter after his first initial defeat by Sweden in 1700.

These challenges from inside could be dealt with in a practical way, especially in a society as deeply divided and as rigidly hierarchical as this. But the rulers of Muscovy faced other less readily tackled problems. One was the cultural and religious conservatism of most Muscovites, so deeply engrained that any kind of change, especially that inspired from abroad, was suspect. Western influences on Muscovy had come first via Poland, producing a violently xenophobic and anti-Catholic reaction clearly apparent well before the Polish threat ended in the 1650s. By then contacts had been made with the Scandinavian Lutheran powers, in particular through the Swedish university founded in Estonia in 1632 and via the many north European mercenaries (including the Scots Alexander Leslie and, after 1661, Patrick Gordon) who took up service in the Muscovite forces. A German drill book was used in Muscovy from 1647, and foreigners continued to play a crucial role in the modernisation and expansion of the Muscovite army. No less influential were the English, Dutch and German merchants who came to constitute the 'German quarter' outside Moscow, regularised by decree in 1652. These contacts, together with those of the influential Office of Embassies dealing with the still non-permanent Russian missions in western capitals, began to bear significant fruit in the later years of Alexis. His second wife, Natalia Naryshkina, was herself of Scottish descent and became an important influence towards liberalisation. Western merchants and manners were still officially regarded askance – witness the restrictive Commercial Code of 1667, or the decree of 6 August 1675 prohibiting the short hairstyles and dress fashions of the west – but the active patronage of men such as Prince Vasily Golitsyn, adviser and later lover of Sofya, ensured some acceptance of western intellectual and literary influences. Golitsyn also introduced an element of humanity into Russian politics, lasting until his fall together with Sofya in 1689.

The hostile conservatism which such change met must not be underestimated, least of all within the Orthodox Church. Nikon, the Metropolitan of Novgorod raised by Alexis to the office of patriarch in 1652, had favoured reform and modernisation of certain aspects of the Orthodox liturgy and beliefs, and had aimed to replace the anti-quated Church Slavonic (otherwise long since extinct) with the vernacular. A patriarchal printing press established in Moscow in 1645 had helped to further some educational progress both within the clergy and more widely; a new printed service book was issued soon after Nikon's promotion, together with a revised psalter intended to bring church discipline and observance more closely into line with that of the Greek Orthodox Church. This generated resis-tance from some of the conservative nobility, the clergy and others. A group of fundamentalists, led by Nikon's erstwhile ally Avvakum, set themselves up as defenders of what later became known as the Old Believers, opposed to all change and to foreign influences generally, including the use of instrumental music and representational art in churches. The remote and well-endowed monastic institution at Solovetsk was openly hostile to reform from 1657 onwards, culmi-nating in a siege by government forces from 1668 to 1676. Clashes of personality and authority between Alexis and Nikon, leading to a clear breach by 1658, added a further complication to this schism (known as the *Raskol*). The church council of 1666–7, excommuni-cating the uncompromising fundamentalists, also formally deposed and exiled Nikon himself for his theocratic beliefs, while accepting many of the reforms he had initiated. This kind of compromise, however, did little to heal the deepening division in Russian spiritual life, and Avvakum and the Old Believers remained a major cause of disaffection and outright revolt, especially in remoter regions and amongst the uneducated clinging to old forms of popular religious observance. In some circles the Tsar himself became equated with Antichrist. This provided religious justification for total non-cooper-ation with the state, and for the political insubordination amongst the less devout, for instance by the *streltsy* in 1682. In 1684 the Government responded by making adherence to the schism a crime under the secular courts punishable by death.[8] In short, government control of the loyal sections of the Church was undoubtedly being strengthened, in anticipation of Peter's more drastic reforms; but the State Church, despite the intentions of the reformers in seeking moral regeneration, was shorn of much of its vitality. And, in contrast to the relationship between absolute monarchs and the Church in the west which we noted in the previous chapter, the beliefs of the Russian Orthodox Church could not simply be incor-porated into the official ideology of a centralising state – rather, open conflict led to the estrangement of an important section of the estab-lished church from tsarist authority, and exclusion of some elements within Russian society from the potential benefits of wider access to new ideas and input from abroad.

Military consolidation and state power

Gradual (if sometimes reluctant or qualified) acceptance that the state was acquiring a kind of monopoly on the exercise of legitimate force was probably the most dramatic aspect of seventeenth-century absolutism. Such a message was reinforced through efforts to confront and reduce particular and corporate power bases within the state, whatever form they took and whenever they appeared to present an active threat to central government. As we observed earlier, it was essential for governments to minimise the risk of armed alliances between provincial magnates and discontented commoners. This in turn required the gradual elimination of aristocratic feuding, the removal of private fortified strongholds within a state and the absorption of private noble armies into those of the state. In France the affirmation of this trend is associated with the period between 1598 and 1672, and especially with the ministry of Richelieu and the early years of Louis XIV. Although, as we have seen, rebellions did not die out immediately, their nature changed: without factional aristocratic leadership, rebels had little chance against the enormous armed forces which Louis XIV could redeploy domestically as well as against foreign enemies. Pacification of a kind is also observable in the Austrian hereditary lands, despite the fact that Leopold's style never matched that of his French counterpart and that he could no longer deal effectively with princely ambitions (territorial absolutism) within the Empire. Even more remarkable, in the aftermath of the upheavals of the middle decades of the century and in the absence of an effective monarch from 1665, is the relative quiescence of the Spanish lands, but there, significantly, aristocratic independence was not checked. In the Scandinavian kingdoms consolidation of a kind had already been achieved in the first quarter of the seventeenth century, reaffirmed later in Danish absolutism after 1660 and in Swedish retrenchment under Charles XI. As we have noted, developments in Russia do not lend themselves readily to European comparisons, yet the extraordinary changes imposed by Peter the Great certainly both reduced the autonomy of the elite and greatly increased the military–naval power of the state. So, allowing for the territorial tendencies prevailing in the Holy Roman Empire and the weakness of the Spanish monarchy, most of Europe except Poland matched the trend towards stronger central government with more effective military control.

By the second half of the century, the age of the uncontrolled military entrepreneur and his freebooting mercenaries was also drawing to a close. It became rarer for troops to pose a real threat to the government that had hired them. There was no successor to Wallenstein, even if lesser heads of state continued to serve as paid junior partners in the conflicts of bigger powers. Admittedly the commanders-in-chief of post-1660 warfare were no less interested in personal profit and no less corrupt than their predecessors, but accountability to the state was an at least theoretical requirement, even for such unpalatable figures as Louvois. The disciplining of troops was not achieved overnight, nor (as the Palatinate discovered) was damage to civilian property a memory of bygone marauding and pillaging mercenaries, but the nature of warfare did change in the century from 1640. Protracted siege warfare became far more common by comparison with pitched battles. The infrastructural and logistic requirements of elaborate fortifications and siegeworks in themselves ensured greater professionalism and technical investment, increasingly making the old feudal military contribution of the nobility redundant and encouraging some standardisation of practices within larger army units.

Private enterprise was by no means eliminated from army supplies, but was increasingly subdivided between different contractors and subjected to at least notional state control. Nor was the hiring of foreign mercenaries abandoned, despite the risk of using men who might casually move from one side to another in search of an employer with money to spend. Yet something resembling state-controlled military conscription came to play a greater role in the supply of reserves and local militias, not just in Sweden through the permanent *indelningsverk* but also on a more random and temporary basis in Denmark in 1676, in Louvois's militias of the later 1680s and in other European states after the turn of the century. The transition was anything but smooth, and the early precedents for compulsory military service revealed many obvious drawbacks in terms of both discipline and popular reaction. Indeed the standards attainable with a regiment of 'adulterers, fornicators, thieves, murderers, drunkards [and] sabbath breakers'[9] might not look promising, and desertion would probably ensure that any achievement was in any case temporary. Morale amongst recruits was further damaged by the fact that, except in periods of starvation, the difference between 'voluntary' enlistments achieved by press-gangs or 'bounty' payments on the one hand, and actual conscription as a social remedy and as kind of labour service to the King on the other, must at times have been anything but obvious. For these reasons a full-scale individual obligation to serve the state could not become established in western Europe until well into the eighteenth century, in France not unequivocally until 1792.

The cost of armies, whatever their provenance, constituted a very large share of the state budget, probably 75 per cent in France in the 1690s and during the War of the Spanish Succession (not counting the navy), and even more it seems in England during the 1650s or in Petrine Russia. Some of the expenditure might have been regarded as long-term investments in security: for example, Vauban's colossal fortifications along the eastern border of France. In peacetime some costs might also have been covered by hiring out regiments to active belligerents, enhancing the already very cosmopolitan nature of most continental armies. But from the 1670s onwards, as the international situation deteriorated, this option was open to fewer and fewer states. The decision of the French government in the 1690s to reduce its direct expenditure on the fleet by relying increasingly on organised privateering, even hiring out its own ships to entrepreneurs in this dubious field, was an attempt to shift the naval burden instead. By contrast, Peter I in 1696 undertook the construction of a new navy from scratch in a prodigious effort of autocratic power-building. The colossal English investment in naval development from mid-century, resulting in a fleet of 323 warships of varying sizes by 1697, may have been more fruitful in terms of employment and technology than the 90,000 troops in English pay by that date, yet here as elsewhere the burden of such large standing commitments required considerable fiscal foundations.

Just how favourably the Ottoman military machinery might have compared with Christian Europe in terms not only of men in the field but also of infrastructure, fiscal support mechanisms and civilian acceptance of the resulting burdens during the seventeenth century is difficult to establish, partly because the basic system was so different. As we noted in chapter 7, the personal military role of the Sultan diminished significantly in the early years of the century, but there was no significant decline of real military power. Effective campaigns were fought in some of the eastern regions of the Empire, even when the European frontier was relatively quiet, and the military revival under the Köprülüs after mid-century demonstrated that the Ottoman state remained one of the most effective militarised states in the world. Unlike in the west, the Ottoman army was built round Janissary regiments consisting of specially trained men who as youths had been collected from all over the Empire (and from all religious denominations) as elite slaves. Highly organised, and motivated by the considerable rewards attainable through distinguished service irrespective of social background, these regiments were supported by a bureaucracy which was still (despite some problems) capable of distributing the huge resources of the Empire effectively. However, the Ottoman educational system may not have facilitated such ready absorption of new military thinking and innovative technology as was possible in the best western armies. Supportive industrial development was also slower than in the most entrepreneurial regions of Europe, and the Empire lacked room for the scale of economic expansion necessary to meet new challenges. However, these problems did not really become apparent to outsiders until after the failure of the siege of Vienna in 1683, and further research is needed before we know whether the subsequent gradual retrenchment in the Balkans led to significantly increased problems of local resistance to state demands.

If the Ottoman system seems not to have exercised much practical influence on other European powers, the extraordinary military and naval escalations of Louis XIV's later years undoubtedly did – sometimes compelling and sometimes tempting monarchs to ignore domestic problems. Ultimately, in Brandenburg and East Prussia, in Burgundy, or in Bohemia, the central government could now successfully deploy troops to secure domestic obedience. Fiscal demands were thus both a cause of popular resistance and (once standing armies were inevitable) the means whereby effective repression could be achieved. The dwindling significance of representative institutions, coupled with the tightening of judicial control in many of the monarchies of Europe, can be regarded as further symptoms of this new militarised absolutism. But even the most self-intoxicated monarch realised that absolutism could never mean autocratic confrontation with the upper ranks of society. As Louis XIV demonstrated in his better years, success depended on a careful mixture of style, strength and appeal to self-interest.

Commercial rivalry in Europe and overseas

The decades after the middle of the seventeenth century also confirmed the wider economic and commercial reorientation in Europe and overseas which had been apparent for some time. The importance of Dutch shipping and financial expertise both in undercutting Mediterranean producers of quality goods and in developing the resources and trade potential of the Baltic have already been emphasised (see chapter 4). This, added to long-standing rivalry with the English overseas (notably in the East Indies, in North America and in the Caribbean), and competition over fishing grounds, was certain to lead to friction between the two maritime powers once the end of the Thirty Years War deprived English merchants of their advantages as neutral wartime traders. Dutch freight rates were still far more competitive than English ones, causing concern even in the North American trade. Following earlier initiatives, the Rump in October 1651 therefore approved a Navigation Act which, in requiring all imported goods to arrive in English vessels or in vessels from the producing country, was a direct attack on the Dutch carrying trade. The first Anglo–Dutch War (1652–4), despite the English seizure of a substantial number of Dutch ships, was fairly inconclusive. In 1660, however, the Convention Parliament passed a Navigation Act which in some respects was more sophisticated in dealing, for instance, with the registered ownership of vessels in order to control Dutch evasion tactics. A treaty with the Dutch in 1662 did not iron out major differences, and in 1663 a Staple

Act imposed equivalent restrictions on goods exported to the English colonies. With various pressure groups at court and in the English East India Company calling for action, the slide into the second Anglo-Dutch War from 1664 was a largely uncontrolled but popular move which the Dutch were not in a position to avoid. New Amsterdam (later New York) was taken by the English in 1664 and, while of little immediate importance, eventually made it easier to reduce Dutch participation in the North American trade. In Europe, however, England was soon isolated. Destructive engagements during the summer of 1666 led to serious and not always realistic criticisms in Parliament, turning to outrage after the Dutch raid up the Medway in June 1667 destroyed docks at Chatham and a large stock of shipping. The second war, for all the prizes taken, also produced a deficit of nearly half a million pounds sterling, which contributed to the financial crisis of the English Crown noted earlier (see p. 386).

Trade wars, it is clear, were from 1660 onwards beginning to loom far larger in international relations than ever before. French resentments against Dutch maritime dominance led to a set of preliminary tariffs imposed by Colbert in 1664 in an effort to strengthen domestic shipping and industry. Tightened in 1667 and during the period 1670–1, these protectionist measures not only hurt the Dutch, whose attempted retaliation in kind was counterproductive given their reliance on free trade in Europe, but also damaged English merchant interests. Yet the temporary European realignment which brought the two maritime powers together in 1668 against Louis XIV predictably did not last, since none of their own underlying resentments had been dealt with. This was apparent in the initial popularity in London of the third Anglo-Dutch War (1672–4) which, despite the wider political and religious implications of the association between Charles and Louis, did not by the time of the indecisive Treaty of Westminster (1674) lead to particularly constructive dialogue between England and the United Provinces. Shared anti-French and anti-Catholic sentiments alone were at the root of the alliance of the maritime powers, yet some positive commercial considerations did ultimately ensure that the respective economic interests of the two maritime powers became genuinely less incompatible in the last decades of the century.

Dutch commercial strength was in part built on circumstances that were not lasting. Although the Dutch were not yet outnumbered in the Baltic trade (see chapter 4), the staples of that trade could be neither controlled nor monopolised. Western demand for grain was less reliable after 1660, with the British Isles, for instance, becoming temporarily self-sufficient. The shipbuilding techniques of the Netherlanders were already being imitated by others, particularly easily by the English after their seizure of a substantial number of vessels in each of the wars. The dynastic conflicts of the period also began to take their toll on the commerce of both maritime powers after 1689, and it was only natural that merchants should seek other routes: Hamburg in particular became a serious rival to Amsterdam as an entrepôt for north-European commerce. On a more fundamental plane, the political developments of the period after 1660, in particular the protectionist tariff systems developed by England and France and increasingly backed by military force, created an environment deeply alien to Dutch priorities and interests. Already, during the second quarter of the century, the Dutch had proved highly vulnerable to organised attack on their shipping interests by the Spaniards. Although the Dutch Republic learnt from Cromwell, it had neither the constitutional framework nor the resources of manpower and taxation to compete on equal military footing in the long run. Even the invasion of England in 1688, and the conclusive harnessing of English foreign policy as part of the anti-French alliance led by William of Orange, failed to produce clear answers for Dutch commercial interests.

A long-term shift in the worldwide economic balance of power towards the British Isles, clear by the eighteenth century, can be traced back to the seventeenth century, not just in terms of these European circumstances but also in the light of various overseas factors. The most significant of these was the growth in north Atlantic trade, involving several triangular routes but pivoting partly on the North American colonies and partly on the West Indies. The New England settlements, created in the 1620s by Puritans wanting to avoid persecution at home, developed a diversified economy; further south the highly successful cultivation of tobacco had turned the initially difficult colonisation of Virginia into a substantial economic success. Both areas, starting completely from scratch, in turn facilitated the development of the lesser West Indian islands, initially through tobacco and later through sugar cane, together with some cotton. Both crops made heavy demands on labour, which was provided partly through the more or less voluntary migration of indentured poor (who were forced to work off their travel costs over a period of years) and partly by means of a rapid growth in the slave trade. Several English ports other than London came to play a decisive role in this trade network, whose growth was spectacularly fast by comparison even with the traditional East Indies trade. By the middle of the seventeenth century, as England began to exclude other nations by force, this north Atlantic trade provided the basis for a rapidly increasing re-export sector to northern and western Europe. As the population of the North American settlements increased (there were probably 275,000 settlers by 1700), a ready market was also created for English exports. The North American colonies turned into a unique economic asset, unusually solid because of the sheer numbers and because of the evolution of strong British-style political institutions locally.

In this system the Dutch, with their emphasis on trade rather than on settlement, were poorly placed to compete, merely serving as recipients in Amsterdam of a large part of the continental re-exports, especially of tobacco. They had not succeeded in the Americas on a scale commensurate with their initial infiltration of the Portuguese and Spanish trading routes. Largely instrumental together with the Portuguese in introducing both sugar and slaves to the West Indies, the Dutch were able to sustain their interests in the European sugar market through their own possessions in the Caribbean. Elsewhere, however, they were not well placed: in 1654 they had even been evicted altogether from Brazil by the local population, and had generally failed to provide the resources and manpower for substantial and permanent settlements both in the north and the south. They never acquired a majority stake in the originally Portuguese-operated slave trade, and after 1660 found themselves hampered by the English Navigation Acts in the lucrative transports to Jamaica and Barbados, where the black population came to outnumber the white by nearly three to one at the end of the century. Even the French, who, apart from the West Indies, were mostly unsuccessful in their colonial ventures in this period, acquired a bigger stake in the slave trade by the end of the century, at a time when the annual average number of slaves transported across the Atlantic to Brazil and the Caribbean was approaching 25,000.

The European powers were more evenly placed in the Indian Ocean and the Far East, where, as the pepper trade levelled off, new commodities such as Indian plain and printed cotton textiles (calicoes) provided a commodity with impressive growth potential alongside spices and other long-standing goods for the open European markets in the later seventeenth century. In South-East Asia the Dutch had become firmly entrenched by taking over from the Portuguese, and had even gained a precarious foothold in Japan, although under sufferance. The Dutch East India Company (the VOC) had, after its establishment in 1602, rapidly built up an impressive but decentralised network of regional many-sided exchange, centring on their stronghold of Batavia on Java. Able to evade public accountability and the kind of annual reckonings to shareholders which limited the scope of, for instance, the English East India Company, the VOC ploughed a considerable amount of capital into the trade in certain high-profit goods. Their turnover increased fivefold between 1620 and the end of the century. In contrast to the ostensible free-trade attitudes of Dutch merchants in Europe, the VOC applied ruthless tactics to secure monopolies on these goods, ruining competitors in the spice trade by massive price-controlling deals or using armed force where necessary (as in the bombardment of Macassar in 1660 and its occupation nine years later, or in the subjugation of the native populations of the

Moluccas to their market control). In much of the east, however, the Dutch presence was relatively superficial, unavoidably so given the generally low level of permanent migration from the Netherlands, and the smallness of the population at home (probably still short of 2 million).

Overseas trade and colonial development, even more than 'normal' life within Europe itself, involved violence at every stage. That of the VOC was particularly unapologetic, since the company had complete authority to negotiate with local rulers, conclude treaties, build fortifications and conduct naval or military operations in the name of the government of the United Provinces. The company directors (the *Heeren*-17) also evaded, or obtained dispensations from, the terms of European peace settlements or truces, for instance in order to be able to continue fighting the Portuguese in the period 1609–21; the Dutch West Indies Company did as much after the truce with Portugal in 1640. In aims and style, the Dutch and English trading companies, like the French ones founded by Colbert, were not far removed from the nominally licensed but privately sponsored privateering which played so prominent a part in early trade wars. Like mercenary entrepreneurs on land, trading companies were essentially a scant disguise for greed and private exploitation. Their success ultimately hinged on physical coercion: the advances in bronze gunfounding which Gustav Adolf had exploited on land could be put to ready use on board merchant shipping, and even the heavier and formerly unwieldy iron cannons were no great problem on the more solid types of ships built by the English. The French fleet had a total of just 1045 pieces of artillery in 1661, but by 1677 Colbert had (with Swedish technical assistance) raised the number to nearly 12,000. Except in the Far East there was no adequate defence against this heavy artillery and, although at first it was only of use in protecting coastal trading stations, sufficient progress was soon made for the Europeans to acquire an incalculable advantage also on land. The dividing line between private and national coercive tactics for a long time remained blurred: state control was only gradually attempted, first over outright piracy in the West Indies in the later seventeenth century (but not yet off the North African coast) and then more generally as the English and French sought to secure exclusive rights to their colonial holdings.[10]

For all participating trading nations, the slave trade was important: it demanded so much capital that a fairly complex if still mostly private organisational structure was necessary, and required detailed planning for not only the barbaric crossing itself but also the encouragement of tribal violence in Africa to secure supplies. Even the system of more or less voluntary indenture (transportation to the colonies in return for tied labour for a period of years) entailed brutality and disappointment for a large proportion of its subjects. In the case of the Irish, wanting to escape from war and devastation in the late 1640s and early 1650s, or in the years 1689–91, the crossing and the subsequent years of virtual slave labour more often than not failed to lead to the promised independence and prosperity. In the English colonies, the system of indenture was further demeaned when it became common after 1655 to turn over convicted criminals to private entrepreneurs for transportation to America on similar terms (in situations where the French, for instance, would impose galley service in the Mediterranean instead). Similarly, those who enlisted as sailors on the long-distance routes, on navy or merchant ships of any nationality, were likely to experience a discipline as brutalising as any in the armed forces.

Last but not least, overseas expansion brought an unsavoury crop of often mutual racial and religious prejudices which the behaviour of European adventurers almost invariably exacerbated. There is no shortage of evidence regarding the prejudices of whites against slaves and coloured people, attitudes which even the eighteenth-century enlightenment did little to challenge. Racial prejudice seemed conveniently consonant with the very hierarchical social thinking of most Europeans, and slavery itself was condoned in religious terms because it could bring the alleged benefit of conversion to Christianity. With no convincing sense of human equality (let alone gender equality) within Europe itself, it would have been surprising indeed to find such sentiments expressed towards the 'other' – the stranger operating according to cultural norms utterly different from anything most Europeans would ever have had the opportunity to encounter – especially since commercial and ultimately colonial relationships depended on exchanges which more recent generations would term 'exploitative'. Yet the evidence is itself in some respects problematic: in this field historians have often unavoidably had to rely almost totally on travellers' accounts, which by definition are subjective, unrepresentative and usually suitably embroidered for the sake of the intended readership. Such accounts can be made to yield a wide array of different interpretations, and (especially where contacts were frequent, as with the Ottoman Empire and the Muslim world of the Middle East) do at times show both the imaginative understanding as well as the critical self-scrutiny which travel can sometimes bring. It is refreshing to find some distinctively independent comments by a Dutch preacher in Amboina in 1615, when explaining how local Muslims in the Moluccas contrasted with the Europeans: 'This black nation, such as they are, are pretty civil, upright, regular and orderly in their daily life and conduct. They do not come home drunk, staggering, raging, bawling, overturning everything, making an uproar, beating the wife and pushing her out of doors, as our own men often do; and this is the reason why none of them want to give their daughters in marriage to us, and why the girls themselves are afraid to do so.'[11]

The public show of justice and punishment

One of the characteristics of central and western European domestic social relations in the seventeenth century was the enormous emphasis placed on law and the sanctity of property. Spaniards with aspirations of rank, and the status-conscious French *parlementaire* establishment, like many others, unreservedly exploited the law for personal or corporate advantage.[12] It may also be argued that western commercial and capitalist society required the service of professional lawyers to an extent unparalleled elsewhere. More important in the present context, however, is the fact that the law invariably tended to protect the haves against the have-nots, and equated the possession of property with social respectability and an entitlement to exercise authority in one way or another. At the highest level, the state was guarantor of the political and social elite, and the supposedly divine attributes of the Prince provided the last link in the great chain of being up to the Creator. Such an ideology was readily used as justification for the brutal repression of rebellion and of communal insubordination which we have just observed. Even more explicit was the imagery and public ceremony accompanying the due process of law and in particular, the implementation of capital and other severe punishments imposed by courts of law. In western Europe capital crimes usually had to be referred to royal or high courts, even where seigneurs or local authorities had substantial jurisdictional rights. The spectacle of justice was accordingly often intended to reinforce the religious and political ideology of seventeenth-century government and to reiterate the state's claim to a monopoly of violence. The desired effect could to some extent always be enhanced through more or less effective censorship and control of the media.

As historians have emphasised,[13] the staging of judicially imposed punishments was very elaborate. For executions in Amsterdam during the seventeenth century the burgomasters, representing the state and dressed in special robes, had a final say in the form which the penalty should take. The scaffold put up for the purpose was accessible from the town hall only, not from the street, and the burgomasters and other magistrates witnessed the proceedings from the town-hall windows. The emphasis on the power of the authorities was underlined in a number of details: magistrates often decided how soon the suffering of the condemned person should be ended, notably if, for instance, he was being broken on the wheel. Similar discretion was exercised in the implementation of non-capital and even symbolic punishments. In order to maximise the public effect, the condemned person was expected to co-operate actively by showing his submission to the magistrates, and preferably by accepting his punishment in a mood of genuine Christian repentance. Refusal to co-operate was a disaster for the authorities second only to a botched execution – the latter might endanger the executioner's own life at the hands of the spectators, or expose the authorities to contempt or even to rioting if no troops were present. The public ceremonial was an integral part of the process, just as it was in instances of symbolic punishment such as simulated beheading or exposure with a noose around the neck. Such visual confirmation of the 'rule of law' conformed to a long tradition which existed, in local variants, everywhere. Similarly, the exposure of the bodies of executed criminals at suitable sites on or outside city walls was intended both as an additional disgrace and as a warning to outsiders and travellers. But the motive of deterrence was most unambiguous when physical punishments were carried out on dead bodies, notably in cases of suicide (still a criminal offence in most of Europe, but not in Amsterdam after 1658) and, in particular, in cases where a condemned person had broken all the rules by taking his own life before the public ceremony.

Ordinary criminal cases, treated essentially in religious and moral terms, gradually generated greater state involvement by virtue of being breaches of the peace. But during the seventeenth century, as the role and the demands of the government itself expanded, offences against the state also came to figure more prominently, including offences such as fraud over taxation or coinage, actual evasion of imposed penalties (a kind of contempt of court), and even treason itself. It is difficult to be precise about the emergence of a concept of 'crime against the state', since offences against a prince had for long been interpreted also as a sin against divine law. But it is no coincidence that the Russian Law Code of 1649 began with an unprecedented definition of political crime against the state. Torture was also used more freely in connection with trials involving the security of the state: in that context it might even be applied after the accused was finally given the death penalty, or to extract ancillary information not central to the ostensible charge.

The Danish Law Code of 1683, between a section on sacrilege and one on discipline within the family, had a section on treason, sedition and abuse of authority in the name of the King. Its first clause specified that anyone insulting or threatening the King and Queen was guilty of a crime against majesty, punishable by loss of honour, life and property: the right hand was to be cut off living, the body quartered and broken on the wheel, and the head and hand exhibited on a stake – and if the culprit had escaped it was all to be done in effigy. That this was no empty threat had already been amply demonstrated in the first years of absolute monarchy, even before the Royal Law had been completed. A nobleman of very high lineage, Kaj Lykke, had admitted making a dishonourable reference to the Queen's morality in a letter to his own mistress, and the judgement passed on him in 1661 by the Supreme Court involved the loss of honour (i.e. noble status), life and 140,000 rigsdalers' worth of property. In his absence a carefully finished and appropriately dressed wax effigy was executed in the presence of the King, although the real Lykke was in fact later partially pardoned and allowed to return to the country. Far more serious were the accusations against the King's brother-in-law, Corfitz Ulfeldt, a long-standing member of the aristocratic council but guilty of corruption and manifest treason first with Sweden, then after his return to Denmark with Brandenburg–Prussia in 1663. He was executed in wooden effigy in 1663, on a scaffold erected immediately below the prison windows of his remarkable wife, Leonora Christina, who (although a daughter of Christian IV) was kept in confinement for 22 years thereafter. Most spectacular of all, however, was the treatment of the author of the Royal Law itself, the commoner Schumacher, ennobled as Griffenfeld and as Great Chancellor, the most powerful man in the kingdom in the early years of Christian V. Griffenfeld's position weakened in 1675 because of disagreements over foreign policy, and well-founded accusations of corruption could now be exploited by his opponents: he was tried before a special commission in 1676 and, after being refused access to documents required for his defence, he was found guilty of *lèse-majesté* and condemned to the full punishment which that entailed. In fact, he had become too powerful and too independent in his exercise of authority for the King's liking, but a formal charge to that effect would of course have been an embarrassment unacceptable to an absolute monarch. Instead, at the very moment that the prescribed punishment was about to be carried out, a pardon was announced and he was instead imprisoned for life. This 'clemency' may have been the result of the doubts of one commissioner about the fairness of the treason charges, but in any case only emphasised the image of the all-powerful monarch.

Treason trials and punishments on this scale were clearly meant to convey the absolute power of the monarchy not only in spiritual but also in secular matters. Contemporary descriptions and comments often appear to suggest that the spectacle worked. But the stakes were high: the trial of Foucquet in France had already demonstrated how tenuous the state-sponsored prosecution could be, and risks had as far as possible to be controlled. Similarly, punishment of lesser offenders could easily turn into a disaster if there was public sympathy for the culprit, if the underlying social climate was tense or if mistakes were made in the staging of the event itself.

The law undoubtedly buttressed the established political order, together with the social hierarchy which relied on it. But it would be a serious oversimplification to regard the law as nothing more than a tool of oppression. As we have already noted in connection with urban society, there was widespread acceptance of, and belief in, the usefulness of legal institutions and rights amongst commoners, and to a lesser extent such beliefs may well also have been significant amongst the peasantry, at least in northern and north-western Europe.

General acceptance of the law as a social regulator would naturally be strongest in those societies where it was least prone to distortion through social and seigneurial privilege. The common law of England had for long enjoyed such acceptance, and awareness of its importance in general terms greatly increased as a result of the confrontations during the period leading up to the outbreak of civil war. Parliament acquired the useful image of a bulwark against the arbitrary exercise of royal power, an image achieved in considerable measure through a widely accepted interpretation of both individual and corporate legal rights, ultimately confirmed, it seemed, in the revolutionary settlement of 1688–9. Moreover, at lower and more practical levels of day-to-day existence the English local courts, like the Scandinavian *ting*, provided (in ways not commonly available in other parts of Europe) a greater scope for participation in the interpretation and implementation of the law. Juries were widely used in the lesser courts in England and, except for the grand juries at assizes and quarter sessions, included men of modest means. Obviously a large proportion of the population were still effectively excluded except as defendants – in particular most women, and also the poor – but the records of church and other courts that have so far been systematically studied suggest that a broad cross-section from the middle ranks of society upwards took part as witnesses and sureties, or served as village constables and in various other official functions.[14] As we noted in connection with the control of poverty-driven crime, local defendants often escaped literal application of the law thanks both to the 'interpretative' role of these community functionaries and to the often open partiality of juries. Indeed, local courts in northern Europe, and even manorial or seigneurial courts elsewhere, often served as a forum for arbitration and settlement to preserve the cohesion of a community, rather than as a vehicle for legal judgement as such.

The participatory element in the higher levels of the English judicial system was undoubtedly strengthened during the commonwealth period – deliberately so, for example, in the adoption of English, rather than Norman French or law Latin, as the formal language. It is some indication of the reactionary nature of the Restoration that this change was immediately reversed: the establishment not surprisingly turned against wider participation in this as in other areas of activity (in the process, incidentally, reviving popular distrust of the legal profession itself). From a different but not unrelated perspective one can also point to the fact that statutory punishment of crimes against property became substantially more draconian over the next century, with the creation of a large number of new capital offences which, though applied with discretion, were designed to deter the unprivileged. This trend towards harshness, interestingly, seems less pronounced in Scotland.

Most important of all in the present context, however, was the greater severity with which political insubordination naturally came to be regarded in English law after the Civil War. Admittedly the procedure for *habeas corpus* was improved in important ways by an act of 1679 which was passed only narrowly. The disappearance of the prerogative courts as a lasting result of the interregnum also in practice helped to secure a politically more autonomous system of justice – even if improvements were far short of modern expectations that juries (imperfect, partial or even ignorant though they sometimes might appear) should not be open to manipulation by the state. Equally, a ruling of 1670 tried to protect juries against the worst forms of pressure from despotic and hectoring judges (in particular, Lord Chief Justice Keeling). But political crime and insubordination unmistakably constituted a delicate area. Despite the exemplary moderation of the Act of Indemnity and Oblivion of 1660, silencing any discussion of the past civil war actions of all but the regicides themselves, notions of what constituted treason were soon very substantially widened by means of judicial construction. This was strikingly apparent in the trial of apprentices which followed the 1668 riot against brothels, with its anti-court and anti-popery slogans;[15] and, less surprisingly, in the aftermath of, for instance, the Monmouth rebellion. Judges such as William Scroggs and George Jeffreys attained notoriety in the late 1670s and the 1680s in their efforts as crown appointees to reconcile the differing concepts of treason and sedition thrust upon them by Parliament and the Crown respectively, in the process departing from what later generations would find acceptable and, incidentally, taking out their own sense of insecurity on sometimes hapless defendants. The Revolution of 1688–9 reduced the danger of blatant manipulation of the law by the monarch but, as subsequent history has shown, the guarantees for the individual offered in the general wording of the Bill of Rights of 1689 were undoubtedly the result more of resentment against crown policies of the 1680s than of any desire to widen the political nation or even to secure egalitarian justice.

By comparison with the Commonwealth, then, the Restoration period involved a distancing of the political and propertied nation from the rest – a distancing of government from governed – not unfamiliar from continental experience, despite its different forms.

Because of the fundamental constitutional issues at stake both in the 1640s and the 1680s, however, the specific trend in England towards firmer control of social and political order through the law and through other restraints cannot be regarded as typical. No major continental power had come as close as England to achieving genuine political change, and no other monarchy (except perhaps in a more narrow sense Sweden) at any stage provided scope for limited but significant participation in the political decision-making process. This may help to explain why, in the last resort, the relatively impersonal power of the British Crown could after 1688 be maintained without recourse to displays of power as dramatic and at times gruesome as those indulged in by continental monarchies.

Critics and public opinion

It will be apparent that state structures and institutions in later seventeenth-century Europe were carefully crafted to convey an image of power and authority – not always as impressive as the propagandists suggested but nonetheless forceful, and certainly designed to discourage insubordination. No doubt the image of absolute or divine-right kingship, particularly when it was promoted with such astonishing extravagance as in the case of Louis XIV,[16] might at times convince even those with inside experience of governmental practice. And compared with earlier forms of Renaissance-style princely authority, central government during the seventeenth century did seem to be expanding and encroaching in unprecedented ways. Those who argued that monarchical power was both theoretically and practically unlimited had a point: Louis XIV was not the only ruler who appeared to act as if the state was his personal property and who could often get away with it.[17] Yet the upheavals of mid-century had irrefutably demonstrated that the reality of royal power was not in fact impregnable: even if the façade of absolutism appeared affirmed after 1660, the notion of a theoretical contract between ruler and subject now implied some degree of accountability which could never again be completely obliterated.

Historians have come to realise the importance of various forms of public opinion in early modern Europe. The unrest, rioting and resistance which we have encountered throughout this book point very clearly not only to widespread awareness of where the line might be drawn between what was fair and what was not but also to collective recognition of matters of social justice throughout most levels of society. Even though the very radical forms of political awareness encountered in the English civil war were to some extent forced underground after 1660, they were not altogether forgotten. Political confrontations elsewhere, though regarded by some as abhorrent and against the divine order, did indicate that unanimity about public affairs could no longer be taken for granted. Admittedly, public discussion of political affairs naturally remained very subdued, and necessarily partially hidden from historical observation because it was often too dangerous to record on paper. Even the huge growth of print culture in the eighteenth century did not succeed in undermining the substantial restrictions on the discussion of domestic politics throughout Europe, and authors had to be adept at exercising considerable self-restraint.[18] But there is no doubt that the later seventeenth century witnessed new levels of political scrutiny amongst a wider public.

Such awareness is most clearly visible in those parts of Europe, such as England and the United Provinces, where a combination of economic prosperity and non-traditional, rather volatile forms of government created more scope for public discussion. The Restoration monarchy in England could never claim the sort of immunity to public scrutiny that Charles I had asserted, and parliamentary enquiries into, for example, the conduct of the Anglo–Dutch war of 1664–7 clearly generated public speculation (even if it was illegal to publish press reports of the proceedings). Whereas petitions, ballads, furtive printing and privately circulated manuscript texts were normally as far as this debate went before 1640, the period from the Restoration through to the extraordinary self-restraint of the 1688–9 revolution was marked by more visible political commentary.[19] By the early eighteenth century, the 'political nation' had became both significantly larger and more independent. In the Netherlands, the decentralised political life of many of the urban communities seems to have enjoyed an even stronger current of debate, though the exact contours have yet to be fully explored.

But even in France itself the government was not immune to substantive, if very discreet, political scrutiny, especially as disillusionment spread in the later years of Louis XIV. Critics who proclaimed alternative values obviously had to exercise considerable caution, and anyone who persisted in opposition could expect disgrace, dispossession, imprisonment or execution for treason. But arguments such as those of Bodin or Hobbes, suggesting that absolute power was the best long-term solution to a number of real political problems, were now tempered in the eyes of some contemporaries by actual observation and critical evaluation. A striking example is found in Fénelon's *Examen de conscience sur les devoirs de la royauté*, a set of confessional promptings written around 1702 for the Duke of Burgundy to teach him that the monarchy itself had duties and collective responsibilities:

Have you taken anything from your subjects solely on your own authority and against the rules? Have you compensated him, as a private person would have done, when you took his house, or enclosed his field in your parklands, or abolished his office, or terminated his pension? Have you examined thoroughly the true needs of the State, to compare them with the inconvenience of taxes, before burdening your people? Have you in regard to such an important matter consulted those men most enlightened, most zealous for the public good, and most capable of telling you the truth with neither flattery nor weakness? Have you ever described as necessity of state that which served merely to flatter your ambition, such as a war launched to make conquests and acquire glory? Have you ever described as necessities of state that which consists of your own pretensions?

These questions were of course directed at the abuses perpetrated by Louis XIV himself, and although the existence of the text became common knowledge only in 1734 when an edition was suppressed, it had already exercised significant influence on the inner circles at court[20] and represented a widespread underground resentment in France which turned to relief when the King finally died. In short, the high point of traditional absolute monarchy in continental Europe was also the start of a new growth in public opinion which would eventually, in the later eighteenth century, acquire formidable political significance. Absolute monarchy may have given some princes authority for which they did not openly have to give account, but its inscrutable mystery always had been, and was now sure to remain, nothing more than a myth.

Concluding remarks

Historians have in recent years devoted much attention to the process of state formation in early modern Europe. For some, the seventeenth century marked the consolidation of the 'tax state', a political and bureaucratic structure shaped in part by the rapidly growing and seemingly insatiable demands for revenue to pay for war. Others have described this process in terms of a growth of the 'power state' or 'military state', in recognition of the fact that the main priorities of early modern government often had to do with the military power needed to survive in the predatory environment of early modern international relations. For some historians, however, the state acquired a more pronounced institutional profile most clearly visible in those monarchies which headed towards what we now often call 'absolute monarchy'.

As we noted in chapter 2, the process of state formation – or the consolidation of absolute monarchy – was hardly a linear process. To contemporary observers in the 1630s and 1640s there were more signs of disintegration than of consolidation, and the political upheavals which disrupted so much of Europe at the time of the economic disasters of the late 1640s reinforced such impressions. The memory of those gloomy years clearly cast a long shadow in the period from 1660 and reinforced the tendency to seek security through enhanced government centralisation. As we have observed in the last two chapters, the foreign policies of Louis XIV were no less brutalising and manipulative than what had gone before, but many rulers now kept a much firmer grip on their lands than had been possible during the Thirty Years War. The term 'absolute monarchy' is of course, in a literal sense, an exaggeration: no ruler could in practice exercise absolute or unlimited power, since the machinery of state was still minuscule by modern standards, and remained largely ineffective over distance. Nonetheless, comparing the French monarchy of Henry IV with that of Louis XIV, or that of Christian IV of Denmark with that of his grandson, huge changes are immediately apparent – changes both of substance and of appearance. Poland aside (and it had remained elective), most of the monarchies in Europe by the 1680s appeared much less likely to disintegrate in the face of internal disruption than they had in the 1630s, and most were well on the way towards having permanent and rationally organised administrative systems located in a fixed political capital, surrounding an often ostentatious and increasingly ritualised royal court.

There were many changes which seemed to follow from (or in some cases promote) this trend. Historians have noted a change from a 'patrimonial' state (reliant on feudal and clientage relationships of an essentially personal kind) to a more 'public' state (where the King represented an abstract and durable unity which functioned by means of a permanent and more depersonalised, even professionalised, bureaucracy). The individual 'subject', expected to offer unquestioning service to the King, began also to aspire to those rudiments of collective self-consciousness which had hitherto been apparent mostly in the great cities of late medieval and early modern Europe. As we noted, there are clear signs of a stronger 'public opinion' during the seventeenth century, still largely loyal and 'patriotic', but no longer necessarily uncritical of how specific political power was exercised on particular occasions. The old society of estates, still maintained as a theoretical construct, was beginning to give way to a more fluid hierarchy where status depended not just on birth but also on wealth, rank, and access to the levers of power. In those areas where economic growth (or recovery) was most pronounced, the spread of consumer culture, a widening access to printed material, and dramatic developments in intellectual life created unprecedented opportunities. By any standards, both the political and the intellectual upheavals of mid-century were extraordinary: in England, the challenges were so profound that, even if the revolution itself was not entirely successful, notions of a contract between ruler and subject became sufficiently well-established to shape all future political developments. Generalisations over a whole continent are bound to be unconvincing when we contrast cases such as England and France, or even Denmark and Sweden; even more so when we remind ourselves that the United Provinces, the Venetian Republic, the independent city of Hamburg, and many other smaller territories within the Holy Roman Empire followed quite different political and social paths. But, overall, the seventeenth century marks a major turning-point in the way Europeans organised themselves.

Not everyone saw these changes as improvements, and for the peasant tax-payer, the conscript soldier or the innumerable poor who thronged all European cities, there was often little scope for optimism. Economic stability remained effectively unattainable in most parts of Europe, and the fear of disease and violence persisted. For most people, ideological conformity was a requirement, and deeply engrained intolerance a fact of life that was hardly even questioned. Yet, at the same time, the seventeenth century witnessed some utterly astonishing works of originality and insight by individual musicians, artists, thinkers and scientists – works which cannot be separated from the violent and at times oppressive environment in which they were created, yet which give this period an unforgettable vitality and richness.

Notes

Chapter 1   The Thirty Years War in the Germand lands

1. G. Benecke, *Society and Politics in Germany 1500–1700* (London, 1974); J. A. Vann and S. W. Rowan (eds), *The Old Reich* (Brussels, 1974); K. Repgen, 'Noch einmal zum Begriff "Dreissigjähriger Krieg" ', *Zeitschrift für historische Forschung*, 9 (1982), 347–52; J. A. Vann, *The Making of a State: Württemberg 1593–1793* (Ithaca, NY, 1984); B. von Krusenstjern and H. Medick (eds), *Zwischen Alltag und Katastrophe: der Dreißigjährige Krieg aus der Nähe* (Göttingen, 1999). N. M. Sutherland, 'Origins of the Thirty Years War and the structure of European politics', *English Historical Review*, 107 (1992), 587–625, has argued that this conflict is merely one stage in a much longer-running European political–dynastic conflict stretching from the Reformation to 1715.

2. Emperor Matthias was childless, and the choice of a younger member of the family – Ferdinand, Archduke in Styria and Carinthia – could not be finalised without a deal with Philip III of Spain, himself a claimant. Matthias had little control over these events, and his advisor Khlesl was ousted and imprisoned in 1618. The context is explained in G. Parker, *The Army of Flanders and the Spanish Road* (Cambridge, 1972); P. Brightwell, 'The Spanish system and the twelve years' truce', *English Historical Review*, 89 (1974), 270–92, and his 'The Spanish origins of the Thirty Years War', *European Studies Review*, 9 (1979), 409–31.

3. The defenestration caused no serious harm to the three, owing to a pile of rubbish below the high window. But the very deliberate act of defiance caught the imagination of observers everywhere, especially since the confrontation involved such basic issues of religious and political self-determination: see the material cited in note 16 below.

4. For a discussion of Ferdinand's entourage, his own beliefs and the attitude of the papacy (which had little significance in the Empire in practical terms), see R. S. Bireley, *Religion and Politics in the Age of the Counter-Reformation* (Chapel Hill, NC, 1981), 46 and *passim*; his *Maximilian von Bayern, Adam Contzen, S.J., und die Gegenreformation in Deutschland, 1624–35* (Göttingen, 1975); and his broader study on *The Jesuits and the Thirty Years War: Kings, Courts and Confessors* (Cambridge, 2003). See also H.Tersch, 'Gottes Ballspiel: der Krieg in Selbstzeugnissen aus dem Umkreis des Kaiserhofes (1619–1650)', in von Krusenstjern and Medick, *Zwischen Alltag und Katastrophe*, 427–65.

5. R. J. W. Evans, *The Making of the Habsburg Monarchy 1550–1700* (Oxford, 1979), 195–234; J. R. Paas, *The German Political Broadsheet, 1600–1700* (vols 1–7, Wiesbaden, 1985–2002)

6. A short survey of the *Kipper- and Wipperjahre* is found in W. Abel, *Massenarmut und Hungerkrisen im vorindustriellen Europa* (Hamburg, 1974), 138–47.

7. Frederick of the Palatinate had been placed under the ban of the Empire in 1621, a step which, like the transfer of the electoral title to Maximilian, was of doubtful constitutional validity, even though Frederick was in open opposition to imperial authority. The meeting of the princes at Regensburg in 1623 was no substitute for proper constitutional procedures, especially since many only sent deputies there. Elector Johann Georg reluctantly recognised Maxmilian's title in 1624.

8. The Empire had in 1512 been divided into ten circles (provinces), each with an assembly (*Kreistag*) and with certain local responsibilities regarding law and order, defence, and taxation for imperial armies. In practice only the southern and western circles had much durable significance, primarily because those areas did not have any single powerful princes. In any case, the circles were affected, like all other imperial institutions, by the confrontational deadlocks around the turn of the century. See also F. Magen, 'Die Reichskreise der Epoche des Dreißigjährigen Krieges', *Zeitschrift für historische Forschung*, 9 (1982), 408–60.

9. The Hansa, a league of north German and northern European ports and trading centres, had flourished in the later Middle Ages, but was already weakened in the sixteenth century by the growth of independent Netherlands and English trade and by the political consolidation of the Nordic kingdoms. The Hansa finally collapsed after the unproductive *Hansetag* (assembly of the Hansa city representatives) in 1669.

10. L. Tandrup, *Mod triumf eller tragedie*, vols 1–2 (Aarhus, 1979); K. J. V. Jespersen, 'Kongemødet i Ulfsbäck præstegård februar 1629', *Historie Jyske Samlinger*, 14 (1982), 420–39; E. L. Petersen, 'Defence, war and finance: Christian IV and the council of the realm', *Scandinavian Journal of History*, 7 (1982), 277–313, and his 'War, finance and the growth of absolutism', in *Europe and Scandinavia: Aspects of the Process of Integration in the 17th century*, ed. G. Rystad (Lund, 1983), 33–49.

11. The debate on a so-called 'military revolution', culminating in the new tactics and equipment of the Swedes in the Thirty Years War, will not be explored in detail here: historians have recently been critical of its general validity, and the related discussions of state formation have taken new directions which will be explored further in chapter 2. For a clear overview, however, see J. Glete, *War and the State in Early Modern Europe: Spain, the Dutch Republic and Sweden as Fiscal–Military States, 1500–1600* (London, 2002), 45–47 and (on Sweden in particular) 174–212.

12. The destruction of Magdeburg became a major atrocity story in its own right, used extensively for propaganda purposes: H. Medick, 'Historisches Ereignis und zeitgenössische Erfahrung: Die Eroberung und Zerstörung Magdeburgs 1631', in von Krusenstjern and Medick, *Zwischen Alltag und Katastrophe*, 377–407.

13. M. Roberts, *Gustavus Adolphus and the Rise of Sweden* (London, 1973), 125–7; S. Lundkvist, 'Gustav Adolf som fältherre', in *Gustav II Adolf* (Stockholm, 1982), 47–60; L. Ekholm in H. Landberg et al., *Det kontinentale krigets ekonomi* (Kristianstad, 1971); R. Nordlund, 'Kontribution eller satisfaktion: Pommern och de svenska krigsfinanserna 1633',

Historisk Tidskrift (Stockholm), 37/94 (1974), 321–402. For a survey of Swedish military organisation until 1632, see Roberts, *Gustavus Adolphus*, vol. 2, 198–271.

14. Decisions on all such matters were to be reached by agreement between Protestant and Catholic blocks (the *corpus evangelicorum* and the *corpus catholicorum*), after each block had debated the issue separately. The *Reichskammergericht* was to retain the Catholic–Protestant equality of membership already agreed in 1635. The confessional–political parity was of course extensively exploited thereafter by princes in their own territorial interests, making the imperial assembly slow and often ineffective.

15. On the significance of the Peace of Westphalia, at a variety of different levels, see V. Press, 'Österreichische Großmachtbildung und Reichsverfassung: zur kaiserlichen Stellung nach 1648', *Mitteilungen des Instituts für Österreichische Geschichtsforschung*, 98 (1990), 131–54; A. Schindling, 'Reichsinstitutionen und Friedenswahrung nach 1648', in *Der Frieden, Rekonstruktion einer europäischen Vision*, vol. 2: *Frieden und Krieg in der Frühen Neuzeit*, ed. R. G. Asch, W. E. Voß and M. Wrede (Munich, 2001), 259–91; a controversial view of the Peace of Westphalia, from a neo-Marxist point of view, can be found in B. Teschke, *The Myth of 1648: Class, Geopolitics and the Making of Modern International Relations* (London, 2003).

16. The pamphlet and fly-sheet literature in Germany during the war has been studied from a number of angles, including that of political propaganda, popular opposition and simple extremist agitation, as well as in terms of its embodiment of literary and pictorial conventions and images handed down from earlier generations. For further discussion, see especially R. W. Brednich, *Die Liedpublizistik im Flugblatt des 15. bis 17. Jhrs.* (Baden-Baden, 1974); G. Rystad, *Kriegsnachrichten und Propaganda während des Dreissigjährigen Krieges* (Lund, 1960); W. A. Coupe, *The German Illustrated Broadsheet in the Seventeenth Century* (Baden-Baden, 1966); J. R. Paas, *The German Political Broadsheet, 1600–1700*, vols 1–7 (Wiesbaden, 1985–2002); D. Böttcher, 'Propaganda und offentliche Meinung im protestantischen Deutschland 1628–1636', *Archiv für Reformationsgeschichte*, 44 (1952); H. Strobach, *Bauernklagen: Untersuchungen zum sozialkritischen Volkslied* (Berlin, 1964). See also A. Ellenius, 'Gustav Adolf i bildkonsten', in Lundkvist, *Gustav II Adolf*, 91–111; T. Schroder, *Das gesamte Werk Jacques Callot*, vols 1–2 (Munich, 1971); and for French newspaper reports, A. Rossel, *Le faux grand siècle* (Paris, 1982).

17. Older works, such as J. V. Polisensky, *Thirty Years War* (London, 1971), 197–208 and 232–53, or G. Franz, *Der Dreissigjährige Krieg* (Stuttgart, 1961), provide detailed surveys and estimates of population losses and migration. For references to the more recent German literature on the subject, combined with a helpful discussion of military discipline itself in the German lands, see R. G. Asch, ' "Wo der soldat hinkömbt, da ist alles sein": military violence and atrocities in the Thirty Years War re-examined', *German History*, 18 (2000), 291–309.

18. W. Crowne, *A true relation of . . . the Travels of . . . Thomas Howard . . . ambassador extraordinary to . . . Ferdinando the Second . . . 1636* (London, 1637), 10–11. For a varied selection of contemporary accounts, see G. Mortimer, *Eyewitness Accounts of the Thirty Years War 1618–48* (Basingstoke, 2002).

Chapter 2   Government in wartime Europe

1. In Denmark the peasantry was nominally present as a Fourth Estate up to 1627, and was called for ceremonial purposes in 1660, but was politically without significance.

2. R. J. Bonney, 'The failure of the French revenue farms, 1600–60', *Economic History Review*, 32 (1979), 11–32, and his *The King's Debts: Finance and Politics in France 1589–1661* (Oxford, 1981). The indirect farmed taxes usually accounted for under one-quarter of total crown revenue in the early seventeenth century; the direct taxes, including the *tailles* which gave between a third and a half of the total revenue, were collected by office-holders in the *pays d'élection*, and by agents of the provincial estates in the *pays d'état*. See also D. Dessert, *Argent, pouvoir et société au grand siècle* (Paris, 1984); J.B. Collins, *Fiscal Limits of Absolutism: Direct Taxation in Early Seventeenth Century France* (Berkeley, CA, 1988).

3. I. A. A. Thompson, *War and Government in Habsburg Spain 1560–1620* (London, 1976), 73. See also his chapter on 'The impact of war and peace on government and society in seventeenth-century Spain', in *Frieden und Krieg in der frühen Neuzeit*, ed. Asch, Voß and Wrede, 161–79.

4. The 'military revolution' thesis was first proposed in 1955 by M. Roberts in an inaugural lecture entitled 'The Military Revolution, 1560–1660', later reprinted in his *Essays in Swedish History* (London, 1967), 195–223. Like so many other relatively gradual changes to which historians have applied the term revolution, this one too has run into major problems of definition and focus. There is now little agreement about what it was, when it happened, or whether such terminology actually helps our understanding either of the military changes themselves or their broader significance. From amongst the extensive literature on the subject, see G. Parker, *The Military Revolution: Military Innovation and the Rise of the West* (Cambridge, 1988), 24–81; C. J. Rogers (ed.), *The Military Revolution Debate: Readings on the Military Transformation of Early Modern Europe* (Boulder, CO, 1995), which cites a number of the key contributions; J. Zunckel, 'Rüstungshandel im Zeitalter des Dreißigjährigen Krieges: "militärische Revolution", internationale Strategien und Hamburger Perspektiven', in *Zwischen Alltag und Katastrophe*, ed. von Krusenstjern and Medick, 83–112; R. G. Asch, 'Kriegsfinanzierung, Staatsbildung und ständische Ordnung in Westeuropa im 17. und 18. Jahrhundert', *Historische Zeitschrift*, 268 (1999), 635–71; J. S. Wheeler, *The Making of a World Power: War and the Military Revolution in Seventeenth-Century England* (Stroud, 1999); and Glete, *War and the State in Early Modern Europe*.

5. G. Parker, 'Mutiny and discontent in the Spanish Army of Flanders', *Past & Present*, 58 (1977), 38–52; Parker, *The Army of Flanders*, esp. 264f.

6. Bonney, *The King's Debts*, ch. 4, esp. 165–8; attempts were also made to farm the *tailles* themselves.

7. W. Beik, *Urban Protest in Seventeenth-Century France: The Culture of Retribution* (Cambridge, 1997), 63–71

8. Y.-M. Bercé, *Histoire des Croquants* (Geneva, 1974), vol. 2, 736f, concerning the Croquants in Saintonge, and his English version, *Peasant Rebellions* (Ithaca, NY, 1989); A. Jouanna, *Le devoir de révolte* (Paris, 1989).

9. J. Bergin, *Cardinal Richelieu: Power and the Pursuit of Wealth* (New Haven, CT, 1985); J.-F. Dubost, 'Absolutisme et décentralisation en Languedoc au xviie siècle (1620–1690)', *Revue d'histoire moderne et contemporaine*, 37 (1990), 369–97; J.B. Collins, *The State in Early Modern France* (Cambridge, 1995), 28–71; and, with particular insights on the military dimension, D. Parrott, *Richelieu's Army: War, Government and Society in France, 1624–1642* (Cambridge, 2001).

10. The traditional view of Castile as the stable heartlands of the Spanish monarchy has recently been qualified, with particular reference to resistance against military demands in the 1630s and 1640s: see R. MacKay, *The Limits of Royal Authority: Resistance and Obedience in Seventeenth-Century Castile* (Cambridge, 1999); and, especially on the economic background, I. A. A. Thompson and B. Y. Casalilla (eds), *The Castilian Crisis of the Seventeenth Century* (Cambridge, 1994). For a very different perspective on Spain from the point of view of outside observers at the time, see J. N. Hillgarth, *The Mirror of Spain, 1500–1700: The Formation of a Myth* (Ann Arbor, MI, 2000).

11. J. H. Elliott, *The Count Duke of Olivares* (New Haven, CT, 1986), 293; and his *Richelieu and Olivares* (Cambridge, 1984). For a more positive analysis of Philip's role in government, see R. A. Stradling, *Philip IV and the Government of Spain, 1621–65* (Cambridge, 1988).

12. R.A. Stradling, 'Olivares and the origins of the Franco–Spanish War, 1627–1635', *English Historical Review*, 101 (1986), 68–94; and his 'Prelude to disaster: the precipitation of the War of the Mantuan Succession, 1627–29', *Historical Journal*, 33 (1990), 769–85.

13. M. Roberts, *The Early Vasas* (Cambridge, 1968), 388.

14. I. Montgomery, 'Gustav Adolf och religionen', in Lundkvist, *Gustav II Adolf*, 61–77; P. Piirimäe, 'Just war in theory and practice: the legitimation of Swedish intervention in the Thirty Years War', *The Historical Journal*, 45 (2002), 499–523. Gustav may have used moral arguments to undermine aristocratic council concerns after 1628, since their debate was only pro forma, but G. Barudio's thesis in his *Gustav Adolf* (Wiesbaden, 1982), that the King was a protagonist of libertarian constitutionalism, may need some qualification in this context.

15. M. Roberts, 'Oxenstierna in Germany, 1633–36', *Scandia*, 48 (1982), 61–105.

16. F. P. Jensen, 'Peder Vinstrups tale ved Christian 4s kroning: et teokratisk indlæg', *Historisk Tidsskrift (Copenhagen)*, 12/2 (1966–7), 375–92.

17. R. Thomsen, 'Den jydske borgerbevægelse 1629', *Historisk Tidsskrift (Copenhagen)*, 11/1 (1944–6), 602–54.

18. S. Heiberg, 'De ti tønder guld: rigsråd, kongemagt og statsfinanser i 1630' erne', *Historisk Tidsskrift (Copenhagen)*, 76 (1976), 25–57; H. B. Madsen, *Det danske skattevæsen 1530–1660* (Copenhagen, 1978), 227–39; and E. L. Petersen, as cited in note 10 to ch. 1. See also *Magtstaten in Norden i 1600-tallet og de sociale konsekvenser*, ed. E. L. Petersen (Odense, 1984), especially the comments on Denmark by Leon Jespersen, 9–40, which are available in an English version in *Scandinavian Journal of History*, 10 (1985), 271–304; and Leon Jespersen, 'The constitutional and administrative situation', in the refreshingly innovative volume, *A Revolution from Above: The Power State of Sixteenth and Seventeenth Century Scandinavia*, edited by him (Odense, 2000), 91–107.

19. J. Engberg, 'Det 17. århundredes generelle politiske krise og striden mellem det danske rigsråd og landkommissærerne 1647–49', *Fortid & Nutid*, 24 (1969–71), 388–411, and his *Dansk finanshistorie i 1640erne* (Aarhus, 1972); L. Jespersen, 'Landkommisærinstitutionen i Christian IVs tid', *Historisk Tidsskrift (Copenhagen)*, 81 (1981), 69–99.

20. The 'revisionist' debate amongst historians is well illustrated in C. Russell, 'Parliamentary history in perspective', *History*, 61 (1976), which includes references to the work of Koenigsberger and others; C. Russell, *Parliaments and English Politics* (Oxford, 1979); T. K. Rabb and D. Hirst, 'Revisionism revised', in *Past & Present*, 92 (1981), 55–99; J. Morrill (ed.), *Reactions to the English Civil War 1642–49* (London, 1982); G. Burgess, 'On revisionism: an analysis of early Stuart historiography in the 1970s and 1980s', *Historical Journal*, 33 (1990), 609–27; J. Kenyon, 'Revisionism and post-revisionism in early Stuart history', *Journal of Modern History*, 64 (1992), 689–99.

21. D. Hirst, *The Representative of the People?* (Cambridge, 1975). The Crown never tampered as blatantly with elections as did, for example, the French Crown before the Estates General of 1614: J. M. Hayden, *France and the Estates General of 1614* (Cambridge, 1974), 77–86. And whereas the French Estates General did not have the unchallenged right to verify its own elections, the English Commons showed that it did, notably over the Buckinghamshire election of 1604, even if, as argued by M. A. Kishlansky, *Parliamentary Selection* (Cambridge, 1986), many English MPs were not elected at all in the modern sense of that word, rather selected by patronage, without contest.

22. An excellent overview of English parliamentary practices is found in D. L. Smith, *The Stuart Parliaments, 1603–1689* (London, 1999).The French Estates General had never met sufficiently frequently to establish regular procedures or institutional identity and, since its decisions were not binding on the constituencies until ratified locally, it was never regarded by the Crown as a fully integrated part of government. In Sweden, the Estates were also quite dependent on the Crown, at least when there was a strong adult king: see M. Roberts, *Sweden as a Great Power* (London, 1968), 7–92.

23. J. P. Kenyon, *The Stuart Constitution* (Cambridge, 1966), 13: King's speech to Parliament, 21 March 1610. See also G. Burgess, 'The Divine Right of kings reconsidered', *English Historical Review*, 107 (1992), 837–61.

24. R. Ashton, *The English Civil War* (London, 1978), 85–97; also his *The City and the Court 1603–43* (London, 1979).

25. That the Crown's religious policy, and especially Charles's attempt forcibly to remove the three-way religious divide between England, Scotland and Ireland, was an issue of fundamental significance in making compromise impossible has been cogently argued by C. Russell, 'The British Problem and the English Civil War', *History*, 72 (1987), 395–415. For Puritanism and the Calvinist Church as a whole, see P. Collinson, *The Religion of Protestants: The Church in English Society 1559–1625* (Oxford, 1982); and the brief overview by J. Spurr, *English Puritanism 1603–1689* (Basingstoke, 1998). For the formation of public opinion, see also R. Cust, 'News and politics in early seventeenth-century England', *Past & Present*, 112 (1986), 60–90; A. Fox, 'Rumour, news and popular political opinion in Elizabethan and early Stuart England', *Historical Journal*, 40 (1997), 597–620.

26. J. Wormald, 'James VI and I: two kings or one?', *History*, 68 (1983), 187–209; M. Lee, *Great Britain's Solomon: King James VI and I in his Three Kingdoms* (Urbana, IL, 1990). Charles appears to have lacked his father's understanding of, and interest in, problems north of the border.

Chapter 3   The framework of life

1. The ideas of the *arbitristas* are discussed by J. H. Elliott, 'Self-perception and decline in early 17th-century Spain', *Past & Present*, 74 (1977), 41–61.

2. For east-central Europe, see E. Fügedi, 'The demographic landscape of east-central Europe', in *East-central Europe in Transition*, ed. A. Maczak et al. (Cambridge, 1985), who suggests that the seventeenth century was a major demographic disaster for this area. For the Ottoman Empire, P. F. Sugar, *Southeastern Europe under Ottoman Rule* (Seattle, WA, 1977), 221–4; and B. McGowan, *Economic Life in Ottoman Europe: Taxation, Trade and the Struggle for Land, 1600–1800* (Cambridge, 1981), 83–7.

3. Increased incidence of disease was not always the consequence of high food prices, and some diseases spread irrespective of the nutritional condition of the recipient. English evidence from the 1690s suggests that the harvest failures then, although not of famine proportions as elsewhere in Europe, were accompanied by low incidence of disease, while the opposite is true of the 1680s, when cereals were plentiful: A. B. Appleby, 'Epidemics and famine in the Little Ice Age', *Journal of Interdisciplinary History*, 10 (1980), 643–53; E. A. Wrigley and R. S. Schofield, *The Population History of England 1541–1871* (London, 1981), esp. 320–55; A. G. Carmichael, 'Infection, hidden hunger and history', *Journal of Interdisciplinary History*, 14 (1983–4), 249–64.

4. For France, see e.g. P. Deyon, *Etude sur la société urbaine au xviie. siècle: Amiens* (Paris, 1967), 498; for Finland, E. Jutikkala, 'The great Finnish

famine of 1696–97,' *Scandinavian Economic History Review*, 3 (1955), 48–63. A. B. Appleby suggested in 'Grain prices and subsistence crises in England and France, 1590–1740', *Journal of Economic History*, 39 (1979), 865–87, that famines were avoided in England because the prices of oats and to some extent of barley were independent of the other cereals – although both wheat and maize were grown in southern France, the wheat was for export only and was always too dear for ordinary local consumption, so that the area did not escape the danger of effective 'monoculture'. On policy, see notably P. Slack, 'Dearth and social policy in early modern England', *Social History of Medicine* 5 (1992), 1–17.

5. J. A. Eddy, 'The Maunder minimum: sunspots and climate in the reign of Louis XIV, in *The General Crisis of the Seventeenth Century*, ed. G. Parker and L. M. Smith (London, 1978); G. Utterström, 'Climatic fluctuations and population problems in early modern history', *Scandinavian Economic History Review*, 3 (1955), 3–47; E. le Roy Ladurie, 'Climat et récoltes aux xviie et xviiie siècles', *Annales*, 15 (1960), 434–65; and some consistent evidence from other approaches to climatic history, presented in the special issue of *Journal of Interdisciplinary History*, 10/4 (1980).

6. There has been some debate over the range of yields obtainable in different parts of Europe, and the figures cited here may be no more than an indication of the more common levels. No general assessment of the burdens on the peasant economy is possible, but for a local one see P. Goubert, *Beauvais et le Beauvaisis* (Paris, 1960), 178–89.

7. G. E. Fussell, 'Low Countries' influence on English farming', *Economic History Review*, 74 (1959), 611–22.

8. See the debate initiated by R. Brenner in *Past & Present* from issue 70 (1976), published in volume form in *The Brenner Debate*, ed. T. Aston and C. Philpin (Cambridge, 1987). See also ch. 8.

9. These urban densities, merely estimates, are not unlike those for postwar British cities, but Glasgow had a net density in 1951 of 400 per hectare, and during the later nineteenth century some of its poorer parishes exceeded twice that density, according to A. Gibb, *Glasgow: The Making of a City* (Glasgow, 1983), 130f and 161.

10. A. Sharlin, 'Natural decrease in early modern cities', *Past & Present*, 79 (1978), 126–38, and the subsequent debate, in *Past & Present*, 92 (1981), 169–80. Cf. P. Clark and P. Slack, *English Towns in Transition 1500–1700* (Oxford, 1976), 85–96. For a more technical approach to urban demography over a longer period, see J. Landers, *Death and the Metropolis: Studies in the Demographic History of London 1670–1830* (Cambridge, 1993).

11. C. D. O. Malley, 'The medical history of LXIV', in *LXIV and the Craft of Kingship*, ed. J. C. Rule (Columbus, OH, 1969), 132–54.

12. C. M. Cipolla, *Public Health and the Medical Profession in the Renaissance* (Cambridge, 1976) and his *Cristofano and the Plague* (London, 1973). Health boards on the Italian model had been attempted in France in the sixteenth century, and became common in other parts of Europe by the seventeenth.

13.   S. K. Cohn, 'The Black Death: end of a paradigm', *The American Historical Review* 107 (2002), 703–38, and his *The Black Death Transformed: Disease and Culture in early Renaissance Europe* (London, 2002). For the early modern period, see also J. N. Biraben, 'La peste en 1720 à Marseilles', *Revue historique*, 247 (1972), 402–26, and his *Les hommes et la peste*, vols 1–2 (Paris, 1975–6); M. W. Flinn, 'Plague in Europe and the Mediterranean countries', *Journal of European Economic History*, 8 (1979), 131–48; P. A. Slack, *The Impact of the Plague in Tudor and Stuart England* (London, 1985).

14.   There is a growing body of literature on the consumer market in early modern Europe, but much of it focuses on the eighteenth century. For this period see J. Brewer and R. Porter (eds), *Consumption and the World of Goods* (London, 1993); L. Weatherill, *Consumer Behaviour and Material Culture in Britain 1660–1760* (2nd edn, London, 1996); S. Pennell, 'Consumption and consumerism in early modern England', *Historical Journal* 42 (1999), 549–64; and J. Styles, 'Product innovation in early modern London', *Past & Present* 168 (2000), 124–69.

15.   H. Phelps Brown and S. Hopkins, *A Perspective of Wages and Prices* (London, 1981) – the most substantial attempt to devise a long-term index, but not fully satisfactory because of the underlying assumptions of continuity in consumption patterns and because of the selective records on which it is based. See also J. de Vries, *The Economy of Europe in an Age of Crisis, 1600–1750* (Cambridge, 1976), 184–7; D. C. Coleman, *The Economy of England 1450–1750* (Oxford, 1977), 99–103; K. Wrightson and D. Levine, *Poverty and Piety in an English Village: Terling 1525–1700* (London, 1979), 39–42; D. Woodward, 'Wage-rates and living standards in pre-industrial England', *Past & Present*, 91 (1981), 28–45; J. Boulton, 'Food prices and the standard of living in London in the "century of revolution", 1580–1700', *Economic History Review* 53 (2000), 455–92; Goubert, *Beauvais*, 547–76; B. S. Pullan, 'Wage-earners and the Venetian economy, 1550–1630', *Economic History Review*, 16 (1964), 408–26; R. T. Rapp, *Industry and Economic Decline in Seventeenth-Century Venice* (Cambridge, MA, 1976), 130–7; A. Perrenoud, *La population de Genève*, vol. 1 (Geneva, 1979), 357–61; M. J. Elsas, *Umriss einer Geschichte der Preise und Löhne in Deutschland*, vols 1–2 (Leiden, 1936–40); J. Bérenger, *Finances et absolutisme autrichien* (Paris, 1975), 182–4. But all figures are necessarily tentative: see M. Sonenscher, 'Work and wages in Paris in the 18th century', in *Manufacture in Town and Country*, ed. M. Berg, P. Hudson and M. Sonenscher (Cambridge, 1983) 147–72. For a different approach, see C. Muldrew, ' "Hard Food for Midas": cash and its social value in early modern England', *Past & Present* 170 (2001), 78–120.

16.   D. V. Glass, 'Two papers on Gregory King', in *Population in History*, ed. D. V. Glass and D. E. C. Eversley (London, 1965), 159–220; G. Holmes, 'Gregory King and the social structure of pre-industrial England', *Transactions of the Royal Historical Society*, 27 (1977), 41–68. See also T. Arkell, 'The incidence of poverty in England in the later 17th century', *Social History*, 12 (1987), 23–47.

17. S. Vauban, *Dîme Royale,* ed. G. Michel (Paris, n.d.), 3f. Sébastien le
Prestre, seigneur de Vauban (1633–1707) completed the manuscript in
1699 but it was not printed until 1707, and then only surreptitiously. It
was immediately banned, a few weeks before Vauban's death.
18. N. Solomon, *La campagne de nouvelle Castile d'après les 'Relaciones
topograficas'* (Paris, 1964), 257–66. H. Kamen, *Spain in the Later
Seventeenth Century* (London, 1980), 276, suggests that Spanish towns
often had 40 per cent poor, of whom half were wholly destitute; cf. J.
Casey, *The Kingdom of Valencia in the Seventeenth Century* (Cambridge,
1979), 37–44.
19. P. Earle, 'The female labour market in London in the later seventeenth
and early eighteenth century', *Economic History Review* 42 (1989),
328–53; J. B. Collins, 'The economic role of women in seventeenth-
century France', *French Historical Studies* 16 (1990), 436–70; S. Woolf
(ed.), *Domestic Strategies: Work and Family in France and Italy,
1600–1800* (Cambridge, 1991).
20. Survey in M. W. Flinn, *The European Demographic System* (Brighton,
1981), 65–75; see also S. Hochstadt, 'Migration in pre-industrial
Germany' *Central European History,* 16 (1983), 195–224.
21. Clark and Slack, *English Towns,* 91–4, 117–21; K. Wrightson, *English
Society 1580–1680* (London, 1982), 26–38, 40–4. For a Swedish case-
study, see S. Lundkvist, 'Rörlighet och social struktur i 1610-talets
Sverige', *Historisk Tidskrift (Stockholm),* 94 (1974), 192–255, with an
English summary 256–8.
22. *The Diary of Samuel Pepys,* ed. R. Latham and W. Matthews (London,
1970–83), II, 1, VI, 341, IV, 357f., VII, 42–125 *passim,* IX, 333, 337.
23. R. Grassby, 'English merchant capitalism in the late 17th century', *Past
& Present,* 46 (1970), 87–107; his 'The personal wealth of the business
community in 17th-century England', *Economic History Review,* 23
(1970), 220–34; and *Puritans and Revolutionaries,* ed. D. Pennington and
K. Thomas (Oxford, 1978), 355–81.
24. Not enough research has been done to show whether this was a general
phenomenon in Catholic Europe. In Italy, for example, many bishoprics
were relatively small and poor, and therefore accessible to members of
the mendicant orders and others of humbler birth. But membership of
the orders (even the Jesuit order) awaits detailed analysis itself. See also
Goubert, *Beauvais,* 198–206. For recent work on clergy further north,
see C. S. Dixon and L. Schorn-Schütte (eds), *The Protestant Clergy of
Early Modern Europe* (Basingstoke, 2003).
25. Information on the Kent village is from Laslett, cited by J. L. Flandrin,
Families in Former Times (Cambridge, 1979), 56–8. See also *Family
Forms in Historic Europe,* ed. R. Wall et al. (Cambridge, 1983), chs 1 and
17; F. Benigno, 'The southern Italian family in the early modern period:
a discussion of co-residential patterns', *Continuity & Change* 4 (1989),
165–94.
26. The literature on this aspect is expanding rapidly; see notably J. Bailey,
*Unquiet Lives: Marriage and Marriage Breakdown in England,
1660–1800* (Cambridge, 2003); L. Gowing, *Domestic Dangers: Women,
Words and Sex in Early Modern London* (Oxford, 1996); M. P.

Sommerville, *Sex and Subjection: Attitudes to Women in Early Modern Society* (London, 1995); D. Underdown, 'The taming of the scold', in *Order and Disorder in Early Modern England,* ed. A. J. Fletcher and J. Stevenson (Cambridge, 1985), 116–36; G. R. Quaife, *Wanton Wenches and Wayward Wives* (London, 1979); and N. Z. Davis, 'Women on top', in her *Society and Culture in Early Modern France* (London, 1975), 1245–51. S. D. Amussen, *An Ordered Society: Gender and Class in Early Modern England* (Oxford, 1988), emphasises regional differences in the status of women, stressing that there was some female economic independence in those areas, for example the pastoral north, where women had a specific role in production and marketing.

27. There is a growing body of literature on infanticide, reflecting both contemporary attitudes and the acutely difficult predicament of single mothers in this period: see notably L. Gowing, 'Secret births and infanticide in seventeenth-century England', *Past & Present* 156 (1997), 87–115; M. Jackson (ed), *Infanticide: Historical Perspectives on Child Murder and Concealment, 1550–2000* (London, 2000).

Chapter 4   Enterprise and profit

1. O. Degn, *Rig og fattig i Ribe* (Aarhus, 1981), vol. 1, 130–44, 272–90.
2. That road transport was totally unsatisfactory in the seventeenth century has been challenged, in the case of England, by J. A. Chartres, 'Road-carrying in England in the 17th century: myth and reality', *Economic History Review,* 30 (1977), 73–94, suggesting a dramatic growth in road usage in the later part of the century.
3. F. Braudel and F. Spooner, 'Prices in Europe from 1450 to 1750', in *The Cambridge Economic History,* vol. 4 (Cambridge, 1967), 378–486; J. J. McCusker, *Money and Exchange in Europe and America 1600–1775* (London, 1978). Silver equivalents can of course only be regarded as a rough comparative standard, since gold and silver were marketable commodities priced according to supply and demand, like everything else.
4. See Further Reading at the end of this volume, and the more specific comments on the impact of colonial trade on Europe in chapter 12.
5. R. T. Rapp, 'The unmaking of the Mediterranean trade hegemony', *Journal of Economic History,* 35 (1975), 499–525, and his *Industry and Economic Decline in Seventeenth-Century Venice* (Cambridge, MA, 1976), *passim,* esp. 107–67.
6. See particularly C. Cipolla, 'The economic decline of Italy', in *The Economic Decline of Empire,* ed. Cipolla (London, 1970); D. Sella, 'Industrial production in 17th-century Italy: a reappraisal', *Explorations in Entrepreneurial History,* 6 (1968–9), 233–53; his *Crisis and Continuity: the Economy of Spanish Lombardy in the Seventeenth Century* (Cambridge, MA, 1979); and his *Italy in the Seventeenth Century* (London, 1997), 19–49; R. Romano, 'Italy in the crisis of the 17th century', in *Essays in European Economic History,* ed. P. Earle (Oxford, 1974), 185–98, emphasises that the agricultural recession in Italy began before the manufacturing one, perhaps as early as the 1580s.

7. W. S. Unger, 'Trade through the Sound in the 17th and 18th centuries', *Economic History Review*, 12 (1959–60), 206–21; P. Jeannin, 'Les comptes du Sund comme source par la construction d'indices généraux de l'activité économique en Europe', *Revue historique*, 231 (1964), 55–102, 307–40, and his 'The seaborne and the overland trade routes of northern Europe in the 16th and 17th centuries', *Journal of European Economic History*, 11 (1982), 5–59.

8. This debate was most pronounced some time ago, but has not been fully resolved: M. Bogucka, 'The monetary crisis of the 17th century in Poland', *Journal of European Economic History*, 4 (1975), 137–52, and her 'The role of the Baltic trade in European development', *Journal of European Economic History*, 9 (1980), 5–20; M. Malowist, 'The economic and social development of the Baltic countries from the 15th to the 17th centuries', *Economic History Review*, 12 (1959–60), 177–89; A. Maczak, 'Money and society in Poland and Lithuania in the 16th and 17th centuries', *Journal of European Economic History*, 5 (1976); J. Topolski, 'Economic decline in Poland from the 16th to the 18th centuries', in *Essays in European Economic History*, ed. Earle, 127–42; A. Attman, *The Russian and Polish Markets in International Trade 1500–1650* (Gothenburg, 1973).

9. Coleman, *Economy of England*, 70. See also K. Wrightson, *Earthly Necessities: Economic Lives in Early Modern Britain* (London, 2002)

10. Coleman, *Economy of England*, 139–42; B. Dietz, 'Overseas trade and metropolitan growth', in *The Making of the Metropolis*, ed. A. L. Beier and R. Finlay (London, 1986), 115–40.

11. J. T. Fuhrmann, *The Origins of Capitalism in Russia* (Chicago, 1972), 123–8, 185–9, with ch. 6 for Peter Marselis, and chs 11–12 for the reception of foreigners; commercial regulation is also discussed by J. M. Hittle, *The Service City: State and Townsmen in Russia 1600–1800* (Cambridge, MA, 1979), 62–76.

12. P. Kriedte, H. Medick and J. Schlumbohm, *Industrialisation before Industrialisation* (Cambridge, 1981), 85–8; R. Houston and K. D. M. Snell, 'Proto-industrialisation: cottage industry, social change and industrial revolution', *Historical Journal*, 27 (1984), 473–92; S. C. Ogilvie and M. Cerman (eds), *European Proto-industrialisation* (Cambridge, 1996); see also Flinn, *European Demographic System*, 35–9, for a summary of the work done to that date to distinguish established peasant life patterns from those of these different economic groups. On the broader issue of artisanal work patterns, see notably G. Crossick, *The Artisan and the European Town, 1500–1900* (Aldershot, 1997), and the wonderful insights into self-perceptions offered by J. Amelang, *The Flight of Icarus: Artisan Autobiography in Early Modern Europe* (Cambridge, 1999).

13. Sugar, *Southeastern Europe under Ottoman Rule*; McGowan, *Economic Life in Ottoman Europe*; and S. Faroqhi, B. McGowan, D. Quataert and S. Pamuk (eds), *An Economic and Social History of the Ottoman Empire*, vol. 2: 1600–1914 (Cambridge, 1997) provide an evolving outline of research issues in the Ottoman economy so far.

Chapter 5   The structure of society: nobility, office-holders and the rich

1. Loyseau was also adopted by the French historian R. Mousnier as a reference point to describe even the reality of early modern society in France, as in his *Les institutions de la France*, vol. 1 (Paris, 1974), 14–23.
2. On Gregory King, see ch. 3, note 16; cf. the discussion of contemporary English perceptions in Wrightson, *English Society*, 16–38; R. Molesworth, *An Account of Denmark as it was in the Year 1692* (1694), 82f [fascimile repr., Copenhagen, 1976].
3. C. Jago, 'The influence of debt on the relations between crown and aristocracy in 17th-century Castile', *Economic History Review*, 26 (1973), 218–36, where he emphasises the extent to which the Castilian nobility had to rely on the Crown for dispensations from the *mayorazgo* system, accounting at least in part for the rapid growth in the number of nobles spending considerable time at court.
4. J. Jørgensen, *Rentemester Henrik Müller* (Copenhagen, 1966), esp. 109–29. It is likely that wholesale alienation of crown land to mostly unwilling creditors damaged the long-term financial credibility of the monarchy and frightened off potential foreign capital. For commoners with social aspirations, however, this type of deal may initially have appeared quite attractive; later on, Müller, despite his attempts to reorganise his estates, was not the only one to complain that the returns from landed property were poor.
5. For a lively commentary at the time, see J. H. Hexter, *Reappraisals in History* (Aberdeen, 1961), and his 'The English aristocracy', *Journal of British Studies*, 8 (1968), 22–78.
6. L. Stone, *The Crisis of the Aristocracy 1558–1641* (Oxford, 1965), 7–8. See also the comments by D. C. Coleman in *History*, 51 (1966), 165–78, by R. Ashton in *Economic History Review*, 22 (1969), 308–22, and the debate in the same journal, 25 (1972), 114f; and S. Woolf, 'The aristocracy in transition', *Economic History Review*, 23 (1970), 520–31.
7. S. Woolf, 'Economic problems of the nobility in the early modern period: the example of Piedmont', *Economic History Review*, 17 (1964–5), 267–83; P. Burke, *Venice and Amsterdam: A Study of Seventeenth-century Elites* (London, 1974), 101–12.
8. C. Jago, 'The influence of debt', and 'The "crisis of the aristocracy" in 17th-century Castile', *Past & Present*, 84 (1979), 60–90; E. Ladewig Petersen, *Danish Nobility*, and his *Fra standssamfund til rangssamfund: det danske samfund 1500–1700* (vol. 3 of *Dansk socialhistorie*), (Copenhagen, 1979), 261–77, 328–32; Engberg, 'Det 17. århundredes politiske krise', 388–411. An advantage for Danish landowners (especially compared with the French) was that fewer peasant rents were commuted to money, and payments in kind were of course immune to inflation: E. Ladewig Petersen, *Christian IVs pengeudlån til danske adelige* (Copenhagen, 1974); O. Fenger and E. Ladewig Petersen, *Adel forpligter* (Copenhagen, 1983).
9. The extensive debate can be followed through a sequence of works, such as J. H. Shennan, *Government and Society in France 1461–1661*

(London, 1969); A. N. Hamscher, *The Parlement of Paris after the Fronde* (Pittsburgh, PA, 1976); R. Bonney, *Political Change in France under Richelieu and Mazarin 1624–61* (Oxford, 1978); R. R. Harding, *Anatomy of a Power Elite: The Provincial Governors of Early Modern France* (New Haven, CT, 1979); J. B. Wood, *The Nobility of the Election of Bayeux 1463–1666* (Princeton, NJ, 1980); Dessert, *Argent, pouvoir et société*; Bergin, *Cardinal Richelieu*; W. Beik, *Absolutism and Society in Seventeenth-Century France: State Power and Provincial Aristocracy in Languedoc* (Cambridge, 1985); and, for a recent perceptive analysis of a complex and dynamic elite, D. Bohanan, *Crown and Nobility in Early Modern France* (Basingstoke, 2001). For the mental world of the French nobility, see notably J. Dewald, *Aristocratic Experience and the Origins of Modern Culture: France 1570–1715* (Berkeley, CA, 1993).

10.   Only paupers were not classified for this tax. For an examination of the ranking within each of the 22 classes of the tax, and the social implications, see A. Guéry, 'Etat, classification sociale et compromis sous Louis XIV: la capitation de 1695', *Annales* (1986), 1041–60.

11.   I. A. A. Thompson, 'The purchase of nobility in Castile 1552–1700', *Journal of European Economic History*, 8 (1979), 313–60; the Crown did make more use of grants in its patronage system, according to J. S. Amelang, 'The purchase of nobility in Castile', *Journal of European Economic History*, 11 (1982), 219–26, but these cannot be described as simple sales.

12.   G. E. Aylmer's major studies of the civil service 1625–60, *The King's Servants: the Civil Service of Charles I* (London, 1961), *The State's Servants: the Civil Service of the English Republic* (London, 1973) and *The Crown's Servants: Government and Civil Service under Charles II* (Oxford, 2002) place venality and purchase on a wider scale of patronage, fee-taking and corruption, seen in terms of contemporary standards of what was deemed acceptable. He accepts that the Long Parliament did genuinely have a stricter attitude to abuses of this kind, even if its practical measures were not always as effective as intended (see latter work, 78ff, 341f and *passim*). After the Restoration, the old practices returned, but the Crown appears to have been more discreet. H. Tomlinson, 'Financial administrative developments in England 1660–88', in *The Restored Monarchy 1660–1688*, ed. J. R. Jones (London, 1979), suggests that the practice of equating certain offices with property declined in the Restoration period, limiting the effects of venality.

13.   The exodus may have been less dramatic than was once assumed: Evans, *Making of the Habsburg Monarchy*, 195ff; J. V. Polisensky, *War and Society in Europe 1618–48* (Cambridge, 1978), 202–16; cf. ch. 1.

14.   Bérenger, *Finances et absolutisme autrichien*, 421–7; G. Benecke, 'Ennoblement and privilege in early modern Germany', *History*, 56 (1971), 360–70. On the Austrian nobility see also *Spezialforschungen und Gesamtgeschichte: Beispiele und Methodenfragen zur Geschichte der frühen Neuzeit*, ed. G. Klingenstein and H. Lutz (Vienna, 1982), part I: 'Der niederösterreichische Adel um 1600'. For grants of titles to townsmen, see notably E. Riedenauer, 'Kaiserliche Standeserhebung für

Reichstädtische Bürger 1519–1740', in *Deutsches Patriziat 1430–1740*, ed. H. Rössler (Limburg, 1968).

15. H. C. Wolter, *Adel og embede* (Copenhagen, 1982); K. J. V. Jespersen (ed.), *Rigsråd, adel og administration 1570–1648* (Odense, 1980); B. B. Jensen, *Udnævnelsesretten i enevældens magtpolitiske system 1660–1730* (Copenhagen, 1987), esp. 283–93; see also the short survey in T. Munck, *The Peasantry and the Early Absolute Monarchy in Denmark 1660–1708* (Copenhagen, 1979), chs 1–2. Alienations in Norway were much less substantial, and had different long-term consequences since a significant proportion of the ultimate owners were the peasantry themselves.

16. Roberts, *Gustavus Adolphus*, vol. 2, 158–60; M. Roberts (ed.), *Sweden's Age of Greatness 1632–1718* (London, 1973), especially sections by S. E. Åstrom, 'The Swedish economy and Sweden's role as a great power', 75–9, and by S. Dahlgren, 'Estates and classes', 119–31; A.F. Upton, *Charles XI and Swedish Absolutism* (Cambridge, 1998), esp. chs 4 and 7.

17. B. Plavsic, 'Seventeenth-century chanceries and their staffs', ch. 2 of *Russian Officialdom: The Bureaucratisation of Russian society*, ed. W. M. Pintner and D. K. Rowney (London, 1980); see also chs 3–4 in the same volume; R. Hellie, *Enserfment and Military Change in Muscovy* (Chicago, 1971), 21–74; R. O. Crumney, *Aristocrats and Servitors* (Princeton, NJ, 1983); J. Keep, 'The Muscovite elite and the approach to pluralism', *Slavonic and East European Review*, 48 (1970), 201–31, and his *Soldiers of the Tsar: Army and Society in Russia 1462–1874* (Oxford, 1985), ch. 2.

18. McGowan, *Economic Life in Ottoman Europe*, 45–79; Faroqhi, McGowan, Quataert and Pamuk (eds), *An Economic and Social History of the Ottoman Empire*, vol. 2, 549–52 and 566–72.

Chapter 6 The structure of society: urban life

1. For a discussion of contemporary usage of the word 'bourgeoisie', and its modern meanings in terms of capital, enterprise and function or mental attitudes, see J. Corcia, 'Bourg, bourgeois, bourgeois de Paris from the 11th to the 18th century', *Journal of Modern History*, 50 (1978), 207–33; cf. R. Mousnier, 'Recherches sur les structures sociales parisiennes en 1634, 1635, 1636', *Revue historique*, 250 (1973), 35–58; P. Earle, *The Making of the English Middle Class: Business, Society and Family Life in London, 1660–1730* (London, 1989); and H. R. French, 'The search for the "middling sort of people" in England, 1600–1800', *Historical Journal* 43 (2000), 277–93.

2. D. R. Ringrose, 'The impact of a new capital city: Madrid, Toledo and New Castile 1560–1660', *Journal of Economic History*, 33 (1973), 761–91, and his *Madrid and the Spanish Economy 1560–1850* (Berkeley, CA, 1983); M. Weisser, 'The decline of Castile revisited: the case of Toledo', *Journal of European Economic History*, 2 (1973), 614–40; L. Martz, *Poverty and Welfare in Habsburg Spain: The Example of Toledo* (Cambridge, 1983).

3. de Vries, *Economy of Europe in an Age of Crisis*, 148–59, and his *European Urbanisation 1500–1800* (London, 1984), which also considers

definition problems in detail; see also his 'Patterns of urbanisation in pre-industrial Europe 1500–1800', in *Patterns of European Urbanisation since 1500*, ed. H. Schmal (London, 1981), 77–109.

4. M. Walker, *German Home Towns 1648–1871* (Ithaca, NY, 1971), 27–31; Clark and Slack, *English Towns*, 17–45 and *passim*.

5. Goubert, *Beauvais*, 256–64.

6. C. R. Friedrichs, *Urban Society in an Age of War: Nördlingen 1580–1720* (Princeton, NJ, 1979), 73–143, 258–87.

7. The term 'patriciate', in the sense used by Walker, *German Home Towns*, 59ff, by P. Burke, 'Patrician culture: Venice and Amsterdam in the 17th century', *Transactions of the Royal Historical Society*, 23 (1973), 135, and by A. F. Cowan, *The Urban Patriciate: Lübeck and Venice 1580–1700* (Cologne, 1986), refers to a fairly small and exclusive group of families with a dominant political lifestyle protected through privileges based on their power. For a wider discussion, see A. Cowan, *Urban Europe 1500–1700* (London, 1998), 51–68.

8. It is noteworthy how frequently an imperial commission intervened in urban disputes, and imperial institutions were evidently still of significance: see O. Brunner, *Neue Wege der Verfassungs- und Sozialgeschichte* (Göttingen, 1968), 294–321; H. Mauersberger, *Wirtschafts- und Sozialgeschichte zentraleuropäischer Städte* (Göttingen, 1960), 113ff; G. Soliday, *A Community in Conflict: Frankfurt Society in the 17th and Early 18th Centuries* (Hanover, NH, 1974); M. Reissmann, *Die hamburgische Kaufmannschaft* (Hamburg, 1975); H. Ruckleben, *Die Niederwerfung der hamburgische Ratsgewalt* (Hamburg, 1970); J. Whaley, *Religious Toleration and Social Change in Hamburg 1529–1819* (Cambridge, 1985), ch. 1. Given the complexity of political connections and of delegated authority in the Empire, it is not surprising that urban conflicts often resulted in the involvement of several princes and other authorities, often with different aims despite nominal allegiance to imperial instructions: see notably C. R. Friedrichs, 'German town revolts and the 17th-century crisis', *Renaissance & Modern Studies*, 26 (1982), 27–51; his 'Urban conflicts and the imperial constitution in 17th-century Germany', *Journal of Modern History*, 58 (1986), suppl. S98–123; and his 'Urban politics and urban social structure in seventeenth-century Germany', *European History Quarterly* 22 (1992), 187–216. For the rather different nature of urban politics in England, see P. D. Halliday, *Dismembering the Body Politic: Partisan Politics in England's Towns, 1640–1730* (Cambridge, 1998).

9. R. Mackenney, *Tradesmen and Traders* (London, 1987), 223–32.

10. B. Lepetit, 'Une création urbaine: Versailles de 1661 a 1722', *Revue d'histoire moderne et contemporaine*, 25 (1978), 604–18.

11. H. Sauval, *Histoire et recherches des antiquités de la ville de Paris* (Paris, 1724), vol. 1, 511, cited in L. Bernard, *The Emerging City: Paris in the Age of Louis XIV* (Durham, NC, 1970), 161. On the wider subject of 'police', it must be noted that the Parisian force, like its imitations elsewhere in Europe (for example in Denmark after 1682) was not at this stage an organisation aimed primarily at crime. Its functions were much wider, ranging over all aspects of orderly community existence, including the

protection of commerce, guilds and the market, together with the preservation of social deference and the sense of hierarchy.

12. Rapp, *Industry and Economic Decline in 17th-Century Venice*, 25–9. Women and children were also used to evade guild regulations: C. R. Boxer, *The Dutch Seaborne Empire 1600–1800* (London, 1965/77), 54f. R. Mackenney, *Tradesmen*, 122–4 and *passim*, has argued for a new look at guilds and their positive role in early modern life.

13. The notion of a subculture, and of some kind of organisational confraternities amongst, for example, rural bandits and urban criminal elements, was a common assumption amongst the better-off at the time. It is not, however, easily substantiated in fact: see H. Kamen, *The Iron Century* (London, 1971), 400–3; P. Burke, 'Perceiving a counterculture', in *The Historical Anthropology of Early Modern Italy* (Cambridge, 1987), 63–75; M. E. Perry, *Crime and Society in Early Modern Seville* (Hanover, NH, 1980), 106–11 and *passim*; J. A. Sharpe, *Crime in Seventeenth Century England* (Cambridge, 1983), 179–81; A. L. Beier, *Masterless Men: The Vagrancy Problem in England 1560–1640* (London, 1985), 123–45.

14. Wrightson and Levine, *Poverty and Piety*, 39–42; cf. T. Wales, 'Poverty, poor relief and the life-cycle', in *Land, Kinship and Life-cycle*, ed. R. M. Smith (Cambridge, 1984), 353–7; my estimates of nutritional content are based on modern recommendations.

15. Vauban, *Dîme royale*, 76–8, 81–3. Estimating wages in the early modern period is very difficult, because of complexities of subcontracting, differences between nominal and real wages once deductions for debts and other obligations to the employer were made, and because other forms of payment (in kind) were common.

16. The nature of early modern rioting has been extensively studied, especially by British and French scholars. For England, see notably J. Walter and K. Wrightson, 'Dearth and the social order in early modern England', *Past & Present*, 71 (1976), 22–42; J. Walter, 'Grain riots and popular attitudes to the law', in *An Ungovernable People*, ed. J. Brewer and J. Styles (London, 1980), 47–84; Fletcher and Stevenson (eds), *Order and Disorder*, 1–40; the short survey by B. Sharp, 'Popular protest in 17th century England', in *Popular Culture in Seventheenth-Century England*, ed. B. Reay (London, 1985), 271–303; and the important analyses by E. P. Thompson, notably his 'The moral economy of the English crowd in the 18th century', *Past & Present*, 50 (1971), 76–136. On France, see notably Beik, *Urban Protest*. See also ch. 12.

17. J. M. Beattie, 'The pattern of crime in England 1660–1800', *Past & Present*, 62 (1974), 47–95, and the same author's books on *Crime and the Courts in England 1660–1800* (Oxford, 1986), chs 5 and 8, and *Policing and Punishment in London 1660–1750* (Oxford, 2001); J. S. Cockburn, 'The nature and incidence of crime in England 1559–1625', in *Crime in England 1550–1800*, ed. J. S. Cockburn (London, 1977), 49–71; R. B. Shoemaker, *Prosecution and Punishment: Petty Crime and the Law in London and Rural Middlesex, c.1660–1725* (Cambridge, 1991). Punishments for theft were often mitigated in practice by deliberate 'miscarriages' of justice, and the harshest sentences were relatively rare:

C. Herrup, 'Law and morality in 17th-century England', *Past &
Present*, 106 (1985), 102–23, and her *The Common Peace: Participation
and the Criminal Law in 17th Century England* (Cambridge, 1987),
155–8, 166–82.

18. Sharpe, *Crime in 17th Century England*, 91–114; H. Kamen, *Spain in the
Later Seventeenth Century* (London, 1980), 168ff; on outlaws and rebels,
see also J. Casey, *The Kingdom of Valencia in the Seventeenth century*
(Cambridge, 1979), ch. 9.

19. P. A. Slack, 'Vagrants and vagrancy in England 1598–1664', *Economic
History Review*, 27 (1974), 360–79; D. Souden, 'Migrants and the popu-
lation structure of later 17th-century provincial towns', in *The
Transformation of English Provincial Towns 1600–1800*, ed. P. Clark
(London, 1984), 133–68; Beier, *Masterless Men*, 14–28.

20. W. K. Jordan, *Philanthropy in England 1480–1660* (London, 1959),
passim; and the discussion of his conclusions by Fiengold in *History of
Education*, 8 (1979), 257–73, by Bittle and Lane in *Economic History
Review*, 29 (1976), 203–10, and the resulting debate in *Economic History
Review*, 31 (1978), 105–28. For a southern-European perspective on
private charity, see S. Cavallo, *Charity and Power in Early Modern Italy:
Benefactors and their Motives in Turin, 1541–1789* (Cambridge, 1995)

21. P. Slack, *Poverty and Polity in Tudor and Stuart England* (London,
1988), 170f., estimates that poor rates in England and Wales by the end
of the century yielded at least £400,000 a year, or three times the
amount collected via charity. See also his excellent *From Reformation to
Improvement: Public Welfare in Early Modern England* (Oxford, 1999).
Francis Brewster's comment, in his *Essays on Trade and Navigation*
(London, 1695), 58, is cited from S. Macfarlane, 'Social policy and the
poor in the later seventeenth century', in *London 1500–1700*, ed. A. L.
Beier and R. Finlay (London, 1986), 253.

22. T. J. McHugh, 'The Hôpital Général, the Parisian elites and crown
social policy during the reign of Louis XIV', *French History* 15 (2001),
235–53. For a new way of looking at why workhouses came to be permanent fixtures in early modern European poor relief policies, see J. F.
Harrington, 'Escape from the Great Confinement: the genealogy of a
German workhouse', *Journal of Modern History* 71 (1999), 308–45.

Chapter 7 Provincial revolts, civil war and crises in
mid-century Europe

1. J. Thirsk (ed.). *The Agrarian History of England and Wales*, vol. 4
(Cambridge, 1967), 815–21. For continental prices, see the index:
Prices.

2. For excellent short surveys see especially T. K. Rabb, *The Struggle for
Stability in Early Modern Europe* (Oxford, 1975), chs 1–6; T. Aston
(ed.), *Crisis in Europe 1560–1660* (London, 1965); Parker and Smith
(eds), *General Crisis of the Seventeenth Century*; H. G. Koenigsberger,
'Die Krise des 17. Jahrhunderts', *Zeitschrift für historische Forschung*, 9
(1982), 143–65, and 'The crisis of the 17th century: a farewell?', in his
Politicians and Virtuosi (London, 1986), 149–68; and for the relevance of

the crisis thesis to central Europe, S. C. Ogilvie, 'Germany and the seventeenth-century Crisis', *Historical Journal*, 35 (1992), 417–41.

3. A. Lossky, 'The general crisis of the 1680s', *European Studies Review*, 10 (1980), 177–97; P. Clark, (ed.), *The European Crisis of the 1590s* (London, 1985), including the stimulating evaluation there by J. H. Elliott, 301–12.

4. Rabb, *Struggle for Stability*, 29–34.

5. Unger, 'Trade through the Sound', 206–21; P. Jeannin, 'Les comptes du Sund', *Revue historique*, 231 (1964), 55–102, 307–40; R. Romano in Parker and Smith, *General Crisis*, ch. 7.

6. A. Wyczanski, 'The system of power in Poland, 1370–1648', in *East Central Europe in Transition*, ed. A. Maczak et al. (Cambridge, 1985), 140–52; A. Maczak, 'The structure of power in the Commonwealth of the 16th and 17th centuries', in *A Republic of Nobles*, ed. J. K. Fedorowicz (1982), esp. 130–2. A particular part of the commonwealth, which escaped Hohenzollern control, has recently been studied in illuminating detail over a longer timespan: K. Friedrich, *The Other Prussia: Royal Prussia, Poland and Liberty, 1569–1772* (Cambridge, 2000), with particular discussion of the 1650s, 121–46.

7. R. I. Frost, ' "Initium calamitatis Regni"? John Casimir and monarchical power in Poland–Lithuania, 1648–68', *European History Quarterly*, 16 (1986), 181–207; his *After the Deluge: Poland–Lithuania and the Second Northern War 1655–1660* (Cambridge, 1993); and his informative discussion of the ambivalent relations between king and nobility in Poland, in 'Obsequious disrespect: the problem of royal power in the Polish–Lithuanian Commonwealth under the Vasas, 1587–1668', in *The Polish–Lithuanian Monarchy in European Context, c.1500–1795*, ed. R. Butterwick (Basingstoke, 2001), 150–71.

8. L. P. Peirce, *The Imperial Harem: Women and Sovereignty in the Ottoman Empire* (Oxford, 1993), offers some striking new insights into the nature of court politics in this period.

9. H. G. Koenigsberger, *Estates and Revolutions* (London, 1971), 253–77; P. Burke, 'The Virgin of the Carmine and the revolt of Masaniello', *Past & Present*, 99 (1983), 3–21; P. Villari, 'Masaniello: contemporary and recent interpretations', *Past & Present*, 108 (1985), 117–32.

10. J. H. Elliott, *The Revolt of the Catalans* (Cambridge, 1963), esp. ch. 16; R. A. Stradling, 'Seventeenth-century Spain: decline or survival?', *European Studies Review*, 9 (1979), 157–94; Stradling, *Europe and the Decline of Spain* (London, 1981), esp. 115–42.

11. Amongst more recent work on the Fronde, see notably R. Bonney, 'La Fronde des officiers', *xviie siècle*, 145 (1984), 323–40; F. Bayard, 'Les financiers et la Fronde', ibid., 355–62, and other articles in the same issue; W. Beik, 'Urban factions and the social order during the minority of Louis XIV', *French Historical Studies*, 15 (1987), 36–67; and O. Ranum, *The Fronde: A French Revolution, 1648–1652* (New York, 1993).

12. D. Parker, *The Making of French Absolutism* (London, 1983), 103–17; see also the very perceptive analysis in Collins, *The State in Early Modern France*.

13. S. A. Westrich, *The Ormée of Bordeaux* (Baltimore, 1972); H. Kötting, *Die Ormée (1651–1653)* (Münster, 1983), argues that the movement involved too broad a social spectrum to make it immune to tactical manipulation and incitation by the political elite. Kötting also discusses the contacts between Bordeaux and the English revolutionaries, 122–36, 155–65, 194–244.

14. One of the most distinguished historians of this period, J. Morrill, concluded already in his 'The religious context of the English civil war', *Transactions of the Royal Historical Society*, 34 (1984), 155–78, that religion was so central an issue in terms of 1642 that the civil war 'was not the first European revolution: it was the last of the Wars of Religion'. See also J. C. Davis, 'Religion and the struggle for freedom in the English Revolution', *Historical Journal*, 35 (1992), 507–30.

15. As in Germany during the Thirty Years War, though generally on a much lesser scale, damage to local economies and the destructive effect of war impositions varied enormously in different parts of England in the 1640s. I. Roy, 'England turned Germany: The aftermath of the Civil War in its European context', *Transactions of the Royal Historical Society*, 28 (1978), 127–44, argues that continental-style practices and exactions were common because of the number of soldiers returning from service abroad; in the west of England, the damage was severe. See also J. S. Morril and J. D. Walter, 'Order and disorder in the English Revolution', in *Order and Disorder*, ed. Fletcher and Stevenson, 137–65. For the effects of the civil war on Scottish towns, and their remarkable resilience in the 1650s, see D. Stevenson, 'The burghs and the Scottish revolution', in *The Early Modern Town in Scotland*, ed. M. Lynch (London, 1987), 167–91. For a recent survey of the impact of the Scots on northern England, see E. M. Furgol, 'The military and ministers as agents of Presbyterian imperialism in England and Ireland, 1640–48', in *New Perspectives on the Politics and Culture of Early Modern Scotland*, ed. J. Dwyer et al. (Edinburgh, n.d.), 95–115.

16. See V. Pearl, 'London's counter-revolution', in *The Interregnum*, ed. G. E. Aylmer (London, 1972), 29–56; R. Brenner, 'The civil war politics of London's merchant community', *Past & Present*, 58 (1973), 53–107.

17. For recent work on this pivotal political step, see S. Kelsey, 'The Trial of Charles I', *English Historical Review*, 118 (2003), 583–616, and his 'The Death of Charles I', *Historical Journal*, 45 (2002), 727–54; for the point of view of this unusually thoughtful monarch, see also K. Sharpe, 'Private conscience and public duty in the writings of Charles I', *Historical Journal*, 40 (1997), 643–65.

18. Ashton, *English Civil War*, 337f; Morrill (ed.), *Reactions to the English Civil War*, 25–7; S. Barber, *Regicide and Republicanism: Politics and Ethics in the English Revolution* (Keele, 1998); D. A. Orr, *Treason and the State: Law, Politics and Ideology in the English Civil War* (Cambridge, 2002); S. Kelsey, *Inventing a Republic: The Political Culture of the English Commonwealth* (Manchester, 1997); and the large recent literature on Cormwell and the Protectorate, including, for example, L. L. Knoppers, *Constructing Cromwell: Ceremony, Portrait and Print 1645–1661* (Cambridge, 2000). On relations between the component

parts of the republic, see D. Hirst, 'The English Republic and the meaning of Britain', *Journal of Modern History*, 66 (1994), 451–86; on the stature of the King over a longer time-span, see K. Sharpe, ' "So hard a text"? Images of Charles I', 1612–1700, *Historical Journal*, 43 (2000), 383–405.

19. B. Reay, 'Quakerism and Society', in *Radical Religion in the English Revolution*, ed. J. F. McGregor and B. Reay (Oxford, 1984), 141–64 and esp. 161ff; B. Reay, *The Quakers and the English Revolution* (London, 1985); C. Hill, *The World Turned Upside Down* (London, 1975); regarding the Ranters, see also G. E. Aylmer, 'Did the Ranters exist?', *Past & Present*, 117 (1987), 208–19. For discussion of the ubiquitous belief in divine presence, see B. Worden, 'Providence and politics in Cromwellian England', *Past & Present*, 109 (1985), 54–99.

20. C. G. A. Clay, *Economic Expansion and Social Change: England 1500–1700* (Cambridge, 1984), ii, 263–6. R. Bonney, 'The English and French Civil Wars', *History*, 65 (1980), 365–82, estimates that in the early 1630s the income of the French Crown had been at least eleven times that of Charles I, for a population around four times the size; this difference in resources was later diminished, however, because of growing problems in the French fiscal system, the costs of administration itself (compared with the many local office-holders in England who were paid nothing by the state), and the crisis of confidence in the French system of venality of offices.

21. Munck, *The Peasantry and the Early Absolute Monarchy in Denmark*, 39–53.

22. Roberts, 'Queen Christina and the general crisis of the 17th century', in his *Essays in Swedish History*, 111–37.

23. Roberts, *Sweden as a Great Power 1611–97*, 44–9, 98–110.

24. S. Dahlgren, 'Estates and revolutions', in *Sweden's Age of Greatness*, ed. Roberts, 102–31.

Chapter 8   The structure of society: peasant and seigneur

1. The three-field system did have a number of important variants, and was not the predominant form in the Netherlands, the arable parts of Scotland or much of southern Scandinavia. For a short survey of some of the complexities of field systems, see Karl-Erik Frandsen, 'Danish field systems in the 17th century', *Scandinavian Journal of History*, 8 (1983), 293–317, which includes comments on the European context; for a broader view, see R. L. Hopcroft, *Regions, Institutions and Agrarian Change in European History* (Ann Arbor, MI, 1999); and T. Kjærgaard, *The Danish Revolution 1500–1800: An Ecohistorical Interpretation* (Cambridge, 1994).

2. *Family and Inheritance: Rural Society in Western Europe 1200–1800*, eds J. Goody, J. Thirsk and E. P. Thompson (Cambridge, 1976), 37–95; J. Blum, *The End of the Old Order in Rural Europe* (Princeton, NJ, 1978), chs 5–7; H. Rebel, *Peasant Classes: The Bureaucratisation of Property and Family Relations under Early Habsburg Absolutism, 1511–1636* (Princeton, NJ, 1983), ch. 5 and *passim*.

3. W. Abel, *Geschichte der deutschen Landwirtschaft* (Stuttgart, 1962), 204f.
4. For a full explanation of these terms, see W. Hagen, 'Village life in East-Elbian Germany and Poland, 1400–1800: subjection, self-defence, survival', in *The Peasantries of Europe*, ed. T. Scott (London, 1998), 145–89, esp. 150f.
5. For a broad sweep, see F. Adanir, 'The Ottoman Peasantries, *c.*1360–*c.*1860', in *Peasantries of Europe*, ed. Scott, 269–310.
6. J. Blum, 'The rise of serfdom in eastern Europe', *American Historical Review*, 62 (1957), 807–36; R. E. F. Smith, *The Enserfment of the Russian Peasantry* (Cambridge, 1968); R. Hellie, *Enserfment and Military Change in Muscovy* (Chicago, 1971); E. Melton, 'The Russian Peasantries', in *Peasantries of Europe*, ed. Scott, 227–66; D. Moon, *The Russian Peasantry 1600–1930: The World the Peasants made* (New York, 1999).
7. R. Hellie, *Slavery in Russia 1450–1725* (Chicago, 1983), 681–9 and *passim*. Slavery also existed especially in the Mediterranean parts of Europe, but was not institutionalised to this extent except in the overseas colonies.
8. A. Kaminski, 'Neo-serfdom in Poland–Lithuania', *Slavic Review*, 34 (1975), esp. 262f; Topolski, 'Economic decline in Poland', in *Essays in European Economic History*, ed. Earle, esp. 131–5; L. Zytkowicz, 'The peasant's farm and the landlord's farm in Poland from the 16th to the 18th century', *Journal of European Economic History*, 1 (1972), esp. 148–52; Z. Kirilly and I. N. Kiss, 'Production de céréales et exploitations paysannes en Hongrie aux xvie–xviie siècles', *Annales*, 23 (1968), 1211–36; L. Zytkowicz, 'Trends of agrarian economy in Poland, Bohemia and Hungary', in *East-central Europe in Transition*, ed. Maczak et al., 59–83; E. Melton, 'Population structure, the market economy, and the transformation of Gutsherrschaft in east central Europe 1650–1800: the cases of Brandenburg and Bohemia', *German History* 16 (1998), 297–327.
9. W. Hagen, *Ordinary Prussians: Brandenburg Junkers and Villagers, 1500–1840* (Cambridge, 2002).
10. Sella, *Crisis and Continuity*, 105–34. The debate on refeudalisation is outlined in Sella, *Italy in the seventeenth Century*, 63–9; on the characteristically composite and often highly developed Italian rural economy, see C. F. Black, *Early Modern Italy: A Social History* (Aldershot, 2001), 43–62.
11. Rebel, *Peasant Classes*, 21–36, 53–76 and *passim*.
12. In theory tenants had security for life, but in practice debts and overburdening led to fairly frequent defaults. Some peasant tenancies were simply enclosed within the demesne (despite legislation to the contrary), but vacant holdings would otherwise still be liable for taxation and hence a burden on the estate as whole. For a fuller discussion, see Munck, *The Peasantry*, 55f, 65–88, 175–96.
13. J. de Vries, *The Dutch Rural Economy in the Golden Age, 1500–1700* (New Haven, CT, 1974), 34f, 214–24.
14. Thirsk (ed.), *Agrarian History of England and Wales*, vol. 4, 232–8; see also Clay, *Economic Expansion and Social Change*, vol. 1, 53–101, for a survey of rural society and the expansion of the commercial sector.
15. Alan MacFarlane has argued that from a sociological or anthropological point of view the term 'peasant' is inappropriate for England. See his

'The peasantry in England before the Industrial Revolution: a mythical model', in *Social Organisation and Settlement*, ed. D. Green et al. (Oxford, 1978), 325–41; or his *The Origins of English Individualism* (Oxford, 1978). His criteria, however, are too restrictive historically for much of continental Europe too, and have accordingly not been adopted. For a critical assessment of his views, see notably Rebel, *Peasant Classes*, 123–5. See also Eva Österberg, ' "Den gamla goda tiden": bilder och motbilder i ett modernt forskningsläge om dett äldre agrarsamhället', *Scandia*, 48 (1982), 31–60.

16. The timing of an 'agrarian revolution' in England has been the object of much controversy: see for example, J. Thirsk, 'Seventeenth-century agriculture and social change', in *Agricultural History Review*, 18 (1970), suppl., 148–77; her discussion in *Agrarian History of England and Wales*, ed. Thirsk, vol. 5, part 2, pp. 533–71; or the short survey in J.V. Beckett, *The Agricultural Revolution* (Oxford, 1990). See also J. Cooper, 'In search of agrarian capitalism,' *Past & Present*, 80 (1978), for reservations about the scale of change in early modern England by comparison with France.

17. Goubert, *Beauvais*, 158–89; and his article 'The French peasantry of the 17th century: a regional example', *Past & Present*, 10 (1956), 66–8.

18. On the growing significance of urban landownership, see especially P. T. Hoffman, 'Taxes and agrarian life in early modern France: land sales 1550–1730', *Journal of Economic History*, 46 (1986), 37–55; on taxation, A. Guéry, 'Les finances de la monarchie française sous l'ancien régime', *Annales*, 33 (1978), 216–37, and, for a wider comparative perspective, R. Bonney, *The Rise of the Fiscal State in Europe* (Oxford, 1999). See also ch. 2.

19. See Munck, *The Peasantry*, 63–5, 218–38; J. T. Lauridsen and T. Munck, 'Retstilstande i Danmark i 1500–og 1600-tallet', *Fortid og Nutid*, 29 (1982), 626–46.

20. Cited in W. Schulze, *Bäuerliche Widerstand und feudale Herrschaft in der frühen Neuzeit* (Stuttgart, 1980), pp. 227–33. For a useful survey in English, see T. Scott, 'Peasant revolts in early modern Germany', *Historical Journal*, 28 (1985), 455–68.

21. Cited from Svenska Riksrådets Protokoll, by S. Dahlgren, 'Estates and classes', in *Sweden's Age of Greatness*, ed. Roberts, 107.

22. The most controversial contributions to the Swedish debate are K. Ågren, *Adelns bönder och kronans: skatter och besvär i Uppland 1650–1680* (Uppsala, 1964), and E. Ernby, *Adeln och bondejorden* (Stockholm, 1975). See also I. Hammarström, 'Kronan, adeln och bönderna under 1600-talet', *Historisk Tidskrift (Stockholm)* (1964), 423–44.

23. See notably S. Cohn, *Popular Protest in Late Medieval Europe: Italy, France and Flanders* (Manchester, 2004); and his forthcoming work on *The Politics of Social Revolt in Medieval Europe, c.1200–1425*, which he has kindly allowed me to read before publication.

Chapter 9   Beliefs, *mentalités*, knowledge and the printed text

1. C. Ginzburg, *The Cheese and the Worms: The Cosmos of a Sixteenth-Century Miller* (London, 1980), *passim*.

2. P. Burke, *Popular Culture in Early Modern Europe* (London, 1978), 65–77 and *passim*; R. Muchembled, *Culture and Elite Culture in France* (Baton Rouge, LA, 1985; French original, Paris, 1978); Ginsburg, *Cheese and Worms*, xiv–xix; R. Chartier, 'Culture as appropriation', in *Understanding Popular Culture*, ed. S. L. Kaplan (Berlin, 1984), 229–53; S. Clark, 'French historians and early modern popular culture', *Past & Present*, 100 (1983), 62–99; B. Reay (ed.), 'Popular culture in early modern England', in *Popular Culture*, 1–30; and, on the enforcement of sexual morality, chs 4–5 in the same volume; B. Reay (ed), *Popular Cultures in England 1550–1750* (London, 1998).

3. There is a very large body of literature on millenarianism in England, but see notably K. Thomas, *Religion and the Decline of Magic* (London, 1971), 156–73; and B. S. Capp, *The Fifth Monarchy Men: A Study in Seventeenth-Century Millenarianism* (London, 1972). For a much less significant but interesting continental manifestation, see R. M. Golden, 'Religious extremism in the mid-17th century: the Parisian *illuminés*', *European Studies Review*, 9 (1979), 195–210.

4. R. Briggs, *Witches and Neighbours: The social and cultural Context of European Witchcraft* (2nd edn, Oxford, 2002), 224–49; L. Roper, *Oedipus and the Devil: Witchcraft, Sexuality and Religion 1500–1700* (London, 1994)

5. This extraordinary outcome of one of the most severe witch hunts on the Franco–Spanish border is analysed by G. Henningsen, *The Witches' Advocate: Basque Witchcraft and the Spanish Inquisition (1609–1614)* (Reno, NV, 1980), esp. chs 11–13; see also G. Parker, 'Some recent work on the Inquisition in Spain and Italy', *Journal of Modern History*, 57 (1982), 519–32.

6. C. Larner, C. H. Lee and H. V. McLachlan, *A Source-book of Scottish Witchcraft* (Glasgow, 1977), 25–39, 120–42. See also C. Larner, *Enemies of God: The Witch-hunt in Scotland* (London, 1981)

7. B. P. Levack, *The Witch-hunt in Early Modern Europe* (London, 1987), 221–4, emphasises the spread of fashionable scepticism as an example of elite withdrawal from popular culture. But the complex impact of power relationships, both within divided local communities and in relation to higher authority, is explored in greater depth in Briggs, *Witches and Neighbours*, 276–320.

8. C. Larner, *The Thinking Peasant: Popular and Educated Belief in Pre-industrial Culture* (Glasgow, 1982), 35.

9. *An Astrological Diary of the Seventeenth Century: Samuel Jeake of Rye 1652–1699*, ed. M. Hunter and A. Gregory (Oxford, 1988), 154f, 175–7, and *passim*.

10. See especially J. Delumeau, *La peur en occident* (Paris, 1978), and his *Le péché et la peur* (Paris, 1983); and, especially for the earlier period, W. G. Naphy and P. Roberts (eds), *Fear in Early Modern Society* (Manchester, 1997). A much more optimistic view of late medieval Christianity is adopted by J. Bossy, notably in *Christianity in the West 1400–1700* (Oxford, 1985), and in 'The Counter-Reformation and the people of Catholic Europe', *Past & Present*, 47 (1970), 51–70.

11. The incident is recounted in D. W. Sabean, *Power in the Blood: Popular Culture and Village Discourse in Early Modern Germany* (Cambridge, 1984), ch. 2.

12. J. Delumeau, *Le catholicisme entre Luther et Voltaire* (Paris, 1971; transl. London, 1977), part III, ch. 4, esp. 290f.

13. B. Lenman, 'The limits of godly discipline in the early modern period with particular reference to England and Scotland', and M. Ingram, 'Religion, communities and moral discipline in late 16th and early 17th-century England', both in *Religion and Society in Early Modern Europe 1500–1800*, ed. K. von Greyerz (London, 1984), 124–45, 177–93.

14. Evans, *The Making of the Habsburg Monarchy 1550–1700*, 362 and ch. 10 *passim*; ominously, von Chaos became the founder of the Austrian military academy! The practice of astrology and alchemy was widespread in the royal and aristocratic houses of Europe. For one of the more enthusiastic cases, see Evans, *Rudolf II and his World* (Oxford, 1973).

15. Reay (ed.), 'Popular religion', in *Popular Culture*, 95.

16. For some of the inherent problems, see D. Spaeth, *The Church in an Age of Danger: Parsons and Parishioners, 1660–1740* (Cambridge, 2001). On the struggle to preserve some flexibility, see J. Coffey, *Persecution and Toleration in Protestant England, 1558–1689* (London, 2000); and J. Sommerville, *The Secularization of Early Modern England: From Religious Culture to Religious Faith* (Oxford, 1992).

17. J. Tazbir, 'The fate of Polish Protestantism in the 17th century', in *Republic of Nobles*, ed. Fedorowicz, 198–217.

18. E. L. Eisenstein, *The Printing Press as an Agent of Change* (Cambridge, 1979), 636–82, argues that the real difference in scientific and intellectual development between Protestant and Roman Catholic Europe can be related directly to the greater freedom of the press in much of the former.

19. R. J. W. Evans, *The Wechel Presses: Humanism and Calvinism in Central Europe 1572–1627* (Oxford, 1975).

20. F. Furet and J. Ozouf, *Lire et écrire: l'alphabétisation des français de Calvin à Jules Ferry*, vol. 1 (Paris, 1977; transl. Cambridge, 1983), esp. 19–27; D. Cressy, *Literacy and the Social Order: Reading and Writing in Tudor and Stuart England* (Oxford, 1980), 62–103, 147 and *passim*; A. Fox, *Oral and Literate Culture in England, 1500–1700* (Oxford, 2000), 1–50 and *passim*; R. A. Houston, *Literacy in early modern Europe* (2nd edn, London, 2002), 141–71. M. Spufford, *Small Books and Pleasant Histories: Popular Fiction and its Readership in Seventeenth-Century England* (Cambridge, 1981), 19–22, has emphasised that, especially amongst women, there may have been significantly more who were able to read than to write. However, some of the former learnt to write their signature and no more, so we may regard signature-based literacy rates as representing estimates standing somewhere between basic reading skills and full literacy: between the higher proportion of people able only to spell their way through texts, and the smaller proportion who were able both to read and to write satisfactorily.

21. A more through discussion is found in T. Munck, 'Literacy, educational reform and the use of print in eighteenth-century Denmark', *European History Quarterly* 34 (2004), 275–303.

22. On French material, see R. Chartier, *The Cultural Uses of Print in Early Modern France* (Princeton, NJ, 1987), 145–239 and elsewhere; for England, see Fox, *Oral and Literate Culture*; and M. Spufford, *Small Books*, especially chs 3–4.

23. H. A. E. van Gelder, *The Two Reformations in the Sixteenth Century* (The Hague, 1961). The debate acquired considerable momentum in the following decades: on England, see for example the wide-ranging discussion on religion and science by C. Hill, H. F. Kearney, T. K. Rabb and B. J. Shapiro in *Past & Present*, from vol. 27 (1964) through to vol. 40 (1968), and by C. Webster, *The Great Instauration: Science, Medicine and Reform, 1626–60* (London, 1975). For more recent work, both on science itself and on the related questions of religious belief, see notably M. J. Osler (ed.), *Rethinking the Scientific Revolution* (Cambridge, 2000); W. G. L. Randles, *The Unmaking of the Medieval Christian Cosmos, 1500–1760: From Solid Heavens to Boundless Aether* (London, 1999); B. M. Dooley, *The Social History of Skepticism: Experience and Doubt in Early Modern Culture* (Baltimore, 1999).

24. C. Ginzburg, 'High and low: the theme of forbidden knowledge in the sixteenth and seventeenth centuries', *Past & Present*, 73 (1976), 28–41.

25. S. Drake, *Galileo* (Oxford, 1980), 53–72, including the citation, 64.

26. P. Redondi, *Galileo: Heretic* (Princeton, NJ, 1988). On the trial itself, see M.A. Finocchiaro, *The Galileo Affair: A Documentary History* (Berkeley, CA, 1989).

27. Drake, *Galileo*, vi.

28. The implications of Cartesianism on religious faith, and the wider repercussions of the gradual rationalisation of the supernatural environment, was explored in P. Hazard, *The European Mind 1680–1715* (1935; trans. London, 1953). See also M. C. Jacob, 'The crisis of the European mind: Hazard revisited', in *Politics and Culture in Early Modern Europe*, ed. P. Mack and M. C. Jacob (Cambridge, 1987), 251–71. For a powerful analysis of the significance of the underlying issues, see J. Israel, *Radical Enlightenment: Philosophy and the Making of Modernity 1650–1750* (Oxford, 2001), 14–29 and *passim*.

29. M. B. Hall, 'Science in the early Royal Society', in *The Emergence of Modern Science*, ed. M. Crosland (London, 1975), 58; and M. B. Hall, *Promoting Experimental Learning: Experiment and the Royal Society, 1660–1727* (Cambridge, 1991). See also M. Hunter, *Science and Society in Restoration England* (Cambridge, 1981), ch. 2; and Hunter, *Establishing the New Science: The Experience of the Early Royal Society* (Woodbridge, 1989).

30. The collapse of political consensus in England in the years leading up to 1642 is, self-evidently, far too complex to reduce to simple primary causes. Nevertheless J. P. Sommerville, *Politics and Ideology in England 1603–1640* (London, 1986), 231–8 and *passim*, has argued persuasively for a recognition of the sheer range of political ideas current among literate Englishmen at the time, and the extent to which these ideas did

influence the choices of many participants when disagreement over the basic constitutional and political principles became open.

31. G. E. Aylmer, *The Levellers in the English Revolution* (Ithaca, NY, 1975), pp. 161–8 and *passim*. For the broader context, a useful introduction is F. D. Dow, *Radicalism in the English Revolution* (Oxford, 1985), chs 2–3.

32. N. Malcolm, 'Hobbes and the European Republic of Letters', in his *Aspects of Hobbes* (Oxford, 2002), 457–545.

33. R. Ashcraft, *Revolutionary Politics and Locke's 'Two Treatises of Government'* (Princeton, NJ, 1986).

Chapter 10   The arts, the value of creativity and the cost of appearances

1. References to this and other material on the musicians serving the court at Dresden are given in my paper on 'Keeping up appearances: patronage of the arts, city prestige and princely power in northern Germany and Denmark 1600–1670', *German History*, 6 (1988). I am grateful to the editors of *German History* for allowing me to use some of the material in that article for the present chapter.

2. The correspondence between Duke August of Brunswick-Lüneburg and his various agents in Germany are a case in point: see R. Gobiet (ed.), *Der Briefwechsel zwischen Philipp Hainhofer und Herzog August d. J.* (Munich, 1984), *passim*. Hainhofer's business; like that of many other Protestants in Augsburg, was severely restricted after the Swedish withdrawal in 1635.

3. *Documents du minutier central concernant l'histoire de la musique, 1600–1650*, ed. M. Jurgens, vol. 1 (Paris, n.d., *c.* 1967), 403–6.

4. Ibid., 9 May 1635, 450–3.

5. Burke, *Popular Culture*, 77–87.

6. Ibid., 92–102, and *passim*, for a survey of the various genres common to many parts of Europe, and for bibliographical references. On the *skomorokhi*, see R. Zguta, *Russian Minstrels* (Oxford, 1978).

7. W. Stahl, 'Franz Tunder and Dietrich Buxtehude, *Archiv für Musikwissenschaft*, 8 (1926), 1–77, esp. 60–4.

8. Monteverdi on 13 March 1620, no. 49, and on 10 September 1627, no. 106, in *The Letters of Claudio Monteverdi*, ed. D. Stevens (London, 1980), 189–93, 355–7. He received altogether three offers of re-employment from the Gonzagas (the last shortly before the dynasty itself came to grief and Mantua was plunged into a bitter war of succession). Monteverdi was naturally concerned to maintain strict confidentiality in these matters (8 March 1620) for fear that the procurators might take it amiss.

9. Monteverdi on 22 May 1627, no. 94, and 9 June 1637, no. 125, *Letters*, 319 and 419 respectively. On the confraternities, see notably D. Arnold, 'Francesco Cavalli: some recently discovered documents', *Music & Letters*, 46 (1965), 50–5; and his 'Music at the Scuola di san Rocco', ibid., 40 (1959), 229–41. See also his article on 'The Monteverdian succession at St Marks', ibid., 42 (1961), 205–11.

10. Opera evidently fulfilled a variety of functions from the start, and was also eminently suitable as a vehicle for political messages of various kinds. See L. Bianconi and T. Walker, 'Production, consumption and political function of seventeenth-century opera', *Early Music History*, 4 (1984), 209–96.

11. As argued by R. W. Scribner, 'Incombustible Luther: the image of the reformer in early modern Germany', *Past & Present*, 110 (1986), 38–68, the Lutheran Church did attach special importance to pictures of Luther himself, at times amounting to a personality cult, but this gave little scope for artistic creativity.

12. For a fuller discussion of these works, see H. Hibbard, *Caravaggio* (London, 1983), 91–148, and *passim*. Some of the very sparse source material relating to Caravaggio is given by W. Friedlaender, *Caravaggio Studies* (Princeton, NJ, 1955), 267ff, but nothing written by himself appears to have survived.

13. F. Haskell, *Patrons and Painters* (New Haven, CT, revised edn, 1980), 31, with the wider context 31–62; see also F. Hammond, *Music and Spectacle in Baroque Rome: Barberini Patronage under Urban VIII* (New Haven, CT, 1994).

14. J. Connors, *Borromini and the Roman Oratory* (Cambridge, MA, 1980), *passim* but esp. 23–8.

15. Haskell, *Patrons and Painters*, 43.

16. R. F. Spear, *Domenichino*, vol. 1 (New Haven, CT, 1982), 7–20.

17. R. Krautheimer, *The Rome of Alexander VII, 1655–1667* (Princeton, NJ, 1985), 5–7, 131–47 and *passim*. In this as in other respects there were obvious parallels with secular patronage: see P. Burke, 'Conspicuous consumption in 17th-century Italy', in his *Historical Anthropology*, 132–49.

18. Haskell, *Patrons and Painters*, 78–85.

19. P. Partner, 'Papal financial policy in the Renaissance and Counter-Reformation', *Past & Present*, 88 (1980), 55–62 and *passim*, providing full references to existing literature on papal financial administration.

20. F. Haskell, 'The market for Italian art in the 17th century', *Past & Present*, 15 (1959), 48–59; and his *Patrons and Painters*, esp. pp. 193–200.

21. B. Roeck, *Elias Holl: Architekt einer europäischer Stadt* (Regensburg, 1985), 186–221 and *passim*. The town hall was destroyed in 1944 and subsequently rebuilt in the same style.

22. For the best analysis, see M. Stein, *Christian den Fjerdes Billedverden* (Copenhagen, 1987), *passim*, on which the following discussion is based.

23. Cited by R. W. Berger, *Versailles: The Château of Louis XIV* (Pennsylvania, PA, 1985), 21. See also R.W. Berger, *A Royal Passion: Louis XIV as Patron of Architecture* (Cambridge, 1994). On the wider problem of decision-making in this project, see G. Walton, *Louis XIV's Versailles* (London, 1986). For an analysis of the more technical side of the building industry, see P. W. Williams, *The Construction of Versailles 1661–1715* (Ph.D. thesis, 1977, University Microfilms International, London) to which Prof. H. M. Scott kindly drew my attention.

24. J. Brown and J. H. Elliott, *A Palace for a King: The Buen Retiro and the Court of Philip IV* (New Haven, CT, 1980), 36, 114f, 141–92 and *passim*; Elliott, 'The court of the Spanish Habsburgs', in *Politics and Culture*, ed. Mack and Jacob (Cambridge, 1987), 5–24. For a broader analytical view of court patronage, see M. Warnke, *The Court Artist: On the Ancestry of the Modern Artist* (Cambridge, 1993).

25. G. Parry, *The Golden Age Restored: The Culture of the Stuart Court, 1603–42* (Manchester, 1981), 153 and *passim* – an excellent introduction to many aspects of Stuart patronage. See also M. Smuts, 'The political failure of Stuart cultural patronage', in *Patronage in the Renaissance*, ed. G. F. Lytle and S. Orgel (Princeton, NJ, 1980), 165–87; J. Goldberg, *James I and the Politics of Literature* (Baltimore, 1983); R. Strong, *Splendour at Court: Renaissance Spectacle and Illusion* (London, 1973), 213–43; D. Howarth, *Images of Rule: Art and Politics in the English Renaissance 1485–1649* (London, 1997); S. Orgel and R. Strong, *Inigo Jones: The Theatre of the Stuart Court*, 2 vols (London, 1973); on the masques, see P. Walls, *Music in the English Courtly Masque, 1604–1640* (Oxford, 1996).

26. K. Sharpe, 'The politics of literature in Renaissance England,' review article in *History*, 71 (1986), 235–47; his *Criticism and Compliment: The Politics of Literature in the England of Charles I* (Cambridge, 1987), 1–39 and *passim*; and his collection of essays, *Remapping Early Modern England: The Culture of Seventeenth-Century Politics* (Cambridge, 2000).

27. See note 1.

28. C. Gould, *Bernini in France* (London, 1981), passim; and the *Diary of Cavalieri Bernini's Visit to France*, by P. Fréart de Chantelou, ed. A. Blunt and M. Corbett (Princeton, NJ, 1985).

29. On the conditions for musicians in France, see M. Benoit, *Versailles et les musiciens du Roi: étude institutionelle et sociale, 1661–1733*; and his *Musiques de cour: chapelle, chambre, écurie 1661–1733* (both Paris, 1971). On Restoration England, see A. Ashbee, *Records of English Court Music*, vol. 1: 1660–85 (Snodland, 1986); and his *Lists of Payments to the King's Musick in the Reign of Charles II (1660–1685)* (Snodland, 1981).

30. This also affected theatre, including even the Comédie-Française, although it had just been turned into a monopoly in 1680. For the social composition of French theatre audiences, and changes in aesthetic standards, see J. Lough, *Paris Theatre Audiences in the Seventeenth and Eighteenth Centuries* (London, 1957), 55–128. On Colbertism in the arts, see the outline by R. M. Isherwood, *Music in the Service of the King* (Ithaca, NY, 1973), 150–203.

31. G. A. Johnson, 'Imagining images of powerful women: Maria de Medici's patronage of art and architecture', in *Women and Art in Early Modern Europe*, ed. C. Lawrence (Philadelphia, PA, 1997), 126–53; M. R. Dunn, 'Spiritual philanthropists: women as convent patrons in seicento Rome', ibid., 154–88.

32. M. D. Garrard, *Artemisia Gentileschi: The Image of the Female Hero in Italian Baroque Art* (Princeton, NJ, 1989), provides detailed documentation.

33. A. Newcomb, 'Courtesans, muses, or musicians? Professional women musicians in sixteenth-century Italy', in *Women Making Music: The*

Western Art Tradition, 1150–1950, ed. J. Bowers and J. Tick (London, 1986), 90–115. Monteverdi's own letters contain frequent references to the qualities he is seeking in the best musicians, including women: see, for example, his letter of 28 December 1610 in *Letters of Claudio Monteverdi*, transl./ed. Stevens, 77.

34.   E. Rosand, 'The voice of Barbara Strozzi', in *Women Making Music*, ed. Bowers and Tick, 168–90.

35.   J. M. Montias, *Artists and Artisans in Delft: A Socio-economic Study of the Seventeenth Century* (Princeton, NJ, 1982), 183–220, 268–71, and *passim*: a pioneering work in this field, analysing not just the functioning of the guild of St Lucas and the state of the market, but also emphasising the dangers of oversupply in a town of some 28,000 inhabitants. See also S. Schama, *The Embarrassment of Riches: An Interpretation of Dutch Culture in the Golden Age* (London, 1987); and J. M. Montias, *Vermeer and his Milieu: A Web of Social History* (Princeton, NJ, 1989). That paintings may not have been as rare in private homes elsewhere in Europe as once assumed is suggested by P. Benedict, 'Towards the comparative study of the popular market for art: the ownership of paintings in 17th-century Metz', *Past & Present*, 109 (1985), 100–17.

36.   Haskell, *Patrons and Painters*, 22f, 142–5.

37.   Jurgens, *Documents du minutier central*, 435–40.

38.   *Roger North on Music*, ed. J. Wilson (London, 1959), 302–5, 352f.

Chapter 11   Absolute monarchy and the return of order after 1660

1.   Danske Lov (1683), in my translation; cf. E. Ekman, 'The Danish Royal Law of 1665', *Journal of Modern History*, 29 (1957), 102–7. The Royal Law remained technically in force until 1848.

2.   This manoeuvre also helped to conceal the greater embarrassment of Mazarin's own colossal fortune, which it was not in the Crown's interests to reveal. See R. Bonney, 'The secret expenses of Richelieu and Mazarin, 1624–1661', *English Historical Review*, 91 (1976), 825–36. For the earlier context, see Bergin, *Cardinal Richelieu*.

3.   Recently, J. Hurt, *Louis XIV and the Parlements: The Assertion of Royal Authority* (Manchester, 2002), has confirmed that royal power was used directly and quite effectively to restrict the Parlements.

4.   Beik, *Absolutism and Society*, esp. chs 12–13; G. Rowlands, *The Dynastic State and the Army under Louis XIV: Royal Service and Private Interest 1661–1701* (Cambridge, 2002); P. Coveney (ed.), *France in Crisis 1620–1675* (London, 1977), 48–54; P. Goubert, *Louis XIV et 20 millions de français* (Paris, 1966; transl. 1970), 72, stresses the smallness of the bureaucracy and the wide range of supervisory duties of the *intendants* over town administration, law-courts, finance, army and navy affairs, forestry, grain supplies and trade – particularly burdensome given the inadequacies of the rudimentary police force of only 2000 men for the whole kingdom. An excellent recent assessment of the

reality of political power in France is provided by Collins, *The State in Early Modern France.*

5. Quoted in O. and P. Ranum, *The Century of Louis XIV* (London, 1972), 111–36, esp. 124.

6. T. J. Schaeper, *The French Council of Commerce 1700–1715* (Columbus, OH, 1983), 59–66, 178–80; J. K. J. Thomson, *Clermont de Lodève 1638–1789* (Cambridge, 1982) discusses an example of an initially highly successful state enterprise; for a survey of the anticipatory ideas of early seventeenth-century French writers, see Parker, *Making of French Absolutism,* 73–81.

7. D. C. Coleman, 'Mercantilism revisited', *Historical Journal,* 23 (1980), 773–91, esp. 790; see also C. Wilson, 'The other face of mercantilism', in *Revisions in Mercantilism,* ed. D. C. Coleman (London, 1969), 118–39; and for a survey of abortive attempts to introduce further regulation in England, Clay, *Economic Expansion,* vol. 2, 203–50.

8. Bérenger, *Finances et absolutisme autrichienne,* 275–96, 353–403.

9. Dessert, *Argent, pouvoir et société.* See also J. Dent, *Crisis in Finance: Crown, Financiers and Society in Seventeenth-Century France* (Newton Abbot, 1973), esp. 232–43; and, in a wider context, Bonney (ed.), *Rise of the Fiscal State.* For the calculations of annual incomes and expenditures under Louis XIV, see A. Guéry, 'Finances de la monarchie française', *Annales,* 33 (1978), 216–39.

10. C. A. Macartney, *The Habsburg and Hohenzollern Dynasties* (London, 1970), 316.

11. Roberts, *Sweden as a Great Power,* 60f.

12. For a full discussion, see A. F. Upton, 'The Riksdag of 1680 and the establishment of royal absolutism in Sweden', *English Historical Review,* 102 (1987), 281–308.

13. As A. F. Upton, 'Absolutism and the rule of law: the case of Karl XI of Sweden', *Parliaments, Estates and Representation,* 8 (1988), 31–46, has demonstrated, no Swedish subject ultimately had any recourse in law against the King himself; but this was not regarded as a problem in a monarchy built on very strong Lutheran traditions of obedience, where the King himself seems to have been a master of understatement and arguably a model of conscientious absolutism.

14. A. F. Upton, *Charles XI and Swedish Absolutism,* 152.

15. Their criticisms have been followed up by J. Miller, 'The potential for "absolutism" in later Stuart England', *History,* 69 (1984), 187–207. The comparison was at least in some respects misleading: the late Stuarts lacked any effective control of local administration comparable to that achieved through, for instance, the French *intendants,* and clearly lacked the fiscal and military autonomy of continental monarchs in dealing with domestic resistance. It is also difficult to see continental-style state-building either in the indolent Charles II or the over-fanatical James. The broader brush adopted by J. Scott, *England's Troubles: Seventeenth-Century English Political Instability in European Context* (Cambridge, 2000) is challenging but not wholly persuasive.

Chapter 12   Power and state-sponsored violence in the later seventeenth century

1. R. Briggs, *Early Modern France 1560–1715* (Oxford, 1977), 150. A more critical perspective by historians on Louis's reign can be dated from Goubert's very influential *Louis XIV et 20 millions de français*.
2. A. L. Beier and R. Finlay (eds), *London 1500–1700: The Making of the Metropolis* (London, 1986), citing in their introduction, 11f, the estimates by others; G. E. Aylmer, *The Crown's Servants: Government and Civil Service under Charles II, 1660–1685* (Oxford, 2002)
3. The practical dangers of anticipating peace were clearly revealed in the Medway raid by the Dutch in 1667, but the financial implications were considerable: see M. Duffy, 'The foundations of British naval power', in *The Military Revolution and the State 1500–1800*, ed. M. Duffy (Exeter, 1980), 49–85, esp. 53–9.
4. Petersen, *Fra standssamfund til rangsamfund 1500–1700*, 336–40.
5. H. Kamen, 'A forgotten insurrection of the seventeenth century: the Catalan peasant rising of 1688', *Journal of Modern History*, 49 (1977), 210–30.
6. A. Olearius, *Des Welt-berühmten Adami Olearii colligirte und viel vermehrte Reise-Beschreibungen* (Hamburg, 1696: revised edition of a text first published in 1647), 113.
7. J. L. H. Keep, *Soldiers of the Tsar: Army and Society in Russia 1462–1874* (1985), 89, where he also warns that these figures are necessarily very approximate.
8. M. Cherniavsky, 'The Old Believers and the New Religion', *Slavic Review*, 25 (1966), 1–20; see also the context in G. Hosking, *Russia: People and Empire 1552–1917* (London, 1997), 64–74.
9. The contemporary description of two of the Covenanters' regiments sent to England in 1640, cited by Parker, *Military Revolution*, 52, quoting from S. Reid, *Scots Armies of the Civil War 1639–1651* (Leigh-on-Sea, 1982), 12.
10. C. Cipolla, *Guns and Sails in the Early Period of European Expansion, 1400–1700* (London, 1965), 57, note 1. Parker, *Military Revolution*, chs 3–4, has demonstrated the effectiveness of resistance against the Europeans in China and Japan, and the ability of, for instance, Indian princes to keep the Europeans at bay well into the eighteenth century.
11. Cited in Boxer, *Dutch Seaborne Empire*, 233. For more recent attempts to make systematic use of travellers' accounts for historical purposes, see notably S. B. Schwartz, *Implicit Understandings: Observing, Reporting and Reflecting on the Encounters between Europeans and Other Peoples in the Early Modern Era* (Cambridge, 1994); M. Daunton and R. Halpern (eds), *Empire and Others: British Encounters with Indigenous Peoples 1600–1850* (London, 1999); L. Colley, *Captives: Britain, Empire and the World 1600–1850* (London, 2002); G. J. Ames and R. S. Love (eds), *Distant Lands and Diverse Cultures: The French Experience in Asia 1600–1700* (Westport, CT, 2003). On mutual understanding in the Near East, see notably S. Faroqhi, 'Die Osmanen und ihre Kenntnisse

über Europa im "langen" 17. Jahrhundert: ein Forschungsbericht', in *Frieden und Krieg in der frühen Neuzeit*, ed. R. G. Asch, W. E. Voß and M. Wrede (Munich, 2001), 485–502.

12. The ubiquity of lawyers and of protracted expensive litigation is a leit-motif in the literature of the period – perhaps with reason, as far as Spain is concerned, although R. L. Kagan has discerned a decline in liti-gation in the course of the seventeenth century caused by a deterioration in the quality of the royal courts themselves: see his 'A golden age of liti-gation: Castile 1500–1700', in *Disputes and Settlements*, ed. J. Bossy (Cambridge, 1983), 160–6; and his *Lawsuits and Litigants in Castile, 1500–1700* (Chapel Hill, NC, 1981), *passim*. Few attempts at quantifica-tion have been made elsewhere, but W. Prest, 'The English bar, 1550–1700', in *Lawyers in Early Modern Europe and America*, ed. W. Prest (London, 1981), 73–80, confirms that there was mounting criti-cism of the legal profession in England before and during the civil war, and that there may have been a stagnation of business. See also W. J. Bouwsma, 'Lawyers and early modern culture', *American Historical Review*, 78 (1973), 303–27; and, more generally, R. O'Day, *The Professions in Early Modern England 1450–1800* (London, 2000).

13. The following discussion is based on some formative recent work: P. Spierenburg, *The Spectacle of Suffering: Executions and the Evolution of Repression, from a Preindustrial Metropolis to the European Experience* (Cambridge, 1984), esp. 43–66, 126–35; R. van Dülmen, *Theater des Schreckens* (Munich, 1985); R. J. Evans, *Rituals of Retribution: Capital Punishment in Germany 1600–1987* (Oxford, 1996); the Danish dimen-sion was explored by Paul Ries of Cambridge University in a unpub-lished paper delivered in 1981; for a gendered approach, see U. Rublack, *The Crimes of Women in Early Modern Germany* (Oxford, 1999).

14. J. Sharpe, 'The people and the law', in *Popular Culture*, ed. Reay, 251–5. On the lesser courts see also K. Wrightson, 'Two concepts of order: justices, constables and jurymen in seventeenth-century England', in *An Ungovernable People*, ed. Brewer and Styles, 21–46; Herrup, *The Common Peace*.

15. Discussed by T. Harris, 'The bawdy house riots of 1668', *English History Review*, 29 (1986), 537–56, and in his study of *London Crowds in the Reign of Charles II: Propaganda and Politics from the Restoration to the Exclusion Crisis* (Cambridge, 1987), 82–91.

16. P. Burke, *The Fabrication of Louis XIV* (New Haven, CT, 1992) is one of the most imaginative analyses of this aspect, but much of the artistic patronage discussed in chapter 10 obviously in part had similar goals.

17. For this concept, see H. H. Rowen, *The King's State: Proprietary Dynasticism in Early Modern France* (New Brunswick, NJ, 1980); D. Parker, 'Absolutism, feudalism and property rights in the France of Louis XIV', *Past & Present*, 179 (2003), 60–96.

18. Discussed more fully in T. Munck, *The Enlightenment: A Comparative Social History 1721–1794* (London, 2000), 64–75 and *passim*.

19. H. W. Weber, *Paper Bullets: Print and Kingship under Charles II* (Lexington, KY, 1996); Fox, 'Rumour, news and popular political opin-ion', *Historical Journal* 40 (1997), 597–620; D. Zaret, *Origins of*

Democratic Culture: Printing, Petitions and the Public Sphere in Early-Modern England (Princeton, NJ, 2000); J. Raymond, 'The newspaper, public opinion and the public sphere in the seventeenth century', in *News, Newspapers and Society in Early Modern Britain,* ed. J. Raymond (London, 1999), 109–40; J. Raymond, *Pamphlets and Pamphleteering in Early Modern Britain* (Cambridge, 2003); M. S. R. Jenner, 'The roasting of the Rump: scatology and the body politic in Restoration England', *Past & Present* 177 (2002), 84–120.

20. François de Salignac de la Mothe-Fénelon (1651–1715) was appointed tutor to the King's grandson, the Duke of Burgundy, in 1689, and became Archbishop of Cambrai six years later. Influenced by the quietist movement, he came into conflict with Bossuet and was removed from court. The passage rendered here is from section XIV.

Further reading

The following is intended as a guide to the most useful and readily available broader secondary material on the period, arranged under the thematic headings most suitable for the text. Much of the material referred to in the notes to each chapter is not listed again here, so readers wanting more specific references should consult the notes.

General surveys

The Cambridge Economic History of Europe, vols. 4–5 (Cambridge, 1967 and 1977)

H. Kamen, *The Iron Century: Social Change in Europe 1550–1660* (London, 1971)

F. Braudel, *Civilisation and Capitalism, Fifteenth to Eighteenth Century* (3 vols., London, 1981–84)

C. Cipolla, ed., *The Fontana Economic History of Europe*, vol. 2 (Glasgow, 1974)

P. Kriedte, *Peasants, Landlords and Merchant Capitalists: Europe and the World Economy 1500–1800* (Leamington Spa, 1983)

I. Wallerstein, *The Modern World System*, vols. 1–2 (London, 1974–80)

T. Ertman, *Birth of the Leviathan: Building States and Regimes in Medieval and Early Modern Europe* (Cambridge, 1997)

R. J. Bonney, *The European Dynastic States 1494–1660* (Oxford, 1991)

W. Doyle, *The Old European Order 1660–1800* (Oxford, 1978; 2nd edn. 1992)

R. Asch & H. Duchhardt, eds., *Der Absolutismus—ein Mythos? Strukturwandel monarchischer Herrschaft 1550–1700* (Cologne, 1996)

D. McKay & H. M. Scott, *The Rise of the Great Powers 1648–1815* (London, 1983)

J. Bergin, ed., *Seventeenth-century Europe* (Oxford, 2001)

A. F. Upton, *Europe 1600–1789* (London, 2001)

D. Sturdy, *Fractured Europe 1600–1721* (Oxford, 2002)

J. Miller, ed., *Absolutism in Seventeenth-century Europe* (London, 1990)

N. Henshall, *The Myth of Absolutism: Change and Continuity in Early Modern European Monarchy* (London, 1992)

J. H. Elliott, 'A Europe of Composite Monarchies', *Past & Present* 137 (1992), 48–71

P. H. Wilson, *Absolutism in Central Europe* (London, 2000)

P. K. Monod, *The Power of Kings: Monarchy and Religion in Europe 1589–1715* (New Haven, 1999)

C. C. Orr, ed., *Queenship in Europe 1660–1815: the Role of the Consort* (Cambridge, 2004)

P. Anderson, *Lineages of the Absolutist State* (London, 1974)

R. Bonney, ed., *Economic Systems and State Finance* (Oxford, 1995)

R. Bonney, ed., *The Rise of the Fiscal State in Europe* (Oxford, 1999)

D. Dessert, *Argent, pouvoir et société au grand siècle* (Paris, 1984)

J. H. Shennan, *Liberty and Order in Early Modern Europe: The Subject and the State 1650–1800* (London, 1986)

A. R. Myers, *Parliaments and Estates in Europe to 1789* (London, 1975)

M. A. R. Graves, *The Parliaments of Early Modern Europe 1400–1700* (London, 2001)

D. L. Smith, *The Stuart Parliaments, 1603–1689* (London, 1999)

T. Aston, ed., *Crisis in Europe 1560–1660* (London, 1965)

G. Parker & L. M. Smith, eds., *The General Crisis of the Seventeenth Century* (London, 1978)

T. K. Rabb, *The Struggle for Stability in Early Modern Europe* (Oxford, 1975)

P. Zagorin, *Rebels and Rulers 1500–1660*, vols. 1–2 (Cambridge, 1983)

Y.-M. Bercé, *Revolt and Revolution in Early Modern Europe* (Manchester, 1987)

Warfare and the Thirty Years War

J. R. Hale, *War and Society in Renaissance Europe 1450–1620* (London, 1985)

M. S. Anderson, *War and Society in Europe of the Old Regime 1618–1789* (London, 1988)

G. Parker, *The Military Revolution: Military Innovation and the Rise of the West 1500–1800* (Cambridge, 1988)

J. Black, *A Military Revolution? Military Change and European Society, 1550–1800* (Basingstoke, 1991)

F. Tallet, *War and Society in Early Modern Europe, 1495–1715* (London, 1992)

C. J. Rogers, ed., *The Military Revolution Debate: Readings on the Military Transformation of Early Modern Europe* (Boulder, 1995)

B. Kroener & R. Pröve, eds., *Krieg und Frieden: Militär und Gesellschaft in der frühen Neuzeit* (Paderborn, 1996)

J. Glete, *War and the State in Early Modern Europe: Spain, the Dutch Republic and Sweden as Fiscal–Military State, 1500–1660* (London 2002)

R. Murphy, *Ottoman Warfare 1500–1700* (London, 1999)

J. A. Lynn, *Giant of the* Grand Siécle; *The French Army 1610–1715* (Cambridge, 1997)

R. Chaboche, 'Les soldats français de la guerre de trent ans', *Revue d'histoire moderne et contemporaine* 20 (1973), 10–24

J. A. Lynn, 'How War Fed War: The Tax of Violence and Contribution During the *Grand Siècle*', *Journal of Modern History* 65 (1993)

T. M. Barker, *Army, Aristocracy and Monarchy: Essays on War, Society and Government in Austria, 1618–1780* (New York, 1982)

M. P. Gutmann, *War and Society in the Early Modern Low Countries* (Assen, 1980)

J. S. Wheeler, *The Making of a World Power: War and Military Revolution in Seventeenth-Century England* (Stroud, 1999)

R. I. Frost, *The Northern Wars: War, State and Society in North-eastern Europe 1558–1721* (London, 2000)

G. Parker, *The Army of Flanders and the Spanish Road 1567–1659* (Cambridge, 19720)

R. A. Stradling, *The Armada of Flanders: Spanish Maritime Policy and European War 1563–1668* (Cambridge, 1992)

F. R. Redlich, *The German Military Enterpriser and his Work Force* (2 vols., Wiesbaden, 1964–65)

J. V. Polisensky, *The Thirty Years War* (London, 1971)

G. Benecke, *Germany in the Thirty Years War* (London, 1978)

G. Parker, eds., *The Thirty Years' War* (London, 1984; 2nd edn. 1996)

J. R. Paas, *The German Political Broadsheet, 1600–1700*, vols. 1–7 (Wiesbaden, 1985–2002)

V. Press, *Kriege und Krisen: Deutschland 1600–1715* (Munich, 1991)

R. G. Asch, *The Thirty Years War* (Basingstoke, 1997)

K. Bussmann & H. Schilling, eds., *1648: War and Peace in Europe*, vols. 1–3 (Munich, 1998)

B. von Krusenstjern & H. Medick, eds., *Zwischen Alltag und Katastrophe: Der Dreißigjährige Krieg aus der Nähe* (Göttingen, 1999)

K. Garber & J. Held, eds., *Der Frieden–Rekonstruktion einer Europäischen Vision* (2 vols., Munich, 2000–01)

G. Mortimer, *Eyewitness Accounts of the Thirty Years War 1618–48* (Basingstoke, 2002)

France and Spain until the 1650s

R. Briggs, *Early Modern France 1560–1715* (Oxford, 1977)

D. Parker, *The Making of French Absolutism* (London, 1983)

J. B. Collins, *The State in Early Modern France* (Cambridge, 1995)

R. Mousnier, *The Institutions of France under the Absolute Monarchy 1598–1789*, vols. 1–2 (Chicago, 1979–84)

M. Greengrass, *France in the Age of Henry IV* (London, 1984)

J. H. Elliott, *Richelieu and Olivares* (Cambridge, 1984)

J. Bergin, *Cardinal Richelieu: Power and the Pursuit of Wealth* (New Haven, 1985)

J. Bergin & L. Brockliss, eds., *Richelieu and his Age* (Oxford, 1992)

D. Parrott, 'The Causes of the Franco–Spanish War of 1635–59', in *The Origins of War in Early Modern Europe*, ed. J. Black (Edinburgh, 1987), 72–111

D. Parrott, *Richelieu's Army: War, Government and Society in France, 1624–1642* (Cambridge, 2001)

R. Bonney, *Society and Government in France under Richelieu and Mazarin 1624–62* (London, 1985)

J. H. M. Salmon, 'Venality of Office and Popular Sedition in Seventeenth-century France', *Past & Present* 37 (1967), 21–43

D. A. Watts, *Cardinal de Retz: the Ambiguities of Seventeenth-Century Mind* (Oxford, 1980)

J. H. Shennan, *The Parlement of Paris* (London, 1968)

O. Ranum, *The Fronde: A French Revolution 1648–1652* (New York, 1993)

W. Beik, *Absolutism and Society in Seventeenth-Century France: State Power and Provincial Aristocracy in Languedoc* (Cambridge, 1985)

S. Kettering, *Patrons, Brokers and Clients in Seventeenth-Century France* (Oxford, 1986)

S. Kettering, *French Society 1589 to 1715* (London, 2001)

J. H. Parry, *The Spanish Seaborne Empire* (London, 1966)

J. Lynch, *The Hispanic World in Crisis and Change 1598–1700* (Oxford, 1992)

J. N. Hillgarth, *The Mirror of Spain, 1500–1700: The Formation of a Myth* (Ann Arbor, 2000)

H. Kamen, *Spain's Road to Empire: The Making of a World Power, 1492–1763* (London, 2002)

G. Parker, 'Spain, her Enemies and the Revolt of the Netherlands', *Past & Present* 49 (1979), 72–95

P. Brightwell, 'The Spanish System and the Twelve Years Truce', *English Historical Review* 89 (1974), 270–92

I. A. A. Thompson, *War and Society in Habsburg Spain* (London, 1992)

R. A. Stradling, *Europe and the Decline of Spain* (London, 1981)

R. A. Stradling, *Spain's struggle for Europe 1598–1668* (London, 1994)

A. Feros, *Kingship and Favouritism in the Spain of Philip III 1590–1621* (Cambridge, 2000)

R. A. Stradling, *Philip IV and the Government of Spain* (London, 1988)

J. H. Elliott, *The Count-Duke of Olivares* (London, 1986)

R. A. Stradling, 'Olivares and the Origins of the Franco-Spanish War, 1627–35', *English Historical Review* 101 (1986), 68–94

R. Mackay, *The Limits of Royal Authority: Resistance and Obedience in Seventeenth-Century Castile* (Cambridge, 1999)

J. H. Elliott, *The Revolt of the Catalans* (Cambridge, 1963)

C. Jago, 'Habsburg Absolutism and the Cortes of Castile', *American Historical Review* 86 (1981), 307–26

England, Scotland and the civil wars

A. G. R. Smith, *The Emergence of a Nation State 1529–1660* (London, 1984)

D. L. Smith, *A History of the Modern British Isles, 1603–1707* (Oxford, 1998)

M. J. Braddick, *State Formation in Early Modern England, c.1550–1700* (Cambridge, 2000)

D. Zaret, *Origins of Democratic Culture: Printing, Petitions and the Public Sphere in Early Modern England* (Princeton, 2000)

K. Sharpe, *Remapping Early Modern England: the Culture of Seventeenth-Century Politics* (Cambridge, 2000)

K. Wrightson, *English Society 1580–1680* (London, 1982)

D. C. Coleman, *The Economy of England 1450–1750* (Oxford, 1977)

C. G. A. Clay, *Economic Expansion and Social Change: England 1500–1700* (2 vols., Cambridge, 1984)

T. C. Smout, *A History of the Scottish People 1560–1830* (Glasgow, 1969)

J. Wormald, *Court, Kirk and Community: Scotland 1470–1625* (London, 1981)

R. Mitchison, *Lordship to Patronage: Scotland 1603–1715* (London, 1983)

R. A. Houston & I. D. Whyte, eds., *Scottish Society 1500–1800* (Cambridge, 1989)

K. Brown, *Kingdom or Province? Scotland and the Regal Union 1603–1715* (Basingstoke, 1992)

J. Morrill, ed., *The Scottish National Covenant in its British Context* (Edinburgh, 1990)

C. Russell, *Parliaments and English Politics 1621–29* (Oxford, 1979)

A. Woolrych, *Britain in Revolution 1625–1660* (Oxford, 2002)

A. Hughes, *The Causes of the English Civil War* (London, 1991)

C. Russell, *The Fall of the British Monarchies, 1637–42* (Oxford, 1991)

G. E. Aylmer, *Rebellion or Revolution: England 1640–1660* (Oxford, 1986)

C. Russell, 'Why did Charles I call the Long Parliament?', *History* 69 (1984), 375–83

J. Richards, ' "His now majestie" and the English Monarchy: the Kingship of Charles I before 1640', *Past & Present* 113 (1986), 70–96

C. Russell, 'The British Problem and the English Civil War', *History* 72 (1987), 395–415

P. Donald, *An Uncounselled King: Charles I and the Scottish Troubles, 1637–1641* (Cambridge, 1991)

K. Sharpe, *The Personal Rule of Charles I* (New Haven, 1992)

J. Morrill, *The Nature of the English Revolution* (London, 1993)

J. Scott, *England's Troubles: Seventeenth-Century English Political Instability in European Context* (Cambridge, 2000)

D. Cressy, 'Revolutionary England 1640–1642', *Past & Present* 181 (2003), 35–71

R. Kishlansky, *The Rise of the New Model Army* (Cambridge, 1980)

G. E. Aylmer, *The Levellers in the English Revolution* (Ithaca, 1975)

M. Mendle, *The Putney Debates of 1647: The Army, the Levellers and the English State* (Cambridge, 2001)

F. D. Dow, *Radicalism in the English Revolution, 1640–1660* (Oxford, 1985)

P. Zagorin, *Milton: Aristocrat and Rebel* (London, 1992)

D. Hirst, 'The English Republic and the Meaning of Britain', *Journal of Modern History* 66 (1994), 451–86

B. Coward, *Oliver Cromwell* (Harlow, 1992)

B. Coward, *The Cromwellian Protectorate* (Manchester, 2002)

The Netherlands and Scandinavia

J. I. Israel, *The Dutch Republic and the Hispanic World 1606–1661* (Oxford, 1982)

J. I. Israel, *The Dutch Republic: Its Rise, Greatness and Fall, 1477–1806* (Oxford, 1995)

J. L. Price, *Holland and the Dutch Republic in the Seventeenth Century: The Politics of Particularism* (Oxford, 1994)

S. Schama, *The Embarrassment of Riches: an Interpretation of Dutch Culture in the Golden Age* (London, 1987)

A. T. van Deursen, *Plain Lives in a Golden Age: Popular Culture, Religion and Society in Seventeenth-Century Holland* (Cambridge, 1991)

G. Parker, 'New Light on an Old Theme: Spain and the Netherlands 1550–1650', *European History Quarterly* 15 (1985), 219–37

J. den Tex, *Oldenbarneveldt*, vols. 1–2 (Cambridge, 1973)

H. H. Rowen, *John de Witt, Grand Pensionary of Holland* (Princeton, 1978)

D. Kirby, *Northern Europe in the Early Modern Period: The Baltic World 1492–1772* (London, 1990)

L. Jespersen, ed., *A Revolution from Above? The Power-state of Sixteenth- and Seventeenth-Century Scandinavia* (Odense, 2000)

P. D. Lockhart, *Denmark in the Thirty Years' War, 1618–1648: King Christian IV and the Decline of the Oldenberg State* (London, 1996)

M. Roberts, *Gustavus Adolphus: A History of Sweden 1611–32*, vols. 1–2 (London, 1953–58)

M. Roberts, *Essays in Swedish History* (London, 1967)

M. Roberts, *Sweden as a Great Power 1611–1697* (London, 1968)

M. Roberts, ed., *Sweden's Age of Greatness 1632–1718* (London, 1973)

M. Roberts, *The Swedish Imperial Experience, 1560–1718* (Cambridge, 1979)

P. D. Lockhart, *Sweden in the Seventeenth Century* (Basingstoke, 2004)

E. Ringmar, *Identity, Interest and Action: A Cultural Explanation of Sweden's Intervention in the Thirty Years War* (Cambridge, 1996)

A. F. Upton, *Charles XI and Swedish Absolutism* (Cambridge, 1998)

R. G. Hatton, *Charles XII of Sweden* (London, 1968)

Central Europe

F. L. Carsten, *Princes and Parliaments in Germany* (Oxford, 1959)

G. Benecke, *Society and Politics in Germany 1500–1750* (London, 1974)

P. H. Wilson, *German Armies: War and German Politics 1648–1806* (London, 1998)

P. Blickle, *Landschaften im alten Reich: die staatliche Funktion des gemeinen Mannes in Oberdeutschland* (Munich, 1973)

J. A. Vann & S. W Rowan, *The Old Reich: Essays on German Political Institutions 1495–1806* (Brussels, 1974)

R. J. W. Evans, *Rudolf II and his World* (Oxford, 1973)

R. J. W. Evans, *The Making of the Habsburg Monarchy 1550–1700* (Oxford, 1979)

C. Ingrao, *The Habsburg Monarchy 1618–1815* (Cambridge, 2000)

H. W. Koch, *A History of Prussia* (London, 1978)

J. A. Vann, *The Making of a State: Württemberg 1593–1793* (Ithaca, 1984)

East Central Europe and Muscovy

N. Davies, *God's Playground: a History of Poland*, vol. 1 (Oxford, 1981)

J. K. Fedorowicz, ed., *A Republic of Nobles: Studies in Polish History to 1864* (Cambridge, 1982)

A. Maczak, H. Samsonowicz & P. Burke, eds., *East-central Europe in Transition* (Cambridge, 1984)

R. Frost, *After the Deluge: Poland-Lithuania and the Second Northern War 1655–1660* (Cambridge, 1993)

R. Butterwick, ed., *The Polish-Lithuanian Monarchy in European Context, c.1500–1795* (Basingstoke, 2001)

K. Friedrich, *The Other Prussia: Royal Prussia, Poland and Liberty, 1569–1772* (Cambridge, 2000)

P. Dukes, *The Making of Russian Absolutism, 1613–1801* (London, 1982)

G. Hosking, *Russia: People and Empire 1552–1917* (London, 1997)

C. S. L. Dunning, *Russia's First Civil War: The Time of Troubles and Founding of the Romanov Dynasty* (Philadelphia, 2001)

J. T. Fuhrman, *Tsar Alexis* (Florida, 1981)

P. Longworth, *Alexis, Tsar of all the Russias* (London, 1984)

E. V. Anisimov, *The Reforms of Peter the Great* (New York, 1993)

L. Hughes, *Russia in the Age of Peter the Great* (New Haven, 1998)

P. Bushkovitch, P*eter the Great: the Struggle for Power 1671–1725* (Cambridge, 2001)

R. Hellie, *Enserfment and Military Change in Muscovy* (Chicago, 1971)

J. L. H. Keep, *Soldiers of the Tsar: Army and Society in Russia 1462–1874* (Oxford, 1985)

W. M. Pinter & D. K. Rowney, *Russian Officialdom: The Bureaucratisation of Russian Society from the Seventeenth to the Twentieth Century* (London, 1980)

M. Cherniavsky, 'The Old Believers and the New Religion', *Slavic Review* 25 (1966), 1–39

J. Cracraft, *The Church Reform of Peter the Great* (London, 1971)

S. Dixon, *The Modernisation of Russia 1676–1825* (Cambridge, 1999)

The Ottoman Empire

S. J. Shaw, *History of the Ottoman Empire and Modern Turkey*, vol. 1 (Cambridge, 1976)

P. F. Sugar, *Southeastern Europe under Ottoman Rule, 1354–1804* (Seattle, 1977)

I. M. Kunt, *The Sultan's Servants: the Transformation of Ottoman Provincial Government 1550–1650* (New York, 1983)

D. Goffman, *The Ottoman Empire and Early Modern Europe* (Cambridge, 2002)

C. Imber, *The Ottoman Empire 1300–1650: the Structure of Power* (Basingstoke, 2002)

S. Faroqhi, *The Ottoman Empire and the World around It* (London, 2004)

B. McGowan, *Economic Life in Ottoman Europe: Taxation, Trade and the Struggle for Land, 1600–1800* (Cambridge, 1981)

H. Inalcik & D. Quataert, eds., *An Economic and Social History of the Ottoman Empire*, vol. 2 (Cambridge, 1997)

A. Wheatcroft, *Infidels: the Conflict between Christendom and Islam, 638–2002* (London, 2003)

Political consolidation and social order after mid-century

P. Goubert, *Louis XIV and Twenty Million Frenchmen* (London, 1970)

P. Goubert, *The Ancien Régime*, vol. 1 (London, 1973)

R. Mettam, *Government and Society in Louis XIV's France* (London, 1977)

R. Mettam, *Power and Faction in Louis XIV's France* (Oxford, 1988)

A. Lossky, *Louis XIV and the French Monarchy* (New Brunswick, 1994)

D. Parker, *Class and State in Ancien Régime France: the Road to Modernity?* (London, 1996)

D. J. Sturdy, *Louis XIV* (London, 1998)

J. Hurt, *Louis XIV and the Parlements: the Assertion of Royal Authority* (Manchester, 2002)

P. Burke, *The Fabrication of Louis XIV* (New Haven, 1991)

B. Lepetit, 'Une création urbaine: Versailles de 1661 a 1722', *Revue d'histoire moderne et contemporaine* 25 (1978)

G. Rowlands, *The Dynastic State and the Army under Louis XIV: Royal Service and Private Interest 1661–1701* (Cambridge, 2002)

J. Smyth, *The Making of the United Kingdom, 1660–1800* (London, 2001)

T. Harris, *Politics under the Late Stuarts: Party Conflict in a Divided Society 1660–1715* (London, 1993)

T. Harris, *London Crowds in the Reign of Charles II* (Cambridge, 1987)

L. K. J. Glassey, ed., *The Reign of Charles II and James VII and II* (London, 1997)

J. Miller, *Restoration England: the Reign of Charles II* (London, 1985)

W. A. Speck, *Reluctant Revolutionaries: Englishmen and the Revolution of 1688* (Oxford, 1988)

G. Holmes, *Augustan England: Professions, State and Society, 1680–1730* (London, 1982)

M. Fulbrook, *Piety and Politics: Religion and the Rise of Absolutism in England, Württemberg and Prussia* (Cambridge, 1983)

R. Vierhaus, *Deutschland im Zeitalter des Absolutismus, 1648–1763* (Göttingen, 1879)

C. A. Macartney, *The Habsburgs and Hohenzollern Dynasties in the Seventeenth and Eighteenth Centuries* (London, 1970)

J. P. Spielman, *Leopold I of Austria* (London, 1977)

T. M. Barker, *Double Eagle and Crescent: Vienna's Second Turkish Siege and its Historical Setting* (New York, 1967)

C. Storrs, *War, Diplomacy and the Rise of Savoy, 1690–1720* (Cambridge, 2000)

G. Symcox, *Victor Amadeus II: Absolutism in the Savoyard State 1675–1730* (London, 1984)

D. Sella, *Italy in the Seventeenth Century* (London, 1997)

H. Kamen, *Spain in the Later Seventeenth Century* (London, 1980)

C. Black, *Early Modern Italy: A Social History* (London, 2001)

Elites and nobility

M. L. Bush, *The European Nobility*, vols. 1–2 (Manchester, 1983–88)

M. L. Bush, ed., *Social Orders and Social Classes in Europe Since 1500: Studies in Social Stratification* (London, 1992)

H. M. Scott, ed., *The European Nobilities in the Seventeenth and Eighteenth Centuries* (London, 1994)

J. Dewald, *The European Nobility 1400–1800* (Cambridge, 1996)

R. G. Asch, *Nobilities in Transition 1550–1700: Courtiers and Rebels in Britain and Europe* (London, 2003)

R. C. Crummey, *Aristocrats and Servitors: the Boyar Elite in Russia 1613–1689* (Princeton, 1984)

J. H. Elliott & L. W. Brockliss, eds., *The World of the Favourite* (New Haven, 1999)

F. Billacois, *The Duel: its Rise and Fall in Early Modern France* (New Haven, 1990)

J. Arlette, *Le devoir de la révolte: la noblesse française et la gestation de l'état moderne* (Paris, 1989)

D. Bohanan, *Crown and Nobility in Early Modern France* (Basingstoke, 2001)

Cities, towns and ports

J. de Vries, *European Urbanisation 1500–1800* (London, 1984)

C. R. Friedrichs, *The Early Modern City 1450–1750* (London, 1995)

A. Cowan, *Urban Europe 1500–1700* (London, 1998)

P. Burke, *Venice and Amsterdam: A Study of Seventeenth-Century Elites* (London, 1974)

R. T. Rapp, *Industry and Economic Decline in Seventeenth-Century Venice* (Cambridge, MA, 1976)

R. Mackenney, *Tradesmen and Traders: The World of the Guilds in Venice and Europe, c.1250–c.1650* (London, 1987)

D. R. Ringrose, *Madrid and the Spanish Economy, 1560–1850* (Berkeley, CA, 1983)

L. Bernard, *The Emerging City: Paris in the Age of Louis XIV* (Durham, NC, 1970)

P. Benedict, ed., *Cities and Social Change in Early Modern France* (London, 1989)

W. Beik, *Urban Protest in Seventeenth-century France* (Cambridge, 1997)

P. Clark & P. Slack, *English Towns in Transition 1500–1700* (Oxford, 1976)

A. L. Beier & R. Finlay, eds., *The Making of the Metropolis: London 1500–1700* (London, 1986)

J. Barry & C. Brooks, eds., *The Middling Sort of People: Culture, Society and Politics in England 1550–1800* (Basingstoke, 1994)

M. Lynch, *The Early Modern Town in Scotland* (London, 1987)

H. Rössler, ed., *Deutsches Patriziat 1470–1740* (Limburg, 1968)

W. Rausch, ed., *Die städte Mitteleuropas im 17. und 18. Jahrhundert* (Linz, 1981)

G. I. Soliday, *A Community in Conflict: Frankfurt Society in the Seventeenth and Early Eighteenth Centuries* (Hanover, NH, 1974)

C. R. Friedrichs, *Urban Society in an Age of War: Nördlingen 1580–1720* (Princeton, 1979)

C. P. Clasen, *Die Augsburger Weber: Leistungen und Krisen des Textilgewerbes um 1600* (Augsburg, 1981)

J. M. Hittle, *The Service City: State and Townsman in Russia 1600–1800* (Cambridge, MA, 1979)

Trade and material life

S. C. Ogilvie & M. Cerman, eds., *European Proto-industrialization* (Cambridge, 1996)

R. S. Duplessis, *Transitions to Capitalism in Early Modern Europe* (Cambridge, 1997)

J. Amelang, *The Flight of Icarus: Artisan Autobiography in Early Modern Europe* (Cambridge, 1999)

P. Musgrave, *The Early Modern European Economy* (Basingstoke, 1999)

M. Greene, 'Beyond the Northern Invasion: The Mediterranean in the Seventeenth Century', *Past & Present* 174 (2002), 42–71

J. de Vries, *The First Modern Economy: Success, Failure and Perseverance of the Dutch Economy, 1500–1815* (Cambridge, 1997)

K. Wrightson, *Earthly Necessities: Economic Lives in Early Modern Britain* (London, 2002)

C. Cipolla, *Guns and Sails in the Early Period of European Expansion, 1400–1700* (London, 1965)

N. Steensgaard, *Carracks, Caravans and Companies: the Structural Crisis in the European–Asian Trade in the Early Seventeenth Century* (Copenhagen, 1973)

H. Furber, *Rival Empires of Trade in the Orient, 1600–1800* (Oxford, 1976)

A. Attmann, *The Bullion Flow Between Europe and the East, 1000–1750* (Göteborg, 1981)

G. V. Scammell, *The First Imperial Age: European Overseas Expansion c.1400–1715* (London, 1989)

C. R. Boxer, *The Dutch Seaborne Empire, 1600–1800* (London, 1965)

J. H. Parry, *The Spanish Seaborne Empire* (London, 1966)

R. Davis, *The Rise of the Atlantic Economies* (London, 1973)

K. G. Davies, *The North Atlantic World in the Seventeenth Century* (Minneapolis, 1974)

D. B. Quinn & A. N. Ryan, *England's Sea Empire 1550–1642* (London, 1984)

N. Canny, ed., *The Oxford History of the British Empire, vol. 1: The Origins of Empire* (Oxford, 1998)

D. Armitage & M. J. Braddick, eds., *The British Atlantic World 1500–1800* (Basingstoke, 2002)

J. M. Postma, *The Dutch in the Atlantic: Slave Trade, 1600–1815* (Cambridge, 1990)

H. Thomas, *The Slave Trade: the History of the Atlantic Slave Trade 1440–1870* (London, 1997)

S. B. Schwartz, ed., *Implicit Understandings: Observing, Reporting and Reflecting on the Encounters between European and other Peoples in the Early Modern Period* (Cambridge, 1994)

Beliefs and cultural life

P. Burke, *Popular Culture in Early Modern Europe* (London, 1978)

P. Burke, *The Historical Anthropology of Early Modern Italy* (Cambridge, 1987)

D. Underdown, *Revel, Riot and Rebellion: Popular Politics and Culture in England 1603–60* (Oxford, 1985)

A. Walsham, *Providence in Early Modern England* (Oxford, 1999)

W. Monter, *Ritual, Myth and Magic in Early Modern Europe* (Brighton, 1983)

J. Sharpe, *Instruments of Darkness: Witchcraft in England, 1550–1750* (London, 1996)

S. Wilson, *The Magical Universe: Everyday Ritual and Magic in pre-modern Europe* (London, 2000)

R. Briggs, *Witches and Neighbours: the Social and Cultural Context of European Witchcraft* (Oxford, 2002)

B. Ankarloo, S. Clark & W. Monter, *Witchcraft and Magic in Europe: The Period of the Witch Trials* (London, 2002)

G. K. Waite, *Heresy, Magic and Witchcraft in Early Modern Europe* (Basingstoke, 2003)

J. Goodare, ed., *The Scottish Witch-hunt in Context* (Manchester, 2002)

L. Roper, *Oedipus and the Devil: Witchcraft, Sexuality and Religion 1500–1700* (London, 1994)

K. Thomas, *Religion and the Decline of Magic* (London, 1971)

J. Delumeau, *Catholicism between Luther and Voltaire* (London, 1977)

J. Bossy, *Christianity in the West* (Oxford, 1986)

D. MacCulloch, *The Reformation: Europe's House Divided* (London, 2003)

C. S. Dixon & L. Schorn-Schütte, eds., *The Protestant Clergy of Early Modern Europe* (Basingstoke, 2003)

C. F. Black, *Church, Religion and Society in Early Modern Italy* (Basingstoke, 2004)

P. Collinson, *The Religion of Protestants: the Church in English Society* (Cambridge, 1983)

J. Spurr, *English Puritanism 1603–1689* (London, 1998)

D. Spaeth, *The Church in an Age of Danger: Parsons and Parishioners 1660–1740* (Cambridge, 2000)

G. Henningsen & J. Tedeschi, *The Inquisition in Early Modern Europe* (Dekalb, IL, 1986)

J. Delumeau, *La peur en occident, xiv–xviii siècles: une cité assiegée* (Paris, 1978)

W. G. Naphy & P. Roberts, eds., *Fear in Early Modern Society* (Manchester, 1997)

P. Camporesi, *Bread of Dreams: Food and Fantasy in Early Modern Europe* (Cambridge, 1989)

K. Stuart, *Defiled Trades and Social Outcasts: Honour and Ritual Pollution in Early Modern Germany* (Cambridge, 1999)

Printing and reading

E. L. Eisenstein, *The Printing Press as an Agent of Change* (Cambridge, 1979)

R. A. Houston, *Literacy in Early Modern Europe: Culture and Education 1500–1800* (2nd edn., London, 2002)

J. Lough, *Writer and Public in France: From the Middle Ages to the Present Day* (Oxford, 1978)

R. Chartier, *The Cultural Uses of Print in Early Modern France* (Princeton, 1987)

M. Spufford, *Small Books and Pleasant Histories: Popular Fiction and its Readership in Seventeenth-Century England* (Cambridge, 1981)

A. Johns, *The Nature of the Book: Print and Knowledge in the Making* (Chicago, 1998)

A. Fox, *Oral and Literate Culture in England 1500–1700* (Oxford, 2000)

J. Raymond, *Pamphlets and Pamphleteering in Early Modern Britain* (Cambridge 2003)

N. Elias, *The Civilizing Process*, vols. 1–2 (Oxford, 1978)

A. Bermingham & J. Brewer, eds., *The Consumption of Culture 1600–1800* (London, 1995)

D. Roche, *A History of Everyday Things* (Cambridge, 2000)

M. Phyllis & M. C. Jacob, *Politics and Culture in Early Modern Europe* (Cambridge, 1987)

G. Parry, *The Golden Age Restor'd: The Culture of the Stuart Court, 1603–42* (Manchester, 1981)

F. Haskell, *Patrons and Painters: A Study in the Relations between Italian Art and Society in the Age of the Baroque* (New Haven, 1980)

H. Raynor, *A Social History of Music from the Middle Ages to Beethoven* (New York, 1978)

Science

A. G. Debus, *Man and Nature in the Renaissance* (Cambridge, 1978)

R. Mandrou, *From Humanism to Science, 1480–1700* (Harmondsworth, 1978)

C. Wilson, *The Invisible World: Early Modern Philosophy and the Invention of the Microscope* (Princeton, 1995)

S. Shapin, *The Scientific Revolution* (Chicago, 1996)

W. G. L. Randles, *The Unmaking of the Medieval Christian Cosmos, 1500–1760* (London, 1999)

M. J. Osler, ed., *Rethinking the Scientific Revolution* (Cambridge, 2000)

B. J. Shapiro, *A Culture of Fact: England 1550–1720* (Cambridge, 2000)

The peasantry

J. Goody, J. Thirsk & E. P. Thompson, *Family and Inheritance: Rural Society in Western Europe 1200–1800* (Cambridge, 1976)

J. Blum, *The End of the Old Order in Rural Europe* (Princeton, 1978)

T. Aston & C. H. E. Philpin, eds., *The Brenner Debate: Agrarian Class Structure and Economic Development in Pre-industrial Europe* (Cambridge, 1985)

T. Scott, ed., *The Peasantries of Europe: From the Fourteenth to the Eighteenth Centuries* (London, 1998)

R. L. Hopcroft, *Regions, Institutions and Agrarian Change in European History* (Ann Arbor, 1999)

J. Blum, *Lord and Peasant in Russia* (Princeton, 1961)

D. Moon, *The Russian Peasantry 1600–1930: The World the Peasants Made* (New York, 1999)

W. Schulze, ed., *Aufstände, Revolten, Prozesse: Beiträge zu bäuerlichen Wiederstandsbewegungen im frühneuzeitlickhen Europa* (Stuttgart, 1983)

R. Mousnier, *Peasant Uprising in Seventeenth-century France, Russia and China* (London, 1971)

E. le Roy Ladurie, 'Peasant Revolts and Protest Movements in France 1675–1788', *Local Historian* 11 (1974)

E. le Roy Ladurie, *Les paysans de Languedoc*, vols. 1–2 (Paris, 1966; abbr. Engl. translation, Urbana, IL, 1977)

P. Goubert, *The French Peasantry in the Seventeenth Century* (Cambridge, 1986)

W. Schulze, *Bäuerlicher Widerstand und feudale Herrschaft in der frühen Neuzeit* (Stuttgart, 1980)

T. Robisheaux, *Rural Society and the Search for Order in Early Modern Germany* (Cambridge, 1989)

T. Munck, *The Peasantry and the Early Absolute Monarchy in Denmark, 1660–1708* (Copenhagen, 1979)

E. A. Wrigley, 'Urban Growth and Agricultural Change: England and the Continent in the Early Modern Period', *Journal of Interdisciplinary History* 5 (1985), 683–728

J. de Vries, *The Dutch Rural Economy in the Golden Age, 1500–1700* (New Haven, 1974)

I. D. Whyte, *Agriculture and Society in Seventeenth-century Scotland* (Edinburgh, 1979)

R. B. Outhwaite, 'Progress and Backwardness in English Agriculture 1500–1650', *Economic History Review* 39 (1986), 1–18

Demographic change

M. W. Flinn, *The European Demographic System 1500–1820* (Brighton, 1981)

J. Walter & R. Schofield, eds., *Famine, Disease and the Social Order in Early Modern Society* (Cambridge, 1989)

J. Dupaquier, *La population française aux xviie et xviiie s.* (Paris, 1979)

E. A. Wrigley & R. S. Schofield, *The Population History of England: A Reconstruction* (London, 1981)

J. Hatcher, 'Understanding the Population History of England', *Past & Present* 180 (2003), 83–130

M. W. Flinn, *Scottish Population History from the Seventeenth Century to the 1930s* (Cambridge, 1977)

A. Sharlin, 'Natural Decrease in Early Modern Cities', *Past & Present* 79 (1978), 126–38

M. Lindemann, *Medicine and Society in Early Modern Europe* (Cambridge, 1999)

J. N. Biraben, *Les hommes et la peste*, vols. 1–2 (Paris, 1975–76)

P. Slack, *The Impact of Plague in Tudor and Stuart England* (London, 1985)

L. M. Beier, *Sufferers and Healers: The Experience of Illness in Seventeenth-century England* (London, 1987)

L. Brockliss & C. Jones, *The Medical World of Early Modern France* (Oxford, 1997)

Family and community

J.-L. Flandrin, *Families in Former Times* (Cambridge, 1979)

J. Gélis, *History of Childbirth: Fertility, Pregnancy and Birth in Early Modern Europe* (London, 1991)

R. Adair, *Courtship, Illegitimacy and Marriage in Early Modern England* (Manchester, 1996)

M. Jackson, ed., *Infanticide: Historical Perspectives on Child Murder and Concealment, 1550–2000* (Aldershot, 2002)

P. Ariès, *Centuries of Childhood* (Harmondsworth, 1962)

L. A. Pollock, *Forgotten Children: Parent–child Relations from 1500–1900* (Cambridge, 1983)

L. Stone, *The family, Sex and Marriage in England 1500–1800* (London, 1977)

R. A. Houlbrooke, *The English Family 1450–1700* (London, 1984)

D. Cressy, 'Kinship and Kin Interaction in Early Modern England', *Past & Present* 113 (1986), 38–69

D. Cressy, *Birth, Marriage and Death: ritual, Religion and the Life-cycle in Tudor and Stuart England* (Oxford, 1997)

R. Houlbrooke, *Death, Religion and the Family in England 1480–1750* (Oxford, 1998)

S. D. Amussen, *An Ordered Society: Gender and Class in Early Modern England* (Oxford, 1988)

A. L. Erickson, *Women and Property in Early Modern England* (London, 1993)

R. Sarti, *Europe at Home: Family and Material Culture 1500–1800* (New Haven, 2002)

R. Phillips, *Putting Asunder: a History of Divorce in Western Society* (Cambridge, 1988)

M. MacDonald & T. R. Murphy, *Sleepless Souls: Suicide in Early Modern England* (Oxford, 1991)

Gender issues

B. S. Andersen & J. P. Zinnser, *A History of their Own: Women in Europe from Prehistory to the Present*, vols. 1–2 (Harmondsworth, 1990)

M. E. Wiesner, *Women and Gender in Early Modern Europe* (Cambridge, 1993; 2nd edn. 2000)

N. Z. Davis & A. Farge, *A History of Women* (vol. 3): *Renaissance and Enlightenment Paradoxes* (Cambridge, MA, 1993)

M. P. Sommerville, *Sex and Subjection: Attitudes to Women in Early Modern Society* (London, 1995)

O. Hufton, *The Prospect before Her: A History of Women in Western Europe* (London, 1996)

M. E. Wiesner-Hanks, *Christianity and Sexuality in the Early Modern World: Regulating Desire, Reforming Practice* (London, 2000)

W. Chadwick, *Women, Art and Society* (London, 2002)

W. Gibson, *Women in Seventeenth-century France* (London, 1989)

M. E. Wiesner, *Gender, Church and State in Early Modern Germany* (London, 1997)

B. S. Capp, *When Gossips Meet: Women, Family and Neighbourhood in Early Modern England* (Oxford, 2003)

R. B. Shoemaker, *Gender in English Society 1650–1850* (London, 1998)

P. Carter, *Men and the Emergence of Polite Society, Britain 1660–1800* (London, 2000)

G. R. Quaife, *Wanton Wenches and Wayward Wives: Peasants and Illicit Sex in Early Seventeenth-century England* (London, 1979)

N. H. Keeble, ed., *The Cultural Identity of seventeenth-century Women: a Reader* (London, 1994)

Poverty and relief

R. Jütte, *Poverty and Deviance in Early Modern Europe* (Cambridge, 1994)

L. Fontaine, *History of Pedlars in Europe* (Cambridge, 1996)

B. S. Pullan, 'Catholics and the Poor in Early Modern Europe' *Transactions of the Royal Historical Society* 26 (1976), 15–34

B. S. Pullan, *Rich and Poor in Renaissance Venice* (Oxford, 1971)

S. Cavallo, *Charity and Power in Early Modern Italy: Benefactors and their Motives in Turin, 1541–1789* (Cambridge, 1995)

R. Chartier, 'Les élites et les gueux: quelques représentations', *Revue d'histoire moderne et contemporaine* 21 (1974), 376–88

J. Depauw, 'Pauvres, pauvres mendiants, mendiants valides ou vagabonds? Les hésitations de la législation royale', *Revue d'histoire moderne et contemporaine* 21 (1974), 401–18

C. Fairchilds, *Poverty and Charity in Aix-en-Provence, 1640–1789* (Baltimore, 1976)

D. Roche, 'A Pauper Capital: some Reflections on the Parisian Poor in the Seventeenth and Eighteenth Centuries', *French History* 1 (1987), 182–209

O. P. Grell & A. Cunningham, eds., *Health Care and Poor Relief in Protestant Europe, 1500–1700* (London, 1997)

A. L. Beier, *The Problem of the Poor in Tudor and early Stuart England* (London, 1983)

P. A. Slack, *Poverty and Policy in Tudor and Stuart England* (London, 1988)

P. Slack, *The English Poor Law 1531–1782* (Basingstoke, 1990)

P. Slack, *From Reformation to Improvement: Public Welfare in Early Modern England* (Oxford, 1999)

T. Arkell, 'The Incidence of Poverty in England in the Later Seventeenth Century', *Social History* 12 (1987), 23–47

R. Mitchison, *The Old Poor Law in Scotland: The Experience of Poverty, 1574–1845* (Edinburgh, 2000)

Repression and crime

R. B. Outhwaite, 'Dearth and Government Intervention in English Grain Markets, 1590–1700', *Economic History Review* 34 (1981), 389–406

R. Schofield, 'The Impact of Scarcity and Plenty on Population Change in England, 1541–1871', *Journal of Interdisciplinary History* 14 (1983–84), 165–91

A. J. Fletcher & J Stevenson, eds., *Order & Disorder in Early Modern England* (Cambridge, 1985)

P. Slack, 'Dearth and Social Policy in Early Modern England', *Social History of Medicine* 5 (1992), 1–17

J. A. Sharpe, *Crime in Early Modern England, 1550–1750* (London, 1984)

J. M. Beattie, *Crime and the Courts in England, 1660–1800* (Oxford, 1986)

M. Gaskill, *Crime and Mentalities in Early Modern England* (Cambridge, 2000)

H. Kamen, 'Public Authority and Popular Crime: Banditry in Valencia 1660–1714', *Journal of European Economic History* 3 (1974), 654–87

E. Oesterberg & D. Lindström, *Crime and Social Control in Medieval and Early Modern Swedish Towns* (Uppsala, 1988)

J. F. Harrington, 'Escape from the Great Confinement: the Genealogy of the German Workhouse', *Journal of Modern History* 71 (1999), 308–45

U. Rublack, *The Crimes of Women in Early Modern Germany* (Oxford, 1998)

P. Spierenburg, *The Spectacle of Suffering: Execution and the Evolution of Repression* (Cambridge, 1984)

P. Spierenburg, *The Prison Experience: Disciplinary Institutions and their Inmates in Early Modern Europe* (New Brunswick, 1991)

R. J. Evans, *Rituals of Retribution: Capital Punishment in Germany 1600–1987* (Oxford, 1996)

Index

481